EUROPE

ASIA

RICA

INDIAN

OCEAN

PACIFIC

OCEAN

AUSTRALIA

# MANAGEMENT

## SIXTH EDITION

### JAMES A. F. STONER
FORDHAM UNIVERSITY

### R. EDWARD FREEMAN
UNIVERSITY OF VIRGINIA

### DANIEL R. GILBERT, JR.
BUCKNELL UNIVERSITY

**PRENTICE HALL**
ENGLEWOOD CLIFFS, NEW JERSEY 07632

Stoner, James Arthur Finch
        Management / James A. Stoner, R. Edward Freeman, Daniel Gilbert.

-
    - 6th ed.
            p.    cm.
        Includes index.
        ISBN 0-13-108747-9
        1. Management.    I. Freeman, R. Edward.    II. Gilbert,
Daniel R.   III. Title
HD31.S6963   1995
658--dc20                                            94-29243
                                                     CIP


Project Manager: *Kristin E. Dackow*
Acquisitions Editor: *Natalie Anderson*
Assistant Editor: *Lisamarie Brassini*
Design Director: *Linda Fiordilino*
Senior Managing Editor, Production: *Fran Russello*
Development Editor: *Burrston House, Ltd./Cathy Crow*
Photo Research: *Burrston House, Ltd./Victoria Gregor*
Cover/Interior Designer: *William Seabright and Associates*
Manufacturing Buyer: *Vincent Scelta*
Editorial Assistant: *Nancy Proyect*
Production Assistant: *Renee Pelletier*

Cover Art: *George Abe*

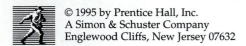

© 1995 by Prentice Hall, Inc.
A Simon & Schuster Company
Englewood Cliffs, New Jersey 07632

Printed in the United States of America

10  9  8  7  6  5  4  3  2  1



ISBN: 0-13-108747-9



Prentice-Hall International (UK) Limited, *London*
Prentice-Hall of Australia Pty. Limited, *Sydney*
Prentice-Hall Canada Inc., *Toronto*
Prentice-Hall Hispanoamericana, S.A., *Mexico*
Prentice-Hall of India Private Limited, *New Delhi*
Prentice-Hall of Japan, Inc., *Tokyo*
Simon & Schuster Asia Pte. Ltd., *Singapore*
Editora Prentice-Hall do Brasil, Ltda., *Rio de Janeiro*

To all those whose efforts have made this book what it is.

    Ed Freeman

    Dan Gilbert

To my coauthors, all those who helped with this book, and to Alexandra, Barbara, and Carolyn who made it possible in their own, unique ways.

    Jim Stoner

# ICON LEGEND:
## ISSUES FOR THE '90S AND BEYOND

QUALITY

SMALL BUSINESS

ETHICS

INTERNATIONAL

DIVERSITY

# Brief Contents

# Contents

## PART ONE: Introduction to Management

# PART TWO:   MANAGEMENT IN THE TWENTY-FIRST CENTURY

# PART THREE:   PLANNING

# PART FOUR: ORGANIZING

CHAPTER   14

# HUMAN RESOURCE MANAGEMENT 374

# PART SIX:  CONTROLLING

# PREFACE

**W**e believe there has never been a more rewarding—or challenging—time to be a manager. The reward comes from knowing that effective, efficient managers can make and are making a real difference in our world. Managers make a difference by influencing the development of new products and services. They make a difference by supporting the personal development of the people who work for them. And, more and more each day, managers make a difference by reconciling organizational activities with ecological, social, and political concerns across the globe. The challenge comes from globalization of the economy, which presents a constantly shifting kaleidoscope of competitive pressures and opportunities. Consider just a few facts. The Berlin Wall is rubble, and scores of U.S. and European companies have launched joint ventures within what used to be Communist countries. Furthermore, organizations such as the European Community and agreements such as the North American Free Trade Agreement are pointing the way for a new set of trade and political alliances. And while U.S. companies and foreign companies are competing for the same customers, they are just as likely to form joint ventures for research and production.

Our goal for this edition then is to make students aware of these environmental changes and to show them how effective managers are adapting. We use the term "dynamic engagement" among peoples around the world to highlight these changes.

Dynamic engagement as a theme is developed in a three-pronged strategy in this book. First, we have grouped six chapters that discuss key aspects of the environment in the second part of the book, where they provide a framework for the traditional discussions of planning, organizing, leading, and controlling.

Second, we pay close attention to business ethics and cultural diversity. If managers are to meet the challenges of today's changing environment, they must draw on their most talented employees—without regard for racial, cultural, or gender differences. Managers must also be sensitive to cultural differences as they deal with their counterparts, employees, and customers from other countries—and increasingly common event. To make these points, we sustain the theme throughout the book that managers deal with *time* and *human relationships,* which set a backdrop for ethics and cultural diversity.

Third, we have placed an even greater emphasis on examples that place the manager on the brink of the twenty-first century and the place for organizations in that fascinating setting. In Chapters 3 through 21, we close with a section entitled "Management 2000 and Beyond."

*Management* was published in its first edition in 1978. Since then, the book has gained tenure as the most widely used and all time best-seller in the Principles of Management field. The book has succeeded not only in the United States but also around the world, in its English edition as well as in its Portuguese, Spanish, Polish, Indonesian, and Bahasa Malaysian translations.

We are humbled by this overwhelming show of trust and we approach this latest edition with renewed enthusiasm, determined to build on the solid foundation that made the first five editions such highly regarded teaching and learning tools.

As always, this book is about the job of the manager. It describes how men and women go about managing the people and activities of their organizations so that the goals of these organizations as well as their own personal goals, can be achieved.

We have attempted in this book to convey the very positive view we have of the manager's job. We believe the job of a manager is among the most exciting, challenging, and rewarding careers a person can have. Individuals can and do make great contributions to society as members of managed organizations—not only businesses but also universities, hospitals, research centers, government agencies, and other organizations. Such organizations bring together the talent and resources that such achievements require. All this highlights a point that we will make a central theme of this book; *management is all about working in and through human relationships.*

In this text, we have chosen to address the reader as a citizen of a world in which management is a pervasive and consequential practice. This book will be valuable to you whether you aspire to be a manager, or do not yet know what that might entail. Regardless, we write in a way that puts you in a manager's shoes from the very beginning. This is done intentionally: we want to encourage the reader to start thinking like a manager as soon as possible. Obviously, the earlier that one learns to think like a manager, the sooner one can understand the practice of management and the meaning of managerial effectiveness. But there is another, more basic reason. All managers—but especially young managers just beginning their careers—are evaluated in large part on how effective they are as employees working for managers. The more successful an individual is as an employee, the more likely that his or her career will be successful. And one of the best ways of learning how to be an excellent employee is to learn how to think like a manager. Thus, addressing the reader as a manager (or at least a prospective manager) is meant to be a helpful way of improving your knowledge about our managerial age, and perhaps your chances for a fulfilling managerial career.

The sixth edition of *Management* would not have been possible without the assistance of an outstanding group of people at Prentice Hall: Kristin Dackow, Project Manager; Linda Fiordilino, Design Director; Vincent Scelta, Manufacturing Buyer; Fran Russello, Managing Editor; Renee Pelletier, Production Assistant; Jo-Ann DeLuca, Marketing Manager; Lisamarie Brassini, Associate Editor; Nancy Proyect and Diane Peirano, Editorial Assistants; Valerie Ashton, Editor-in-Chief; and, finally, Natalie Anderson, Senior Executive Editor.

In addition, we wish to recognize the able assistance of Burrston House, in particular: Glenn Turner, President; Meg Turner; Victoria Gregor; Kelly Doolittle; and—most especially—our Development Editor, Cathy Crow.

The new, improved look of this Sixth Edition is due to the able hand of William Seabright of William Seabright and Associates and George Abe the part opener and cover designer.

Research assistance was provided by Jason Boulette, Douglas Kirkman, Kim Dyer, Lay Bolen, Matthew Bacchetta, G. Lindsay Perkins, Sunil Kakodker. We would like to give special credit to Tara Radin, who oversaw research on this edition.

We would like to thank our reviewers for their many excellent suggestions during the preparation of the Sixth Edition:

| | |
|---|---|
| Medina Thomas | University of Texas |
| David Grisby | Clemson University |
| Tim Query | Indiana State University |
| Stan Elsea | Kansas State University |
| Durwood Hofler | Northeastern Illinois University |
| Judy Neal | University of New Haven |
| Elizabeth Cooper | University of Rhode Island |
| Coral Snodgrass | Canisius College |

| | |
|---|---|
| Robert Keating | University of North Carolina—Wilmington |
| Eileen Aranda | Aranda & Associates, Phoenix, AZ |
| Charles B. Shrader | Iowa State University |
| Anne C. Cowden | California State University—Sacramento |
| Eugene J. Calvasina | Auburn University—Montgomery |
| LaVelle Mills | Tarleton State University |
| John Hall | University of Florida |
| Marylou Lockerby | College of DuPage |
| Kenneth Bass | East Carolina University |
| Ken Dunegan | Cleveland State University |
| Debra Arvanites | Villanova University |
| Chi Archibong | North Carolina A & T |
| Nick Mathys | DePaul University |
| Carol Moore | California State University—Hayward |
| Paul Thacker | Macomb Community College |

We express gratitude to Anne C. Cowden of California State University at Sacramento for many contributions to the Sixth Edition, including research on numerous in-text and annotated examples.

# MANAGEMENT

SIXTH EDITION

# INTRODUCTION TO MANAGEMENT

CHAPTER 1 **MANAGING AND MANAGERS**

CHAPTER 2 **THE EVOLUTION OF MANAGEMENT THEORY**

# INTERSECTION

## 1

**M**illions of men and women around the world spend their days as managers in organizations. They confront endless challenges as they strive to complete their daily tasks. The purpose of this book is to prepare the managers of tomorrow by introducing them today to the issues they will face. In Part I we introduce the practice of management and trace its evolution. In Part II we explore in depth the current issues that frame the workplace: environment and environmental awareness; ethics and social responsibility; globalization; entrepreneurship; culture, diversity, and multiculturalism; and quality. We also recognize the common roles and responsibilities that managers share. With this in mind, we devote a part of the text to each of the primary elements of management: planning (Part III), organizing (Part IV), leading (Part V), and controlling (Part VI).

Two chapters comprise Part I. In Chapter 1 we explore what the practice of management is about. We discuss the reasons for studying management and examine the interconnectedness of time and human relationships. In Chapter 2 we trace the history of management theories and describe the current area as one of *dynamic engagement.* Thus we use this first section of the text to address general issues and concerns and prepare for the more in-depth discussion that follows.

## CHAPTER 1

# MANAGING AND MANAGERS

**Upon completing this chapter, you should be able to:**

1. Explain the importance of organizations and management.

2. Define the four principal activities of the management process.

3. Describe different categories of managers.

4. Discuss the different skills that managers must have and the roles they can fill.

5. Understand why managers need to be concerned with vision, ethics, cultural diversity, and the changing workplace.

# A TYPICAL DAY IN THE WORK LIFE OF NATALIE ANDERSON

Natalie Anderson is an acquisitions editor for textbooks in the field of management at Prentice Hall (PH). PH, the largest textbook publisher in the world, is a division of Simon & Schuster publishing, which, in turn, is part of Viacom, Inc. Viacom is a conglomerate that also owns Paramount Studios, the New York Knicks, Madison Square Garden, MTV, Nickelodeon, and Showtime.

One typical Friday morning, Natalie arrives at the office at about 8:30 a.m. Checking her voice mail messages, she sees there are three: one, time-stamped 9:30 the night before, from a West Coast author who's writing the study guide to accompany a new introductory management text; another from a PH production editor; and the third from a Miami sales representative, asking for the publication date of an environmental management textbook listed on her laptop instock report.

While listening to voice mail, Natalie hooks up her laptop computer to the printer and phone line and prints out new e-mail messages. Once she's off the phone she reads through them. There are five messages, four from sales representatives in search of information and one from the electronically inclined author of PH's new principles of management text, Joan Pankovsky. After putting the four messages from the sales staff in her "out" box for her assistant to respond to, Natalie puts the message from Joan on top of her desk, where it joins a number of other messages and files.

*The opening graphics are stunning—just like MTV!*

Before the cafeteria shuts down at 9:00 a.m., Natalie heads downstairs for a bagel and a cup of coffee. As she stands in line, her marketing manager, Franco Limani, joins her. "Hey, Franco, how is the Pankovsky ad coming along? Do we have the design finalized yet?"

"Well, we did until your boss got hold of it. Vladimir asked us to include additional sample pages, since the text design is so stunning. But that will add some time to our schedule. And it'll add some costs, of course," Franco responds. Natalie asks how that will affect the advertising budget, and he says they have some money left over from another book whose publication was delayed.

After stopping in the hall to chat briefly with the Pankovsky production editor, who is currently overseeing the copy editing and typesetting process, Natalie returns to her office. Her editorial assistant, Diane Petrossian, is waiting for her: "You're going to be late for your 10:00 a.m. appointment with Glenn in the city, unless you step on it. Here are the files you'll need. Joan Pankovsky called a few minutes ago; I told her you would get back to her this afternoon. And I e-mailed the sales representatives who sent us messages last night."

"Thanks, Diane, I would be lost without you," Natalie responds gratefully, putting on her coat and stuffing the files into her briefcase. As she zips out the door, she asks Diane, "Would you mind calling the Pankovsky production editor and setting up a scheduling meeting on the book for Monday afternoon? And check with Lisa, Vladimir, and Franco to make sure they can attend. Bye!"

It's 9:20 a.m. and her appointment is for 10:00 in town. The all-news radio station says bridge traffic is backed up for five miles due to a jackknifed tractor-trailer, so she opts for the tunnel. On the drive in, Natalie reflects on one aspect of the Pankovsky *Principles of Management* plan. Both she and the author feel strongly that there should be a major multimedia component in the package for her book. Pankovsky believes they

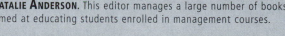

**NATALIE ANDERSON.** This editor manages a large number of books aimed at educating students enrolled in management courses.

5

should do a laser disk, and that the content should be totally educational. Glenn Burrston, the multimedia developer for the project, disagrees; he proposes a glitzy-looking, high-tech compact disk that has only a few educational video clips.

To help strike a compromise between these two strong-minded professionals, and to identify the most effective promotional tool, last night on her way out of the building Natalie had stopped in to see Seth Speekes, in the Market Research department. According to Seth, PH's recent survey of business professors showed that 15 percent have access to laser disk players. Ten percent have access to CD players hooked up to computers. However, the percentage of professors who believe they will have access to CD players in the next two years is significantly higher than the percentage who expect to have laser disk players. Seth's vote is for a CD.

Glenn is waiting in the lobby when Natalie hurries into the City Hotel at 10:15. They spend two hours over coffee in a small conference room discussing the format and content of the multimedia disk. Glenn shows her the opening graphics for the disk, which he has commissioned a computer graphics artist to design. They are stunning—just like MTV! Hopefully, Vladimir won't be upset when he sees how much this glitz is costing us, Natalie muses.

It takes only 30 minutes to get back to the office. On the way into the building, Natalie stops in the cafeteria for some pickings from the salad bar. And more coffee. →

NATALIE ANDERSON practices as a manager in a large organization. In this chapter, we will introduce you to the *practice of management*—what it involves and how it is changing—and the connection between organizations and management. Managing in organizations is what Natalie, and millions of men and women worldwide, do in their working lives.

## ORGANIZATIONS AND THE NEED FOR MANAGEMENT

**organization:**

Two or more people who work together in a structured way to achieve a specific goal or set of goals.

**goal:**

The purpose that an organization strives to achieve; organizations often have more than one goal; goals are fundamental elements of organizations.

For most of our lives, we are members of one **organization** or another—a college, a sports team, a musical or theatrical group, a religious or civic organization, a branch of the armed forces, or a business. Some organizations, like the army and large corporations, are structured very formally. Others, like a neighborhood basketball team, are more casually structured. But all organizations, formal or informal, are put together and kept together by a group of people who see that there are benefits available from working together toward some common goal. So a very basic element of any organization is a **goal** or purpose.* The goal will vary—to win a league championship, to entertain an audience, to sell a product—but without a goal no organization would have a reason to exist.

All organizations also have some program or method for achieving goals—a *plan*. The plan might be to practice playing skills, to rehearse a certain number of

---

* When we say that organizations have goals, we use this phrase as a shorthand way of saying that people who are members of an organization have some shared purpose. Organizations, it is important to note, do not have goals in the same sense that human beings have goals. This is what we have in mind when we say "organizations and their goals."

**management:**

The process of planning, organizing, leading, and controlling the work of organization members and of using all available organizational resources to reach stated organizational goals.

**manager:**

People responsible for directing the efforts aimed at helping organizations achieve their goals.

times before each performance, or to manufacture and advertise a product. Whatever it is, without some plan for what it must do, no organization is likely to be very effective.

Organizations must also acquire and allocate the *resources* necessary to achieve their goals. Perhaps a playing field or rehearsal hall must be available, or money must be budgeted for wages. All organizations depend on other organizations for the resources they need. A team cannot play without the required equipment; manufacturers must maintain contracts with suppliers. Natalie Anderson, for example, depends on graphic artists to design texts, specialists to develop media, etc.

**MANAGING ORGANIZATIONS. Management** is the practice of consciously and continually shaping organizations. All organizations have people who are responsible for helping them achieve their goals. These people are called **managers**. These managers—coaches, conductors, sales executives—may be more obvious in some organizations than in others, but without effective management, organizations are likely to founder.

This book is about how organizations are managed. More specifically, it is about how managers can best help their organizations set and achieve goals. Our emphasis will be on the so-called *formal* organizations—such as businesses, religious organizations, government agencies, and hospitals—that provide goods or services to their customers or clients and offer career opportunities to their members. But no matter how formal or informal, all managers in all organizations have the same basic responsibility: to help other members of the organization set and reach a series of goals and objectives.

As part of this process, managers can set the tone, influencing the attitude that employees have about their work. At Southwest Airlines, for example, CEO Herb Kelleher has developed a loyal and committed staff built on three values: 1) Work should be fun...it can be play...enjoy it; 2) Work is important...don't spoil it with seriousness; and 3) People are important...each one makes a difference.[1]

## WHY STUDY ORGANIZATIONS AND MANAGEMENT

Organizations are in the news and in our conversations every day. On September 11 and 12, 1993, for example, the headlines of *The New York Times* were filled with references to organizations:[2]

- Random House Children's Books Headed for PCs
- Microsoft to Charge for Technical Help
- NASA is Preparing, Again, for Shuttle Launching
- M.T.A. Proposes Free Bus-Subway Transfer for Commuters

Your conversations with friends, parents, classmates, and co-workers are probably filled with talk about organizations such as colleges, musical ensembles, athletic teams, and companies where you work.

In a world where organizations are everywhere, there are three compelling reasons for studying them and the practice of management. In each case—involving the past, present, and future—the effects of people collaborating as an organization, under the guidance of managers, can be far-reaching.

**LIVING IN THE PRESENT.** First, organizations contribute to the present standards of living of people worldwide. We rely on organizations daily for food, shelter, clothing, medical care, communications, amusement, and employment. The Red Cross, for example, is an organization that is particularly focused on the present as it offers assistance to specific groups of people in times of need.

**O**RGANIZATIONS CONTRIBUTE TO PRESENT STANDARDS OF LIVING. Organizations all over the world make available a wide range of goods for consumers. Here, clothes shoppers browse in a hypermart in Mexico City.

**O**RGANIZATIONS BUILD THE FUTURE. Increased recycling has created a need for ways to use recycled plastic. Floyd Hammer, founder of Hammer's Plastic Recycling Corp., patented a process for converting recycled plastic into weather-resistant park benches, parking lot curbs, and landscaping timbers.

**BUILDING THE FUTURE.** Second, organizations build toward a desirable future and help individuals do the same. New products and practices are developed as a result of the creative power that can emerge when people work together in organizations. Organizations have an impact—positive or negative—on the future status of our natural environment, on the prevention and treatment of disease, and on war around the globe. In this text we will discuss a number of organizations that are addressing concerns about the future in their products and practices, such as Tom's of Maine, which produces a line of all-natural personal-care products with environmentally sensitive packaging.[3]

**REMEMBERING THE PAST.** Third, organizations help connect people to their pasts. Organizations can be thought of as patterns of human relationships. Every day that we work with others adds to the history of the organization and to our own history. We often define ourselves in terms of the organizations we have been a part of—whether schools, teams, political groups, or businesses. In addition, organizations maintain records and value their own history, keeping traditions alive in our minds. Often it is through the records and history of organizations that we know about the past.

## MANAGEMENT AS A SPECIALTY IN TIME AND HUMAN RELATIONSHIPS

Management is a specialty in dealing with matters of *time* and *human relationships* as they arise in organizations. We have just seen how organizations affect the past, present, and future. Our idea about time in organizations has several elements:

1. Management is an attempt to create a *desirable future*, keeping the past and the present in mind.
2. Management is practiced in and is a reflection of a *particular historical era*.
3. Management is a practice that produces consequences and effects that *emerge over time*.

The importance of human relationships also involves several ideas:

1. Managers act in relationships that are *two-way streets*; each party is influenced by the other.
2. Managers act in relationships that have *spillover effects* for other people, for better and for worse.
3. Managers juggle *multiple simultaneous relationships*.

We emphasize these twin themes of time and human relationships throughout the book because we believe they can greatly aid your learning about management. Managers think about time and human relationships all the time. *And so do you*. The college years, regardless of your age, are a period in your life when you envision a new or revised future for yourself. These are also years when you may develop new relationships (or modify existing relationships) with spouses, friends, teachers, and employers. Since you are "living" these two themes every day, we appeal to that personal experience when we define management as a specialty in time and human relationships.

## MANAGERIAL AND ORGANIZATIONAL PERFORMANCE

**managerial performance:**
The measure of how efficient and effective a manager is—how well he or she determines and achieves appropriate objectives.

Management is the principal activity that *makes a difference* in how well organizations serve people affected by them.

How successfully an organization achieves its objectives, and satisfies social responsibilities as well, depends to a large extent on its managers. If managers do their jobs well, an organization will probably achieve its goals.

How well managers do their jobs—**managerial performance**—is the subject of much debate, analysis, and confusion in the United States and many other countries.[4] So is **organizational performance**—the measure of how well organizations do *their* jobs.[5] Therefore we will be discussing many different concepts and criteria for evaluating managers and organizations.[6]

**organizational performance:**
The measure of how efficient and effective an organization is—how well it achieves appropriate objectives.

## EFFICIENCY AND EFFECTIVENESS*

**efficiency:**
The ability to minimize the use of resources in achieving organizational objectives: "doing things right."

**effectiveness:**
The ability to determine appropriate objectives: "doing the right thing."

Underlying many of these discussions are two concepts suggested by Peter Drucker, one of the most respected writers on management: efficiency and effectiveness.[7] As he puts it, **efficiency** means "doing things right" and **effectiveness** means "doing the right thing."

Efficiency—the ability to do things right—is an "input-output" concept. An efficient manager is one who achieves outputs, or results, that measure up to the inputs (labor, materials, and time) used to achieve them. Managers who are able to minimize the cost of the resources needed to achieve goals are acting efficiently.

Effectiveness, in contrast, involves choosing *right* goals. A manager who selects an inappropriate goal—say, producing mainly large cars when demand for small  cars is soaring—is an ineffective manager, even if the large cars are produced with maximum efficiency. Managers at General Motors learned this lesson the hard way. When the demand for fuel-efficient, smaller cars increased in the 1970s, GM ignored the competition created by the Japanese and Germans, believing that the trends were an aberration and that Americans, loyal to American products, would not continue to buy foreign cars. As a consequence, they continued to produce large, fuel-inefficient cars, and in so doing lost enormous competitive ground to these new rivals.[8]

---

* We acknowledge that there is an ongoing debate about the usefulness of these two terms.

**E**FFICIENCY MEANS DOING THINGS RIGHT. Solectron Corp.'s concurrent engineering team is geared to move products quickly and efficiently from initial design into full production. Solectron is a 1991 winner of the Malcolm Baldrige National Quality Award. (Baldrige winners are featured in various photos throughout the text; the award is discussed in Chapter 8.)

No amount of efficiency can make up for a lack of effectiveness. In fact, Drucker says, effectiveness is the key to an organization's success. Before we can focus on doing things efficiently, we need to be sure we have found the right things to do.[9]

## **T**HE MANAGEMENT PROCESS

**S**ince the late nineteenth century, it has been common practice to define management in terms of four specific functions of managers: planning, organizing, leading, and controlling. Although this framework has come under some scrutiny, it is still generally accepted.[10] We can thus say that management is the process of planning, organizing, leading, and controlling the efforts of organization members and of using all other organizational resources to achieve stated organizational goals.[11]

**process:**
A systematic method of handling activities.

A **process** is a systematic way of doing things. We refer to management as a process to emphasize that all managers, regardless of their particular aptitudes or skills, engage in certain interrelated activities in order to achieve their desired goals. In the rest of this section, we will briefly describe these four main management activities and how they involve relationships and time.

## PLANNING

**planning:**
The process of establishing goals and a suitable course of action for achieving those goals.

**Planning** implies that managers think through their goals and actions in advance and that their actions are based on some method, plan, or logic rather than on a hunch. Plans give the organization its objectives and set up the best procedures for reaching them. In addition, plans are the guides by which (1) the organization obtains and commits the resources required to reach its objectives; (2) members of the organization carry on activities consistent with the chosen objectives and procedures; and (3) progress toward the objectives is monitored and measured so that corrective action can be taken if progress is unsatisfactory.

The first step in planning is the selection of goals for the organization. Goals* are then established for each of the organization's *subunits*—its divisions, departments, and so on. Once these are determined, programs are established for achieving goals in a systematic manner. Of course, in selecting objectives and developing programs, the top manager considers their feasibility and acceptability to the organization's managers and employees.

Relationships and time are central to planning activities. Planning produces a picture of desirable future circumstances—given currently available resources, past experiences, etc. Natalie Anderson plans for the future when she deals with the promotional campaign for the Pankovsky book, an endeavor involving many relationships.

Plans made by top management charged with responsibility for the organization as a whole may cover periods as long as five or ten years. In a large organization, such as a multinational energy corporation like British Petroleum, those plans may involve commitments of billions of dollars. On the other hand, planning in particular parts of the organization spans much shorter periods. For example, such plans may be for the next day's work, or for a two-hour meeting to take place in a week. Planning will be discussed in more detail in Part Three.

## ORGANIZING

**organizing:**
The process of engaging two or more people in working together in a structured way to achieve a specific goal or set of goals.

**Organizing** is the process of arranging and allocating work, authority, and resources among an organization's members so they can achieve the organization's goals.

Different goals require different structures. An organization that aims to develop computer software, for example, needs a different structure than does a manufacturer of blue jeans. Producing a standardized product like blue jeans requires efficient assembly-line techniques, whereas producing software requires organizing teams of professionals such as systems analysts and programmers. Although these professionals must interact effectively, they cannot be organized like assembly-line workers. Thus, managers must match an organization's structure to its goals and resources, a process called *organizational design*.

Relationships and time are central to organizing activities. Organizing produces a structure for the relationships in an organization, and it is through these structured relationships that future plans will be pursued. For instance, Natalie Anderson coordinates the work of various people and structures time in organizing the production process for the Pankovsky book. Another aspect of relationships that is part of organizing is seeking new people to join the structure of relationships. This search is called *staffing*. Organizing will be discussed in more detail in Part Four.

---

\* Some writers distinguish between *goals* and *objectives*. While there may be reasons for doing so, for the sake of simplicity we treat them as synonymous.

**LEADERS MOTIVATE.** General manager Mead D'Amore led Westinghouse's Commercial Nuclear Fuels Division to win the Baldrige Award in 1988, the first year the award was offered.

## LEADING

**leading:**
The process of directing and influencing the task-related activities of group members or an entire organization.

**Leading** involves directing, influencing, and motivating employees to perform essential tasks. Relationships and time are central to leading activities. In fact, leading gets to the heart of managers' relationships with each of the people working for them. Managers lead in an attempt to persuade others to join them in pursuit of the future that emerges from the planning and organizing steps. By establishing the proper atmosphere, managers help their employees do their best. Natalie Anderson leads, for instance, when she praises Diane for her assistance and prods Franco about the ad design. Leading will be discussed in more detail in Part Five.

## CONTROLLING

**controlling:**
The process of ensuring that actual activities conform to planned activities.

Finally, the manager must be sure the actions of the organization's members do in fact move the organization toward its stated goals. This is the **controlling** function of management, and it involves these main elements: (1) establishing standards of performance; (2) measuring current performance; (3) comparing this performance to the established standards; and (4) taking corrective action if deviations are detected. Through the controlling function, the manager keeps the organization on track. Increasingly, organizations are establishing new ways to build in quality to the control function. One popular approach is *Total Quality Management (TQM)*, which we discuss in more detail in Chapter 8. TQM focuses management on the continuous improvement of all operations, functions, and, above all, processes of work. Meeting the customers' needs is a primary concern.[12]

Relationships and time are central to controlling activities. The reason managers must worry about control is that, over time, the results of organized relationships do not always work out as planned. Natalie Anderson controls when she reviews and follows up on the activity reports submitted to her by Diane and others. She also has controlling on her mind when she anticipates Vladimir's response to the costs of the ad design. Controlling will be discussed in more detail in Part Six.

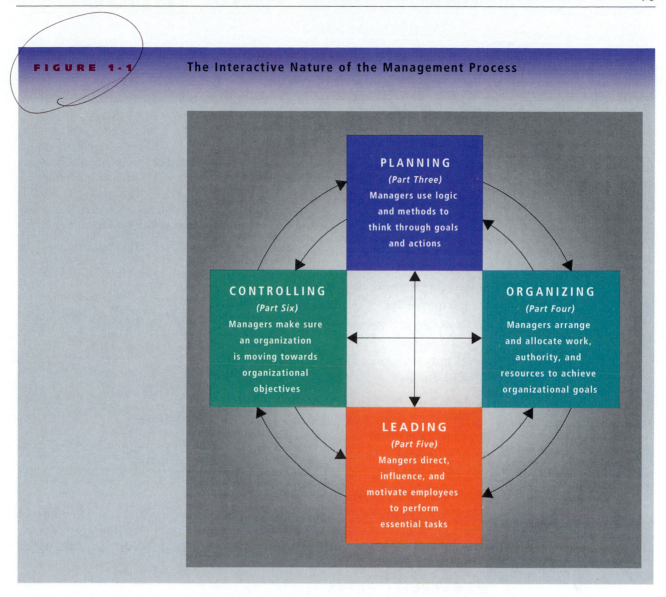

**FIGURE 1-1** The Interactive Nature of the Management Process

**PLANNING**
*(Part Three)*
Managers use logic and methods to think through goals and actions

**CONTROLLING**
*(Part Six)*
Managers make sure an organization is moving towards organizational objectives

**ORGANIZING**
*(Part Four)*
Managers arrange and allocate work, authority, and resources to achieve organizational goals

**LEADING**
*(Part Five)*
Mangers direct, influence, and motivate employees to perform essential tasks

**model:**

A simplified representation of the key properties of an object, event, or relationship; can be verbal, physical, or mathematical.

## THE MANAGEMENT PROCESS IN PRACTICE

It is easier to understand a process as complex as management when it is broken down into parts and the basic relationships between the parts are identified. Descriptions of this kind, known as **models**, have been used by students and practitioners of management for decades. A model is a description used to convey complex relationships in easy-to-understand terms. In fact, we used a model—without identifying it as such—when we said that the major management activities are planning, organizing, leading, and controlling. These are four ways to deal with formal relationships that evolve over time. But the relationships we described are more intertwined than our model implies. For example, we said that standards are used in evaluating and controlling employees' actions, but establishing such standards is an inherent part of the planning process and an integral factor in motivating and leading subordinates. And taking corrective action, which we introduced as a control activity, often involves adjusting plans.

In practice, the management process does not involve four separate or loosely related sets of activities but a group of *interrelated* functions. Figure 1-1 presents a more complete management model, because the arrows showing relationships all point in two directions. Planning, organizing, leading, and controlling are the simultaneous and interconnected actions that keep managers like Natalie Anderson very busy.

## DEMING'S FOURTEEN POINTS

Sometimes the four functions of management can be clearly identified in today's practice of management. Often, however, you have to look beneath the surface to identify them in particular management efforts. Consider, for example, the fourteen points that W. Edwards Deming, one of the major leaders of the quality movement, proposed as a guideline for top managers. Can you identify which function or functions (planning, organizing, leading, or controlling) underlie each point?

1. Create constancy of purpose for improvement of product and service.
2. Adopt the new philosophy.
3. Cease dependence on mass inspection.
4. End the practice of awarding business on price tag alone.
5. Constantly and forever improve the system of production and service.
6. Institute modern methods of training on the job.
7. Institute leadership.
8. Drive out fear.
9. Break down barriers between staff areas.
10. Eliminate slogans, exhortations, and targets for the work force.
11. Eliminate numerical quotas.
12. Remove barriers to pride of workmanship.
13. Institute a vigorous program of education and training.
14. Take action to accomplish the transformation.[13]

We will say more about Deming in Chapter 8. For now, it is interesting to note that although his books and articles have preached the "quality crusade" for decades, Deming was for years virtually unknown in the United States, his own country.

## MANAGERIAL ROLES

We have discussed management in terms of four broad functions. We can look beyond these functions to identify a number of specific roles that managers may fill at various times. You are already familiar with some of the crucial roles required of managers—because you are already a veteran of many different relationships that have evolved over your life thus far! In your ties with your family, friends, classmates, and co-workers, sometimes you *lead*, sometimes you act as a go-between or *liaison*, and sometimes others look to you as a *symbol* of some worthwhile trait such as honesty or willingness to work hard. In these same relationships, you *monitor* what is going on outside the relationship, *share information* with your partners, and even act as a *spokesperson* for them. Furthermore, you sometimes take the *initiative*, sometimes *handle disagreements*, sometimes *allocate resources* such as money, and sometimes *negotiate* with your collaborators.

Henry Mintzberg has carefully studied what managers do. In his book *The Nature of Managerial Work* he describes the manager's agenda as consisting of precisely the ten activities discussed above.[14] Mintzberg refers to the first three as *interpersonal* roles of a manager, the next three as *informational* roles, and the final four as *decisional* roles. We can identify several of these roles in our case about Natalie Anderson. For example, we find her acting as:

- *Liaison* (interpersonal role), presiding over the conference call involving Franco and Joan;

- *Monitor* (informational role), checking with Seth about market projections, and
- *Negotiator* (decisional role), debating with Glenn about the book's various media.

Increasingly, today's organizations are seeing that many managerial roles need not be confined to traditional managers. As the organizational environment becomes increasingly competitive, companies are looking for ways to improve quality. Often this means people who once had very narrow, nonmanagerial roles are asked to expand their range of activities. At Stone Construction Equipment, Inc., Stan Gerhart makes cowls—metal engine covers for light machinery. At  one time, his workday involved just one job: he cranked out cowls and put them on the shelf all day, then punched out and went home. New management at Stone asked Gerhart to redesign his job from the ground up and to run his one-man department as its own small business within a small business. His new job required him to deal with his own suppliers and customers elsewhere in the shop. Gerhart has been free to implement many time-saving and quality-building ideas he has developed. He says, "It makes my job a whole lot easier because I control my own destiny."[15]

A key point about the role of managers is that they must be very versatile when it comes to dealing with human relationships. You already know that about your own relationships, no doubt! The specialization that we call *management practice* builds upon the versatility that we have just described.

### INNOVATIVE DEVELOPMENTS IN SMALL BUSINESSES

Versatility is clearly an asset in small businesses. When both managers and employees can expand their roles, companies benefit. And sometimes smaller businesses can implement changes faster than larger ones. In fact, many small businesses have developed interesting and unique management practices that larger companies can learn from.

- At W. L. Gore & Associates Inc., the Gore-Tex-fabric producer based in Newark, Delaware, management reorganized the company by abolishing titles and management levels, giving employees unprecedented leeway in defining their own jobs.
- Quad/Graphics Inc., a fast-growing printing company with headquarters in Pewaukee, Wisconsin, has a long list of training courses for employees, an on-site sports center, and a stock-ownership program. In structuring its operations, Quad set up each press crew as an autonomous profit center responsible for its own operations.
- Prime Technology, a machine distributor in Grand Rapids, Michigan, with 30 people on the payroll, has team-based management, generous bonus programs, and an open-book policy of sharing business operations information with employees.
- At both Phelps County Bank in Rolla, Missouri, and Intuit Software in Palo Alto, California, employees are encouraged to search out new ways of improving operations—meaning that no one need be limited by the boundaries of the job. Work at both places provides an opportunity for employees to develop the versatility of management practices that workers need in today's challenging work environment.[16]

# TYPES OF MANAGERS

**first-line (or first-level) managers:**
Managers who are responsible for the work of operating employees only and do not supervise other managers; they are the "first" or lowest level of managers in the organizational hierarchy.

**middle managers:**
Managers in the midrange of the organizational hierarchy; they are responsible for other managers and sometimes for some operating employees; they also report to more senior managers.

**W**e have been using the term *manager* to mean anyone who is responsible for carrying out the four main activities of management in relationships over time. One way to grasp the complexity of management is to see that managers can practice at different *levels* in an organization and with different *ranges* of organizational activities. After looking at the level and scope of various kinds of managers, we will go on to see how different skills and roles are emphasized in different types of management.

## MANAGEMENT LEVELS

**FIRST-LINE MANAGERS.** The lowest level in an organization at which individuals are responsible for the work of others is called **first-line** or **first-level management**. First-line managers direct non-management employees; they do not supervise other managers. Examples of first-line managers are the foreman or production supervisor in a manufacturing plant, the technical supervisor in a research department, and the clerical supervisor in a large office. First-level managers are often called "supervisors." A school principal is also a first-level manager, as is the manager of a major league baseball team.

**MIDDLE MANAGERS.** The term **middle management** can include more than one level in an organization. Middle managers direct the activities of lower-level managers and sometimes those of operating employees as well. Middle managers' principal responsibilities are to direct the activities that implement their organizations' policies and to balance the demands of their managers with the ca-

**A FIRST-LINE MANAGER.** First-line managers direct the work of non-management employees.

pacities of their employers. Natalie Anderson is a middle manager: she has managers such as production editors reporting to her, and she reports, in turn, to Vladimir.

**top managers:**

Managers responsible for the overall management of the organization; they establish operating policies and guide the organization's interaction with its environment.

**TOP MANAGERS.** Composed of a comparatively small group of people, **top management** is responsible for the overall management of an organization. These people are called executives. They establish operating policies and guide the organization's interactions with its environment. Typical titles of top managers are "chief executive officer," "president," and "vice president."

## FUNCTIONAL AND GENERAL MANAGERS

**functions:**

A classification referring to a group of similar activities in an organization, such as marketing or operations.

Another major classification of managers depends on the scope of activities they manage. Organizations are often described as a set of **functions**. A function, in this sense, is a collection of similar activities.[17] The marketing function, for example, commonly consists of sales, promotion, distribution, and market research activities. At Coca Cola, the marketing function is responsible for TV ads, and the research and development function is responsible for Coke's special formula. On college campuses, the athletic department is a function, because the activities of its members differ from what, say, the members of the philosophy department do.

**functional manager:**

A manager responsible for just one organizational activity, such as finance or human resources management.

**FUNCTIONAL MANAGERS.** The **functional manager** is responsible for only *one* functional area, such as production, marketing, or finance.

**general manager:**

The individual responsible for all functional activities, such as production, sales, marketing, and finance, for an organization such as a company or a subsidiary.

**GENERAL MANAGERS.** The **general manager**, on the other hand, oversees a complex unit, such as a company, a subsidiary, or an independent operating division. He or she is responsible for *all* the activities of that unit, such as its production, marketing, and finance.[18] A small company may have only one general manager— its president or executive vice president—but a large organization may have several, each heading a relatively independent division. In a large food company, for example, there may be a grocery-products division, a refrigerated-products division, and a frozen food-products division, with a different general manager responsible for each. Like the chief executive of a small company, each of these divisional heads is responsible for all the activities of the unit. Even if she doesn't have the title, Natalie Anderson performs the tasks of a general manager as she oversees and links several different functions.

It is important to remember that functional and general managers alike plan, organize, lead, and control relationships over time. The difference, again, is in the scope of activities that they oversee.

## MANAGEMENT LEVEL AND SKILLS

**technical skill:**

The ability to use the procedures, techniques, and knowledge of a specialized field.

**human skill:**

The ability to work with, understand, and motivate other people as individuals or in groups.

**conceptual skill:**

The ability to coordinate and integrate all of an organization's interests and activities.

Robert L. Katz, a teacher and business executive, has popularized a concept developed early in this century by Henri Fayol, a famous management theorist we will meet again in Chapter 2. Fayol identified three basic kinds of skills: technical, human, and conceptual. Every manager needs all three. **Technical skill** is the ability to use the procedures, techniques, and knowledge of a specialized field. Surgeons, engineers, musicians, and accountants all have technical skills in their respective fields. **Human skill** is the ability to work with, understand, and motivate other people as individuals or in groups. **Conceptual skill** is the ability to coordinate and integrate all of an organization's interests and activities. It involves seeing the organization as a whole, understanding how its parts depend on one another, and anticipating how a change in any of its parts will affect the whole.

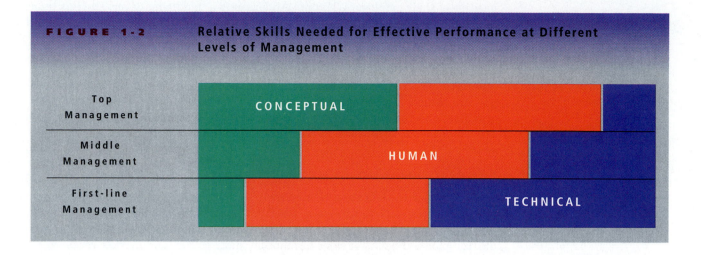

**FIGURE 1-2**    Relative Skills Needed for Effective Performance at Different Levels of Management

Fayol and Katz suggest that although all three of these skills are essential to a manager, their relative importance depends mainly on the manager's rank in the organization (see Figure 1-2). Technical skill is most important in the lower levels. Human skill, although important for managers at every level, is the primary skill needed by middle managers; their ability to tap the technical skills of their subordinates is more important than their own technical proficiency. Finally, the importance of conceptual skill increases as one rises through the ranks of a management system. At higher and higher organizational levels, the full range of relationships, and the organization's place in time, are important to understand. This is where a manager must have a clear grasp of the big picture.*

## THE CHALLENGE OF MANAGEMENT

You are studying management in a time and place where many people are rethinking what management is all about. The impetus for this reevaluation comes from the increasing pace of change both in organizations and in the larger world. Think about the momentous events that have occurred in this country and around the world since you entered first grade—or even since you entered high school or college or the workforce. In this complex and dynamic environment, managers must continually adjust to changing conditions. It should come as no surprise, then, that today's managers look at change as a constant in their lives. We conclude this overview of management practice with three concurrent challenges that confront managers as they deal with a changing world on the doorstep of the twenty-first century.

### THE NEED FOR VISION

The world is shrinking. New telecommunications technologies continue to expand our reach and speed up our communications. In addition, the world is being reshaped, both by technologies—such as genetic engineering, automated manufacturing, lasers, and computer chips—and by changing political boundaries and

---

* In the fast changing, global, restructured world of today, it may be questionable wheter Katz's model continues to apply to the complexity of managerial tasks. In Part Two we explore these issues.

# THE DAY CONTINUES . . .

Returning to her office, Natalie notes that Diane must be at lunch—she's not at her desk, and there is a pile of phone messages and photocopying on Natalie's chair (the only spot at Natalie's desk not usually covered with manuscripts). She leafs through the memos, and identifies one she can delegate immediately. Henrietta Hersch, from PH's United Kingdom office, called to inquire about foreign rights for the International edition of Pankovsky. The author is well known abroad, so her book is expected to sell well overseas. Natalie walks around the corner to the office of her assistant editor, Ann-Marie Caby, and asks her to return Henrietta's call first thing in the morning, since it is already past office hours in England. They spend 15 minutes discussing how to handle the foreign publishing rights. Natalie suggests that Ann-Marie call the international marketing manager for additional guidance.

A good two hours are spent making return phone calls, the lengthiest one to Professor Pankovsky. At 4:00 p.m., Franco joins in for a conference call on the marketing strategy for the new text. Forty-five minutes later, the three participants have agreed on a multi-pronged marketing plan, which includes capitalizing on the Glenn Burrston compact disk. Back at her desk, Natalie switches gears and skims the weekly activity reports submitted by Diane and other staff members. She puts them aside; they'll reappear later as her Sunday afternoon reading. →

**NATALIE ANDERSON (STANDING) WITH PROJECT MANAGER KRISTIN DACKOW.** These two team members work together in selecting photographs to appear in this textbook.

alliances. Since the previous edition of this book the Soviet Union has ceased to exist. These new technologies and new global political alignments mean that managers face new possibilities for forging relationships that will carry their organizations into the future. For example, Andrew Dressel, a founder of MapInfo, an *INC*. 500 company in Troy, New York, that manufactures software, wanted a new challenge and developed a new vision with an international focus. He has put his entrepreneurial expertise to work in a business "incubator" in Kiev, Ukraine, to help aspiring Ukrainian entrepreneurs develop their own businesses. The goal is to share his company-building skills and to explain how capitalism works.[19]

A vision for living through and benefiting from these changing circumstances is important to any manager. For most of this century, for example, it was heresy to talk about joint ventures between American and Japanese auto manufacturers. Today there are many alliances. Managers with vision created those new relationships. In the publishing industry, the very idea of publication is changing. Natalie Anderson and her associates find themselves envisioning what various new technologies such as CDs can bring to the distribution of information. They can no longer simply equate "publication" with a book.

## NUMMI—AN EXPERIMENT IN A NEW ERA

The first of the joint ventures between American and Japanese auto manufacturers was New United Motor Manufacturing Inc.—NUMMI for short. The Fremont, California, facility was originally a GM plant characterized by tense labor–management relations. When GM closed the plant in 1982, it suffered from low productivity, poor quality, drug and alcohol abuse, and absenteeism over 20 percent. Wildcat strikes and sickouts had brought the plant to a standstill four times in 20 years.

In 1983 GM and Toyota reached a deal to reopen the plant as NUMMI. Using time-and-motion studies and selective hiring to increase productivity, NUMMI was able to create world-class productivity and quality as well as an increase in worker motivation and satisfaction. The plant produces quality automobiles for both companies, such as the GEO prism, Toyota Corolla, and Toyota trucks.

The success of NUMMI is built on its management of human resources. NUMMI has three goals: 1) to serve management by improving overall quality and productivity; 2) to serve the workers by involving them in the design

**A GROUNDBREAKING JOINT VENTURE.** The groundbreaking ceremony for New United Motor Manufacturing Inc. (NUMMI) marked the first joint venture between U.S. and Japanese auto manufacturers. Both GM and Toyota products are produced at the Fremont, California, plant.

and control of their own work, thereby increasing motivation and satisfaction in the work; and 3) to serve the interest of the entire organization by creating a formal system to encourage learning, to seize and communicate innovation, and to systematize continuous improvement. These ends are reached successfully through the Toyota Production System's operating philosophy:

1. *Kaizen,* the never-ending search for perfection (continuous improvement).
2. *Kanban,* the reduction of costs, through its "just-in-time" system.
3. Development of full human potential.
4. Building mutual trust.
5. Developing team performance.
6. Treating every employee as a manager.
7. Providing a stable livelihood for all employees.

Union relationships are built on management-worker cooperation. The collective bargaining agreement is committed to employee security. Layoffs, for example, may occur only in severe economic times, and management salaries and contracted work will be reduced before layoffs.

At NUMMI, the continuous search for quality has been quite successful and has provided GM with experiences in management techniques that it has applied elsewhere, such as in its Saturn plant (featured in Chapter 18).[20] ■

## THE NEED FOR ETHICS

The decisions made by managers in organizations have a broad reach both inside and outside the organizations. Thus managers must be concerned with values and ethics. Sometimes things go awry in the course of organizational activity. Our increasing alarm over industrial pollution is just one reminder that managers inevitably allocate advantages and disadvantages no matter what they do—or fail to do. For example, Nike has developed a technological process capable of recyling every type of shoe the company makes except for cleated models. Now discarded shoes, rather than taking up landfill space, can be recycled to provide products that can be used to make new shoes. Nike's recycling efforts come from a combination of corporate responsibility and the original purpose of the company: a passion for the environment that marks not only Nike's home state of Oregon, but also the company's founders and first customers, runners.[21]

The study of who is—and should be—benefited or harmed by an action is called *ethics*. Ethics deals with both conflict and opportunity in human relationships. Ethical questions are among the most difficult ones any person faces. These questions deal with right and wrong where the magnitude of the decision is often great. Ethics provides the glue that holds our relationships, and the larger society, together. Our emphasis on human relationships throughout this book provides an opportunity to bring ethics into the discussion time and again. Natalie Anderson's job involves dealing with ethical concerns. When she deals with foreign rights to publish and with the representation of Pankovsky's ideas as author, Natalie is deciding about benefits and harms. Because business ethics is a major concern today, we will devote Chapter 4 to its study.

## THE NEED FOR RESPONSIVENESS TO CULTURAL DIVERSITY

Education, travel, telecommunications, changing immigration policies, the end of the Cold War, and several decades of peacetime have combined to break down intercultural barriers to an extent not seen in the past. Organizations, reflecting modern life, have been permeated by these changes. Exciting new relationships and new possibilities are now available. Look around your college classroom and snackbar, or your workplace. Look at the people in the media and the leaders of your community and country. The change is probably obvious.

The workplace, like the classroom, is very different from what it was thirty years ago. One very prominent example of this is the influx of women, bringing not just numbers, but talent and perhaps different approaches to relationships. In short, managers of today's organizations must be prepared to deal with diversity in their organizations and to draw on the talents of all of their employees. Indeed, from a global perspective, immigrants to this country, who present distinct multicultural issues and training needs, make up as much as 40 percent of the annual growth in the U.S. workforce. In order to compete, companies must learn to manage these new workforce entrants successfully.[22]

As Avon Chairman and CEO Jim Preston puts it, "Talent is color blind. Talent is gender blind. Talent has nothing to do with dialects, whether they're Hispanic or Irish or Polish or Chinese. And we need talent—all we can get. If America is to regain its competitive supremacy in the world, we won't do it just by restoking the blast furnaces in Pittsburgh, or cranking out more automobiles in Detroit. We'll do it by harnessing the human power of all the diverse groups that make up this country."[23]

Many managers are already deeply immersed in this challenge. With minorities and women comprising two-thirds of America's workforce, managers are finding  it necessary to rethink traditional policies to accommodate the varying interests and needs of diverse groups of people. At the accounting firm Deloitte & Touche, for example, managers have introduced dependent-care benefits, such as a child-care hotline offering suggestions about day-care options and an education hotline assisting parents in their evaluations of

# AND THE DAY ENDS

It is 5:00 p.m. and Natalie decides it's time for a bit of MBWA—management by walking around. Diane has gone home, so Natalie bypasses her desk and heads for the open door to Ann-Marie's office. She finds Ann-Marie swearing at her computer; she's just lost some files that she spent the afternoon developing. "Put a call in to the Help Desk," Natalie suggests. Ann-Marie seems relieved to hear a friendly voice. They chat while they wait for a computer specialist to arrive. Ann-Marie proudly brings Natalie up to date on the fortunes of her softball team in the company league.

Once the specialist shows up, Natalie is off to see Vladimir, her supervisor. Vladimir has at least ten book covers spread out on his office floor. He and several editors are surveying the display. There is no shortage of assistance coming Vladimir's way. Prompted for an opinion, Natalie contributes her two cents' worth: "I hate yellow."

Then she moves on to see Franco. When it appears that he has left for the golf game he mentioned yesterday, Natalie takes the cue and heads out of the building. It is past 6:00 p.m. Tonight, she will try to catch up on her personal correspondence and squeeze in an hour at the health club.

For Natalie, it has been a full day of working through relationships throughout Prentice Hall. She has interacted with long-time co-workers sitting just around the corner from her office, and she has developed working ties to relative strangers from around the nation and the globe. In all these relationships, Natalie has constantly been conscious of time: her time, their time, the history and future possibilities of each relationship and of their organizations.

public and private schools for their children. In addition, Deloitte & Touche managers provide a flexible work schedule for partners in order to increase productivity and reduce the departure rate of women. In 1993, they went further in breaking tradition by allowing a partner in the firm to work part-time so she could spend more time with her children.[24]

At Baxter International, a multinational health-care company, managers have initiated the "Inside Advantage" program to deal with employees' mobility within the organization. Nathaniel Thompkins, Director of Diversity Management at Baxter, says this program confronts "critical issues of workplace diversity: the way people have access to opportunity." [25] The mere fact that a company has a director of diversity management is a telling sign of how managers are beginning to face the challenge of diversity in a positive and proactive way.

**M A N A G E M E N T   2 0 0 0**

# THE NEED FOR NEW MANAGERS

The very nature of work—what people do as members of organizations—is rapidly changing. Robert Reich, U.S. Secretary of Labor, calls this the phenomenon of "new work":[26]

"New work involves less rote repetition and more problem-solving. Value is added by customizing and continuously improving a product or service to meet customer needs. New work is enhanced, not imperiled, by technology. And it cannot be instantly duplicated overseas, because it depends on the one resource within the nation that remains durably *here* with us—our minds."

A recent analysis published in *Fortune* magazine painted this picture of the workplace in the year 2000:[27]

- The average company will become smaller, employing fewer people.

- The traditional hierarchical organization will give way to a variety of organizational forms, the network of specialists foremost among these.

- Technicians, ranging from computer repairmen to radiation therapists, will replace manufacturing operatives as the worker elite.

- The vertical division of labor will be replaced by a horizontal division.

- The paradigm of doing business will shift from making a product to providing a service.

- Work itself will be redefined: constant learning, more high-order thinking, less nine-to-five mentality.

These changes demonstrate yet another way in which the world of relationships and their evolution over time is taking on new meaning and holding new opportunities for the managers of the twenty-first century and their organizations.

## SUMMARY

1. **Explain the importance of organizations and management.**

   Organizations have profound effects on our lives, our standard of living, and our future. Because organizations endure in time, they help us connect our pasts, presents, and futures. Organizations, both formal and informal, have plans and goals. How well organizations achieve their goals depends on managerial performance—the manager's effectiveness and efficiency.

2. **Define the four principal activities of the management process.**

   The management process includes the interrelated activities of planning, organizing, leading, and controlling. All of these activities involve human relationships and time.

3. **Describe different categories of managers.**

Managing is living in the middle of the relationships that make up and sustain an organization. Managers can be classified by level—first-line, middle, or top. They can also be classified by organizational activity—functional managers are responsible for only one activity, and general managers are responsible for all the functions in an organizational unit.

4. **Discuss different skills that managers must have and the roles they can fill.**

In moving organizations toward their goals, managers adopt a wide range of interpersonal, informational, and decision-making roles. Time and human relationships are crucial parts of these roles. Managers at different levels need different types of skills. Lower-level managers need technical skills more than higher-level managers, who rely more on conceptual skills. Managers at all levels need human skills.

5. **Understand why managers need to be concerned with vision, ethics, cultural diversity, and the changing workplace.**

In a rapidly changing world, managers have reason to infuse their planning, organizing, leading, and controlling expertise with vision, ethical analysis, responsiveness toward cultural diversity, and a new understanding of the very idea of work and the workplace.

## REVIEW QUESTIONS

1. What sorts of effects do organizations have on our lives?
2. What are the four main activities of the management process?
3. What do managers do?
4. What is the role of time and human relationships in management?
5. What is the importance for managers of ethics, cultural diversity and the changing workplace?

## KEY TERMS

| | |
|---|---|
| Organization | Controlling |
| Goal | Model |
| Management | First-line (first-level) managers |
| Manager | Middle managers |
| Managerial performance | Top managers |
| Organizational performance | Functions |
| Efficiency | Functional manager |
| Effectiveness | General manager |
| Process | Technical skill |
| Planning | Human skill |
| Organizing | Conceptual skill |
| Leading | |

# THE VICE PRESIDENT, THE PRODUCT MANAGER, AND THE MISUNDERSTANDING[28]

Tom Brewster, one of the field sales managers of Major Tool Works, Inc., was promoted to his first headquarters assignment as an assistant product manager for a group of products with which he was relatively unfamiliar. Shortly after he undertook this new assignment, one of the company's vice presidents, Nick Smith, called a meeting of product managers and other staff to plan marketing strategies. Brewster's immediate superior, the product manager, was unable to attend, so the director of marketing, Jeff Reynolds, invited Brewster to the meeting to help orient him to his new job.

Because of the large number of people attending, Reynolds was rather brief in introducing Brewster to Smith, who, as vice president, was presiding over the meeting. After the meeting began, Smith—a crusty veteran with a reputation for bluntness—began asking a series of probing questions that most of the product managers were able to answer in detail. Suddenly he turned to Brewster and began to question him quite closely about his group of products. Somewhat confused, Brewster confessed that he did not know the answers.

It was immediately apparent to Reynolds that Smith had forgotten or had failed to understand that Brewster was new to this job and was attending the meeting more for his own orientation than to contribute to it. He was about to offer a discreet explanation when Smith, visibly annoyed with what he took to be Brewster's lack of preparation, announced, "Gentlemen, you have just seen an example of sloppy staff work, and there is no excuse for it!"

Reynolds had to make a quick decision. He could interrupt Smith and point out that he had judged Brewster unfairly; but that course of action might embarrass both his superior and his subordinates. Alternatively, he could wait until after the meeting and offer an explanation in private. Inasmuch as Smith quickly became engrossed in another conversation, Reynolds decided to follow the second approach. Glancing at Brewster, Reynolds noted that his expression was one of mixed anger and dismay. After catching Brewster's eye, Reynolds winked at him as a discreet reassurance that he understood and that the damage could be repaired.

After an hour, Smith, evidently dissatisfied with what he termed the "inadequate planning" of the marketing department in general, abruptly declared the meeting over. As he did so, he turned to Reynolds and asked him to remain behind for a moment. To Reynolds' surprise, Smith himself immediately raised the question of Brewster. In fact, it turned out to have been his main reason for asking Reynolds to remain behind. "Look," he said, "I want you to tell me frankly, do you think I was too rough with that kid?" Relieved, Reynolds said, "Yes, you were. I was going to speak to you about it."

Smith explained that the fact that Brewster was new to his job had not registered adequately when they had been introduced and that it was only some time after his own outburst that he had the nagging thought that what he had done was inappropriate and unfair. "How well do you know him?" he asked. "Do you think I hurt him?"

For a moment, Reynolds took the measure of his superior. Then he replied evenly, "I don't know him very well yet. But, I think you hurt him."

"Damn, that's unforgivable," said Smith. He then telephoned his secretary to call Brewster and ask him to report to his office immediately. A few moments later, Brewster returned, looking perplexed and uneasy. As he entered, Smith came out from behind his desk and met him in the middle of the office. Standing face to face with Brewster, who was 20 years and four organization levels his junior, he said, "Look, I've done something stupid and I want to apologize. I had no right to treat you like that. I should have remembered that you were new to your job. I'm sorry."

Brewster was somewhat flustered but muttered his thanks for the apology.

"As long as you are here, young man," Smith continued, "I want to make a few things clear to you in the presence of your boss's boss. Your job is to make sure that people like myself don't make stupid decisions. Obviously we think you are qualified for your job or we would not have brought you in here. But it takes time to learn any job. Three months from now I will expect you to know the answers to any questions about your products. Until then," he said, thrusting out his hand for the younger man to shake, "you have my complete confidence. And thank you for letting me correct a really dumb mistake."

1. What do you think was the effect of Smith's outburst on the other managers at the meeting?

2. Was it necessary for Smith to apologize to Brewster? Why?

3. How would you respond to the kind of apology that Brewster received?

4. What would it be like to have Smith working for you? To work for Smith?

5. How does Smith define Brewster's responsibilities as an assistant product manager? How does he define his own role as a top manager?

## VIDEO CASE STUDY

### FOREVER YOUNG:
### MTV POISED FOR THE 1990S[29]

MTV was born at 12:01 on August 1, 1981, when it broadcast the Buggles' "Video Killed the Radio Star" to 2.1 million subscribers around the country. At that time, MTV was little more than the videos it broadcast, occasionally interrupted by a video jockey commenting on the music. By the end of the year, though, it was named *Fortune*'s product of the year. MTV had transformed pop culture from an aural into a visual medium and made it even more exciting in the process.

The inaugural video and the many that followed were perhaps forgettable, but their vehicle, MTV, has proved enduring. As of January 1994, MTV was reaching into 233 million homes in more than 75 countries. "A lot of people thought MTV wouldn't last," noted Tom Freston, chairman of MTV Networks, "and now we're accepted as an institution on the TV dial."[30] MTV no longer finds it such a struggle to remain hip; MTV is now credited for defining what's hip.

Essential to MTV's success has been the vision clearly articulated and followed by its managers. "Early on we made a key decision that we would be the voice of Young America," said Robert Pittman, MTV's former president and CEO. "We would not grow old with our audience."[31] MTV instead accepted the reality that older viewers would grow out of MTV as newer ones grew into it, and adapted its approach accordingly. Recognizing that the appeal of MTV tended to extend only to 12- to 34-year-olds, MTV

Networks—actually a trilogy of channels, including Nickelodeon and VH-1 as well as MTV—designed a strategy to at least keep viewers in the family. Nickelodeon hooks potential MTV-viewers at an early age, then MTV gets them, until they are then passed on to VH-1.

The people at MTV have been integral to maintaining this vision. Recognizing the importance of people to the company's success, Pittman personally interviewed every employee in the original programming group. "We were building more than just a channel; we were building a culture," asserted Pittman. "I was looking for a unique blend—smarts and ignorance. We put together a group of smart, aggressive people, yet not any of them had ever done the job he or she was hired to do. Everyone was ignorant of the traditions and conventions of the job, freeing us all to do it a new way."[32]

In hiring new employees, MTV managers have been forced to keep open minds. Margie Bynoe, former vice president of human resources at MTV Networks, understood that people's idiosyncracies played an important role in MTV's corporate culture and business success. Interviewees who arrived in electric ties and punk hair-dos were taken as seriously as more traditional candidates. At MTV, the diversity of the workplace refers not only to race and gender, but also to an endless number of personality traits.

At MTV, youth appeal is not something artificially fabricated: MTV is young. Most of the staff is in their 20s or 30s, with the exception of Kurt Loder, co-anchor of MTV News, who is 47. "A lot of the staff is of a fairly tender age," said Doug Herzog, senior VP of programming and president of MTV Productions. "So we're in touch with the audience. Many here are, as they say, in the demographic."[33] According to "MTV News" co-anchor Tabitha Soren, "[MTV] is the perfect place for me...because I'm young and they're young."[34] And young people continue to flock to the network in search of jobs. Top graduates from all disciplines, including political science and economics from such schools as Harvard and Princeton, send resumes for jobs that pay in the neighborhood of $15,000 a year.

Creativity and a youthful attitude go hand-in-hand at MTV. Management encourages a "play-around" atmosphere in offices that resemble college dorms, more than traditional offices, with posters and paraphernalia lining the walls. In Soren's office, friends' pictures occupy a metal bookcase and all sorts of concert passes, pins and buttons camouflage a bulletin board. Elvis hovers on the wall, standing guard. In the office of MTV's vice president for news, Dave Sirulnick, a surfboard partially blocks the downtown view from his 24th-floor Manhattan window. "The worst thing that could happen to us," warned Judy McGrath, president/creative director, "is a bunch of guys in suits sitting around in a room saying, 'What are those kids talking about these days?'"[35] There's little fear of that, considering the younger generation, or at least younger attitude, at the helm. Even Sumner Redstone, chairman of parent company Viacom, joined in an MTV party in January 1992 held at Viva Zapata, a hot spot in Key West, Florida. The 69-year-old put aside his traditionally reserved demeanor and downed tequila shots with the best of them.

Keeping its finger on the pulse of the youth and their tremendous buying power, MTV has made change one of the few constants at the network. "We would change before the audience was ready for us to change," noted Pittman. "We would continually reinvent MTV so that it didn't look like it belonged to the last generation of viewers—or even worse, that it looked accessible to 40- and 50-year olds. We would stay ahead of the audience—not follow the TV programming tradition of mirroring the audience."[36] This has resulted in a variety of programming innovations: "The Real World," a soap opera-esque documentary of seven young adults hired to live together

and be filmed; "Beavis and Butt-head," a cartoon featuring the moronic misadventures of two dim-witted heavy metal maniacs; "Big Picture," a preview show of current movies, critiqued MTV-style; "House of Style," a report on the most up-to-date fashions and trends hosted by Cindy Crawford; "MTV Sports," in which host Dan Cortese attempts weird and dangerous exploits; and "Speed Racer," the revival of a 60s cartoon about a race-car driver who combats evil around the world.

"MTV News," another programming innovation, fills an important void, for it interprets the news and puts it in terms that make it significant to young people. It's not necessarily *what* is covered on MTV News that differentiates it from other networks' news—though that varies as well—it's *how* it is covered. "Our audience looks to us for news presented in a way that is relevant to their lives," indicated assignment editor Ann Hartmayer.[37] "Everything is set to music, the rhythms are important. The thing has to move, has to have a meter," asserted senior producer Michael Alex. "The music is part of our point."[38] In addition, MTV documentaries rarely feature adults or "suit-and-tie" experts. "Kid-in-the-street" interviews take their place. "There are no criminologists, sociologists, legislators, mayors or other experts that young people will tune out," said producer Ivano Leoncavallo. "We make an effort to communicate in the most direct way."[39]

Now almost 15 years young, MTV translates into much more than a video jukebox. "MTV is the only place that really has as its mission to serve this audience [of young people] all day, every day," Sara Levinson, president/business director, pointed out.[40] Still, competitors are entering the scene. In its first decade, MTV won the trust of the youth; the challenge for the network now lies in keeping it. According to Freston, "The ongoing, creative challenge for us is to stay fresh and relevant for our viewers."[41] To stay young....

## CASE QUESTIONS

1. How does management style influence the working environment at MTV?
2. What sort of processes operated at MTV?
3. What sort of roles do managers take on at MTV?
4. How does MTV handle diversity?

## CHAPTER 2

# THE EVOLUTION OF MANAGEMENT THEORY

**Upon completing this chapter, you should be able to:**

1. Explain the setting in which management theory first developed.

2. Describe the ways in which a theory can be useful.

3. Distinguish the scientific management school, the classical organization theory school, the behavioral school, and the management science school of management theory.

4. Understand the historical context in which the systems approach, the contingency approach, and the dynamic engagement approach to management theory have developed.

# THE APOSTLE OF MASS PRODUCTION[1]

Henry Ford and the Model T have long been symbols of the modern industrial age. Even the subsequent growth and success of Ford's rival, General Motors, was due in large part to GM's need to find an innovative response to the Model T. In large measure, the managerial approach of Henry Ford, as well as his preferences in managerial theory, is a paradigm of much that was constructive and much that was imperfect—in early approaches to management.

The son of a poor Irish immigrant, Henry Ford was born in 1863 and grew up on a farm in rural Michigan. He was fascinated by machinery and was quite skilled in repairing and improving almost any machine. He started the Ford Motor Company in 1903, and by 1908, the Model T was built.

In the early part of the century when automobiles were introduced, they were a symbol of status and wealth, the near-exclusive province of the rich. Ford intended to change that: the Model T was to be for the masses—a car that virtually anyone could afford. He understood that the only way to make such a car was to produce it at high volume and low cost. Ford focused his factory efforts on efficiency, mechanizing wherever possible, and breaking down tasks into their smallest components. One worker would perform the same task over and over, producing not a finished part, but one of the operations necessary for the production of the whole; the incomplete part would then be passed on to another worker, who would contribute a successive operation. Ford was able to achieve remarkable efficiencies: Although the first Model T took over 12 $\frac{1}{2}$ hours to produce, only 12 years later, in 1920, Ford was producing one Model T every minute. By 1925, at the peak of the car's popularity, a Model T was rolling off Ford's assembly lines at the rate of one every 5 seconds.

*Ford simply decided to double wages in order to get the best people...*

However, mechanization of the plant had some adverse effects. The faster Ford pushed his workers, the more disgruntled they became. In 1913, turnover was 380 percent, and Ford had to hire ten times more workers than he needed just to keep the line moving. In an action that at the time was unprecedented, Ford simply decided to double wages in order to get the best people and motivate them to work even harder. In the days following the announcement that wages were being doubled, thousands and thousands of men came to the Ford plant in search of work. Police had to be called in to control the crowds.

When he died in 1945, Ford was worth over $600 million. He left an indelible mark on both American industry and society. His name is synonymous with mass production and the development of modern management theory. →

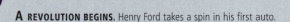

**A REVOLUTION BEGINS.** Henry Ford takes a spin in his first auto.

**M**ost people associate Henry Ford with the Model T, the affordable mass-produced automobile that changed society. But Ford is also important as a management thinker because he developed ideas about how organizations function. Moreover, Ford hired theorists, such as Frederick Winslow Taylor, and gave them the chance to develop their management theories. In this chapter we will see how different management theories developed and continue to evolve. But first we will look at some early ideas about how to run organizations effectively.

## EARLY THINKING ABOUT MANAGEMENT

**P**eople have been shaping and reshaping organizations for many centuries. Looking back through world history, we can trace the stories of people working together in formal organizations such as the Greek and Roman armies, the Roman Catholic Church, the East India Company, and the Hudson Bay Company. People have also long been writing about how to make organizations efficient and effective—since long before terms such as "management" came into common usage. Two prominent and instructive examples are the writings left for us by Niccolo Machiavelli and Sun Tzu.

### MACHIAVELLI AND SUN TZU: EARLY STRATEGISTS

Although the adjective "Machiavellian" is often used to describe cunning and manipulative opportunists, Machiavelli was a great believer in the virtues of a republic. This is evident in *Discourses,* a book Machiavelli wrote in 1531 while he lived in the early Italian republic of Florence. The principles he set forth can be adapted to apply to the management of organizations today:[2]

1. An organization is more stable if members have the right to express their differences and solve their conflicts within it.
2. While one person can begin an organization, "it is lasting when it is left in the care of many and when many desire to maintain it."
3. A weak manager can follow a strong one, but not another weak one, and maintain authority.
4. A manager seeking to change an established organization "should retain at least a shadow of the ancient customs."

Another classic work that offers insights to modern managers is *The Art of War,* written by the Chinese philosopher Sun Tzu more than 2,000 years ago. It was modified and used by Mao Zedong, who founded the People's Republic of China in 1949. Among Sun Tzu's dictums are the following:[3]

1. When the enemy advances, we retreat!
2. When the enemy halts, we harass!
3. When the enemy seeks to avoid battle, we attack!
4. When the enemy retreats, we pursue!

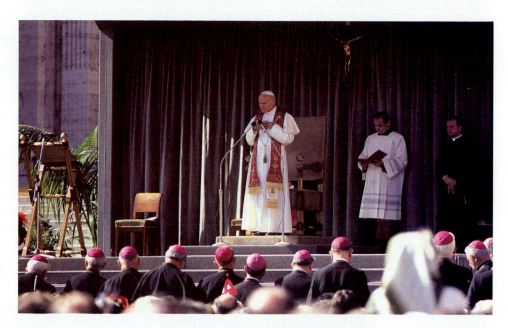

**AN ORGANIZATION WITH A LONG HISTORY.** The Roman Catholic church is an organization with a formal structure and hierarchy that existed long before the term "management" came into common usage.

Although these rules were meant to guide military strategy, they have been used when planning a strategy to engage business competitors. Keep Sun Tzu in mind as you study the chapter about strategy and planning.

Although neither Machiavelli nor Sun Tzu was trying to develop a theory of management per se, their insights teach us an important lesson about history. Management is not something that originated in the United States in this century. We must be careful not to put on historical and cultural blinders when, from the perspective of this particular time and place, we think about the management of organizations. ▬

Before going on to our discussion of the major management theories, let's take a moment to look at the reasons studying management theory will help you understand management and today's complex organizations.

## **W**HY STUDY MANAGEMENT THEORY?

**theory:**
Coherent group of assumptions put forth to explain the relationship between two or more observable facts and to provide a sound basis for predicting future events.

**T**heories are perspectives with which people make sense of their world experiences. Formally, a **theory** is a coherent group of assumptions put forth to explain the relationship between two or more observable facts. John Clancy calls such perspectives "invisible powers" to emphasize several crucial uses of theories, the "unseen" ways in which we approach our world.[4]

First, theories provide a *stable focus* for understanding what we experience. A theory provides criteria for determining what is relevant. To Henry Ford, a large and compliant work force was one relevant factor as he theorized about his business. In other words, his theory of management included, among other things, this assumption about the supply of labor.

Second, theories enable us to *communicate efficiently* and thus move into more and more complex relationships with other people. Imagine the frustration you would encounter if, in dealing with other people, you always had to define even the most basic assumptions you make about the world in which you live! Because Ford and his managers fully understood Ford's theory about manufacturing automobiles, they could interact easily as they faced day-to-day challenges.

Third, theories make it possible—indeed, challenge us—to *keep learning* about our world. By definition, theories have boundaries; there is only so much that can be covered by any one theory. Once we are aware of this, we are better able to ask ourselves if there are alternative ways of looking at the world (especially when our theories no longer seem to "fit" our experience) and to consider the consequences of adopting alternative beliefs. Two cases are instructive.

One example involves world politics. For years, what might be called a theory of the Cold War dominated diplomatic activity between the United States and the Soviet Union. During those years, most diplomats and military officials did not consider what the world would be like if the Cold War ended. Now, however, the "Cold War" theory no longer fits our experience, and government and military officials, as well as managers of other organizations, are scrambling to develop new theories for dealing with former enemies on a more cooperative basis.[5] For example, the breakup of the Soviet Union and Russia's struggles toward financial stability have left some of the world's top scientists unemployed, struggling with poor equipment, and willing to work for little pay. In this breach U.S. firms such as Corning, American Telephone and Telegraph, and United Technologies have capitalized on the opportunity this presents by funding research facilities in Russia.[6]

The other case takes us back to Henry Ford. Ford has been criticized for not using his approach as a way to learn about better ways to run his company. While Ford was giving his customers no choice about anything other than price (which *was* attractive!) Alfred Sloan was transforming General Motors. Beginning in the 1920s, Sloan rejected part of Ford's theory about running a business in favor of alternative ways to design automobiles and organize manufacturing and distribution.[7] GM's marketing strategy had always been to market nationwide with cars of interest to different segments of the public. Sloan set up separate divisions, with central direction from headquarters, to market the Buick, Oldsmobile, Pontiac, Cadillac, and Chevrolet lines. In contrast to Ford, each type of car has its own distinction and price differential.[8]

In this chapter, we will focus on four well-established schools of management thought.[9] the *scientific management school,* the *classical organization theory school,* the *behavioral school,* and the *management science school.* Although these schools, or theoretical approaches, developed in historical sequence, later ideas have not *replaced* earlier ones. Instead, each new school has tended to complement or coexist with previous ones. At the same time, each school has continued to evolve, and some have even merged with others.[10] This takes us to three recent integrative approaches: the *systems approach,* the *contingency approach,* and what we call the *dynamic engagement approach* to management. Figure 2-1 shows the approximate date when each of these theoretical perspectives emerged, as well as key historical events that signaled the emergence of each way of thinking about organizations and management.

## THE EVOLUTION OF MANAGEMENT THEORY

Management and organizations are products of their historical and social times and places. Thus, we can understand the evolution of management theory in terms of how people have wrestled with matters of *relationships* at particular *times* in history. One of the central lessons of this chapter, and of this book as a whole, is that we can learn from the trials and tribulations of those who have preceded us in steering the fortunes of formal organizations. As you study management theory you will learn that although the *particular* concerns of Henry Ford and Alfred Sloan are very different from those facing managers in the mid-1990s, we can still

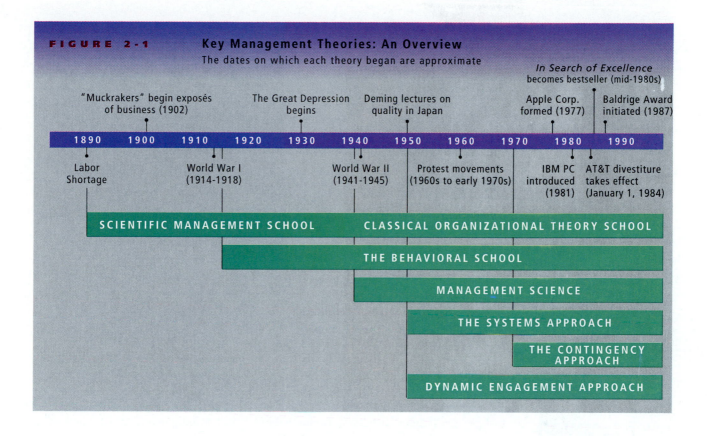

**FIGURE 2-1    Key Management Theories: An Overview**
The dates on which each theory began are approximate

*In Search of Excellence* becomes bestseller (mid-1980s)

"Muckrakers" begin exposés of business (1902)

The Great Depression begins

Deming lectures on quality in Japan

Apple Corp. formed (1977)

Baldrige Award initiated (1987)

| 1890 | 1900 | 1910 | 1920 | 1930 | 1940 | 1950 | 1960 | 1970 | 1980 | 1990 |

Labor Shortage

World War I (1914-1918)

World War II (1941-1945)

Protest movements (1960s to early 1970s)

IBM PC introduced (1981)

AT&T divestiture takes effect (January 1, 1984)

SCIENTIFIC MANAGEMENT SCHOOL

CLASSICAL ORGANIZATIONAL THEORY SCHOOL

THE BEHAVIORAL SCHOOL

MANAGEMENT SCIENCE

THE SYSTEMS APPROACH

THE CONTINGENCY APPROACH

DYNAMIC ENGAGEMENT APPROACH

see ourselves continuing the traditions that these individuals began long before our time. By keeping in mind a framework of relationships and time, we can put ourselves in their shoes as students of management.

Imagine that you are a manager at an American steel mill, textile factory, or one of Ford's plants in the early twentieth century. Your factory employs thousands of workers. This is a scale of enterprise unprecedented in Western history. Many of your employees were raised in agricultural communities. Industrial routines are new to them. Many of your employees, as well, are immigrants from other lands. They do not speak English well, if at all. As a manager under these  circumstances, you will probably be very curious about how you can develop working relationships with these people. Your managerial effectiveness depends on how well you understand what it is that is important to these people. Current-day challenges parallel some of those faced in the early twentieth century. In the 1980s 8.7 million foreign nationals entered the U.S. and joined the labor market. They often have distinct needs for skills and language proficiency, much as those before them at the advent of the industrial age.[11]

Early management theory consisted of numerous attempts at getting to know these newcomers to industrial life at the end of the nineteenth century and beginning of the twentieth century in Europe and the United States. In this section, we will survey a number of the better-known approaches to early management theory. These include scientific management, classical organization theory, the behavioral school, and management science. As you study these approaches, keep one important fact in mind: the managers and theorists who developed these assumptions about human relationships were doing so with little precedent. Large-scale industrial enterprise was very new. Some of the assumptions that they made might therefore seem simple or unimportant to you, but they were crucial to Ford and his contemporaries.

# THE SCIENTIFIC MANAGEMENT SCHOOL

**scientific management theory:**
A management approach, formulated by Frederick W. Taylor and others between 1890 and 1930, that sought to determine scientifically the best methods for performing any task, and for selecting, training, and motivating workers.

Scientific Management theory arose in part from the need to increase productivity. In the United States especially, skilled labor was in short supply at the beginning of the twentieth century. The only way to expand productivity was to raise the efficiency of workers. Therefore, Frederick W. Taylor, Henry L. Gantt, and Frank and Lillian Gilbreth devised the body of principles known as **scientific management theory**.

## FREDERICK W. TAYLOR

Frederick W. Taylor (1856-1915) rested his philosophy on four basic principles:[12]

1. *The development of a true science of management,* so that the best method for performing each task could be determined.
2. *The scientific selection of workers,* so that each worker would be given responsibility for the task for which he or she was best suited.
3. *The scientific education and development of the worker.*
4. *Intimate, friendly cooperation between management and labor.*

Taylor contended that the success of these principles required "a complete mental revolution" on the part of management and labor. Rather than quarrel over profits, both sides should try to increase production; by so doing, he believed, profits would rise to such an extent that labor and management would no longer have to fight over them. In short, Taylor believed that management and labor had a common interest in increasing productivity.

Taylor based his management system on production-line time studies. Instead of relying on traditional work methods, he analyzed and timed steel workers' movements on a series of jobs. Using time study as his base, he broke each job down into its components and designed the quickest and best methods of performing each component. In this way he established how much workers should be able to do with the equipment and materials at hand. He also encouraged employers to pay more productive workers at a higher rate than others, using a "scientifically correct" rate that would benefit both company and worker. Thus, workers were urged to surpass their previous performance standards to earn more pay. Taylor called his plan the **differential rate system.**

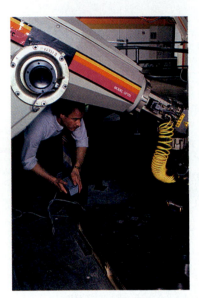

**A SCIENTIFIC MANAGEMENT LEGACY.** A General Electric engineer uses a teaching box to train an industrial robot to perform tasks that have been analyzed using motion studies.

**differential rate system:**
Frederick W. Taylor's compensation system involving the payment of higher wages to more efficient workers.

## CONTRIBUTIONS OF SCIENTIFIC MANAGEMENT THEORY

The modern assembly line pours out finished products faster than Taylor could ever have imagined. This production "miracle" is just one legacy of scientific management. In addition, its efficiency techniques have been applied to many tasks in non-industrial organizations, ranging from fast-food service to the training of surgeons.[13]

## LIMITATIONS OF SCIENTIFIC MANAGEMENT THEORY

Although Taylor's methods led to dramatic increases in productivity and to higher pay in a number of instances, workers and unions began to oppose his approach because they feared that working harder or faster would exhaust whatever work was available, causing layoffs.

Moreover, Taylor's system clearly meant that time was of the essence. His critics objected to the "speed up" conditions that placed undue pressures on employees to perform at faster and faster levels. The emphasis on *productivity*—and, by extension, *profitability*—led some managers to exploit both workers and customers. As a result, more workers joined unions and thus reinforced a pattern of suspicion and mistrust that shaded labor-management relations for decades.

### HENRY L. GANTT

Henry L. Gantt (1861-1919) worked with Taylor on several projects. But when he went out on his own as a consulting industrial engineer, Gantt began to reconsider Taylor's incentive system.

Abandoning the differential rate system as having too little motivational impact, Gantt came up with a new idea. Every worker who finished a day's assigned work load would win a 50-cent bonus. Then he added a second motivation. The *supervisor* would earn a bonus for each worker who reached the daily standard, plus an extra bonus if all the workers reached it. This, Gantt reasoned, would spur supervisors to train their workers to do a better job.

Every worker's progress was rated publicly and recorded on individual bar charts—in black on days the worker made the standard, in red when he or she fell below it. Going beyond this, Gantt originated a charting system for production 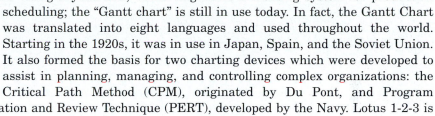 scheduling; the "Gantt chart" is still in use today. In fact, the Gantt Chart was translated into eight languages and used throughout the world. Starting in the 1920s, it was in use in Japan, Spain, and the Soviet Union. It also formed the basis for two charting devices which were developed to assist in planning, managing, and controlling complex organizations: the Critical Path Method (CPM), originated by Du Pont, and Program Evaluation and Review Technique (PERT), developed by the Navy. Lotus 1-2-3 is also a creative application of the Gantt Chart.[14]

### THE GILBRETHS

Frank B. and Lillian M. Gilbreth (1868-1924 and 1878-1972) made their contribution to the scientific management movement as a husband-and-wife team. Lillian and Frank collaborated on fatigue and motion studies and focused on ways of promoting the individual worker's welfare. To them, the ultimate aim of scientific management was to help workers reach their full potential as human beings.

In their conception, motion and fatigue were intertwined—every motion that was eliminated reduced fatigue. Using motion picture cameras, they tried to find the most economical motions for each task in order to upgrade performance and reduce fatigue. The Gilbreths argued that motion study would raise worker morale because of its obvious physical benefits and because it demonstrated management's concern for the worker.

# CLASSICAL ORGANIZATION THEORY SCHOOL

**classical organization theory:**

An early attempt, pioneered by Henri Fayol, to identify the principles and skills that underlie effective management.

Scientific management was concerned with increasing the productivity of the shop and the individual worker. **Classical organization theory** grew out of the need to find guidelines for managing such complex organizations as factories.

### HENRI FAYOL

Henri Fayol (1841-1925) is generally hailed as the founder of the classical management school—not because he was the first to investigate managerial behavior, but because he was the first to systematize it. Fayol believed that sound manage-

**EXHIBIT 2-1**   **Fayol's 14 Principles of Management**

1. *Division of Labor.* The most people specialize, the more efficiently they can perform their work. This principle is epitomized by the modern assembly line.

2. *Authority.* Managers must give orders so that they can get things done. While their *formal* authority gives them the right to command, managers will not always compel obedience unless they have *personal* authority (such as relevant expertise) as well.

3. *Discipline.* Members in an organization need to respect the rules and agreements that govern the organization. To Fayol, discipline results from good leadership at all levels of the organization, fair agreements (such as provisions for rewarding superior performance), and judiciously enforced penalties for infractions.

4. *Unity of Command.* Each employee must receive instructions from only one person. Fayol believed that when an employee reported to more than one manager, conflicts in instructions and confusion of authority would result.

5. *Unity of Direction.* Those operations within the organization that have the same objective should be directed by only one manager using one plan. For example, the personnel department in a company should not have two directors, each with a different hiring policy.

6. *Subordination of Individual Interest to the Common Good.* In any undertaking, the interests of employees should not take precedence over the interests of the organization as a whole.

7. *Remuneration.* Compensation for work done should be fair to both employees and employers.

8. *Centralization.* Decreasing the role of subordinates in decision making is centralization; increasing their role is decentralization. Fayol believed that managers should retain final responsibility, but should at the same time give their subordinates enough authority to do their jobs properly. The problem is to find the proper degree of centralization in each case.

9. *The Hierarchy.* The line of authority in an organization—often represented today by the neat boxes and lines of the organization chart—runs in order of rank from top management to the lowest level of the enterprise.

10. *Order.* Materials and people should be in the right place at the right time. People, in particular, should be in the jobs or positions they are most suited to.

11. *Equity.* Managers should be both friendly and fair to their subordinates.

12. *Stability of Staff.* A high employee turnover rate undermines the efficient functioning of an organization.

13. *Initiative.* Subordinates should be given the freedom to conceive and carry out their plans, even though some mistakes may result.

14. *Esprit de Corps.* Promoting team spirit will give the organization a sense of unity. To Fayol, even small factors should help to develop the spirit. He suggested, for example, the use of verbal communication instead of formal, written communication whenever possible.

*Source:* Henri Fayol *Industrial and General Administration*, J.A. Coubrough, trans. (Geneva: International Management Institute, 1930).

ment practice falls into certain patterns that can be identified and analyzed. From this basic insight, he drew up a blueprint for a cohesive doctrine of management, one that retains much of its force to this day.

With his faith in scientific methods, Fayol was like Taylor, his contemporary. While Taylor was basically concerned with *organizational functions*, however,

**A SUCCESSFUL BUREAUCRACY.** United Parcel Service (UPS) is a bureaucratic organization marked by a clear division of labor, a fixed hierachy of authority, and clearly defined regulations. Automation, computerization, and scientific management principles add to its efficiency.

Fayol was interested in the *total organization* and focused on management, which he felt had been the most neglected of business operations. Exhibit 2-1 lists the 14 principles of management Fayol "most frequently had to apply."[15] Before Fayol, it was generally believed that "managers are born, not made." Fayol insisted, however, that management was a skill like any other—one that could be taught once its underlying principles were understood.

## MAX WEBER

**bureaucracy:**
Organization with a legalized formal and hierarchical structure; also refers to the formal structural process within an organization.

Reasoning that any goal-oriented organization consisting of thousands of individuals would require the carefully controlled regulation of its activities, the German sociologist Max Weber (1864-1920) developed a theory of bureaucratic management that stressed the need for a strictly defined hierarchy governed by clearly defined regulations and lines of authority.[16] He considered the ideal organization to be a **bureaucracy** whose activities and objectives were rationally thought out and whose divisions of labor were explicitly spelled out. Weber also believed that technical competence should be emphasized and that performance evaluations should be made entirely on the basis of merit.

Today we often think of bureaucracies as vast, impersonal organizations that put impersonal efficiency ahead of human needs. We should be careful, though, not to apply our negative connotations of the word *bureaucracy* to the term as Weber used it. Like the scientific management theorists, Weber sought to improve the performance of socially important organizations by making their operations predictable and productive. Although we now value innovation and flexibility as much as efficiency and predictability, Weber's model of bureaucratic management clearly advanced the formation of huge corporations such as Ford. Bureaucracy was a particular pattern of relationships for which Weber saw great promise.

Although bureaucracy has been successful for many companies, in the competitive global market of the 1990s organizations such as General Electric and Xerox have become "bureaucracy busters," throwing away the organization chart and replacing it with ever-changing constellations of teams, projects, and alliances with the goal of unleashing employee creativity.[17]

## MARY PARKER FOLLETT

Mary Parker Follett (1868-1933) was among those who built on the basic framework of the classical school. However, she introduced many new elements, especially in the area of human relations and organizational structure. In this, she initiated trends that would be further developed by the emerging behavioral and management science schools.

Follett was convinced that no one could become a whole person except as a member of a group; human beings grew through their relationships with others in organizations. In fact, she called management "the art of getting things done through people."[18] She took for granted Taylor's assertion that labor and management shared a common purpose as members of the same organization, but she believed that the artificial distinction between managers (order givers) and subordinates (order takers) obscured this natural partnership. She was a great believer in the power of the group, where individuals could combine their diverse talents into something bigger. Moreover, Follett's "holistic" model of control took into account not just individuals and groups, but the effects of such environmental factors as politics, economics, and biology.

Follett's model was an important forerunner of the idea that management meant more than just what was happening inside a particular organization. By explicitly adding the organizational environment to her theory, Follett paved the way for management theory to include a broader set of relationships, some inside the organization and some across the organization's borders. A diverse set of modern management theories pays homage to Follett on this point.

## RELATIONSHIPS AND QUALITY AT HOME DEPOT

Home Depot, America's largest home-improvement retailer, practices much of what Follett had in mind. Before Home Depot opens a new store, all employees receive about four weeks of training. To maintain contact and to reinforce information about the company, the retailer holds quarterly Sunday morning meetings for its 23,000 employees using satellite TV hook-ups in each store. The sessions are know as "Breakfast with Bernie and Arthur" (the founders of Home Depot). The telecast is interactive, allowing for exchange of information and permitting employees to phone the company's top executives to ask questions. Home Depot also has an in-house TV station that produces programs designed to teach the Home Depot "service spirit" to new store employees.

Home Depot also educates customers. Stores offer clinics, taught by staff or by supplier representatives, on how to do a variety of home improvement projects. Home Depot also strives to make improvements based on customer experiences and suggestions. For instance, when contractors requested a special checkout area near the lumber racks, Home Depot complied, finding that the change speeded "front-of-store" check out. The team spirit, sharing of information, and quality customer service that define Home Depot has made it the dominant power in the $115 billion home improvement industry. In 1993, among 404 major corporations in the U.S., Home Depot was ranked as the second most admired company.[19] ▪

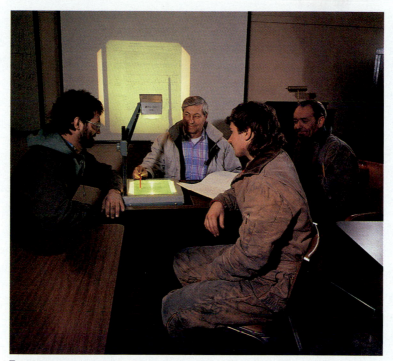

**THE IMPORTANCE OF THE GROUP.** Follett was ahead of her time in recognizing the power that comes from combining diverse talents in a group such as this team from Globe Metallurgical, a 1988 winner of the Baldrige award.

## CHESTER I. BARNARD

Chester Barnard (1886-1961), like Follett, introduced elements to classical theory that would be further developed in later schools. Barnard, who became president of New Jersey Bell in 1927, used his work experience and his extensive readings in sociology and philosophy to formulate theories about organizations. According to Barnard, people come together in formal organizations to achieve ends they cannot accomplish working alone. But as they pursue the organization's goals, they must also satisfy their individual needs. And so Barnard arrived at his central thesis: An enterprise can operate efficiently and survive only when the organization's goals are kept in balance with the aims and needs of the individuals working for it. What Barnard was doing was specifying a principle by which people can work in stable and mutually beneficial relationships over time.

For example, to meet their personal goals within the confines of the formal organization, people come together in informal groups such as cliques. To ensure its survival, the firm must use these informal groups effectively, even if they sometimes work at purposes that run counter to management's objectives. Barnard's recognition of the importance and universality of this "informal organization" was a major contribution to management thought.

Barnard believed that individual and organizational purposes could be kept in balance if managers understood an employee's **zone of indifference**—that is, what the employee would do without questioning the manager's authority. Obviously, the more activities that fell within an employee's zone of indifference (what the employee would accept), the smoother and more cooperative an organization would be. Barnard also believed that executives had a duty to instill a sense of moral purpose in their employees. To do this, they would have to learn to think beyond their narrow self-interest and make an ethical commitment to society. Although Barnard stressed the work of *executive* managers, he also focused considerable attention on the role of the individual worker as "the basic strategic factor in organization." When he went further to emphasize the organization as the cooperative enterprise of individuals working together as *groups,* he set the stage for the development of a great deal of current management thinking.[20]

**zone of indifference (area of acceptance):**

According to Barnard and Simon, respectively, inclinations conditioning individuals to accept orders that fall within a familiar range of responsibility or activity.

# EFFICIENCY AND THE FACTORY

[Taking the advice of efficiency expert Walter Flanders in 1908,] Ford bought grounds in Highland Park, where he intended to employ the most modern ideas about production, particularly those of Frederick Winslow Taylor. Those would bring, as Taylor had prophe-

sied, an absolute rationality to the industrial process. The idea was to break each function down into much smaller units so that each could be mechanized and speeded up and eventually flow into a straight-line production of little pieces becoming steadily larger. The process began to change in the spring of 1913. The first piece on the modern assembly line was the magneto coil assembly. In the past, a worker—and he had to be a skilled worker—had made a flywheel magneto from start to finish. A good employee could make 34 or 40 a day. Now, however, there was an assembly line for magnetos, divided into 29 different operations performed by 29 different men. In the old system it took 20 minutes to make a magneto; now it took 13.

Ford and his men soon moved to bring the same rationality to the rest of the factory. Quickly, they imposed a comparable system for the assembly of motors and transmissions. Then, in the summer of 1913, they took on the final assembly, which, as the rest of the process had speeded up, had become the great bottleneck. The workers [now maneuvered] as quickly as they could around a stationary metal object, the car they were putting together. If the men could remain stationary as the semifinished car moved up the line through them, less of the workers' time—Ford's time—would be wasted.

Charles Sorensen, who had become one of Ford's top production people, [initiated the assembly line by pulling] a Model T chassis slowly by a windlass across 250 feet of factory floor, timing the process all the while. Behind him walked six workers, picking up parts from carefully spaced piles on the floor and fitting them to the chassis...[Soon,] the breakthroughs came even more rapidly...[By installing an automatic conveyor belt,] Ford could eventually assemble a car in [93 minutes].... Just a few years before, in the days of stationary chassis assembly, the best record for putting a car together had been 728 hours of one man's work. Ford's top executives celebrated their victory with a dinner at Detroit's Pontchartrain Hotel. Fittingly, they rigged a simple conveyor belt to a five-horsepower engine with a bicycle chain and used the conveyor to serve the food around the table. It typified the spirit, camaraderie, and confidence of the early days.

Nineteen years and more than fifteen million cars later, when Ford reluctantly came to the conclusion that he had to stop making the T, the company balance was $673 million. And this was not merely a company's success; it was the beginning of a social revolution. Ford himself [believed] he had achieved a breakthrough for the common man. "Mass production," he wrote later, "precedes mass consumption, and makes it possible by reducing costs and thus permitting both greater use-convenience and price-convenience."

[Not surprisingly,] the price of the Model T continued to come down, from $780 in the fiscal year 1910-11 to $690 the following year, then to $600, to $550, and, on the eve of World War I, to $360. At that price, Ford sold 730,041 cars, outproducing everyone else in the world....

Henry Ford, immigrant's son and one-time machinist's apprentice, had indeed become a very rich man. Obviously, he had become so by being a venturesome and successful theorist of industrial management. But both his practices and his personality drew fire from those who were critical of his implicit attitude toward those "masses" for whom he had originally perfected and prized the Model T. For example, his widely publicized doubling of wages for employees in 1914 was seen by some as a trailblazing maneuver in management-labor relations, by others as a scheme to solidify Ford's paternalistic power over those who depended upon him for a living. In addition, Ford stubbornly resisted the unionization of his employees long after his major competitors had made agreements with union organizations. Repression on the part of company police against union "agitators" was common on the company's grounds until, finally, having lost an election conducted by the National Labor Relations Board [a government agency established in 1935 to affirm labor's right to bargain collectively], Ford contracted with the United Auto Workers in 1941. →

**INFORMAL GROUPS EXIST IN EVERY ORGANIZATION.** In identifying the "informal organization," Barnard promoted the effectiveness of recognizing and using informal workplace groups such as this one.

For example, companies are increasingly using teams. In fact, some advocate using teams as the building blocks of the organization. Because teams are generally self-managing, supervisory roles are limited. Management provides direction by giving each team a common purpose and holds the teams accountable for measurable performance goals. Companies such as Motorola, DuPont, AT&T, and General Electric are moving in this direction.[21] We will discuss teams more fully in Chapter 18.

# THE BEHAVIORAL SCHOOL: THE ORGANIZATION IS PEOPLE

**behavioral school:**

A group of management scholars trained in sociology, psychology, and related fields, who use their diverse knowledge to propose more effective ways to manage people in organizations.

The **behavioral school** emerged partly because the classical approach did not achieve sufficient production efficiency and workplace harmony. To managers' frustration, people did not always follow predicted or expected patterns of behavior. Thus there was increased interest in helping managers deal more effectively with the "people side" of their organizations. Several theorists tried to strengthen classical organization theory with the insights of sociology and psychology.

## THE HUMAN RELATIONS MOVEMENT

**human relations:**

How managers interact with other employees or recruits.

**Human relations** is frequently used as a general term to describe the ways in which managers interact with their employees. When "employee management" stimulates more and better work, the organization has effective human relations; when morale and efficiency deteriorate, its human relations are said to be ineffective. The human relations movement arose from early attempts to systematically discover the social and psychological factors that would create effective human relations.

**THE HAWTHORNE EXPERIMENTS.** The human relations movement grew out of a famous series of studies conducted at the Western Electric Company from 1924 to 1933. These eventually became known as the "Hawthorne Studies" because many of them were performed at Western Electric's Hawthorne plant near Chicago. The Hawthorne Studies began as an attempt to investigate the relationship between the level of lighting in the workplace and worker productivity—the type of question Frederick Taylor and his colleagues might well have addressed.

In some of the early studies, the Western Electric researchers divided the employees into test groups, who were subjected to deliberate changes in lighting, and control groups, whose lighting remained constant throughout the experiments. The results of the experiments were ambiguous. When the test group's lighting was improved, productivity tended to increase, although erratically. But when lighting conditions were made worse, there was also a tendency for productivity to increase in the test group. To compound the mystery, the control group's output also rose over the course of the studies, even though it experienced no changes in illumination. Obviously, something besides lighting was influencing the workers' performance.

In a new set of experiments, a small group of workers was placed in a separate room and a number of variables were altered: Wages were increased; rest periods of varying length were introduced; the workday and work week were shortened. The researchers, who now acted as supervisors, also allowed the groups to choose their own rest periods and to have a say in other suggested changes. Again, the results were ambiguous. Performance tended to increase over time, but it also rose and fell erratically. Partway through this set of experiments, Elton Mayo (1880-1949) and some associates from Harvard, including Fritz J. Roethlisberger and William J. Dickson, became involved.

In these and subsequent experiments, Mayo and his associates decided that a complex chain of attitudes had touched off the productivity increases. Because they had been singled out for special attention, both the test and the control groups had developed a group pride that motivated them to improve their work performance. Sympathetic supervision had further reinforced their motivation. The researchers concluded that employees would work harder if they believed management was concerned about their welfare and supervisors paid special attention to them. This phenomenon was subsequently labeled the **Hawthorne effect.** Since the control group received no special supervisory treatment or enhancement of working conditions but still improved its performance, some people (including Mayo himself) speculated that the control group's productivity gains resulted from the special attention of the researchers themselves.

The researchers also concluded that informal work groups—the social environment of employees—have a positive influence on productivity. Many of Western Electric's employees found their work dull and meaningless, but their associations and friendships with co-workers, sometimes influenced by a shared antagonism toward the "bosses," imparted some meaning to their working lives and provided some protection from management. For these reasons, group pressure was frequently a stronger influence on worker productivity than management demands.

To Mayo, then, the concept of "social man"—motivated by social needs, wanting rewarding on-the-job relationships, and responding more to work-group pressures than to management control—was necessary to complement the old concept of "rational man" motivated by personal economic needs.[22] All these findings might seem unremarkable today. But compare what Mayo and his associates considered relevant with what Ford and Weber found relevant, and you see what a change these ideas brought to management theory.

**Hawthorne effect:**

The possibility that workers who receive special attention will perform better simply because they received that attention: one interpretation of studies by Elton Mayo and his colleagues.

## APPLYING QUALITY CONCEPTS TO HUMAN RELATIONS THEORIES

The application of these human relations theories can be seen in today's competitive environment. For example, with the restructuring of today's competitive global economy, many companies have made the decision to "downsize" or reduce the numbers of managers and workers. However, some companies, well aware of the dynamics pointed out by the Hawthorne studies, have approached employee reductions with great care. At Sky Chiefs, a $450 million airline in-flight services corporation, the problems experienced by the airlines industry such as price wars, brisk competition from foreign airlines, aging fleets, and the increasing cost of new planes, were directly affecting the company. Forced to reduce staff, management realized that if it managed the process poorly and didn't take into consideration the needs of employees, those who remained after the downsizing would be less loyal and cohesive as a group.

To minimize potential problems after the downsizing, the management adopted "total quality leadership" to provide the company with a framework for implementing the restructuring. It spent thousands of hours and dollars to fund training and improvement processes related to total quality leadership. The key to the success of the restructuring was that instead of management dictating what would happen and to whom, employees, seen as the backbone of the company, were empowered to facilitate the process. For example, prior to the restructuring process, employees participated in evaluating all headquarters functions. An employee-managed restructuring committee was selected by management to assemble, interpret, and evaluate the data. Then smaller action teams were created to address the downsizing. To help those who were to be let go, extensive counseling and outplacement services were provided, including group workshops on networking, interviewing techniques, and hiring, and employees were videotaped to help with future interviews.

Now, after the restructuring, productivity and operating profits are increasing. The remaining employees have accepted their new roles and responsibilities, and morale continues to improve.[23]

## FROM HUMAN RELATIONS TO THE BEHAVIORAL SCIENCE APPROACH

Mayo and his colleagues pioneered the use of the scientific method in their studies of people in the work environment. Later researchers, more rigorously trained in the social sciences (psychology, sociology, and anthropology), used more sophisticated research methods and became known as "behavioral scientists" rather than "human relations theorists."

The behavioral scientists brought two new dimensions to the study of management and organizations. First, they advanced an even more sophisticated view of human beings and their drives than did Mayo and his contemporaries. Abraham Maslow and Douglas McGregor, among others, wrote about "self-actualizing" people.[24] Their work spawned new thinking about how relationships can be beneficially arranged in organizations. They also determined that people wanted more than "instantaneous" pleasure or rewards. If people were this complex in the way they led their lives, then their organizational relationships needed to support that complexity.

Second, behavioral scientists applied the methods of scientific investigation to the study of how people behaved in organizations as whole entities. The classic example is the work of James March and Herbert Simon in the late 1950s.[25] March and Simon developed hundreds of propositions for scientific investigation, about patterns of behavior, particularly with regard to communication, in organizations. Their influence in the development of subsequent management theory has been significant and ongoing.

According to Maslow, the needs that people are motivated to satisfy fall into a hierarchy. Physical and safety needs are at the bottom of the hierarchy, and at the top are ego needs (the need for respect, for example) and self-actualizing needs (such as the need for meaning and personal growth). In general, Maslow said, lower-level needs must be satisfied before higher-level needs can be met. Since many lower-level needs are routinely satisfied in contemporary society, most people are motivated more by the higher-level ego and self-actualizing needs.

Some later behavioral scientists feel that even this model cannot explain all the factors that may motivate people in the workplace. They argue that not everyone goes predictably from one level of need to the next. For some people, work is only a means for meeting lower-level needs. Others are satisfied with nothing less than the fulfillment of their highest-level needs; they may even choose to work in jobs that threaten their safety if by doing so they can attain uniquely personal goals. The more realistic model of human motivation, these behavioral scientists argue, is "complex person." Using this model, the effective manager is aware that no two people are exactly alike and tailors motivational approaches according to individual needs.

**theory X:**
According to McGregor, a traditional view of motivation that holds that work is distasteful to employees, who must be motivated by force, money, or praise.

**theory Y:**
According to McGregor, the assumption that people are inherently motivated to work and do a good job.

As American corporations increasingly do business with other cultures, it is important to remember that theories can be culturally bounded. For example, Maslow's hierarchy of needs is not a description of a universal motivational process. In other nations the order of the hierarchy might be quite different depending on the values of the country. In Sweden, quality of life is ranked most important, while in Japan and Germany, security is ranked highest.[26]

McGregor provided another angle on this "complex person" idea. He distinguished two alternative basic assumptions about people and their approach to work. These two assumptions, which he called **Theory X** and **Theory Y,** take opposite views of people's commitment to work in organizations. Theory X managers, McGregor proposed, assume that people must be constantly coaxed into putting forth effort in their jobs. Theory Y managers, on the other hand, assume that people relish work and eagerly approach their work as an opportunity to develop their creative capacities. Theory Y was an example of a "complex person" perspective. Theory Y management, McGregor claimed, was stymied by the prevalence of Theory X practices in the organizations of the 1950s. As you are already able to see, the roots of Theory X can be traced to the days of scientific management and the factories based on these principles. In accordance with McGregor's thinking, General Electric CEO Jack Welch argues that people must forget the old idea of "boss" and replace it with the idea that managers have the new duties of counseling groups, providing resources for them and helping people think for themselves. "We're going to win on our ideas," he says, "not by whips and chains."

**A THEORY Y ATTITUDE.** At Baldrige-Award-winning Westinghouse, employee Spencer Douglas says it best: "There's so much pride here and everybody here wants to do their very best.... They hate to work on a product and pass it on to the next person and find something that they've missed."

# THE MANAGEMENT SCIENCE SCHOOL

**A**t the beginning of World War II, Great Britain desperately needed to solve a number of new, complex problems in warfare. With their survival at stake, the British formed the first operational research (OR) teams. By pooling the expertise of mathematicians, physicists, and other scientists in OR teams, the British were able to achieve significant technological and tactical breakthroughs. When the

**operations research:**
Mathematical techniques for the modeling, analysis, and solution of management problems. Also called *management science*.

**management science school:**
Approaching management problems through the use of mathematical techniques for their modeling, analysis, and solution.

Americans entered the war, they formed what they called **operations research** teams, based on the successful British model, to solve similar problems. The teams used early computers to perform the thousands of calculations involved in mathematical modeling.

When the war was over, the applicability of operations research to problems in industry gradually became apparent. New industrial technologies were being put into use and transportation and communication were becoming more complicated. These developments brought with them a host of problems that could not be solved easily by conventional means. Increasingly, OR specialists were called on to help managers come up with answers to these new problems. Over the years, OR procedures were formalized into what is now more generally called the **management science school**.[27]

The management science school gained popularity through two postwar phenomena. First, the development of high-speed computers and of communications among computers provided the means for tackling complex and large-scale organizational problems. Second, Robert McNamara implemented a management science approach at Ford Motor Company in the 1950s and 1960s. (Later, he brought the same approach to his assignment as Secretary of Defense in the Johnson Administration.)[28] As McNamara's so-called "Whiz Kids" proteges moved to management positions at Ford and across American industry, the management science school flourished. If you find yourself working in an organization where "crunching the numbers" is the central way that management decisions are reached and justified, you can thank McNamara and his generation.

Today the management science approach to solving a problem begins when a mixed team of specialists from relevant disciplines is called in to analyze the problem and propose a course of action to management. The team constructs a mathematical model that shows, in symbolic terms, all relevant factors bearing on the problem and how they are interrelated. By changing the values of the variables in the model (such as increasing the cost of raw materials) and analyzing the different equations of the model with a computer, the team can determine the effects of each change. Eventually, the management science team presents management with an objective basis for making a decision.[29]

Management science offered a whole new way to think about time. With sophisticated mathematical models, and computers to crunch the numbers, forecasting the future based on the past and present became a popular activity. Managers can now play with the "what if the future looks like this?" questions that previous management theories could not handle. At the same time, the management science school pays less attention to relationships per se in organizations. Mathematical modeling tends to ignore relationships as data, emphasizing numerical data that can be relatively easily collected or estimated. The criticism is thus that management science promotes an emphasis on only the aspects of the organization that can be captured in numbers, missing the importance of people and relationships.

# RECENT DEVELOPMENTS IN MANAGEMENT THEORY

Theories are powerful influences. The longer we use a given theory, the more comfortable we become with it and the more we tend to not seek out alternative theories unless events force us to change. This helps explain why "modern" management theory is really a rich mosaic of many theories that have endured over at least the past century. One benefit of understanding this concurrent popularity of many points of view about organizations is that it prepares you for your own organizational experiences. If this chapter has not already brought to mind different managerial styles to which you have been exposed, it will prepare you for the day when, for example, you work for a "management science" manager who in turn works for a manager who practices by one of the theories to follow in the next section! Or if you have already experienced such managers, it will help you understand their perspectives better.

While it is impossible to predict what future generations will be studying, at this point we can identify at least three additional perspectives on management theory that can grow in importance: the systems approach, the contingency approach, and what we call the dynamic engagement approach.

## THE SYSTEMS APPROACH

**systems approach:**
View of the organization as a unified, directed system of interrelated parts.

**R**ather than dealing separately with the various segments of an organization, the **systems approach** to management views the organization as a unified, purposeful system composed of interrelated parts. This approach gives managers a way of looking at the organization as a whole and as a part of the larger, external environment (see Chapter 3). Systems theory tells us that the activity of any segment of an organization affects, in varying degrees, the activity of every other segment.[30]

Production managers in a manufacturing plant, for example, prefer long uninterrupted production runs of standardized products in order to maintain maximum efficiency and low costs. Marketing managers, on the other hand, who want to offer customers quick delivery of a wide range of products, would like a flexible manufacturing schedule that can fill special orders on short notice. *Systems-oriented* production managers make scheduling decisions only after they have identified the impact of these decisions on other departments and on the entire organization. The point of the systems approach is that managers cannot function wholly within the confines of the traditional organization chart. They must mesh their department with the whole enterprise. To do that, they have to communicate

**SYNERGY AT CNN.** Organizational synergy is possible at CNN through a global network of correspondents and camera crews who feed reports to the Atlanta anchor desk.

not only with other employees and departments, but frequently with representatives of other organizations as well.[31] Clearly, systems managers grasp the importance of webs of business relationships to their efforts.

## SOME KEY CONCEPTS

Many of the concepts of general systems theory are finding their way into the language of management. Managers need to be familiar with the systems vocabulary so they can keep pace with current developments.

**subsystems:**

Those parts making up the whole system.

**SUBSYSTEMS.** The parts that make up the whole of a system are called **subsystems.** And each system in turn may be a subsystem of a still larger whole. Thus a department is a subsystem of a plant, which may be a subsystem of a company, which may be a subsystem of a conglomerate or an industry, which is a subsystem of the national economy, which is a subsystem of the world system.

**synergy:**

The situation in which the whole is greater than its parts. In organizational terms, synergy means that departments that interact cooperatively are more productive than they would be if they operated in isolation.

**SYNERGY.** Synergy means that the whole is greater than the sum of its parts. In organizational terms, **synergy** means that as separate departments within an organization cooperate and interact, they become more productive than if each were to act in isolation. For example, in a small firm, it is more efficient for each department to deal with one finance department than for each department to have a separate finance department of its own.

**open system:**

A system that interacts with its environment.

**closed system:**

A system that does not interact with its environment.

**OPEN AND CLOSED SYSTEMS.** A system is considered an **open system** if it interacts with its environment; it is considered a **closed system** if it does not. All organizations interact with their environment, but the extent to which they do so varies. An automobile plant, for example, is a far more open system than a monastery or a prison.

**system boundary:**

The boundary that separates each system from its environment. It is rigid in a closed system, flexible in an open system

**SYSTEM BOUNDARY.** Each system has a boundary that separates it from its environment. In a closed system, the **system boundary** is rigid; in an open system, the boundary is more flexible. The system boundaries of many organizations have become increasingly flexible in recent years. For example, managers at oil companies wishing to engage in offshore drilling now must consider public concern for the environment. A trend is that American communities are demanding more and more environmental responsibility from companies. For example, Santa Rosa, California, a city of 125,000, treats environmental violations such as "off-gassing" a waste product, that is, allowing it to evaporate into the atmosphere, as a potential criminal offense.[32]

**flows:**

Components such as information, material, and energy that enter and leave a system.

**FLOW.** A system has **flows** of information, materials, and energy (including human energy). These enter the system from the environment as *inputs* (raw materials, for example), undergo transformation processes within the system (operations that alter them), and exit the system as *outputs* (goods and services).

**feedback:**

The part of system control in which the results of actions are returned to the individual, allowing work procedures to be analyzed and corrected.

**FEEDBACK. Feedback** is the key to system controls. As operations of the system proceed, information is fed back to the appropriate people, and perhaps to a computer, so that the work can be assessed and, if necessary, corrected.[33] For example, when Aluminum Company of America began feeding production data back to the factory floor, workers in the Addy, Washington, magnesium plant quickly observed ways to improve operations, boosting productivity by 72 percent.[34] Figure 2-2 shows the flows of information, materials, energy, and feedback in an open system.

Systems theory calls attention to the dynamic and interrelated nature of organizations and the management task. Thus, it provides a framework within which

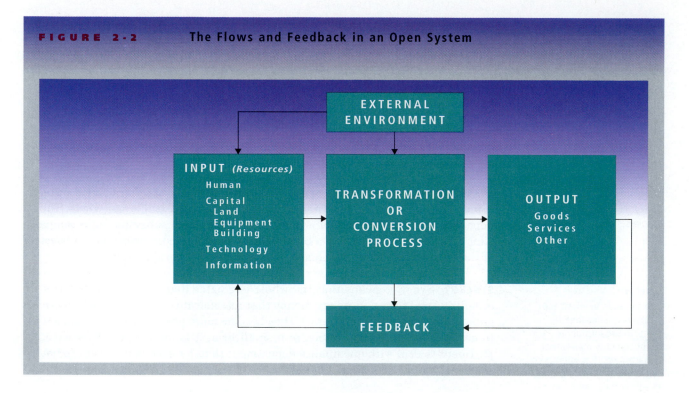

**FIGURE 2-2**    The Flows and Feedback in an Open System

we can plan actions and anticipate both immediate and far-reaching consequences, while allowing us to understand unanticipated consequences as they develop. With a systems perspective, general managers can more easily maintain a balance between the needs of the various parts of the enterprise and the needs and goals of the whole firm.

# THE CONTINGENCY APPROACH

The well-known international economist Charles Kindleberger was fond of telling his students at MIT that the answer to any really engrossing question in economics is: "It depends." The task of the economist, Kindleberger would continue, is to specify *upon what* it depends, and in what ways.

"It depends" is an appropriate response to the important questions in management as well. Management theory attempts to determine the predictable relationships between situations, actions, and outcomes. So it is not surprising that a recent approach seeks to integrate the various schools of management thought by focusing on the interdependence of the many factors involved in the managerial situation.

**contingency approach:**

The view that the management technique that best contributes to the attainment of organizational goals might vary in different types of situations or circumstances; also called the *situational approach*.

The **contingency approach** (sometimes called the *situational approach*) was developed by managers, consultants, and researchers who tried to apply the concepts of the major schools to real-life situations. When methods highly effective in one situation failed to work in other situations, they sought an explanation. Why, for example, did an organizational development program work brilliantly in one situation and fail miserably in another? Advocates of the contingency approach had a logical answer to all such questions: Results differ because situations differ; a technique that works in one case will not necessarily work in all cases.

According to the contingency approach, the manager's task is to identify which technique will, *in a particular situation, under particular circumstances, and at a particular time,* best contribute to the attainment of management goals. Where workers need to be encouraged to increase productivity, for example, the classical theorist may prescribe a new work-simplification scheme. The behavioral scientist may instead seek to create a psychologically motivating climate and recommend some approach like *job enrichment*—the combination of tasks that are different in scope and responsibility and allow the worker greater autonomy in making decisions. But the manager trained in the contingency approach will ask, "Which method will *work best here*?" If the workers are unskilled and training opportunities and resources are limited, work simplification would be the best solution. However, with skilled workers driven by pride in their abilities, a job-enrichment program might be more effective. The contingency approach represents an important turn in modern management theory, because it portrays each set of organizational relationships in its unique circumstances.

For example, when managers at Taco Bell addressed the question of what would work best for its restaurants, they redefined business based on the simple premise that customers value food, service, and the physical appearance of the restaurant. To implement the new customer-focused goals, the company recruited new managers who were committed to creating or delivering goods that customers value and who could coach and support staff in the new direction. To concentrate on customers, Taco Bell outsourced much of the assembly-line food preparation, such as shredding lettuce, allowing employees to focus on customers. As a result, it has enjoyed a 60 percent growth in sales at company-owned stores.[35] Other fast food restaurants might base their business on different situational factors, by the contingency view.

## ENTERING AN ERA OF DYNAMIC ENGAGEMENT

All of the preceding theories have come down to us in the late twentieth-century world of organizations and management. Here they are practiced against a backdrop of rapid change and profound rethinking about how management and organizations will evolve in the next century. At the heart of this rethinking, which is really occurring in numerous ways at the same time, are new ways of thinking about relationships and time.

As boundaries between cultures and nations are blurred and new communications technology makes it possible to think of the world as a "global village," the scope of international and intercultural relationships is rapidly expanding. The pace of organizational activity picks up dramatically. These trends indicate a heightened level of *intensity* in organizations and management today.

**dynamic engagement:**
The view that time and human relationships are forcing management to rethink traditional approaches in the face of constant, rapid change.

To emphasize the intensity of modern organizational relationships and the intensity of time pressures that govern these relationships, we call this flurry of new management theory the **dynamic engagement** approach. "Dynamic engagement" is our term. In times when theories are changing, it is often true that the last thing that happens is that someone assigns a name to the new theory. We use *dynamic engagement* to convey the mood of current thinking and debate about management and organizations. It is quite likely that twenty years from now, well into your organizational lives, you will look back and call this period of movement by some other name.

Dynamic—the opposite of static—implies continuous change, growth, and activity; engagement—the opposite of detachment—implies intense involvement with others. We therefore think the term *dynamic engagement* best expresses the vigorous way today's most successful managers focus on human relationships and quickly adjust to changing conditions over time.

Six different themes about management theory are emerging under the umbrella that we call dynamic engagement. To emphasize their importance to your understanding of management in the 1990s and beyond, and to highlight the differences between them, we devote a chapter in Part Two to each of them.

### NEW ORGANIZATIONAL ENVIRONMENTS (Chapter 3)

The dynamic engagement approach recognizes that an organization's environment is not some set of fixed, impersonal forces. Rather, it is a complex, dynamic web of people interacting with each other. As a result, managers must not only pay attention to their own concerns, but also understand what is important to other managers both within their organizations and at other organizations. They interact with these other managers to create jointly the conditions under which their organizations will prosper or struggle. The theory of competitive strategy, developed by Michael Porter, focuses on how managers can influence conditions in an industry when they interact as rivals, buyers, suppliers, and so on. Another variation on the dynamic engagement approach, most notably argued by Edward and Jean Gerner Stead in *Management for a Small Planet,* places ecological concerns at the center of management theory.

### ETHICS AND SOCIAL RESPONSIBILITY (Chapter 4)

Managers using a dynamic engagement approach pay close attention to the values that guide people in their organizations, the corporate culture that embodies those values, and the values held by people outside the organization. This idea came into prominence with the publication in 1982 of *In Search of Excellence* by Thomas Peters and Robert Waterman. From their study of "excellent" companies, Peters and Waterman concluded that "the top performers create a broad, uplifting, shared culture, a coherent framework within which charged-up people search for appropriate adaptations."[36]

Robert Solomon has taken this idea a step further, arguing that managers must exercise moral courage by placing the value of *excellence* at the top of their agendas. In dynamic engagement, it is not enough for managers to do things the way they always have, or to be content with matching their competitors. Continually striving toward excellence has become an organizational theme of the 1990s. Because values, including excellence, are ethical concepts, the dynamic engagement approach moves ethics from the fringe of management theory to the heart of it.

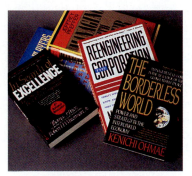

**CURRENT MANAGEMENT WRITING.** The dynamic engagement approach is evident in much of the current literature in the field of management.

### GLOBALIZATION AND MANAGEMENT (Chapter 5)

The dynamic engagement approach recognizes that the world is at the manager's doorstep in the 1990s. With world financial markets running 24 hours a day, and even the remotest corners of the planet only a telephone call away, managers facing the twenty-first century must think of themselves as global citizens. Kenichi Ohmae makes this point as he describes a "borderless" world where managers treat all customers as "equidistant" from their organizations.[37]

A simple comparison illustrates how things have changed. If you were to look through Alfred Sloan's autobiography about his long career as General Motors chairman through the 1940s, you would find very little about international factors—with good reason in that time and place. Today, however, if you tune into a CNN broadcast you will notice that the reporters do not use the word "foreign" at all. Or, consider the poster on the wall of Honda dealerships, which says the idea of an "American car" doesn't make any sense in an era when a single car contains parts made by people from all over the globe.

### INVENTING AND REINVENTING ORGANIZATIONS (Chapter 6)

Managers who practice dynamic engagement continually search for ways to unleash the creative potential of their employees and themselves. A growing chorus of theorists are urging managers to rethink the standard organization structures to which they have become accustomed. Peters is once again at the forefront. His concept of "liberation management" challenges the kinds of rigid organization structures that inhibit people's creativity. Peters' heroes succeed in spite of those structures.[38] Michael Hammer and James Champy have made their concept of **"reengineering** the corporation" into a bestseller. Hammer and Champy urge managers to rethink the very processes by which organizations function and to be courageous about replacing processes that get in the way of organizational efficiency.

**Reengineering**

This occurs when an organization conducts a significant reassessment of what it is all about.

### CULTURES AND MULTICULTURALISM (Chapter 7)

Managers who embrace the dynamic engagement approach recognize that the various perspectives and values that people of different cultural backgrounds bring to their organizations are not only a fact of life but a significant source of contributions.

Joanne Martin has pioneered the cultural analysis of organizations. She explains how differences create unprecedented challenges for modern managers. Charles Taylor is a prominent proponent of the so-called "communitarian" movement. Taylor claims that people can preserve their sense of uniqueness—their authenticity—only by valuing what they hold in common and seeking to extend what they hold in common in the organizations and communities in which they live. Cornel West grabs our attention to different cultures with the very title of his book, *Race Matters*. Martin, Taylor, and West all want us to see the benefits that come from welcoming and understanding differences among people. Still, none of them say that acceptance of different cultures will be easy. Multiculturalism is a moving target as more and more people become conscious of their particular cultural traditions and ties. Here is where both "dynamic" and "engagement" clearly come together as we envision the organizations of the twenty-first century.

### QUALITY (Chapter 8)

By the dynamic engagement approach, Total Quality Management (TQM) should be in every manager's vocabulary. All managers should be thinking about how every organizational process can be conducted to provide products and services that are responsible to tougher and tougher customer and competitive standards. Strong and lasting relationships can be fruitful byproducts of a "quality" frame of mind and action, by this view. Total Quality Management adds one more dynamic dimension to management, because quality, too, is always a moving target.

Dynamic engagement is an example of the changing face of management theory. Not everyone we have mentioned in this overview of the dynamic engagement approach calls himself or herself a management theorist. Some are philosophers and some are political scientists. As we bring this chapter to a close, we want to point out an important lesson in this lineup of dynamic engagement theorists. The dynamic engagement approach challenges us to see organizations and management as integral parts of modern global society. This was not always a tenet of management theory. Once the door is opened between organizations and the larger world, however, many new influences can come to bear on questions about management theory and relationships.

# REMEMBER TO CHANGE WITH THE TIMES

We have discovered two basic things in this chapter. First, theorists, whatever their fields of endeavor, tend to be people and products of their times. Second, management theories, like theories in all fields, tend to *evolve* to reflect everyday realities and changing circumstances. By the same token, managers must be sensitive to changing circumstances and equally willing to change. If they do not, they must be surpassed by more flexible competitors.

Both of these ideas apply to Henry Ford, the man who boldly embraced the ideas of scientific management, revolutionizing the auto industry and our society in the process.

Yet many of Ford's managerial practices were conservative or unresponsive to changing times, and his hold on the automotive market was eventually wrested from him by companies more farsighted in their managerial theories and practices. Hostile to the banking community, for example, Ford refused outside investments in his company throughout his lifetime, borrowing capital only when absolutely necessary and preferring to finance corporate activities solely through the company's own income. He was also inclined to ignore the dynamics of the industry that he had largely founded. Although he opened up branch factories to cater to a growing European market, he long failed to follow managerial advice to retool for both the hydraulic brake and six- or eight-cylinder engine; he also resisted management counsel regarding the advances in gearshift and transmission technology and even put off introducing color variety into his product line (Ford preferred his cars to be black). His disinterest in consumer demands for comfort and style ultimately cost him his industry's leadership, which passed to General Motors, a conglomerate assembled from over 20 diverse firms by founder William Durant and a second generation of American industrial organizers.

**MANAGEMENT 2000 AND BEYOND**

# A COMPANY OF BUSINESSPEOPLE

For most of the twentieth century, the terms that have been used for relationships between people in the workplace have been supervisor/worker, manager/employee, the company/the union or us/them. It was expected that owners and managers would run the company, and workers would follow directions. Because of the dynamic marketplace changes of the past 20 years, many people are questioning whether this old thinking still works. Part of the story can be told in the recent history of failed American businesses and others that are struggling mightily.

Meanwhile, a number of pathbreaking managers in both large and small companies are ignoring old ideas—as well as the latest innovations such as TQM. Instead, these managers are creating a wholly different mind-set about business and a different way of organizing work, one in which "us versus them" is a thing of the past. Whatever the differences—and there are many—the key lies not in a company of employees and managers but in "a company of businesspeople."

These new-generation companies are scattered across any number of industries. Examples include Wabash National, which makes truck trailers, to LifeUSA, which writes insurance, to Springfield Remanufacturing Corp., which rebuilds engines. Larger companies represented in this movement include Southwest Airlines and Wal-Mart. Some are tiny, such as 18-employee Jamestown Advanced Products, a metal parts maker. What they have in common is a way of doing business and a way of thinking about business that is dramatically different from others. The key component: a new conception of how people in a company work together. In the mind-set created by these next-generation companies, the traditional corporate pyramid goes out the window. Everyone is freed to think like an owner, and this attitude becomes a part of everyday life. At Wal-Mart, associates, all of them shareholders, get weekly and monthly data on their stores' performance, including detailed matters such as profit margins for each item and delivery times. At Chaparral, a steel company, compensation is tied to individual performance and company profits, and employees are encouraged to redesign jobs. At Southwest Airlines, financial information key to performance, such as revenue passenger miles and fuel usage, as well as the regular profit-and-loss statements, are circulated to all employees. Each of these companies has been honored for its quality and success many times.

To become competitive in an increasingly changing market, many current-day organizations might wish to look into this new organizational mind-set to prepare for the future which is, as never before, fast approaching.[39]

## SUMMARY

1. **Explain the setting in which management theory first developed.**

   Human beings have been making plans and pursuing goals through organizations, and accomplishing all kinds of feats, for thousands of years. Management theory, however, is generally considered a relatively recent phenomenon that emerged with the industrialization of Western Europe and the United States in the nineteenth century.

2. **Describe the ways in which a theory can be useful.**

   Management theory, like any social theory, provides a stable focus for people's experiences. It enables people to communicate efficiently about what they consider to be relevant aspects of management and organizations. And, because theories may not provide all the answers, they encourage us to keep learning.

3. **Distinguish the scientific management school, the classical organization theory school, the behavioral school, and the management science school of management theory.**

   Scientific management sought to determine scientifically the best methods for performing any task, and for selecting, training, and motivating workers. Classical organization theory grew out of the need to manage complex organizations and focused on management, attempting to identify the principles and skills that underlie effective management. The behavioral school grew out of attempts to understand better and manage workers, using insights from sociology and psychology. The management science school emerged as computers became available and involves the use of mathematical techniques for modeling, analyzing, and solving management problems.

4. **Understand the historical context in which the systems approach, contingency approach, and dynamic engagement approach to management theory have developed.**

These more integrative approaches are useful in thinking about management in today's fast-paced world, where change is a constant and relationships (inside and outside the organization) are more numerous and more complex than ever before. In this context, the systems approach gives managers a way of looking at the organization as a whole and as a part of the larger, external environment. The contingency approach focuses on the interdependence of the many factors involved in the management situation. And the dynamic engagement approach is an unfolding set of challenges to the way we think about management and organizations on the eve of the twenty-first century.

## REVIEW QUESTIONS

1. Why is the study of theory important?
2. What environmental factors influenced the development of these schools of management theory: scientific management, classical organization theory, behavioral, and management science?
3. How pertinent today is Taylor's assumption that management and labor had a common cause? Why?
4. Why did Follett believe that individual freedom and self-control should come through the activities of the group?
5. Which of Fayol's principles of management do you observe in use in organizations today?
6. What is the Hawthorne effect and why is it important to managers?
7. How does the management science school differ from the behavioral school of management?
8. Where in organizations do you see the management science school in use?
9. What is the major task of the manager according to the contingency approach?
10. What assumptions about the contemporary world set the dynamic engagement approach apart from the other management theories presented in this chapter?

## KEY TERMS

| | |
|---|---|
| Theory | Management science school |
| Scientific management theory | Systems approach |
| Differential rate system | Subsystems |
| Classical organization theory | Synergy |
| Bureaucracy | Open system |
| Zone of indifference | Closed system |
| Behavioral school | System boundary |
| Human relations | Flows |
| Hawthorne effect | Feedback |
| Theory X | Contingency approach |
| Theory Y | Dynamic engagement |
| Operations research | Reengineering |

# THEORY AND POLICY ENCOUNTER POWER AND MOTIVATION AT CONSOLIDATED AUTOMOBILE[40]

On Tuesday morning at 6:00 a.m., two young automobile assembly-line workers, disgruntled over failing to get their supervisor transferred, shut off the electric power supply to an auto-assembly line and closed it down at Consolidated Automobile Manufacturers, Inc.

The electric power supply area, containing transformers, switches, and other high-voltage electrical equipment, was positioned near the center of the plant in a 6-by-7 foot area. Enclosing this area was a 10-foot-high chain-link fence with a [protective cage] around the facility and provided a measure of security.

The two assembly-line workers, William Strong and Larry Kane, gained access to the electric power supply area by scaling the fence. Once inside, they halted the assembly line by opening the switches and cutting off the electrical power.

Strong and Kane, who worked as spot welders, had taken matters into their hands when the union's grievance procedure had not worked fast enough to satisfy them. Co-workers, idled by the dramatic protest and the motionless assembly line, grouped themselves around the fenced area, shouting encouragement to the two men inside. In response, Strong and Kane were chanting, "When you cut the power you've got the power." They were in the process of becoming folk heroes to their co-workers.

Sam Winfare, who supervised Strong and Kane and who was the target of their protest, had been supervisor for only a short time. In explaining the events that led to the protest, Winfare said that production on the assembly line had been chronically below quota before he took charge, and the plant manager had plainly told him that his job was to improve the production rate. Production has improved markedly in the short time that Winfare had been supervisor.

Winfare advised the plant manager that his transfer would only set a serious long-term precedent. "The company's action to remove me would create a situation where the operations of the plant would be subject to the whims of any employee with a grudge," he argued. His contention was confirmed by the comments of a union steward, who said there were other conditions in the plant that needed improving—such as the cafeteria food and relief from the more that 100-degree heat in the metal shop. Moreover, the steward said, there was at least one other supervisor who should be removed. He implied that, if successful, the power cage protest would achieve two goals—namely, employees could dictate the company's problem-solving agenda and simultaneously undermine its power to determine decision-making priorities. The union steward's final comment was that two men on the unauthorized, wildcat strike might accomplish the same thing as a full-blown strike.

Each passing minute was costing the company a production loss of one automobile unit valued at $6,000; the cost of each lost production hour, therefore, was $360,000.

As he began a staff meeting to resolve the dilemma, the plant manager felt pressure to accomplish two objectives: (1) to restore production on the profitless assembly line (a solution about which he was uncertain), and (2) to develop policies for preventing future interruptions by assembly-line workers.

## CASE QUESTIONS

1. What is the primary problem in this case?
2. How would each of the approaches to management in this chapter analyze the case?
3. How should the plant manager restore production on the assembly line?
4. What policy, if any, should be developed to prevent future production interruptions?
5. If there is an underlying struggle for power in this situation, precisely where does it lie? Which theoretical approach to management policy is best suited to answer this question?

## KESSLER AT THE FDA HELM:
## STREAMLINING A MAMMOTH[41]

There are pills that can reduce a woman's chance of becoming pregnant by 75 percent if she takes a dose within 72 hours of having sex. Few women realize this, though many have been taking the pills for years as a means of birth control, because drug companies lack the approval of the Food and Drug Administration (FDA) to market them as "morning after" pills. While drug manufacturers have been assured that FDA approval would be granted, they are reluctant to spend the requisite time and money on the FDA's notoriously lengthy application process. Unfortunately, this is not an isolated situation. FDA red tape has prevented many potentially beneficial products from entering the U.S. market. This is a serious problem, considering the wide scope of the FDA's jurisdiction, over food, food additives, drugs and medical devices, TVs, microwave ovens, and pet products—accounting for $960 billion worth of goods.

Dr. David A. Kessler, who took over as commissioner in 1990, made it his mission to turn things around at the FDA. In addition to bringing FDA practices up to speed, Kessler confronted the difficult task of restoring the agency's credibility and morale after the 1989 generic drug scandal which ended in the conviction of four FDA employees for taking "illegal gratuities." In order to restore faith in the agency, his first steps included cracking down on everything from falsely labeled "fresh" orange juice to allegedly dangerous breast implants.

Then came the formidable challenge of streamlining the cumbersome bureaucracy that had traditionally plagued the FDA. Kessler began by delegating authority to the 21 field offices, empowering the lower-level FDA managers, and reducing the frequency of review by headquarters. This enabled the FDA to expedite enforcement actions and drug reviews. Moreover, the time necessary to process injunction requests was reduced by 60 percent. Kessler also acquired congressional approval to bill companies for drug evaluations, and thereby increased the FDA's 1993 budget to $826 million, up 8.7 percent from the previous year. Extra reviewers were then hired in an effort to cut the average drug approval time from 22 months to 12 months by 1997.

In order to transform the FDA into a more efficient regulator, Kessler borrowed what he called "the best practices of the private sector." This has involved rehiring, reorganizing, and restructuring. From 1990 to 1993, total staff grew from 7,800 to 9,000. "The first day I got here, I was called to the Health & Human Services Dept. [the FDA's parent]," recalled Kessler. "For a whole day, nothing else got done."[42] He immediately put five deputies in place to oversee policies, manage crises, deal with Congress and the outside world, handle daily operations and, overhaul the agency's ancient communications systems. "In the past, management [at the FDA] meant doing the budget, allocating office space, and doling out parking spots," remarked Kessler. "The agency never asked how work should get done."[43] Under Kessler, this has changed.

In addition, Kessler has focused the FDA's centers for biologics and foods on product approval by reorganizing them around products instead of scientific disciplines. This resulted in the on-time implementation of the 1990 Nutritional Labeling & Education Act. Instead of having food-labeling expertise scattered throughout the FDA, Kessler's restructuring placed it all in a single division. "We would never have gotten food labeling done had it not been for the reorganization," said Food Safety center director Fred R. Shank.[44]

Kessler has also made the FDA more user-friendly. Each agency center previously had its own forms and requirements for companies wishing to report adverse reactions to products. Now, all of the centers share the same forms and requirements, and interaction is encouraged between similar divisions who formerly worked autonomously. Moreover, Kessler has refused to accept substandard applications in an attempt to force companies to submit better ones. In fact, 30 percent of applications are now refused, whereas applications were rarely refused previously.

But there could be a downside to a more efficient FDA. Many people have expressed concern that expediting the FDA's approval process will result in an increase in potentially harmful drugs being made available. "The public has traditionally expected FDA to keep unsafe and ineffective drugs from being approved and marketed," John Petricciani, vice-president for medical and regulatory affairs for the Human Health Services Association, pointed out. "[T]here has been a growing recognition of the other side of consumer protection, and that is to approve safe and effective drugs in a timely manner.... As the Agency begins to move towards more rapid approvals, there will also be heightened expectations of the FDA to monitor the safety and efficacy of drugs after approval."[45]

Recognizing this, Kessler has responded with the implementation of MEDWatch, a program designed to encourage voluntary reporting of adverse reactions by health professionals. "[This] is not just a new FDA system," Kessler noted, "it is a way of making reporting of adverse events and product problems a part of the culture of healthcare providers. Physicians, nurses, and others who care for patients are the first to know when a drug or medical device does not perform as it should. The sooner they report it to FDA, the faster the agency can analyze the problem and take corrective action."[46] MEDWatch is designed to correct for the fact that health professionals are not legally required to report and that as many as 50 percent are not even aware that they can report. The goal of MEDWatch is therefore to make health professionals aware that they can report and to make the process easy.

MEDWatch is symbolic of the great strides taken by the FDA under Kessler's influence. "The changes have been excellent first steps," noted Kenneth P. Berkowitz, a vice-president at drugmaker Hoffmann-La Roche Inc. "Kessler has planted the seeds for a more effective FDA."[47]

# Management in the Twenty-First Century

# INTERSECTION

# 2

In Part I we introduced *dynamic engagement,* our term that expresses how today's most successful managers emphasize human relationships and rapidly adapt to changing conditions over time. Six themes about management theory are emerging under the umbrella of dynamic engagement, and it is these themes that we explore in Part II.

We begin with a discussion of the environment, for changes in the external environment are constantly altering how organizations conduct business. In Chapter 3 we discuss the elements of the organizational environment, giving special emphasis to the natural environment, and explore how organizations manage their total environment. Then, in Chapter 4, we recognize the interconnectedness between organizations and their environment and delve into how managers approach ethics and social responsibility. The international dimension cannot be ignored, and that is what we address in Chapter 5. Then, in Chapter 6, we approach the value of inventing and reinventing organizations. In Chapter 7 we introduce the challenge of culture, diversity, and multiculturalism; and in Chapter 8 we explore quality. All of these themes are significant in today's business world, and they promise to become increasingly significant tomorrow and the day after.

## CHAPTER 3

# ORGANIZATIONAL AND NATURAL ENVIRONMENTS

**Upon completing this chapter, you should be able to:**

1. Explain the importance of the external environment.

2. Distinguish natural and organizational environments.

3. List and discuss the elements of the direct-action environment.

4. Identify the stakeholders of an organization.

5. Explain how organizations can use stakeholder networks and coalitions to influence stakeholders.

6. List and discuss the four variables that make up the indirect-action environment.

7. List the natural environment challenges that we face.

8 Explain how organizations can respond to the natural environment.

# MCDONALD'S: GREENING THE GOLDEN ARCHES[1]

n 1990, McDonald's found itself in the middle of an animated debate surrounding its food packaging. At the heart of this debate lay the famous polystyrene (styrofoam) "clamshells" used to package McDonald's hamburgers and other food products. Clamshell opponents argued that this was not an environmentally responsible packaging method, and that "greener" methods were available. The Citizens Clearinghouse for Hazardous Waste even organized a boycott against McDonald's, with picketers in "Ronald McToxic" clown suits.

This was not the first criticism levied against the clamshell. McDonald's had previously confronted public outcries in the late 1980s when voices were raised against the clamshell for its use of chlorofluorocarbons (CFCs)—chemicals considered capable of destroying the stratospheric ozone layer. The fate of the clamshell initially was in doubt, but, on August 5, 1987, McDonald's announced that it could save the clamshell by having suppliers switch to a non-CFC production process.[2]

Despite this change, as environmental awareness climbed between 1988 and 1990, the clamshell was reexamined by the public. Of particular concern was the alarming rate at which landfills were being filled: it was anticipated that, by 1995, available landfill space would fall to 80 percent of what was available in 1980. Incineration, once thought a viable alternative, also proved problematic in light of concern for air quality and ash disposal. Other alternatives were explored. The Environmental Protection Agency (EPA) and several state governments developed a "waste management hierarchy" that placed incineration and landfill disposal as last-resort alternatives. Preferred choices included reducing, reusing, and recycling—in that order.

*The McDonald's clamshell became a casualty of the growing environmental consciousness of the American public.*

According to a survey by packaging designers Gerstman & Meyers, 60 percent of the respondents *believed* that plastic packaging was the source of most of the solid-waste disposal problem. Considering the amount of polystyrene the company used—about 80 million pounds each year to package its Big Macs, Quarter Pounders, Egg McMuffins, breakfast pancakes, McChicken sandwiches and Chicken McNuggets—McDonald's, with 1990 sales exceeding $18 billion, became an easy target for angered environmentalists. Finally, the McDonald's clamshell became a casualty of the growing environmental consciousness of the American public.

**MCDONALD'S GOES GREEN.** The home of the golden arches has responded to public concern with a "green" approach.

The irony is that consumer perception was at odds with reality. Actually, plastic accounted for only 8 percent (by weight) of total municipal solid waste, whereas paper accounted for 40 percent. Indeed, fast-food containers comprised less than one-half of one percent of total landfill volume. Environmentalists could have focused their attention more effectively elsewhere.

Nevertheless, at stake was the "golden" image McDonald's had worked so hard to achieve, often through charity to child-related causes. "Twenty years ago, we decided we wanted an image beyond food, based on strong virtues," explained McDonald's chief marketing officer Paul D. Schrage. "It makes us dependable."[3] McDonald's had spent millions of dollars in support of such efforts, most notably its Ronald McDonald Houses, which offer near-hospital lodging to families of children hospitalized with cancer, and the affiliated Ronald McDonald Children's Charities. In addition, McDonald's sponsored the World's Largest Concert, a 1989 worldwide sing-along that aired on PBS, and the May 1990 *Life Magazine* special issue on children. Given McDonald's interest in preserving its good public image, the cries against the clamshell, whether warranted or not, had to be heard and answered. →

THE MCDONALD'S case illustrates many of the changes that organizations have confronted in recent years. New relationships have been forged—sometimes with groups that didn't even exist a few years ago—and managers have had to develop a new sense of the time frame for their decisions. In today's world many organizations survive by anticipating and responding intelligently to external change. The purpose of this chapter is to provide frameworks for understanding the many changes that the external world thrusts upon organizations.

## THE IMPORTANCE OF ORGANIZATIONAL AND NATURAL ENVIRONMENTS

In Chapters 1 and 2 we suggested that management is currently undergoing a substantial rethinking. One of the main reasons for this reexamination is the change brought about by forces and pressures that are external to organizations. In the 1970s the world reeled from the shock of quadrupled prices for petroleum, and organizations from General Motors to the Post Office had to decide how to reconfigure themselves to take this external event into account. The 1980s saw a dramatic shift from a local to a global playing field as strong organizations from Japan, Korea, Europe, and other areas intensified competition for markets across the world. In the 1990s new technologies for communication and information processing (ranging from inexpensive fax machines and notebook computers to superpowerful new computers) and geopolitical upheavals have revolutionized the way we think about organizations. Indeed, all of these factors, and many others, are part of the organizational environment that managers must take into account.

At the same time worldwide concern about the natural environment has emerged, spurred by environmental disasters, the discovery of a hole in the ozone

**PUBLIC ACTIVISM.** External groups with particular agendas are often organized and powerful. People demonstrate on a wide variety of issues such as abortion, animal research, and human rights. Here, opponents of animal research demonstrate on a university campus.

layer that covers the earth, and an increase in pollution and other forms of environmental degradation. A new environmentalism has swept the globe—symbolized by the 1992 Earth Summit in Rio de Janeiro, which drew unprecedented attention to the environmental problems that we all share.

Traditional ways of thinking about management pay little detailed attention to either organizational or natural environments—for good reasons. When most of the management theorists discussed in Chapter 2 were alive, the external environment of organizations was primarily stable and unchanging. And there was little concern about the natural environment; citizens of the world simply assumed that the earth's resources were inexhaustible. Today the world is very different. External groups with particular agendas are often organized and powerful, and many organizations depend on them for support. Technological, political, economic, and social trends can have major effects on whether or not organizations are successful. And, finally, today's managers must pay attention to the natural environment if we are to preserve the world for future generations. While it is difficult to separate "organizational" and "natural" environments because they are ultimately connected, in the following sections we will present some ways to understand, analyze, and manage the changes that organizations face in today's topsy-turvy world.

## ORGANIZATIONAL ENVIRONMENTS

**external environment:**
All elements outside an organization that are relevant to its operation; includes direct-action and indirect-action elements.

← ch.2, p. 46

**inputs:**
Resources from the environment, such as raw materials and labor, that may enter any organizational system.

**outputs:**
Transformed inputs returned to the external environment as products or services.

**direct-action elements:**
Elements of the environment that directly influence an organization's activities.

**indirect-action elements:**
Elements of the external environment that affect the climate in which an organization's activities take place, but do not affect the organization directly.

**stakeholders:**
Those groups or individuals who are directly or indirectly affected by an organization's pursuit of its goals.

**external stakeholders:**
Groups or individuals in an organization's external environment that affect the activities of the organization.

To understand organizational environments we must borrow some concepts from systems theory. As we saw in Chapter 2, one of the basic assumptions of systems theory is that organizations are neither self-sufficient nor self-contained. Rather, they exchange resources with and are dependent upon the **external environment,** defined as all elements outside an organization that are relevant to its operations. (Some of these elements connect the organization to the physical world. Because of its current importance, we will treat this topic separately in a section on natural environments.) Organizations take **inputs** (raw materials, money, labor, and energy) from the external environment, transform them into products or services, and then send them back as **outputs** to the external environment.

The external environment has both **direct-action** and **indirect-action elements.*** Direct-action elements, also called **stakeholders,** include shareholders, unions, suppliers, and many others who directly influence an organization. Stakeholders are discussed in more detail in the next section. Indirect-action elements, such as the technology, economy, and politics of a society, affect the climate in which an organization operates and have the potential to become direct-action elements. Figure 3-1 outlines an organization's environmental picture and shows the influence of both direct- and indirect-action elements. The roles of each type of element are discussed in the next two sections.

## ELEMENTS OF THE DIRECT-ACTION ENVIRONMENT

The direct-action environment is made up of stakeholders—individuals or groups that are directly or indirectly affected by an organization's pursuit of its goals. Stakeholders fall into two categories. **External stakeholders** include such

---

* Some people refer to "direct action" as the "task environment" and "indirect action" as the "general environment." We prefer the language of action and relationships for the reasons given in Chapter 1.

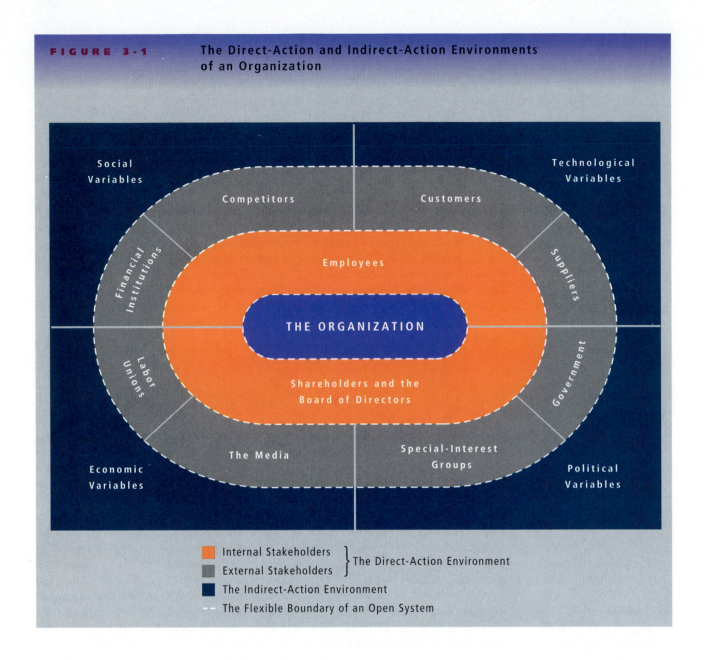

**FIGURE 3-1**    The Direct-Action and Indirect-Action Environments of an Organization

Social Variables
Technological Variables
Competitors
Customers
Financial Institutions
Employees
Suppliers
THE ORGANIZATION
Labor Unions
Government
Shareholders and the Board of Directors
The Media
Special-Interest Groups
Economic Variables
Political Variables

Internal Stakeholders
External Stakeholders  } The Direct-Action Environment
The Indirect-Action Environment
-- The Flexible Boundary of an Open System

**internal stakeholders:**

Groups or individuals, such as employees, that are not strictly part of an organization's environment but for whom an individual manager remains responsible.

groups as unions, suppliers, competitors, customers, special-interest groups, and government agencies. **Internal stakeholders** include employees, shareholders, and the board of directors.* The roles stakeholders play may *change* as organizational environments *evolve* and *develop*. Managers must be sensitive to this fact when they are tracing the various influences on an organization's behavior and recommending responses to environmental change.

Both the internal and the external stakeholder groups of most organizations have changed substantially over the past few years. In the rest of this section, we will outline the stakes of various elements in each category and examine how they have shifted.

---

* The internal-external stakeholder distinction is useful up to a point. Managers *may* have more influence with internal stakeholders than external ones. On the other hand, internal stakeholders are organization members, while external stakeholders are not.

## EXTERNAL STAKEHOLDERS

External stakeholders, which affect an organization's activities from outside the organization, include customers, suppliers, governments, special-interest groups, the media, labor unions, financial institutions, and competitors.

**CUSTOMERS.** Customers exchange resources, usually in the form of money, for an organization's products and services. A customer may be an institution, such as a school, hospital, or government agency; or another firm, such as a contractor, distributor, or manufacturer; or an individual. Selling tactics vary according to customer and market situations. Usually, a marketing manager analyzes the potential customers and market conditions and directs a marketing campaign based on that analysis.

A small business may target a narrow "niche" of customers. For example, Mark Nelson started his medical software business, CD Plus, as a one-person operation. Assessing the pressure placed on the healthcare industry, he developed user-friendly software for doctors and medical researchers. By following simple, straightforward directions on the screen, even people unfamiliar with medical terminology and computers can access the latest literature on a particular drug, symptom, disease, or treatment. In the beginning, Nelson was innovator, marketer, distributor, receptionist, security guard, and customer service representative. By 1992, his CD Plus had sales of over $11 million and employed 70 people.[4]

In recent years, as non-U.S. firms have challenged the dominance of American business by offering customers more choices and setting new standards of quality, competition has begun to change customer relationships. For example, when Japanese television manufacturers found it difficult to set up service networks for their products in the United States, they responded by making televisions that were less likely to malfunction. Before, a customer's relationship with a television manufacturer was cemented by the local dealer and repair shop. Now customers are able to buy televisions at large discount retailers, without having to worry about service. This change had a major impact on the American television industry inventors of the product. Although in the 1950s there were about 30 American-owned companies making televisions sets, in the 1980s there was only one.[5]

Personal computers are sold the same way today. Dell, Gateway, and others pioneered the direct-mail method of selling to individual customers. Both companies staff 24-hour 800 numbers to help customers. The emphasis in these examples is on finding new ways to establish and maintain customer relationships.

**SUPPLIERS.** Every organization buys inputs—raw materials, services, energy, equipment, and labor—from the environment and uses them to produce output. What the organization brings in from the environment—and what it *does* with what it brings in—will determine both the quality and the price of its final product. Organizations are therefore dependent upon suppliers of materials and labor and will try to take advantage of competition among suppliers to obtain lower prices, better-quality work, and faster deliveries.

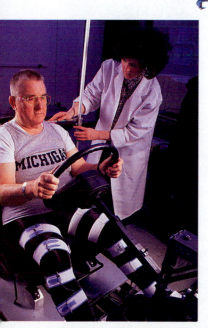

**TAKING THE CUSTOMER'S MEASURE.** Ford Motor Co. used tips from a "mature-driver's advisory committee" plus physical measurements to be sure Ford Taurus controls could be operated safely by drivers with arthritis.

Some organizations, such as Tandem Computers, have found that they can control quality better over the long run by developing more long-lasting, supportive relationships with their suppliers. When a supplier designed a defective chip, rather than drop the supplier and do business with a competitor, Tandem worked with the company and gave it another chance to design a chip for Tandem's most recent computer. The supplier came through, and the relationship is now a successful one.[6]

Advances in inventory control and information processing have also changed supplier relationships. Under the conventional system, the manufacturer was usu-

EXHIBIT 3-1

**MAJOR FEDERAL REGULATORY AGENCIES**

*Consumer Product Safety Commission* Establishes and enforces federal safety standards for the content, construction, and performance of thousands of manufactured goods.

*Environmental Protection Agency* Establishes and enforces federal standards for environmental protection, especially from industrial pollution.

*Equal Employment Opportunity Commission* Administers and enforces Title VIII (the fair employment practices section) of the Civil Rights Act of 1964 and the Equal Employment Opportunity Act of 1972.

*Federal Aviation Administration* Regulates and promotes air transportation safety; sets standards for the operation of airports and the licensing of pilots.

*Federal Communication Commission* Regulates interstate and foreign communication by radio, television, telegraph, and telephone.

*Federal Deposit Insurance Corporation* Insures bank deposits; has authority to examine bank practices and approve bank mergers.

*Federal Reserve System* Regulates the nation's banking system; manages the nation's money supply.

*Federal Trade Commission* Ensures free and fair competition in the economy and protects consumers from unfair or deceptive practices.

*Food and Drug Administration* Administers federal laws regarding food purity, the safety and effectiveness of drugs and medical devices, the safety of cosmetics, and the safety and honesty of packaging.

*Interstate Commerce Commission* Enforces federal laws concerning the transportation of goods and people across state lines.

*National Labor Relations Board* Prevents or corrects unfair labor practices by either employers or unions.

*Nuclear Regulatory Commission* Licenses and regulates the design, construction, and operation of nonmilitary nuclear facilities.

*Occupational Safety and Health Administration* Develops and enforces federal standards and regulations ensuring safe and healthful working conditions.

*Securities and Exchange Commission* Administers federal laws concerning the buying and selling of securities.

ally responsible for all of the inventory necessary for production capability. Today, however, some companies keep zero inventory, relying on several "just-in-time" deliveries each day. Suppliers such as Baxter Healthcare Corporation have used new information technology to put computer terminals on customers' premises so that each customer can directly order a product whenever it is needed. Emery Air Freight provides its regular customers with personal computer systems that not only weigh packages, calculate charges, and generate air bills, but also consolidate shipments, give the customers a direct link to Emery's computer tracking system, and generate management reports about their shipping activity.

**GOVERNMENT.** The doctrine of laissez-faire, developed in the eighteenth century, holds that a government should exert no direct effects on business, but should limit itself to preserving law and order, allowing the free market to shape the economy. By the beginning of the twentieth century, however, abuses of business power led the U.S. government to take on the role of "watchdog," regulating organizations to protect the public interest and ensure adherence to free-market principles. As Exhibit 3-1 shows, Congress has passed many laws creating regulatory agencies, which establish and enforce the ground rules within which businesses must operate. In addition, court decisions have played a major role in shaping the

**SPEAKING OUT.** Special interest groups may apply public pressure in an attempt to influence the policies and practices of organizations. This billboard is part of a campaign undertaken by a group that sees alcohol advertising as demeaning to women when it portrays them as sex objects.

strategies and policies of the modern business organization. State and local governments, too, have assumed the role of watchdog and passed laws concerning the operation of businesses within their boundaries.

A good example is the recent debate about healthcare policy in the United States. The approach adopted by government will directly affect the cost of benefits for all organizations. For some organizations, such as Blue Cross Insurance and Kemper Insurance, the action of government may directly determine their chance of survival.

Government policies may also have a major effect on the tobacco industry. For example, in March, 1994, top executives of the seven tobacco companies were grilled by a congressional subcommittee on health in the wake of the government's consid-

eration of labeling nicotine an addictive drug. Opponents of tobacco were proposing higher taxes on tobacco (President Clinton's health plan includes a tax increase on tobacco to fund health care reform), further restrictions on the places where people can smoke, and tougher health-related regulations on the industry. Such policies could have a dramatic impact on the tobacco industry's financial stability and public image in the United States.[7]

Governments also act to aid and protect industries. In recent years the United States government has bailed out the savings and loan industry with billions of dollars and the creation of a new organization, The Resolution Trust Corporation, to save and restructure the industry. In Japan, where government support for industry is a matter of national policy, the Ministry of International Trade and Industry actively assists some industries.

**special-interest groups (SIGs):**

Groups of people who organize to use the political process to advance their position on particular issues, such as abortion and gun control.

**political action committees (PACs):**

Groups organized to lobby and make campaign contributions to influence legislators.

**SPECIAL-INTEREST GROUPS.** Special-interest groups (SIGs) use the political process to advance their position on a particular issue such as gun control, abortion, or prayer in the public schools. Managers can never be sure whether an ad hoc group will form to oppose the company on some issue—selling nonstandard infant formula in the Third World, for example, or investing in South Africa. In the McDonald's case, the Citizens Clearinghouse for Hazardous Waste is a good example of how SIGs can influence an organization.

Special-interest politics is hardly a new phenomenon. What is new is the way that modern communications technology and election financing have allowed SIGs to flourish in our time.[8] The media can give such groups instant national attention, and the **political action committees** (PACs) of the groups use campaign contributions to influence legislators.[9] Managers must take both present and future spe-

**WALL STREET WEEK.** *Wall Street Week* is just one of several television shows that provide extensive and sophisticated coverage on business and economic issues.

cial-interest groups into account when setting organizational strategy. Among the most important special-interest groups are *consumer advocates* and *environmentalists* (which we shall comment on later).

**CONSUMER ADVOCATES.** The modern consumer movement dates from the early 1960s, with President Kennedy's announcement of a "Consumer Bill of Rights" and Ralph Nader's crusade against General Motors' Corvair.

One framework for understanding the consumer movement is Hirschmann's model of exit, voice, and loyalty.[10] Dissatisfied customers can choose either to *exit*—that is, to take their business elsewhere—or to *voice* their complaints; the customers' *loyalty* to the organization will determine which option is used. Exit, of course, can cripple an organization by removing its customer base without giving managers time to make changes. Voice, in contrast, is a political strategy designed to seek redress for grievance. Filing lawsuits requesting the intervention of a regulatory agency and lobbying a lawmaking body are examples of the exercise of voice.

It is important to note that the use of voice can be constructive rather than adversarial. Recognizing the costs of government intervention, consumer leaders often prefer negotiation. At the same time, progressive managers welcome voice as an opportunity to understand customer needs and to learn about changes in the marketplace.

Many companies, such as AT&T, have learned to work with consumer advocates and to listen to their suggestions for improvements in quality and service. Some companies such as Xerox have formed their own customer-advocate groups (or user-groups) in an effort to improve this relationship.

**MEDIA.** The economy and business activity have always been covered by the media, because these topics affect so many people. Today, though, mass communications allow increasingly extensive and sophisticated coverage, ranging from general news reports to feature articles to in-depth investigative exposés. The coverage is also more immediate, due to the increasing use of communication satellites.

Today, managers at most large organizations realize they operate in a fishbowl, where every action may be the subject of media scrutiny. To improve their communication with both internal and external audiences, they have developed sophisticated public relations and marketing departments. In addition, executives who regularly deal with the media often seek professional coaching to improve their ability to present information and opinions clearly and effectively. Some organizations provide training for all employees to help them respond capably in situations that may arise. United Airlines, for example, holds regular drills to prepare all employees—from emergency workers to media relations workers—to deal effectively with the aftermath of an airplane crash.

**LABOR UNIONS.** Personnel specialists generally deal with an organization's labor supply, sometimes supplemented by other managers with specific hiring and negotiating responsibilities. They use multiple channels to locate workers with the various skills and experience the organization needs. When an organization employs labor union members, union and management normally engage in some form of **collective bargaining** to negotiate wages, working conditions, hours, and so on.

Dramatic changes in labor relations have come about in recent decades. Both personnel staff and union management have been professionalized. Also, employers generally accept the collective bargaining process and cooperate with unions to increase worker responsibility and participation. The sit-down strikes and violence that so often characterized the unions' early days are for the most part over. Instead, unions urge stock-ownership, profit-sharing, and gain-sharing programs that give the workers a stake in the organization, and quality-of-worklife programs that give them more control over what they do and how they do it.[11]

**collective bargaining:**
The process of negotiating and administering agreements between labor and management concerning wages, working conditions, and other aspects of the work environment.

## A QUALITY UNION RELATIONSHIP AT ARMCO

Union relationships have become an important factor in the total quality efforts of firms, because total quality involves having workers take on a new level of commitment and involvement in the company's success. However, the movement away from traditional adversarial relationships is not easy. The "we versus them" mentality, still found in many unionized companies, can undermine quality efforts. At Armco Worldwide Grinding Systems in Kansas City, Missouri, the union-management relationship was described as one of "periodic noncooperation." Then, in 1992, the company implemented its "TeamWorks" program. TeamWorks is an effort by the company to give all its employees an equal voice in developing ideas to make Armco more profitable, more productive, and more satisfying for its workers. This was the last step in a quality process that had been ongoing for ten years.

With TeamWorks, employees volunteer to serve on seven-member teams that research and suggest ideas to improve quality and productivity as well as to reduce expenses and generate added revenue. When the company accepts an idea, team members earn recognition and awards. The results are impressive: close to $4 million in cost savings has been realized through team ideas; 80 teams have submitted nearly 500 ideas for review; and grievances have declined by 40 percent. Prior to TeamWorks, employees focused attention on "how the company was going to get me next" rather than concentrating on developing working solutions to business problems. Managers mandated all programs and work changes. Now, employees manage the programs and work changes. With the development of the teams, encouragement of open discussion, and the financial awards to employees for the savings generated from their ideas, Armco has been able to turn the situation around.[12]

**FINANCIAL INSTITUTIONS.** Organizations depend on a variety of financial institutions, including commercial banks, investment banks, and insurance companies, to supply funds for maintaining and expanding their activities. Both new and well-established organizations may rely on short-term loans to finance current operations and on long-term loans to build new facilities or acquire new equipment. Because effective working relationships with financial institutions are so vitally important, establishing and maintaining such relationships is normally the joint responsibility of the chief financial officer and the chief operating officer of the organization.

**COMPETITORS.** To increase its share of the market, an organization must take advantage of one of two opportunities: (1) it must gain additional customers, either by garnering a greater market share or by finding ways to increase the size of the market itself; or (2) it must beat its competitors in entering and winning in an expanding market. In either case, the organization must analyze the competition and establish a clearly defined marketing strategy in order to provide superior customer satisfaction.[13]

Airline companies such as American, TWA, United, and USAir and their non-U.S. counterparts are clearly competitors in the American air-carrier market. But competition can also come from organizations that provide substitute products or services. In the northeast corridor, for example, Amtrak metroliners compete with airlines for intercity shuttle service. Video conferencing can also compete with the airlines by substituting for face-to-face meetings, thus eliminating the need for travel in some situations.

In recent years, the competition facing U.S. organizations has broadened to include non-U.S. firms. In the 1950s, the label "Made in Japan" implied "junk" or "cheap"; by the 1980s, it had become a hallmark of quality. The success of  Japanese products, ranging from cars to cameras, has been enormous. Many products, such as VCRs, are not even made in the United States today, and there is competition from abroad in almost every "U.S.-dominant" industry. For example, Taiwan's up-and-coming companies are supplying the world's personal computer giants. These Taiwanese computer makers, such as Twinhead, First International Computer, and Compal, are playing a critical behind-the-scenes role as designers and manufacturers of the world's PCs and peripherals, many of which are eventually marketed under more well-known brand names. In the last few years, Taiwan has passed South Korea as the world's top producer of color monitors. It also leads in computer mice and keyboards. Dozens of well-known computer makers, including IBM, Dell, Packard Bell, and Apple, are stocking up in Taipei with finished PCs and notebook computers. In 1992 the Taiwanese sales of hardware were $6.6 billion.[14]

**OTHER STAKEHOLDER GROUPS.** Each individual organization has a host of different stakeholders. For instance, a hospital will have to consider the American Hospital Association; groups of doctors, nurses, and other caregivers; and, of course, patients. Every organization has a particular stakeholder map that is in essence a picture of the direct-action component of its external environment. Figure 3-2 is a stakeholder map for McDonald's.

## INTERNAL STAKEHOLDERS

Even though, strictly speaking, internal stakeholders are not part of the *organization's* environment (because they are part of the organization itself), they are a part of the environment for which an *individual manager* is responsible.

**EMPLOYEES.** The nature of the work force is changing in most organizations, partly because of demographic factors. The so-called baby-boom generation is getting

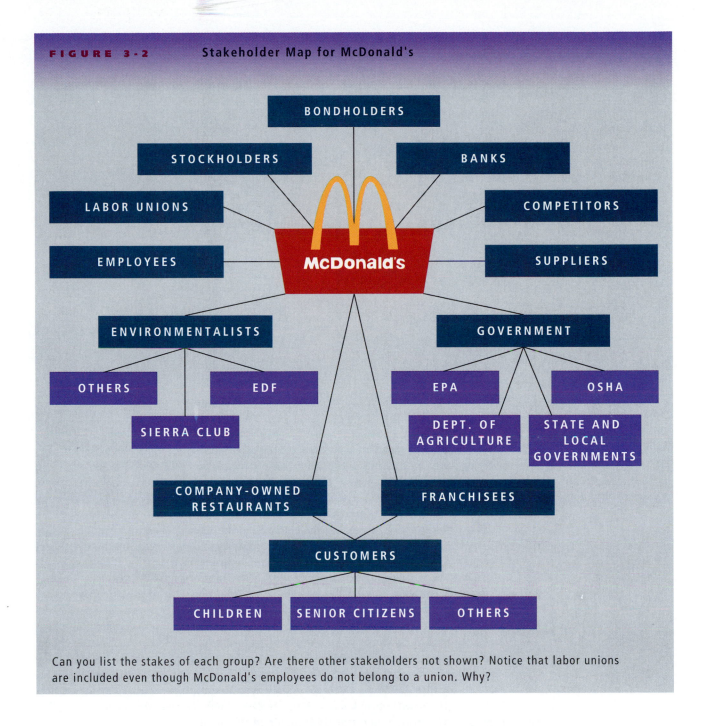

**FIGURE 3-2**     Stakeholder Map for McDonald's

Can you list the stakes of each group? Are there other stakeholders not shown? Notice that labor unions are included even though McDonald's employees do not belong to a union. Why?

older and the declining birth rate means that the United States will soon face a labor shortage. At the same time, the skills needed by employees are changing. As companies find it necessary to experiment with quality programs, team approaches, and self-managed work groups, they need employees who are better educated and more flexible.

**SHAREHOLDERS AND BOARDS OF DIRECTORS.** The governing structure of large public corporations allows shareholders to influence a company by exercising their voting rights. Traditionally, however, shareholders have been interested primarily in the return on their investment and have left the actual operation of the organization to its managers.

**STAKEHOLDERS VOICE CONCERN.** Shareholders have been increasingly active in voicing their opinions about corporate policies and actions. Exxon, for instance, had to respond not only to the larger community but to its own stockholders following the *Exxon Valdez* oil spill.

In recent years, however, certain groups of social activists have begun purchasing small quantities of stock for the purpose of forcing votes on controversial issues at annual corporate meetings.[15] Ralph Nader pioneered the technique in 1969, when he launched "Campaign GM." The strategy was that an ad hoc group bought two shares of General Motors stock with the intention of waging a proxy fight on social and business issues, including the need for public transportation, the rights of women and minorities, product design for safety, and emissions control.[16] Although a Securities and Exchange Commission ruling in 1983 made this particular tactic more difficult to carry out,[17] the tactic of buying up shares to seize control of entire companies continues to be common business policy. Although mergers and hostile takeovers are often spurred by the legitimate need to reorganize American manufacturing, they involve large expenditures of capital that are usually justified by cutting back operations and liquidating assets. In the 1980s, many managers were on the defensive; sometimes they harmed the long-term health of their organizations in their efforts to keep profits and stock prices up so as to discourage takeover attempts.[18] One noted example was the takeover of RJR Nabisco, which was chronicled in a best-selling book, *Barbarians at the Gate: The Fall of RJR Nabisco,* and the HBO movie of the same title.[19]

Moreover, direct ownership of stocks by individuals is on the decline; individuals are now more likely to hold shares through investments in mutual funds, contributions to retirement plans, and membership in company and state pension plans. In fact, approximately 40 percent of the common stock of the country's largest and many middle-size businesses is controlled by pension funds.[20] These large blocks of shares are managed by professionals who can emphasize financial performance, putting greater pressure on managers to produce short-term results. Recently many of these institutional investors were instrumental in forcing the resignations of CEOs at General Motors, IBM, and Kodak. Among the reasons given were the inability of the CEO to adjust to the changing environment or to deliver needed changes quickly enough (the case of Robert Stempel at General Motors), or an unwillingness to follow board direction.[21]

# McCHANGE AT McDONALD'S

Initially, McDonald's responded to public concern by boosting polystyrene recycling endeavors. In October 1989, McDonald's introduced a plan at 450 New England restaurants to recycle polystyrene plastic and corrugated cardboard garbage. McDonald's outfitted the restaurants with special recycling bins. It made available posters and pamphlets explaining the rationale for the recycling endeavor; efforts to educate the public frequently accompanied its recycling efforts.

In spite of mixed reviews of the program, McDonald's expanded it in 1990 to a few cities outside New England. Then in April, McDonald's announced "McRecycle," the company's commitment of $100 million to buying recycled materials for restaurant construction, remodeling, and operations. Ed Rensi, chief operating officer and president of McDonald's USA, asserted, "We challenge suppliers to provide us with these recycled products."[22]

McDonald's was reluctant to replace the clamshell unless it was absolutely necessary. In addition to its recycling efforts, McDonald's agreed to work with the Environmental Defense Fund (EDF), a nonprofit advocacy group, to set up a strategic alliance. A joint McDonald's/EDF task force was set up to consider solid waste issues within the McDonald's system more thoroughly. According to Jackie Prince, EDF staff scientist, "What made the experiment bold was not just the virtually unprecedented notion of a partnership between an environmental advocacy organization and a major U.S. corporation seen by many as a symbol of our disposable society, but also the thoroughness of the undertaking: a top-to-bottom examination of materials improvement and waste reduction opportunities throughout the McDonald's system and a comprehensive examination of its network of more than 600 suppliers."[23]

The task force was charged with coming up with "a framework, a systematic approach, and a strong scientific basis for McDonald's solid waste decisions." The task force arrived at a program of 42 initiatives to reduce McDonald's waste and soften the impact of some practices. One result, for example, was that McDonald's switched to using recycled paper bags. Another was that, finally, the clamshell was abandoned. It had served as a useful packaging device, both for aesthetic and functional rea- sons, but it had become a focal point for environmentalists. Furthermore, EDF Executive Director Fred Krupp told Ed Rensi that the EDF would publicly refuse to endorse the recycling program. All things considered, McDonald's decided to phase

out foam sandwich packaging in all U.S. McDonald's within 60 days. The paper packaging used to replace the clamshell is not recyclable but it is nonetheless better for the environment and was expected to reduce the volume of waste by 90 percent. Richard Denison, senior scientist for the EDF, asserts, "It was absolutely the right thing to do."[24] →

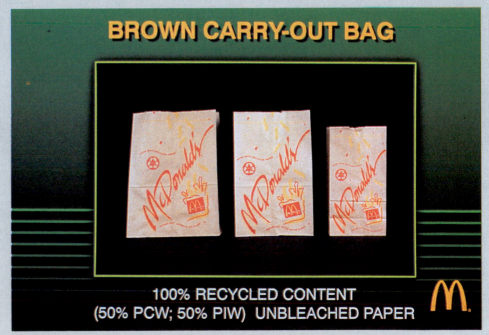

**BROWN CARRY-OUT BAG**

**100% RECYCLED CONTENT (50% PCW; 50% PIW) UNBLEACHED PAPER**

**NEW McBAGS.** McDonald's switched to recycled, unbleached paper for its bags.

# MANAGING MULTIPLE STAKEHOLDER RELATIONSHIPS

The stakeholder framework is a method for understanding and influencing the direct-action environment. (It might be interesting to draw a map for your college or workplace and list the key challenges.) Organizations devise plans, organize themselves, lead, and control ways to interact with key stakeholders. For example, Bell Atlantic devised a plan to offer cable-TV service which required influencing key stakeholders such as government, banks, customers, and even other companies in the industry.

The stakeholder framework raises issues that affect many organizations.

## NETWORKS AND COALITIONS

A complex network of relationships links stakeholders with one another as well as with the organization. For example, consumer advocates may have contacts with an organization, its employees, and a government regulatory agency; in turn, the regulatory agency will affect both the organization and its competitors.

A particular issue may unite several stakeholders in support of or in opposition to organizational policy.[25] For example, special advocacy groups might join with labor unions, the media, and legislators to block the introduction of a new technology that could cost workers jobs as well as pollute the environment. On occasion, such coalitions outlive the initial issue and continue to work together on others.

## MULTIPLE ROLES

A single individual or group may have multiple relationships with an organization.[26] A toy company employee, for example, may also be a parent who purchases the company's products, a shareholder with an investment in the company, a member of a consumer group lobbying for stricter safety codes for children's products, or a member of a political party with pronounced ideas about free trade and protectionism. Stakeholders may therefore have to balance conflicting roles in deter-

**MULTIPLE STAKEHOLDER RELATIONSHIPS.** Individuals may need to balance conflicting roles and values when they work for an organization, use its products, perhaps own stock in the company, and live and raise their families nearby. Such multiple stakeholder relationships are not uncommon.

mining what action they want the organization to take. This is especially true of management, as we will see in the next section.

### THE SPECIAL ROLE OF MANAGEMENT

Management has its own stake in the organization. All employees do, of course, but management is responsible for the organization as a whole, a responsibility that often requires dealing with multiple stakeholders and balancing conflicting claims. Shareholders, for example, want larger returns, while customers want more investment on research and development; employees want higher wages and better benefits, while local communities want parks and day-care facilities. To ensure the survival of the organization, management must keep the relationships among key stakeholders in balance over both the short and the long term.[27] In the McDonald's case managers had to weigh the relative importance of stakeholders, each of whom wanted McDonald's to change.

## ELEMENTS OF THE INDIRECT-ACTION ENVIRONMENT

The indirect-action component of the external environment affects organizations in two ways. First, forces may dictate the formation of a group that eventually becomes a stakeholder. Second, indirect-action elements create a climate—rapidly changing technology, economic growth or decline, changes in attitudes toward work—in which the organization exists and to which it may ultimately have to respond. For example, today's computer technology makes possible the acquisition, storage, coordination, and transfer of large amounts of information about individuals, and banks and other business firms use this technology to maintain, store, process, and exchange information about the credit status of potential buyers. Individuals concerned about the misuse of such data might form a special-interest pressure group to seek voluntary changes in bank business practices. If this group were to organize a successful boycott of a particular bank, it would become a stakeholder of that bank and enter its direct-action environment.

Fahey and Narayanan have grouped these complex interactions into four broad factors that influence the organization and must be considered by its managers: social, economic, political, and technological.[28]

### SOCIAL VARIABLES

Fahey and Narayanan divide **social variables** into three categories: demographics, lifestyle, and social values. Demographic and lifestyle changes affect the composition, location, and expectations of an organization's labor supply and customers. Social values underlie all other social, political, technological, and economic changes and determine all the choices that people make in life.

**DEMOGRAPHICS.** The demographics, or makeup, of the U.S. population has undergone major changes since World War II. Although the population as a whole is growing slowly, some segments of the population, such as Hispanics and blacks, are growing much faster than others. In fact, organizations are increasingly reflective of these demographics. From 1983 to 1993 the percentage of male, white professionals and managers in the workforce declined from 55 percent to 47 percent, while for white women, the per-

**social variables:**
Factors, such as demographics, lifestyle, and social values, that may influence an organization from its external environment.

**FIGURE 3-3**     **The Aging Population:
Percentage of the Population 65 Years and Over**

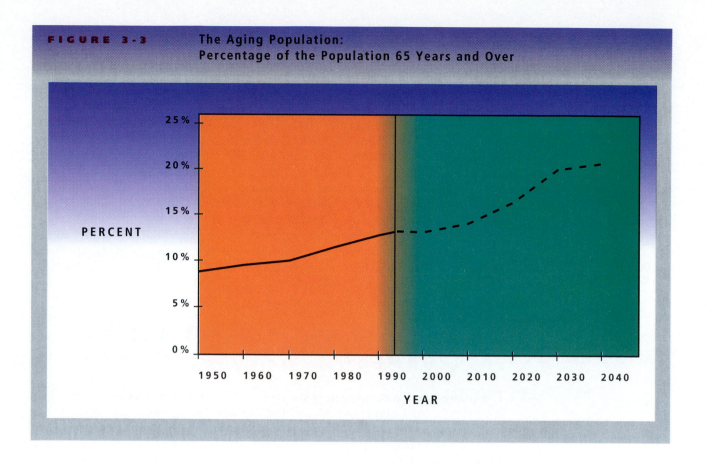

centage increased from 37 percent to 42 percent. According to the U.S. Labor Department, through the year 2005 half of all labor force entrants will be women and more than one-third will be Hispanics, African Americans, and other races.[29]

Figure 3-3 shows the aging of the American population in terms of the number of people 65 years or older. Americans are also living longer; by 2010 the average life expectancy for men will be 74.4 years, as opposed to just 53.6 years in 1920. There have also been dramatic shifts in age structure—that is, the relative sizes of different age groups. The "baby boomers"—those people born between 1946 and 1964—account for more than a third of the country's population, and as this cohort has grown up, society has naturally reflected its interests and demands. Moreover, despite the increase in fertility that occurred as the baby boomers became parents, the median age of the population continues to rise.

Why are these changes so important to managers? First, they affect the size of the labor supply. In recent years, for example, the relatively small number of teenagers has forced fast-food restaurants and other traditional employers of teenagers to turn to retirees and women with families who want to reenter the workforce to fill their part-time jobs. Meanwhile, the rising median age means that managers may face a shortage of skilled workers in the future, once the baby boomers start to retire.

Second, changes in the makeup of the population create social issues that affect managers. Today, for example, many employees are finding themselves in the "sandwich generation"—caught between the demands of caring for their own children and the need to help their aging parents. As a result, many major corporations, including IBM, Johnson & Johnson, and Mobil, have set up special programs

**INFLUENCE OF SENIOR CITIZENS.** Increases in life expectancy and the aging of the "baby boomers" are two factors that are increasing the percentage and influence of senior citizens.. Organizations need to be aware of such demographic changes.

to help their employees deal with elder care.[30] Third, demographics shape the markets for many products, as indicated by the baby boomers' influence.

**LIFESTYLES.** According to Fahey and Narayanan, lifestyles are the "outward manifestations of people's attitudes and values."[31] In recent decades, change rather than stability has characterized Americans' lifestyles. For example, "traditional" families account for a shrinking proportion of U.S. households. Fewer and fewer U.S. families include married couples, and households consisting of single adults and one-parent families are becoming more numerous.

**SOCIAL VALUES.** In recent years, changing social values have affected our commitment to equality of opportunity and the regulation of industry, altered our assessments of the costs and benefits of new technology such as life-support systems for the seriously ill, and increased the social and economic expectations of consumers, women, and minorities.

Perhaps more important for managers is the way in which values affect our attitudes toward organizations and work itself. For example, employee participation in managerial decision making was once seen as simply a means of improving worker morale and productivity; now it is regarded by some observers as an ethical imperative.[32]

Naturally, social values vary from one country to another. In Japan, for example, where many employees work for the same company all their lives, low-level workers participate in policy and decision making more freely than American workers do. French organizations, which operate in a society where relationships are somewhat formal, tend to be more rigidly structured than their American and Japanese counterparts. In Germany, where worker and union rights are guaranteed by law, em-

ployees are known as *Soziale Partner* or "social partners." Strong unions are involved at all levels of business from the local plants to the corporate boardrooms. Moreover, labor costs are higher than in the United States and vacations are three times as long. Next to Japan, Germany is America's greatest competitive threat. Even though it has a fraction of the resources and less

**EXHIBIT 3-2**    **COMMON ECONOMIC INDICATORS**

National Income and Product
   Gross national product
   Personal income
   Disposable personal income
   Personal consumption expenditures
   Retail sales
Savings
   Personal savings
   Business savings
Investment
   Industry investment
   Investment expenditures
   New equipment orders
   Inventory investment
   Housing starts
Prices, Wages, and Productivity
   Inflation rate
   Consumer price (index) changes
   Producer price (index) changes
   Raw material price (index) changes
   Average hourly earnings

   Output per hour per business sector
Labor Force and Employment
   Numbers employed by age/sex/class
    of work
   Unemployment rate
Government Activities
   Federal surplus/deficit
   Expenditures by type
   Government purchases of goods and
    services
   State and local expenditures
   Defense expenditures
   Money supply changes
International Transactions
   Currency exchange rates
   Exports by type
   Imports by type
   Balance of trade
    Merchandise
    Goods and services
   Investment abroad

Source: Reprinted by permission from *Macroenvironmental Analysis for Strategic Management* by Liam Fahey and V.K. Narayanan. Copyright 1986 by West Publishing Company. All rights reserved.

than one-third the population of the United States, it produces internationally competitive products in key manufacturing sectors.[33]

## ECONOMIC VARIABLES

**economic variables:**
General economic conditions and trends that may be factors in an organization's activities.

Obviously, general economic conditions and trends are critical to the success of an organization. Wages, prices charged by suppliers and competitors, and government fiscal policies affect both the costs of producing products or offering services and the market conditions under which they are sold. Each is an **economic variable**.

   Common economic indicators measure national income and product, savings, investment, prices, wages, productivity, employment, government activities, and international transactions (see Exhibit 3-2). All these factors vary over time, and managers devote much of their organizations' time and resources to forecasting the economy and anticipating changes. Because economic change is now the norm rather than the exception, this task has become more complicated.

## POLITICAL VARIABLES

**political variables:**
Factors that may influence an organization's activities as a result of the political process or climate.

Will a government agency adopt a rigorous or a lenient stance toward the management of a company with which it is dealing? Will antitrust laws be rigidly enforced or ignored? Will government policy inhibit or encourage management's freedom to act? These sorts of questions concern **political variables,** and their answers depend largely on the nature of the political process and on the current political climate. The political process involves competition between different interest groups, each seeking to advance its own values and goals. For example, out of the general political debate about the environment, groups emerged which had a direct impact on McDonald's products and services.

**technological variables:**
New developments in products or processes, as well as advances in science, that may affect an organization's activities.

**BIOTECHNOLOGY AT WORK.** Calgene's "Flavr Savr" tomato, a product of biotechnology, reached supermarkets in 1994.

## TECHNOLOGICAL VARIABLES

**Technological variables** include advances in basic sciences such as physics, as well as new developments in products, processes, and materials. The level of technology in a society or a particular industry determines to a large extent what products and services will be produced, what equipment will be used, and how operations will be managed.

Major changes are on the horizon in the field of biotechnology, and Japanese corporations are mounting a powerful new challenge to American dominance in biotechnology products. Although we are only beginning to see the applications of this new technology, it is already a multibillion-dollar industry, with products ranging from genetically improved farm animals and grains to cancer treatments and biodegradable plastics. The real focus in this rapidly growing field, however, is a battle between Japan and the United States for prominence in research and development (R&D).

By helping to finance basic research conducted in other countries, Japanese companies gain access to technological breakthroughs outside their country, in effect augmenting their research efforts while freeing their own resources for perfecting products that have the best chance of dominating markets around the world. Takeda, for example, which has a joint venture with Abbott Labs and alliances in West Germany, France, and Italy, funds research at Harvard University. Fujisawa acquired LyphoMed and a former joint venture with SmithKline. Chugai bought Gen-Probe, Inc., for $110 million and has stakes in Genetics Institute, Inc., and British Bio-technology.[34]

## MANAGING THE INDIRECT-ACTION ENVIRONMENT

Managers monitor the indirect-action environment for early-warning signs of changes that will later affect their organization's activities. For example, rather than waiting for sales to fall, an alert manager will reduce production of luxury items when he or she first spots a downward trend in general consumer spending.

Information about the indirect-action environment comes from many sources: an industry's grapevine, managers in other organizations, the data generated by an organization's own activities, government reports and statistics, trade journals, general financial and business publications, on-line computer data-bank services, and others. Hints, predictions, statistics, gossip—any of these may alert a manager to a trend that should be monitored. The manager can then order further research to clarify potential important developments. By using statistical *forecasting* techniques, managers can anticipate change in social, economic, political, and technological variables and so prepare alternate plans for the future.

For example, businesses that want to appeal to affluent customers need to be aware of the so-called yucas—young, upwardly mobile Cuban Americans. Unlike other ethnic groups that have sought to blend into the U.S. culture, the yucas switch between English and Spanish publications and media to find the best quality and remain actively involved in the mainstays of Cuban culture. Because Cuban American young people tend to live at home until they are married, yucas can spend more on consumer goods such as clothing, cars, and consumer electronics. Another up-and-coming group that will have a profound impact on change is teenagers. While society has been focused on the baby boomers, the number of teenagers has started to grow again. In 1992, the U.S. population aged 13 to 19 inched up by 70,000 to 24.08 million, ending a 15-year decline. The pace of growth is picking up as boomers' babies grow up and new immigrants arrive. During the next decade the teen population will grow at close to twice the rate of the overall population. This puts teenagers at the leading edge of a demographic wave that will wash over America during the next two decades, transforming our culture and economy. As teens' spending power and influence increase, they will change the way marketers of everything from apparel to cars to soft drinks will do business in the years to come.[35]

# NATURAL ENVIRONMENTS

In recent years concerns about damaging the natural environment have taken on new importance. Many Americans now classify themselves as concerned about the environment. This increased focus on environmental issues is having a profound impact on many organizations, which must deal not only with changes required by specific laws and regulations, but with public perceptions. It has also created opportunities: Many organizations today are involved in developing new processes and new products that either do no environmental damage or clean up environmental damage that has already occurred. At McDonald's, the clamshell debate is a prime example.

Increasingly, managers are confronting a number of questions about the environment. What are the primary areas of concern? How far can (or should) organizations go in helping to protect and clean up the Earth? And who should bear the costs?

## THE RISE OF THE ENVIRONMENTAL MOVEMENT

It is standard thinking to believe that the environmental movement in the United States is a recent phenomenon coming from the social activists in the 1960s.[36] But this is not true. The Sierra Club, a well-known activist organization, actually began in 1896 and spawned a host of groups who were concerned with the conservation of the land and natural resources. Relying on the thinking of John Muir and others, conservationists argued that we must try to curtail the negative impact of humans and human technologies on the Earth.

The 1960s did provide a renewed sense of importance to the environmental movement. Rachel Carson published a book in 1960, *The Silent Spring,* that argued that the continued use of toxic chemicals and pesticides was damaging to the land and humans who lived off the land. This book marshalled attention on the relationships between technology, science, and human interaction with the natural world.

During the same time frame of the late 1960s and early 1970s the United States government was leading an effort by industry to develop a supersonic transport airplane (SST) that flew at three times the speed of sound and used the very

**THREAT OF POLLUTION.** The pollution of this creek is a small but eloquent example of the need for strong environmental regulations, aggressive enforcement, and provisions for clean-up of polluted sites.

latest technology. The SST became a symbol for the environmental movement and it coalesced many different groups to effectively stop further development. It was one of the few times in United States history that technological development was slowed or stopped because of environmental damage.

Responding to the public pressure in the 1970s, President Richard Nixon and the Congress passed the Clean Air Act, the Clean Water Act, and began the Environmental Protection Agency. While the initial targets of the EPA were the steel and automobile industries, the agency soon moved to affect virtually every major organization in the country. Rules were developed, standards were set and companies had to comply with new environmental regulations or face fines, delays, or lawsuits.

In the 1980s, the environmental movement broadened substantially. In the United States, the government looked more to free market solutions to pollution, waste disposal, and other issues. In the rest of the developed world, environmentalism became a political force. The Green Party was formed and elected members to a number of European parliaments.

One market-oriented solution tried in the United States was the issuing of permits to pollute. These permits capped the total amount of pollutants at a certain level, and if a company could clean up its plant to produce less, then it could sell the "right to pollute" to other companies. Criticized heavily by some environmentalists, such a system tried to give incentives to companies to clean up their act, and by setting the total amount of pollutants to be released at a fixed level, the government tried to insure that companies polluted as little as possible.

## CURRENT ENVIRONMENTAL CONCERNS

The litany of environmental problems is long. Organizations—as well as individuals—contribute to these problems and can have an impact on their resolution.

**POLLUTION.** Pollution comes in many forms.[37] There are hazardous substances such as PCBs (polychlorinated biphenyls) which are used as cooling fluids in electric power transformers. Chlorinated solvents are a major concern as contaminants to drinking water. Pesticides accumulate in the environment over time. Lead, found in pipes, and asbestos, used in earlier construction, are both toxic. Hazardous waste such as nuclear waste and toxic chemicals are byproducts of industry and government and must be stored safely. Solid waste is any unwanted or discarded material that is not liquid or gas, and must be disposed of in incinerators, landfills, or by other means. Acid rain is a form of air pollution that damages soil, water, and vegetation in certain areas.

### MAKING A PROFIT "IN MY BACKYARD"

For the past few decades most cities, counties, and states seem to have adopted the slogan NIMBY—not in my backyard—when it comes to the disposal of hazardous and solid waste, making the disposal of such byproducts of industry and consumption difficult. An exception is Tooele County, Utah, where the slogan could be IMBY—in my back yard. The county, roughly the size of Connecticut, is mostly desert. At the Tooele Army Depot nearly half of the nation's nerve gas is in storage, awaiting permanent disposal. The county also accepts nuclear waste for disposal. In 1993 United States Pollution Control Inc., a subsidiary of Union Pacific, completed building within the county a $150 million

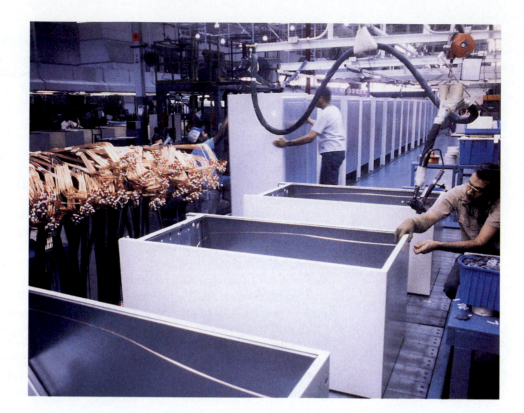

**ENVIRONMENTALLY RESPON- SIBLE MANUFACTURING.**
Whirlpool won an industry competition and a $30 million prize with its development of a CFC-free, high-efficiency refrigerator.

commercial incinerator, the nation's largest. The incinerator disposes of such elements as paint sludge and PCB-contaminated soil brought in from all over the country.

It was in 1988 that the county decided to go against the tide of sentiment against solid and hazardous wastes and seize an opportunity to create jobs and income for its 28,000 residents. To accomplish this the county set aside a 100-square-mile hazardous-waste-disposal district. There, three private disposal companies have created about 500 new jobs. Local property taxes have not gone up, largely because of the special "mitigation fee" the companies pay the county to compensate for the stigma of having a "dirty" reputation for being associated with hazardous waste disposal. In 1992 the county collected almost 20 percent of its revenues from the mitigation fees. So far the residents have not seen any signs of the pollution affecting them other than beneficially in jobs and tax revenues.[38]

**CLIMATE CHANGES.** We have to worry about human-induced climate changes such as global warming. Some scientists have suggested that global warming poses a severe threat to life as we know it. A small rise of several degrees in the average temperature would be enough to set off major changes in climate. Greenhouse gases which are emitted from the burning of carbon-based fuels such as gasoline serve to trap warmth in the atmosphere, and some scientists predict a global average temperature increase of 1.5 to 4.5 degrees centigrade over the next century unless current trends abate.[39]

**OZONE DEPLETION.** When chlorofluorocarbons (CFCs) are released into the atmosphere and break down, they release chlorine molecules, which destroy ozone molecules—resulting in the degradation of the ozone layer surrounding the earth. If the earth's protective ozone layer gets too thin, then damaging ultraviolet radiation will lead to an increase in skin cancers. Ozone depletion has led to an international agreement to limit the production of CFCs and to ban CFCs altogether in some countries.

**OTHER GLOBAL ISSUES.** Finally, we have to worry about large global issues such as biodiversity, adequate water supplies, population, and food security. The recent debacle in Somalia has been called an environmental crisis by some, since the nomadic way of life of the Somali people is no longer sustainable given devegetation, population increases, and the scarcity of food.

Confusing the issue is the fact that for each scientific "gloom and doom" projection, there are other scientific studies that conclude that environmental problems are not severe. Managers must decide how to act *before* all of the scientific facts are in. They must rethink their organizations from top to bottom if they are to respond effectively to the environmental crisis—if there is indeed a crisis. Although the science is unclear, two facts *are* clear. First, we have not lived in an environmentally friendly way and continuance on the same path may have devastating effects. Secondly, as McDonald's concluded, today's managers have to be concerned not only with the scientific facts, but with public perception.

It is also important to note that, on a global scale, the environment is becoming one of the hottest issues for business in the 1990s. The export market for "green" goods, services, and technologies is rapidly expanding. Stricter regulatory standards are being adopted globally as developing regions such as Asia discover  that high rates of industrial expansion and economic growth are compromising the quality of the environment. Thus, there is a greater demand for American technologies and know-how to tackle and solve environmental problems in the Pacific and Asia. The market for U.S. environmental exports includes Latin American, Asia, eastern Europe, and the countries of the former Soviet Union. It has been estimated that on a worldwide basis spending on environmental protection will reach $590 billion by the year 2000, with a growth rate of 6.7 percent annually.[40]

## FRAMEWORKS FOR THINKING ABOUT THE NATURAL ENVIRONMENT

Given the pervasiveness of environmental impacts on organizations, we need some kind of framework for evaluating action in response to environmental concerns. We will consider two such frameworks in this chapter, but you should know that many people are inventing new frameworks even as this book is being written.

**THE COST-BENEFIT FRAMEWORK.** Organizations take raw materials and produce products and services. If the cost of producing the output is greater than the price customers are willing to pay, then the organization cannot make enough profit to stay in business for very long. Organizations sustain themselves by creating value over and above the costs of the inputs. If the benefits to those willing to pay outweigh the costs, then the organization creates a surplus and can continue to produce its goods and services. Such "cost-benefit" thinking has ruled the business world from early times.

The **cost-benefit model** has been the dominant mode of thinking about environmental solutions for the last 30 years, especially in the minds of environmental regulators. Simply put, if the benefits of a proposed environmental regulation outweigh its costs, then the regulation should be implemented. But if the costs of a particular environmental rule outweigh its perceived benefits, then the rule should not be enforced.

For example, if good refrigerators without CFCs can be produced for a price that's not too much more than before, then the benefit—not contributing to ozone depletion—is greater than the increased cost. Alternatively, if these new products do not function as well as the old type, or if they are prohibitively expensive, then the costs may be seen as greater than the benefits.

The problem with cost-benefit thinking is that not all benefits and costs are easily quantifiable. For example, what is the benefit to our children of the ozone layer not being destroyed? Such a benefit is difficult to measure. Because we have ignored the natural environment for so long, it is now difficult to simply add "environmental costs" to the normal business equations. For some site-specific and local environmental issues this thinking can help guide us towards solutions that

**cost-benefit model:**

A traditional approach to thinking about environmental solutions that says a proposed environmental regulation should be implemented if the potential benefits outweigh the potential costs.

**RAINFOREST DESTRUCTION CONTINUES.** Rainforests continue to be ravaged at an alarming rate. Economic development that destroys rainforests is completely at odds with the concept of sustainable development.

make sense, but applying it on a global basis simply doesn't work very well. We have too little understanding of the real, long-term costs and benefits of environmental action and inaction.

**THE SUSTAINABLE DEVELOPMENT FRAMEWORK.** Moving beyond cost-benefit thinking and taking into account the fact that many environmental costs and benefits accrue over a long period of time, a number of thinkers have begun to develop a new framework based on the concept of **sustainable development.** The logic of this framework is very simple: engage in those organizational activities that can be sustained for a long period of time or that renew themselves automatically. Economic development that destroys resources such as old growth forests, or rainforests, cannot be sustained, for if such development continues, the very process of life itself may be threatened.

**sustainable development:**
A more modern approach to thinking about environmental issues that says that organizations should engage in activities that can be sustained for a long perod of time or which renew themselves automatically.

The concept of sustainable development has long been a source of concern and was emphasized in the Bruntland Commission Report to the United Nations, which called for a radically new way of encouraging economic development to preserve the environment. It was defined as development which "meets the needs of the present without compromising the ability of future generations to meet their own needs."[41] In 1990, Maurice Strong, Secretary General of the United Nations Conference on Environment and Development, sponsored the formation of the Business Council for Sustainable Development (BCSD) to work out how businesses could adopt sustainable development as a standard operating procedure.[42]

Again, let us look at the example of CFCs and the destruction of the ozone layer. Sustainable development thinking would tell us that if we continue to produce CFCs, then we will "compromise the ability of future generations," since the destruction of the ozone will lead at least to more skin cancers, and possibly to even worse effects.[43] Sustainable development therefore tells us to coordinate our actions across companies, geographies, and political entities such as national governments to adopt a treaty such as the Montreal Protocol, which banned the production of CFCs after a certain date.

Applying sustainable development thinking to individual firms is trickier. It is easy for each organization to believe that sustainable thinking must be left up to government, and that no one business should have to incur costs for sustainable development that its competitors—who may be in other countries with laxer regulations—do not have. So, if sustainable development is to provide a new way to think about individual organizational action, it must be more fully developed in line with the organizational environment concepts in this chapter.

## A MOVEMENT TO CLEAN UP THE WORLD

A movement started in Australia to encourage individuals to come together to clean up the world in teams. It was begun by yachtsman Ian Kiernan, who represented his country in the BOC challenge, a solo around-the-world yacht race, in 1987. On that trip he began to take note of the plastic garbage floating in the sea. The racers themselves had agreed beforehand to keep their garbage on board rather than throwing it overboard, the traditional means of disposal at sea. When he returned home to Sydney, Kiernan noticed broken glass on the beaches where he swam and decided to do something about it. Kiernan and a public relations consultant friend teamed up and launched Clean Up Sydney Harbor Day. On the designated day, 40,000 citizens picked up 5000 tons of trash. Jubilant over their success, the two expanded their efforts and launched Clean Up Australia Days in January of 1990. In March of 1993, 400,000 Australians gathered 25,500 tons of garbage at more than 5,000 waterways, parklands, and roadside crossings across the continent. In September 1993 the two promoted a worldwide cleanup effort. More than 7,000 communities in 79 countries took part in the three-day cleanup, with individuals combing parks, beaches, roadsides, and city streets. It is estimated that as many as 30 million people participated. Ecologically-minded citizens were found in the Philippines, Mexico, Nepal, Costa Rica, Malaysia, and Burkina Faso. While these projects have received some corporate sponsorship, Kiernan hopes the success of the first worldwide cleanup will bring more companies on board.[44]

## THE GREENING OF ORGANIZATIONS

One way to think of how organizations can begin to apply sustainable development to individual decisions is to see how much stakeholders care about the natural environment. Today, environmental awareness is at an all-time high. We are sure that you have considered recycling at least some of your waste and that you have made at least one purchasing decision during the last year where the natural environment was a factor in your decision. There are at least four postures that organizations can adopt to become more sensitive to the environment.[45]

1. *The legal posture.* Organizations can adopt a posture that they will obey any laws, rules, and regulations about the environment willingly and without legal challenge. Such a posture means that the organization will try to use the law to its own advantage. For instance, if an organization can invent a technology or a process to make it more efficient and satisfy environmental regulations, then it will have an advantage. Indeed, Harvard Professor Michael Porter has suggested that countries which

have strict environmental regulations produce firms which are more competitive on a global basis. The reason is simple: these firms must innovate to find ways to satisfy strict laws while remaining competitive with firms that have no such rules.

2. *The Market Posture.* Organizations can adopt a posture that they will respond to the environmental preferences of their customers. Some industrial customers of manufacturers require that the manufacturers meet certain environmental standards for their products and their manufacturing processes. In some markets, customers want products that can easily be recycled, or that are made from recycled paper. The pulp and paper industry has undergone dramatic shifts as the move to using recycled paper has increased. Many companies have investments in old plant and equipment, but have had to make new investments in equipment to use recycled paper rather than new pulp from forests.

3. *The Stakeholder Posture.* This posture takes the market posture one step further to include responding to multiple stakeholder groups on environmental issues. Paying attention to recyclable material in consumer packaging, educating employees on environmental issues, participating in community efforts to clean up the environment, and appealing to investors who want to invest in green companies are all a part of the stakeholder posture. And these multiple stakeholder policies seem to go together. Dupont's CEO Edgar Woolard has tried to make Dupont more sensitive to stakeholder environmental concerns by adopting a policy of "Pollute as little as possible," in part to turn around Dupont's reputation as a large polluter. When he announced that a plant would have to close if it couldn't meet the company-imposed pollution requirements, the plant engineers busily reinvented the processes at the plant to meet the requirements. When Woolard asked them how much money it would cost Dupont to invest in the new technologies and processes, the engineer replied that if they did it the new way, Dupont would actually save money.[46]

4. *The Dark Green Posture.* Some organizations are beginning to experiment with adopting environmental values that tell us we should live in a manner that is more in harmony with the earth. We should not exploit the earth's resources for our own gain, and certainly not in a non-renewable, non-sustainable fashion. We should not treat animals cruelly or use them for unimportant experimentation such as cosmetics testing, and we should live in a way that sustains and respects the earth. Based on a group of ideas known as "deep ecology," from the Scandinavian philosopher Arne Naess, this posture is very hard to imagine in our present state of environmental awareness. Perhaps some of the best examples are companies such as Ben and Jerry's and The Body Shop.

Ben and Jerry's ice cream has long promoted saving the rainforest with contributions from the sale of its popular "rainforest crunch" ice cream. Nuts for the ice cream are bought from rainforest tribes to give the tribes a way to make a living that does not require cutting down the forests. A number of utilities have contributed to save the rainforest programs to try and offset any damage that they may do by burning coal. Similarly, the Body Shop has built a large retail business based on consumer preferences to the environment. As we will see in the Chapter 7 case, Anita Roddick believes strongly in responding to customers who want to recycle, and who want to participate in sustainable economic development in the developing world. In order to enable the Body Shop to live by these dark green principles as much as possible, Roddick has announced energy audits for each store and the construction of wind farms to replace the energy that The Body Shop uses. While it is unclear how to manage organizations based on dark green principles, there are a number of companies that are responding to the challenge with innovative ideas all aimed at respecting and preserving the earth.

**BEN & JERRY'S CARING CAPITALISM.** By buying the nuts for its Rainforest Crunch ice cream from rainforest tribes, Ben and Jerry's gives the tribes a way to make a living without resorting to cutting down the forests. The company also donates part of the profits from the sale of this popular flavor to rainforest

**ENVIRONMENTAL PRESSURE GROUPS.** During the 1970's, protesters helped close many nuclear plants with claims that the utilities were more interested in profits than in the future safety of the planet.

# MANAGING ORGANIZATIONAL AND NATURAL ENVIRONMENTS

**A**s you can see from this chapter, the external forces and pressures that managers face today are unprecedented. Yet there is still a tendency to focus on the internal workings of an organization and ignore the importance of new stakeholders or new trends in the external environment. Once again we meet our old friends *time* and *relationships*.

Many activist stakeholder groups, from consumers to environmentalists to special-interest groups, are giving managers signals that certain relationships have been ignored or that a different time frame is necessary. For example, several external events in the past few years put managers on notice that the relationship between the genders is changing, and that the time horizon for change is short: the confirmation hearings for Supreme Court nominee Clarence Thomas, the Navy's Tailhook scandal, and the 1993 Supreme Court ruling, *Harris v. Forklift Systems* (1993), on "hostile environments" for employees in the workplace. As a result, many corporations adopted new policies, or began to implement training programs to respond to these external events. Those who do not respond will face a number of challenges, including legal actions from their employees. Sexual harassment can cost corporations billions of dollars a year in lawsuits, turnover, lost productivity, low morale, and absenteeism. Some research has shown that 90 percent of *Fortune* 500 companies have dealt with sexual harassment complaints, 33 percent have been sued at least once, and about 25 percent have been sued repeatedly. One estimate is that the problem costs the average large corporation $6.7 million a year.[47]

Similarly, environmental pressure groups have given the signal that they will use any available means, from legal challenges to civic protests such as "tree spiking," to get organizations to pay attention to how they may be damaging the environment. Increased concern about the natural environment means that new human relationships must enter the organizational equation, and the move from cost-benefit thinking to the sustainable development concept means that the time frame has changed to become more immediate.

The challenge is clear. Managers today must reinterpret what they do, in response to external environmental signals that new relationships and a new time horizon have become essential to strong organizational leadership. McDonald's has certainly gotten that message, and the message is beginning to spread, as we can see from the close of this chapter's illustrative case.

**MANAGEMENT 2000 AND BEYOND**

# CAN BUSINESS REALLY SAVE THE EARTH?

One of the themes of this chapter has been that organizations can adopt a posture that helps to protect and clean up the environment. Companies like McDonald's have begun that process. But how far should a business go? After all, businesses must be profitable in order to survive. Is it possible to be profitable and adopt an approach such as sustainable development?

Entrepreneur and author Paul Hawken suggests that business has no other choice. In his recent best seller, *The Ecology of Commerce: A Declaration of Sustainability,* he argues that every act of commerce, every business deal or transaction, helps to destroy the environment.[48] Many times, acts that are meant to help protect the earth end up hurting it, and Hawken believes that we have to think about business differently. He thinks that everyday business actions should be made to help preserve the environment, but this cannot occur with the kind of economic thinking that we currently have.

Hawken proposes a set of "green fees" to replace all of the taxes that we currently have. Such a redesign of basic economic structures would be far reaching to say the least. Hawken says, "The whole key to redesigning the economy is to shift incrementally most, if not all, of the taxes presently derived from 'goods' to 'bads', from income and payroll taxes to taxes on pollution, environmental degradation, and nonrenewable energy consumption. Because green taxes are incorporated into the price a company or customer pays for a resource, product, or service, they create powerful incentives to revise and constantly improve methods of production, distribution, and consumption, as well as a means to reconsider our wants and needs."[49]

Hawken asks us to imagine the result of very high taxes on gasoline, say $2 per gallon. Such a tax would raise $220 billion in the United States, equivalent to one half of the total income taxes currently paid . People and companies would have incentives to use different modes of transportation to avoid these taxes, creating more value by doing so, and avoiding the pollution that comes from using carbon based fuels. He thinks that taxing heavy metals would lead to an end to mining and a move to capture these metals from the wastestreams of current industries.

Paul Hawken isn't just another theorist. He has used his ideas to start several businesses aimed at helping to protect and preserve the environment. He believes that business can in fact bring out the very best in people. He says, "The vision that informs green taxes...assumes that human beings are enormously adaptive and creative, and that there is great untapped potential and goodwill that is repressed and inactive in our current economic culture."[50] He thinks that green taxes can be used to make our society better.

Can you think of other taxes that could be levied on goods and services that would result in taking care of the environment? Managers in the next century will undergo a green revolution taking the environment into account in their decision making on a routine basis.

# THE COST OF CONSCIENCE

It is interesting to note that since the "greening" of McDonald's and replacement of the clamshell, the fight against polystyrene has lost a great deal of its venom. Don Jacobs, executive director of hospitality services at the University of Pennsylvania, switched back to polystyrene cups after six years of doing without. Paper has proved inferor to polystyrene, particularly with regard to warm beverages such as coffee, and the improved image of plastic has made customers more amenable to using it.

The teaming of EDF with McDonald's demonstrates the value of stakeholders working together to protect the environment. It has prompted other similar efforts, such as a project between EDF and Prudential, Johnson & Johnson, Time-Warner, Nationsbank, Duke University, and McDonald's to promote the use of recycled (or otherwise environmentally preferable) paper. Currently, only 6 percent of the 22 million tons of printing handwriting paper produced annually is recycled. Stepping up paper recycling is important, as the American Paper Institute has noted, because every ton recycled reduces the use of landfills by three cubic yards.

In August of 1993, it was announced that, by the end of the decade, products such as Time-Warner magazines, Band-Aid boxes, and Prudential insurance policies would all be made of environmentally preferable paper. This endeavor reflects a trend toward coalition-building, away from resorting to legal and regulatory channels. In addition, it provides for workable solutions. "The real value of the task force is that we are working with actual users of these products," said John Ruston of the EDF. "You find what works in a business setting."[51]

> *The fight against polystyrene has lost a great deal of its venom.*

According to Ruston, the specific goal of the task force lies in prompting paper companies to recognize the ready market for recycled paper. "The paper industry is the most capital-intensive one in the United States," noted Ruston. "They are not going to invest in new technology without the assurance of demand."[52] The fact that companies such as Prudential (which spends $300 million on paper each year) are turning to recycled paper, coupled with the Clinton Administration's directive that federal agencies (which buy 300,000 tons of paper each year) increase their usage of recycled paper, sends a clear signal to paper companies that their investment in recycling efforts will pay off.

Time-Warner's membership in the task force is worth underscoring; if the numerous publications put out by Time-Warner turn over to recycled paper, it could prompt similar changes throughout the industry, which, unlike the newspaper industry, has confronted significant hurdles in its efforts to use recycled paper. In its November/December 1990 issue, *Sierra* became the first consumer magazine in the United States to print entirely on recycled coated paper. *Buzzworm* came next with its January/February 1991 issue. As of early 1993, apart from *Buzzworm* and *Sierra*, only a few small magazines and catalogs have turned to printing on recycled paper.

A basic problem lies in cost. Because recycled paper suitable for such publishing is generally more expensive, publishing on recycling paper often costs publications a 15 percent to 20 percent premium. Outmoded machinery and a shortage of de-inking facilities contribute to the expense. A sort of vicious cycle emerges: the problems are not easily fixed until demand increases, but demand will not increase until more, cheaper recycled paper is readily available. The task force aims at putting an end to the cycle.

# SUMMARY

1. **Explain the importance of the external environment.**

   The many rapid changes taking place in the external environment of organizations require increasing attention from managers. The external environment contains numerous resources upon which organizations rely. This means that organizations are inevitably affected by what goes on in the environment.

2. **Distinguish natural and organizational environments.**

   Managers must recognize the elements of internal organizational environments, such as stakeholders. In addition, managers must also understand the relationship of elements of the natural environment that can affect the organization.

3. **List and discuss the elements of the direct-action environment.**

   The direct-action component of the environment consists of the organization's stakeholders—that is, the groups with direct impact on the organization's activities.

4. **Identify the stakeholders of an organization.**

   Stakeholders are the people and groups of people who have an interest in what goes on in the organization. External stakeholders include customers, suppliers, governments, special-interest groups, the media, labor unions, financial institutions, and competitors. Internal stakeholders include employees, shareholders, and the board of directors.

5. **Explain how organizations can use stakeholder networks and coalitions to influence stakeholders.**

   Stakeholders often work together to influence the behavior of an organization. Managers, as stakeholders, must balance their own concerns against the competing concerns of other stakeholders. They may be able to use the network of relationships among the stakeholders and the organization to influence stakeholders individually. For their part, stakeholders may unite in coalitions to exert influence over the organization. Individual stakeholders may also hold conflicting stakes in an organization.

6. **List and discuss the four variables that make up the indirect-action environment.**

   The indirect-action component of the environment consists of social, economic, political, and technical variables that influence the organization indirectly. These variables create a climate to which the organization must adjust, and they have the potential to move into the direct-action environment

7. **List the natural environment challenges that we face.**

   Concern about damage to the natural environment has taken on an increasingly important role in recent years. People are concerned about problems ranging from pollution to global warming and ozone depletion.

**8. Explain how organizations can respond to the natural environment.**

Some organizations have taken on active roles in promoting environmental awareness. Some managers choose merely to adhere to the legal requirements, while others go so far as to assert environmental values through their organizations' products and marketing. Managers—especially at higher levels—must monitor the external environment and try to forecast changes that will affect the organization. They may use strategic planning and organizational design to adjust to the environment.

## REVIEW QUESTIONS

1. What is the importance of the external environment?
2. What is the difference between natural and organizational environments?
3. What are the elements of the direct-action environment?
4. Who are the stakeholders of an organization?
5. How can organizations use stakeholder networks and coalitions to influence stakeholders?
6. What are the four variables that comprise the indirect-action environment?
7. What natural environment challenges do we face?
8. How can organizations respond to the natural environment?

## KEY TERMS

External environment
Inputs
Outputs
Direct-action elements
Indirect-action elements
Stakeholders
External stakeholders
Internal stakeholders
Special-interest groups

Political action committees
Collective bargaining
Social variables
Economic variables
Political variables
Technological variables
Cost-benefit model
Sustainable development

## TRI-STATE TELEPHONE[23]

John Godwin, chief executive of Tri-State Telephone, leaned back in his chair and looked at the ceiling. How was he ever going to get out of this mess? At last night's public hearing, 150 angry customers had marched in to protest Tri-State's latest rate request. After the rancorous shouting was over and the acrimonious signs put away, the protesters had presented state regulators with some sophisticated economic analyses in support of their case. Additionally, there were a number of emotional appeals from elderly customers who regarded phone service as their lifeline to the outside world.

Tri-State Telephone operated in three states and had sales of over $3 billion. During the last five years, the company had experienced a tremendous amount of change. In 1984, the AT&T divestiture sent shock waves throughout the industry, and Tri-State Telephone had felt the effects, as pricing for long-distance telephone service changed dramatically. The Federal Communications Commission instituted a charge to the effect that customers should have "access" to long-distance companies whether or not they were in the habit of making long distance calls. Consumer groups, including the Consumer Federation of America and the Congress of Consumer Organizations, had joined the protest, increasing their attention on the industry and intervening in regulatory proceedings wherever possible. The FCC was considering deregulating as much of the industry as possible, and Congress was looking over the commissioner's shoulder. Meanwhile, the Department of Justice and Judge Harold Greene (both of whom were responsible for monitoring the AT&T divestiture) continued to argue about what business companies like Tri-State should be engaged in.

In addition, technology was changing rapidly. Cellular telephones, primarily used in cars, were now hand-held and could be substituted for standard phones. Digital technology was going forward, leading to lower costs and requiring companies like Tri-State to invest to keep up with the state of the art. Meanwhile, rate increases negotiated during the inflationary 1970s were keeping earnings higher than regulators would authorize. New "intelligent" termi-nals and software developments gave rise to new uses for the phone network (such as using the phone for an alarm system), but as long as customers paid one flat fee, the phone company could not benefit from these new services.

Godwin's company has recently proposed a new pricing system whereby users of local telephone services would simply pay for what they used rather than a monthly flat fee. All of the senior managers were convinced that the plan was fairer, even though some groups who used the phone with notable frequency (like real estate agents) would pay more. It would give the company an incentive to bring new services to their customers, and customers would be able to choose which ones to buy. None of them had anticipated the hue and cry from the very customers who would save money under the new plan. For instance, Godwin's studies showed that the elderly were very light users of local service and could save as much as 20 percent under the new plan.

After the debacle at the hearing the previous night, Godwin was unsure how to proceed. If he backed off the new pricing plan, he would have to find a different way to meet the challenges of the future—maybe even different businesses to augment company income. Alternatively, the company could not stand the negative press from a protracted battle, even though Godwin thought that the regulators were favorably disposed toward his plan. In fact, Godwin himself believed the company should help its customers rather than fight with them.

### CASE QUESTIONS

1. Who are the stakeholders in this case?
2. Which stakeholders are most important?
3. What are the critical trends in Tri-State's environment?
4. Why do you think Tri-State's customers are so upset?
5. What should John Godwin do?

## ENVIRONMENTAL AWARENESS PAYS OFF AT
## FARMERS INSURANCE[54]

In 1989, California passed the Clean Air Act in an attempt to combat the increasing levels of air pollution that had made cities such as Los Angeles synonymous with smog. Because much of the state's pollution problems were as a result of the phenomenal number of Californian commuters, the act called upon businesses in the state to take an active role in reducing the number of cars on the road. Companies with 100 employees or more at one site were told to submit "rideshare" plans to California's Air Quality Management District (AQMD) each year. The rideshare plans were to be centered on achieving an employee average vehicle ridership (AVR) of 1.5, or 3 employees to every 2 cars on site, by 1999. And to ensure that the Clean Air Act would be taken seriously, the AQMD was authorized to fine companies without approved rideshare programs up to $25,000 a day. Needless to say, this left most companies scrambling to find ways to get their employees to share rides.

Farmers Insurance Group is one California company that is not only succeeding in complying with the Act, but excelling. "In one year we went from an average vehicle ridership of 1.17 to 1.30, and we're still growing," Debbie Dala, employee transportation coordinator at Farmers, stated proudly.[55] "We used the opportunity presented by the Clean Air Act to develop a comprehensive employee-incentive program to encourage ridesharing and strengthen our commitment to the environment."[56]

Getting employees to rideshare is not as easy as Dala makes it sound, however. Many companies offering everything from cash to preferred parking for employees who rideshare have met with results less spectacular than those seen at Farmers. Victoria Collins, vice president of marketing for the promotional company JSI West, points out that Farmers' success is not typical. "Companies come to us having implemented a program for a year or more and having an AVR as low as 1.06. For Farmers to increase its ridership to 1.3 in one year is pretty good," says Collins.[57] While JSI provided the rideshare incentive program for Farmers, the real reason for their success, says Collins, has been the aggressive participation of Dala herself. "She markets the program, sets up activities and events, and publishes a newsletter," she says. "You need a person who has a sense of which types of awards are right for your employees."[58]

In order to arouse interest in ridesharing, Farmers set up an incentive program that enables employees to earn points that can be redeemed for merchandise ranging from a bird feeder to an inflatable catamaran. "One woman used her points for a flashlight for her husband's car, in case of a road emergency. Then she decided that she needed one for herself," recalled Dala.[59] To be eligible for the ridesharing award program, employees must share rides for at least half of the distance between home and the office, and they must share rides at least one day a week. They earn one point for every day they rideshare, and employees who earn 20 points in a month receive five bonus points. Employees who receive 60 points in a quarter receive 10 bonus points. Additional bonus points can be earned by recruiting co-workers. With the points earned, employees then shop from a special catalog that includes a variety of electronic equipment, sports equipment and tools. It only takes 25 points—the equivalent of just one month's ridesharing—to get an AM/FM Walkman radio. For 150 points, an employee can purchase a Sony Mega Watchman or, for 340 points, a Toshiba 20″ color television. "[Employees] really enjoy the awards and find the levels attainable," says Dala.[60]

During her early days of administrating the rideshare program at Farmers, Dala concentrated most of her attention on organizing a foundation for the program. Once the program became established, though, she was able to shift her efforts more toward recruiting new hires. "Human resources provides me with a 10- to 15-minute segment during the new-hire orientation, so I can explain the program to the new employees," says Dala. "This gets them before they've established habits."[61] She gives a history of the Clean Air Act and Farmers' support of it and then explains the point system. She also shows off the merchandise catalog. For those new hires who are interested, Dala uses a list of employees currently ridesharing, typical arrival and departure times, and zip codes to put ridesharers in contact with one another.

It is not enough, though, for Dala merely to sign up new recruits. "Companies need to do something to stimulate interest in the program and keep employees in the program until it becomes a habit," Collins asserted. "The first year of a rideshare program is the hardest."[62] Dala's efforts are therefore also aimed at continually promoting the program in order to keep participating employees on board. "We have a bulletin board, which I change once a month," she pointed out. "It has a new-member section and a section from the catalog. I put out flyers to remind people, and put on a slogan and jingle contest once a month."[63] In addition, when employees pick up their awards, Dala puts their pictures on the bulletin board. "It never fails," she remarked. "Right after that, two more people come down from the same department to look at the catalog."[64]

Dala's efforts have paid off. Employees enjoy using the points to purchase goods, and some even appreciate the social aspect of the ridesharing experience. "People seem to like to rideshare. They make friends with their rideshare partners," Dala explained.[65] Under Dala's leadership Farmers has been able to implement one of the most successful ridesharing programs in the country. Ridesharing has also reduced some employees' stress, which, in turn, could lead them to work more productively. But Dala has even greater expectations for the program, "I'm waiting for two people who rideshare together to get married—now *that* would be something."[66]

## CASE QUESTIONS

1. How have environmental concerns influenced policies at Farmers Insurance?

2. What stakeholders can ridesharing affect?

3. How has ridesharing influenced the organizational environment at Farmers Insurance?

## CHAPTER 4

# SOCIAL RESPONSIBILITY AND ETHICS

**Upon completing this chapter, you should be able to:**

1. Discuss the basic principles of Andrew Carnegie's *The Gospel of Wealth.*

2. Evaluate the criticisms of Carnegie's gospel.

3. Explain Milton Friedman's position on corporate social responsibility.

4. Compare and contrast Carnegie's views with those of Friedman.

5. Explain the concept of enlightened self-interest.

6. List and define the key terms used in ethics.

7. Discuss the issues a manager must consider in applying ethics.

8. Evaluate the challenge of relativism to moral reasoning.

# KINKO'S: ETHICS, RESPONSIBILITY AND COPYRIGHT LAWS[1]

Radio Ad
Anncr: (Music background) "Managing Your Business Trip" presented by Kinko's Copy Centers. (Music fades)

(Conversation over the phone between two colleagues)
Voice 1: My plane didn't get in till 10:00.
Voice 2: That late? What about our presentation....
We made changes after you left...
Voice 1: Jim faxed them to me.
Voice 2: Where?
Voice 1: At our branch office.... I made the changes there.
Voice 2: Twenty copies?
Voice 1: All collated, spiral bound...
Voice 2: Color charts?
Voice 1: Done.
Voice 2: Great! (Hesitantly) We don't have a branch office...
Voice 1: Sure we do.
Anncr: Kinko's... Your Branch Office. Twenty-four hours a day, seven days a week. Over 600 locations. For the Kinko's near you, call 1-800-743-COPY.

*Twenty-four hours a day, people can be found at a Kinko's.*

Across the street from virtually every major college and university in the United States there is a Kinko's® copy center. Twenty-four hours a day, people can be found at a Kinko's, pasting-up and copying documents for their academic, personal, and professional purposes. Imagine a typical scene: In one corner, a community leader sits at a Macintosh, putting together a newsletter for a local charity organization. In another part of the room stand a handful of students, gathered around several copy machines. A few are copying notes, stapling the different sets. Another is cutting out pictures from magazines and pasting them onto a collage. Over near the cash register, a businessperson waits for a Kinko's worker to finish reducing a 10-page document that will then be faxed to someone waiting in the Kinko's office in Japan. This is what Kinko's is about: meeting the demands of the information age by providing a full range of services for a diverse array of customers, from students to professionals.

The Kinko's copy centers we know today as "branch offices" capable of performing any business demand began primarily as a service for students and professors.

**COPIES AT KINKO'S.** Kinko's copy centers can be found throughout the United States, ready to assist customers with their document needs from creation to communication.

Ever since Paul Orfalea, nicknamed "Kinko" for his frizzy hair, opened the first Kinko's (an official trademark of Kinko's Graphics Corporation) in 1970 in Santa Barbara, California, the copy shop has exhibited a strong customer focus. Orfalea strategically located the first shop near the campus of the University of California at Santa Barbara to bring service to the students and faculty, instead of waiting for them to come to him. The shop's physical layout continues to serve the customer with easy access provided to the desktop publishing, paste-up, and copying facilities. Kinko's now numbers somewhere around 650, with locations in all 50 states as well as Canada and London. All Kinko's copy shops are owned by a few closely-held corporations, with Orfalea having a hand in all of them. Because control and consistency are essential to the Kinko's philosophy, Kinko's is not franchised. →

Kinko's mission lies in serving the customer from the point a document is created until the point it is completed. What this means has changed over the years, and continues to change, but it basically translates into offering both self-serve and full-serve desktop publishing and copying; free access to supplies such as staplers, tape, paper cutters, rubber cement, and glue; stationery supplies for sale, and faxing capabilities.

By the mid-1980s, Kinko's realized that it could expand its business and serve its customers better by working more closely with the faculty at neighboring colleges and universities. Noticing that professors are often unsatisfied with the single textbooks available and, therefore, may create syllabi that incorporate chapters from any number of books, Kinko's saw a role it could play in working with professors to create custom-made packets for students.

Kinko's thus identified a market that was not currently being served, and offered a publishing service that enabled professors to put together tailor-made anthologies for their students. The professors could request that selected excerpts from books be copied and included in specially bound volumes that could then be sold to students as course "packets." In keeping with the theme of bringing the business to the customer, Kinko's actually solicited reading lists from faculty members at local colleges and universities at the beginning of each semester so the anthologies could be compiled. This provided a cost-effective and efficient alternative to the previous standard procedures—students' buying all of the individual books, or professors placing desired books on reserve in the library so students could check them out and copy the pertinent sections.

The Kinko's practice called into question the issue of copyright. Most, if not all, of the sources for these anthologies were already-published works. This meant that they were copyrighted, and could not be copied legally without the permission of the publisher. Obtaining permission took time, however, which Kinko's did not always have; professors often worked up until the very last minute, creating and revising their syllabi. Still, it was the practice—and the responsibility—of Kinko's to obtain the necessary copyright permissions and pay any necessary royalty fees, passing the cost along in the price of the bound volume.

A copyright is something of value to the owner, just as is a title to land, even though the copyright protects "intellectual" property as opposed to "real" property. However, because a copyright is tied to intellectual, intangible matter, it is more difficult to protect. Of particular concern are out-of-print works. Owners of the copyrights on such works rely exclusively on the royalties for financial returns on their investment.

As it turned out, not all Kinko's stores were attentive in obtaining the necessary copyright permission. Indeed, in 1989, eight publishing companies—Basic Books, Harper & Row, John Wiley & Sons, McGraw-Hill, Penguin Books, Prentice Hall, Richard D. Irwin, and William Morrow & Co.—discovered that copyright permission had not been obtained for the material in some of the volumes sold by at least two Kinko's stores in New York, and they joined together in a suit against Kinko's for copyright infringement. If these were the only two instances where copyright permission had not been obtained, it might not have been a concern; however, the size of the market that Kinko's was serving—thousands of students at hundreds of colleges and universities around the country—suggested that these were not isolated incidents. Thus the issue was extremely significant. →

**corporate social responsibility:**
What an organization does to influence the society in which it exists, such as through volunteer assistance programs.

The purpose of this chapter is to explain the evolution of a concern with ethics and social responsibility in organizations, and to present some frameworks for analyzing ethical decisions. For many years managers and theorists have talked about an organization's responsibility to society. **Corporate social responsibility** focuses on what an organization does that affects the society in which it exists. More recently, managers and theorists have broadened their concerns to include basic ethical questions such as, "How should we live in relation to each other?" We de-

**ethics:**
The study of rights and of who is—or should be—benefited or harmed by an action.

fine **ethics** broadly and simply as the study of how our decisions affect other people.* It is also the study of people's rights and duties, the moral rules that people apply in making decisions, and the nature of the relationships among people.

# ETHICS AND SOCIAL RESPONSIBILITY TODAY

**E**thics and social responsibility are concepts that are fundamentally about the quality of our relationships over time. The Kinko's dilemma makes it clear that many organizational decisions involve knotty problems where organizational interests affect the interests of others. The stock market scandals in the United States and Japan, the corruption between business and government in Italy, the possibilities and consequences of new technologies, and the increasing interplay of different cultures are just some of the issues that have brought questions about the social responsibility and ethics of business to the forefront.

Companies and managers that ignore moral concerns are saying to those affected, "We don't want to invest in making this relationship better." And, even though unethical behavior may sometimes pay today, those who ignore ethical issues are heading for trouble over the long run. From the 60-year-old Credo of Johnson & Johnson to AT&T's new statement of values, called "Our Common Bond," companies are using their past experiences and values and the concerns of the present in setting new moral visions for the future.

Today there are many examples of how people can manage with corporate social responsibility and ethics in mind:[2]

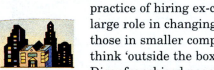

- Elliot Hoffman, owner of Just Desserts, a San Francisco bakery, instituted a practice of hiring ex-convicts. "I really believe that business has to play a large role in changing our society," he says. "Businesspeople, especially those in smaller companies, know how to get things done. We tend to think 'outside the box'. We need to bring that creativity to our community. Disenfranchised people need on-ramps into society. Those aren't going to come from the federal government."
- In response to the homeless situation, one of Ben & Jerry's answers was to open a store in Harlem and employ homeless people to serve ice cream.
- For every UPC code mailed in by consumers, Scott Paper donates five cents to Ronald McDonald Houses. According to spokeswoman Laura Boyce, "We get a chance to spotlight a worthy organization, and it creates awareness among consumers, too."
- Paul Newman earmarks all of the profits from *Newman's Own* food products for various charities, such as the Hole in the Wall Gang, a camp for children with terminal cancer.
- The Campbell Soup Company has sponsored a long-running program, "Labels for Education," that involves supplying equipment to schools based on the number of Campbell and Swanson labels sent in by consumers during the school year.
- Burger King, along with IBM, operates a similar program. Through "Burgers and Bytes," computers are donated to schools according to the number of cash-register receipts generated. Burger King also operates Burger King Academy to provide education and social services for dropouts and truants.

---

* Some writers make a further distinction between "ethics" and "morals," but we believe that this is needlessly confusing.

**EDUCATING COLGATE KIDS.** School children created this playground map at their school using a kit supplied by Colgate Palmolive—just one of the company's socially responsible ventures.

- In Louisiana in 1991, Colgate-Palmolive kicked off its "Partners in Education" program, which doubled as a marketing endeavor and a philanthropic measure. In return for retailers putting up their display, the company gave the retailers Map Playground Kits, which included materials for students to paint their own maps. The stores then dispersed the kits to local grade schools.

- Reebok ended up launching a new product in 1991—the BlackTop line of outdoor basketball shoes. Part of the profits from the shoes are used to renovate basketball courts, such as a court in South Dade County, Florida, devastated by Hurricane Andrew and renovated in 1993. "Our involvement in Court Renewal gives us a lot more credibility for the [BlackTop line], so I'd say it's a major factor in the product's success," according to spokesman Dave Fogelson. "But it started because we wanted to do something for inner-city kids."

## THE CHANGING CONCEPT OF SOCIAL RESPONSIBILITY

**B**ig businesses have always been criticized. Beginning around the turn of the century, crusading journalists—the "muckrakers"—shocked the nation with exposés of corrupt business practices, touching off a wave of government regulation. Other waves of government regulation were created in the wake of the Great Depression of the 1930s and then again in the 1960s and 1970s, when the civil rights and consumer movements held corporations responsible for a growing list of social problems.

## ATTITUDES TOWARD BIG BUSINESS AND BIG GOVERNMENT

In examining attitudes about business and government in the United States, it is interesting to take a look at history. The rise of big business created a set of relationships that our society and its founders had not envisioned. By 1890 each of the several railroads employed over 100,000 workers, and organizations such as John D. Rockefeller's Standard Oil Company had grown into huge multinational corporations. Through mergers and internal expansions, tobacco companies also grew rapidly around the turn of the century. This became a symbol of giantism in the American economy, one originally based on small farmers and shopkeepers. Government was small and very limited in comparison to its regulatory capacity today. One of the distinguishing characteristics that still prevails today when we compare U.S. regulatory relationships between the public and private sectors to other nations, particularly European countries, is that the United States stands alone of all major market economies in having big business precede big government. In countries such as Britain, France, Germany, and Japan well-established government bureaucracy was embedded in the culture and provided a counterbalance to big business. In America there was no such culture; in fact, the culture was founded on the value of rejecting the interference of government into the affairs of business, big or small. This legacy has made the relationship of the two sectors around issues of regulation quite often an adversarial and costly process. ▬

Government regulations provide some ground rules for managers, but they do not answer some pressing questions: Where does an organization's social responsibility begin? Where does it end? To answer these questions, we need to take a closer look at different views of corporate social responsibility and responsiveness that have developed over the past century.

## ANDREW CARNEGIE AND THE GOSPEL OF WEALTH

In 1899, Andrew Carnegie (1835-1919), founder of the conglomerate U.S. Steel corporation, published a book called *The Gospel of Wealth,* which set forth the classic statement of *corporate social responsibility.* Carnegie's view was based on two principles: the charity principle and the stewardship principle. Both were frankly paternalistic; they saw business owners in a parent-like role to childlike employees and customers who lacked the capacity to act in their own best interests.[3]

**charity principle:**
Doctrine of social responsibility requiring more fortunate individuals to assist less fortunate members of society.

The **charity principle** required the more fortunate members of society to assist its less fortunate members, including the unemployed, the handicapped, the sick, and the elderly. These unfortunates could be aided either directly or indirectly, through such institutions as churches, settlement houses, and (from the 1920s onward) the Community Chest movement. Of course, well-to-do people themselves decided how much to contribute, and initially charity was considered an obligation of individuals, not of business itself. By the 1920s, however, community needs outgrew the wealth of even the most generous wealthy individuals, and business was expected to contribute its resources to charities aiding the unfortu-

**THE STEWARDSHIP PRINCIPLE.** Some nuclear power plants have shown that nuclear plants can operate without jeopardizing the environment or their human neighbors.

**stewardship principle:**

Biblical doctrine that requires businesses and wealthy individuals to view themselves as stewards, or caretakers, holding their property in trust for the benefit of the whole society.

nate.[4] Carnegie himself practiced what he preached by giving away millions of dollars for charitable and civic purposes.

The **stewardship principle,** derived from the Bible, required businesses and wealthy individuals to view themselves as the stewards, or caretakers, of their property. Carnegie's idea was that the rich hold their money "in trust" for the rest of society and can use it for any purpose that society deems legitimate. However, he also saw it as the role of business to multiply society's wealth by increasing its own through prudent investments of the resources under its stewardship.[5]

U.S. Steel, acting on Carnegie's ideas, embarked upon an active program of philanthropy. It was the exception rather than the rule; between the Civil War and the Great Depression, most management commitments to social welfare were in response to legal requirements or labor-movement pressure.[6]

Not until the Great Depression of the 1930s did large numbers of executives take an independent interest in the social impact of business. In 1936, for example, Robert Wood (the CEO of Sears, Roebuck) pointed proudly to his "stewardship" of "those general broad social responsibilities which cannot be presented mathematically and yet are of prime importance."[7] By the 1950s and 1960s, the charity and stewardship principles were widely accepted in American business as more and more companies came to recognize that "power begets responsibility." Even companies that did not subscribe to these principles realized that if business did not accept social responsibilities of its own free will, it would be forced to accept them by the government.

There are many examples of the applications of these principles today. The charity principle could be seen after the Los Angeles riots, when many corporations gave cash to individual church relief efforts. Fame Assistance Corp., the nonprofit human services arm of the First African Methodist Episcopal Church of Los Angeles, tripled its annual budget as a result of such charitable contributions. Donors included Atlantic Richfield, at $100,000, and AT&T Foundation, Wells Fargo, and First Interstate Bank of California Foundation, at $25,000 each. In addition, companies including American Express, Northern Trust of California, and Merrill Lynch instituted employee matching programs.

Giving to individual religious units generally proves to be problematic for companies, though, for if you give to one denomination, all others want a share as well.

According to Stanley C. Wright, director of Eastman Kodak's corporate contributions, "Once you start down the religious path, you better hit 'em all because they all buy cameras and film." Many companies have thus instituted a general prohibition against giving to individual religious efforts, and instead give only to umbrella groups. The donations to individual efforts in the wake of the Los Angeles riots thus represented a deviation from the norm.[8]

One problem with the concept of social responsibility had to do with the specifics of its implementation. Some critics suggested that there was no guideline for the appropriate magnitude of corporate concern, nor was there any suggestion of how a company should weigh its social responsibilities against its other responsibilities. For example, when Ford was developing the Pinto model, the company discovered that the gas tank was unusually prone to catching fire in crashes. The company undertook a cost-benefit analysis to see if fixing the problem would be worthwhile. The analysis showed that the company could make the car much safer by installing an $11 shield for the gas tank, but Ford decided not to do this. In effect, it decided that the human lives disrupted and destroyed by the faulty gas tanks were worth less than $11 per Pinto.[9]

Finally, some critics charged that the notion of "social responsibility" permitted business executives to choose their corporations' social obligations according to their own convictions. According to these critics, the notion of corporate responsibility became a smoke screen for the personal values of a few powerful individuals.

## MILTON FRIEDMAN'S ARGUMENT

In the 1970s and 1980s, the convergence of a number of economic forces led some scholars to reexamine the notion of corporate social responsibility. Business was reeling from the one-two punch of rising energy costs and the expense of complying with legislation designed to reduce pollution, protect consumers, and ensure equal opportunity. In addition, inflation and the national debt were soaring—a legacy of the Vietnam War, the Great Society programs of the 1960s, and the shifting balance of trade. Many held that if businesses were to survive, they must be relieved of inappropriate social responsibilities and allowed to get back to basics: making money. This is not a new idea. Its leading proponent in recent years has been the economist Milton Friedman, who argues that a business's primary responsibility is to maximize profits.

According to Friedman, "There is one and only one social responsibility of business: to use its resources and energy in activities designed to increase its profits so long as it stays within the rules of the game...[and] engages in open and free competition, without deception and fraud."[10] Friedman contends that corporate officials are in no position to determine the relative urgency of social problems or the amount of organizational resources that should be committed to a given problem. He also insists that managers who devote corporate resources to pursue personal, and perhaps misguided, notions of the social good unfairly tax their own shareholders, employees, and customers. In short, he argues, businesses should produce goods and services efficiently and leave the solution of social problems to concerned individuals and government agencies.

Friedman's views represent one extreme on a continuum that recognizes some division of social responsibility among the various segments of society, including government and the business community. Most managers and other people believe that both the government and the business community do have some responsibility to act in the interest of society. As the two most powerful institutions in the country, the sheer size of business and government obliges them to address problems of public concern. Both corporations and government depend upon acceptance by the society to which they belong.

For instance, businesses are subject to the regulations of the Occupational Safety and Health Administration (OSHA), the federal agency charged with en-

**GOVERNMENT RESPONSIBILITY.**
Gerard F. Scannell developed a reputation as a vigouous enforcer of workplace safety standards as head of the Occupational Safety and Health Administration (OSHA), the federal agency charged with ensuring safe and healthful working conditions in the United States.

suring safe and healthful working conditions. One of its projects was to prepare guidelines to eliminate repetitive-motion disorders, the cause of half of all workplace illnesses and disabilities. It has considerable power: In one case, OSHA chief Robert Scannell, former head of safety at Johnson & Johnson, levied fines of $7.3 million against USX for safety, health, and record-keeping violations, and pushed Ford Motor Co. to institute a company-wide program to reduce repetitive-motion hazards on the assembly line.

Another way in which social responsibility issues can affect corporate pocketbooks is through lawsuits brought by employees or others, which can cost organizations a great deal of money. For example, Fibreboard and its insurers approached settling their asbestos-litigation problems by setting aside a fund of $3 billion to pay for all pending and future claims brought by victims of asbestos injuries. This fund creates one of the largest single funds for asbestos victims in American history. Another example comes from the Exxon corporation. In the wake of the 1989 Alaskan oil spill and the subsequent controversy surrounding Exxon's efforts to clean up the spill, Exxon has sued more than 250 insurers seeking to recover some of its $3.6 billion in expenses from the accident. At the same time, Lloyd's of London and other insurers are suing Exxon in an effort to avoid paying claims related to the spill. The management of social responsibility can be a complex and challenging arena for companies.[11]

## ENLIGHTENED SELF-INTEREST

**enlightened self-interest:**
Organizations' realization that it is in their own best interest to act in ways that the community considers socially responsible.

Keith Davis has said that there is "an iron law of responsibility which states that in the long run those who do not use power in a manner that society considers responsible will tend to lose it."[12] So it may be that it is in the **enlightened self-interest** of organizations to be socially responsible—or at least *responsive* to social forces. For instance, if Kinko's does not act in an enlightened manner regarding copyright, its self interest may be jeopardized.

One example of how social responsibility can be in a company's self-interest is provided by the Dayton-Hudson Corp. of Minnesota. For years Dayton-Hudson has belonged to "the 5% Club"—a group of companies that donate 5 percent of their pretax profits to charity. While Friedman and others may argue that this money should go to the shareholders, others would point out that Dayton-Hudson's positive community image helped it get an anti-takeover law passed by the Minnesota legislature when it was in danger of a takeover.

## CORPORATE SOCIAL RESPONSIVENESS

**corporate social responsiveness:**

A theory of social responsibility that focuses on how companies respond to issues, rather than trying to determine their ultimate social responsibility.

The study of **corporate social responsiveness**—how organizations become aware of and then respond to social issues—takes two basic approaches. On the one hand, it deals with how individual companies respond to social issues. On the other hand, the theory deals with the forces that determine the social issues to which businesses should respond. These two approaches can be combined to classify the ways in which corporations can and do respond to specific social issues. Robert Ackerman was among the first to suggest that *responsiveness,* not responsibility, should be the goal of corporate social endeavors. Ackerman pointed out that corporate response to social issues has a life cycle, starting with corporate recognition of the problem, continuing through study of the problem and consideration of ways to deal with it, and concluding with implementation of a solution.[13] Implementation often comes slowly and at some point a company may lose the initiative as government or public opinion forces it to act. Ackerman advises managers to be responsive to problems early to retain the largest amount of managerial discretion.

For example, it has recently been suggested that women who spend a great deal of time working at video display terminals stand a higher-than-average chance of having problem pregnancies. The research is confusing and disputed by some investigators. Ackerman's point is that as this issue unfolds, and as more actors and competing interests become involved, managers could lose the power to handle the issue at their own discretion. We can easily imagine several studies confirming these early indications and the resulting drama of congressional hearings, work stoppages, lawsuits, and bureaucratic regulation. In Ackerman's model of social responsiveness, options are developed early in the life cycle of such an issue. It may be in the enlightened self-interest of companies to make the best information available to their employees, encourage them to ask questions, and even give transfers or retraining to workers who request them. Being responsive may well be the best course of action in the long run.

## CORPORATE SOCIAL PERFORMANCE

**corporate social performance:**

A single theory of corporate social action encompassing social principles, processes, and policies.

In 1979, Archie Carroll combined the philosophical ideas of social responsibility and social responsiveness into a single theory of corporate social action called **corporate social performance.**[14]

According to this theory, the arena of social responsibility debates is shaped by economic, legal, and ethical principles. In this country, for example, we support free enterprise (an economic principle), the public's right to a safe workplace (a legal principle), and equal employment opportunity (an ethical principle). Together these principles create a "social contract" between business and society that permits companies to act as moral agents.

At individual companies, managers try to implement the principles of the social contract in their decision-making *processes* and in their company *policies.* Their decisions and policies can reflect one of four stances:[15]

- *Reactive*—the company responds to a social issue only *after* it has challenged company goals
- *Defensive*—the company acts to ward off a challenge
- *Accommodative*—the company brings itself into line with government requirements and public opinion
- *Proactive*—the company anticipates demands that have not yet been made.

Corporate social performance is an important consideration for many investors, who believe that an organization's good social performance is not only socially responsible but leads to good financial performance. More than a dozen "social conscience" mutual funds exist that choose securities for investment purposes according to the companies' records in social responsibility—that is, in protecting the environment, helping the community, etc. What's interesting is that each fund uses its own standards in determining which securities are acceptable.[16]

The existence of so many different standards and ideas of social performance means that we must look to the underlying assumptions about organizations and society. Ultimately we have to turn to ethics as the study of the basic underlying values of people, organizations and society.

## ETHICS IN EASTERN THINKING

In discussing both social responsibility and ethics the underlying values of the culture are particularly crucial. In Asia the teachings of Confucius as well as other ancient scholars still have profound impact on thinking. Kong Fu Ze, whom the Jesuit missionaries renamed Confucius, was a high civil servant in China around 500 B.C. His teachings are lessons in practical

**SOCIALLY RESPONSIVE EMPLOYEES.** Organizations may promote socially responsible activities among employees. These bank employees added to the image of their company through their participation in a fund-raising "sports challenge" in their community.

ethics and have no religious content; Confucianism is not a religion but a set of pragmatic rules for living everyday life. Confucius drew his lessons from what he saw in Chinese history. The key principles of Confucian teachings are:

1. The stability of society is based on unequal relationships between people.
2. The family is the prototype of all social organizations.
3. Virtuous behavior toward others consists of treating others as one would like to be treated oneself. (This basic human benevolence does not, however, extend as far as the Christian injunction to love thy enemies.)
4. Virtues with regard to one's task in life include trying to acquire skill and education, working hard, not spending more than necessary, and being patient and persevering. Conspicuous consumption is taboo, as is losing one's temper. Moderation is enjoined in all things.

In line with this philosophy Chinese decision makers still consider dependability, loyalty, and job experience as important qualities and tend to reward these behaviors over such U.S. values as merit and performance (although, under the new economic reforms in China, there is some movement away from strict Confucian ethics). Much of the recent surge in Asian countries may have developed from the tenets of Confucius. These tenets provide a set of ethics for organizations that underlie the cultural attitudes and values of Chinese organizations.[17] ▬▬▬

## THE SHIFT TO ETHICS

Many critics say that we live in the time of "the ethics crisis." We see headlines that touch upon it daily. Controversies about influence peddling in Italy, Japan, and the United States; aftereffects of silicone breast implants; overcharging for rental cars; and unfair trade practices by large retailers have fueled a renewed concern about the role of ethics in business. All of this is in addition to the Wall Street scandals and the S & L crisis of the 1980s, which tarnished the reputation of many organizations. Not surprisingly, pollster Louis Harris reported that 70 percent of the public answers no to the question, "Does business see to it that its executives behave legally and ethically?"[18]

The Gallup polling organization reported similar findings from an earlier poll, done in 1983. According to that poll, nearly 50 percent of all Americans thought that business ethics had declined during the previous ten years. Executives themselves are unhappy about the current business climate: Close to 40 percent say superiors have at some point asked them to do something they considered unethical.[19]

Although public opinion polls, especially different ones done at different times, cannot be taken as definitive reflections of business conditions, all recent polls point in the same direction: Public confidence in business ethics has declined. As a result, many theorists are calling for a broader examination of business ethics. Because most business decisions have an ethical component (i.e., they affect the intentions of others), managers must add ethics to their understanding of organizations.

Many companies have made a commitment to ethics in business. For example, in the winter of 1993 Benetton ran a campaign to collect used clothing, in association with the International Red Cross and Coritas, a clothing charity. More than 90 percent of the 7,000 Benetton stores worldwide were equipped with brightly colored clothes bins during February and the beginning of March. This campaign, which replaced Benetton's AIDS campaign, kicked off with an ad of a naked retailer, clothed only in large text reading "I want my clothes back."[22]

# WAS KINKO'S USE FAIR?

In response to the suit brought by the publishing companies against Kinko's, Kathlene Karg, assistant copyright director of the Washington, D.C.-based Association of American Publishers, pointed out that "publishing houses have had enough, especially with out-of-print works where permission fees are the only royalty an author or publisher will get.... It is just not fair for some to comply and others not."[20] Authors often pour abundant resources into their works, in terms of time, creative inspiration, and money—just as a farmer pours money into the development of crops on his land. If a thief trespasses onto a farmer's land and steals the growing produce, the legal system punishes the thief for depriving the farmer of his or her returns. The publishing companies initiated the suit against Kinko's to ensure that copyright owners receive the just returns from the use of their intellectual property.

The Copyright Act of 1976 forbids the illegal copying of published material. This is a broad ban, generally aimed at protecting copyright owners from substantial copying for commercial purposes. A "fair use" exception was carved into the Copyright Act to protect insubstantial, educational copying. The student who copies a few pages at the library for personal use is not considered to be doing anything illegal. However, a business that derives profits from copying entire chapters for thousands of students at hundreds of colleges and universities around the country *is* doing something illegal if that business does not first obtain the requisite permission from the publishers of the copyrighted works.

In the action against Kinko's, the court held that the copying by Kinko's, in the absence of permission from the publishers, constituted illegal copyright infringement. Although Kinko's argued that its use constituted "fair use," in that it was serving the academic community, the court refused to look beyond the underlying financial incentives and the profits Kinko's received. The court found, "Although Kinko's tries to impress this court with its purportedly altruistic motives, the facts show that Kinko's copying had the intended purpose of supplanting the copyright holders' commercially valuable right."[21] The court thus fined Kinko's, but refrained from issuing a final order until Kinko's and the publishing companies were able to come to terms with an overall agreement as to how things would be handled in the future. In the end, Kinko's agreed to a $1.9 million settlement, covering both fines and court costs.

Kinko's attempt to be responsive to the needs of the academic community ran into a complicated legal and ethical issue. This case illustrates why focusing solely on social responsibility fails to capture the full complexity of major organizational decisions. This is where a broader ethical analysis is needed. →

## WHAT IS ETHICS?

We have defined *ethics* as the study of how our decisions affect other people. As previously noted, it is also the study of people's rights and duties, the moral rules that people apply in making decisions, and the nature of the relationships among people.[23]

**SOCIAL RESPONSIBILITY IN ADVERTISING.** During the 1990s, many companies have coordinated their advertising programs with support of social issues. Esprit's "What would you do?" campaign included ads promoting a number of causes, including the rights of the disabled.

## FOUR LEVELS OF ETHICAL QUESTIONS IN BUSINESS

We cannot avoid ethical issues in business any more than we can avoid them in other areas of our lives. In business, most ethical questions fall into one or more of four categories: societal, stakeholder, internal policy, or personal (see Figure 4-1).

**SOCIETAL.** At the *societal* level, we ask questions about the basic institutions in a society. The problem of apartheid in South Africa was a societal-level question: Is it ethically correct to have a social system in which a group of people—indeed, the majority—is systematically denied basic rights? Although recent changes in South Africa have ended the apartheid system, it is difficult to project how smoothly the transition to equality will go. Companies wishing to do business there still face a complex set of issues as political, economic, and social dynamics change; the situation can still present an ethical conundrum for many companies. [24]

Another societal-level question concerns the merits of capitalism. Is capitalism a just system for allocating resources? What role should the government play in regulating the marketplace? Should we tolerate gross inequalities of wealth, status, and power? For some people, the relatively huge increases in executive compensation in the past decade or so in the United States are part of this issue. For example, in the United States from 1980 to 1990, while worker pay increased 53 percent and corporate profits 78 percent, CEO pay rose by 212 percent. In 1980 the chief executive's average pay was $624,996, with total compensation 42 times the pay of a factory worker. In 1992 the average CEO made a record $3,842,247 in total pay—157 times what factory workers earned. By way of contrast, in Japan

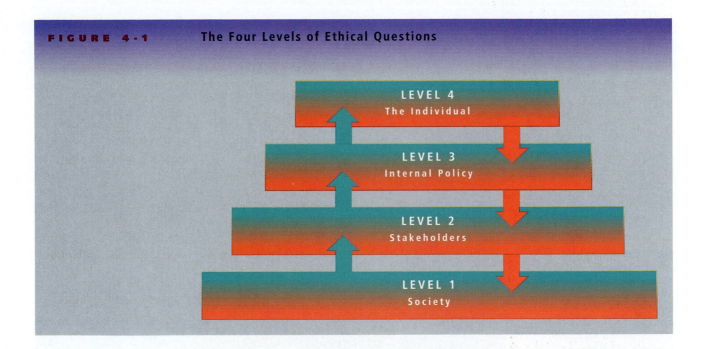

**FIGURE 4-1** **The Four Levels of Ethical Questions**

LEVEL 4
The Individual

LEVEL 3
Internal Policy

LEVEL 2
Stakeholders

LEVEL 1
Society

CEOs make less than 32 times as much as the rank-and-file. In 1992 there were only eight Japanese CEOs whose compensation was over a million dollars.[25]

Societal-level questions usually represent an ongoing debate among major competing institutions. As managers and individuals, each of us can try to shape that debate. Andrew Carnegie (along with other early theorists of corporate social responsibility) worked at this level when he argued that the proper role of a business such as his own U.S. Steel was to apply the principles of charity to assist the poor and unfortunate.

← ch. 3, p. 63

**STAKEHOLDER.** The second kind of ethical questions concerns stakeholders—suppliers, customers, shareholders, and the rest. Here we ask questions about how a company should deal with the external groups affected by its decisions, as well as how the stakeholders should deal with the company.

There are many stakeholder issues. Insider trading is one; another is a company's obligation to inform its customers about the potential dangers of its products. What obligations does a company have to its suppliers? To the communities where it operates? To its stockholders? How should we attempt to decide such matters? Kinko's managers face the ethical question of whether to respect the rights of copyright holders as stakeholders.

**INTERNAL POLICY.** A third category of ethics might be called "internal policy." Here we ask questions about the nature of a company's relations with its employees. What kind of employment contract is fair? What are the mutual obligations of managers and workers? What rights do employees have? These questions, too, pervade the workday of a manager. Layoffs, benefits, work rules, motivation, and leadership are all ethical concerns here.

**PERSONAL.** Here we ask questions about how people should treat one another within an organization. Should we be honest with one another, whatever the consequences? What obligations do we have—both as human beings and as workers who fill specific work roles—to our bosses, our employees, and our peers? These questions deal with the day-to-day issues of life in any organization. Behind them lie two broader issues: Do we have the right to look at other people primarily as means to our ends? Can we avoid doing so?

**STAKEHOLDER LEVEL.** What obligations does a company have to the communities where it operates? Here, Little League fields and basketball courts next to an industrial site are reminders that businesses need to think about being good neighbors.

One example of meeting ethical obligations is Kidd & Co. When a fire destroyed family-owned Kidd & Co.'s Nevada marshmallow factory, vice president John Kidd and his older brother Charlie decided to pay all 63 employees while they were rebuilding, honoring an obligation to employees and other stakeholders. In turn, the employees performed community service work.

## THE TOOLS OF ETHICS

Consciously or unconsciously, we engage in some kind of ethical reasoning every day of our lives. To improve our ethical reasoning, we must analyze it explicitly and practice it daily.* The key terms of the ethical language are *values, rights, duties, rules,* and *relationships.* Let's consider each in turn.

### VALUES

**values:**

Relatively permanent desires that seem to be good in themselves.

When you value something, you want it or you want it to happen. **Values** are relatively permanent desires that seem to be good in themselves, like peace or goodwill.

Values are the answers to the "why" questions. Why, for example, are you reading this book? You might reply that you want to learn about management. Why is that important? To be a better manager. Why do you want that? To be promoted and make more money sooner. Why do you need more money? To spend it on a VCR. Such questions go on and on, until you reach the point where you no longer want something for the sake of something else. At this point, you have arrived at a value. Corporations also have values, such as size, profitability, or making a quality product.

Recently AT&T CEO Robert Allen articulated a set of values called "Our Common Bond," intended to serve as the anchors for the future. The telecommunications industry is changing so fast that it is difficult to make decisions on common management principles, so Allen turned to values for an answer. Our

---

* Our framework here begins the complex process of applying ethical reasoning to business. Many vague, grey areas remain.

Common Bond lists respect for the individual, teamwork, dedication to customers, innovation, and integrity as the ground rules for AT&T and its subsidiaries.

## VALUES LEAD TO QUALITY IMPROVEMENTS AT L. L. BEAN

Two important values at L. L. Bean are providing top-quality customer service and employee development. Over the years, employees of this mail-order and retail dealer in Freeport, Maine, have gone above-and-beyond to carry out Bean's tradition of quality service, sustaining the company's reputation for quality. For example, when a customer in New York failed to receive his canoe in time for a weekend trip, an L. L. Bean sales representative drove the canoe to the customer. That was not the end of it, however; the incident made company managers question why the canoe did not arrive on time. They discovered that although company employees were committed to customer service, they were not empowered to make the type of decisions necessary to prevent such occurrences, nor did they have the necessary knowledge of processes elsewhere in the company that affect such situations.

To correct the system, L. L. Bean employed a total quality management approach. However, rather than focusing on process improvement, as most companies do when starting on this type of change, L. L. Bean centered its efforts on employee development. Bean's definition of total quality reflects its valuing of employees: "Total quality involves managing an enterprise to maximize customer satisfaction in the most efficient and effective way possible by totally involving people in improving the way it is done." The total quality approach also involved challenging all the company's assumptions and redesigning its processes. The change has been very successful, leading to higher profits and increased customer satisfaction.[26] ◼

### RIGHTS AND DUTIES

**rights:**
Claims that entitle a person to take a particular action.

A **right** is a claim that entitles a person the "room" in which to take action. In more formal terms, one might call this room a person's "sphere of autonomy" or, more simply, his or her freedom. Rights are rarely absolute; most people would agree that the scope of individual rights is limited by the rights of others. Ordinarily, you have a right to speak your mind freely—until you make slanderous statements about another person.

**duties:**
Obligations to take specific steps or obey the law.

Moreover, rights are correlated with duties. Whenever someone has a right, someone else has a duty to respect it. A **duty** is an obligation to take specific steps—to pay taxes, for example, and to obey the law in other respects.

### MORAL RULES

**moral rules:**
Rules for behavior that often become internalized as moral values.

**Moral rules** guide us through situations where competing interests collide. You might think of moral rules as "tie breakers"—guidelines that can resolve disagreements. Moral rules, which are rules for behavior, often become internalized as values.

### HUMAN RELATIONSHIPS

Every human being is connected to others in a web of relationships. These relationships exist because we need one another for mutual support and to accomplish our goals. From a small child's relationship with parents to a manager's relationship

**PROMISE KEEPING.** Many business agreements are initially sealed on the strength of a handshake. Business would grind to a halt without the simple convention of promise keeping, part of the rules of common morality.

**common morality:**
The body of moral rules governing ordinary ethical problems.

with an employee, relationships are a pervasive aspect of moral life. We constantly decide how to maintain and nurture them. These decisions reflect our values and our concern for ethics. So, when we say that management is about relationships (see Chapter 1), we are claiming that it has a large ethical component.

## COMMON MORALITY

**Common Morality** is the body of moral rules governing ordinary ethical problems. These are the rules we live by most of the time, and which we can use to understand managerial problems in ethical terms. Let's briefly examine some basic principles of common morality to see how they work.*

**PROMISE KEEPING.** Most people want to have some assurance that other people will do what they say. Without the simple convention of promise keeping, social interaction would grind to a halt; business would be impossible. Every moral theory thus asserts, at the very least, that human beings should keep most of their promises most of the time. Insider trading became such a scandal in part because those who were caught had promised not to engage in such activities.

**NONMALEVOLENCE.** Among other things, rights and duties provide ways of preventing violent conflict. If we constantly had to worry about our basic physical safety, we would be much less willing to trust other people and to engage in complex dealings that might involve disputes with them. Most moral theories thus require that most people, most of the time, refrain from harming other human beings.

There are, of course, exceptions. We allow the police to use force to subdue criminals; we accept wars that we regard as just; and we let people defend themselves when they are attacked without cause. But morality requires us to avoid violence in settling disputes.

**MUTUAL AID.** Human communities are sustained by the recognition that people depend on each other and help each other. Blood donation and the United Way are good examples. According to the principle of mutual aid, individuals should help one another if the cost of doing so is not great.

---

\* There is disagreement about the scope of common morality, especially when this concept is applied across cultures.

| TABLE 4-1 | Key Differences in the Justice and Care Perspectives | |
| --- | --- | --- |
| | **JUSTICE** | **CARE** |
| Orientation | Separation; autonomy | Attachment; interdependence |
| Mode of thinking | Formal; abstract | Contextual; narrative |
| Idea of morality | Fairness; rights; equality | Care; responsibility |
| | Primacy of individual | Primacy of relationship |
| | "Formal logic of fairness" | "Psychological logic of relationships" |
| | Separation justified by ethic of rights | Attachment required by ethic of care |
| Conflict resolution | Balancing rights; adversarial adjudication | Communication; protecting relationships |
| Responsibility | Limiting aggression and protecting rights | Extension of care and nuturing of relationships |
| Images of violence | Closeness | Isolation |
| Metaphor of relationship | Hierarchy or balance | Network or web |

*Source:* Rebecca Villa, Andrew Wicks, and R. Edward Freeman, "A Note on the Ethics of Caring" (Charlottesville: Darden Graduate Business School Foundation, UVA-E-068, 1990).

**RESPECT FOR PERSONS.** Common morality also requires us to regard other people as ends in themselves, not as mere means to our own ends. Treating people as ends involves taking them seriously, accepting their interests as legitimate, and regarding their desires as important.

**RESPECT FOR PROPERTY.** Property plays a prominent role in capitalism. Underlying the idea of property is the principle that most people, most of the time, should get the consent of others before using their property. If you think of people as owning their own bodies, respect for property is a corollary of respect for individuals. At Kinko's, the issue is the respect for copyright holders and their copyright as property.

## THE MORALITY OF CARE

Recent theorists such as Carol Gilligan and Nell Noddings have argued that common morality—the morality of rules and justice—is only one perspective for reasoning about morality.[27] They have suggested an alternative mode of reasoning called "the ethics of care." Gilligan proposes that there are two strands of moral theory— the "justice" perspective and the "care" perspective—with the justice perspective more typical of men and the care perspective more common among women.

People operating from the justice perspective emphasize separateness from others and an autonomous life. They see the solutions to moral problems as a balancing of competing rights in a formal and abstract manner. In contrast, the care perspective is characterized by a sense of connection to others, a life of love and caring, and a view that moral problems arise from conflicting responsibilities, which often require subtle interpretation of relationships.

People who take the justice perspective fear entangling connections to others. They want to protect the rights that preserve separation. Those operating from the care perspective, on the other hand, fear that a morality based on rights and noninterference will sanction indifference and unconcern. People who take the justice perspective criticize the care perspective as being inconclusive, ambiguous, and inconsistent because of its situational emphasis. Those who operate from the care perspective see the justice orientation as unfeeling, unemotional, and afraid of commitments. The main differences between these two perspectives are summarized in Table 4-1.

---

**EXHIBIT 4-1**

**12 Questions for Examining the Ethics of a Business Decision**

1. Have you defined the problem accurately?
2. How would you define the problem if you stood on the other side of the fence?
3. How did this situation occur in the first place?
4. To whom and to what do you give your loyalty as a person and as a member of the corporation?
5. What is your intention in making this decision?
6. How does this intention compare with the probable results?
7. Whom could your decision or action injure?
8. Can you discuss the problem with the affected parties before you make your decisions?
9. Are you confident that your decision will be as valid over a long period of time as it seems now?
10. Could you disclose without qualm your decision or action to your boss, your CEO, the board of directors, your family, society as a whole?
11. What is the symbolic potential of your action if understood? If misunderstood?
12. Under what conditions would you allow exceptions to your stand?

*Source:* Laura L. Nash, "Ethics Without the Sermon." Harvard Business Review 59 (November-December 1981):78–90.

---

It is important to realize that both perspectives are used. Perhaps eventually a more comprehensive theory will integrate the two views. For now, we must strive to understand people with a perspective different from our own and try to reach mutually satisfactory solutions.

## APPLYING ETHICS

Managers at modern organizations sometimes establish rules that may conflict with the rules of common morality. For example, invoking the principle of mutual aid to assist a person who needs help might draw sneers from corporate managers if the distressed party is a competitor. We must know *how* to apply the principles of common morality and the language of ethics to business situations. Exhibit 4-1 lists twelve questions for examining the ethics of a business decision.

## INSTITUTIONALIZING ETHICS

CEOs do not have to confront ethical questions in a vacuum. Instead, they can institutionalize the process of ethical decision making by ensuring that each moral decision builds upon preceding decisions. Ways of institutionalizing ethical policy include corporate codes of conduct, ethics committees, ombudsman offices, judicial boards, ethics-training programs, and **social audits**.

**social audit:**
Report describing a company's activities in a given area of social interest, such as environmental protection, workplace safety, or community involvement.

One survey found that more than 90 percent of the companies that have tried to institutionalize ethics have created codes of ethics that require and prohibit specific practices. Although no more than 11 percent of these companies actually display their codes in offices and factories, most of them will dismiss, demote, or reprimand employees who intentionally violate those codes.[28]

In Europe companies are looking more closely at their approach to ethics. While the strongest trend is in the United States, the United Kingdom (UK) companies are also recognizing the need for ethical codes. Once rare, codes of ethics are becoming increasingly common. According to

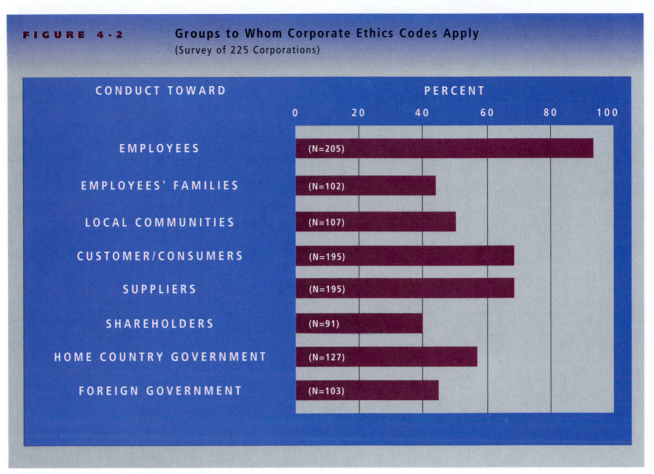

**FIGURE 4-2**     **Groups to Whom Corporate Ethics Codes Apply**
(Survey of 225 Corporations)

*Source:* Ronald Berenbeim, *Corporate Ethics* (New York: The Conference Board, 1987), p.15.

one report, almost a third of leading British companies have a written code—up from 18 percent in 1987. Many others are considering developing an ethics code.[29] In Spain, subsequent to charges of corrupt dealings with the government, Blanco Biblao Vizcaya recently published the country's first explicit code of conduct; Fiat is doing the same in Italy. Although the French remain skeptical concerning the usefulness of written codes, which they tend to regard as an Anglo-Saxon gimmick, they have become more reflective about their practices.

Even though another survey reports that "codes have a limited effect in deterring the misbehavior of intentional wrong-doers," many companies feel that codes of ethics notify employees that business decisions should take account of ethical as well as economic considerations. "More importantly," the study concludes, codes of conduct remind employees "that the company is fully committed to stating its standards and is asking its work force to incorporate them into their daily activities."[30] Figure 4-2 indicates the groups to whom corporate ethics codes apply.

Many companies trying to institutionalize ethical policy have created specific organizations to enforce that policy. Of these companies, more than 40 percent have also set up programs to teach their employees how to confront moral problems in business. Some 18 percent have set up ethics committees; 3 percent have appointed an ombudsman (an officer to investigate decisions from an ethical point of view); and 3 percent have judicial boards that rule on ethical questions.[31] Ethics training programs very often include discussion programs and workshops in which employees thrash out hypothetical moral problems. Participating companies report that "the give-and-take of these programs helps to sensitize employees to ethical issues, broaden and deepen employee awareness of code directives, and underscore the commitment of the company to its ethical principles."[32]

## Our Credo

We believe our first responsibility is to the doctors, nurses and patients,
to mothers and fathers and all others who use our products and services.
In meeting their needs everything we do must be of high quality.
We must constantly strive to reduce our costs
in order to maintain reasonable prices.
Customers' orders must be serviced promptly and accurately.
Our suppliers and distributors must have an opportunity
to make a fair profit.

We are responsible to our employees,
the men and women who work with us throughout the world.
Everyone must be considered as an individual.
We must respect their dignity and recognize their merit.
They must have a sense of security in their jobs.
Compensation must be fair and adequate,
and working conditions clean, orderly and safe.
We must be mindful of ways to help our employees fulfill
their family responsibilities.
Employees must feel free to make suggestions and complaints.
There must be equal opportunity for employment, development
and advancement for those qualified.
We must provide competent management,
and their actions must be just and ethical.

We are responsible to the communities in which we live and work
and to the world community as well.
We must be good citizens — support good works and charities
and bear our fair share of taxes.
We must encourage civic improvements and better health and education
We must maintain in good order
the property we are privileged to use,
protecting the environment and natural resources.

Our final responsibility is to our stockholders.
Business must make a sound profit.
We must experiment with new ideas.
Research must be carried on, innovative programs developed
and mistakes paid for.
New equipment must be purchased, new facilities provided
and new products launched.
Reserves must be created to provide for adverse times.
When we operate according to these principles,
the stockholders should realize a fair return.

*Johnson&Johnson*

*Source:* Courtesy of Johnson & Johnson

**moral relativism:**

The idea that we cannot decide matters of right and wrong, good and evil, in any rational way.

**naive relativism:**

The idea that all human beings are themselves the standard by which their actions should be judged.

## INSTITUTIONALIZING ETHICS AT JOHNSON & JOHNSON

A well-known company that has become famous for its institutionalization of ethics is Johnson & Johnson. In its beginnings, when it specialized in baby powder and bandage products, Johnson & Johnson was a highly centralized organization. Now it is both highly diversified, operating more than 160 businesses in over 50 countries, and highly decentralized. The process of decentralization started under a son of one of the company's three founders, General Robert Wood Johnson, who took over in 1932. Today each business has a president or managing director who reports to a company group chairperson but who generally manages his or her particular company with a fair amount of independence. Because Johnson & Johnson's decentralized structure depends so heavily on individual autonomy and decision making, the company established a "Credo" in 1943 (see Exhibit 4-2), not only to ensure its essential dedication to product quality, but also to encourage personal commitment to the goals of a loosely structured organization. Former Chairman James Burke believes that the Credo is a unifying factor among employees.

During the Tylenol crisis, when seven people died after taking Extra-Strength Tylenol® capsules that had been tampered with, Johnson & Johnson relied on the credo to eventually reintroduce the product and regain the public trust. According to Burke, chairman during the crisis, the credo represents 100 years of accumulated public trust.[33]  ■

## THE CHALLENGE OF RELATIVISM

**F**inally, we must confront the challenge of relativism to ethics in general. There are many versions of **moral relativism,** but all of them hold that we cannot decide matters of right and wrong, good and evil, in any rational way.

Moral relativism seems to imply that since right and wrong are relative to whoever is making the decision, there are only individual answers to any moral question. It also suggests that constructive moral argument is impossible, for each person will do what is right for himself or herself. Though we may agonize over moral problems, we have no sure way of deciding that one decision is morally better than another.

### NAIVE RELATIVISM

Perhaps the most widespread form of relativism might be called **naive relativism**—the idea that all human beings are themselves the standard by which their actions should be judged. The naive relativist believes that because ethical decisions are personal, important, and complex, only the decision maker's opinion is relevant.

However, it does not follow from the personal and serious nature of morality that we can't reason about it—quite the contrary. Precisely because morality is so vital to our lives, we must do our very best thinking in this area, and for this we need the help of people who are engaged in the process of moral reasoning. If we reject the idea that one's moral beliefs have to stand up to scrutiny and criticism, how will anyone get better at making moral choices? If there are no standards for deciding whether one moral decision is better or worse than another, how can we believe that morality is important?

Tolerance of others is necessary and good, but naive relativism takes tolerance too far. People often disagree about moral questions, but we should not therefore conclude that there can never be any reason for anything we do, or that one course of action is always just as good as another. Instead, we must try to sort things out, because if we don't, we have admitted defeat in coming to terms with our own lives. Besides, the naive relativist's tolerance for all points of view is a contradiction in that it is itself an absolute point of view: "We must always be tolerant."

There is an even more compelling argument against naive relativism. In insisting that the moral test of any action is whether or not the person believed it to be correct, naive relativism tells us that we need not check on the *content* of a particular action; we need only find out if the person acted in accord with his or her beliefs. Therefore, any judgment about an action taken regarding such issues as abortion, infanticide, civil liberties, and capital punishment is necessarily suspended. The real failing of naive relativism is its laziness: It is not a belief, but rather an excuse for having no beliefs. It is hard to marshal facts and construct theories about many ethical questions, and the naive relativist just doesn't want to bother. Such moral laziness exacts a price. It requires giving up any hope of living in a better world or becoming a better human being.

## CULTURAL RELATIVISM

**cultural relativism:**

The idea that morality is relative to a particular culture, society, or community.

A second form of moral relativism, **cultural relativism,** claims that morality is relative to particular cultures, societies, or communities. It further asserts that no standards can help us *judge* the morality of a particular culture, and that the best anyone can hope to do is to *understand* the moral codes and customs of a given society.

Cultural relativism tells us to try to understand, for example, Kenyan morality or Middle Eastern morality, but not to judge them. If norms and customs are shared by the members of any society, what right do we have to criticize them from an external standpoint? Why should other parts of the world be obliged to accept our ideas of morality?

The implications of cultural relativism for business are vast, because more and more corporations operate in a global marketplace today, with employees who maintain allegiances to many different nations, races, and creeds. Managers who have to do business in such dissimilar places as Japan, Korea, Saudi Arabia, France, Mexico, China, and Brazil confront a diversity of cultural norms, from different table manners to different religions and moral principles. For example, cultural factors businesspeople should know about prior to doing business in Saudi Arabia are 1) the predominance of Islam—Muslims pray five times a day, virtually close their businesses during Hajj, the month of pilgrimage, and Ramadan, the month of fasting, and have strict regulations regarding alcohol and drugs, pornography, and the separation of the sexes; 2) there is potential for instability in the area; 3) Saudis honor the boycott against companies that have a tie to Israel; and 4) women are restricted by social and religious customs, although enlightened Saudi businessmen will accord an idea or product the consideration it deserves.[34]

If the cultural relativists are right, the search for common morality in the business arena is over. Managers are obligated merely to obey local customs, codes, and laws. But are the cultural relativists right? Can American managers in Saudi Arabia ethically treat Saudi women as the Saudis do, without a second thought?

**CULTURAL DIFFERENCES.** Business people must be aware of numerous cultural differences that affect views of morality around the world. The differences in dress between these businessmen are just an outward sign of broad cultural differences that each must be sensitive to.

Even as policies change, can American managers in South Africa accept white South African attitudes toward blacks without a qualm? Or consider the People's Republic of China. Should a corporation operating there accept the denial of basic political freedoms? And what if companies find themselves torn between the requirements of two different governments and legal systems? For instance, the government of France once instructed the French subsidiary of U.S.-based Dresser Industries to sell the Soviet Union materials for a gas pipeline linking it to Western Europe, while the United States government was forbidding Dresser and all of its subsidiaries to sell such materials to the Soviets.

When companies find themselves caught between conflicting moral and legal demands from more than one culture, the only advice a cultural relativist can offer is this: Do whatever you like, because you will violate legal strictures whatever you do. So, far from helping Dresser out of a difficult situation, cultural relativism would only confirm the realization that the company cannot possibly escape the dilemma.

The second problem with cultural relativism is that most cultures are fairly diverse. Therefore, what may appear to be the prevailing norms may not reflect the values of all of the population, or even the majority. Relativism does offer one contribution to the debate on ethics in business: It reminds us of the interplay between individuals and the community—a basic requirement for ethical thinking.

The challenge of relativism illustrates the depth and complexity of ethics. There is a temptation to take the easy way out that relativism provides. Once we have decided that management has a large ethical component, there is no escape from the complex conversation that is ethics. By explicitly talking about how ethics and management are connected, managers can improve their ability to reason about ethics.

**MANAGEMENT 2000 AND BEYOND**

# TOM CHAPPELL AND THE SOUL OF A BUSINESS

Tom Chappell is one of the many new entrepreneurs who refuse to accept the old ways of thinking about business—especially the old ways that say that business and ethics are contradictory. In his recent book, *The Soul of a Business: Managing for Profit and the Common Good,* he tells the story of how he built his company, Tom's of Maine, around a line of products anchored by their famous natural toothpaste.[35] But Chappell was disenchanted with his success. He took some time out and returned to the university. At Harvard Divinity School, he discovered some deeply held values in himself. With his new focus, he then returned to Tom's and reoriented the company to make it possible for others to live true to their values.

According to Chappell,

> Each of us performs and feels. In many companies, only one side of us takes on the challenge of doing the job to meet its goals (sales, production, or profit); the other side is put on hold, wanting to share its pain, confusion, or joy with others. At Tom's of Maine we want to see both sides of every person working together; we want to know one another as warehouse worker/father/husband; as vice-president/wife/mother/citizen.

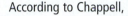

Chappell has used many of the concepts in this chapter to build an organization that is oriented around individual autonomy and caring relationships with others. His management method, which he calls "the Middle Way," is an all-out integration of profit and the common good. The Middle Way is a Buddhist notion of taking a path between the two extremes of just making money and caring about people but being unprofitable. It is also a Western idea; Aristotle's Principle of the Golden Mean gives similar advice.

Tom Chappell believes that managers in the next century will have to "manage by values." He articulates these values in a Tom's of Maine mission statement, which proclaims the company's mission "to be a profitable and successful company while acting in a socially responsible manner."[36] He specifies this mission in a long-range objective "to become the choice of customers who care about health, the natural world, and their communities."[37] And these values of profits and the common good have helped the company focus on what it knows how to do. Tom says, "We had gone from zero to $12.5 million by being ourselves. Three years later, after refining our identity—who and what we were—and committing ourselves even more strongly to the common good, we are heading toward $20 million. My current objective is to aim for $100 million by doing what Tom's of Maine does best: BE TOM'S OF MAINE—that is, a company committed to people and the environment."[38] Chappell shows us how to practice business *and* ethics, as he leads the way towards twenty-first century thinking.

# AFTER THE COURT SPOKE

At first, the court's decision in the case against Kinko's complicated the educational process it had initially facilitated. Sabine Von Dirke, an associate professor at the University of Pittsburgh, felt frustrated by what happened. Von Dirke pointed out, "I've had to eliminate several articles.... I wanted students to use and read because the copyright fee would have been too high." She added, "You have to have your decision about what you're going to include...much earlier, and it means that frequently, I cannot be as up-to-date as I would like to be....If publishing houses shaped up and reacted more quickly, it would be a lot better."[39]

What happened was that faculty members and copy shops recognized that they were going to have to take responsibility for their actions. Boston University sent a memo in October 1991, warning that faculty members were going to be "held to a stricter standard." In addition, to help accommodate their customers further, Kinko's and other stores interested in the professor publishing market worked with publishers to streamline the process of requesting and receiving copyright permission. New companies, such as PUBNET Permission, have sprung up to facilitate this process.

With regard to Kinko's competitors, the effect of the court decision was a sort of dual-edged sword. On the one hand, it forced competitors to scrutinize their own behavior more carefully. One competitor remarked, "It sends a message to Kinko's and everybody else that publishers are willing to go after companies that disregard the law."[40] At the same time, however, it did make competition more fair. Doug Arthur, director of the bookstore at the University of Wisconsin-Milwaukee, noted, "The state has very strict regulations about obtaining copyright permission on any material we custom-publish.... As a result, it was hard to compete on price with firms that weren't paying copyright royalties."[41]

The Kinko's case illustrates that ethics issues have broad consequences for copyright holders, competitors, professors, and students. Ethical analysis can help us understand and manage the competing interests.

## SUMMARY

1. **Discuss the basic principles of Andrew Carnegie's *The Gospel of Wealth*.**

   The classic statement of corporate social responsibility was created by Andrew Carnegie in his *The Gospel of Wealth* (1899). Carnegie's gospel was based on the charity principle (society's more fortunate members are obligated to help the less fortunate) and the stewardship principle (the rich are the caretakers of wealth and public property). Carnegie was a noted philanthropist and his philosophy inspired a concern for corporate social responsibility between the 1930s and 1960s.

2. **Evaluate the criticisms of Carnegie's gospel.**

   The drawbacks of Carnegie's gospel were that it preserved the status quo and protected business from other forms of pressure, and that the term *social responsibility* was so vague that it left too much to individual discretion.

to maximize its own profits, within the limits of the law. A company's contribution to the general welfare should be the efficient production of goods and services. Social problems should be left to concerned individuals and government agencies.

4. **Compare and contrast Carnegie's views with those of Friedman.**

Carnegie and Friedman represented opposing views of social responsibility.

5. **Explain the concept of enlightened self-interest.**

Enlightened self-interest is the idea that it is in an organization's own best interests to act in ways the community considers socially responsible.

6. **List and define the key terms used in ethics.**

To engage in ethical reasoning, we need to understand ethical language, including the terms *values, rights and duties, moral rules,* and *relationships.*

7. **Discuss the issues a manager must consider in applying ethics.**

We must also understand the basic tenets of common morality, ranging from promise keeping to respect for property. In addition, we need to comprehend the distinction between the justice perspective men commonly use and the care perspective women commonly use in making moral decisions.

8. **Evaluate the challenge of relativism to moral reasoning.**

Managers must be aware of and avoid the temptations of naive relativism—the idea that human beings are themselves the standard by which they should be judged—and cultural relativism—the idea that morality is relative to a particular culture. Relativism's main contributions to the debate on ethics in business is to remind us of the interplay between individuals and the community—a basic requirement for ethical thinking.

## REVIEW QUESTIONS

1. What are the basic principles of Andrew Carnegie's *The Gospel of Wealth*?
2. What are the criticisms of Carnegie's gospel?
3. What is Milton Friedman's position on corporate social responsibility?
4. What are the similarities and differences between Carnegie's and Friedman's views on social responsibility?
5. What is enlightened self-interest?
6. What are the key terms in ethics?
7. What are the four levels to ethical questions?
8. What issues must a manager consider when applying ethics?
9. What is the challenge of relativism to moral reasoning?
10. What is cultural relativism?

## KEY TERMS

Corporate social responsibility
Ethics
Charity principle
Stewardship principle
Enlightened self-interest
Corporate social responsiveness
Corporate social performance
Values

Rights
Duties
Moral rules
Common morality
Social audit
Moral relativism
Naive relativism
Cultural relativism

## CASE STUDY

# ALEXANDER GAVIN'S DILEMMA: CULTURAL RELATIVISM AND BUSINESS AS USUAL[42]

April 10, 1983

Dear Professor Hennessey:

I have not talked with you since my participation in The Executive Program at Tuck School in the summer of 1978. Many times I've hoped I might come back to visit but my life has been one surprise after the other, and I have been too busy to take any vacations in recent years.

I want to tell you about a situation that happened to me recently. I know you will be interested in it, and if you have time I'd like you to tell me what you would have done had you been in my position.

As I think you know, I am Senior Project Manager for the El Sahd Construction Company in Kuwait. The company is a prosperous one, with an excellent reputation for producing in a timely and cost-effective way on major construction projects in the Middle East. The Chairman and Chief Executive Officer is a well-known Kuwaiti and my direct boss is another American expatriate who is Senior Vice President for urban construction projects.

Two months ago, we put in a bid to be the principal subcontractor on a project in Iran. Our bid was $30 million, and we expected to bargain with Ajax, Ltd., the British-based company asking for the bids. We had built a heavy profit into the $30 million.

I was asked to go to Tehran on March 3rd to talk with the Ajax manager of the major project. That manager told me that we were going to get the job. I was delighted. The job meant a lot to us. We had put a great deal of planning into it, and it was exactly the kind of work that we do best.

Then came the surprise. I was told our bid had to be $33 million. My response was that we can always raise our price but that I would like to know why we were being asked to do so. The reply was, "Our way of doing business requires that because $1 million will go directly to the Managing Director of our Company in London. I will get $1 million and you, Alexander, will get $1 million in a numbered Swiss account." "Why me?" I asked. "Because we need to have you on the hook as insurance that you will never talk about this with anybody else."

I went back to Kuwait to ponder the matter. I was particularly disturbed because I had heard of cases like this in which, should the bidder fail to cooperate, the next message was that physical harm might be part of the exchange. I had been involved in "pay-offs" before. They are a common part of doing business in the Middle East, but I had never been in a situation where I was being coerced into taking a "cut" myself. I didn't like that. It went against my ethics.

At that point, I really didn't know what to do. I thought, among other things, how helpful it would have been to put my dilemma before a Tuck class and listen to the discussion.

Sincerely,
Alexander Gavin

## CASE QUESTIONS

1. What rights are at stake in this case?

2. What decision rule should Mr. Gavin use?

3. Will this rule work in different cultures?

## KMART EMPLOYEES: UNDER WATCHFUL EYES[43]

When his position at Kmart's facility in Fort Wayne, Indiana, was terminated, Lewis Hubbell confronted the challenge of relocating himself and his family. He was reassigned to the company's distribution center in Manteno, Illinois, where he began the painful process of starting over. "Leaving Indiana was the hardest thing I've ever done," Hubbell recalled. "I had to leave my friends, my church, my son—even my cemetery plot is back there."[44] Perhaps more difficult than leaving, though, was accepting what he found in his new "home."

At first, Hubbell readjusted to his new life and new job. He found an apartment as a temporary residence while he waited for his wife and daughter to join him. Perhaps more important, he made a friend: Al Posego. Posego, a fellow Kmart employee, initiated the friendship by inviting Hubbell and several other Kmart workers to join him for a beer after work. Within months, getting together after work at a nearby American Legion Hall had become a weekly ritual. Posego visited Hubbell at his apartment a couple of times, and even offered to help Hubbell move into a new house.

Then, the local Teamsters Union received an anonymous package containing some disturbing information. The package included invoices and copies of weekly reports that had been prepared for Kmart management by Confidential Investigative Consultants (CICs). According to the Teamsters, the reports covered a wide range of personal information about various Kmart employees, including their dating experiences, drinking habits, and living arrangements. "Kmart violated every standard of decency you can think of in spying on these workers' lives," contended Teamsters President Ron Carey. "No employer should be allowed to snoop around in employees' personal affairs."[45]

Perhaps what hit Hubbell the hardest, though, was that Posego was identified as one of the undercover investigators hired by Kmart to spy on the activities of employees. "We worked together and talked together on the job and stopped off maybe once a week to have a beer," Hubbell remarked. "If you asked me if I had made one friend since moving to Illinois, I would have said Al."[46] He recalled, "When I found out he was a company spy, I really felt betrayed." Hubbell recalled. "I was really afraid that I'd walked into something too big."[47]

Outraged, the Teamsters Union filed a suit on behalf of several employees who worked at the plant that was investigated. The suit charged Kmart with violations of the Illinois privacy law, fraud, deceit, and breach of contract. "Kmart's spies posed as the workers' friends while they poked into their private lives and thoughts, and even followed them into their homes," charged Carey. "Kmart has exploited the workers' trust and violated their good faith."[48]

Kmart argued that the spies were hired to investigate a suspected theft ring, which was broken up as a result of the investigation. Nevertheless, the Teamsters believed that the company had gone too far. "The kind of information in these reports bears no legitimate business or security concerns for Kmart," asserted Phil Snelling, a partner at Johnson, Jones & Snelling, the law firm that represented the plant workers. "They are simply way over the line claiming any kind of business justification for a pervasive spy system."[49]

The Teamsters were also concerned about the timing of the investigation, which took place shortly before their July election that made the Manteno plant Kmart's first unionized distribution site. Although Kmart denied any relationship between the investigation and the election, Tom Johnson, another partner at Johnson, Jones & Snelling, disagreed. "This appears to be different from a surveillance program aimed at ferreting out theft," he noted. "The reports we've seen talk about who was shopping at Kmart and who was shopping at Wal-Mart, who was living with whom and who was signing up for a union card."[50]

If companies want to conduct employee surveillance employees, it is essential that they do it correctly. "When it's done correctly it's a tremendous tool, but it also has its potential for abuse," pointed out Charles Carroll, president of ASET Corp., a vendor of drug investigation and education services. "Oftentimes a corporation will call us and there's a hidden agenda: They want to look at union efforts or troublemakers."[51] Those are the jobs ASET turns down. U.S. law strictly prohibits investigating union activities, and companies found to be in violation of this law face serious penalties.

Monitoring workplace activity is not in and of itself illegal, however, and Kmart is not alone in its use of spies to investigate employees. Internal investigations using undercover "agents" are widespread among American businesses. A survey by *Macworld* revealed that approximately 20 million employees in the U.S. are subject to some form of electronic surveillance.

Employee surveillance is especially prevalent among retailers whose narrow profit margins can be destroyed by employee theft. According to the National Retail Federation, employee theft accounted for an estimated 41 percent of the $27 billion in shortages reported by American retailers in 1992. In a statement Kmart issued in response to the charges against it, the company declared, "Theft is a serious problem as it has a direct impact on Kmart's ability to remain competitive and offer customers merchandise at the best price possible."[52]

Spying on employees has a serious downside, however, aside from legal complications. Most important is the breakdown of trust. "The spy isn't just watching the guilty employee, the spy is spying on everybody and it's a massive deceit," said Lew Maltby, director of the American Civil Liberties Union's project on employee privacy issues. "Every company has problems, that's why God invented managers.... But any manager who can't find out what's going on in the company without hiring spies ought to be fired."[53]

A breakdown of trust within a company can prove far more expensive than any theft ring. Employees may lose faith in both the company and their purpose in it. Hubbell, who has worked for the company for 28 years, asserted, "I feel betrayed by the company, and I feel that we have no choice but to fight back [in court]. Kmart was wrong to spy on working people who are just trying to feed their families. I was loyal to Kmart, but they weren't loyal to me."[54]

## CASE QUESTIONS

1. Whose rights are at stake?
2. Would different cultures consider this situation differently?
3. If surveillance is legal, does that mean it is ethical?
4. How would common morality evaluate Kmart's actions?

## CHAPTER 5

# GLOBALIZATION AND MANAGEMENT

**Upon completing this chapter, you should be able to:**

1. Identify different aspects of globalization.

2. Explain the meaning and importance of competitiveness.

3. Trace the historical evolution of globalization of business.

4. Discuss the important conditions that managers must consider in the globalization of their actions.

# AN UNMANAGED CHOKEPOINT AT SUMITOMO[1]

During the summer of 1993, a July 4 explosion that gutted a Japanese plastics plant awakened the international electronics industry to its vulnerability. The factory that burned down, owned by Sumitomo Chemical Company, manufactured approximately 65 percent of the world's supply of epoxy, the chemical used to seal most computer chips in their plastic packages. Spot prices for computer memory chips immediately rose 50 percent, and computer buyers around the world saw prices shoot upward.

Having a single supplier responsible for so much of the manufacture of a critical electronic component means that there are "chokepoints" in the electronics industry. A chokepoint exists where a limited number of suppliers provide key items to an entire industry. It exposes the entire industry and its customers, as well as the broader economy, to increased risk.

In the electronics industry, such chokepoints do not appear to have been intended. As a result of intense competition, cost-cutting and global consolidation, though, suppliers of components have dropped out of the market, in some instances leaving only a few remaining. Through fierce protection of intellectual property rights and heavy investments in research and development, some of the larger manufacturers actually forced smaller players out of the market.

It is possible to argue that the problem lies not with the chokepoints, but with the management of companies positioned at the chokepoints. "What do you do, recommend that [Sumitomo Chemical] diversify production and raise costs?" asked Peter Wolff, an analyst at Kidder, Peabody & Co. in Tokyo. Having a single industry supplier, or only a limited few, can boost that company up its experience curve and efficiently drive down costs. "It's a lot cheaper if we ask them to install sprinklers," added Wolff.[2]

*A chokepoint...exposes the enti[re] industry...to increased risk.*

Concern emerges with the realization that many chokepoints are hidden. "The fact that epoxy resin was concentrated in one plant was a big surprise to us," noted Kenichi Tsuji, a purchasing manager at NEC Corp.[3] To complicate matters further, some companies able to point out chokepoints are not willing to help. Hitachi Chemical, for example, refused to identify the suppliers that it relies on for more than 50 percent of any one electronics chemical. An aide explained that the company was afraid that answering the question might "cause undue concern on the part of our customers."[4]

Looking back, Sumitomo now admits that its efforts toward keeping other players out of the market backfired. The company's relationships with other Japanese businesses prevented price increases and thus stunted the epoxy resin's profitability. Therefore, not only was the epoxy resin supply concentrated almost entirely in one supplier, but profitability concerns caused that supplier to concentrate its production in a single plant. When that plant exploded, the supplier and the surrounding industry suffered drastically. →

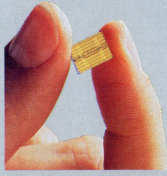

**A COMPUTER CHIP.** The price of computer memory chips soared when a Sumitomo plastics plant burned down in the summer of 1993.

**T**HE GLOBALIZATION of management is a fact of life. The daily press is filled with reminders of how organizations have taken on a global focus. News reports frequently mention such matters as international trade balances and currency fluctuations. It is common to read about Japanese companies making inroads in United States markets or American companies making inroads in Japanese markets. There are stories about managers from the former "Iron Curtain" nations training in Western Europe or the United States, and American and British companies teaming up to provide new telecommunications and airline travel services. Today, no manager can afford to assume that his or her organization is isolated from all of this global activity. Customers for Sumitomo's chips, such as Hewlett-Packard, can attest to that.

Today it is not unusual for a global organization headquartered in the United States to oversee manufacturing operations in, say, the United States, Germany, and Singapore; to sell its product in dozens of countries; and to face competition from companies based in the so-called "Four Tigers"—Hong Kong, Singapore, South Korea, and Taiwan.

It is not just large corporations that have a global focus. Increasingly, small businesses are going global. A poll of the 1993 *INC.* magazine 500 showed that 38 percent were doing business globally, with an average of 15 percent of sales from other countries. The most popular trading venues are Canada and Mexico, though 25 were doing business in Latin America, 115 in Europe, 73 in Asia and 30 in Australia. According to the U.S. Department of Commerce, most exporters are not very large. "Very small" companies employing 20 or fewer employees accounted for $30 billion or 12 percent of U.S. exports in 1987.[5]

This chapter surveys the global environment for organizations and managers. We will discuss the meaning of *globalization* and the related idea of *competitiveness;* consider the central role of governments in global business; look at the modern history of global business; examine the economic, political, technological, and social factors that global managers must take into account; and consider why and how organizations internationalize. And, as in the previous chapters, relationships and time will be recurring themes as we introduce you to the spread of globalization in all its complexity and possibilities.

## **W**HAT GLOBALIZATION MEANS

**W**hat do we mean by the **globalization** of business? We see the phenomenon of globalization as consisting of three interrelated factors—*proximity, location,* and *attitude.* Taken together, these three facets of globalization emphasize the unprecedented lineup and complexity of relationships that confront a global manager.

**globalization:**
The recognition by organizations that business must have a global, not local focus.

### PROXIMITY

First, managers now operate in much closer proximity than ever before to a greater number and range of customers, competitors, suppliers, and government regulators. This proximity, a function of the "shrinking globe," is partly a matter of time, as today's telecommunications technology allows people around the world to share voice, video, and facsimile information in minutes. The increasing technological and managerial capabilities of people around the globe is another aspect of proximity. Managers find themselves competing—or even collaborating—with a new cast of global players. Honda, for example, moved nearly sixty American specialists to Japan for several years to work with their Japanese counterparts on design for the 1994 Honda Accord.[6]

To emphasize this new spirit of closer ties and the insignificance of miles in today's business world, Kenichi Ohmae, a longtime consultant to global business organizations, urges managers to treat all customers as "equidistant" from their organizations.[7]

**NISSAN IN TENNESSEE.** Jimmy Haynes selects bumper fascias at the Smyrna, Tennessee, Nissan factory, just one of a number of Japanese auto assembly plants now operating in the United States.

## LOCATION

Second, the location and integration of an organization's operations across several international boundaries is part of globalization. For example, American Telephone & Telegraph (AT&T) telephones and telephone switching computers are designed in the United States, manufactured in Singapore and the United States, and sold worldwide—to customers who use the equipment to connect with AT&T long-distance services that reach all corners of the globe. In 1990, companies based in the United States employed 2.8 million people in Western Europe, 1.8 million in Asia, and 1.3 million in Latin America.[8] Toyota, Nissan, and Honda operate auto assembly plants in the United States. In fact, in September, 1993, Honda managers announced plans to manufacture all Honda Accords and Civics sold in the United States in Honda's plants in Ohio.[9] And (as discussed in Chapter 1) Toyota and General Motors have jointly operated the NUMMI (New United Motor Manufacturing Inc.) plant in Fremont, California, since 1984. Christopher Bartlett and Sumantra Ghoshal use the term *transnational management* to describe this growing practice of spreading an organization's operations across many nations.[10]

### TOYOTA FINDS U.S. WORKERS THAT SHARE ITS VALUES

Japanese automobile firms that have established operations in the U.S. have brought with them their ideas, processes, and management of quality. Although not all methods that work in Japan have been transplantable to the U.S. culture, many are—especially if employees are carefully selected. One firm that has used a careful screening process successfully is Toyota Motor Manufacturing Inc. of U.S.A., located in Georgetown, Kentucky.

Toyota builds its quality efforts around its employees, recruited almost exclusively from within Kentucky. In order to match the needs of the organization with the interests of the potential employees, Toyota conducts an exhaustive value-based hiring process that allows the company to identify potential workers with the types of skills it needs—problem-solving and interpersonal skills. These skills are compatible with the company's basic values. The company wants people who can think for themselves and solve problems; it also wants people who can work on a team. Toyota managers see each employee selection as a long-term investment decision.

At Toyota, value-based hiring follows the following guidelines:

1. Select employees whose values are compatible with those of the firm.
2. Design an exhaustive screening process.
3. Don't just look for job knowledge or technical skills—try to match the person's values with those of the firm's.
4. Always provide candid, realistic previews of what working at the firm will be like and what the entry job entails.
5. Self-selection is important.

These guidelines help Toyota managers find workers who have skills and qualities compatible with Toyota's needs. The firm's production system is based on consensus decision making, job rotation, and flexible career paths. The use of Kaizen, or continuous improvement, explains Toyota's commitment to hiring intelligent, educated workers.[11] You might compare this approach and process to the one used by Henry Ford and Taylor that was presented in Chapter 2. What are the identifiable values in each approach? ▆

### ATTITUDE

Third, globalization refers to a new, open attitude about practicing management internationally. This attitude combines a curiosity about the world outside one's national borders with a willingness to develop the capabilities for participating in the global economy. Ohmae, once again, makes this point clear in the simple statement, "Nothing is 'overseas' anymore." [12]

Attitudes change over time. Recall from Chapter 2, for example, how efficiency was the byword of Henry Ford, Frederick Taylor, and their contemporaries as they wrestled with the idea of mass production in the early years of this century. Now, as the century draws to a close, what Ohmae, Bartlett, Ghoshal, and many others are saying is that globalization has emerged as a crucial frame of reference for managers in the mid-1990s.

The globalization of business, in all three aspects, has been accompanied by a prominent new concern about *competitiveness*. We now turn to a discussion of the meaning of competitiveness, the part that governments play in debates about it, and the modern history of globalization and competitiveness.

## GLOBALIZATION AND COMPETITIVENESS

**competitiveness:**
The relative standing of one competitor against others.

Competitiveness is a frequent topic of conversation these days among managers and government officials and in the news media. We define **competitiveness** as the relative standing of one competitor against other competitors. Competitiveness is like the game of musical chairs: There are a finite number of places to sit, and some are more desirable than others.

Competitiveness is an idea that applies in a number of different settings. For decades, managers at the so-called Big Three American automakers—General Motors, Ford, and Chrysler—have worried about their organizations' relative standing in the U.S. automobile marketplace. Merchants in many small towns

**"NOT MADE IN U.S.A."** These shoppers are out of luck if they hope to buy an American-made VCR. Although the technology for these machines was originally developed and patented in the United States, videocassette recorders have never been manufactured here.

the world economy has declined over the past two decades.[17] The commission concluded that both government and business need to place a higher priority on international competitiveness. Among specific recommendations, the commission suggested that responsibility for formulating international trade policy and encouraging exports (now fragmented among multiple government agencies) should be unified.

Global managers thus operate in a climate marked by more aggressive government efforts to influence how they run their organizations. According to Porter, those efforts have influenced global competitiveness:[18]

> With striking regularity, firms from one or two nations achieve disproportionate worldwide success in particular industries. Some national environments seem more stimulating to advancement and progress than others.

Porter traces that success, to a significant degree, to the economic climate, institutions, and policies attributable to government actions. With a touch of irony, Porter concludes that in this era of globalization, what happens in a company's "home country" is more important than ever.[19] Sumitomo's global activities, coming at a time of changing banking regulations in Japan, is a case in point. We now turn to consider specific worldwide examples of significant government influence in the global contest of business.

## THE BLURRING OF PUBLIC AND PRIVATE SPHERES OF INFLUENCE

Because international competition has increased, government has played an increasingly active role in the post-World War II marketplace. In the United States, this role crystallized when the federal government bailed out the Chrysler Corporation in 1980 by guaranteeing its loans. Shortly thereafter, the government exempted a number of computer manufacturers from antitrust laws so they could perform joint research and development, increasing their ability to compete with the Japanese.

One outcome is SEMATECH, the Semiconductor Manufacturing Technology consortium, which was established in 1987 on the belief that how and where semiconductors are manufactured is important. SEMATECH is a collaborative effort among the nation's leading companies in partnership with government. The goal of the consortium is to improve U.S. semiconductor manufacturing proficiency to equal or exceed the world's best, both in design and in the manufacturing process itself. It is a valuable example of the use of joint development consortia to strengthen competitiveness and has been singled out as the role model for industry-government cooperation by the Clinton Administration.[20]

Under President Reagan, a major tax-reform bill led to an enormous influx of venture capital into the economy. The Reagan administration also promoted American business over international competitors in defense contracting. For example, a low foreign bid to install a glass cable between New York and Washington was rejected in favor of AT&T's bid on the grounds that the cable had national defense implications.

This blurring of public policy and private enterprise is not limited to the United States. In Japan, the Ministry of International Trade and Industry actively assists some industries rather than others, and government takes an active role in the economy. The Group of Five (representatives of the United States, West Germany, Japan, France, and the United Kingdom) routinely meet to plan their monetary policy in concert. And since the October 19, 1987, stock market crash, there have been suggestions that the stock markets in these nations should be coordinated.

# THE CHANGING INTERNATIONAL SCENE

Political changes, shifts in government policies, and new agreements among nations are all having an impact on the global marketplace. In this section we will discuss the changing business scene in a number of areas around the world.

## THE COMING OF THE EUROPEAN COMMUNITY

The European Community (EC) was established in 1992.[21] The EC's goal is to eliminate trade barriers among member nations, creating a single market of 300 million people and fostering political unity in Europe.

The EC is an evolution of the Common Market, which was created in 1957 by the Treaty of Rome. The original members—Belgium, France, Italy, Luxembourg, Netherlands, and West Germany—have been joined by Denmark, Great Britain, and Ireland (1973), by Greece (1981), and by Spain and Portugal (1986) (see Figure 5-1). In theory, the Common Market was to coordinate economic policies and eliminate trade barriers among member nations. In reality, the Common Market had little authority and trade barriers proliferated. Meanwhile, strong American and Japanese multinational companies threatened to leave Europe behind in the increasingly global economy.

Europe responded with the Single Europe Act of 1987, which amended the Treaty of Rome and created the EC, conferring real power on the largely symbolic European Parliament. Many areas of cooperation have been established, such as a commitment to eliminate trade barriers by 1992, end custom formalities by 1993, and create a central European bank by 1994, paving the way for a single European currency in the late 1990s.

The EC has a number of dramatic implications for business. First, it should increase efficiency. Under the Common Market, trade barriers sometimes forced firms to modify a product design or manufacturing facilities. Under the EC, these

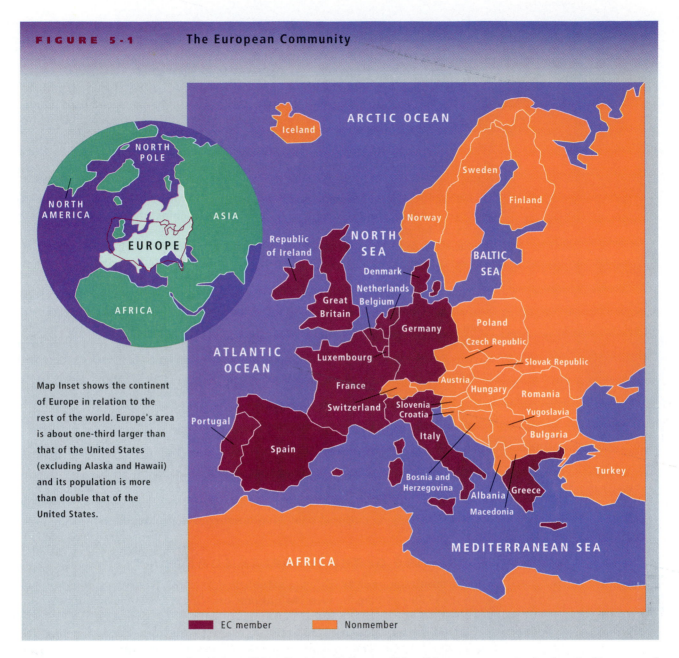

**FIGURE 5-1**    The European Community

Map Inset shows the continent of Europe in relation to the rest of the world. Europe's area is about one-third larger than that of the United States (excluding Alaska and Hawaii) and its population is more than double that of the United States.

■ EC member    ■ Nonmember

barriers will be eliminated; firms will be able to create a single plan for Europe and to consolidate manufacturing in strategically located plants. Second, European companies should become more formidable competitors in the global economy, since they will be developing within a more cooperative system. In addition, the EC will unify European markets, and the increased profit potential should encourage innovation. Third, the EC will encourage businesses to focus on their relationship with the EC, rather than with domestic governments. This will heighten political unity in Europe.

Many dreaded the 1992 changes and feared that they would create a "Fortress Europe," in which the EC would erect trade barriers to American and Japanese companies. Others claim that a united Europe will exist on paper only. It will take a great deal of time and effort to overcome so many differences.

## ECONOMIC EXPERIMENTS IN THE PEOPLE'S REPUBLIC OF CHINA

In 1980, the People's Republic of China launched a series of unique economic experiments—unique, that is, for a nation that had relied on a planned economy for

40 years. Under Mao Zedong, the government had set the nation's economic goals and owned almost all the means of production and distribution. Managers were chosen for their devotion to Mao, not for their skill or experience. In fact, "sound management" was condemned as "bourgeois revisionism." To reorient their thinking, educated people were often sent to work alongside peasants in the fields. Despite this antimanagement bias, China met its goal of feeding, housing, clothing, and educating a population of one billion people between 1950 and 1976.

After Mao's death, China's new generation of leaders announced an ambitious new goal—economic growth—and a series of economic reforms to be phased into virtually all of China's state-owned enterprises. These reforms promoted entrepreneurship *within* state-owned businesses, permitted certain businesses to experiment with restructuring, and allowed entrepreneurs to start small, privately owned businesses.

Throughout the 1980s, China accelerated its reform program, hoping to become an increasingly viable player in the world economy. And companies such as Reebok, Nike, Squibb, and Ingersoll-Rand responded by investing in joint ventures with Chinese companies. Attracted by untapped market opportunities as well as the productive capacities of an industrious, if not yet industrialized, economy.

Growing pains have accompanied China's economic growth, however. To transform a predominantly agricultural society into one poised to reap the benefits of twentieth-century technology and innovation, China's leaders have chosen to *modify,* not abandon, its planned economy. This means trying to keep the economy from expanding too quickly, to avoid the predictable effects of inflation—upward-spiraling wages and prices—which could be worsened by a planned economy that essentially violates the law of supply and demand. Many leaders believed the changes were coming too fast and were especially alarmed when university students demanded democratic reforms on top of the economic reforms.

In May 1989, tanks rumbled into Tiananmen Square, signaling an end to the period of liberalization. While the world watched, party hard-liners staged a bloody crackdown on the students. Some fear this violence signals a lasting retreat from economic reforms. Others are more optimistic and accept the 1987 assessment of the Congressional Office of Technology that China will become increas-

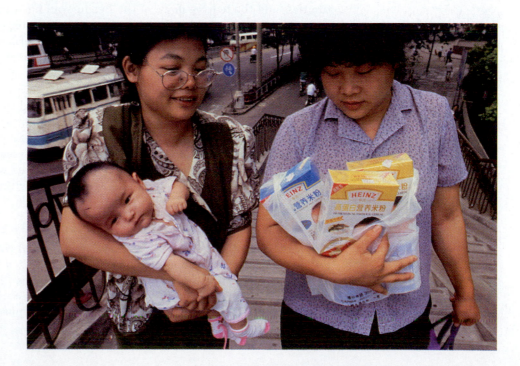

**A HEINZ BABY.** The Heinz baby food purchased by these Chinese mothers comes from an H.J. Heinz factory in China operated as a joint venture with two Chinese partners. Available in China since 1986, precooked rice cereal and other Heinz baby food products are popular among China's working parents.

ingly important to the United States as its economic, technological, and military strength grows.

In fact, by 1993 there were 3000 Chinese businesses authorized to deal with foreigners. The Chinese government has also designated 300 "open cities" in which citizens are free to conduct business with foreign traders and investors.[22]  Looking ahead to 1997, when Hong Kong reverts to Chinese rule, many U.S. firms continue to invest in China. Among them is Motorola, Inc., which has built a new factory outside Hong Kong, just 30 minutes from the Chinese border.[23] One example of a small business that has done very well in China is tiny Conveyant Systems Inc., a distributor of PC-based telephone communications gear. Conveyant is very competitive with much larger world competitors such as AT&T, Siemens, Northern Telecom, and others. Strengthening its position in China by becoming a 60-percent owner of Tiachi Telecommunications Corporation in Tianjin, China, Conveyant had by 1993 garnered a 3 percent slice of the enormous Chinese domestic market for digital private-branch-exchange (PBX) products.[24]

## AFTER THE SOVIET UNION

*Perestroika,* the Soviet version of economic restructuring announced by President Mikhail Gorbachev in 1988, called for a gradual end to central economic coordination for the Soviet Union. When the Soviets showed an interest in embracing foreign investments, European, Japanese, and American companies were quick to respond. A consortium of top-notch U.S. companies—including Chevron, RJR Nabisco, Eastman Kodak, Johnson & Johnson, and Archer Daniels Midland—was formed to invest $5 billion to $10 billion in the former U.S.S.R. over a 15-year period through a number of joint ventures.[25] McDonald's has already opened its doors in Moscow, and Pepsi has become a favorite Soviet beverage. Taken together, the 700-plus joint ventures exceed the $500 million mark.

The collapse of the Soviet Union and Gorbachev's departure from office—hastened by a coup attempt in August 1991—have cast considerable uncertainty over global business opportunities in that part of the world. Boris Yeltsin, a rival of Gorbachev and the President of the new Russian Republic, has vowed to continue with democratic reform and promotion of a freer market economy.

Formerly under Soviet influence, Eastern European countries also hold opportunities, and the tearing down of the Berlin Wall has come to symbolize the bold  moves toward democracy. German reunification has assured the restructuring of the economy in what was East Germany, and investments by General Electric and General Motors in Hungary and other projects in Poland have the entire Eastern Bloc in a flurry of economic activity.[26] An issue facing many businesses attempting to work in the newly opened countries is human resources and staffing. Beyond the language and cultural barriers lie some of the biggest challenges, including an absence of an efficient business and communication infrastructure; a lack of employees with the combination skills; limited local knowledge of the human resources profession as it is understood in the West (because most hiring decisions were previously made by the government); and difficulty in finding managers willing to relocate.[27]

## THE NORTH AMERICAN FREE TRADE AGREEMENT

The Northern American Free Trade Agreement (called NAFTA) was negotiated in the early 1990s by officials representing United States President George Bush, Canadian Prime Minister Brian Mulroney, and Mexican President Carlos Salinas de Gortari. NAFTA provides for the phased removal of tariffs and other barriers to trade among companies and individuals in the United States, Canada, and

Mexico. There is already a longstanding history of trade among the three nations: in 1992 alone, Mexican purchases of U.S. goods totalled $40.6 billion.[28]

In fact, some people consider NAFTA merely a formal christening of a trade relationship that has existed already for some time. One example is provided by Buckman Laboratories. Based in Memphis, Tennessee, Buckman Laboratories manufactures microbiocides used to control corrosion, scale, and slime for the paper, leather, and paintmaking industries. The privately-held company has found a  global niche. Buckman derives 50 percent of its $200 million in annual sales from outside the United States and maintains more than 50 percent of its company assets outside the United States as well. The company's international expansion began three years after its founding, when it formed a Canadian subsidiary in 1948, long before NAFTA's arrival. Moreover, Robert H. Buckman, President and CEO, believes that his company's trade with Mexico will increase regardless of NAFTA's success. "I see tremendous expansion in trade with Mexico—with or without NAFTA—and Latin America," said Buckman. "In fact, it's already started. NAFTA is simply a recognition of reality."[29]

Still, NAFTA was a subject of controversy in Canada and the United States throughout the Congressional debate that led to its passage in the Fall of 1993. Both new United States President Bill Clinton and new Canadian Prime Minister Jean Chretien had to defend NAFTA to their own constituencies.

The controversy over NAFTA is an object lesson in the effects of government policy and regulation, part of the second concern about competitiveness discussed earlier in this chapter. Recall Michael Porter's observation that government officials and managers are now more conscious than ever of the fact that economic and

**NAFTA PROTESTERS.** The North American Free Trade Agreement was the subject of much controversy throughout the congressional debate leading to its passage in the fall of 1993. Protesters feared the NAFTA would lead to lower wages and the loss of jobs in the United States.

# KEIRETSU IN COMMAND

The Sumitomo Group began as a copper mining company nearly 300 years ago. Today, the group is comprised of 20 core companies and dozens of smaller businesses located in a variety of industries around the world, including computers, metals, steel, glass, coal, real estate, beer, consumer electronics, and life insurance. The group is tied together first and foremost by ritual and behavior. For example, each year the presidents of all 20 companies come together with the Sumitomo family at a special temple-like hall that commemorates the group's founders. In addition, the presidents meet separately each month in what is called a *"Hakusuikai"* or "white water group" to discuss business matters from planning new ventures to providing support for ailing group members.

The Sumitomo Group is one example of a *keiretsu*—a huge business conglomerate. Often labeled "the corporate equivalent of blood brotherhood," these "business families" underlie many Japanese business arrangements. Members of a *keiretsu* are often obligated to show preference to one another, regardless of what other opportunities might exist. At times, *keiretsu* loyalties thus preempt otherwise beneficial relationships with companies from different countries or different *keiretsus*.

Such a business structure defies American practices, grounded firmly in the encouragement of head-to-head competition among companies in the marketplace. Anti-trust laws actually prohibit the sort of behavior and anti-fair play that *keiretsus* promote. In the U.S., the view is that "if you build a better mousetrap, the world will beat a path to your door." In Japan, it appears to depend more on who your friends are.

The *keiretsu* system has placed foreign companies at a serious disadvantage in Japan. Most of the conglomerates are focused around a major bank, something prohibited by law in the United States. The six largest *keiretsus* cluster around Sumitomo, Mitsubishi, Mitsui, Dai Ichi Kangyo, Fuji and Sanwa banks. The Dai Ichi *keiretsu* is the largest of these, and claims sales five times larger than the most powerful American companies, such as General Motors and Exxon.

*Keiretsu* arrangements account for roughly one-sixth of Japan's sales and profits. In addition, intercompany holdings keep 60 percent to 80 percent of *keiretsu* stock from being publicly traded. As mentioned earlier, many of the *keiretsu*s are organized around large Japanese banks. This enables the group companies to take on financial losses without having to worry about the lowering of their credit ratings—they will always be able to turn to the group's bank. In the electronics industry, this situation has proved especially disadvantageous to foreign firms. Japanese electronics companies such as NEC, Hitachi and Fujitsu compete on price without having to worry about rising financial losses. This prevents foreign competitors from engaging in head-to-head competition with the Japanese; it hurts foreign businesses, and the global consumer.

The Sumitomo *keiretsu* has come to the rescue of members on numerous occasions. "Sumitomo Bank is the absolute expert in arranging its peanut shells to make the problem disappear," said Alicia Ogawa, an analyst at S. G. Warburg Securities.[30] One example occurred when Sumitomo Bank bailed Mazda out during the early 1970s and brought the company back from the brink of bankruptcy. Members of the Sumitomo *keiretsu* rescued Mazda by offering the ailing company financial support and hiring former Mazda employees who had been laid off. All members of the Sumitomo *keiretsu* purchased only Mazda cars for the duration of the company's recovery.

Sumitomo Bank was also involved in bailing out troubled computer manufacturer NEC. Before NEC had become a manufacturer of mainframe computers, Sumitomo relied upon equipment made by NCR. When the bank chose to upgrade its computer systems, however, it replaced its existing NCR machines with NEC mainframes. "NEC is close to us and is part of our group," explained a Sumitomo Bank manager. "We hope our order will lead to more NEC mainframes being used in banks. We want their business to expand."[31] Switching costs amounted to more than $1 billion as a result of hardware and software changes, but the bank absorbed the expense out of loyalty to NEC as a member of the Sumitomo Group.

Japanese officials claim that the influence of *keiretsus* has dwindled as a result of modernization and deregulation of the economy. Evidence of Sumitomo's protectionism, however, suggests that the *keiretsu* system does in fact continue to be an influence on the decision-making process in the Japanese market as well as interfere with the business of foreign companies in Japan. →

political conditions can support "winning" industries in the world markets. NAFTA has raised consciousness about such differences in conditions among the three nations involved. Of particular concern in the United States and Canada was the possibility that companies based in either of the other countries might seek **competitive advantage** by following more relaxed labor relations or environmental practices. Accordingly, so-called "side agreements" on these two issues were negotiated in 1993.[32]

**competitive advantage:**
A capability or circumstance that enables a corporation to earn higher-than-average profits in a particular industry.

## RECAP ABOUT GOVERNMENT INFLUENCE

The effects of government on business in all the countries and areas we have discussed underscore how important it is that managers see themselves as parties to relationships with government officials, both in their "home" countries and, increasingly, around the globe. Of course, it is true that in any given nation government policy has long influenced business in such areas as taxes, licenses, and hiring. It is also true that international agreements such as the General Agreement on Tariffs and Trade (GATT) have long influenced international management. What is highlighted here is the new level of intensity of management-government relations. To each party, the stakes are higher than ever before.

# A BRIEF MODERN HISTORY OF GLOBALIZATION

International business has existed in some sense since prehistory, when flint blanks, ceramics, and other goods were traded across great distances. Even during the Roman Empire, traders carried goods to consumers around the world. However, multinational enterprises—as we know them today—were great rarities until the nineteenth century. By then, U.S. companies like General Electric, International Telephone and Telegraph, and Singer Sewing Machine Company had started to invest in overseas manufacturing facilities, as had West European companies like Ciba, Imperial Chemicals, Nestle, Siemens, and Unilever.

## THE AFTERMATH OF WORLD WAR II

When World War II ended, the United States was the only major country that had not been devastated by war. The size of the U. S. economy had almost doubled during the war, and the United States dominated the world economically, politically, and militarily. In this climate, many U.S. firms started making substantial direct investments in foreign primary industries such as oil production and mining. Technological development and product design remained focused on the United

**GLOBAL EXPANSION.** Avis "tries harder" around the world. Avis has operations in more than 140 countries, offering a familiar name for travelers as well as providing service for the local populations.

States market at home; American-owned multinationals generally viewed the rest of the world as a source of raw materials, cheap labor, and supplemental markets.

In the mid-1950s, U.S. companies started to make substantial direct investments in foreign manufacturing facilities. In the 1960s, it was American service firms—banks, insurance companies, marketing consultants, and the like—that expanded overseas. In time, however, as purchasing power increased abroad, especially in Europe and Japan, their domestic production prospered. Eventually overseas producers expanded beyond their national boundaries, entering the international marketplace. Although these foreign competitors initially relied on U.S. technology, lower costs eventually gave them a competitive advantage. Today, they have taken the initiative in developing and improving technology, and this has furthered their competitiveness.[33]

Western Europe's firms—particularly in such industries as chemicals, electrical gear, pharmaceuticals, and tires—started to respond in the late 1960s by setting up and acquiring U.S. affiliates. So did the gigantic Japanese trading companies—particularly during the 1980s, when they were trying to circumvent protectionist U.S. legislation that would cut their access to the American market. To lower their manufacturing costs, Japanese and U.S. companies also started to invest in facilities in newly developing nations.

As a result, international trade and competition both have intensified in recent years. More than one-quarter of all the goods produced in the world now cross national boundaries, while nearly three-quarters of the goods produced in the United States face foreign competition.[34] As Lester Thurow notes, we now live in a world where transportation costs are so unimportant that everything that can be traded soon will be.[35] In this global market, organizations must fight to capture overseas markets while defending their home markets from foreign competition.

One of the more recent markets to open up to U.S. interests is Vietnam. In a move fraught with emotion and bitter memories more than two decades old,

President Clinton lifted the 19-year embargo against Vietnam. This has created a rush among American firms anxious to do business with the 72 million people of Vietnam. Among more than 30 companies with established representative offices in Vietnam are Digital, BankAmerica, IBM, Caterpillar, General Electric, Motorola, and Philip Morris. GM, Ford, and Chrysler are considering establishing assembly plants to tap into Vietnam's educated workforce. The U.S. companies have plenty of competition from other countries that have a selling head start, such as Australia, Taiwan, France, Hong Kong, and Japan. But a hidden U.S. advantage is the million or so Vietnamese who have settled in the United States and have already invested in small businesses in the south of Vietnam who are likely to do more now that it is legal.[36]

## THE ROLE OF THE MULTINATIONAL ENTERPRISE (MNE)

Companies and individuals can own foreign assets in two fundamental ways. They can purchase shares in the companies that own those assets. Foreign **portfolio investment** of this sort gives those companies and individuals a claim on profits, but no right to participate in management. Or they can engage in **direct investment,** the buying and management of foreign assets.[37]

Direct investment goes beyond *exporting, licensing,* and even *franchising,* all of which are avenues to globalization that will be discussed later in the chapter. Direct investment is characterized by an active involvement in the management of foreign investments, typically through a **multinational enterprise (MNE),** a large corporation with operations and divisions spread over several countries but controlled by a central headquarters.[38] Table 5-1 gives an idea of just how large some multinational firms have grown. In making investment decisions, managers in MNEs must assess three factors. The first is the economies of different nations. An important issue involves evaluating a country's **infrastructure,** the facilities needed to support economic activity. The infrastructure includes transportation systems, communication systems, schools (important for providing workers with adequate skills), hospitals, power plants, and sanitary facilities. The second factor is the political risk, which refers to the possibility that political changes, in either the short or the long run, will affect its activities abroad. The third factor is the appropriateness of technology to different cultures. Production technologies that work well in Japan might not work well in Ecuador. Moreover, the Ecuadorians and their government might resent being forced to adapt to new technology, a change that is often traumatic. Any technological change is difficult, and the support of the host government may be nearly essential.

**THE IMPACT OF MNES ON HOST COUNTRIES.** MNEs are not necessarily welcome participants in national economies around the world. MNEs are courted by some host country governments and viewed with suspicion in other potential host countries. Thus, global managers must not assume that a beneficial relationship between the MNE and people in the host country will automatically result.

A substantial amount of research has been conducted regarding the effects of MNEs.[39] Christopher Korth, for instance, has identified some of the potential benefits and costs that the operations of an MNE may have on a host country.[40] Note that the benefits and costs listed below are *potential*. Whether they actually occur in a specific situation depends on the environment (including government actions) and the actual behavior of the MNE involved. Some of the major potential benefits are transfer of capital, technology, and entrepreneurship to the host country; improvement of the host country's balance of payments; creation of local job and career opportunities; improved competition in the local economy; and greater availability of products for local consumers.

These benefits may occur in any given situation. Many MNE managers and some analysts believe that they usually do. But each potential benefit may incur a

---

**portfolio investment:**
Investment in foreign assets whereby a company purchases share in companies that own those assets.

**direct investment:**
Investment in foreign assets whereby a company purchases assets that it manages directly.

**multinational enterprise (MNE):**
A large corporation with operations and divisions spread over several countries but controlled by a central headquarters.

**infrastructure:**
Physical facilities needed to support economic activity; includes transportation and communication systems, schools, hospitals, power plants, and sanitary facilities.

**TABLE 5-1**        **The World's Largest MNEs**

### SALES

| | BILLIONS OF U.S. DOLLARS |
|---|---|
| 1. Itochu | $180.0 |
| 2. Sumitomo Corp. | 168.3 |
| 3. Mitsubishi Corp. | 166.1 |
| 4. Marvbeni | 161.8 |
| 5. Mitsui & Co. | 160.2 |
| 6. Exxon | 117.0 |
| 7. General Motors | 113.0 |
| 8. Nissho Iwai | 105.6 |
| 9. Ford Motor | 100.0 |
| 10. Toyota Motor | 94.9 |

### PROFITS

| | BILLIONS OF U.S. DOLLARS |
|---|---|
| 1. Philip Morris | $4.94 |
| 2. Exxon | 4.80 |
| 3. Royal Dutch/Shell Grp. | 4.78 |
| 4. General Electric | 4.31 |
| 5. AT&T | 3.85 |
| 6. Dupont | 2.69 |
| 7. Merck | 2.45 |
| 8. Unilever | 2.23 |
| 9. Toyota Motor | 2.22 |
| 10. Chevron | 2.21 |

| RANK 1993 | RANK 1992 | BILLIONS OF U.S. DOLLARS | | MARKET VALUE |
|---|---|---|---|---|
| 1 | 2 | Nippon Telegraph & Telephone | Japan | 140.52 |
| 2 | 9 | American Telephone & Telegraph | USA | 82.40 |
| 3 | 1 | Royal Dutch/Shell Group | Neth/Britain | 81.59 |
| 4 | 3 | Exxon | USA | 81.35 |
| 5 | 6 | General Electric | USA | 79.34 |
| 6 | 16 | Mitsubishi Bank | Japan | 73.56 |
| 7 | 16 | Sumitomo Bank | Japan | 65.97 |
| 8 | 6 | Wal-Mart Stores | USA | 64.07 |
| 9 | 20 | Industrial Bank of Japan | Japan | 63.21 |
| 10 | 23 | Sanwa Bank | Japan | 61.19 |
| 11 | 21 | Fuji Bank | Japan | 60.81 |
| 12 | 19 | Dai-Ichi Kangyo Bank | Japan | 57.67 |
| 13 | 11 | Toyota Motor | Japan | 56.97 |
| 14 | 7 | Coca-Cola | USA | 54.23 |
| 15 | 26 | Sakura Bank | Japan | 49.49 |
| 16 | 25 | Tokyo Electric Power | Japan | 46.26 |
| 17 | 4 | Philip Morris | USA | 44.97 |
| 18 | 8 | Merck | USA | 43.78 |
| 19 | 13 | British Telecommunications | Britain | 40.70 |
| 20 | 43 | Nomura Securities | Japan | 39.56 |

Source: "The Global 1000: A Topsy-Turvey Year for Giants," *Business Week*, July 12, 1993, pp. 52-53.

cost. For example, the MNE may use local financing, thereby absorbing capital that might have financed indigenous companies. Or a few well-advertised, standardized consumer products may drive many locally produced products from the market, thereby reducing consumer choice.

Clearly, there were abuses on the part of some MNEs in the past. United Fruit, for example, is generally acknowledged to have engaged in extensive political and economic interference in Latin America in the years between the two World Wars. In the early 1970s, officials of ITT were accused of conspiring with the CIA to prevent the election of Salvador Allende Gossens, a Marxist, to the presidency of Chile.[41] More recently, the Japanese electronics giant, Hitachi, admitted stealing proprietary technology from IBM. Today, MNEs have high political visibility and, despite their size and power, are vulnerable to punitive actions by local governments. Under such conditions, few companies are likely to risk even the appearance of unethical behavior.

**THE IMPACT OF MNES ON HOME COUNTRIES.** The debate over the impact of MNEs on their home countries is less intense, probably due to the absence of such highly charged emotional issues as political interference, cultural disruption, and economic dependence. We have already discussed the potential benefits that lead companies to go international, so we will focus here on the potential negative effects of MNEs on home countries.

One drawback is that the outflow of foreign investments, coupled with reduced income from exports, may weaken the national balance of payments. In the long run, these losses may be more than compensated for by the flow of income from dividends, licensing fees, royalties, and sales of components for foreign assembly. Still, there is the risk that the home country will suffer a loss of technological advantages, especially when joint ventures and global strategic partnerships are involved.[42]

The most volatile issue on the home front is whether an MNE's foreign investment (most obviously in manufacturing) causes the loss of domestic jobs. On the surface, moving factory production overseas would certainly seem to cause job loss at home, but some observers feel this job displacement is inevitable, whether or not organizations decide to invest overseas. Even if one organization ignores the possible cost benefits of moving its production overseas, its competitors will not. This will put the stay-at-home company at a competitive disadvantage, cause it to lose business, and eventually force it to reduce its work force anyway.[43] If Sumitomo decides to build a factory in Indonesia to have more competitive costs, are jobs lost in Japan?

# GLOBAL BUSINESS PRACTICE

Time plays two important roles in global management. In each instance, patience and a sense of history are involved. First, managers cannot simply transform their organizations into global participants overnight. It takes time and careful deliberation to establish a global position (in the second sense of globalization—location— that we discussed at the beginning of this chapter). In this section, we will discuss reasons for seeking global positions and possible paths for doing so.

Second, the globalization of business has resulted in relationships among managers whose cultural traditions not only differ, but have evolved down those different paths for hundreds, if not thousands, of years. Thus, it is unrealistic to expect global business relationships to evolve without considerable effort and adaptation. A classic case in point is the historical and cultural divide between the United States and Japan, which we will survey later in this section.

In an effort to bridge the cultural differences inherent in a global economy, The Gillette Corporation has developed a quality training program to ensure a supply of global talent through its International Graduate Trainee Program. Every year Gillette identifies and interviews top graduates from prestigious universities in Columbia, Japan, Mexico, and other countries in which Gillette operates. Some of these students become part of an 18-month training program, the first six months of which are spent in the home country, followed by a year at the Boston headquarters. In 1993, 25 students participated in the program from such diverse locations as Poland, Russia, the People's Republic of China, England, and Singapore. Of the 113 individuals who graduated from the training program from its inception in 1987 to 1993, 60 were still with the company in 1993, a 53% retention rate.[44]

## HOW COMPANIES GO INTERNATIONAL

Few organizations start out multinational. More commonly, an organization proceeds through several stages of internationalization, where each stage represents a way of conducting business with closer proximity and contact to customers in other countries.

**exporting:**
The selling of domestically produced goods in foreign markets.

The first two stages involve **exporting,** the selling of domestically produced goods in foreign markets. Companies at the first stage of internationalization have only passive dealings with foreign individuals and organizations.[45] At this point, for example, a company may be content with filling overseas orders that come in without any serious selling effort on its part. International contacts may be handled by an existing department. Third parties, such as agents and brokers, often act as go-betweens for companies at the first stage of internationalization.

In the second stage, companies deal directly with their overseas interests, though they may also continue to use third parties. At this point, most companies do not base employees abroad, but domestic employees regularly travel abroad on business.

In the third stage, international interests shape the company's overall makeup in an important way. Although still essentially domestic, the company has a direct hand in importing, exporting, and perhaps producing its goods and services abroad.

**licensing:**
The selling of rights to market brand-name products or to use patented processes or copyrighted materials.

**franchise:**
A type of licensing arrangement in which a company sells a package containing a trademark, equipment, materials, and managerial guidelines.

It is at this juncture that managers face the possibility of establishing formal contractual relationships with managers in the other countries. They can use **licensing,** the selling of rights to market brand-name products or use patented processes or copyrighted materials, or they can sell **franchises,** a special type of license in which a company sells a package that contains a trademark, equipment, materials, and managerial guidelines. Franchising is the primary way McDonald's, Pizza Hut, and other fast-food chains have expanded into international markets.

Although licenses and franchises give corporations access to foreign revenues, their role in management is limited. To gain a greater say in management, organizations have to turn to direct investment. At this, the fourth stage, they either create a foreign subsidiary or buy a controlling interest in an existing foreign firm.

**joint venture:**
Business undertaking in which foreign and domestic companies share the costs of building production or research facilities in foreign countries.

Another option is the **joint venture,** in which domestic and foreign companies share the cost of developing new products or building production facilities in a foreign country. A joint venture may be the only way to enter certain countries where, by law, foreigners cannot own businesses. In other situations, joint ventures let companies pool technological knowledge and share the expense and risk of research that may not produce marketable goods.

Hitachi, Ltd. president Tustomu Kanai oversees Hitachi joint ventures with Texas Instruments (memory chips), General Electric (selling lighting products in Japan), Hewlett-Packard (RISC computer chips), and Boehringer-Mannheim (medical equipment).[46]

**global strategic partnership:**
Alliance formed by an organization with one or more foreign countries, generally with an eye toward exploiting the other countries' opportunities and toward assuming leadership in either supply or production.

**ethnocentric manager:**
Attitude that the home country's management practices are superior to those of other countries and can be exported along with the organization's goods and services.

**polycentric manager:**
Attitude that since a foreign country's management policies are best understood by its own management personnel, the home organization should rely on foreign offices.

**geocentric manager:**
Attitude that accepts both similarities and differences between domestic and foreign management policies and so attempts to strike a balance between those that are most effective.

**OVERSEAS FRANCHISES.** Dairy Queen is one of a number of familiar names that can be found on businesses throughout the world. Franchising is a popular way for U.S. companies to expand into international markets.

Finally, Howard V. Perlmutter and David A. Heenan, who have studied international cooperation,[47] argue that a true **global strategic partnership** among companies must be international, "extending beyond a few developed countries" to include newly industrializing, less-developed, and socialist nations.[48] Firms that forge these strategic alliances will try either to assume "leadership as low-cost suppliers" or to come forward with the best possible product or service, or both.

The emergence of strategic alliances and partnerships has affected the influence of *keiretsu* such as Sumitomo. By forming alliances, companies can strengthen their ability to compete with Sumitomo.

## GLOBALIZATION ACROSS DIFFERENT CULTURES

An MNE's ultimate success often hinges on its skill in fitting into the social fabric created by another country's values and culture. This is especially important for managers who must motivate and lead employees from different cultures with varying concepts of formality and courtesy—even different ideas about when a 10:00 a.m. meeting should start.[49]

## MANAGERS AND PREJUDICE

Dealing with employees from other countries often forces managers to confront their own prejudices. Howard Perlmutter and David D. Heenan have identified three primary attitudes among the managers of international companies: ethnocentric, polycentric, and geocentric.[50] **Ethnocentric managers** see foreign countries and their people as inferior to those of the home country. These managers believe that the practices of the home country can be exported along with its goods and services. A **polycentric manager** sees all countries as different and as hard to understand. Such managers tend to leave their foreign offices alone, believing local managers are most likely to understand their own needs. **Geocentric managers** recognize similarities as well as differences among countries. Such managers attempt to draw on the most effective techniques and practices, wherever they originate.

Firms with foreign interests are likely to have managers with each of these perspectives. Perlmutter and Heenan believe that geocentric attitudes are the most suitable kind for managers of multinational companies, but they are also the hardest to learn and accept.

## WOMEN IN THE INTERNATIONAL WORK FORCE

Since the 1950s, the United States has witnessed profound changes in women's prospects at work and in society. Once our culture identified men predominately with public or work life and linked women to private and home life. Gradually, the patriarchal society and women themselves began to change their attitudes and values about the roles of women in society. The women's movement, economic necessity, and the greater avenues opened up by court cases and legislation enabled women to seek education and employment in great numbers. Women began to redefine their roles in society, and society was forced to adjust—though not without resistance on the part of traditional women and men. How far women have actually come is debatable, given their virtual absence from the upper echelons of management, but few would disagree that American women have many more options today than they did 40 years ago.

Yet in international management, women frequently encounter stifling reminders of a more patriarchal past. Dealing directly with Asian and Middle Eastern firms can be quite awkward for women executives. In these cultures, women are traditionally excluded from or thought incompetent to hold positions of authority outside the home. In some cases, Asian and Middle Eastern business*men* have been reluctant to work with American business*women*. Yet, in many other situations local businessmen work quite well with foreign businesswomen, seeming to "make an exception" for foreign women that they are not yet ready to make for their own wives and daughters.

## WWB PROVES SMALL-BUSINESS LOANS TO WOMEN ARE GOOD BUSINESS[51]

At the 1975 United Nations International Women's Year Conference in Mexico City, it was pointed out that women performed more than 65 percent of the world's work, but earned only 10 percent of the income and owned less than 1 percent of the property. Michaela Walsh, who was attending as an observer for the Rockefeller Brothers Fund, met with a group of delegates to discuss how they could help women overcome the legal, financial, and cultural hurdles that prevent them from achieving economic self-sufficiency. They resolved to establish an organization that would support women who had entrepreneurial skills but lacked start-up capital and management skills to build fruitful businesses.

The organization they envisioned, Women's World Banking, was incorporated in 1979 under Dutch law (to confirm its international identity) "to advance and promote the full participation of women and their families in local and global economies." Walsh got grants of $250,000 each from the United Nations and the U.S. government to cover start-up costs, and secured $10 million in capital from individual contributors.

In many parts of the world, including the United States, women find it difficult to secure loans from banks for their business ideas. As Nancy Barry, president of WWB, explains, "Most commercial bankers still think a guy in a three-piece suit, regardless of his credit rating, is a better credit risk than a poor, black, brown, yellow, or white woman."[52] Moreover, many women lack sufficient collateral to back the loans they need to start their businesses. WWB sought to break this circular problem so that women could participate as full members in the business community. "The idea is to help women have access to finance, business, markets and banks," explains Ela Bhatt, global chair of Women's World Banking. "It means helping women in whatever way necessary to have access to the formal banking system."[53]

As of 1993, WWB affiliates in 51 countries had made more than 500,000 small loans to poor women. The repayment rate on these loans is a staggering 95 percent, a better track record than that of most major commercial banks. Although the average loan amount appears small (slightly more than $200), these loans have a tremendous impact on the lives of the borrowers and their communities. For example, a small loan of $300 to a group of 12 women in Uganda for an agricultural cooperative ultimately benefitted more than 100 women, men, and children in their village as a result of the increased production and income. WWB pursues a broad range of endeavors, from giving a woman in Maine the money to harvest the herbs needed for her teas and tonics to lending money to help a woman buy a cart for selling vegetables in an Indian marketplace. WWB has directly helped at least 250,000 women worldwide get started in business and has indirectly reached many more. ■

## THE HOFSTEDE STUDIES

The Dutch management scholar Geert Hofstede conducted studies in 40 countries and drew some conclusions about the relationship between national character and employee motivation.[54] He concluded that people vary a great deal, and those variations seriously challenge the rules of effective managerial practice based on Western theories and peoples. Hofstede cites four dimensions he feels describe important aspects of a national culture.[55]

1. *Individualism versus collectivism* measures an individual's relationship with other people and the degree to which the desire for personal freedom is played off against the need for social ties.

2. *Power distance* evaluates the way a particular society handles inequality among people. On one end of the scale are countries and people that play down inequality as much as possible. At the other end are cultures that accept and support large imbalances in power, status, and wealth.

3. *Uncertainty avoidance* measures how a society deals with the uncertainty of the future. A weak uncertainty-avoidance society is one that does not feel threatened by the uncertainty of the future, but is generally tolerant and secure. A strong uncertainty-avoidance culture, on the other hand, tries to overcome future uncertainties by developing legal, technological, and religious institutions that create security and avoid risk.

4. *Masculinity versus femininity* refers to the rigidity of sex roles. Hofstede defines a society as masculine if there are extensive divisions of social roles by sex and as feminine if these divisions are relatively small. Another way of looking at it is that masculinity versus femininity refers to differences in approaches to the quantity versus quality of life: Masculine refers to a national orientation towards assertiveness and acquisition of money and material goods, while feminine refers to an orientation towards caring for others and the quality of life.

In light of the differences he found between nations, Hofstede feels that it is unrealistic to expect any single management approach to be applicable worldwide.

## APPLYING JAPANESE APPROACHES ABROAD

While Hofstede has expressed serious doubts about applying American/Western management practices in other countries, some observers have become very excited about the effectiveness of Japanese practices. The study of "Japanese management" enjoyed significant popularity in the 1980s.

William G. Ouchi is among those who have studied Japanese business in the hope that it might provide solutions to some American problems.[56] Table 5-2 lists some of the characteristics he noted that distinguish Japanese organizations from American ones.[57]

These differences in organizational characteristics are associated with differences in managerial behavior. Naturally, there are wide variations in how individual Japanese managers act, yet there are a number of ways in which the *average* Japanese manager appears to differ from the average American manager. Overall, Japanese managers seem to be more concerned with the longer-term implications of their decisions and actions and more willing to make current sacrifices for future benefits. They are also more likely to encourage subordinates to participate in decision making and to welcome and acknowledge suggestions from subordinates. Partly because of this participation, they are less likely to make quick, unilateral decisions. In addition, communication between managers and subordinates is more indirect and subtle than in the United States. Managers try hard to avoid embarrassing co-workers in public or in private. They get to know their co-workers well as individuals and show concern for their welfare outside the workplace.

The interpretations of Ouchi and others offered valuable insights into what many Japanese managers were doing on a day-to-day basis. More recently, some observers have come to the conclusion that what was initially interpreted as a

| TABLE 5-2 | Characteristics of Japanese and American Organizations | |
| --- | --- | --- |
| | **JAPANESE ORGANIZATIONS** | **AMERICAN ORGANIZATIONS** |
| | Lifetime employment | Short-term employment |
| | Slow evaluation and promotion | Rapid evaluation and promotion |
| | Non-specialized career paths | Specialized career paths |
| | Implicit control mechanisms | Explicit control mechanisms |
| | Collective decision making | Individual decision making |
| | Collective responsibility | Individual responsibility |
| | Wholistic concern | Segmented concern |

Source: William G. Ouchi, *Theory Z: How American Business Can Meet the Japanese Challenge* (Reading, Mass.: Addison-Wesley, 1981), p. 58.

management style unique to the Japanese culture is also successfully used by managers in many other countries. "Japanese management" may more usefully be interpreted as a way of managing that is widely applicable in many, perhaps all, countries, industries, and companies—a "global management" style.[58]

**MANAGEMENT 2000 AND BEYOND**

# ACHIEVING GLOBAL PROXIMITY[59]

Tomorrow's organizations may take a cue on communication in the global economy from what is happening today at VeriFone. This California-based business manufactures the small in-store terminals through which credit cards are read and runs the networks that provide authorization for purchases. At VeriFone, the globalization of business in all its aspects—proximity, location, and attitude—takes on new meaning.

An emphasis on physical proximity to its customers was part of founder William Melton's original vision for the company. So, besides having major operations in California, Honolulu, India, and Taiwan, VeriFone has smaller offices in 25 locations around the world, putting all customers within reasonable distance. Even so, about one-third of all employees travel more than half the time. Even technical staff travels, checking details of their efforts with customers. All this contact pays off. "I have my marketing tentacles everywhere," boasts CEO Hatim Tyabji. "There's no opportunity we don't find out about before our customers do." Tyabji himself visits every major prospect and customer and many smaller ones regularly.

All this travel would seem to be at odds with the other part of Melton's original vision: that all of his employees would constantly interact and share information. Maximum, creative use of computer networking and portable computers has provided the solution. Electronic mail and on-line databases now keep everyone in "virtual proximity." Tyabji notes, "Being at headquarters is irrelevant to me." Indicating toward his laptop computer, he explains, "There is my office." Almost everyone at VeriFone is on-line almost all of the time. Indeed, new employees get laptops before they get desks. And they constantly tap in, from hotel rooms, airports, meetings, or wherever they are. For VeriFone employees, E-mail is as natural as talking. VeriFone managers receive an average of 60 messages a day over the company's VAX-mail system and the Internet communications network, which links all employees. Employees respond to their own messages; there are no secretaries at VeriFone. In fact, ordinary paper mail is forbidden internally. Customers are also encouraged to use E-mail, but when paper mail is received it is relayed overnight to traveling employees rather than waiting on their desks. Nothing is left waiting on desks for VeriFone employees to return to their offices.

Adding to VeriFone's mastery of global communication are the creative ways it has found to use the communication network. Nearly all of VeriFone's work processes are carved up and electronically distributed in order to speed activities up and utilize maximum expertise. And VeriFone employees are within minutes of expert advice. For example, a salesperson in a difficult negotiation with a client might use a break to send out a description of the problem via laptop. Before long, a range of managers will have responded with advice.

International time zones often are perceived as a hassle in doing business, but not at VeriFone. VeriFone has figured out a way for the time zone difference to serve as an advantage. For example, when a group at one facility working on a time-crucial project is ready to leave work, it hands off everything from engineering specifications to customer data to a group in a time zone perhaps eight hours earlier in its day. By transferring work from San Francisco to Taipei to London and then back to San Francisco, VeriFone can maintain a project 24 hours a day without the need for overtime work. One advantage of this approach is the ability to respond very quickly to proposals. VeriFone recently won 80 percent of the business of a consortium of German banks when it responded to a proposal just days after the banks had issued the request for proposals. All the other bidders were left to compete over the remaining 20 percent.

The communications network also allows employees access to important information which includes shipments, booking, revenues, detailed personnel data, everyone's travel schedules, order status, progress with sales, and articles of interest gathered from various news sources. Although this worldwide perspective of instant communication, shared data and work collaboration is a cultural shock initially for many newcomers, the advantages are readily apparent. As Tyabji has said: "If you give good people the kinds of tools we've given our people...then all you have to do is get the hell out of their way."

Even as communications technology accelerates us onto the "information superhighway," a big issue is how to use it most effectively. The technology VeriFone employees use is no longer even leading-edge, but they benefit from using it fully and creatively. VeriFone gives us just a glimpse of how we might start to rethink the office and communication in the twenty-first century. "Other companies have everything we have," Tyabji says. "They just don't know how to use it."

## SUMMARY

1. **Identify different aspects of globalization.**

   Globalization is one of the most important changes to the external environment of most businesses. Globalization refers to a new perspective, or attitude, about relationships with other people in other nations. Globalization refers to the unprecedented scope, shape, number, and complexity of business relationships conducted across international boundaries.

2. **Explain the meaning and importance of competitiveness.**

   Competitiveness, the relative standing of one competitor against others, can refer to an organization or to a nation. Globalization has heightened the role of governments in influencing competitiveness between nations. Governments can influence competitiveness through economic climate, institutions, and policies.

# THE MOVE TO INTERNATIONAL BANKING

To cope with changing dynamics in the domestic and international banking environment, Japanese-based Sumitomo decided to branch out internationally. The bank became particularly involved in leveraged buyouts and merger and acquisition deals in the United States and Europe. It served as the adviser to Yamanouchi for its $395 million takeover of San Francisco-based Shaklee, it arranged Japanese financing for Campeau's buyout of Federated Department Stores and it acquired a loan commitment fee of $2.5 million from Paramount in its failed bid for Time, Inc. Sumitomo has also played an integral role in pushing for greater Japanese involvement in shaping international fiscal policy.

In 1986, the bank made a large and aggressive acquisition of its own—12.5 percent of Goldman, Sachs & Company, a New York investment bank. Many bankers were intrigued by the move, since Sumitomo's role is strictly limited by the Federal Reserve Board. The Fed has already expressed concern that the arrangement might further erode the Glass-Steagall Act, which separates commercial banks from investment banks. Sumitomo may not increase its stake in Goldman, Sachs, nor have any management role or engage in joint venture with Goldman, Sachs. The relationship is important, however, because Sumitomo needs at least a tentative toehold in the United States if it is to keep pace with the increasing globalization of business. Sumitomo's purchase also reflects a number of the reasons MNEs turn to international investments.

Faced with a slow-growing and more competitive domestic market, for example, Sumitomo has turned to international ventures to gain a higher rate of return on its investments and to increase its share of the world's banking market. In addition, even the partial acquisition of Goldman, Sachs signals Sumitomo's ambition to became a major force in international banking.

3. **Trace the historical evolution of globalization of business.**

The pace of internationalization began to quicken after World War II, when the strong U.S. economy and technological advances in communication and transportation made it feasible to buy and manage foreign assets. By the 1960s, though, economic growth in Europe and Japan had spawned competitors for American firms. That competition now also comes from North American trading partners, Canada and Mexico, and the so-called "Four Tigers"—Hong Kong, Singapore, South Korea, and Taiwan.

4. **Discuss the important conditions that managers must consider in the globalization of their actions.**

Global business relationships are affected by a host of economic, political, and technological conditions that differ from nation to nation. Above all, the global manager has reason to be patient with the evolution of global business relationships. This stems primarily from the fact that globalization has brought together people whose cultures have differed for centuries and even millennia.

## REVIEW QUESTIONS

1. What does globalization mean for managers?
2. What does competitiveness mean to managers and government officials?
3. How do government actions influence the competitiveness of companies and nations?
4. What recent political and economic changes have dramatically altered the face of global business?
5. What is the difference between portfolio investment and direct investment?
6. What are some of the positive influences of multinational corporations?
7. Why is international business activity attractive to some organizations?
8. What is the progression from minimal involvement in global business to significant involvement?
9. Why are cultural differences important for organizations competing globally?
10. Why might new kinds of organizations emerge for the conduct of global business?

## KEY TERMS

Globalization
Competitiveness
Competitive advantage
Portfolio investment
Direct investment
Multinational enterprise
Infrastructure
Exporting

Licensing
Franchise
Joint venture
Global strategic partnership
Ethnocentric manager
Polycentric manager
Geocentric manager

## PIER 1 EXPORTS SUCCESS TO FOREIGN MARKETS[60]

**N**umerous companies have confronted the challenge of exporting American retail shops abroad and have failed. Pier 1, though, plans on succeeding. With a well thought out, rational strategy, the 31-year-old, $700 million novelty store has ventured overseas with The Pier in the United Kingdom. It is planning more international expansion during the next few years.

At the heart of Pier 1's overseas strategy lies a strong customer focus, which guides the company's domestic strategy as well. According to director of merchandising Adrian Long, Pier 1 has a tradition of "moving with the customers." As the customer has matured, so has Pier 1.

Opportunities in the United States appear to be dwindling, though. Sales were up only 7 percent from 1991 to 1992, contrasted with double-digit growth rates during the late 1980s. Pier 1 is not abandoning its domestic efforts—actually, the company plans to open 300 new outlets during the next ten years—but it is keenly looking abroad for more exciting opportunities. The Pier in the United Kingdom is merely a first step, followed by two stores in Puerto Rico opened in 1993. Next on the list are stores in Mexico and Central and South America. At the same time, the company is looking eagerly toward the Far East for additional possibilities. By the year 2000, Pier 1 hopes to have about 250 stores abroad, outside the United States and Canada.

Pier 1 is not expanding overseas blindly. To hedge its risk, the company is working primarily through mechanisms, such as joint ventures and licensing arrangements, that minimize the risk to which it is exposed. Pier 1 owns only 50 percent of United Kingdom-based The Pier.

In order to be competitive in foreign markets, Pier 1 has made several significant changes in its international strategy, particularly with regard to product mix. In the United Kingdom, Pier 1 is offering products more in line with local tastes. The size and lay-out of European homes tend to dictate different needs. For example, since built-in and walk-in closets are rare in the United Kingdom, closet wardrobes tend to sell well there. Similarly, since European homes tend to be smaller than American homes, furniture items sold in the U.S. market, such as bedside tables, are too large and must either be modified or discontinued.

Color preferences also vary overseas as a result of the quality of outdoor light. In the United Kingdom, warm colors tend to prevail, such as pale yellows, warm greens, and peaches. In warmer climates such as Spain and Greece, however, whites, azure blues, bright yellows, and reds tend to be preferred.

With regard to other goods, Pier 1 is finding it necessary to accommodate a variety of cultural appetites. In the United Kingdom, Indian goods sell well as a result of the trading history between the two countries.

Even with its attention to cultural details, what Pier 1 recognizes is that the company is not about the specific goods that lines the shelves; rather, the company is about the shopping experience it provides, buoyed by colorful, exotic merchandise. Pier 1 can thus remain true to its central role without offering the same goods in every store around the globe. "You can live the rest of your life and never go into a Pier 1 store, because we don't sell anything that you have to have," says President Marvin J. Girouard.[61] But the goods are so enticing that the customer often cannot help but make a purchase.

The key to Pier 1's international success lies in getting close to customers abroad, an ambition that falls squarely in line with its domestic strategy. Pier 1 must become acclimated into the cultures in which new stores are located to be able to determine what those customers consider exotic and clever, so that the new Pier 1 outlets can stock items unusual in those cultures, sold at moderate prices and displayed in an integrated fashion—as the outlets in the United States successfully do with goods that Americans consider unique.

### CASE QUESTIONS

1. What risks did Pier 1 face in going international?
2. How were the risks managed?
3. What problems may arise if Pier 1 were to decide to open stores in Japan?

## MOVING BACK TO SOUTH AFRICA:
## A RISK TOO GREAT?[62]

South Africa has long been shunned by the global marketplace for its repressive racial practice of apartheid. During the mid-1980s, economic sanctions were imposed by numerous countries throughout the world in protest of apartheid, and as a result, scores of companies divested themselves of any and all economic interests in South Africa. Between 1985 and 1990, 209 companies in the United States sold or closed their offices and subsidiaries in South Africa. A clear message had been sent: Apartheid will not be tolerated.

As company after company pulled out of South Africa, the sanctions began taking their toll. The National Party, which had dominated the government since 1948, began to realize that South Africa could not survive unless democracy was embraced. After years of promoting racial exclusivity and encouraging the concentration of wealth in the hands of a select (white) few, the National Party began reforming its ways.

One step toward reform was the release of Nelson Mandela after 27 years of imprisonment. Mandela was President of the African National Congress (ANC), the National Party's primary opposition. The ANC, which fought against the National Party for nearly half a century, was founded in 1912 as a liberal lobby for the democratization of South Africa. First through legal means, and later through armed insurrection, the ANC sought to overthrow the racist government created by the National Party. Mandela's release thus signaled a first step toward a racially integrated South Africa.

As more widespread reform slowly began to take root in South Africa, the governments of many countries decided to lift the economic sanctions they had previously imposed. But while national governments gave the green light to businesses to reinvest, many local governments still resisted. In the United States, for example, then-President Bush lifted the ban on American investment in South Africa in July 1991. Nevertheless, approximately 140 state and local governments continued to impose sanctions against businesses with holdings in South Africa. Moreover, while South Africa appeared to be moving in the direction of democracy, the country still suffered from unrest and politically-motivated violence. Political strife, and the frequent, violent confrontations that resulted from it, placed in jeopardy the future of South Africa.

Then, in September 1993, a truly momentous step toward a unified South Africa took place: Constitutional negotiators from both the National Party and the ANC met in Johannesburg to form the Transitional Executive Council (TEC). The TEC provided for a power-sharing government that would run the country until a multiracial election could be held the following year. South Africa announced that it would hold the first truly democratic election in its history on April 27, 1994. The government elected by that ballot was to author a new constitution based on the ideals of democracy, equality, and national unity.

With true reform underway, Mandela made an appeal to the United Nations: "We believe the time has come when the international community should lift all economic sanctions against South Africa."[63] With this announcement, Mandela heralded a new beginning for South Africa. "Before [the announcement], South Africa was untouchable," asserted William Moses, senior analyst at Investor Responsibility Research Center (IRRC). "You had to know you were going to make a hell of a lot of money and have an overwhelming interest in the market because you had the anti-apartheid people against you and the state against you."[64] Moses predicted that all remaining local sanctions against South African investment would be lifted by 1994. "There's no real resistance," he noted. "It's just a matter of getting around to it."[65]

With the removal of the social and economic stigmas, South Africa is once again open for business. In spite of a deep recession, the country has much in its favor. For example, it boasts numerous natural resources. South Africa contains 44 percent of the world's gold reserves, 69 percent of its platinum group metals, and 25 percent of its diamonds. In addition, South Africa has a well-developed infrastructure of modern telecommunications, airports, railways, and ports, making it relatively easy for companies to set up offices and subsidiaries. Also, the country's GNP of more than $70 billion, larger than that of all the other African countries combined, demonstrates its purchasing power. And, perhaps most important, South Africa is geographically positioned as a potential springboard for companies looking to expand throughout the continent.

Acknowledging such benefits, several European and Asian companies have begun taking steps to reenter the South African marketplace. In fact, Japanese and South Korean consumer electronics marketers have been actively competing to secure a foothold in South Africa's growing, $2.4 billion high-technology market. In particular, the market for such products as televisions and telephones, denied to blacks during the years of apartheid, is particularly enormous. Firms such as South Korea's Daewoo and Japan's Sony are therefore moving quickly to take advantage of the new demand.

Strangely, however, American firms have been slow to reenter South Africa. "The U.S. is waking up a bit late to this market," observed Tony van der Schuyf, director of the new Products Laboratory, a market research company in Johannesburg.[66] This is especially confusing considering the presence of several key advantages that U.S. companies in particular would have in South Africa. "South Africans speak English, they can afford food, and probably hold American products in higher esteem than most Americans," Moses pointed out. "They know our brands, and they're eager to buy them. South Africa isn't out of the woods yet, but clearly it's a market that could be very, very lucrative."[67] While American companies hesitate, foreign competitors are making significant inroads into the South African marketplace that threaten the ability of American companies ever to catch up.

But American companies are not willing to ignore the volatile political climate that still remains unsettled. "The potential for an extremely bloody civil war exists, and until that is addressed, there are some real reasons many people will be leery," commented Douglas Templeman, senior vice president of Parsons Environmental Corp.[68] Parsons, a $1.6 billion engineering and construction company, recognizes the tremendous potential that lies in moving into a country in desperate need of new housing and environmental engineering, but is not willing to accept the accompanying risks. "The political scene is highly charged and unpredictable," Templeman remarked. "It's clear to us that if and when a stable political solution is reached that South Africa will be a very, very attractive market."[69] H. J. Heinz, who has been carefully tracing South Africa's 40 million consumers for some time, has also adopted a "wait-and-see" approach and has stated that it will not invest until South Africa becomes "a stable political entity with a majority government."[70] Stanley Works, which pulled out of South Africa in 1986, is approaching the situation even more cautiously. "There will be no hurry to move into an area that poses difficulties for employees and in fact is very unstable," said Patricia McLean, Stanley's manager of corporate communications.[71]

Parsons, Heinz, and Stanley Works echo the concerns of many American businesses, but not all. Companies such as Microsoft, Lotus, Federal Express, and Pillsbury have already made significant efforts to reinvest, though at a slower pace than foreign competitors. According to the IRRC, a total of 152 U.S. companies had employees or direct investments in South Africa by April 1994. For the most part, however, U.S. firms are choosing to open a sales office "or something small, rather than going full steam ahead with a factory," said Moses. "That makes sense almost anywhere, to open a sales office before you open a factory. But in South Africa you have the added concern of the country's stability."[72]

## CASE QUESTIONS

1. What are the factors influencing companies' decisions about whether to invest in South Africa?
2. How does investment in South Africa influence companies' global competitiveness?
3. What role does timing play in investing in South Africa?
4. Do you agree that it is almost always better to open a sales office in a new region before opening a factory there? Why?

## CHAPTER 6

# INVENTING AND REINVENTING ORGANIZATIONS

**Upon completing this chapter, you should be able to:**

1. Understand the importance of small business.

2. Define entrepreneurship.

3. Draw a distinction between entrepreneurship and management.

4. Explain key psychological traits of entrepreneurs.

5. Discuss the importance of reinventing organizations.

# IF YOU BUILD IT, THEY WILL COME . . .[1]

f you build it, they will come." So spoke the voice that actor Kevin Costner heard in the movie *Field of Dreams,* provoking him to build the baseball field he had dreamed about. The statement also reflects the philosophy of Howard Schultz, restaurant entrepreneur and chairman and CEO of Starbucks, a company that sells premium coffee through 300 retail stores and coffee bars in the United States. Beginning with a dream, Schultz took a business with $10 million in sales and built it into the country's largest roaster and retailer of specialty coffee. In 1992, Starbucks reported more than $90 million in sales and a compounded annual growth rate of 80 percent over the past three years.

Named for the first mate in Melville's *Moby Dick,* Starbucks began in 1971 when three young entrepreneurs—Jerry Baldwin, Zev Siegl and Gordon Bowker—began selling whole-bean coffee in Seattle's Pike Place Market. By 1982, it had grown into a thriving Seattle enterprise with five retail stores, a small roasting facility, and a wholesale business that sold coffee to local restaurants. It was then that Schultz was invited to join the business. At the time he was vice president of U.S. operations in New York for Hammarplast, a Swedish housewares company. Anxious to leave New York, Schultz agreed to manage retail sales and marketing for Starbucks and he and his wife packed up and headed west to Seattle.

*"The Italian starts his day at the coffee bar and sees his friends there later on..."*

Shortly after joining Starbucks, Schultz began to feel discontented. After working for the company for only a year, he found himself in Italy on business, where he was overwhelmed by a vision: What he saw was the possibility of a caffeinated American culture. "I saw the relationship Italian culture has with coffee and the romance of the beverage," he recalled. "The Italian starts his day at the coffee bar and sees his friends there later on. It struck me that this was also possible in America. It had never been done—and we could do it because the quality of Starbucks' coffee is unsurpassed." And so began Schultz's romanticization of coffee.

Schultz became increasingly frustrated by the disparity between what he was doing at Starbucks and what he wanted to be doing: His dream had turned into an obsession. Schultz then left Starbucks. He wrote a business plan for a new company, and even returned to Italy to see again what had first inspired him. He visited coffee bar after coffee bar, watching, thinking, and dreaming all the time.

And so Schultz opened his first coffee bar in April 1986. Named Il Giornale, after the Italian newspaper, the coffee bar was an instant success in Chicago. It served Starbucks coffee. Schultz then opened a second Il Giornale in Seattle and a third in Vancouver. A year later, Schultz bought Starbucks from his former employers for about $4 million. He merged the existing Il Giornale and Starbucks businesses, dropping the Il Giornale name. So began the business of Starbucks as we know it today.

Starbucks today encompasses a range of outlets, from kiosks in airports to small espresso bars to 2,000-square-foot flagship stores, as well as a direct-mail-order business. Between 1991 and 1992, sales climbed 61 percent, to $93 million. As of 1993, the company operated more than 185 retail outlets, and had set a pace of opening a store a week. Most of the stores were sprinkled along the West Coast, but Starbucks had made its East Coast debut in Washington, D.C.

Schultz's transformation of Starbucks was about having a dream and taking a chance. "Those were scary times," recalled his wife. "But I knew if he didn't take a chance, he would never be happy."

Schultz's relentless pursuit of "happiness" has translated into resounding success. Within a year of going public, Starbucks stock climbed from $17 per share to $40 per share. "I think Starbucks could easily top a billion dollars in sales by the end of the decade," said Christopher E. Vroom, a retail analyst with securities firm Alex, Brown & Sons, Inc. "Starbucks is single-handedly changing the way consumers think about coffee." →

ORGANIZATIONS come and go. In the authors' lifetimes, such organizations as Pennsylvania Railroad, Nash, the Civil Aeronautics Board, the World Football League, and Pan American World Airways have disappeared from the landscape. Others have been swallowed up into other organizations: People Express, the Baltimore Colts, the Seattle Pilots, and Republic Airlines are cases in point. In the United States last year alone, an estimated 600,000 new businesses were formed.[2] If history is any guide, most of those will disappear within a few years. For every Howard Schultz, there are many whose dreams do not become reality. Many more organizations are undergoing changes, as managers wrestle with questions about products, markets, organizational forms, global competitive pressures, and so on. In short, the story of organizations today is the story of managers inventing and reinventing organizations. That is the subject of this chapter.

## SMALL BUSINESS

**small business:**
Businesses that are locally owned and managed, often with very few employees working at a single location.

Small business plays a central role in our lives because we conduct much of our own personal economic activity with people running small businesses. Whenever you have your bicycle repaired, get your hair cut, or visit your dentist, you are part of the small business economy. The same holds true when you go for a late-night snack at your neighborhood "Mom and Pop" pizzeria, buy the morning newspaper, or browse for Mother's Day and Father's Day greeting cards at a local shop. **Small business** refers to businesses locally owned and managed, often with very few employees working at a single location. By customary U.S. government definition, a "small" business is one with fewer than 500 employees. By this definition, Starbucks was, but is no longer, a small business.

Small business is easy to overlook as you think about the world of organizations and management. You are not alone if the names of such large organizations as IBM, Exxon, and MTV come to mind more readily than do those listed in Table 6.1, which identifies the fastest-growing small businesses in the United States.[3] But small business is *where it all begins*. Consider the following facts:

- More than 36 million Americans work for organizations with fewer than 100 employees. In 1992, 53 percent of all jobs in America were held by people working in organizations with fewer than 500 employees—small businesses. Between 1988 and 1990, for example, while large organizations accounted for a net loss of 500,000 jobs in the United States, organizations with fewer than 20 employees accounted for a net gain of 4 million net new jobs.[4]
- According to a Dun & Bradstreet analysis of the two million businesses formed in 1991, 20 percent were one-person or two-person operations, a significant increase from past patterns. As Bruce Kirchhoff, former chief econo-

**TABLE 6-1**          **Fortune's Ten Fastest-Growing Companies, 1993**

| | | SALES | |
|---|---|---|---|
| | | ANNUAL GROWTH RATE 3-5 YEARS | |
| 1 | WELLFLEET COMMUNICATIONS | 243% | A leader in high-performance products for local and wide area computer networks; specializes in large and complex systems. |
| 2 | BE AEROSPACE | 207% | Builds seats, ovens, and cof-feemakers for commercial air-craft. Tapping new market for individual video players for pas-sengers. |
| 3 | PRESIDENT RIVER-BOAT CASINOS | 201% | Mississippi River gambling, on a 297-foot boat cruising in Iowa and dockside in Biloxi; now ren-ovating a moored boat in St. Louis. |
| 4 | GRANCARE | 181% | Relentless acquirer of nursing homes in the West and Midwest; also pushing into faster-growing areas like home health care. |
| 5 | CISCO SYSTEMS | 159% | A major supplier of large, compli-cated computer networks to businesses around the world. NEC resells its products in Japan. |
| 6 | COLUMBIA HOSPITAL | 149% | Its planned merger with Galen Health Care will create a giant that owns 99 hospitals in 19 states, with revenues of more than $5 million. |
| 7 | U.S. LONG DISTANCE | 148% | Provides operators for long-dis-tance calls from pay phones and hotels; sells direct-dial service in four states; handles billing for companies. |
| 8 | OUTBACK STEAKHOUSE | 147% | A chain of 117 casual steak restau-rants with Aussie theme, American food. Mainly in the Southeast, about one-third franchised. |
| 9 | QUAL-MED | 138% | Growing by acquisition, its HMOs cover some 335,000 people in six Western states; bidding for large Defense Department con-tracts. |
| 10 | PHYCOR | 131% | Operates 16 medical clinics in ten states with primary care and up to 29 specialities; the 550 affili-ated doctors work in Phycor clinics. |

*Source:* Andrew E. Serwer, "America's 100 Fastest Growers," *Fortune,* August 9, 1993, p. 40.

mist of the Small Business Administration, observes: "A tremendous shift to self-employment is under way." Some of this growth is driven by people who are concerned about the downsizing of large corporations. Some have started their own businesses after having been laid off. Others are interested in the freedom of being one's own boss.[5]

- The well-known "giant" organizations of the mid-1990s all had humble beginnings. Consider the origins of Wal-Mart, AT&T, and General Motors (GM). Wal-Mart began as a single store that Sam Walton opened in 1962 in Rogers, Arkansas.[6] AT&T had its beginnings in the tinkering of Alexander Graham Bell, who was a teacher, not a financier or business tycoon. With the telephone patent that he received in 1876, Bell and his advisers awarded franchises to people with the money and local political clout necessary to start local telephone systems. When Bell's patents expired at the end of the nineteenth century, thousands of companies emerged to threaten a fledgling AT&T in the American market. It was not until the 1930s that AT&T took the organizational shape that endured as a unique monopoly for fifty years.[7] Alfred Sloan, who is credited with shaping and leading the modern General Motors, started out with Hyatt Roller Bearings in Newark, New Jersey, after his graduation from MIT. As Sloan tells the story, Hyatt had twenty-five employees, and one ten-horsepower motor ran the factory's machinery.[8] Twenty-five years later, after Sloan bought Hyatt and, in turn, sold it to General Motors, Sloan moved into upper management at GM.

Joseph Schumpeter, an Austrian economist, wrote in the early 1940s that a healthy economic system was one frequently buffeted by a "perennial gale of creative destruction."[9] The phrase still aptly describes today's world of small business.

In the next section, we will explore in depth the process of creating new organizations—more specifically, small businesses. That process is known as *entrepreneurship*.

## THE MEANING OF ENTREPRENEURSHIP

**entrepreneur:**
The originator of a new business venture and a new organization for that venture.

The function that is specific to **entrepreneurs** is the ability to take the factors of production—land, labor, and capital—and use them to produce *new* goods or services. The entrepreneur perceives opportunities that other business executives do not see or do not care about.

Some entrepreneurs use information that is generally available to produce something new. Henry Ford, for example, invented neither the automobile nor the division of labor, but he applied the division of labor to the production of automobiles in a new way—the assembly line. Other entrepreneurs see new business opportunities. Akio Morita, the president of Sony, the Japanese consumer electronics giant, saw that his company's existing products could be adapted to create a new one—the Walkman personal stereo. "Basically, the entrepreneur sees a need and then brings together the manpower, materials, and capital required to meet that need."[10] Grinding coffee beans and selling brewed coffee are not new. What is new is the quality and ambience that Starbucks gives to these activities. Essentially an entrepreneur creates an organization as a way of offering something new to customers, employees, or other stakeholders.

The greeting card industry offers an example of how entrepreneurs can find a niche by offering something different. In the $5.3 billion retail card market, the biggest three companies—Hallmark Cards, American Greeting, and Gibson Greeting—have 85 percent of the sales. However, more than a thousand smaller publishers are trying to outdo each other with creativity and innovation for the remaining 15 percent. Responding to complaints of the sometimes boring nature of traditional cards, some start-ups target particular niches in the market. One such company is Send Inc., one of the small number of African American-owned U.S. greeting card companies. The founder, Mark Norris, started his company in response to frustration with the quality and variety of greeting cards available to ethnic consumers. His cards are sold in card shops, museums, and up-scale retailers on four continents, and he has plans to expand the company's focus to include the general market. Cardthartic of Chicago is a company aimed at the gay and lesbian market. Its first line of cards addresses such occurrences as adoptions by same-sex couples or the loss of someone to AIDS. Its president, Jodee Stevens, launched the venture with $90,000 in personal funds and posted first year revenues of less than $100,000. Stevens expects the company to break even in two to three years.[11]

## PRO FASTENERS: MEETING THE QUALITY DEMANDS OF INDUSTRIAL CUSTOMERS

One of the major trends driving many companies of any size is the increasingly high standards of industrial customers (both domestic and international), who demand exceptional quality from vendors who supply them with materials and components. In this demanding, competitive environment Pro Fasteners Inc., a 55-employee San Jose, California, distributor of industrial hardware and components to the electronics industry, has emerged as a market leader, a world-class competitor, and a model for others. Since its beginnings a decade ago it has thrived, snapping up market share in a very competitive market. From 1990 to 1992 Pro garnered more than 50 quality awards. It has won acceptance as a prime vendor to A-list customers such as Applied Materials Inc., a big semiconductor-equipment manufacturer. Applied is a world-class producer that operates on tight just-in-time schedules and demands world-class quality levels. To meet the needs of such customers, Pro must produce no more than a few wrong or faulty or late parts out of every million shipped.

Managers at Pro appear to be making all the right moves, using a continuous-improvement quality push to achieve records of near-perfect performance. To accomplish this level of quality, Pro uses a state-of-the-art computer system, promotes communication and training, and utilizes cross-functional teams. All of this has not been accomplished without growing pains, as the company reinvents itself as it goes along, and everyone adjusts to new ways of managing. As more and more organizations strive to enter the arena of world-class quality, much can be learned from both the successes and the growing pains of companies like Pro Fasteners.[12] ■

## ENTREPRENEURSHIP VERSUS MANAGEMENT

**entrepreneurship:**
The seemingly discontinuous process of combining resources to produce new goods or services.

**Entrepreneurship** is different from management. Paul H. Wilken explains that entrepreneurship involves *initiating changes* in production, whereas management involves the ongoing coordination of the production process. He states, "entrepreneurship is a discontinuous phenomenon, appearing to initiate changes in the production process . . . and then disappearing until it reappears to initiate another change."[13]

Entrepreneurship is, above all, about change. "Entrepreneurs see change as the norm and as healthy. Usually, they do not bring about the change themselves (that is, they are usually not inventors). But—and this defines entrepreneur and entrepreneurship—*the entrepreneur always searches for change, responds to it,*

**EXPLOITING AN OPPORTUNITY.** The imposition of building-wide smoking bans at an increasing number of institutions created an opportunity for Duo-Gard Industries Inc. of Westland, Michigan. The company had little success selling its freestanding, greenhouse-like sunrooms—until president and founder Albert Miller decided to market them as smoking shelters. A diverse list of customers includes Champion Spark Plug, General Motors Corp., the University of Louisville, and more than 100 Veterans Administration hospitals.

*and exploits it as an opportunity.*"[14] These words were written by Peter Drucker, a well-known contemporary management writer, but they might just as easily have come from the pen of Schumpeter, the economist quoted earlier, who popularized the term "entrepreneurship." For Schumpeter, indeed, the whole process of economic change depended on the person who makes it happen—the entrepreneur.[15]

# THE IMPORTANCE OF ENTREPRENEURSHIP

**E**ntrepreneurship is currently a very popular topic among students of management and economics. It was not always so. Before 1960, most economists had understood its importance, they tended to underrate it. To begin with, the attention then devoted to big companies obscured the fact that most new jobs are created by newer, smaller firms. Moreover, the function of the entrepreneur—organizing new productive resources to expand *supply*—seemed unimportant to the dominant school of economics, which was chiefly interested in managing consumer *demand* by inducing consumers to buy more products. (A classic example of managing consumer demand was the American auto industry practice of model changes from year to year.)[16]

In the 1970s, the mood changed again when economics concerned primarily with consumer demand failed to prevent the constant inflation of that decade. Economists began to worry about the fact that productivity was increasing much less rapidly than it had earlier. This made them more interested in the *supply* of goods and services—the entrepreneur's sphere—and less interested in managing demand. The Japanese (Nissan) and German (Volkswagen) challenges to the American auto industry's "Big Three" (Chrysler, Ford, and General Motors) doomed the management of consumer demand as a manager's byword.

Slower growth in general made those sectors of the economy that were still rapidly growing stand out: medical services, electronics, robotics, genetic engineering, and a few others. These are all high-tech industries in which many companies are small **start-ups** founded by people who wanted to change the business world—entrepreneurs. What George Gilder calls the "heroic creativity of entrepreneurs"[17]

**start-up:**
Business founded by individuals intending to change the environment of a given industry by the introduction of either a new product or a new production process.

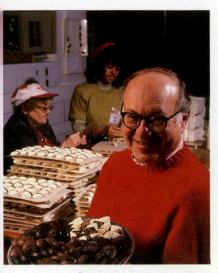

**SWEET SUCCESS.** Harbor Sweets, a homemade chocolate shop in Boston, is just one of the many small businesses that fuel the economy. Four-fifths of all new employment openings come from small businesses.

came to seem essential to our economic well-being, especially in a global economy. In this section, we want to look at the ways entrepreneurship benefits society.

## THE BENEFITS OF ENTREPRENEURSHIP

Entrepreneurship has at least four social benefits. It fosters economic growth; it increases productivity; it creates new technologies, products, and services; and it changes and rejuvenates market competition.[18]

**ECONOMIC GROWTH.** One reason economists started paying more attention to small new firms is that they seem to provide most of the new jobs in our economy. In an important U.S. industry, electronics, a trade association study showed that companies that have survived for 5 to 10 years hire more than 50 times as many people as do companies that have been around for more than 20 years.[19]

Moreover, one researcher, David Birch, has estimated that in the United States more than four-fifths of all new employment openings come from small businesses. Of these openings, upwards of 30 percent are provided by companies that are less than 5 years old. But Birch adds, "Not all small businesses are job creators. The job creators are the relatively few younger ones that start up and expand rapidly in their youth, outgrowing the 'small' designation in the process."[20] Birch has also found that new companies—and therefore the jobs they create—are increasingly found in the service sector of the economy rather than in the manufacturing sector.[21]

**PRODUCTIVITY. Productivity**—the ability to produce more goods and services with less labor and other inputs—increased much less rapidly in the United States during the 1970s than it had in the 1950s and 1960s. Many economists concluded, and still believe, that this is the most fundamental problem of our economy. One reason

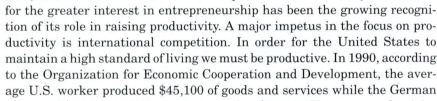

for the greater interest in entrepreneurship has been the growing recognition of its role in raising productivity. A major impetus in the focus on productivity is international competition. In order for the United States to maintain a high standard of living we must be productive. In 1990, according to the Organization for Economic Cooperation and Development, the average U.S. worker produced $45,100 of goods and services while the German worker averaged $37,580 and the Japanese worker $34,500. However, productivity gains in Germany, Japan, and other countries place pressure on America to continue to strive for increased productivity in the race for global business.[22]

Higher productivity is chiefly a matter of improving production techniques, and this task, according to John Kendrick, is "the entrepreneurial function par excellence." Two keys to higher productivity are **research and development (R&D)** and investment in new plant and machinery. According to Kendrick, "there is a close link between R&D and investment programs, with a higher entrepreneurial input into both."[23]

**productivity:**
Measure of how well an operations system functions and indicator of the efficiency and competitiveness of a single firm or department.

**research and development (R&D):**
Entrepreneurial function devoting organizational assets to the design, testing, and production of new products.

**NEW TECHNOLOGIES, PRODUCTS, AND SERVICES.** Another consequence of the association between entrepreneurship and change is the role that entrepreneurs play in promoting innovative technologies, products, and services. Many people who have developed new technologies, products, or services were employees of large corporations that refused to use the new inventions—forcing the inventors to become entrepreneurs. Take Gore-Tex fabric, now a staple of winter sportswear. When Gore-Tex was first developed, no established garment manufacturer wanted to use it, and it was ignored until a struggling smaller firm decided to experiment with it. Table 6-2 lists other contributions, ranging from the zipper to titanium, that have resulted from the innovative efforts of entrepreneurs over the past several decades.

Sometimes one entrepreneurial innovation gives rise to many others. The most famous and important case comes from the very start of the Industrial Revolution

**TABLE 6-2**    **Some Contributions of Independent Inventors and Small Organizations**

| | | |
|---|---|---|
| Digital computer | Air Conditioning | Cyclotron |
| Xerography | Ball-point pen | Titanium |
| Laser | Tungsten carbide | Cotton picker |
| Insulin | Velcro | Dacron polyester fiber |
| Turbojet engine | Fiberglass surfboards | Automatic transmission |
| Magnetic recording | String trimmers | Mercury dry cell |
| Oxygen steelmaking process | Magnetic core memory | Power steering |
| | Flexible soda straws | Color photography |
| Gyrocompass | Vacuum tube | Polaroid camera |
| Rocketry | FM radio | Cellophane |
| Shell molding | Penicillin | Bakelite |
| Shrink-proof knitwear | Petroleum catalytic crack-ing | Hovercraft |
| Zipper | | Metal-laminated skis |
| Self-winding wristwatch | Fiber optics | Fiberglass snow skis |
| Continuous hot-strip steel | Heterodyne radio | Prince tennis racket |
| | Streptomycin | Geodesic domes |
| Helicopter | | |

*Sources:* Adapted from Jacob Rabinow, National Bureau of Standards. Reprinted from Karl H. Vesper, *Entrepreneurship and National Policy* (1983). Walter E. Heller International Corporation Institute for Small Business.

during the second half of the eighteenth century. Early in that century, imported cotton fabric from India gave some British entrepreneurs the idea of producing such fabric in Britain. At first, the raw cotton (mostly from the American South) was spun into yarn by hand-operated machines and then woven, also by hand-operated machines, into fabric. But a problem arose: the machines that did the spinning worked too slowly to produce enough yarn to keep all the weaving machines fully occupied. Spinning, therefore, was a bottleneck. Before long, inventors were working to unjam it. In the mid-1760s, James Hargreaves invented the spinning jenny, a machine that could produce up to 11 threads of cotton simultaneously. Later in the century, the spinning jenny was linked to the steam engine, so that it no longer had to be worked by the operator's foot. The overall effect of these innovations was to increase still further the amount of cotton thread produced. Now there was too much thread and not enough weaving capacity—exactly the opposite of the old problem. Again, inventors went to work. In 1785, an English clergyman invented the power loom, a weaving machine powered by a steam engine.

Even Starbucks is leading a trend toward a rapid increase of gourmet coffee shops. In the small city of Charlottesville, Virginia, four new gourmet coffee retailers opened in 1993.

**MARKETPLACE CHANGE.** Entrepreneurs stir up the waters of competition in the marketplace. Zoltan Acs calls small businesses created by entrepreneurs "agents of change in a market economy."[24] Examples are everywhere: Steve Jobs and Steve Wozniak upset the computer market with the Apple Computer, the Wankel engine got the attention of managers in the auto industry, Donald Burr changed the rules of airline price competition with People Express, Al Neuharth changed the sports pages of American newspapers with *USA Today,* and MTV changed the way rock music is promoted.[25] You can imagine that if you were running a small coffee shop and bakery, and Starbucks moved in across the street, you'd soon be thinking about the competitiveness of your business! And Schultz faces competition from bookstores such as Borders that have opened coffee bars.

← Ch. 5, p. 129

The international market also provides entrepreneurial opportunities for companies. Cascade Medical Inc., for example, knew there was a large potential mar-

 ket in Saudi Arabia for its blood-glucose home monitoring system. Saudi Arabia has 700,000 diabetics. It joined with a Saudi trading partner and now competes with foreign health-care companies—all giants—and has snapped up 20 percent of the Saudi home-glucose-monitoring market.[26]

# THE ENTREPRENEUR

**B**ecause entrepreneurs have the potential to contribute so much to society, researchers have tried to analyze their personalities, skills, and attitudes, as well as the conditions that foster their development. Research has shown that certain psychological and sociological factors are characteristic of entrepreneurs.

## PSYCHOLOGICAL FACTORS

Like most people, entrepreneurs are complex, and no one theory can explain all of their behavior. Perhaps the first and certainly the most important theory of entrepreneurship's psychological roots was put forward in the early 1960s by David McClelland, who found that people who pursued entrepreneur-like careers (such as sales) were high in *need-achievement,* the psychological need to achieve. People with high need-achievement like to take risks, but only reasonable ones, and such risks stimulate them to greater effort. Moreover, McClelland found that certain societies tended to produce a larger percentage of people with high need-achievement. Other researchers have studied the entrepreneur's motives and goals, which seem to include wealth, power, prestige, security, self-esteem, and service to society.[27]

In the mid-1980s, Thomas Begley and David P. Boyd studied the psychological literature on entrepreneurship in an effort to distinguish between entrepreneurs and people who manage existing small businesses. They ultimately identified five dimensions:

1. *Need-achievement.* Entrepreneurs are high in McClelland's concept of need-achievement.

2. *Locus of control.* This is the idea that individuals—not luck or fate—control their own lives. Entrepreneurs and managers both like to think they are pulling their own strings.

3. *Tolerance for risk.* Entrepreneurs who are willing to take moderate risks seem to earn higher return on assets than entrepreneurs who either take no risks or take extravagant risks.

4. *Tolerance for ambiguity.* To some extent, every manager needs this, because many decisions must be made with incomplete or unclear information. But entrepreneurs face more ambiguity, since they may be doing certain things for the first time—ever—and because they are risking their livelihood.

5. *Type A behavior.* This refers to the drive to get more done in less time and—if necessary—despite the objections of others. Both founders and managers of small businesses tend to have much higher rates of Type A behavior than do other business executives.[28]

Ellen Fagenson provides a different angle on the psychological differences between entrepreneurs and managers.[29] Entrepreneurs, she has learned, tend to value *self-respect, freedom,* a *sense of accomplishment,* and an *exciting lifestyle.* Managers, on the other hand, tend to value *true friendship, wisdom, salvation,* and *pleasure.* She concludes, "Entrepreneurs want something different out of life than managers."[30]

Clearly, the entrepreneur needs self-confidence, drive, optimism, and courage to launch and operate a business, without the safety of a steady paycheck. Sometimes, entrepreneurs decide to launch a new venture because they cannot

**A MINORITY BUSINESSWOMAN.** Minority entrepreneurs are increasingly common in today's business world, where forming their own companies gives them the latitude to create and thrive. Women, in fact, are forming small businesses at twice the rate that men are.

ignore their dream, their vision, and they are willing to risk security for financial gain. In other cases, they are pushed by circumstances beyond their control such as a corporate cutback (an increasingly common phenomenon today), or frustrated by limited opportunities for advancement, or driven by the need to coordinate personal and professional goals. Faced with these circumstances, many individuals find the courage and confidence to take control of their professional fate.

## SOCIOLOGICAL FACTORS

Often members of minority groups feel employers discriminate against them—either directly or indirectly. (And in fact, if we look at the progress of the various groups which make up our heterogenous nation and the spate of lawsuits brought against corporations, their feelings are often based in reality.) To succeed in the corporate culture, some minorities feel they must "sell their souls" by giving up their racial, ethnic, or sexual identity. Others bump their heads against the "glass ceiling." (New studies indicate that less than 5 percent of the top executive jobs in the United States are held by minorities.) These frustrations have left many minorities thirsting for an environment that suits their needs and allows them the latitude to create and thrive. This desire, coupled with the perennial enticements of entrepreneurship, have made minority entrepreneurs common in today's business world.[31]

For African Americans this can mean an opportunity to move out of what has been a white, male-dominated corporate structure. Increasingly African Americans are seeing the new service sector-businesses ranging from advertising to architectural services—as a place of opportunity and growth. One advantage of the small business service area is that it is less capital-intensive. Another benefit is that more and more corporations are contracting out services traditionally provided in-house.

Today, women are forming small businesses at nearly twice the rate that men are. In the United States in 1994, women owned or controlled about 6.5 million small businesses—nearly one-third of the total. Currently, one in ten workers is employed by a woman-owned company.[32] One such entrepreneur is Fran Greene. At 52 years of age, she left a big electronics-component supplier and struck out on her own, feeling that her age and gender translated to a dead end in corporate America. She established Sun State Electronics, a Winter Springs, Florida, distribution company that sells high-tech gear to the aerospace and defense industries. In 1993 the company was a $2.5 million venture employing 10 people. Another is Ella Williams, who left Hughes Electronics to establish her own engineering and consulting firm, Aegir Systems.[33]

Another minority-owned business is the Artemis Capital Group, which deals in municipal bonds. Artemis is the creation of six women who left good positions at prestigious Wall Street firms to start their own business. The group is made up of Phyllis Esposito, Robin Wiessmann, Sandra Alworth, Aimee Brown, Deborah Buresh, and Toberta Connolly. They all share the title of "principal." Although they are young (mostly mid- to late-30s), they have a broad range of experience, from investment banking to debt restructuring, sales, and syndicate management.

## BARRIERS TO ENTREPRENEURSHIP

**business plan:**
Formal document containing a mission statement, description of the firm's goods or services, a market analysis, financial projections, and a description of management strategies for attaining goals.

Recognizing a need and having an idea of how to fill it are rarely a strong enough basis for launching a new venture, particularly if the would-be entrepreneur needs to borrow capital. Most successful entrepreneurs also create a **business plan,** a formal document that contains a statement of purpose, a description of the products or services to be offered, a market analysis, financial projections, and some management procedures designed to attain the firm's goals. Before they can write a business plan, though, entrepreneurs must be aware of the barriers to entry.

Why do entrepreneurs fail? The most common reason, says Karl Vesper, is "lack of a viable concept."[34] Another common problem is a lack of market knowledge. Sometimes it is hard to attract the people with the best information because they already have good jobs, are chained to their present employers by "golden handcuffs," or are too complacent to feel a need to do truly first-rate or important work. Even a lack of technical skills can be a problem, says Vesper.

Then, too, there is the difficulty of finding the $25,000 to $100,000 a start-up typically needs. Capital is even harder for women to come by, because women often start businesses in the service sector where, although start-up costs are lower, banks make less money on the smaller loans. Women borrowers also complain about discrimination, especially among venture capitalists. Some banks, seeing the growing number of women-owned business as a potentially lucrative market, have risen to the demand and set up special loan programs for women and minorities with existing businesses. Bank of America and Harris Trust are among the banks with such programs.[35]

A certain number of entrepreneurs fail after start-up because they lack general business know-how. Some would-be entrepreneurs are deterred from entering certain lines of work—for example, housecleaning—by what they see as a social stigma. In all, Vesper lists twelve common barriers to entrepreneurship, which are shown in Figure 6.1.

Stiff competition from large, entrenched corporations can also present a formidable obstacle to an entrepreneur. Here is where the *new competitive relationships* created by entrepreneurs are plain to see. There is no reason to believe that managers already in a particular market will take lightly the entrance of a start-up company. Ben Cohen and Jerry Greenfield, of Ben & Jerry's Homemade, learned this lesson.

## THE ICE-CREAM WARS: DAVID AND GOLIATH

Battle lines have been drawn in a modern version of David and Goliath: Ben & Jerry's Homemade and Häagen-Dazs are fighting over the market for super-premium ice cream, which has become big business. During the last decade, Americans began to consume

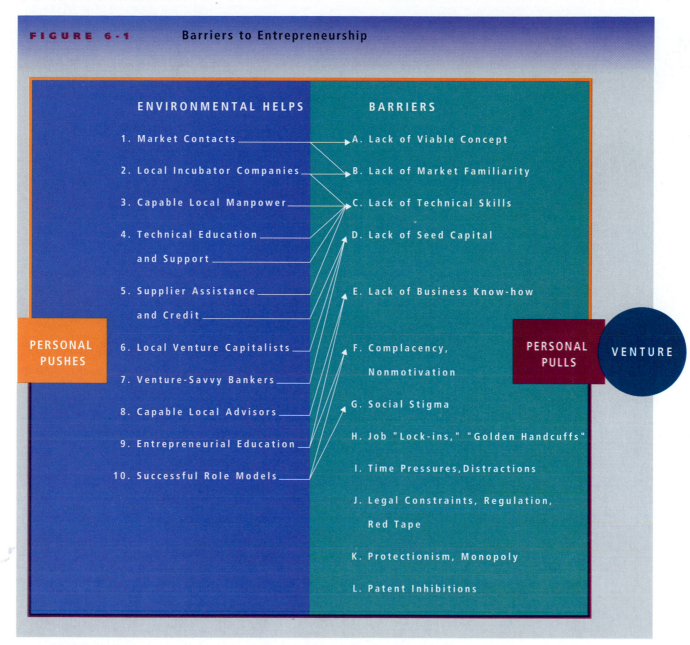

**FIGURE 6-1**    Barriers to Entrepreneurship

ENVIRONMENTAL HELPS

1. Market Contacts
2. Local Incubator Companies
3. Capable Local Manpower
4. Technical Education and Support
5. Supplier Assistance and Credit
6. Local Venture Capitalists
7. Venture-Savvy Bankers
8. Capable Local Advisors
9. Entrepreneurial Education
10. Successful Role Models

BARRIERS

A. Lack of Viable Concept
B. Lack of Market Familiarity
C. Lack of Technical Skills
D. Lack of Seed Capital
E. Lack of Business Know-how
F. Complacency, Nonmotivation
G. Social Stigma
H. Job "Lock-ins," "Golden Handcuffs"
I. Time Pressures, Distractions
J. Legal Constraints, Regulation, Red Tape
K. Protectionism, Monopoly
L. Patent Inhibitions

PERSONAL PUSHES

PERSONAL PULLS

VENTURE

*Source:* Karl H. Vesper, *Entrepreneurship and National Policy* (1983). Walter E. Heller International Corporation Institute for Small Business.

the high-fat, low-air treat in ever-increasing amounts. By 1993, the domestic ice cream industry reached $10 billion.[36]

Not surprisingly, this boom in demand has flattened and resulted in the introduction of numerous brands and fierce competition for market shares.[37] Ice cream companies are having to explore exotic flavors, such as cookie dough, in order to hang on to market share. In 1992, supermarket sales of ice cream rose barely 1 percent and production fell from 882 million gallons in 1988 to 863 million gallons in 1991.[38]

In the beginning was Häagen-Dazs, begun by a Brooklyn immigrant who sold his company to Pillsbury as the market was expanding. Before long, other brands emerged on the scene, including Ben & Jerry's, which was originally developed by Ben Cohen and Jerry Greenfield to cater to the college population in Vermont. Although there are several other brands on the market, these two are now the major competitors in one of the business world's fiercest battles for consumers. Market leaders Häagen-Dazs and Ben & Jerry's were only 1 percent apart in market share for 1992, with Häagen-Dazs barely holding on to its lead.[39]

**BEN AND JERRY.** Ben Cohen and Jerry Greenfield have built Ben & Jerry's from a small ice-cream shop in a Vermont college town to a major national competitor in the premium ice-cream market.

As a subsidiary of a large company, Häagen-Dazs has enjoyed national distribution. Ben & Jerry's has now expanded to the point that it is currently distributed in all 50 states, with more than 100 shops in 18 states. Initially, much of their distribution has been threatened by a Häagen-Dazs move to create exclusive distributorship: Häagen-Dazs would like to require that distributors and retailers who handle its product handle no other ice cream in the super-premium class. The practice is widespread in some segments of the food market—for example, Coke and Pepsi each require that its bottlers handle only one of the two. However, in market segments where there are only a few competitors, this practice can severely affect the competition and effectively lock the smaller company out of the market. In this case, the maneuver can also be interpreted as a violation of the Sherman and Clayton Acts, which mandate fair trade.

As Ben & Jerry's began to expand from local sales in Vermont to distribution throughout New England, Häagen-Dazs sent letters to the independent dealers who sold its product stating that they could not sell both Häagen-Dazs and Ben & Jerry's. Ben & Jerry's believed this ploy denied them the chance to compete and were ready to take Pillsbury to court over it. They also took their complaint to the public, distributing ads that told the story and printing bumper stickers that asked, "What's the doughboy afraid of?" Eventually, Pillsbury and Ben & Jerry's reached an out-of-court settlement that prohibited exclusive dealership for two years in any new market into which Ben & Jerry's chooses to venture.

Another up-and-comer, San Francisco-based Double Rainbow, has not had the same luck fighting giant Häagen-Dazs. Double Rainbow battled Häagen-Dazs's exclusive dealership arrangement from 1985 until 1990, but the courts proved unsympathetic. Now owned by a British conglomerate, Häagen-Dazs argued that it had only 2 percent of the highly competitive ice-cream market. Double Rainbow countered that the 2 percent figure is misleading because it represented Häagen-Dazs's share of the *total* ice-cream market, not of the smaller market segment of super-premium ice creams, where competition for freezer space is especially intense. Although Double Rainbow's critically acclaimed ice cream has been extremely successful in San Francisco, national sales have sagged as a result of its being "frozen out" of many markets. Meanwhile, Häagen-Dazs's profits have soared nationally. ▄▄▄

Entrepreneurship is yet one more example of how people in the business world move and shape relationships in a particular time and place. Entrepreneurs shake up patterns of relationships and must react quickly (time, again) to the reactions of their new counterparts in the market. Clearly, entrepreneurship is not easy. Here is how Charles Burck, writing in *Fortune*, portrayed the trials that entrepreneurs live through:[40]

> This is life without a safety net—thrilling and dangerous. Misjudgments are punished ruthlessly. When competition gets tougher, small businesses feel it first. Financing is hard to find, sometimes impossible. Regulatory costs hurt more in companies with less fat—one reason growth is slow. Owners lie awake at night worrying. . . . Yet the entrepreneurial sector thrives.

Entrepreneurs *invent* organizations. Once organizations are established, however, this spirit of change and danger should not end, as we now consider under the heading, "reinventing organizations."

## REINVENTING ORGANIZATIONS

**O**nce an organization is up and running through the process of entrepreneurship, the fun and challenge of management begins in earnest. More and more managers these days are concerned with what happens once organizational members settle

# THE SECRET OF STARBUCKS' SUCCESS

No single factor can be credited with the success of Starbucks. Perseverance, timing, careful planning and a touch of luck have all contributed to the lucrative business that exists today.

To Schultz, dreaming and vision required caution; to be an entrepreneur does not mean acting recklessly and taking unnecessary risks. On the contrary, Schultz articulated an initial vision for the company that he has since adhered to faithfully.

Schultz's goal was for Starbucks to become the leading North American retailer of specialty coffee. Toward this end, he focused on cautious growth. He began "by taking many steps backward," recalled Schultz. "We were willing to lose money for however long it took to build a foundation ... rather than sacrifice long-term integrity and values for short-term profit." And he did. Starbucks suffered through three consecutive years of losses, with more than $1 million lost in 1989 alone. "But we had tremendous conviction that this was the way to build a company and that the losses were going to end," said Schultz.

And they did. Soon Starbucks was back on track toward financial success. And without having to take shortcuts that would have undercut Schultz's vision. For example, Starbucks could have adopted franchising agreements—many people approached Schultz, but he turned them all down, so as not to "dilute the integrity of the product and our people," said Schultz.

At the same time, demographic trends supported Schultz's vision. "Baby boomers have money, they're sophisticated, and they're consuming less alcohol," said John Rohs, a restaurant analyst at Wertheim Schroder & Company Inc. "Now, baby boomers can name-drop coffees such as Jamaican Blue Mountain instead of wines like Chateauneuf-du-Pape."

Starbucks sees itself as competing in the markets for both true gourmet coffee and premium coffee. Between 1983 and 1989, the gourmet coffee market grew from almost $210 million to just over $675 million, and was expected to grow to $1.05 billion in 1994. Between 1983 and 1989, the premium coffee market grew from not quite $90 million to more than $275 million, and was expected to surpass $680 million by 1994.

Starbucks competes against a vast array of rivals, including supermarkets, specialty retailers and specialty coffee stores, as well as against all restaurant and beverage outlets that serve coffee, including espresso stands, carts and stores.

The tenet, "only perfection will do," lies at the heart of Starbucks' management. Last year, 80,000 pounds of coffee beans were given to charity because the beans no longer met the company's standards for freshness. Starbucks employees search the world over for top-quality arabica beans, from the best, high-altitude farms. →

into routines for dealing in relationships with one another, as well as relationships with customers, suppliers, and others "outside" the organization. Organizational routines and experiences inevitably set precedents that can become difficult to change if the need arises. Ira Kantrow calls attention to this phenomenon by distinguishing "doing the correct thing" from "doing what the past dictates."[41]

As we saw in Chapter 1, more and more managers believe in the apparent paradox that *change is a constant* in and around their organizations. Howard Schultz lives with this realization every day. It is no wonder then that they are concerned with the possibility of lethargy and stagnation in their organizations. It can take considerable effort by managers and their organizational colleagues just to keep up, or cope, with the changes in the world around them. What that could mean, warns Peter Senge, is that organizational members can become so preoccupied with coping that they have no energy left to create new ideas, products, and relationships.[42]

Senge distinguishes between *adaptive* learning in organizations—that is, coping with change—and *generative* learning—that is, creativity coming from joint effort among organizational members.[43] James Brian Quinn refers to the promise of "the intelligent enterprise" in this same spirit.[44] Senge and Quinn are joined by many managers and business commentators who all argue that it is generative learning that holds the greatest hope for organizations of the twenty-first century.

An organization that has subscribed to the "learning organization" concept that Senge and Quinn promote is Tandem Computers. Tandem uses a technique called "double loop" learning. Double loop learning is learning that corrects errors by looping back to examine the underlying values and policies of the organization in the decision-making process; it questions whether the operating norms of the organization are appropriate. Most U.S. organizations use "single loop" learning, in which errors are corrected by changing routine behavior. For instance, management analyzes a work problem and directs workers to respond to the management solution. Double loop learning might identify that the workers are more directly involved in the actual work and have a better solution than management. This type of learning can lead to much greater teamwork and a more effective organization.[45]

## INTRAPRENEURSHIP

In today's fast-paced economy, companies that do not keep up may go the way of the dinosaur. Many large companies have lost the entrepreneurial spirit that they started with. As they have grown larger, their ability to be innovative and flexible may have been stifled by the very size and success of the organization. But large, established corporations can find ways of keeping up and competing with smaller, more nimble companies. Many terms have been coined to describe how managers can keep organizations from stagnating, make organizations adaptive, and promote organizational climates that support creative learning. Perhaps the most widely used term for this process is **intrapreneurship.** Intrapreneurship, an obvious play on "entrepreneurship," is the practice of beginning and developing new business ventures *within the structure of an existing organization.*[46]

**intrapreneurship:**
Corporate entrepreneurship, whereby an organization seeks to expand by exploring new opportunities through new combinations of its existing resources.

The development of entrepreneurs and intrapreneurs boils down to a fairly simple principle: Human beings are endowed with the urge to create—to bring into being something that has never existed or never worked so well before. It follows, then, that corporations can foster profit-making innovations by encouraging employees to think like intrapreneurs, and then giving them the freedom and flexibility to pursue their projects without bogging down in bureaucratic inertia. Many companies have been successful in creating and fostering intrapreneurial ventures, including Merck, 3M, Rubbermaid, Johnson & Johnson, Corning, General Electric, Raychem, Compaq, and Wal-Mart.

## BAIT AS AN INTRAPRENEURIAL VENTURE

One of the firms that has had success with internal innovation and development is Du Pont. An interesting venture was the creation of a new multimillion dollar crawfish bait business within the existing company. The idea for the venture originated at a Du Pont polymer plant in Louisiana with a plant employee who loved crawfish. When he set out his bait traps, he had to replace them every two days because the bait would disintegrate. It occurred to the crawfish lover that Du Pont polymer could be used to hold the bait together longer. He worked with one of the plant's chemists, who provided him with samples. The collaboration resulted in development of bait that would not disintegrate for five days. The product was marketed using Du Pont's agricultural product division to manage distribution and sales. Although the financial risk was low, the project clearly involved a new market and entrepreneurial management.

At Du Pont such activities can lead to both nonfinancial and financial recognition. After-the-fact discretionary bonuses are awarded to venture champions as well as teams. Du Pont is known for giving organizational support to its members. There is voluntary support, both formal and informal, from different parts of the organization as well. Innovators are encouraged to seek assistance from people outside their immediate area of activity. Often people will actually perform technical work on a voluntary basis.[47] ■

Intrapreneurship requires special attention from managers, because *by design* it cuts against the grain of established organizational activities. Thus, we might expect that the following are important to support intrapreneurship:[48]

1. Explicit goals for intrapreneurial processes.
2. A system of information exchange between managers and intrapreneurs.
3. An emphasis on individual responsibility and accountability.
4. Rewards for creative effort.

More recently, "innopreneurship" has been used to describe what others call intrapreneurship; still others refer to "internal corporate venturing."[49] Senge talks about new "disciplines" of leadership that managers can employ to shape their organizations in times of flux.[50] No matter what you call it, the central idea is that managers must be capable of *reinventing the patterns of relationships* that make up their organizations.

An example of an organization that is reinventing itself is the San Diego Zoo, which is moving to become a prototype learning organization. The world-renowned  zoo has dedicated itself to becoming an organization that educates visitors about animals and their habitats and about conservation. To accomplish this mission, zoo managers have designed new formats which display an animal's environment in the most natural manner possible. This change has led zoo personnel to discover new ways of coordinating their complex work. To bring together a diverse variety of functions and skills, extensive use is made of cross-functional teams. The teams set their own budgets and schedules and participate in the hiring process. The result is that employees and managers have found that they are more productive than ever. The goal of becoming an educational organization has led the Zoo to develop a new approach towards visitors, who keep coming back because they learn something new every visit.[51]

**MANAGEMENT 2000 AND BEYOND**

# REENGINEERING THE CORPORATION

The most widely publicized recent approach to reinventing organizations is the practice of "reengineering the corporation," as Michael Hammer and James Champy titled their book.[52] Reengineering involves a significant reassessment of what a particular organization is all about. Hammer and Champy urge managers to ask a very basic question about what they do: "If I were re-creating this company today, given what I know and given current technology, what would it look like?"[53] In other words, managers should imagine that they are starting with a "clean piece of paper."[54]

Hammer and Champy observe that organizations can tend to stagnate when organizational members—including managers—focus on their own immediate "neighborhoods"—such as their jobs and departments—rather than on the larger patterns of relationships in which they work and influence the lives of others. Reengineering thus involves *redefining processes as patterns of relationships* connecting organizational members with people outside the organization. Hammer and Champy present many examples of organizations that have reengineered simple organizational tasks—such as processing a customer's order—that used to take weeks, even months, to do. Reengineering becomes necessary when, despite the fact that *individual jobs* are well-defined and well-performed, the *sum effect on other people* of those efforts is inefficient for the organization and unsatisfactory for customers and others.

According to Hammer, "Reengineering means radically rethinking and redesigning those processes by which we create value [for customers] and do work." He lists speed, quality of service, and overhead costs as today's important competitive issues that reengineering can address. Aetna Life and Casualty, Taco Bell, and AT&T are just a few of the companies Hammer points to whose leaders have gone out on a limb to say, "This cannot stand! We must do it differently." He argues, "The hallmark of a really successful company is its willingness to abandon what has been successful in the past. There is no such thing as a permanently winning formula."[55]

As a college student, you can probably think of administrative processes at colleges and universities that might need a reengineering analysis. Suppose that it took you days and days to get the necessary signatures for something like taking a course overload in a semester, or studying abroad, or declaring a double major. Despite the fact that each approval, considered separately, might make perfect sense, a reengineering project could make life a lot more productive for all concerned.

In fact, administrators at many colleges and universities have conducted what amount to reengineering projects to put together the complex orientation program for first-year students. Orientation involves everything from—and everyone concerned with—registering for the first semester of classes to receiving instructions about social regulations on campus. Thinking about how to ensure the coherence, efficiency, and effectiveness of orientation is quite a task, and thinking this way about *the entire process* is the hallmark of reengineering.

Reengineering implies that organizations are shifting patterns of *relationships,* not fixed entities like machines and buildings. Tom Peters, co-author of the best-selling *In Search of Excellence,* has studied dozens of cases where organizational members are "empowered" to create new ideas and products and relationships. That *empowerment* (see Chapter 13), which he calls *liberation management,* comes from flexible organizations and, more importantly, *a management attitude biased toward creative human efforts.* About the frenzied pace of modern competition, Peters writes, "Those who would survive, managers and nonmanagers alike, will simply 'have to make their own firm,' create their own projects."[56] Many managers, Peters relates, pay attention to reinventing their organizations every day.

# INTRODUCING LATTELAND

"One double-tall skinny no foam, walking latte. Next. One decaf mocca Grande. Next. One short latte, hit of almond, with foam to go. Next. . . . " The orders reverberate through the small store. Customers hand over a couple of dollars for each order, sprinkle their coffee with chocolate, nutmeg or cinnamon powder, and head off, back to business.

Part of the mystique involves a new caffeine vocabulary that has become standard in the Northwest. Coffee preparers are "baristas," Italian for bartender. Drinks are ordered in three sizes: short, tall and grande. Two shots of espresso is a "doppio." Espresso with steamed milk is "latte."

The Starbucks lingo emphasizes the fact that Starbucks stores are targeted to customers, for good reason. More than one million people pass through Starbucks stores each week, with more than a quarter of a million in the Seattle area alone. Each Starbucks is designed to fit into the neighborhood, whether as coffee houses outfitted with counters, stools, and tables or as stands where customers can grab a coffee, an espresso, or a cappuccino on the way to work. At night, featuring jazz music, sleek black stools and counters with mahogany trim, Starbucks can offer the ambiance of a bar, without the pressure of consuming alcohol. In Seattle, coffee has become so integral a part of the day that Jean Godden, a columnist for *The Seattle Times,* dubbed the city "Latteland." Schultz's dream is to turn the United States into an entire "Latteland" through Starbucks.

Underlying the company's focus on consideration for customers is an internal, entrepreneurial consideration for how employees—termed "partners"—are to be treated. Indeed, even the company mission statement places the partner first, the customer second, and the shareholder third. "Our people come first, then customers, then shareholders," said Schultz. "It may sound out of order, but we can't exceed the expectations of our customers unless we exceed it for our employees first."

"Our only sustainable competitive advantage . . . is the quality of our workforce," said Schultz. "We're building a national retail company by creating pride in—and a stake in—the outcome of our labor." Starbucks offers to all partners—full-time and part-time—a generous employee-benefits package that covers health care, stock options, training programs, career counseling and products discounts. The health benefits include a deductible-exempt $300 allowance for annual physicals, as well as provisions for dental and vision care. "No one can afford not to provide these kinds of benefits," added Schultz. "The desire to scrimp on these essentials helps reinforce the sense of mediocrity that seeps into many companies. Without them, people don't feel financially or spiritually tied to their jobs."

Schultz's commitment to partners is rooted in his family upbringing. "When my father retired, he had no pension, no insurance, no anything," recalled Schultz. "I was always struck by how little his life's work was valued. That has had a powerful effect on how I treat people."

What Starbucks seeks is partner loyalty. Its renowned benefits package—well beyond industry norms, especially for part-timers—helps it earn this loyalty. The company has avoided industry norms for employee turnover, which typically ranges in the triple digits for food retailers. Starbucks boasts a turnover of less than 50 percent. A strong culture and employee incentives also build loyalty. "We realize that if we can reinforce the culture and reduce the turnover in part-time employees, all shareholders will be better off," noted Craig Foley, a director (Witt Wickham Capital Corp.) in New York City, and the largest Starbucks shareholder before the public offering.

Generous benefits go hand-in-hand with high standards for employees. Only 19 people have qualified to roast coffee for Starbucks in 22 years. "Learning to roast is a tremendous privilege," said Schultz.

All of this translates into soaring success for Starbucks. Thus the shareholder is far from neglected. "The future of Starbucks lies in increasing shareholder value," said Schultz, "and increasing employee value will increase shareholder value."

But the future of Starbucks' latteland is far from certain. "Anyone can buy coffee beans and espresso machines," pointed out Barton Weitz, director of the Center for Retailing Education and Research at the University of Florida in Gainesville. "These ideas aren't patented. . . .  The issue in retail ventures is: How easy is it to copy?"

The newfound popularity of coffee, espresso and the like around the country, now that it is being offered in many types of coffee cafes and stands, indicates that a tough road may lie ahead for Starbucks. Starbucks has developed a strong brand recognition, particularly on the West Coast, but will that be enough?

In spite of the company's current astounding success, Schultz is already wondering. "It's hard for me to celebrate success," he said. "I'm always feeling: I want more, the next market, the next site."

## SUMMARY

1. **Understand the importance of small business.**

   Organizations come and go, change, endure, and change again. At the start and heart of this evolution is the often-overlooked phenomenon of small business. Over 50 percent of Americans employed in 1990, for example, worked in organizations with fewer than 500 employees—the conventional dividing line between "small" and "large" business. Our lives are touched daily by the output of small business.

2. **Define entrepreneurship.**

   The practice of taking an idea and inventing an organization for developing that idea is known as entrepreneurship. The entrepreneur, who sees environmental change as an opportunity, uses the factors of production to produce new goods and services. Entrepreneurship is different from management because it focuses on initiating change. Entrepreneurship can occur when an individual or group of individuals start a new business.

3. **Draw a distinction between entrepreneurship and management.**

   Entrepreneurship is now an important area of study and contributes to a society's economic growth and productivity, to its supply of technologies, products, and services, and to the rejuvenation of competition in marketplaces. Entrepreneurship differs from management in that entrepreneurship involves initiating changes in production and creation of a new organization whereas management involves the ongoing coordination of the production process at an existing organization.

4. **Explain key psychological traits of entrepreneurs.**

The psychological characteristics of entrepreneurs have been studied widely. The most important theory of entrepreneurship's psychological roots was put forward by McClelland, who found that certain types of people had high need-achievement and that certain types of societies tended to create high need-achievement. Begley and Boyd identified five dimensions—need-achievement, locus of control, tolerance for risk, tolerance for ambiguity, and Type A behavior—that seemed to distinguish the founders and managers of small businesses from the typical executive. In addition, social circumstances, such as lack of opportunity for advancement or salaried employment, tend to push certain individuals into entrepreneurship.

5. **Discuss the importance of reinventing organizations.**

Once organizations are up and running, it is important that managers pay attention to renewing the relationships that make up the organization. This is a managerial practice dealing with reinventing existing organizations. The best known term for this is intrapreneurship, which is as vital to existing organizations as entrepreneurship is to the steady stream of new small businesses. Reinventing organizations is an emphasis on both overcoming complacency and fostering creative human efforts in organizations.

## REVIEW QUESTIONS

1. What is small business and why is it important?
2. How does entrepreneurship differ from management?
3. Why is entrepreneurship important?
4. What are some of the difficulties that entrepreneurs face?
5. What kind of persons are well-suited to become entrepreneurs?
6. What is intrapreneurship?
7. Why is it important for managers to look for ways to reinvent organizations?
8. What does reengineering an organization involve and why might it be difficult to do?

## KEY TERMS

| | |
|---|---|
| Small business | Productivity |
| Entrepreneur | Research and development |
| Entrepreneurship | Intrapreneurship |
| Start-up | Business plan |

## FRESH IDEAS AT FRESH FIELDS[57]

Fresh Fields may be a supermarket, but what it's super at selling is its image: "Good for you foods."

A New Age grocery store, Fresh Fields falls somewhere between a health food store and a traditional supermarket. It is not merely a health food store, because it carries a wider variety of foods including fresh pasta, baked goods, seafood and deli selections. What distinguishes Fresh Fields from supermarkets lies in what is absent from the shelves, rather than what is present, for Fresh Fields shoppers will not find foods containing lots of preservatives and artificial flavorings, such as Jell-O and Oreos, that they can purchase at other supermarkets. What Fresh Fields offers is "organic and conventional produce, meats, seafood, dairy products, baked goods from an in-store bakery, deli items, gourmet and vegetarian prepared foods, a wide array of cheese, a full grocery department, an extensive selection of supplements, skin enriching cosmetics and natural health care products and environmentally friendly household goods."[58]

The arrival of Fresh Fields coincides with that of the New Age, health-conscious trend of the 1990s, and the company has not hesitated in taking advantage of consumers' new shopping preferences resulting from the trend. According to a 1992 survey by HealthFocus, a Pennsylvania-based research firm, 90 percent of shoppers say that health has become a factor in determining the food they buy. This perhaps accounts for why many Americans are willing to pay up to 20 percent more for natural foods. Actually, the Fresh Fields premium tends to hover closer to 5 percent, and when in season, Fresh Fields' locally grown organic produce can even cost less than produce sold at other supermarkets.

A team of entrepreneurs began Fresh Fields in 1991. The team included 33-year-old Mark Ordan, former Goldman Sachs investment banker, as CEO and president; 75-year-old Leo Kahn, founder of Staples, the prosperous office-supply stores, as chairman; and 44-year-old Jack Murphy, former manager of the Heartland supermarket chain in New England, as chief operating officer.

Within the first 19 months, five Fresh Fields locations opened in Maryland and Virginia. Expanding into Pennsylvania and Illinois, by mid-1994 Fresh Fields had opened a total of 14 stores in the four states, with more in the planning stages.

Much of Fresh Fields' success can be attributed to the fact that the company offers only the freshest produce, often from local growers. The company screens growers to find those who use natural methods of pest management and apply the least amount of agricultural chemicals. In addition, Fresh Fields seeks meat and poultry from farms, not factories, to avoid the growth-promoting drugs often used. Fresh Fields also makes an effort to get to know the people who catch the seafood, and seeks out fish caught in deep, clean waters, not from coastal waters threatened by pollution.

According to Kahn, though, the key to Fresh Fields' success lies in pleasing the customer. "Everybody says the same thing: please the customer—but while everybody says it, not too many practice it. The customer is smarter than all of us. Here we're building an organization that zeroes in and keeps customer satisfaction in mind."[59]

Instilled in Fresh Fields is a warm, friendly, caring culture that begins with Kahn and travels through to all stakeholders: employees, suppliers, customers, community members. Whereas at other stores, such as Wal-Mart, there is a single, symbolic greeter by the door, every employee at Fresh Fields is a sort of "greeter," and he or she looks up, smiles and says "hello" to shoppers as they pass by. Within the company, there are no employees, there are only "associates," many of whom Kahn knows by name.

Much of what Fresh Fields is about is relationship-building. The warm relationship between the company and associates lies at the heart. From there, associates build relationships with suppliers to add the personal touch that is integral to the Fresh Fields quality image.

As shoppers walk through the stores, numerous samples are offered. "Originally, I bought organic produce and spent $25 to $30 every week or two," says Merri Mukai, a homemaker in Annandale, Virginia. "Then I tried the baked goods and upped my spending by $60. Now I'm buying meats and eyeing the fish. They've definitely got me hooked."[60]

Says Fresh Fields, "We guarantee your satisfaction unconditionally. You can consider our guarantee as an opportunity to be adventurous and to try new products, without risk. If for any reason you are less than completely satisfied with something you purchase at Fresh Fields, we will cheerfully offer you a full refund."[61]

## CASE QUESTIONS

1. What economic and social factors should Fresh Fields managers watch?
2. Suppose you manage a local supermarket and Fresh Fields comes to town. How would you reinvent your organization to meet the challenges posed by Fresh Fields?

## VIDEO CASE STUDY

### TAKEOUT TAXI DELIVERS[62]

In 1987, when Stephen Abt was a new product development executive with U.S. Sprint, he and his wife had their first child. Suddenly, their lives changed drastically. "It was just like everyone said: Kaboom, everything changed," Abt recalled. "We used to go out four to six times a month. I don't think we went out four to six times that entire first year after our daughter was born."[63] Yet they didn't always want to cook. Abt and his wife were not alone; the success of Domino's in pioneering prepared food delivery reflected the real need that home deliverers served. "[P]eople were desperate for the convenience of prepared meals for home delivery."[64] But many people wanted more than pizza.

Seeing an opportunity, Abt left his $100,000-a-year management position at Sprint and started Takeout Taxi, a third-party food deliverer. Unlike Domino's, Takeout Taxi is not in any way involved in food preparation; rather, it contracts with local restaurants to field orders for meals and delivers those meals to customers at their homes, offices, or hotels. Takeout Taxi focuses its energy on areas often neglected by restaurants. "We're not a food delivery service," Abt asserted. "We're a marketing company that delivers.... Most restaurant owners are busy running the business. They don't have the time or the skills to do targeted marketing," Abt noted. "Their primary form of marketing is through location. They don't do much else."[65]

But Takeout Taxi does. "We can build computer databases of dine-in customers, including names, addresses, birthdays, and anniversaries," Abt pointed out. "We use these to drive direct-mail programs with trackable forms like coupons and registration."[66]

Through delivery orders and in-store promotions, Takeout Taxi captured names and personal information in a database that included more than 200,000 restaurant customers by the end of 1993. This database enabled Takeout Taxi to design incredibly effective targeted marketing programs to help increase restaurant sales. "When we do a marketing promotion for them through the mail for their in-house business, we can have a 40, 50, 60 percent response rate," Abt pointed out. "These response rates are unheard of."[67]

Many restaurant owners initially did not respond favorably to the prospect of third-party home delivery. Takeout Taxi requires a wholesale discount rate on the food it delivers; its revenues derive from the difference between the wholesale rate and the menu price that the customer pays. Some restaurant owners have argued that it would hurt their profits to sell at the discount rate and have therefore been hesitant to deal with Takeout Taxi. "They get in their minds that a 30 percent discount will hurt them and they fail to see home-delivery as an additional service that doesn't add to staff or physical plant," said Chuck Kersio, owner of the Tortilla Factory. "When I think about the fact that the only costs I have are food and packaging, even if I include some staffing costs it's still more profitable than my dining room."[68]

In addition, some restaurant owners feared that entering the delivery market could jeopardize the perceived quality of their food. Protective of their core dine-in business, many restaurant owners have been reluctant to relinquish control over their meals. "Their biggest fear is customers not getting a meal of the same quality," said Ron Paul, president of

Technomic Inc. in Chicago, Illinois. "Someone goes to a restaurant and says, 'Wow, what great ribs,' and then later they call up and order the ribs for delivery. But when they get there, they're not so good, and then that customer doesn't go back to the restaurant."[69] To maintain food quality, Takeout Taxi not only delivers the food in thermal containers, but it also strategically limits the service area for each restaurant it represents. "The real secret to this is we are set up in certain zones where the maximum drive time to the farthest house is 15 minutes," explained John Addison, a Kansas City franchisee. According to Paul, however, it's not all about delivery time. "Some of it is ego," he asserted. "The $25 prime rib experience cannot be delivered."[70]

Those restaurants that have decided to work with Takeout Taxi appear to have benefited significantly. "I personally was questioning how it would work," said Mary Sue Kintzer, Manager of the Country Oven in Linglestown, Pennsylvania. "I couldn't imagine a system that would be as organized as it is, that would make us look as good as it makes us look."[71] According to R. D. Frye, a manager at T.G.I. Friday's, Takeout Taxi has successfully brought about increased customer interest in the restaurants served. The average restaurant affiliated with Takeout Taxi has exhibited a 3 percent to 12 percent increase in revenue, in an industry with zero growth. "We have a very small restaurant—only about 75 seats—and on weekends the wait for a table can stretch up to two hours," said Rob Cotton of Iguana Cantina in Waltham, Massachusetts. "Now I'm able to serve another crowd of people at checks of $14, through delivery."[72]

Takeout Taxi shares in the success it has brought the restaurants it assists. Since 1991, when the company began franchising, it has increased its annual deliveries from 83,000 to 958,000, with sales multiplying from $2 million nationwide to more than $23 million. The store in Herndon, Virginia, served a market of about 30,000 households, and made an average of 2,000 deliveries each week, at about $25 apiece. By the end of 1993, Takeout Taxi was delivering meals for approximately 750 restaurants in the 66 markets where it was conducting business.

Although Abt initially saw the market as being comprised of busy, two-income families, he has come to realize that it's much broader. "Everyone gets lazy at least one time a month."[73] In a survey conducted by the National Restaurant Association in the early 1990s, 41 percent of the respondents said that they would order food to be delivered from a table-service restaurant if it were available. Abt has thus tailored service to provide "small indulgences." "This isn't about gourmet food. This is an It's-Monday-night-and-I-don't-feel-like-cooking thing," Abt said. "We don't want to deliver chateaubriand for two. This is a small indulgence for just about anyone."[74]

## CASE QUESTIONS

1. What sorts of opportunities does Takeout Taxi take advantage of?
2. How has Takeout Taxi changed the marketplace?
3. What reinvention opportunities does Takeout Taxi have?

## CHAPTER 7

# CULTURE AND MULTICULTURALISM

**Upon completing this chapter, you should be able to:**

1. Identify the major elements of organizational culture.

2. Discuss the linkage between organizational success and culture.

3. Define multiculturalism and diversity along a number of dimensions.

4. Recognize some barriers to making a corporate culture sensitive to multiculturalism.

5. Identify some ways of managing in a multicultural world.

# MANAGEMENT:
# THE PERSONAL TOUCH[1]

Anita Roddick, founder and managing director of The Body Shop International, demonstrates how much a manager's personality and values can actually define the manager's role and help to shape an organization. The Body Shop sells products that "cleanse and polish the skin" and, while it may appear to be a "boutique, cosmetics company," it is really quite different.

The Body Shop was founded in 1976 by Roddick and her husband Gordon. At that time, the couple formed the business so Anita would have a means of supporting herself and their two children while her husband Gordon fulfilled his dream of riding on horseback from Buenos Aires to New York City. When Gordon left, Anita was operating a single shop in England; when he returned ten months later there were two shops, with another one soon to follow.

By the early 1990s, The Body Shop had blossomed into a financial success. In 1992, The Body Shop boasted earnings of $265 million worldwide and enjoyed a 23 percent growth rate for the first half of 1993. As of November 1993, nearly 1000 Body Shop stores were located around the world in 43 countries.

Many of Roddick's personal values have influenced The Body Shop's corporate culture. Indeed, the company is driven by her intense commitment—what she calls "electricity and passion"—that can't help but engender enthusiasm and boost employee, customer, and community morale. At the same time, Roddick also focuses on her specific managerial responsibilities, primarily (though not exclusively) product development and marketing.

*The company is driven by her...electricity and passion.*

Roddick's use of marketing tends to distinguish The Body Shop not only from direct competitors but also from most other companies. The Body Shop does not spend money on consumer advertising. The organization is premised upon the belief that consumers are underwhelmed by the commercial hype already clouding the marketplace. The Body Shop therefore allocates promotional money to social activism instead of consumer advertising. "In the old days we couldn't afford [to advertise]," recalled Roddick. "Now we would be deeply embarrassed to."[2] In a way, the organization's refusal to advertise has become an element of the corporate culture.

Roddick does not market the company in a traditional way. Instead, she aggressively pursues avenues through which the company can enjoy media coverage for free. In this way, the marketing of The Body Shop resembles a political campaign. "I'm always available to the press," noted Roddick. "I fervently believe that passion persuades, and I emit a lot of enthusiasm."[3] Clearly, Roddick recognizes the value of media coverage of The Body Shop. "[I]f I put our poster for Colourings [a line of makeup] in the shop windows, that creates sales and profits," asserted Roddick. "A poster to stop the burning of the rain forest doesn't. It creates a banner of values, it links us to the community, but it will not increase sales. What increases sales is boring *Glamour* magazine saying Princess Diana uses Body Shop products. Then we'll get 7,000 bloody phone calls asking for our catalog. You can measure the effect."[4]

Roddick has also found that she must market herself as well as the company, and that the image she conveys is one that falls in line with the values she articulates. "The staff doesn't want me in fur coats or in big cars or acting like I've got the million dollars that I have," said

**ANITA RODDICK.** The dynamic personality and strong values of Body Shop founder Anita Roddick are central to The Body Shop's uniqueness and success.

Roddick. "They want me to be as I am. Other people, the City [London's Wall Street], want me to be respectable. So you are dealing with multitudes of different people. There are so many planks in the platform of running a business."[5]

It is Roddick who controls the press coverage, though, not the other way around. She demonstrated her ability to create favorable coverage early on when The Body Shop first opened. Roddick opened the first store next door to a funeral home. When she received a formal letter of complaint from the neighboring undertakers, she leaked it to the press that they were ganging up on her—a struggling, female shopkeeper. The day the story ran, Roddick rang up $200 in sales.

Attention to communication has played a major role in Roddick's management of The Body Shop's success. In the early days, Roddick felt it necessary to hide her true financial woes. "I used to have friends call me when a potential franchisee was arriving so I could have an absolutely ridiculous conversation. Ring, Ring. 'Oh, yes, this is where you'd like the franchisee, Barry Street, Edmonds? No, I don't think it's the right town for that. Besides, we've already had 14 other applications.' That went on all the time." This image of success that she fabricated soon turned into reality.[6] →

**ONE ASPECT OF CULTURE.** Differences in dress and attitudes around the globe are just one aspect of culture that organizations must be sensitive to. Other aspects include cultural differences within our own society and the organizational culture.

**B**EING part of an organization entails being part of its *culture*. As the case study shows, "how we do things around here" has a profound impact on the performance of an organization. How people interact in an organization and the basic assumptions they make are part of the organization's culture. Anita Roddick has challenged some of the prevailing ideas in her industry. At the Body Shop the culture emphasizes the valuing of women, entrepreneurialism, and the natural environment.

Given the changes in the global landscape that we outlined in Chapters 3 and 5, today's organizations face the challenge of adopting an *organizational* culture that is not only flexible, but also sensitive to the many cultural differences that organization members face both within and between societies.

Cultural differences within American society have been highlighted during the past few years as more groups have gained access to the mechanisms of political voice. Many people are more sensitive to the need to appreciate differences of race, gender, physical abilities, sexual orientation, and ethnic identity.

As today's organizations take part in the global economy, we as organization members must also be sensitive to the differing cultural views that we encounter as we expand our horizons beyond our own country. The purpose of this chapter is to look at the concept of organizational culture, to uncover how it works, and to understand the challenges and opportunities of multiculturalism at home and abroad as they relate to organizations today.

## DEFINING CULTURE IN ORGANIZATIONS

**culture:**

The complex mixture of assumptions, behaviors, stories, myths, metaphors, and other ideas that fit together to define what it means to be a member of a particular society.

**Culture** has been an important concept in understanding human societies and groups for a long time. Many people remember poring over photos of exotic "cultures" pictured in *National Geographic*, or reading about anthropologist Margaret Mead's study of the native culture on the island of Samoa. Culture, in this anthropological and historical sense, is the heart of a particular group or society— what is distinctive about the way members interact with one another and with outsiders—and how they achieve what they do.

## ORGANIZATIONAL CULTURE

**organizational culture:**

The set of important understandings, such as norms, values, attitudes, and beliefs, shared by organizational members.

← Ch. 2, p. 49

During the last fifteen years the concept of **organizational culture** has been expanded by students of organizations to explain much of what goes on in organizations. Why do managers at IBM wear white shirts? Why do Procter & Gamble members write memos of only one page? Why do most meetings at DuPont start with a talk about safety? Are these mysterious tribal rituals? Surely these things are not completely explainable in terms of the traditional schools of management theory discussed in Chapter 2.

Until the early 1980s, coincident with the rise of the influences we call dynamic engagement, it seemed to many that it was enough to understand an organization's strategy (part of planning) and its structure (part of organizing) in order to have a good explanation for what it did. But many thinkers began to see that much more was going on in organizations than just developing new products and services and paying attention to hierarchy and power. Researchers, spurred in part by their efforts to understand organizations that were not U.S.-based and that operated on some rather different basic assumptions, began to use the concept of culture from anthropology to understand some of these basic differences.

For instance, it was an assumption within many large Japanese firms that the worker had a lifetime contract and was not to be fired even in times of low sales. Further, Japanese firms assumed that promotion to key spots in the hierarchy should be based on both age and ability, not necessarily just ability, as many American firms assumed. Today, these assumptions are much less frequently correct. But in the early 1980s, these kinds of assumptions started researchers thinking about how what looked to be a very different way of organizing a firm could be successful when it flew in the face of all their organizational "knowledge." For some, the answer seemed to lie in the concept of culture.

Indeed a strong, widely recognized corporate culture is frequently cited as a reason for the success of such companies as GE, Johnson & Johnson, and Procter & Gamble. Conversely, a strong, unchanging culture is just as often cited as the reason for the recent troubles of companies such as General Motors and IBM.

A number of organizations cultivate a particular culture. At Mary Kay Cosmetics, the ceremonies, rewards, decor, and other symbolic forms of communication are features of a corporate culture that guides the actions of organization members. At Apple Computer, as the company quickly advanced to a leading position in its industry, managers worked hard to maintain the informality and personal relationships characteristic of a small company. Even in its marketing, they touted Apple as the small-company alternative to IBM and other industry giants. Tandem Computers emphasizes a culture of employee-centered incentives, and Minnesota Mining and Manufacturing (3M) gears its corporate culture toward innovation.

### CORPORATE CULTURE: A WOMAN'S VIEW OF CHANGE

The traditional culture of corporate America developed in a time when women had little influence in organizations. In her recent book, *Our Wildest Dreams: Women Entrepreneurs Making Money, Having Fun and Doing Good,* Joline Godfrey argues that as more and more women strike out on their own, forming small businesses, they are abandoning elements of the traditional culture in favor of an alternative set of values in which success is defined in more than one way. Godfrey outlines a new set of values, different from traditional corporate values, that herald the development of a new business culture exemplified in such businesses as The Body Shop:

- Work, live, love, learn—rather than work, work, work
- Seek meaning and money—rather than money alone
- Build networks of relationships—rather than hierarchies of power
- "Do no harm"—rather than "let the buyer beware"
- Sustain resources—rather than "use it or lose it"
- Grow naturally—rather than grow fast
- Embrace work *and* family—rather than work *or* family

Although some large organizations, such as Levi Strauss and Johnson & Johnson, embrace some of the new rules, in general it is easier for small, new businesses to develop this type of culture from the start than for large, established organizations to change an existing culture. And although women do not have a monopoly on cultural change (this text discusses many organizations, such as Tom's of Maine and Ben and Jerry's, where men embrace new values), Godfrey highlights the role of women in fostering this kind of change:

> Many women are leaving the giants of the *Fortune* 500 to start their own businesses. Others choose never to enter the ranks of the giants. No longer content to spend their most productive years in organizations sealed off by a glass ceiling, no longer willing to work for companies that greedily consume all the hours of their life (leaving nothing for self, family, or friends), no longer able to blindly accept old assumptions about what business is and must be, women are voting with their feet. We are closing the door on corporate rigidity and inventing companies in which we can make good money, do good, and have fun. We are creating stuff of our wildest dreams.[7]

Although some aspects of an organization's culture are readily apparent, many other aspects are less visible. Figure 7-1 compares organizational culture to an iceberg. On the surface are the overt, or open, aspects—the formally expressed organizational goals, technology, structure, policies and procedures, and financial resources. Beneath the surface lie the covert, or hidden, aspects—the informal aspects of organizational life. These include shared perceptions, attitudes, and feelings as well as a shared set of values about human nature, the nature of human relationships, and what the organization can and will remember.

Edgar Schein has defined culture as:

> A pattern of shared basic assumptions that [a] group learned as it solved its problems of external adaptation and internal integration, that has worked well enough to be considered valid and, therefore, [desirable] to be taught to new members as the correct way to perceive, think, and feel in relation to those problems.[8]

Culture, therefore, is how an organization has learned to deal with its environment. It is a complex mixture of assumptions, behaviors, stories, myths, metaphors, and other ideas that fit together to define what it means to work in a particular organization. When we say that there is a culture of safety at DuPont, a culture of service at Dell, and a culture of innovation at 3M, we are saying that people at each of these organizations has learned a particular way to deal with a lot of complex issues.

## THREE BASIC ELEMENTS OF CULTURE

Schein suggests that culture exists on three levels: artifacts, espoused values, and underlying assumptions (see Figure 7-2).

**FIGURE 7-1**   The Iceberg of Organizational Culture

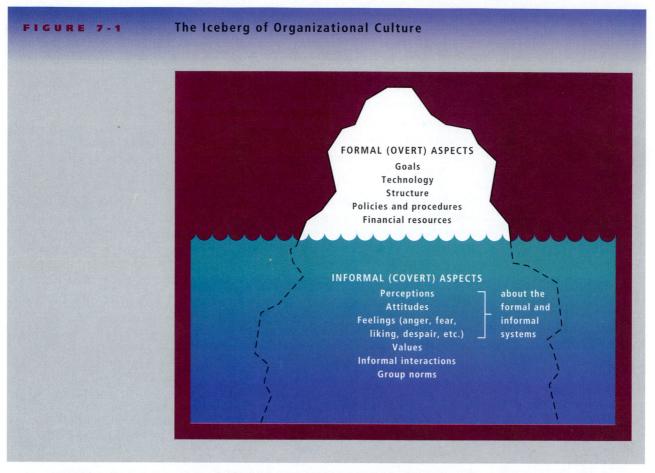

*Source:* Adapted from Stanley N. Herman, "TRW Systems Group," in Wendell L. French and Cecil H. Bell, Jr., *Organization Development: Behavioral Science Interventions for Organization Improvement*, 3rd ed., p. 19. © 1984. Used by permission of Prentice Hall, Englewood Cliffs, N.J.

**FIGURE 7-2**   Schein's Levels of Culture

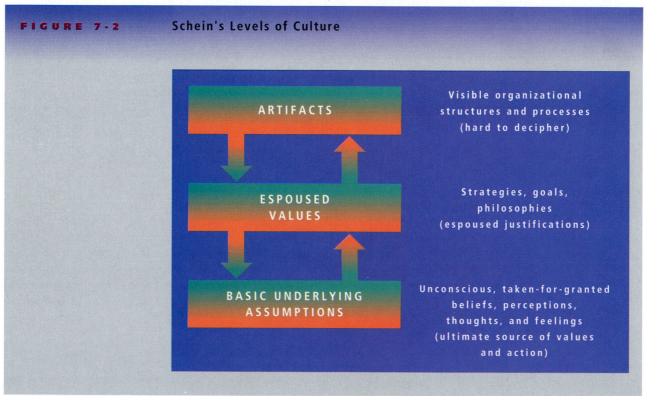

*Source:* Edgar H. Schein, *Organizational Culture and Leadership,* 2nd ed. San Francisco: Jossey-Bass Publishers, 1992; p. 17.

**artifacts:**

The things that come together to define a culture and reveal what the culture is about to those who pay attention to them; they include products, services, and even behavior patterns of the members of an organization; according to Schein, the first level of organizational culture.

**ARTIFACTS. Artifacts** are the things that "one sees, hears, and feels when one encounters a new group with an unfamiliar culture."[9] Artifacts include products, services, and even behaviors of group members. For example, if you walk into the headquarters of one large multibillion-dollar computer company, you will notice that the CEO is dressed casually, while at a competitor the CEO will be wearing an expensive, dark blue suit. These differing artifacts are evidence of two very different organizational cultures.

Artifacts are everywhere, and we can learn about a culture by paying attention to them. Think about some of the artifacts at your college or university. Is there a certain way that people dress? Are there certain courses or methods of study that are deemed to be important? Do most students live on or near campus, or is yours a commuter campus? Do most students have jobs? Is there a small or large percentage of "returning" students? Is there much or little athletic activity? Is your school a "football" school? A "basketball" school? Is there an equal amount of athletic activity available to men and women? All of these artifacts and many others will define in part the culture of your school.

**espoused values:**

The reasons given by an organization for the way things are done; according to Schein, the second level of organizational culture.

**ESPOUSED VALUES.** Schein calls the second level of culture **espoused values.** In Chapter 4 we saw that values were things worth doing, or the reasons for doing what we do. Espoused values are the reasons that we give for doing what we do. Schein argues that most organizational cultures can trace their espoused values back to the founders of the culture. At DuPont, for example, many procedures and products are a result of the espoused value of safety. No surprise, for originally DuPont was in the business of making gunpowder; in the words of a recent DuPont chairman, "Either you make gunpowder safely, or you don't make it for very long."[10] The value of safety still pervades the DuPont culture, long after the days when the manufacture of gunpowder was central to the business. New members learn these espoused values, and learn their meaning in the organizational context.

The Darden School at the University of Virginia has an espoused value of being a "teaching school" and having the faculty always available for consultation with students. New faculty members learn the importance of "Coffee," a 25-minute break between classes where all of the faculty and all of the students congregate to talk informally about everything from the morning business news to classroom performance to new initiatives for the school. When potential students or faculty members are interviewed, they are always told about coffee and often taken to experience it. While 25 minutes of communal coffee doesn't by itself make the school a "teaching school," it does serve to focus the attention of faculty and students on issues important to their school's mission to be a leading school of business.

**basic assumptions:**

The beliefs that are taken for granted by the members of an organization; according to Schein, the third level of organizational culture.

**BASIC ASSUMPTIONS. Basic assumptions,** Schein's third level of organizational culture, are the beliefs that organization members take for granted. Culture prescribes "the right way to do things" at an organization, often through unspoken assumptions.

Before 1980, managers at AT&T took as a basic assumption that any service they offered had to be available (or at least planned) for all customers. It simply could not conceive of making a service available to only a limited range of customers. Managers at newcomer MCI, however, had a different basic assumption, one that was partly responsible for the ensuing revolution in telecommunications. By putting up just two microwave towers, one in St. Louis and the other in Chicago, MCI was able to "skim" part of AT&T's market. It acted by questioning a basic belief of AT&T.

Many cosmetic companies have assumed that the appropriate marketing strategy focuses on advertising and promotions about how their products enhance beauty. Anita Roddick and The Body Shop have questioned these basic assump-

**THE COFFEE BREAK.** At The Darden School at the University of Virginia, a 25-minute coffee break has become  part of the school's culture.  The daily break offers an excellent opportunity for students and faculty to get to know one another outside the classroom.

tions, building marketing around The Body Shop's political activity, environmen-talism, and skepticism about the traditional idea of beauty.

# CORPORATE CULTURE AND PERFORMANCE

Artifacts, espoused values, and basic assumptions form the basics of understand-ing organizational culture. According to Eliott Jacques, an organizational culture is"the customary or traditional ways of thinking and doing things, which are shared to a greater or lesser extent by all members of the organization [and] which new members must learn and at least partially accept in order to be accepted into the service of the firm."[11]

In other words, organizational culture is a framework that guides day-to-day be-havior and decision making for employees and directs their actions toward comple-tion of organizational goals. Indeed, culture is what gives birth to and defines the organizational goals. Culture must be aligned with the other parts of organizational actions, such as planning, organizing, leading, and controlling; indeed, if culture is not aligned with these tasks, then the organization is in for difficult times.

## THE KOTTER AND HESKETT STUDY

In a study of more than 200 companies, Harvard Business School researchers John Kotter and James Heskett tried to determine which factors make some organiza-

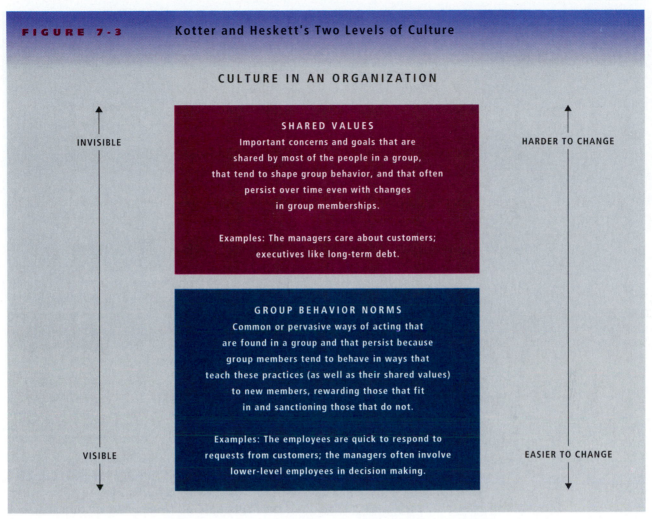

**FIGURE 7-3**    Kotter and Heskett's Two Levels of Culture

### CULTURE IN AN ORGANIZATION

INVISIBLE

HARDER TO CHANGE

**SHARED VALUES**
Important concerns and goals that are
shared by most of the people in a group,
that tend to shape group behavior, and that often
persist over time even with changes
in group memberships.

Examples: The managers care about customers;
executives like long-term debt.

**GROUP BEHAVIOR NORMS**
Common or pervasive ways of acting that
are found in a group and that persist because
group members tend to behave in ways that
teach these practices (as well as their shared values)
to new members, rewarding those that fit
in and sanctioning those that do not.

Examples: The employees are quick to respond to
requests from customers; the managers often involve
lower-level employees in decision making.

VISIBLE

EASIER TO CHANGE

*Source:* John P. Kotter and James L. Heskett, *Corporate Culture and Performance.* New York: The Free Press, 1992, p. 5.

tional cultures more successful than others.[12] If success factors could be isolated, they reasoned, then companies could embark on programs to change their cultures in order to be more successful.

Kotter and Heskett identified two levels of culture (see Figure 7-3), one visible and one invisible (much like the iceberg view we discussed earlier). First, on the visible level, are the behavior patterns and styles of the employees. Second, on the invisible level, are the shared values and assumptions that are held over a long period of time. This second level is the more difficult to change. Kotter and Heskett argue, however, that changes in the first level—in behavior patterns and styles—over time can lead to a change in the more deeply held beliefs. In this way, cultural change is something like "momentum" in athletics: it emerges out of behavior. In sports, trying to "get the momentum" is a coaching recipe for failure; trying to "execute the little details" is effective—and the momentum sometimes follows.

The results of the Harvard study indicate that culture has a strong—and increasing—impact on the performance of organizations. The study had four main conclusions:

1) Corporate culture can have a significant impact on a firm's long-term economic performance.
2) Corporate culture will probably be an even more important factor in determining the success or failure of firms in the next decade.
3) Corporate cultures that inhibit strong long-term financial performance are not rare; they develop easily, even in firms that are full of reasonable

| TABLE 7-1 | Adaptive vs. Unadaptive Corporate Cultures | |
|---|---|---|
| | **ADAPTIVE CORPORATE CULTURES** | **UNADAPTIVE CORPORATE CULTURES** |
| *Core Values* | Most managers care deeply about customers, stockholders, and employees. They also strongly value people and processes that can create useful change (e.g., leadership up and down the management hierarchy) | Most managers care mainly about themselves, their immediate work group, or some product (or technology) associated with that work group. They value the orderly and risk-reducing management process much more highly than leadership initiatives. |
| *Common Behavior* | Managers pay close attention to all their constituencies, especially customers, and initiate change when needed to serve their legitimate interests, even if that entails taking some risks. | Managers tend to behave somewhat insularly, politically, and bureaucratically. As a result, they do not change their strategies quickly to adjust to or take advantage of changes in their business environments. |

*Source:* John P. Kotter and James L. Heskett, *Corporate Culture and Performance.* New York: The Free Press, 1992, p. 51.

and intelligent people.

4) Although tough to change, corporate cultures can be made more performance enhancing.[13]

Kotter and Heskett discovered that some corporate cultures are good at adapting to changes and preserving the performance of the organization, while others are not. They distinguished between "adaptive" and "unadaptive" corporate cultures, and they defined the core values and common behaviors in each kind of culture. Table 7-1 summarizes these distinctions.

Family Dollar exemplifies the financial success that a strong culture can help build. "A bell rings whenever a customer enters, creating a homey atmosphere," says president and chief operating officer (COO) Peter J. Hayes. "There is usually at least one person up front to greet customers not only with a 'Hello' but also with eye contact."[14] This customer-oriented, personable culture contributed to the company's $1.2 billion in sales for 1992.

Similarly, The Limited, Inc., offers an example of the close connection between culture and financial performance. The culture at The Limited is deeply imbued with the underlying values of the chairman, Leslie H. Wexner, who asserts, "A 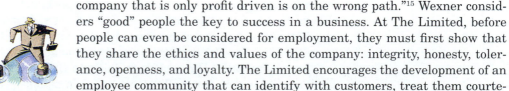 company that is only profit driven is on the wrong path."[15] Wexner considers "good" people the key to success in a business. At The Limited, before people can even be considered for employment, they must first show that they share the ethics and values of the company: integrity, honesty, tolerance, openness, and loyalty. The Limited encourages the development of an employee community that can identify with customers, treat them courteously, and be friendly to the point of making them feel at home. "I don't believe in having people pay allegiance to a monolithic $19 billion or $20 billion enterprise....It's much more effective when it's broken down into units that people can identify with and that can capture their imagination as individuals."[16] Managers at The Limited call employees "associates," because, according to Wexner, "they really are associated with the success of the business."[17] The culture at The Limited thus emphasizes the relationships—between the company, employees, and customers—that ground its financial success.

## TAKING CHARGE OF CORPORATE CULTURE

Managers at many companies have tried to take charge and direct their corporate culture. Anita Roddick is living proof. Indeed, many of the case examples in this book involve companies in the middle of culture changes. Kotter and Heskett claim that a critical element in successful culture change is leadership from the top. At GE, Jack Welch has been a relentless champion of making GE number 1 or number 2 in all of its businesses. Bob Allen has tirelessly led AT&T toward quality management and employee participation. At Con Agra, Mike Harper emphasized "results for shareholders through satisfying customer needs." At Nissan Motors, Yutaka Kume changed a large, bureaucratic organization by giving power to those much further down in the organization. In each of these cases, cultural changes have led to periods of renewed financial performance.[18]

Patagonia, a designer and distributor of technical outdoor clothing, embraces a classic culture that reflects the persona of its founder. Yvon Chouinard is a mountain climber and an environmental activist who spends up to eight months of the year away from the company, testing new products. According to former CEO Kris McDivitt, who applauds his efforts, "It's all about how you form relationships with people."[19] And whether Chouinard is working on reforestation in Chile, skiing with dealers in Japan, or meeting with random mountain climbers he encounters during his travels, that is just what he is doing: building relationships.

Initially, however, as his company grew, Chouinard (like many other entrepreneurs) ran into some problems. He found that the "professional managers" he hired did not fit in with the culture. "This is a unique culture, extremely unique. Not everyone fits here," remarked Chouinard. "I've found that rather than bring in businessmen and teach them to be dirt bags, it's easier to teach dirt bags to do business....We realize we don't need any managers. The company is now divided into small working groups. The solutions come from all the people working together."[20] The vision of the founder has thus created a culture of connection and working together. It works only because the founder takes care to hire compatible employees and teach them the culture. This is taking charge of the culture.

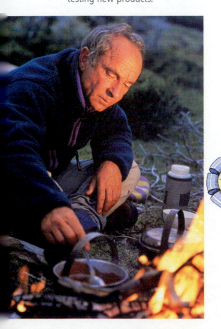

**A TASTE FOR ADVENTURE.** Yvon Chouinard, the founder of Patagonia, spends a good part of the year mountain climbing and testing new products.

## THE ROLE OF EDUCATION AND SHARING

When employees join an organization, the manager introduces them to the culture of the organization during training sessions, or more commonly, during the job interviews themselves. Through words and actions the manager conveys the written and unwritten rules that all employees must follow. When employees join Family Dollar, for example, they attend a one-week school to train them in all procedures. Although this policy requires training more than 1,200 employees each year, the leaders believe the expense is worthwhile, because it keeps the employees connected to one another and increases productivity.

Mere education is not enough—culture is constantly reinforced through the creation of stories, heroes, rites, and ceremonies. The greeter at a Wal-Mart store stands as a symbol of the company's culture of frugality, hard work, and service to customers. Company slogans also serve to reinforce cultures. They carry simple messages, but adeptly convey the companies' vision, strategy, and values. For example, the Ford slogan "Quality is Job One," reflects a major effort at cultural change involving a focus on building better-quality cars and being much more responsive to customers.

Even the architecture of a company's buildings and grounds can reflect its corporate culture. The Nike World Campus, on 74 acres of pine groves in Beaverton, Oregon, breathes the energy, youth, and vitality associated with Nike's products and links quality and fitness—the hallmark values of Nike. Similarly, the new downtown Manhattan headquarters of the National Audubon Society is a hundred-year-old building on lower Broadway, recently renovated using environmen-

# SUPPORTING SOCIAL ACTIVISM

"Taking a high profile in the community is a better marketing effort than trying to outspend the competition," asserts Anita Roddick.[22] Toward this end, The Body Shop has taken on an aggressive role espousing social activism. "Our business is about two things: social change and action, and skin care," said Roddick. "Social change and action come first."[23]

Essentially, Roddick believes in applying morality to business. "I believe quite passionately that there is a better way," she said. "I think you can rewrite the book on business. I think you can trade ethically; be committed to social responsibility, global responsibility; empower your employees without being afraid of them. I think you can really rewrite the book. That is the vision, and the vision is absolutely clear."[24] Roddick has thus *humanized* business. "It's creating a new business paradigm," she said. "It's showing that business can have a human face, and God help us if we don't try. It's showing that empowering employees is the key to keeping them, and that you empower them by creating a better educational system. It's showing that you forsake your values at the cost of forsaking your workforce. It's paying attention to the aesthetics of business. It's all that. It's trying in every way you can. You may not get there, but goddammit, you try to make the journey an honorable one."[25]

According to Roddick, it is important that stores adhere closely to the values articulated, even if it means altering plans. Because of the company's environmental policy, in Oregon, The Body Shop had to forego the use of a seemingly brilliant ingredient, a plant called "meadow foam," which seemed promising in shampoo, but was an endangered species.

Roddick's social activism and environmental consciousness have been securely woven into the very fabric of the organization. To her, business "relationships" are what are important—they are what has been going on for centuries. "It's just buying and selling, with an added bit for me, which is the magical area where people come together—that is, the shop," said Roddick. "It's trading. It's making your product so glorious that people don't mind buying it from you at a profit. Their reaction is, 'I love that. Can I buy that?' You want them to find what you are doing so wonderful that they are happy to pay your profit."[26] →

tally sound materials. Conveying a sense of an inspiring and healthy workplace, it parallels the Audubon image.[21]

## FROM CULTURE TO MULTICULTURALISM

**A**nita Roddick has used a strong corporate culture built on social activism to establish The Body Shop as a successful organization. While corporate culture can be a strong force for financial performance, the strength of the concept of culture is also its potential weakness. Culture is difficult to change, especially at the level of underlying assumptions and values. In today's world many of the assumptions and values that operate are quite different from those of a generation ago. Indeed, the very nature of the workforce has changed by revolutionary proportions. The average employee in the United States is no longer a white male who hopes to work his way up the organizational ladder. Today's workforce is multicultural: a mix of people from many different cultures, ethnicities, and lifestyles. If organizations are to adapt to this reality they must better understand multiculturalism and its impacts. An exercise in multicultural understanding is presented in Exhibit 7-1.

**EXHIBIT 7-1**

**An Exercise in Multicultural Understanding**

1. Imagine that Jack, a young, white, male graduate from your college, is entering a management training program with a large manufacturing firm or a large bank. Can you list some barriers that may prevent Jack from reaching the very top position in the organization? For starters, consider that there is a relatively large number of people like Jack competing for a very few spots at the top of any organization.

2. Suppose that Jack is African American, or Hispanic American, or Asian American. What additional barriers does he face? How do these barriers impact Jack's chances of making it to the top?

3. Suppose that the new management trainee isn't Jack, but Tara, a young, white woman who has graduated from your school. What are the barriers to the top for Tara? What are the differences between Tara and either version of Jack?

4. Suppose that Tara is African American, or Hispanic American, or Asian American. What additional barriers does she face?

5. What would be the barriers if Tara or Jack came from France? Haiti? Japan? Brazil?

6. Suppose that Tara or Jack is gay; what are the additional barriers?

7. Suppose that Tara or Jack has a physical disability and must use a wheelchair. What are the additional barriers?

8. Suppose that Tara or Jack is older than 50?

## DEFINING MULTICULTURALISM

**Multiculturalism** as it applies to management can be defined as the view that there are many different cultural backgrounds and factors that are important in organizations, and that people from different backgrounds can coexist and flourish within an organization. Usually multiculturalism refers to cultural factors such as ethnicity, race, gender, physical ability, and sexual orientation, but sometimes age and other factors are added. Robert Hughes has argued that multiculturalism is a basic premise of American society.[27] Contrary to those who claim that concern with multiculturalism is the foundation for the current emphasis on "political correctness," Hughes suggests that the belief that people from many different backgrounds can work together is fundamental to democracy and the American way of life. While Anita Roddick believes in such coexistence, her view is not universally accepted.

## THE WORKFORCE 2000 REPORT

While many of the issues surrounding multiculturalism and diversity have been around for a long time, many organizations adopted a renewed concern with the publication of the Hudson Institute's 1987 report, entitled *Workforce 2000*.[28] The report identified four key trends expected to become more important as the 20th century draws to a close. First, the report predicted that renewed productivity growth will lead to a healthier U.S. economy. Second, manufacturing will become a smaller part of that economy as service jobs become a bigger factor in creating wealth and new jobs. Third, these new service industry jobs will require a high level of skill, leading to employment for the educated and unemployment for the uneducated. Finally, the demographic composition of the workforce in the U. S. will become older, more female, and more disadvantaged. The percentage of white males in the workforce was 47 percent in 1987 when the report was issued, but the report predicted the percentage of new white males entering the workforce will be greatly reduced. Estimates have varied from 15 to 30 percent.

The Hudson Institute suggested six policy initiatives to cope with these changes:

1. Stimulate balanced world economic growth.

**multiculturalism:**

As applied to the workplace, the view that there are many different cultural backgrounds and factors that are important in organizations, and that people from different backgrounds can coexist and flourish within an organization.

**CHANGING DEMOGRAPHICS.**
One key trend identified by the Workforce 2000 report is that the U.S. workforce will be relatively older in the years to come.

2. Increase efforts to stimulate productivity in service industries.

3. Maintain the adaptability and flexibility of the aging workforce.

4. Help resolve the often conflicting needs of women in relation to work and family.

5. Work to integrate African American and Hispanic American workers more fully into the economy.

6. Improve the education of all workers.

Concurrent with the release of the "Workplace 2000" report, many organizations began to worry more than ever about how to manage such a diverse workforce. How could women, Hispanic Americans, African Americans, and others with cultural heritages different from white males be integrated into the workforce? Many organizations began to have "diversity programs" or "multiculturalism programs."

In a more recent study, William Johnston concluded that the labor supply is becoming more global. This will ensure that any particular company has an even more diverse labor pool from which to draw its workers.[29] Most of the population growth is occurring in "developing economies," where the workforce is relatively young and the educational level is rapidly improving. Over 570 million of the 600 million new workers entering the workforce will come from these developing economies such as Mexico, Indonesia, Philippines, etc. Although the statistics on women in the workforce vary widely by country, many more women will enter the workforce all over the world. Organizations will have more choices about where to locate their facilities to take advantage of particular labor markets, and will thus be forced to learn to accommodate many different cultural factors into their individual organizational cultures.

## GENDER ISSUES IN MULTICULTURALISM

One important dimension of diversity in organizations is gender diversity. The Workforce 2000 studies point out that the workforce is rapidly moving from being male-dominated to one of equality in numbers between men and women.

**THE GLASS CEILING.** Women in top executive positions are scarce. Although more and more women have managerial positions, invisible barriers still prevent most from climbing to the highest corporate levels.

Nevertheless there remain many barriers for women seeking equal treatment in most organizations.

**GLASS CEILING.** While there are more women in the workforce than ever before, they are still largely in junior positions. Only a handful of women are chief executives of large companies. Studies estimate that men hold 97 percent of the top positions, and women comprise fewer than 0.5 percent of the highest-paid officers and directors positions in the top 1000 U.S. companies.[30]

Getting hired is merely an initial step for women (and minorities as well); getting promoted within a company often proves a more imposing challenge. For senior positions, promotions are very hard to achieve. This is commonly referred to as the **glass ceiling syndrome**—women and minorities can see opportunities for senior management positions but are blocked by seemingly invisible barriers from reaching them. Much of the decision to promote someone to a senior position is based on such intangibles as how comfortable the senior team is with that person. It is quite normal to be more comfortable with those who are similar to us in interests and background. Inadvertently, the glass ceiling is maintained because women may be excluded from activities that have traditionally been almost all male such as golf and sports conversations.

**glass ceiling syndrome:**

The view that even though women and minorities can get hired into organizations, they have difficulty getting promoted, particularly to senior levels; it's as if there's an invisible barrier; they can see opportunities above, but they cannot reach them.

**sexual harassment:**

As applied in the workplace, any unwanted sexual behavior that can involve, for example, words, gestures, sounds, actions, or physical touching.

**SEXUAL HARASSMENT.** In addition, many women face **sexual harassment** in the workplace.* Sexual harassment consists of any unwanted sexual behavior, including but not limited to suggestive looks, sexual jokes, touching, or pressure for sexual favors. The Equal Employment Opportunity Commission (EEOC) has defined two types of sexual harassment in the workplace. The first, labeled *quid pro quo* harassment, occurs when sexual favors are requested or demanded in exchange for tangible benefits—advancement, pay increases—or to avoid tangible harm—loss of job, demotion. The second type of harassment is labeled *hostile environment*. It is more complex because claims of this type can be made for unwelcome sexual conduct, either physical or verbal, that "unreasonably interferes with an individual's job performance" or that can be said to "create an intimidating, hostile, or offensive working environment."[31]

It is difficult to pinpoint exactly what a hostile environment is; sensitivities differ and what is offensive to one woman is not necessarily offensive to another. Sheri Poe, president and CEO of Ryka Inc., maker of women's athletic footwear,

---

\* Men also face sexual harassment, but the overwhelming majority of harassment complaints are from women about men.

**TABLE 7-4**      **Six Arguments for Managing Cultural Diversity**

| | |
|---|---|
| 1. Cost Argument | As organizations become more diverse, the cost of a poor job in integrating workers will increase. Those who handle this well, will thus create cost advantages over those who don't. |
| 2. Resource-Acquisition Argument | Companies develop reputations on favorability as prospective employers for women and ethnic minorities. Those with the best reputations for managing diversity will win the competition for the best personnel. As the labor pool shrinks and changes composition, this edge will become increasingly important. |
| 3. Marketing Argument | For multinational organizations, the insight and cultural sensitivity that members with roots in other countries bring to the marketing effort should improve these efforts in important ways. The same rationale applies to marketing to subpopulations within domestic operations. |
| 4. Creativity Argument | Diversity of perspectives and less emphasis on conformity to norms of the past (which characterize the modern approach to management of diversity) should improve the level of creativity. |
| 5. Problem-solving Argument | Heterogeneity in decision and problem solving groups potentially produces better decisions through a wider range of perspectives and more thorough critical analysis of issues. |
| 6. System Flexibility Argument | An implication of the multicultural model for managing diversity is that the system will become less determinant, less standardized, and therefore more fluid. The increased fluidity should create greater flexibility to react to environmental changes (i.e., reactions should be faster and at less cost). |

*Source:* Taylor H. Cox, Jr., and Stacy Blake, "Managing Cultural Diversity: Implications for Organizational Competitiveness," *Academy of Management Executive*, vol. 5, issue 3, August 1991, p. 47.

investment it has made in them. In addition, if multicultural issues aren't managed well, then people are not as comfortable as they could be in the work environment and they spend time and energy worrying about discrimination, harassment, and other issues rather than their jobs.

The *resource acquisition argument* says that companies that handle multiculturalism well will have an advantage over other companies in hiring multicultural workers—an increasingly important advantage in an era of Workforce 2000 demographics. For example, a recent book discussed the best places to work for women and African Americans. The impact has been positive for companies listed, including Merck, Xerox, Syntex, Hoffman LaRoche, and Hewlett Packard.[42]

The *marketing argument* says that organizations that manage multicultural issues well have an insight into markets consisting of minority group members and women. Markets, too, are diverse, and cultural issues have some effect on the buying decisions of customers. Nancy Woodhull, president of Gannett News Media,

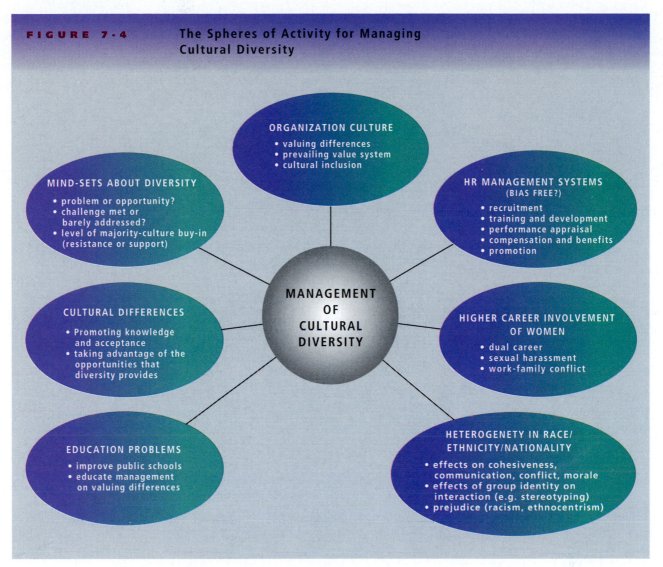

**FIGURE 7-4**     The Spheres of Activity for Managing Cultural Diversity

*Source:* Taylor H. Cox, Jr., and Stacy Blake, "Managing Cultural Diversity: Implications for Organizational Competitiveness," *Academy of Management Executive*, vol. 5, issue 3, August 1991, p. 51.

claims that USA Today is successful precisely because it has a variety of people from different cultural backgrounds involved in daily news meetings.[43]

The *creativity and problem-solving arguments* hold that groups of people from diverse backgrounds can be more creative than groups with homogeneous backgrounds, and are better at solving problems. However, steps must be taken to realize these benefits; in particular, team members must become aware of possible attitude differences in others. And there must be a core of shared beliefs or shared values around which people can express their differences.

Finally, the *system flexibility* argument says that the ability to manage diversity increases the adaptability and flexibility of an organization. External and internal issues can be responded to more quickly. In addition, to manage diversity successfully, an organization must question outdated policies and procedures that emerged in days when multiculturalism was not a large concern for the organization.

## MANAGING DIVERSITY

To reap the benefits just listed, managers must take positive steps to manage the issue of diversity. Figure 7-4 outlines seven spheres of activity that together provide a comprehensive approach to managing diversity issues.

**MANAGEMENT 2000 AND BEYOND**

# MORE DIMENSIONS OF DIVERSITY TO COME

R. Roosevelt Thomas, Jr., a renowned diversity consultant, believes that the corporate world has made a great deal of progress on the issues we have discussed in this chapter. He also believes that in the future we must deal with diversity on even more dimensions. In an introduction to a new book by Harvard Business School professor Mary Gentile, Thomas writes:

> [W]e will begin to focus more on the collective mixture of differences and similarities, rather than on the differences themselves. The task of managing diversity is not only to address issues that have resulted in individuals being underutilized or excluded, but also to consider those who traditionally have been fully utilized and included....Managing diversity does not simply mean white males grappling with the opportunities and challenges of diversity. It also encompasses the incorporation of white male experiences along with those of other visible and invisible contributors to the diversity 'stew' into the mixture of similarities and differences that is known as today's work force.[44]

Thomas suggests that there are a number of guidelines for managing diversity, but he proposes one test that is controversial. He calls it the "Special Consideration Test."

The test consists of one question: Does this program, policy, or principle give special consideration to one group? Will it contribute to everyone's success, or will it only produce an advantage for blacks or whites or women or men? Is it designed for them as opposed to us? Whenever the answer is yes, you're not yet on the road to managing diversity.[45]

Thomas argues that such a test does not rule out addressing concerns that affect a particular group, but it asks that managers be sure that the concerns don't affect other groups as well. For instance, a group of women managers might find a lack of mentors or role models in a company. To address this concern using the Special Consideration Test, a manager would first check to be sure that a lack of mentoring is not a problem for other groups as well. Thomas believes that programs that give special consideration to one group do not really get at the real causes of prejudice and can in fact lead to more prejudice and inequality.

He summarizes his view of managing diversity in this way:

> In a country seeking competitive advantage in a global economy, the goal of managing diversity is to develop our capacity to accept, incorporate, and empower the diverse human talents of the most diverse nation on earth. It's our reality. We need to make it our strength.[46]

Making a strength of diversity will be a necessity for the successful manager operating in the global economy in the next century. As managers think through these issues—the complex mosaic of culture and multiculturalism—they need to examine their own beliefs about diversity and whether or not affirming diversity can help them become more effective.

# EDUCATION AT THE HEART

"There's no scientific answer for success," said Roddick. "You can't define it....You've simply got to live it and do it." And that is what she has done. Roddick has treated The Body Shop as an extension of herself. She has built upon her own background and taken an approach that builds upon her strengths. "I've just taken what every good teacher knows," said Roddick, a former teacher herself. "You try to make your classroom an enthralling place. When I taught history, I would put brilliant graphics all around the room and play music of the period we were studying. Kids could just get up, walk around, and make notes from the presentation. It took me months to get it right, but it was stunning. Now, I'm doing the same thing. There is education in the shops. There are anecdotes right on the products, and anecdotes adhere. So I've really gone back to what I know how to do well."[47]

Roddick places great emphasis on employee empowerment. Inasmuch as training is a prerequisite for empowerment, The Body Shop opened a training school in 1985. It features courses on employee relations, employment law, and time management. It was important to Roddick that the staff know more about The Body Shop products than the customers, and that they be able to answer all the questions "they hoped they would never be asked."[48]

Unlike similar schools sponsored by other companies, The Body Shop's schools accept anyone affiliated with the company—including franchisees and their employees—and students attend for free. However, people must be admitted, and currently the school is not able to meet the demand for its courses.

Roddick considers such an educational investment in the community to be integral. "If you think education is expensive, try ignorance," she asserted. "Education is at the very heart of The Body

**SOCIAL RESPONSIBILITY SELLS PRODUCTS.** The Body Shop sells a wide range of beauty and health care products for men, women, and children, including bath oils and gels, soaps, sponges, and makeup.

Shop. We encourage the development of the human spirit as well as the mind."[49] Whereas some companies "train for sale," at The Body Shop, according to Roddick, "We train for knowledge."[50]

This education and information serve to motivate The Body Shop employees. According to Roddick, "They're much more motivated and they actually enjoy their jobs....We find that people who are not trained are less motivated in their jobs, which is why we place such a heavy emphasis on training." In addition, Roddick said, "We did not want our staff...to stop learning just because they had started working."[51]

Together, the company's education and social activism have enabled Roddick to motivate employees beyond their own expectations. "I'd never get that kind of motivation if we were just selling shampoo and body lotion," said Roddick. "I'd never get that sort of staying late, talking at McDonald's after work, bonding to customers. It's a way for people to bond to the company. They're doing what I'm doing. They're learning. Three years ago I didn't know anything about the rain forest. Five years ago I didn't know anything about the ozone layer. It's a process of learning to be a global citizen. And what it produces is a sense of passion you simply won't find in a Bloomingdale's department store."[52]

Most important to Roddick is that she encourage employees to put their best foot forward. "I want them to understand that this is no dress rehearsal," said Roddick. "You've got one life, so just lead it. And try to be remarkable."[53]

The aspiration statement has served to bridge the gap between tradition and timely change.

Management support has proved crucial to the success of the new Levi Strauss philosophy, for it has emphasized to employees that their work is not just "getting pants out the door," that it also includes the articulated values. Management's "walking the talk" sends the message to employees to take ownership themselves. "To create an environment that supports teamwork and trust, you can't just talk about it," said Thompson. "Fundamentally, it requires a personal commitment. Bob Haas can't do it by himself. The executives can't do it by themselves. Each employee has to step up and put a stake in the ground."[60]

The culture at Levi Strauss that values equality and non-discrimination extends beyond the employees to community stakeholders as well. For example, in 1991, when the company learned that the Boy Scouts' parent organization excludes homosexuals and requires its members to recite an oath to God, Levi Strauss discontinued its support, even though it had given $200,000 to local scouts during the previous five years. Representatives unsuccessfully attempted to organize a boycott in California, but Levi Strauss remained committed to its corporate policy and values.

With regard to its relationship with employees, Levi Strauss maintains numerous programs that facilitate diversity in the workplace. For example, it is one of the few companies that offer flexible working arrangements to accommodate employees with family responsibilities. In addition, it has a widely recognized policy of offering medical coverage to employees' sexual partners, regardless of their gender. While many employers offer medical coverage to employees' heterosexual partners, few recognize homosexual partners.

The result at Levi Strauss is a multicultural environment that values its employees. According to Haas, often in companies there is a gap between the articulated values and what the working environment is actually like. "The more you can narrow that gap," said Haas, "the more people's energies can be released toward company purposes."[61] Levi Strauss has already taken great strides toward narrowing the gap, and more can be anticipated in the future.

## CASE QUESTIONS

1. How would you describe the culture at Levi Strauss?
2. How does Levi Strauss manage diversity?
3. How do managers at Levi Strauss fight stereotypes?
4. What would you do to manage diversity at Levi Strauss?

## RESPONDING TO ALLEGATIONS OF RACISM: FLAGSTAR AND THE PLEDGE[62]

The 1990s have witnessed an increased emphasis on valuing diversity. With both the marketplace and the workforce becoming more and more diverse, many managers have redesigned their companies' cultures to reflect and encourage multiculturalism. Changing a company's culture, however, is often more difficult than managers might first believe. At Denny's, for example, promoting multiculturalism required a reworking of its corporate culture from top to bottom.

In the early 1990s, Denny's found itself the target of numerous allegations of racism, by both customers and employees. Black customers asserted that they were not receiving the same treatment at Denny's as white customers. Some complained that they were either forced to wait for their food longer than white customers or denied service entirely; others said that they were forced to pre-pay for their meals while white customers in the restaurant were not. There were also allegations that Denny's engaged in "black-outs," where Denny's restaurants would close if there were too many black customers. In addition, Denny's was accused of discriminatory hiring practices as well as preventing blacks and other minorities from reaching management and franchise positions. None of this garnered much attention, however, until a suit was filed on March 24, 1993, by a group of minority customers in San Jose, California, who made the all-too-familiar allegation that Denny's had required cover charges and pre-payment of meals from minority customers, but not from white customers.

In response to these charges, Denny's parent company, Flagstar, formally apologized to the customers, and Flagstar CEO Jerry Richardson dropped the cover charge and pre-payment policies and explained that they had been intended to prevent late night "dine-and-dash" theft and that any discriminatory implementation of them was in direct violation of corporate policies. Richardson admitted, however, that he had been unaware that the cover charge and pre-payment policies even existed within the company. Furthermore, Richardson began talks with civil rights groups such as the NAACP. Flagstar also signed a consent decree issued by the Justice Department that required spot testing of Denny's restaurants for discriminatory practices as well as an anti-discrimination training program for all Denny's staffers. "Our company does not tolerate discrimination of any kind," Richardson assured all, and his actions seemed to support his words.[63]

Then, on May 24, 1993, six black Secret Service agents filed suit against Denny's for allegedly having denied them service at a Denny's in Annapolis, Maryland. The six men claimed that while they received deliberately slow service, their white counterparts were served in a timely fashion. "Hearing the allegations made yesterday by six African-American Secret Service agents on national television that they were not treated fairly at Denny's was a painful experience for our company," Richardson admitted.[64]

The highly publicized suit served as a catalyst that set off a whirlwind of changes throughout Flagstar. In late May Richardson issued an internal memo that marked the beginning of Richardson's pledge to change: "I am distressed that some people in our company haven't gotten the message that we will not tolerate unfair treatment of customers," he wrote. "The past year has been a trying experience, particularly for many of our African-American em-

ployees who are embarrassed by what happened. This is my personal pledge to them to restore their pride in Denny's."[65]

Richardson stopped promising change and started creating it. On July 1, 1993, Flagstar reached an historic agreement with the NAACP. The agreement, which was the most far-reaching arrangement the civil-rights organization had ever signed, represented a breakthrough in relations between minorities and businesses. The plan targeted several specific problem areas within Flagstar. For example, of Flagstar's more than 120,000 workers, 20 percent were black, but only 4.4 percent of its managers were black. Under the agreement, at least 12 percent of Flagstar's managers will be black by the year 2000. The company also wanted to increase the number of black-owned franchises; only one of Denny's 405 franchises was owned by a black person as of 1993, but Flagstar planned to have at least 53 black-owned franchises by 1997. Flagstar also agreed to direct more marketing funds toward minority advertising and to begin purchasing more goods and services from minority-owned businesses. In addition, Flagstar promised to appoint at least one minority to its board of directors. In all, the plan will direct more than one billion dollars in jobs and economic benefits to minority workers and companies by the year 2000.

Richardson also undertook efforts to restore Denny's reputation as well as his own. At the forefront of his efforts was "The Pledge." "The Pledge" was the name given to a 60-second TV spot, which aired in 41 television markets and on the Black Entertainment Television network during a two-week period in June 1993. In it, Jerry Richardson and a representative sample of Flagstar's 46,000 employees endorsed a solemn pledge to treat customers with "respect, dignity, and fairness." "The whole idea for the 'Pledge' started with our desire to express support for our own employees," explained David Hurwitt, Flagstar's senior vice president of marketing. "These people have been very much under the gun. We chose television for this special campaign because we felt it was important to show people exactly who the Denny's employees are."[66] Overall, response to "The Pledge" was favorable. "Our phone has been ringing off the hook since Denny's aired this ad," said W. Gregory Wims, president of the NAACP in Rockville, Maryland, the largest branch in the Washington, D.C., area. "About 90 percent of our members approve of the commercials and the steps Denny's has been taking to improve relations with people of color."[67]

# THE QUALITY REVOLUTION AT MOTOROLA[1]

Motorola, a global electronics company with record sales of $17 billion in 1993, had also posted a particularly good year in 1979 as measured by profits and sales. At a meeting of its senior management, however, Arthur Sundry, senior sales manager for the Communications Sector, stood up and said, "Our quality stinks and we ought to do something about it."[2] Such a statement would signal the end of a career at many companies but, at Motorola, a company founded upon a culture of innovation, employees are encouraged to speak their minds. Then CEO Robert Galvin, son of Motorola founder Paul Galvin, took Sundry's words to heart, particularly considering that they were coming from the national sales manager of Motorola's largest, fastest-growing, and most profitable product line. According to Galvin, managers looked at each other and said, "If Art thinks that's true, it must be true. We'd better do something about it."[3]

"So we had a very personal, a very emotional buy-in, almost on an instantaneous basis, which got us started," recalled Galvin. Finding the path to quality was neither easy nor smooth. "We muddled and stumbled for a good period of time," he reported.[4] Managers reached out and listened to anyone inside or outside the company with ideas and Galvin implemented a top-to-bottom review of Motorola quality.

*The key to achieving total customer satisfaction lay in empowering employees...*

The review indicated that Motorola's products generally enjoyed a superior rating for long-term reliability, but many new products frequently failed during their first three to nine months of service. The failure of new products damaged Motorola's quality reputation. In addition, the internal company review located problems in manufacturing and product delivery.

In response to such problems, Motorola management began a series of continuous improvement initiatives in 1981 with a goal of increasing quality and customer satisfaction tenfold within five years. Many employees thought that the goal was unattainable.

Motorola management determined that the key to achieving total customer satisfaction lay in empowering employees with the authority and responsibility to improve manufacturing processes throughout the company. Before Motorola could empower its employees, however, the company needed to give its workers the tools to improve quality. "We went to the intellectual experts, the people in academia…[and] learned a great deal from them," recalled Gavin. "We brought in consultants, talked to our customers…. We began a process of reaching out to learn from every source we could. Finally we engaged in a very formal training to teach ourselves all manner of the new ways and means."[5] Teams of trained and empowered employees would lead to higher quality.

A $10 million, 88,000-square foot training center, dubbed Motorola University, became the cornerstone of an intensive employee education program. The company reorganized its traditional training and education unit into a

**RECOGNITION OF WORLD-CLASS QUALITY.** Then-CEO George Fisher accepts congratulations from President Ronald Reagan upon Motorola's winning the Baldrige award in 1988.

worldwide facility with its own board of directors. Management set target levels of education and skills for every job description in the organization. Motorola believed that it could reach its product quality goals only by consistently improving employee education. The university became the nerve center for constant reeducation and retooling of the workforce.

By the mid 1980s every department was required to devote 1.5 percent of its budget to education and employees had to take a minimum of 40 hours of training each year. Overall the Schaumberg, Illinois, electronics giant was spending $70 million a year on training, with 40 percent targeted at quality instruction. Motorola did not limit its training programs to rank-and-file workers; the company's top 1,200 executives were compelled to attend two weeks of training each year.

Quality improvement programs often fail without deep top-management commitment. According to George Fisher, Motorola CEO from 1988 to 1993, "We learned the hard way…that unless you start at the top with your training programs, you have a phenomenon where people are going back to their jobs after taking a course, they want to implement some new process or procedure, and they're all enthusiastic to do it, and, lo and behold, they go in and talk to their boss, and he doesn't know what they're talking about."[6] With Galvin spending more than 50 percent of his time on quality issues, this problem was not at issue at Motorola.

Motorola also developed new human resources policies and a vision statement for personnel management. Whenever productivity improvements eliminate jobs, the company offers retraining for new positions. Job security became part of Motorola's quality culture.

Empowered employees on the factory floor were able to make many of the changes necessary to improve quality. Ten months after implementing the program at the Seguin, Texas, plant, defect rates dropped 70 percent. Employees enthusiastically embraced their newly found freedom. Without a direct monetary incentive, workers submitted over 2 million written process improvement suggestions a year, an average of 24 per employee. They also formed over 4,000 teams to reduce cycle time, cut defects, or improve customer satisfaction in some innovative way. "Empowered to change the way they work, these teams are the backbone of Motorola's quality movement," asserted Motorola vice-president and Senior Quality Assurance Manager, Bill Smith.[7]

Motorola won the Malcolm Baldrige National Quality Award in 1988, the first year it was awarded. The company reached its five-year quality goal. Sundry, the Motorola manager who publicly called attention to the company's problems with quality, was promoted to executive vice-president before his retirement in 1990. →

To BE SUCCESSFUL in today's business environment, organizations like Motorola must pay attention to quality. Indeed, one of the most important developments of recent years is a renewed attention to the concept of "quality," also dubbed "total quality management" or "total quality control."* The purpose of this chapter is to explain the reasons for the emphasis on quality and describe the main approaches to "the quality movement."

---

* There are a variety of definitions of these terms and some authors see important nuances and differences among them. For the purposes of this chapter, however, we will sometimes use them interchangeably.

**"INSTITUTE LEADERSHIP."** At Baldrige-winning Marlow Industries, CEO Raymond Marlow's vision and leadership are a powerful force for quality.

tomer service. Focusing on quality, not quantity, enables the company to attract profitable, full-fare business fliers. For more than ten years, revenues of the Alaska Air Group have grown at a rate of more than 24 percent a year, to $1.05 billion in 1990.

## 12.  REMOVE BARRIERS TO PRIDE OF WORKMANSHIP

Deming maintains that annual rating or merit systems should be eliminated. If people inherently want to perform well, as Deming assumes, then they do not need such incentive systems. What they need is assistance in overcoming obstacles imposed by inadequacies in materials, equipment, and training. Systems that endeavor to remove such obstacles should replace systems that attempt to coerce performance by making workers feel that they are always being judged, ranked, and rated.

A lean workforce of 150 fully empowered employees produces air conditioner compressors in Carrier Corporation's Arkadelphia, Arkansas, plant. Empowered plant employees do not punch a time clock or have to prove illness if absent.

The empowered, team-based workforce in Carrier's highly automated plant is extremely flexible. Workers are trained in several job assignments and can fill in at numerous points on the assembly line. Often, employees interview their prospective manager. The manager will not be hired if employees decide the compatibility between the manager and workers is not just right.[32]

## 13.  INSTITUTE A VIGOROUS PROGRAM OF EDUCATION AND TRAINING

Deming emphasizes training. This includes a thorough foundation in the tools and techniques of quality control, as well as additional instruction in teamwork and the philosophy of a TQM culture.

Infiniti, the luxury car division of Nissan Motor Company, runs a six-day camp for dealer personnel. The goal of the innovative training program is to make Infiniti dealerships unequalled in the treatment of customers. The car maker requires that all dealer employees, even clerks and receptionists, attend the training program conducted every other year in Phoenix, Arizona. Attendees are taught to change their attitudes and no longer think of dealership visitors as "tire kickers" or mere customers. Instead, potential car buyers are to be treated as honored guests. In Japan, honored guest and customer are defined by a single word, *okyakusama.* In 1991, Infiniti tied Toyota's Lexus for first place in J. D. Powers and Associates' annual customer satisfaction survey. While Lexus was rated first in car quality, Infiniti won the overall title for its treatment of customers.[33]

## 14. TAKE ACTION TO ACCOMPLISH THE TRANSFORMATION

According to Deming, the entire organization must work together to enable a quality culture to succeed. As top managers design and implement the strategy, workers can then cooperate in the pursuit of a TQM culture.

Zytec, a 1991 Baldrige winner, has revamped its entire strategic planning process in order to achieve the highest level of quality possible. The company uses formal and informal means to collect data from customers for market research and  to help it improve its own operations. A five-year strategic plan is developed by six cross-functional teams, and then reviewed and critiqued by about 20 percent of the company (150 employees)—from all shifts, departments and expertises. Feedback on the plan is also solicited from a handful of customers and suppliers before it is finalized by Zytec executives.[34]

## TQM: THE MAIN IDEAS

While Deming, Juran and others have specific, detailed approaches to TQM, five main ideas provide the context for these approaches and seem to apply to any TQM method. The five ideas are:

1. A Systems Approach
2. The Tools of TQM
3. A Focus on Customers
4. The Role of Management
5. Employee Participation

### A SYSTEMS APPROACH

The TQM approach depends on understanding organizations as systems. Dobyns and Crawford-Mason delineate three main systems for which managers are responsible: the social or cultural system, the managerial system, and the technical system. Figure 8-2 diagrams these systems.

A **system** is "a series of functions or activities...within an organization that work together for the aim of the organization."[38] Parts of the system must work to support each other. People must cooperate for the good of the whole system or else "suboptimization" occurs. When parts of an organization do not support other parts, then the organization cannot focus on total quality management. A task of management involves having everyone focus on the system aim.

The **cultural system,** also referred to as the *social system,* is the set of beliefs and the resulting behaviors that are shared throughout the organization, as

**system:**

In an organization, the functions and activities that work together to fulfill the purposes of the organization.

**cultural system:**

The set of beliefs and the resulting behaviors that are shared throughout the organization; also called the *social system.*

# SIX SIGMA SIGNALS QUALITY

Everybody at Motorola was proud when they reached their lofty five-year quality goals in 1987. But Motorola management was not satisfied with the new level of quality. When executives visited electronic plants in Japan, they were shocked to find Japanese factories producing at quality levels 2,000 times better than Motorola's factories in the United States.

The company had already relinquished consumer electronics to the Japanese, to focus on industrial applications. When Motorola sold its Chicago television plant to Matsushita in 1974, defects ran at a rate of 150 for every 100 sets produced. By 1979, Matsushita reported a mere four defects for every 100 televisions, using the same American workforce. Motorola could not afford to lose the current competitive battle as a result of quality. The company had to reintensify its quality efforts. "So you look at the competitive threat, and you look closely at what you can offer," advised Galvin, "and you decide you better really renew your organization on the subject of quality."[35]

In 1987, Galvin demanded a more dramatic improvement in quality: to improve from 6,000 defects per million to "Six Sigma" by 1992. Six Sigma defines the concept of achieving approximately zero defects (more precisely, 3.4 defects per million or 99.999 percent defect-free manufacturing). The first step in Motorola's "second generation" quality program was another tenfold quality improvement. Galvin set a timetable to improve product and service quality 10 times by 1989, improve them at least 100 times by 1991 and then hit the Six Sigma goal by 1992.

The quality program's ultimate objective was not only to move toward zero manufacturing defects, but also to improve all levels of customer satisfaction. Motorola named its quality program after its ultimate goal: Total Customer Satisfaction (TCS). TCS provides for continuous improvement in price, delivery, performance, quality, and total customer experience. Of these, quality stands as the linchpin of Motorola's Total Customer Satisfaction program. According to Motorola's Bill Smith, "It includes all the ways in which customers interact with a company, such as receiving an understandable and accurate invoice, obtaining prompt responses to requests for information or technical support, and getting courteous and professional treatment from salespeople."[36]

Motorola set up a process called the "Six Steps to Six Sigma" to deal with the non-manufacturing, more subjective aspects of quality. Steps one and two are to determine the product you make and who your customers are. Step three looks at the suppliers you need to make the product. In step four, workers map out the process to fulfill your mission. Step five involves evaluating the process and eliminating the non-value-added steps or the sources of error. And the sixth step is the establishment of measurement criteria and the drive for continuous improvement.

Motorola doubled its efforts aimed at "designing-in" quality and improving supplier quality. Recognizing that much of the success of their quality improvement efforts rested with their suppliers, Motorola implemented the Certified Supplier Program to improve supplier quality. The program virtually eliminates the need for incoming quality inspections of suppliers' components. By cutting out supplier inspections, Motorola reduces overhead costs and increases its competitive advantage. Motorola also requires pursuit of the Malcolm Baldrige quality award by all of its suppliers.

Engineering, manufacturing, and marketing personnel started working together from day one, to design-in quality. "That design process increasingly has to integrate what the customer feels with what our suppliers can provide," said CEO George Fisher. "So there are two major external forces in addition to getting the parts of the company working together. No longer do you have a situation where you can design a product and throw it over a wall and expect a manufacturing organization to simply make it. We marry our technology development with a deep understanding of our customer needs."[37] →

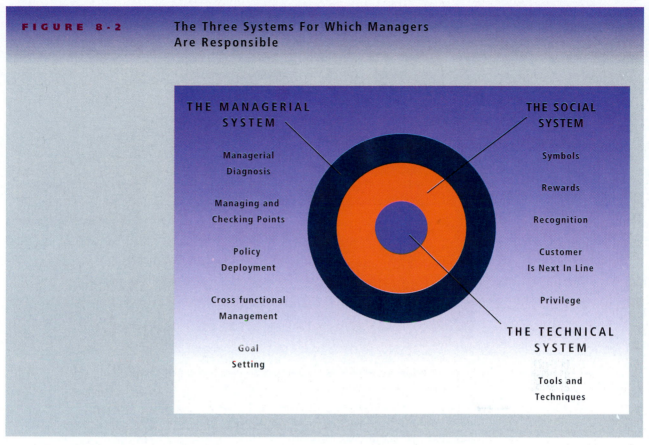

**FIGURE 8-2**  **The Three Systems For Which Managers Are Responsible**

THE MANAGERIAL SYSTEM

Managerial Diagnosis

Managing and Checking Points

Policy Deployment

Cross functional Management

Goal Setting

THE SOCIAL SYSTEM

Symbols

Rewards

Recognition

Customer Is Next In Line

Privilege

THE TECHNICAL SYSTEM

Tools and Techniques

pointed out in Chapter 7.[39] Some companies begin to implement their quality initiatives by trying to change the cultural system.

In 1987, Union Pacific Railroad was reeling from the effects of changing marketplace demands and deregulation. The railroad's large clients were increasing the amount of freight they shipped by truck, and deregulation forced the railroad to compete not only on price, but also on service. After decades of regulation, the railroad had forgotten how to talk to customers. Eight layers of company bureaucracy separated the customer from the executive vice-president for marketing and sales. To recover business, senior managers realized they needed to implement a total quality program; they also recognized that they would first have to change 125 years of stodgy, "set in their ways" railroad culture.

Toward this end, Union Pacific CEO Mike Walsh instituted a mandatory top-to-bottom quality training program, and demonstrated the leadership and commitment coming from the top of the organization. The sustained, ongoing nature of the training enabled the company to overcome the employee skepticism that initially plagued the program. Training was the centerpiece of an eight-pronged Union Pacific Total Quality Strategy, as the company overcame not only the conservative culture of the railroad, but also the lingering cultural differences that had resulted from the merger between Union Pacific and two other railroads.

Union Pacific management successfully installed a "quality" culture. Productivity, as measured by a million gross ton miles per employee, more than doubled. The cost arising from poor quality, such as damaged products and train derailments, decreased from 26 percent of total revenue in 1987 to 12 percent in 1992. Net income grew from $440 million in 1987 to $602 million in 1991.[40]

The **technical system** is "composed of such factors as the technologies used and the physical infrastructure (including ergonomic considerations, computer

**technical system:**
The factors, such as the technology and the physical infrastructure, and the capital investments necessary for an organization to achieve its goals.

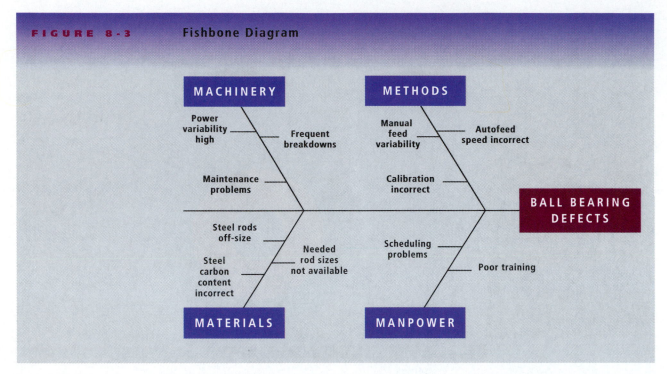

**FIGURE 8-3**     **Fishbone Diagram**

*Source:* Marshall Sashkin and Kenneth J. Kiser, *Putting Total Quality Management to Work* (San Francisco: Berrett-Koehler Publishers, 1993), p. 39. Used with permission.

software, and hardware configurations, and the capital investments needed to accomplish the company's mission)."[41]

Japan's commuter railway, *Shinkansen,* carries 500,000 passengers every day in 1,000 bullet trains over 730 miles of track. The computer system that controls this complex network of fast moving trains requires error-free software. Designers called on Hitachi Software Engineering Corporation to develop the railroad's traffic control system. The Hitachi-developed software has flawlessly controlled the bullet train since 1972. Hitachi Software maintains a comprehensive continuous quality improvement process with a goal of zero defects. The software designer has reduced customer-reported defects from more than 100 per 1000 computers in 1978 to less than four in 1990.[42]

**management system:**
The processes through which an organization manages its human and physical resources and assets.

The **management system** "defines the effectiveness of those processes by which an organization manages its human and physical assets."[43] Continuous quality improvement and worker empowerment translate into smaller, not larger, quality departments. The responsibility for improving quality is given to everyone from workers on the factory floor to senior executives. Motorola typifies this approach. While quality control departments typically measure quality through inspections at the end of the manufacturing process, Total Quality Management requires that workers incorporate attention to quality at every step in the manufacturing process and that managers seek out root causes of variations. Car enthusiasts consider BMW one of the world's most highly engineered and carefully crafted automobiles. BMW's Quality Department shrank from 1,200 people in 1976 to 65 in 1991, while quality simultaneously improved.[44]

**fishbone diagram:**
Diagram used to organize and show visually the possible causes of a problem or event; also called the *cause-and-effect diagram* and the *Ishikawa diagram.*

## THE TOOLS OF TQM

We have already discussed statistical quality control as an important tool and key insight of quality management. But there are other equally important tools. Kaoru Ishikawa popularized a way of diagraming how various factors determine a good or bad outcome in the **fishbone diagram** (Fig. 8.3), also referred to as the *cause-*

**benchmarking:**

The process of finding the best available product features, processes, and services and using them as a standard for improving a company's own products, processes, and services.

*and-effect diagram.* Figure 8-3 is a fishbone diagram that helps to show possible causes of a problem.

Another tool of TQM is **benchmarking,** or comparing your own products and processes against the very best in the world. Xerox uses benchmarking to improve the quality of its products and its customer service.

### BENCHMARKING: A KEY TO CONTINUOUS IMPROVEMENT AT XEROX

In the late 1970s, Xerox turned to benchmarking when it found that foreign competition could sell its equivalent copier at a price equal to Xerox's manufacturing cost. To find a benchmark, Xerox used its Japanese affiliate, Fuji Xerox, as a window into the competition. By observing the efficient processes of selected competitors, Xerox was able to streamline its own operations without compromising service or quality. For instance, Xerox found that it could cut the number of steps in storing and handling material from four to two, saving time and money.

Although Xerox managers looked to the competition in the early days of their benchmarking efforts, they have focused their more recent benchmarking efforts on firms outside the industry. The reason? Managers believe they find their most innovative ideas studying seemingly unrelated firms. In addition, if attention is focused only on the competition, "playing catch-up is the best you can do," according to Robert C. Camp, manager of benchmarking, competency, quality, and customer satisfaction.

For ideas on how to improve their processes for filling customer orders, Xerox turned to L.L. Bean in the early 1980s. Like Xerox, the Freeport, Maine, company ships products that do not come in standard size packages. Additionally, L. L. Bean selects its orders manually, like Xerox, only three times faster. Xerox found that L. L. Bean had superior systems for processing and filling orders.

Xerox has also looked internally for benchmarks, identifying the locations or units within its own organization that have the best processes, then bringing the other locations or units up to the same performance level. This process has improved understanding of operations at Xerox, providing the necessary perspective to make external comparisons valuable.

Since the early 1980s, benchmarking has enabled Xerox to cut manufacturing costs in half and reduce in-process inventories by two-thirds. In addition, it has reduced service labor costs and substantially raised the productivity rate of its distribution organization. In its second decade of benchmarking, Xerox is focusing on improving processes rather than solving problems. The company is firmly committed to continuing use of this tool as an important part of its drive toward continuous improvement.[45] ▪

### A FOCUS ON CUSTOMERS

Many early attempts to improve quality systematically failed precisely because managers became enamored of the tools of quality. They spent a great deal of time creating diagrams, doing statistical process control and benchmarking. If customer needs are not the starting point, though, using the tools of quality may result in products and services that no one wants to buy. Joseph Juran defined quality as "fitness for use"—the ability of a product or service to satisfy a customer's real needs. By focusing on real needs, Juran believes managers and workers can concentrate their efforts where it really matters.

Ford Motor Co. installed a single, nationwide, toll-free customer service telephone system to get a continuous pulse of customer satisfaction. In doing so, the company scrapped a system of regional customer service telephone lines that was frustrating customers with slow response time and frequent busy signals. Customer satisfaction pays. Ford estimates that attracting a new customer costs the company five times more than retaining an old one.[46]

Toyota's focus on customer satisfaction has led to impressive results. While industry sales were dropping in the United States market, Toyota's market share was increasing. Toyota's improvement in customer satisfaction began with a deep commitment from top management. Managers implemented a business plan called "The Toyota Touch," which calls for a "commitment to excellence, concern for superior quality, and caring for people based on communication and cooperation.[47] Toyota also created a corporate-level customer relations organization that reports directly to top management. The company established a Customer Assistance Center whose primary goal is the measurement of customer satisfaction. Forty employees at the center handle over 300,000 calls each year.[48] In addition, the company appoints "Action Dealers" to handle customer complaints. The action dealer has two days to contact the customer and 15 days to resolve the problem. Toyota turns up the heat on poorly performing dealers by assigning them to their "Bottom 20 Dealer Program." Bottom 20 dealers must submit action plans to headquarters that outline their strategy to improve quality.[49]

In 1988, University Microfilms Inc., the country's largest publisher of doctoral dissertations, embarked on a quality improvement program hoping to reduce a growing backlog of 8,000 dissertations. UMI formed quality teams that reduced thesis process time from 150 to 60 days and lowered the backlog to 1,500. Similarly, customer complaints fell 17 percent to a rate of 9 per 1,000 disserta-

**KEEPING CUSTOMERS SATISFIED.** Ford emphasizes keeping existing customers like this one satisfied. High levels of customer satisfaction pay off, because attracting new customers costs five times more than retaining old ones.

tions. Further, UMI intends to increase its output by 30 percent without hiring additional workers. The increase in productivity goes right to bottom-line profits.[50]

## THE ROLE OF MANAGEMENT

Many managers begin with the assumption that where there is a quality problem, the workers or some individual (manager or worker) is to blame. One of the hallmarks of a TQM approach is the questioning of that assumption. TQM implies that when there is a quality problem it begins in the boardroom and in the offices of the senior managers and others who do not take quality seriously enough. For instance, Deming believes that until the system that is the cause of a particular failure in quality can be identified, management cannot do its job. It is every manager's job to seek out and correct the *causes* of failure, rather than merely identify failures after they occur and affix blame to someone. Probably the most famous of all Deming's sayings is that 85 percent of an organization's problems come from the systems and 15 percent from the workers.

When asked why Ford had made such progress on quality, Deming responded that the senior managers believed it was the most important part of their job, and acted on that belief.[51] At Motorola, then-CEO Robert Galvin ensured that quality issues were placed first on all executive board meeting agendas. He would leave shortly after quality issues were discussed, before company financial performance was briefed. Galvin insists he spent 50 percent of his time on quality issues. The former CEO of Xerox, David Kearns, would hold up product launches for the most minor quality flaws, despite protests from his sales organization. Roger Milliken, the CEO of Milliken and Company, made certain that senior management, himself included, received comprehensive quality training before training lower-level employees.[52]

## EMPLOYEE PARTICIPATION

Having the support and attention of senior management remains a necessary condition for making TQM work in an organization, but without empowered employees it won't go very far. **Empowerment** stands for a substantial change that businesses are implementing. It means letting employees make decisions at all levels of an organization without asking for approval from managers. The idea is quite simple: the people who actually do a job, whether it is running a complex machine or providing a simple service, are in the best position to learn how to do that job the best way. Therefore, when there is a chance to improve the job or the systems of which a job is a part, people should make those improvements without asking for permission.

In 1985, there were 23 people in Velcro's quality department. Most employees believed that quality was the responsibility of the quality department. To change this attitude top management empowered rank-and-file workers with the authority and tools necessary to improve quality. Velcro management opened channels of communication with workers on the factory floor. Quality became everyone's job. By 1988, waste had been reduced by over 73 percent as a percentage of total manufacturing expenses. During the same time period, the number of people in the quality department dropped to 12 and their responsibilities shifted from inspection to teaching, coaching, and empowering.[53]

The new GM Saturn plant in Tennessee represents GM's all-out effort to outdo Japanese competitors by implementing American TQM. Decisions are made by teams of people who will be affected by the decision. Every decision must receive at least 70 percent support from all of the team members; failing this, all parties must bring additional facts to the meeting. If the company does not meet its qual-

**empowerment:**
The act of providing authority, knowledge, and resources to individuals so they can achieve work objectives.

**WHO'S JOB IS QUALITY?** Once, quality control meant assigning people to inspect finished work and reject defective products, much like these Hershey workers are doing near the end of the Hershey's Kisses assembly line. With TQM, quality is everyone's job and the goal is to avoid defects from the start.

ity goals, all members, including managers, can lose up to 20 percent of their pay. In addition, employees can receive rewards for exceeding goals.[54]

Seattle-based Satisfaction Guaranteed Eateries empowers its front-line employees to take responsibility for actions once reserved for managers. Employees of the company's five restaurants have been given the authority to do what it takes to satisfy disgruntled customers. This policy, applying even to busboys, allows front-line employees to order free drinks or even pick up the entire dinner check for dissatisfied customers.[55]

## THE BALDRIGE AWARD

**Baldrige award:**
An award given to manufacturing companies, service enterprises, and small businesses to recognize outstanding achievements in the area of quality; it is the greatest honor of its type that an organization can receive in the United States.

A recent commitment to quality in the United States is reflected by the Malcolm Baldrige National Quality Award, referred to commonly as the **Baldrige award** or just "the Baldrige." This award, named after a former secretary of commerce, was created in 1987 to recognize businesses that have made outstanding contributions through their quality efforts. Separate awards are bestowed upon businesses in the areas of manufacturing, service, and small business. In the United States, it is the greatest honor of its type that an organization can receive.

Applicants are judged according to a series of criteria in seven major areas: leadership, effectiveness in collecting and analyzing information, planning, human resources utilization, management of process quality, quality and operational results, and customer focus and satisfaction. Applicants are screened on the basis of a written application and then inspected by a team of examiners who observe operations and interview employees and managers at all levels. Past winners have included Motorola, Federal Express, Xerox Business Products and Systems Group, Solectron, and two AT&T divisions.

The emergence of the Baldrige award has developed a "language of quality" that has provided a general impetus for managers to encourage quality awareness and quality-improvement methods.[56] Far more important than the handful of awards conferred each year is the overall impact of its existence. "It is hard to imagine that the Baldrige process is disruptive to a company," remarked Reimann. "The beauty of it is that it is a self-assessment experience, a self-education program that is wrapped around an award, rather than an award with elaborate criteria."[57] Many companies that do not plan to apply for the award use the application guidelines to guide their own internal quality improvement programs and look to award winners as models. "The Baldrige is a road map to help you improve quality," asserted Patrick Mene, director of quality for Ritz-Carlton Hotel. "It helps you set values and show the cause-and-effect linkage between delivering quality service, satisfied customers, improved productivity and higher profits."[58] Juran, who has defined TQM as consisting of "those actions needed to get to world-class quality," has stated that the Baldrige criteria are the most complete list of what those actions are.[59]

## TIME AND RELATIONSHIPS

We have emphasized how the work of management and managers revolves around time and relationships. Another way of explaining the TQM revolution is to say that it focuses attention on a new sense of time and relationships. Doing the job right the first time requires investing resources in understanding systems and enabling people to improve processes continuously. While you may be able to make a larger quantity of a product by focusing on how many can be produced per unit of time, TQM asks you to focus on increasing the quality of what is produced.

The result of this different sense of time is usually a larger quantity and better quality.

This new sense of time goes hand in hand with a rethinking of what relationships are most important in organizations. First and foremost, the relationship with employees must be rethought. Employees, according to TQM, want responsibility, want to learn and improve, and want to demonstrate self-mastery and achievement. This is a far cry from treating employees as those who need to be helped and motivated to produce quality goods and services.

**MANAGEMENT 2000 AND BEYOND**

# TOM PETERS AND BEYOND QUALITY

In a recent provocative book, *The Tom Peters Seminar: Crazy Times Call for Crazy Organizations,* management guru Tom Peters has challenged managers to think even more creatively about the ideas of dynamic engagement that we have outlined in Chapters 3 through 8. He lists nine areas where managers need to go beyond current thinking, and he claims that "crazy times call for crazy organizations."[60] Exhibit 8-2 presents a table of contents for Peters' book. We want to pay special attention to the idea of "beyond TQM."

Peters' view is that business is in a state of flux. Given the changes we have described in the last few chapters, corporations are in a constant mode of experimentation and change. Hence, the traditional ways of thinking about companies need a similar "revolution," as indicated with the notion of going beyond ideas like TQM. Peters sees the corporation as evolving toward a group of people who call their own shots, who contract with each other and work together in a network to accomplish their ends. The only way to survive today is through creativity and imagination. Companies as diverse as 3M, Microsoft, and

| **EXHIBIT 8-2** | **BEYOND CHANGE: TOWARD THE ABANDONMENT OF EVERYTHING** |
|---|---|

Beyond Decentralization: Disorganizing to unleash imagination
Beyond Empowerment: Turning every job into a business
Beyond Loyalty: Learning to think like an independent contractor
Beyond Disintegration: The corporation as Rolodex
Beyond Reengineering: Creating a Corporate talk show
Beyond Learning: Creating the curious corporation
Beyond TQM: Toward WOW
Beyond Change (Redux): Toward Perpetual Revolution

*Source:* Tom Peters, *The Tom Peters Seminar: Crazy Times Call for Crazy Organizations,* New York: Vintage Press, 1994.

# SUCCESS IN SPITE OF FAILURE

Motorola managers faced the challenge of losing market share because their quality did not match the quality of the competition. The electronics giant had already forfeited one market and was threatened in their last stronghold. The company responded by implementing the quality initiatives advocated by Deming, Juran, and others.

In 1992, Motorola reached a quality level of 5.7 Sigma. Although short of its Six Sigma target, Motorola's results were nonetheless impressive. Sales per employee rose from $62,600 in 1986 to more than $111,000 in 1992. Defects per million fell from 6,000 in 1981 to 40 in 1992. Net cash from operations, sales, capital expenditures, and share price have all more than doubled. While some companies argue that quality costs too much, Motorola proved that quality can be profitable. Richard Buetow, Motorola's Director of Corporate Quality, estimates that the company has saved $1.5 billion as a direct result of its quality commitment.

Customer quality expectations continue to rise. "The world is converging on products that don't fail during their useful life," said Buetow. The quality director predicts that Motorola will target a defect rate of less than two per billion by the year 2001. "We will have to think in terms of perfection even though we may not get there."[61] And, at Motorola, as in other quality leaders, the ways of pursuing quality evolve and change. In 1993, Motorola established a new quality-related goal: reducing the cycle time for everything the company does by a factor of ten over the next five years.

Asea Brown Boveri (ABB) all have come to the realization that it is "brainpower" that separates the winners from the losers.

Unleashing the power of employees to make decisions and think for themselves is a hallmark of TQM systems, especially as advocated by the thinkers in this chapter. Peters suggests that the leading-edge companies today have shifted the focus of their quality programs from Things Gone Wrong (TGW) to Things Gone Right (TGR). The same TQM systems and ideas need to be shifted to allow employees to bring emotion and passion to the workplace to create "things gone right." The experiences to be strived for are "wow" or "gee whiz" ones that employees and customers remember. Peters says in his characteristic style:

> Know what the numbers are, but then explode beyond mechanistic TGW-reduction programs to "wow," "glow," and "tingle." Get closer (much, much closer) to the customer, while remembering that tomorrow's triumphant product is much more likely to emerge from the quirky mind of an inspired lunatic than a buttoned-down, Brooks Brothers male, age 46.5 years, who is trying to cope with the statistical revelation that women are making most of the important buying decisions.[62]

Will the business world of the year 2000 be a bunch of "crazy lunatics" trying to outdo each other in terms of giving customers "peak experiences"? Who knows? Tom Peters envisions more serendipity and creativity and joy than humorless bureaucracy. Perhaps we will have to change our perception that "doing business" is separate from "having fun." In the world of tomorrow, having fun may just be what business is all about.

# SUMMARY

1. **Explain Total Quality Management.**

   Quality has become a factor that organizations can no longer ignore. Managers today are aiming for Total Quality Management, which occurs when an entire organizational culture becomes focused on quality and customer satisfaction through an integrated system of tools, techniques, and training.

2. **Describe the history of quality.**

   Many Japanese companies were successful in achieving revolutionary rates of quality improvement after the second world war. Since that time, quality has become a global standard.

3. **Discuss Deming's fourteen points and other frameworks for guiding management's pursuit of quality.**

   Deming's fourteen points provide an all-encompassing framework for guiding management's pursuit of quality. The Malcolm Baldrige National Quality Award criteria and Juran's trilogy also provide valuable frameworks.

4. **Discuss the role of top management in quality improvement.**

   Top management commitment and leadership are necessary to attain and sustain revolutionary rates of quality improvement.

5. **Discuss the roles of benchmarking and focusing on customers in quality programs.**

   Benchmarking and focusing on customers are two important things managers can do to increase quality.

6. **Explain how employees can be supported in pursuing quality.**

   Empowerment of employees—giving employees the authority, knowledge, and resources to do what is necessary to fulfill their jobs—is part of creating quality within an organization.

## REVIEW QUESTIONS

1. What is Total Quality Management and how does it represent a challenge to prior management practices?
2. What is the historical link between quality concerns and World War II?
3. What are some of the differences between the approaches recommended by Deming and Juran?
4. What is the Juran trilogy?
5. What themes unite Deming's Fourteen Points?
6. What similarities do you see between Deming's Fourteen Points and the human relations model that emerged in the same era?
7. What are the seven key areas covered in the application for the Malcolm Baldrige National Quality Award?

8. What is the relationship between TQM and dealing with customers?

9. How can managers encourage quality?

10. How might managers at a restaurant and a newspaper practice benchmarking?

11. What factors might managers and employees miss if they worked with a "things done wrong" perspective?

12. How can employees be encouraged to pursue quality?

## KEY TERMS

Quality
Total Quality Management
Statistical process control
Quality circle
Constancy of purpose
Continuous improvement
System

Cultural system
Technical system
Management system
Fishbone diagram
Benchmarking
Empowerment
Baldrige award

## CASE STUDY

## RITZ-CARLTON SAYS, MOVE HEAVEN AND EARTH FOR THE CUSTOMER[63]

The Atlanta-based Ritz-Carlton Hotel Corporation operates 23 luxury hotels in the United States and two in Australia. The hotel chain, which employs 11,500 people, claims distinctive facilities and an unusual environment, highly personalized services, and exceptional food and beverages. With average room rates higher than $150 per night, Ritz-Carlton realized it must do more than just please its customers in order to succeed. The hotel, known simply as "The Ritz," did what many experts thought no hotel chain could accomplish: in 1992, the Ritz became the first hotel to win the coveted Malcolm Baldrige National Quality Award.

While the name "Ritz" has been synonymous with quality for years, the luxury hotel chain did not actively begin its quest for total quality management until 1989. It was then that Horst Schulze, Ritz President and CEO, told senior managers that he was not satisfied with hotel quality. He believed that the only reason the chain was considered the leading luxury hotel in the industry was that everyone else was even more unsatisfactory. Schulze therefore introduced a total quality initiative grounded in participatory executive leadership, thorough information gathering, and coordinated planning and execution. A trained, empowered, and committed workforce was another essential element. All employees learn the company's "Gold Standards"—the Ritz's minimum set of standards for premium service.

Schulze and a team of the chain's 14 top executives form the senior management quality team, which meets weekly to review performance and set standards. "They spend a lot of time working on ways to improve our product by talking to as many guests and employees as possible," reported corporate director of quality Patrick Mene.[64]

Ritz-Carlton carefully selects and trains its employees to be quality engineers capable of spotting defects and immediately correcting them. Employees receive 126 hours of annual training on quality issues. Ritz management believes that high-quality personnel reduce costs because they do the job right the first time. The company reinforces its employee improvement program by recognizing superior individual performance. Annual raises are tied to the individual's level of performance, and work teams share in bonus pools when solutions they recommend for quality issues are successfully implemented.

Management empowers employees to "move heaven and earth" to satisfy customers. Whenever a customer complains or a service problem arises, employees are expected to take immediate corrective action. Employees have total authority to do what it takes to satisfy customer needs without waiting for management direction. The Ritz gathers quality data on all aspects of a guest's stay to determine if the customer's expectations are being met. The chain surveys more than 25,000 guests each year to determine where improvements are necessary. Ritz computers maintain data on the likes and dislikes of more than 240,000 repeat customers.

Ritz-Carlton won 121 quality-related awards in 1991, and earned the industry-best ranking by all three major hotel-rating organizations. Surveys indicate that 95 percent of the Ritz's customers rate their stay as a "memorable visit" exceeding their expectations. The 1992 Baldrige Award told Ritz customers and employees what they already knew—the Ritz means quality.

### CASE QUESTIONS

1. How has the Ritz emphasized quality?
2. How has the Ritz benefited from its quality initiatives?
3. Discuss the Ritz in light of Deming's fourteen points.
4. What else could the Ritz do to improve quality?

**THE RITZ-CARLTON CATERS TO ITS CUSTOMERS.** A customer enjoys the peace and beauty of a Ritz-Carlton lobby.

---

## VIDEO CASE STUDY

### THE TOYOTA WAY[65]

At Toyota, quality is about catering to customers. The business plan is called *The Toyota Touch,* because it calls for a long-term philosophy placing the customer *first.*

In achieving quality, Toyota pays close attention to the people it brings into the fold. At Toyota Motor Manufacturing Canada, applicants had to demonstrate communication skills, departmental flexibility, the ability to work in teams, and the initiative to seek out weaknesses and improve them. "We wanted people who wanted to do things differently," recalled Bill Taylor, Toyota's vice-president of manufacturing.[66] Experience in the auto industry was not a prerequisite. In fact, Taylor was among the few employees who could claim any such experience.

The plant in Canada is responsible for part of Toyota's success there. It is equipped with up-to-date machinery and is clean and well-lit. Local competitors, such as Honda Canada Inc., Hyundai, and Cami Automotive Inc. (a joint venture between GM and Suzuki Motor Co.) do not enjoy the same benefits.

Most important, however, is *The Toyota Touch* philosophy, which is interwoven into all operations. Decorating the wall are signs such as, "Customer satisfaction starts at the process" and "Customer satisfaction: the heart of our business."[67] "These may be corny values," remarked Taylor, "but if you believe in them, they pay big dividends."[68]

At Toyota, though, "customer" is a word defined very generally. Managers do not expect initial line workers to be thinking about the end-user all the way down the line. "My customer is the person in front of me," noted line worker Victoria Schumacher. "And I'm the customer of the person before me."[69] This focus on internal customers gives workers a real person to cater to in their own performance.

Respect for co-workers accompanies the attention to the customer. For example, when an error occurs, the line stops and the workers together attempt to fix it. There is no blame-throwing or sulking. "What is significant is what the team does with the problem after the line is stopped," explained Taylor. "No one points a finger at the worker responsible for the problem. Instead the team focuses its energy on the problem. You have to give people room to solve problems themselves. Otherwise you stymie their initiative."[70]

At the same time, Toyota uses errors to the company's benefit through the Japanese process of *kaizen,* or continuous improvement. "When a team sees a problem, they *kaizen* [used as a verb by the Canadians] it and come up with a better way to do the job," noted Adriaan Korstanje, manager of public affairs.[71]

Evidence of *kaizen* is scattered throughout the Toyota plant. For example, the air-driven tracks from which power tools hang—within workers' comfortable reach—resulted from a worker's suggestion.

And it was the company's maintenance team that built the tracks. Workers also came up with the idea for the set of rollers that batteries slide down, making the job easier for the workers who install batteries in cars.

*Kaizen* has also come in the form of challenges to employees. Unlike other North American auto manufacturers, Toyota does not employee a single industrial engineer. Instead, Toyota relies on Toyota employees. In 1990, when the company wanted to increase productivity from 50,000 to 65,000 cars a year, management challenged employees to make it happen. Through *kaizen,* employees were able to improve processes and reduce total production time by 30 seconds a car, a significant reduction.

The philosophy of *kaizen* extends also to the administrative offices. A sense of community exists among the 200 administrative employees, most of whom work in a single open room approximately the size of a gymnasium. "It took some adjustment," commented Bill Easdale, senior vice-president of administration and former vice-president of personnel and industrial relations at de Havilland Aircraft of Canada Ltd. "I came from an organization where the executive offices were big and leather-lined, and had their own washrooms. We had secretaries who watched over our appointments. Here, if people have a question, they just walk up to your desk. It gets a little noisy at times, but I welcome the change. The biggest difference is that my own productivity has dropped, but the productivity of the people who work with me has gone way up. And that's the way it should be."[72]

At Toyota, quality is not about superficial glamour inside the plant. Rather, it is about the way managers treat employees, co-workers treat one another, and the company treats its customers. It is a way of life.

### CASE QUESTIONS

1. What are the factors that lead to Toyota's success in achieving high levels of quality?

2. In what other organizations or types of organizations would *kaizen* work well? Where might it fail?

3. What should Toyota consider doing better?

# PLANNING

# INTERSECTION 3

The themes discussed in Part II are what managers must keep in mind as they make strategic decisions and plan for the future of their organizations. This is what Part III addresses—planning. Through the art of decision making, managers constantly shape and reshape their organizations. They decide in what direction they want their organizations to go, and make the plans and decisions to get them there.

In Chapter 9, we discuss the art of decision making in general and point out the challenges and difficulties that can emerge. We then devote Chapter 10 to planning, which is a particular type of decision making. Planning does not have a specific beginning and end; rather, it is an ongoing process. Then, having discussed how managers arrive at suitable strategies for their organizations through the planning and decision-making processes, we move on to Chapter 11, where we consider the keys to successfully implementing these strategies. Dynamic engagement remains an important concern in Part III, for it is by drawing from past experiences that managers are able to guide future actions more successfully.

## CHAPTER 9

# DECISION MAKING

Upon completing this chapter, you should be able to:

1. Connect decision making with the idea that managers deal with time and human relationships.

2. See decision making as a complex problem of psychology and of understanding one's world.

3. Distinguish programmed decisions from nonprogrammed decisions.

4. Explain the rational decision making process.

5. Put rational decision making in perspective as a process affected by bounded rationality, satisficing and heuristics.

6. Explain how game theory and chaos theory describe the larger context in which managers decide.

# THE END OF AN ERA . . . OR IS IT[1]?

On October 6, 1993, 30-year old Michael Jordan, the Chicago Bulls' gravity-defying basketball star, retired from the National Basketball Association (NBA). In the wake of the untimely death of his father, he decided to put an end—for the time being, at least—to his professional basketball career.

Philip H. Knight, founder and CEO of Nike, could not help but wonder how Jordan's decision would affect Nike. After all, Michael Jordan's endorsement of Nike athletic shoes has substantially contributed to the company's tremendous success. Although Jordan retired from the NBA, not from his relationship with Nike, Knight was left to ponder how Jordan's decision would affect Nike, and how the shoe company should respond.

The Nike/Jordan story began in the mid-1980s, when Nike managers felt the company slipping from its position as the leading athletic shoe maker in the United States. In 1984, company earnings dropped for the first time in a decade. In 1985, competitor Reebok even captured the market share lead for a short period of time.

Although the fitness craze of the early 1980s had given the athletic shoe market a boost, by the mid-1980s the market was experiencing a general slowdown. In addition, Nike managers realized that they had lagged behind their competitors in responding to demands for increasingly specialized shoe types. Knight knew the company needed a jump start. Enter Jordan.

*Nike people concentrated their efforts on a single goal: Air Jordan.*

Teaming up with Jordan coincided with Nike's underlying specialization strategy, which included focusing on products such as basketball shoes. What Jordan brought to Nike was *image*. Although Jordan was still a rookie with the Chicago Bulls at that time, he had already made a name for himself, both

No bird soars too high,
If he soars with his own wings.
—William Blake

in college basketball with the University of North Carolina and through the 1984 Olympic basketball team triumph in Los Angeles. And that was what Nike was banking on. About the success of spokespeople, Louis Stern, professor of marketing at Northwestern's J. J. Kellogg Graduate School of Management, has said, "It's not as if advertising spokespeople just emerged. . . . It's that these people are so significant in our lives because of the media, and that their image seems to radiate far beyond their presence as mere human beings."[2]

After striking a deal with Nike, Jordan went on to become one of the most celebrated sports figures of all time, both as an athlete and as a product endorser. The "Air Jordan" line of basketball shoes is a product inextricably linked to a star. With Jordan on board, Nike was able to introduce and carry out one of the most successful marketing strategies ever. Nike people concentrated their efforts on a single goal: Air Jordan. "We pointed all our guns in the same direction, firing all at once-the product, the athlete, TV and print ads, point-of-purchase displays," recalled Ron Parham, Nike's director of investor relations. "Every corporate marketing resource was aligned and timed to coincide [with] and support the introduction of Air Jordans."[3]

In one of the greatest marketing stories of all times, Jordan "rescued" Nike from six consecutive quarters of declining earnings. "He changed the game completely," remarked Parham. "He changed basketball and he changed the endorsement game."[4] Nike expected to sell 100,000 pairs of Air Jordan basketball shoes in the first year they were introduced; actual sales reached closer to three or four million pairs. "Air Jordan has become our Cabbage Patch doll," said the Nike spokesman. "It's one of the best things that's ever happened to us."[5] →

**decision making:**

The process of identifying and selecting a course of action to solve a specific problem.

**M**ANAGEMENT IS THE practice of consciously and continually shaping formal organizations, and the art of decision making is central to doing that. ***Decision making**—identifying and selecting a course of action to deal with a specific problem or take advantage of an opportunity—is an important part of every manager's job. We all make decisions, of course. What sets the practice of management apart is the systematic, specialized attention that managers give to decision making. Decision making is Philip Knight's specialty as chief executive officer at Nike.

In this chapter, we will describe the traditional process of decision making, the factors that go into decision making, and some of the difficulties that can arise in selecting a course of organizational action. We will conclude with an overview of two emerging approaches to decision making—game theory and chaos theory.

## TIME AND HUMAN RELATIONSHIPS IN DECISION MAKING

**T**ime and human relationships are crucial elements in the process of making decisions. Decision making connects the organization's present circumstances to actions that will take the organization into the future. Decision making also draws on the past; past experiences—positive and negative—play a big part in determining which choices managers see as feasible or desirable. Objectives for the future are thus based, in part, on past experiences. For instance, declining sales of Nike products helped turn managers' attention to basketball and Michael Jordan.

In some cultures, human relationships take on even more importance in deciding about business dealings than they do in the United States. For example, the  Chinese believe that even the most comprehensive plan will always involve unforeseen problems. To solve these, one must rely on a network of relationships. Therefore, the Chinese are more interested in a long-standing and sincere commitment to working together than in apparently perfect contracts that appear to contain no loopholes. The Chinese believe that a signed contract marks the end of the first stage in business dealings, not a final agreement. With his or her signature, a signatory to any contract automatically establishes himself or herself as a "friend" with a responsibility to help maintain a "win-win" agreement if difficulties arise. It is considered not only a business necessity, but also a matter of reputation and face.[6]

A manager, of course, does not make decisions in isolation. While he or she is making decisions, other decisions are being made by people both within the same

---

\* Many textbooks sharply distinguish decision making from problem solving. Solving problems often requires making more than one decision.

organization and outside, at other businesses, government offices, and social organizations. When managers project possible consequences of their own decisions, they must be conscious that other people's decisions may conflict or interact with their own. Decision making, in short, is a process that managers conduct in relationship with other decision makers. For instance, Knight and his colleagues at Nike were making their decisions at the same time that Michael Jordan (a businessperson in his own right) was making his own business decisions. This phenomenon is highlighted in the emerging approaches known as game theory and chaos theory, discussed in "Management 2000 and Beyond" at the end of the chapter.

# PROBLEM AND OPPORTUNITY FINDING

**problem:**
Situation that occurs when an actual state of affairs differs from a desired state of affairs.

**D**ecision making deals with problems. A **problem** arises when an actual state of affairs differs from a desired state of affairs. In many cases, a problem may be an opportunity in disguise. The *problem* of customer complaints about slow delivery of orders could, for example, also be seen as an *opportunity* to redesign production processes and customer service. Because managers face many problems and opportunities, we will begin our discussion by looking at the factors that help effective managers recognize both problems and opportunities. Then we will look at the circumstances that lead managers to act.

For 35 African-American farmers, members of a Georgia small-farm association, recognizing a problem was the first step to identifying an opportunity. With most of their soybeans sold as animal feed for a modest profit, the farmers were just scraping by. Thinking globally, the farmers contacted 84-year-old long-time Atlanta resident Seiho Tajiri. He agreed that if they were to grow a better grade of soybean, there could be an opportunity for them in his native Japan, which produces only a small portion of the soybeans it needs. With Tajiri's assistance, a group of the farmers traveled to Japan in 1993 and negotiated an order for 200 tons of soybeans from Takano Foods, the largest maker of natto, a fermented soybean dish that is a favorite of the Japanese. Now the farmers are looking towards increasing their global trade opportunities. As third-generation farmer Lucious Abrams says, "They need the soybeans, we need the market."[7]

## THE PROBLEM-FINDING PROCESS

William Pounds has argued that the problem-finding process is often informal and intuitive. Four situations usually alert managers to possible problems.[8]

1. A *deviation from past experience* means that a previous pattern of performance in the organization has been broken. This year's sales are falling behind last year's; expenses have suddenly increased; employee turnover has risen. Events such as these are signals to the manager that a problem has developed.

2. A *deviation from a set plan* means the manager's projections or expectations are not being met. Profit levels are lower than anticipated; a department is exceeding its budget; a project is off schedule. Such events tell the manager that something must be done to get the plan back on course.

3. *Other people* often bring problems to the manager. Customers complain about late deliveries; higher-level managers set new performance standards for the manager's department; employees resign. Many decisions that managers make daily involve problems presented by others.

4. The *performance of competitors* can also create problem-solving situations. When other companies develop new processes or improvements in operating procedures, the manager may have to reevaluate processes or procedures in his or her own organization.

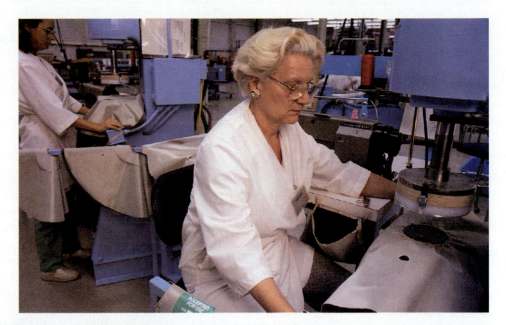

**PROBLEM RECOGNITION.**
Problem recognition can not be separated from the historical time in which managers make decisions. In the early years of the auto industry, passenger safety was less a concern than it is today, as we can see in the development of air bags.

## IDENTIFYING A PROBLEM AT COCA-COLA

Coca-Cola USA managers in Atlanta identified a training problem in 1992. They had launched a massive quality training program in 1989 in which all 1,500 workers learned techniques such as problem solving, statistical-process control, and process management. But three years later, most employees had completely forgotten the tools they had learned. The problem: They had never had a chance to use those tools in the workplace. In 1993, Coca-Cola managers modified the training program to address this problem. Employees were provided with training as they needed it instead of all at once. Ken Levine, Atlanta division manager of continuous improvement, explains:

> Rather than training all associates in the beginning of a TQM initiative to understand a myriad of tools they may never use, it's useful to train teams as they form. Using this just-in-time approach, real problems can be used to illustrate tools and techniques. This will accelerate the ability of teams to begin to solve problems and improve processes.[9]

Coca-Cola learned the hard way that the maxim "If you don't use it, you lose it" is painfully accurate. In this case, the problem was found through a deviation from a set plan (that is, employees were not using the TQM tools).

Alert managers often sense problems early. A study by Marjorie A. Lyles and Ian I. Mitroff included data from case histories from upper-level managers of major organizations. Eighty percent of these managers said they had become aware of the existence of a major problem before it showed up on financial statements or in other formal indicators—and even before it was presented to them by others. "Informal communication and intuition" were described as the sources of their information.[10]

Problem finding is not always straightforward. Sara Kiesler and Lee Sproull have identified some of the most common errors managers make in sensing problems. They describe three main categories of pitfalls that managers often encounter: false association of events, false expectation of events, and false self-perceptions and social image. For example, during the 1960s and early 1970s, managers at mainframe computer manufacturers had false expectations: They believed that a significant demand for personal computers did not and probably never would exist. Their expectations were at odds with the reality that developed.[11] Here is a case where these managers' past experiences were not a reliable guide to future events. The past can play an important part in decision making, but that does not mean that what happened in the past will automatically continue to happen in the future.

## OPPORTUNITY FINDING

**opportunity:**
Situation that occurs when circumstances offer an organization the chance to exceed stated goals and objectives.

**dialectical inquiry method:**
A method of analysis in which a decision maker determines and negates his or her assumptions, and then creates "countersolutions" based on the negative assumptions; also called the *devil's advocate method* .

It is not always clear whether a situation faced by a manager presents a problem or an opportunity. As we have noted, the two are often intertwined. For example, missed opportunities create problems for organizations, and opportunities are often found while exploring problems.[12] David B. Gleicher, a management consultant, provides a useful distinction between the two terms. He defines a problem as something that endangers the organization's ability to *reach* its objectives, and an **opportunity** as something that offers the chance to *exceed* objectives.[13]

The **dialectical inquiry method,** sometimes called the *devil's advocate method,* is useful in problem solving and opportunity finding.[14] In this method, the decision maker determines possible solutions and the assumptions they are based on, considers the opposite of all of the assumptions, and then develops countersolutions based on the negative assumptions. This process may generate more useful alternative solutions and identify unnoticed opportunities.

An enormous amount of research has been devoted to problem *solving,* whereas very little research concerns problem *finding* and even less concerns opportunity finding. Yet, as Peter Drucker makes clear, opportunities—rather than problems—are the key to organizational and managerial success. Drucker observes that solving a problem merely restores normality, whereas progress "must come from the exploitation of opportunities." Drucker links exploitation of opportunities to effectiveness—finding "the right things to do, and . . . [concentrating] resources and efforts on them."[15] When decision making is linked to opportunity finding, it clearly involves choosing actions that can help make a future for the organization. At Nike, Knight and his colleagues turned a problem into an opportunity when they used the NBA rule about the acceptable color of basketball shoes as an opportunity to market the shoe more cleverly.

Among those who have identified an opportunity to exploit are young entrepreneurs Todd Holmes and Louis Amorosa. Noting that many people seemed to be drinking less beer but experimenting with and enjoying a wider range of beers, the two friends founded "Beer Across America," a microbrewery beer-of-the-month club, in 1991, when they were 23. By 1994 theirs was one of a half dozen beer clubs around the country allowing access to a wide range of brewers and beers. Members receive selected beers, both domestic and imported, via UPS, for about the same price as charged by retailers. In 1993 Beer Across America reported $12 million in sales.[16]

## DECIDING TO DECIDE

The idea that managers are problem solvers may conjure up the image of managers sitting behind desks, calmly deciding what to do about every problem that arises. In fact, managers differ widely with regard to what they consider to be a problem and how they elect to deal with it.

**OPPORTUNITY FINDING.** Household recycling stations are just one of many products now on the market that capitalize on the emergence of recycling as a major trend.

## THRESHOLDS FOR PROBLEM RECOGNITION

How big is the gap between the actual and desired state of affairs? How does this gap affect our chances of reaching or exceeding goals for the organization? If this gap is a problem, how hard will it be to fix? How quickly do we need to move to fix the problem or to take advantage of an opportunity? These are the sorts of questions managers ask when defining a situation as either a problem or an opportunity. Some of the answers can be found in standards for performance that managers set for their organizations. To answer such questions effectively, managers must use their judgment based on their knowledge of the environment for their organizations. That is why *information gathering,* through either formal or informal systems, is such an important role of an effective manager.

As William Guth and Renato Tagiuri have noted, though, the information gathered is filtered through managers' values and backgrounds. Their values and backgrounds also influence the types of problems and opportunities they choose to work on.[17] If managers are motivated primarily by economic values, they usually want to make decisions on practical matters, such as those involving marketing, production, or profits. If they are particularly concerned about the natural environment, they might aggressively seek out problems and opportunities with ecological implications. If their orientation is political, they may be more concerned with competing with other organizations or with their own personal advancement.

← Ch. 8, p. 225

With the current importance of quality and continuous improvement, benchmarking is one type of information gathering that is assuming increasing importance for organizations. For instance, in 1990 top managers at Digital Equipment Corporation decided to adopt benchmarking to improve every functional area. In the public relations department, a team was appointed to work with 25 practitioners under the guidance of a benchmarking manager. They established five areas of study, such as media relations, and identified 20 companies (including Whirlpool, Apple, and Hewlett-Packard) to interview by telephone to gather information. Even competitors cooperated in answering their 25 questions; in today's climate of strategic alliances and partnerships, industries are more willing to open up and share information. Of the 20 companies, 4 were selected to be visited in order to get more in-depth answers in areas of expertise. After all the data was assembled and analyzed, DEC used the information as a basis for decisions on new ideas and approaches.[18]

The backgrounds and expertise of managers will also influence what they see as problems and opportunities. A study of executives by De Witt C. Dearborn and Herbert A. Simon found that managers from different departments will define the same problem in different terms.[19] In their study, individual executives tended to be sensitive to those parts of an issue that related to their own departments, defining opportunities and problems from their own particular perspectives. For example, marketing managers want inventory to be high and view low inventory as a problem situation. Finance managers, on the other hand, view a high-inventory situation as a problem, preferring low inventory in most cases.[20]

**SETTING PRIORITIES.** No manager can possibly handle every problem that arises in the daily course of business. It is important, therefore, that managers learn to establish priorities. These priorities can help a manager determine how quickly, how intensively, and how collaboratively he or she must deal with the problem. When doing this, some questions can be useful guides:

**IS THE PROBLEM EASY TO DEAL WITH?** A manager who gives the same level of attention to every problem will get very little work done. Most problems, however, require only a small amount of the manager's attention. Even if the decision turns out to be wrong, correcting it will be relatively speedy and inexpensive. To avoid getting bogged down in trivial details, effective and efficient managers reserve formal decision-making techniques for problems that truly require them.

**TALKING IT THROUGH.** Most decisions are not made in isolation. Rather, they are made in the context of relationships with others. Managers are finding that the best results emerge through teamwork, where people contribute varied insights.

**MIGHT THE PROBLEM RESOLVE ITSELF?** Managers find that an amazing number of time-wasting problems can be eliminated if they are simply ignored. Therefore, managers should rank problems in order of importance. Those at the bottom of the list usually take care of themselves or can be dealt with by others. If one of these problems worsens, it moves to a higher-priority level on the list.

**IS THIS MY DECISION TO MAKE?** When confronted with an important problem requiring a decision, a manager must determine if he or she is actually responsible for making the decision. Here a general rule can be of help: The closer to the origin of the problem the decision is made, the better. Usually, those who are closest to a problem are in the best position to decide what to do about it. This rule has two corollaries: (a) pass as few decisions as possible to those higher up in the organization, and (b) pass as many as possible to those lower down in the organization.

When managers refer an issue to someone higher up for a decision, they have to be sure they are not simply passing the buck instead of being properly cautious. How can managers decide when they should pass a problem on? If our basic rule and its corollaries do not supply the answer, managers can supplement them with a few other questions. Does the issue affect other departments? Will it have a major impact on someone else's area of responsibility? Does it require information available only from a higher level? Does it involve a serious breach of our departmental budget? Is this problem outside my area of responsibility or authority? A "yes" answer to any of these questions indicates the issue should probably be referred to someone higher ranking in the organization.

Note that these questions once again suggest that a manager makes decisions in the context of relationships with others. Sitting alone at a desk is not a useful, or realistic, image of decision making.

# THE NATURE OF MANAGERIAL DECISION MAKING

**D**ifferent problems require different types of decision making. Routine or minor matters, such as a return of merchandise, can be handled by a set procedure, a

**NONPROGRAMMED DECISION MAKING.** While there are generally policies and procedures in place to guide decision making in an emergency, havoc resulting from the 1994 Los Angeles-area earthquake, such as the collapse of sections of the Santa Monica freeway, clearly call for nonprogrammed decision making.

type of *programmed decision.* More important decisions, such as the location of a new retail outlet, require a *nonprogrammed decision,* a specific solution created through a less structured process of decision making and problem solving. Because all decisions involve future events, managers must also learn to analyze the *certainty, risk,* and *uncertainty* associated with alternative courses of action.

## PROGRAMMED AND NONPROGRAMMED DECISIONS

**programmed decisions:**
Solutions to routine problems determined by rule, procedure, or habit.

**Programmed decisions** are made in accordance with written or unwritten *policies, procedures,* or *rules* (see Chapter 11) that simplify decision making in recurring situations by limiting or excluding alternatives. For example, managers rarely have to worry about the salary range for a newly hired employee because organizations generally have a salary scale for all positions. Routine procedures exist for dealing with routine problems.[21]

Programmed decisions are used for dealing with recurring problems, whether complex or uncomplicated. If a problem recurs, and if its component elements can be defined, predicted, and analyzed, then it may be a candidate for programmed decision making. For example, decisions about how much inventory of a given product to maintain can involve a great deal of fact-finding and forecasting, but careful analysis of the elements in the problem may yield a series of routine, programmed decisions. For Nike, buying television advertising time is a programmed decision.

To some extent, programmed decisions limit our freedom because the individual has less latitude in deciding what to do. However, programmed decisions are actually intended to be liberating. The policies, rules, or procedures by which we make programmed decisions save time, allowing us to devote attention to other, more important activities. For example, deciding how to handle customer complaints on an individual basis would be time-consuming and costly, but a policy stating "exchanges will be permitted on all purchases within 14 days" simplifies matters considerably. The customer service representative is then freed to deal with thornier issues.

**nonprogrammed decisions:**
Specific solutions created through an unstructured process to deal with nonroutine problems.

**Nonprogrammed decisions** deal with unusual or exceptional problems. If a problem has not come up often enough to be covered by a policy or is so important that it deserves special treatment, it must be handled as a nonprogrammed deci-

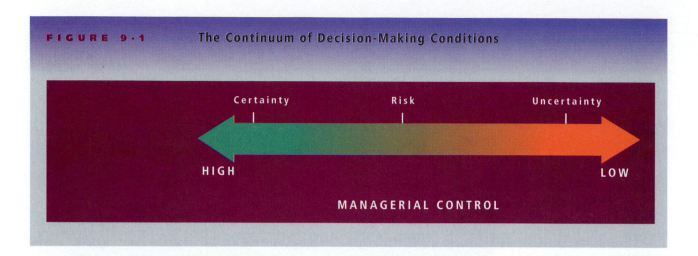

**FIGURE 9-1**    The Continuum of Decision-Making Conditions

Certainty          Risk          Uncertainty

HIGH                                          LOW

MANAGERIAL CONTROL

sion. Problems such as how to allocate an organization's resources, what to do about a failing product line, how community relations should be improved—in fact, most of the significant problems a manager will face—usually require nonprogrammed decisions. How to design and market newer, more advanced basketball shoes is an example of a nonprogrammed decision at Nike. Knight enters uncharted waters when it comes to creating the sequel to Air Jordans.

As one moves up the organizational hierarchy, the ability to make nonprogrammed decisions becomes more important. For this reason, most management-development programs try to improve managers' abilities to make nonprogrammed decisions, usually by teaching them to analyze problems systematically and to make logical decisions.

More and more organizations have made their commitment to social responsibility a matter of policy involving both programmed and nonprogrammed decisions.

For example, Lotus, the computer software company, has a policy of donating one percent of its profits to philanthropic events and organizations. Thus how much to spend on charity is a programmed decision. Exactly how the money is spent, however, is a nonprogrammed decision. A committee made up of all ranks of employees decides where the money will be allocated. Past projects have included the funding of the television documentary on the civil rights movement, "Eyes on the Prize," and sponsorship of the 1991 AIDS Walk in Boston. The committee's focus is to concentrate on underfunded projects.[22]

## CERTAINTY, RISK, AND UNCERTAINTY

In making decisions, all managers must weigh alternatives, many of which involve future events that are difficult to predict, such as a competitor's reaction to a new price list, interest rates in three years, or the reliability of a new supplier. Decision-making situations are frequently categorized on a continuum ranging from *certainty* (highly predictable), through *risk,* to *uncertainty* (highly unpredictable) (see Figure 9-1).[23]

**certainty:**
Decision making condition in which managers have accurate, measurable, and reliable information about the outcome of various alternatives under consideration.

**CERTAINTY.** Under conditions of **certainty,** we know our objective and have accurate, measurable, reliable information about the outcome of each alternative we are considering. Consider, for example, the director who must order programs for a storytelling festival. She knows the objective—get programs printed—and can easily compare representative samples from local printers and the prices they quote for printing varying quantities of programs. With this information, she can select a printer and know with certainty what the printing will cost. This information will *not* help her make a more difficult decision, though: *How many* programs should she order? In making this decision, she must consider the fact that, while she doesn't want to run short of programs, ordering too many wastes money that could be better spent ordering high-margin souvenir items such as tee-shirts or sweatshirts. The director now moves from conditions of certainty to conditions of risk or uncertainty. Unfortunately, such conditions are far more common than conditions of certainty.

**risk:**
Decision-making condition in which managers know the probability a given alternative will lead to a desired goal or outcome.

**probability:**
A statistical measure of the chance a certain event or outcome will occur.

**RISK. Risk** occurs whenever we cannot predict an alternative's outcome with certainty, but we do have enough information to predict the **probability** it will lead to the desired state. (If you have ever flipped a coin to make a decision or played a roulette wheel, you have dealt with probabilities.) If this is the tenth annual story-telling festival held in this town at this time of the year, the director can analyze the data available to determine, albeit with some risk, the number of programs likely to be needed. If this is the event's first year, though, the director faces *uncertainty.*

When Bank of America and Security Pacific banks merged in 1992, experts predicted the combination would crush the competition. But what was seen as a "certainty" turned out to be uncertain. As the banks combined operations, over 450 branches were closed. Other, smaller California banks took advantage of the opportunity this presented, advertising increased security and availability of branches. For example, Great Western Bank used actor Dennis Weaver in TV ads: "Used to be a bank here. One day it was in business; next day it was gone." The Bank of Fresno, Redlands Federal, and Sanwa Bank of California are among those who have lured customers with a variety of tactics. Sanwa, for instance, set up sidewalk card tables across the street from closing branches to sign up new customers.[24]

**uncertainty:**
Decision-making condition in which managers face unpredictable external conditions or lack the information needed to establish the probability of certain events.

**UNCERTAINTY.** Under conditions of **uncertainty,** little is known about the alternatives or their outcomes. Uncertainty arises from two possible sources. First, managers may face external conditions that are partially or entirely beyond their control, such as the weather—an important factor for a three-day festival held in outdoors tents. Second and equally important, the manager may not have access to key information. If this is a new festival, perhaps the director has not formed a network with other festival directors who could share valuable information about likely attendance records. Or perhaps no one can accurately predict the turnout for a new storytelling festival held in the fall, when many families are busy with school activities and other events.

## NORWEST: PLAYING IT SAFE IN GLOBAL LENDING

At Minneapolis-based Norwest Corporation, managers prefer to operate in an area between certainty and risk, avoiding uncertainty. The old adage "nothing ventured, nothing gained" has never held any wisdom for Lloyd Johnson, chairman and chief executive officer. For years Lloyd Johnson has avoided risk and expanded only into areas of banking that produce fees without consuming capital. In 1990, while the nation's top banks were reeling from bad debt, Norwest posted record profits. Earnings rose 37 percent to $281 million, producing a powerful 19.6 percent return on equity and a 1.06 percent return on assets. In the same year Norwest's assets rose nearly $7 billion. Norwest's reserves are at 160 percent of nonperforming loans. Can this success really be attributed to playing it safe? It would seem so.

Norwest has not made a nonguaranteed Third World loan since 1984. Of the company's 1990 income, 37 percent came from no-risk, non-interest sources such as fees. For example, when a Norwest technology client asked for $11 million in trade finance

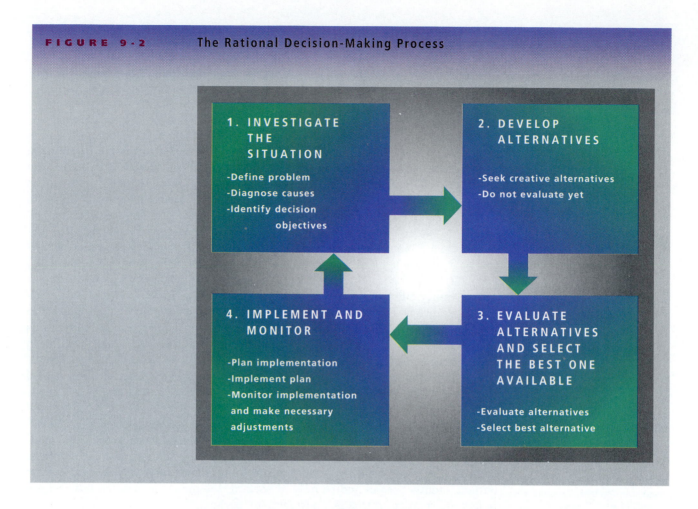

**FIGURE 9-2**    The Rational Decision-Making Process

1. INVESTIGATE THE SITUATION
-Define problem
-Diagnose causes
-Identify decision objectives

2. DEVELOP ALTERNATIVES
-Seek creative alternatives
-Do not evaluate yet

4. IMPLEMENT AND MONITOR
-Plan implementation
-Implement plan
-Monitor implementation and make necessary adjustments

3. EVALUATE ALTERNATIVES AND SELECT THE BEST ONE AVAILABLE
-Evaluate alternatives
-Select best alternative

for a deal in China, the company refused to lend a dime. Instead, Norwest organized a consortium of banks that gave the client the capital required. "In the old days we would have provided all the money ourselves and made about $170,000 on the deal," says Darin Narayana, executive vice president in charge of international banking. "Instead we made $85,000 in fees—at no risk."[25]

# THE RATIONAL MODEL OF DECISION MAKING

**rational model of decision making:**
A four-step process that helps managers weigh alternatives and choose the alternative with the best chance of success.

**M**anagers who weigh their options and calculate optimal levels of risk are using the **rational model of decision making.**[26] This model is especially useful in making nonprogrammed decisions. It helps managers go beyond *a priori reasoning,* the assumption that there is an obvious solution already existing and simply waiting to be found.[27]

No approach to decision making can guarantee that a manager will always make the right decision. But managers who use a rational, intelligent, and systematic approach are more likely than other managers to come up with high-quality solutions. This belief has guided managers for many, many years. It is an article of faith that we can trace to the managerial approaches of Henry Ford, Henri Fayol, and Chester Barnard (see Chapter 2).

The basic process of rational decision making involves the four stages shown in Figure 9-2 and discussed in the following sections.[28]

## STAGE 1: INVESTIGATE THE SITUATION

A thorough investigation has three aspects: problem definition, diagnosis, and identification of objectives.

**DEFINE THE PROBLEM.** Confusion in problem definition arises in part because the events or issues that attract the manager's attention may be symptoms of another more fundamental and pervasive difficulty. A manager may be concerned about an upsurge in employee resignations, but this is not a problem unless it interferes with the achievement of organizational objectives. If the individuals resigning are relatively low performers, and more qualified replacements can be readily found, the resignations may represent an opportunity rather than a problem. Curing the turnover problem, then, may be the last thing the manager should do. Defining the problem in terms of the organizational objectives that are being blocked helps to avoid confusing symptoms with problems.

**DIAGNOSE THE CAUSES.** All this underscores the importance of diagnosing the causes of the problem. Managers can ask a number of diagnostic questions. Each involves, in some way, human relationships: What changes inside or outside the organization may have contributed to the problem? What people are most involved with the problem situation? Do they have insights or perspectives that may clarify the problem? Do their actions contribute to the problem?

Causes, unlike symptoms, are seldom apparent, and managers sometimes have to rely on intuition to identify them. Different individuals, whose views of the situation are inevitably shaped by their own experiences and responsibilities, may perceive very different causes for the problem. It is up to the manager to put all the pieces together and come up with as clear a picture as possible.

 At Ruiz Foods, a California-based Mexican-food company, founder and CEO Fred Ruiz realized that one cause of difficulty for immigrant employees was the language barrier. His solution, offering classes in English literacy, is just part of a larger picture of concern for employees and employee development.

Ruiz started his small, family-run business with his mother's recipes, her freezer and MixMaster, and a small commercial stove that he built. His is a family-oriented business that he tries to run as a Mexican-American role model for its employees, other minority-owned businesses, and the community. Embracing the concept of *familia* (family), the company actively encourages the recruitment and hiring of family members—both members of the Ruiz family and those of current employees. English literacy classes (80 percent of the employees speak Spanish) are just part of the training offered to Ruiz employees, who are encouraged to grow both personally and professionally. Training in math skills, computer skills, and management development has not only benefited the employees, but has helped Ruiz Foods more than triple its sales.[29]

**IDENTIFY THE DECISION OBJECTIVES.** Once the problem has been defined and the cause(s) diagnosed, the next step is to decide what would constitute an effective solution. Most problems consist of several elements, and a manager is unlikely to find one solution that will work for all of them.

If a solution enables managers to achieve organizational objectives, it is a successful one. However, more ambitious objectives may be appropriate. The immediate problem may be an indicator of future difficulties a manager can prevent by taking early action. Or the problem may offer the opportunity to improve, rather than merely restore, organizational performance.

What should be noted about all three aspects of problem investigation is the importance of a manager's education about the world and his or her imagination!

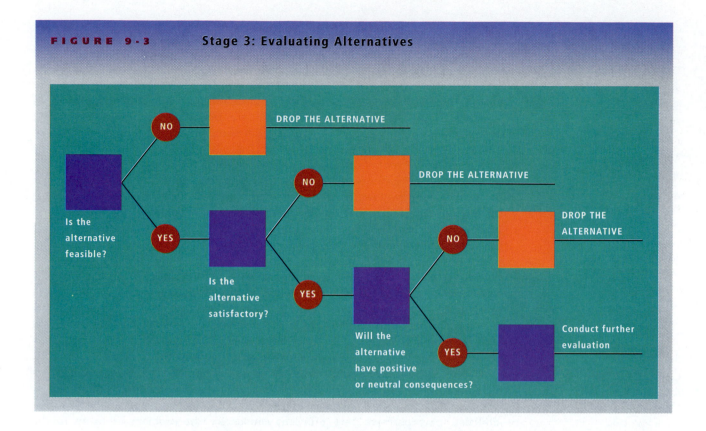

**FIGURE 9-3**     Stage 3: Evaluating Alternatives

Is the alternative feasible?

NO → DROP THE ALTERNATIVE

YES → Is the alternative satisfactory?

NO → DROP THE ALTERNATIVE

YES → Will the alternative have positive or neutral consequences?

NO → DROP THE ALTERNATIVE

YES → Conduct further evaluation

**brainstorming:**
Decision making and problem solving technique in which individuals or group members try to improve creativity by spontaneously proposing alternatives without concern for reality or tradition.

## STAGE 2: DEVELOP ALTERNATIVES

This stage may be reasonably simple for most programmed decisions but not so simple for complex nonprogrammed decisions, especially if there are time constraints. Too often the temptation to accept the first feasible alternative prevents managers from finding the *best* solutions for their problems. To prevent this, no major decision should be made until several alternatives have been developed. To increase their creativity at this task, some managers turn to individual or group **brainstorming,** in which participants spontaneously propose alternatives even if they seem unrealistic or fantastic.

## STAGE 3: EVALUATE ALTERNATIVES AND SELECT THE BEST ONE AVAILABLE

Once managers have developed a set of alternatives, they must evaluate each one on the basis of three key questions (see Figure 9-3).

**1. IS THIS ALTERNATIVE FEASIBLE?** Does the organization have the money and other resources needed to carry out this alternative? Replacing all obsolete equipment might be an ideal solution, but it is not feasible if the company is already near bankruptcy. Does the alternative meet all the organization's legal and ethical obligations? Closing a plant to save costs, for example, involves a complicated web of legal and ethical obligations to displaced workers. Is the alternative a reasonable one given the organization's strategy and internal politics? Any solution is only as effective as the support it wins within the organization. Therefore, in evaluating an alternative, managers must try to anticipate what would happen if employees fail to support and implement it wholeheartedly.

**2. IS THE ALTERNATIVE A SATISFACTORY SOLUTION?** To answer, managers need to consider two additional questions. First, does the alternative meet the decision objectives? Second, does the alternative have an acceptable chance of succeeding? (This assumes the chance can be calculated; in conditions of uncertainty, of course, this may be extremely difficult or impossible.) Managers should realize, too, that the definition of "acceptable" may differ from organization to organization and from person to person, depending on the organization's culture and the risk-tolerance of those involved in the decision.

### 3. WHAT ARE THE POSSIBLE CONSEQUENCES FOR THE REST OF THE ORGANIZATION?

Because an organization is a system of interrelated parts and exists among other systems, managers must try to anticipate how a change in one area will affect other areas—both now and in the future. Cutting back research and development, for example, might save money in the short term but could cripple the organization in the long run. If the decision might affect people in other departments, they too should be consulted.[30] Competitors may also be affected by the decision; their reactions will have to be taken into account. Can competitors respond to a new marketing strategy or a new product? Alternatives with negative consequences should be eliminated, of course, and alternatives with positive consequences will usually be favored over those with merely neutral consequences.

An investigation of a problem situation in this way clearly proved advantageous for managers at J.B. Hunt Transport Services. "Everywhere you go opportunities are hanging like big, ripe fruit" says Johnnie Bryan Hunt, founder of the company. Executives at J.B. Hunt Transport may start to say, "There was a problem with . . ." only to correct themselves midsentence: "No, there was an *opportunity* for us because. . . ." And J.B. is more than just talk.[31] In the late 1980s Hunt Transport was feeling the effects of higher fuel and labor costs and lower freight rates. At the same time, railroads, a major transport rival, were becoming more responsive to customer demands. Then in 1989, Santa Fe Railway approached Hunt with a proposal for a combined effort on transporting goods across certain routes. Hunt jumped at the opportunity to merge the cheaper fuel and labor of trains with the faster, more reliable services of his trucks, making his company one of the first major trucking companies to join railroads in intermodal shipping. After the initial agreement with Santa Fe, Hunt went on to join forces with six other major railroads. The results were positive. Hunt's intermodal division alone made $160 million in 1992; CEO Kirk Thompson projected it would comprise half the company's business by 1995.

## STAGE 4: IMPLEMENT AND MONITOR THE DECISION

Once the best available alternative has been selected, managers are ready to make plans to cope with the requirements and problems that may be encountered in putting it into effect.[32] Implementing a decision involves more than giving appropriate orders. Resources must be acquired and allocated as necessary. Managers set up budgets and schedules for the actions they have decided upon, allowing them to measure progress in specific terms. Next, they assign responsibility for the specific tasks involved. They also set up a procedure for progress reports and prepare to make corrections if new problems should arise. Budgets, schedules, and progress reports are all essential to performing the management functions of control.

Potential risks and uncertainties that have been identified during the earlier evaluation-of-alternatives stages must also be kept in mind. There is a natural human tendency to forget possible risks and uncertainties once a decision is made. Managers can counteract this failing by consciously taking extra time to reexamine their decisions at this point and to develop detailed plans for dealing with these risks and uncertainties.

After managers have taken whatever steps are possible to deal with potential adverse consequences, actual implementation can begin. Ultimately, a decision (or a solution) is no better than the actions taken to make it a reality. A frequent

# FROM A HUMBLE BEGINNING

The Nike organization grew out of an idea Philip Knight expressed in a graduate school paper he wrote in 1962 while he was getting his M.B.A. at Stanford. In 1964, he and Bill Bowerman, Knight's former track coach from the University of Oregon, started an athletic shoe company called Blue Ribbon Sports, to evoke the image of a winner. That year they sold 1,300 pairs of running shoes at local track meets from the trunk of a car. In the meantime, Knight also worked as a C.P.A. and an accounting professor until 1969, when he decided to devote himself full-time to Blue Ribbon Sports. Then, in 1972, Blue Ribbon Sports became Nike, named after the mythological goddess of victory.

Between 1972 and 1990, Nike experienced tremendous growth. Sales in 1972 were $2 million. By 1982, sales had reached $694 million, with an average annual growth rate of 82 percent. In 1990, sales reached $2 billion, with part of this phenomenal growth due to Michael Jordan's endorsement. Even before Jordan stunned the sports world with his retirement announcement, however, Knight and his managers had reason to be on the lookout for future opportunities. After all, they knew that as unique as his talents are, Jordan would not play professional basketball forever.

**NIKE TOWN, CHICAGO.** How do you handle the challenge when the superstar focal point of your marketing effort leaves the court?

One new venture was the "Nike Town" concept. A "Nike Town" was part sports museum, part store, and part amusement park, and was intended as a celebration of Nike's "energy and youth and vitality" product image. Nike Towns feature 3-D commercials, giant tropical fish tanks, and basketball courts. Initially Nike built two Nike Towns, one in Portland, Oregon, and the other in Chicago, Illinois, but was planning for more throughout the world. "It's part of a whole program of imagemaking," said David Manfredi, partner in Elkus/Manfredi Ltd., the Boston-based firm that designed a similar store for Sony. "This is an opportunity to have direct control over how your company is presented to the world."[33] The idea here was to focus on image, not cost; merchandise was not discounted. When the Chicago Nike Town opened, it attracted 5,000 customers a week who spent approximately $50 each.

To keep up with the changing marketplace, Nike managers have already started diversifying. In 1992, Nike opened retail outlets in which apparel, shoes, and Nike paraphernalia are sold. Nike managers attribute a $100 million increase in gross profits in 1992 to its retail sales division, which operates 30 Nike-owned outlets for factory seconds and the two Nike Town stores. A far cry from the company's humble beginnings with shoes being sold from the trunk of a car. The stores promote the growth of the Nike apparel business, which is experiencing much faster growth than the athletic shoe business. →

error of managers is to assume that once they make a decision, action on it will automatically follow. Even if a decision is a good one, if others are unwilling or unable to carry it out, then the decision will not be effective.

Actions taken to implement a decision must be monitored. Are things working according to plan? What is happening in the internal and <u>external environments</u>

← Ch. 3, p. 65

as a result of the decision? Are people performing according to expectations? What is the competition doing in response? Decision making is a continual process for managers—and a continual challenge of dealing with other human beings over time. At Nike, even after choosing Michael Jordan as a spokesperson, Knight had every reason to watch the sales patterns of Air Jordans very closely in 1984 and 1985. With many managers trying to gain endorsements from NBA stars, Nike products were vulnerable to competition from Reebok products.

# THE RATIONAL MODEL IN PERSPECTIVE

**bounded rationality:**
The concept that managers make the most logical decisions they can within the constraints of limited information and ability.

**satisfice:**
Decision-making technique in which managers accept the first satisfactory decision they uncover.

**heuristic principles:**
A method of decision making that proceeds along empirical lines, using rules of thumb, to find solutions or answers.

The rational model conjures up an image of the decision maker as a super calculating machine. But we know that managers must make decisions within tight time constraints and with less information than they would like to have. Three concepts have emerged over the years to help managers put their decision making in perspective: bounded rationality and satisficing, heuristics, and biases. These concepts are neither good nor bad per se. Rather, they help us keep in mind that we human beings do have limits as we use our minds to confront the world.

## BOUNDED RATIONALITY AND SATISFICING

In trying to describe the factors that affect decision making, Herbert Simon, among others, has proposed a theory of **bounded rationality.** This theory points out that decision makers must cope with inadequate information about the nature of the problem and its possible solutions, a lack of time or money to compile more complete information, an inability to remember large amounts of information, and the limits of their own intelligence.

Instead of searching for the perfect or ideal decision, managers frequently settle for one that will *adequately* serve their purposes. In Simon's terms, they **satisfice,** or accept the first satisfactory decision they uncover, rather than *maximize,* or search until they find the best possible decision.[34] What the effective decision maker learns to do is satisfice with a clear sense of goals for the organization in mind.

## HEURISTICS

Research by Amos Tversky and Daniel Kahneman has extended Simon's ideas on bounded rationality. They have demonstrated that people rely on **heuristic principles,** or rules of thumb, to simplify decision making.[35] Loan officers, for example, may screen mortgage applicants by assuming people can afford to spend no more than 35 percent of their income on housing. Three heuristics show up repeatedly in human decision making.[36] These are general cognitive guides people use intuitively.

**AVAILABILITY.** People sometimes judge an event's likelihood by testing it against their memories. In principle, it is easier to recall frequently occurring events. Thus, events that are more readily "available" in memory are assumed to be more likely to occur in the future. This assumption is based on the experience of a lifetime, and it seems reasonable enough. However, human memory is also affected by how *recently* an event occurred and how *vivid* the experience was. Thus, a risk manager recently caught in a flood is likely to overestimate the importance and frequency of flooding the next time he or she procures insurance.

**REPRESENTATIVENESS.** People also tend to assess the likelihood of an occurrence by trying to match it with a preexisting category. For example, employers may rely on stereotypes of sexual, racial, or ethnic groups to predict an individual job candidate's performance. In a similar way, product managers may predict the perform-

**A VIVID MEMORY.** According to the heuristic principle of availability, someone who has experienced first-hand a vivid event such as a fire is likely to have that memory highly available and be overly sensitive to the possibility of fire in future situations.

ance of a new product by relating it to other products with proven track records. In fact, however, each individual or product is a new commodity, not just the representative of a group, and should be judged accordingly.

**ANCHORING AND ADJUSTMENT.** People do not pull decisions out of thin air. Usually, they start with some initial value, or "anchor," and then make adjustments to that value in order to arrive at a final decision. Salary decisions, for example, are routinely calculated by assuming last year's salary to be an initial value to which an adjustment must be made. Unfortunately, depending heavily on the single factor of initial value tends to obscure relevant criteria. In addition, different initial values lead to different decisions.

In extending the Nike product line from shoes to other types of sports equipment, Nike managers rely on a heuristic that athletes will be drawn to the Nike name and logo. They also assume that customers will choose Nike products on the basis of heuristics—for reasons of availability (*"I recall Nike ads."*), representativeness (*"Nike sells shoes, so they probably know something about socks and shirts"*), and anchoring (*"I had a good pair of Nikes once"*).

**game theory:**
The study of people making interdependent choices.

**chaos theory:**
The study of dynamic patterns in large social systems.

## DECIDING WHO DECIDES

The rational model provides no guidance in who should make a decision, and often "Who will decide?" is the first decision a manager must make. This decision can be complicated. If a number of different people will be affected by the decision—as is often the case—the decision process must be guided by the prospects of their accepting the decision.

Traditionally, the final responsibility for making decisions belongs to managers. But this approach is not always appropriate. Even a well-thought-out managerial decision may fail if the manager is unable to convince others to carry it out willingly. And sometimes others have excellent reasons for resisting a decision; perhaps they are aware of alternatives or relevant factors that were not considered in the original analysis. On the other hand, employees may implement a decision loyally even though they disagree with it—with poor results because the decision is poor. Thus, more and more often employees are being involved in the decision-making process. This aspect of decision making is important enough that we will devote an entire chapter to it (see Chapter 13: Authority, Delegation, and Decentralization).

**MANAGEMENT 2000 AND BEYOND**

# DECIDING ADAPTIVELY

Rational decision making proceeds on the belief that managers can transform a complicated web of facts, assumptions, objectives, and educated guesses into a clear decision that people at the organization can act on. There is a strong faith in all this that the world can be influenced through managers' mental capabilities. Decision making, then, is an effort to exercise control over the organization's destiny. This has been a distinctive management belief for more than a century.

This faith has been challenged in recent years. More and more, an *adaptive approach* to decision making has emerged as a way to think about what managers can and cannot expect to accomplish. This adaptive approach turns on the assumption that the link between an organizational action (the result of a decision) and the consequences of that action is far messier and far more unpredictable than rational decision makers believe. According to adaptive thinking, the results of a decision action are *jointly produced* by what your organization does *and* what other organizations are doing at the same time.

A classic example of a jointly-produced outcome has been occurring in recent years in the U.S. passenger airline industry. Airlines often fly relatively empty planes. Yet airline companies have to pay for expensive jet aircraft and for large numbers of highly-trained employees whether flights are full or not. So, for any one airline, it might make rational sense to cut air fares to induce more passengers to fly on that airline. What happened in the spring of 1992, however, is that managers at several leading airlines—including American, United, Delta, and Northwest—all decided to cut fares at the same time. But there was not sufficient growth in the total number of passengers flying to make up for the forgone revenue from lower airfares. The jointly-produced result of these separate, rationally-derived decisions at each individual company was a so-called "price war" in which *every* airline suffered financial losses![37]

Two versions of the adaptive approach to decision making are game theory and chaos theory.

*Game theory* is the study of people making interdependent choices. A *game* is a situation involving at least two people in which each person makes choices based, in part, on what he or she expects the other to do. Game theory highlights the explicit role of human relationships and interactions in decisions.[38]

Games were first used in planning nuclear armament build-ups after World War II. Currently, game theory is used in such business decisions as competitive pricing.[39] We experience games all the time. Two people must "play" a game when they meet at a revolving door at the same time, or when one is driving on a freeway and another attempts to enter the flow of traffic.[40] For our understanding of decision making, the key point is that in a game the outcome is jointly produced. We make it through the revolving door, or we get delayed, because you do something and I do something.

Hence, a game theory perspective requires that we view decision making as a process of two decision makers adapting to each other's presence at the same time. Each can decide rationally but also adaptively. This is what we were just describing about the modern U.S. airlines industry.

*Chaos theory* is the study of dynamic patterns in large social systems.[41] Chaos theory thus is a descendant of systems theory. Chaos theorists pay close attention to the *turbulence* of a system. Under conditions of turbulence, not only is the future completely unpredictable, but present circumstances are likely unstable, too. In this way, turbulence differs from certainty, risk, and uncertainty, which are comparatively stable conditions under which managers can at least choose an attainable objective.

Ralph Stacey argues that chaos is a pattern of three states: equilibrium, disequilibrium, and bounded instability.[42] The task of decision makers is to keep the organization in the third state because that is where organizations can innovate. Decision making becomes a continual process of *adaptation* to forces largely beyond a decision maker's control. It is like surfing a huge wave off Diamond Head, a wave that never hits shore!

## Summary

1.  **Connect decision making with the idea that managers deal with time and human relationships.**

    Decision making—the process of identifying and selecting a course of action to deal with a problem or take advantage of an opportunity—is an important part of the manager's job. Managers draw on past performances, present circumstances, and future expectations when making a decision. In addition, when managers project possible consequences of their decisions, they must be conscious that other people's decisions may conflict or interact with their own.

# A SHIFT OF FOCUS: WOMEN ENTER THE GAME

In 1993, Nike managers expanded their marketing strategy to focus on growing audiences, such as women. In conjunction with New York-based Conde Nast Publications, Nike has created in-store events, called "Dialogue," that have taken place in major retail outlets across the country. "Dialogue" events include fashion shows of Nike sports apparel and feature motivational speakers such as biathlon champion Liz Downing and marathon runner Priscilla Welsh. These endeavors are designed to further increase Nike sales to women, which had already increased 25 percent in 1990 and 1991 and 28 percent in 1992.

Target marketing to women reflects the Nike managers' understanding that the marketplace is changing and that they must rethink and expand their strategies. According to Nancy Woodhull, president of Nancy Woodhull & Associates, a Washington, D.C.-based company that specializes in helping organizations understand women consumers, "These campaigns [such as Nike's] work because you have to bond with women on an emotional level, no matter what type of product you are selling, or what type of program you decide to launch."[43]

The decision to focus on women was not made haphazardly. Getting support for this new strategy took a lot of effort, particularly on the part of then–women's marketing director Kate Bednarski, who was part of a team working to increase Nike's share of the women's athletic shoe market. Some managers were concerned that such a move might cannibalize sales in the men's market. According to Bednarski, "many seemed to fear that growing the women's business would somehow undermine the company's image and decrease its appeal to men."[44]

Once Nike was convinced that a viable market was available, though, the women's team set to work. Through long hours of brainstorming, the team eventually arrived at a series of ads featuring women as powerful, capable people. "[They] address the issue of what it feels like always to be told that you can't do something simply because you're a woman," said Bednarski.[45]

The immediate response within the company was not particularly favorable. However, the advertising team convinced management that, considering the low initial investment, the campaign was worth at least trying out. The campaign represented a departure from Nike's successful strategy of linking products with stars like Michael Jordan. Through persistence and creativity, however, Bednarski and her team were able to convince her supervisors to take a chance.

The women's marketing and advertising team, their supervisors, and their "competitors" within Nike's organization are all making decisions in the context of each other's making decisions. By game theory, the decision to proceed with Dialogue is the joint result of their individual decisions. At the same time, this resulting decision is being played out in a world where forces of turbulence are at work. Jordan's retirement is one manifestation. By chaos theory, Nike managers must see themselves as adapting—and adapting some more. As they move from what looks relatively stable—Air Jordan and now Dialogue—to what looks relatively unstable—life after Air Jordans—they do well to understand their own satisficing, heuristics, and biases. That is what modern decision making has become.

2. **See decision making as a complex problem of psychology and of understanding one's world.**

Four informal and intuitive situations usually alert managers to a problem's existence: performance deviates from past experience; performance deviates from a plan; other people express dissatisfaction; or the performance of competitors challenges an organization. Whether managers recognize a situation as a problem depends upon their threshold for problem recognition, which is determined by their understanding of goals, plans, and acceptable standards of performance, as well as by their personal values and backgrounds. No manager can solve every problem. Instead, managers must learn to set priorities in deciding which decisions to handle and which ones they should delegate to lower-ranking employees or refer to higher-ranking managers.

3. **Distinguish programmed decisions from nonprogrammed decisions.**

Decisions can be thought of as programmed or nonprogrammed. Programmed decisions involve routine matters and can be handled by written or unwritten policies, procedures, and rules. Nonprogrammed decisions involve unusual or exceptional problems. Because most decisions involve some element of the future, managers must be able to analyze the certainty, risk, or uncertainty of each situation. Under conditions of certainty, managers can predict the results of each alternative. Under conditions of risk, the probable outcome of each alternative can be predicted. Under conditions of uncertainty, the outcome probabilities cannot be predicted.

4. **Explain the rational decision making process.**

The rational model of decision making (and problem solving) assumes the most effective decisions result when managers follow a four-step process of investigating the situation, developing alternatives, evaluating alternatives and selecting the best one, and then implementing the decision and following it up. The rational model has a long history in management practice and management education.

5. **Put rational decision making in perspective as a process affected by bounded rationality, satisficing and heuristics.**

Human beings can only juggle so much information in their minds, and often must make decisions under significant time pressures. The concepts of bounded rationality, satisficing, and heuristics put these constraints in perspective. With these ideas, managers can better understand rational decision making.

6. **Explain how game theory and chaos theory describe the larger context in which managers decide.**

Two recent approaches to decision making emphasize that decision makers must adapt to what other decision makers are doing at the same time. Game theory and chaos theory highlight decision making as something done in relationships where the various individual decision makers jointly produce outcomes that they did not necessarily intend.

## REVIEW QUESTIONS

1. What is the principal difference between problem finding and opportunity finding?
2. What four situations usually alert managers to the existence of a problem?
3. What factors affect a manager's threshold for problem recognition?
4. What questions can managers use to set priorities in decision making?
5. Contrast programmed and nonprogrammed decisions and give an example of each.
6. Explain with examples from your life the difference between making decisions under conditions of certainty, risk, and uncertainty.

7. Describe the four basic stages in the rational model of decision making and problem solving.

8. When do bounded rationality, satisficing, and heuristics enter your own decision making for better? For worse?

9. What are some examples in modern world politics that can be explained by game theory and or chaos theory?

## KEY TERMS

Decision making
Problem
Opportunity
Dialectical inquiry method
Programmed decisions
Nonprogrammed decisions
Certainty
Risk

Probability
Uncertainty
Rational model of decision making
Brainstorming
Bounded rationality
Satisfice
Heuristic principles

## CASE STUDY

## A NEW BLOCKBUSTER IMAGE[46]

In the fall of 1993, Chairman H. Wayne Huizenga of Blockbuster faced a host of difficult decisions concerning the future of the company. Should he slow down the diversification of the company? Was his approach too scattered? A year earlier, in 1992, Blockbuster was merely a video-rental giant. Steps taken in the past months, however, had set Blockbuster on a course toward becoming a full-fledged entertainment company. But the steps taken were not without a few stumbles, and criticism about Huizenga's decisions was multiplying. As 1993 drew to a close, Huizenga had reason to consider rethinking what he wanted for the company.

Blockbuster began in 1985 with one store. Within three years, there were 415 stores around the country. As of October 1993 there were more than 3,200 stores in 10 countries around the world. In a word, Blockbuster has enjoyed tremendous success.

According to former McDonald's marketing executive Tom Gruber, chief marketing officer at Blockbuster in 1990, the key to the company's success lies in its "McMarketing" principles: fast service, convenient locations, family orientation, and kid appeal. "The same factors at work in fast-food retailing

are at work in video retailing," said Gruber. By 1989, Blockbuster capitalized on its image as "America's Family Video Store."[47]

But by 1993 Blockbuster was seeking a new image—that of a multimedia company. The video chain with $1.2 billion in sales considered itself stuck in a market promising little or no growth in the near future. Although more than 66 percent of U.S. households own at least one VCR, the advent of interactive technologies including 500-channel TV and video-on-demand calls into question the future of video rentals. So Huizenga took numerous measures to diversify Blockbuster.

In the meantime, however, the video-rental business is thriving. Herein lies one of the reasons opponents criticize Huizenga's diversification strategy; not all people believe that the video-rental business is doomed. Even Huizenga predicts that it will remain healthy for the next decade. During the first half of 1993, revenues in existing Blockbuster locations climbed 6.1 percent, and analysts expect 1993 revenues to soar 75 percent.

But Huizenga is not waiting for the market to evaporate before acting. He started transforming

Blockbuster's business in 1992, heralded by the sponsorship of Paul McCartney's concert tour. In 1993 the company sponsored Rod Stewart's tour. "We wanted to signal to everyone who had anything to do with Blockbuster that we are a big-time entertainment company," asserted current chief marketing officer James L. Hilmer.[48]

In the meantime, Huizenga has already taken deliberate steps to turn Blockbuster into "a global entertainment company with different forms of distribution." In November 1992, Huizenga entered music retailing by acquiring Sound Warehouse and Music Plus chains. Today, Blockbuster is the No. 3 music retailer in the United States. In December 1992, a joint venture was formed with Virgin Retail Group to open "megastores" in the United States, Europe, and Australia. Then, in February 1993, Huizenga turned his attention to television and film, buying Republic Pictures, then in April acquiring a majority interest in Spelling Entertainment Group. Also in April, Huizenga bought 21 percent of Discovery Zone, an operator and franchiser of indoor children's play centers, and rights to open 50 new Discovery centers. In August, Huizenga changed gears again with the buyout of the two largest video-store franchises. September witnessed a $600 million investment in Viacom, in support of its bid for Paramount Communications.

Plans are in the works for indoor neighborhood entertainment centers. The company recently revealed plans for Blockbuster Entertainment Village, a 2,600-acre entertainment and sports complex in south Florida. In addition, there are plans to create "game zones" within video stores that will feature video games. Sega of North America Inc. already rents video games through Blockbuster and uses the stores to try out leading-edge hardware, such as the new virtual-reality goggles.

### CASE QUESTIONS

1. Which of Huizenga's decision alternatives appear particularly feasible and particularly unfeasible, given what you know about these markets?
2. Where does it make sense for Huizenga to satisfice?
3. Who else is making decisions that it is crucial for Huizenga to factor into his analysis?

## VIDEO CASE STUDY

### HAS FOX FUMBLED?[49]

In early 1994, Fox Broadcasting Company agreed to pay $1.58 billion for the television rights to the next four seasons of the National Football Conference (NFC), home to powerhouse teams such as the Dallas Cowboys and the Washington Redskins. In addition, Fox hired sports commentator John Madden, in a four-year, $32 million deal that more than doubled what Madden had been earning at CBS. In addition, it included a high-priced contract for Madden's CBS co-commentator, Pat Summerall. Fox also hired away legendary quarterback Terry Bradshaw by offering him more than twice his CBS salary.

Many in the television industry gleefully surmised that the previously up-and-coming "fourth network" was on its way down. They believed Fox had made a drastic error in buying NFC rights for an amount that CBS, the next highest bidder, considered to be at least 25 percent more than it was worth. They saw the generous contracts Madden, Summerall, and Bradshaw as compounding the error. Industry analysts projected that Fox would lose hundreds of millions of dollars over the duration of the contract. Clearly, Rupert Murdoch, chairman of News Corporation, Fox's parent company, had made a mistake.

Or had he?

Looking beyond the financial bottom line of the football deal itself reveals numerous other benefits. "There are so many more things that play into our plan," pointed out Fox's Chairperson, Lucie Salhany. "We're just seven years old and this will really put us on the map. It will increase our affiliates, increase our ability to promote our other programs to a new audience, and draw new advertisers. After the announcement [that Fox had won the NFC broadcast rights], our phones started ringing immediately."[50]

The move also left CBS without football for the first time since the network began broadcasting in 1956. With CBS potentially weakened, Fox is now positioned as a serious challenger to the "big three"—CBS, ABC, and NBC—and the ratings balance of power is threatened. "The only way to justify the current investment in NFL football [by Fox] is to see what it does for the overall Fox Network," asserted Christopher Dixon, media analyst at Paine Webber. "Sunday afternoon football can provide a promotional base and give Fox much more credibility in the eyes of the public, and even more important, with advertisers."[51]

Aside from transforming Fox from an upstart into a contender, Sunday afternoon NFC games will also support Fox's other programming. Fox commentators will be able to give plugs for the Sunday evening line-up following the games, just as CBS commentators did. *Murder, She Wrote* and *60 Minutes* benefitted enormously from being slotted after football and being promoted during the games. The impact promises to be even more dramatic for Fox, which, through the football deal, will be attracting many new viewers to the network. Viewers who tune in to Fox for football will become familiar with its schedule—and not just for Sunday night. They will become accustomed to switching to Fox more frequently. Said Stacey Marks-Bronner, general manager of Chicago's WFLD, a UHF station, "The hardest problem is not being a habit. So now we're going to be a habit."[52]

Thus the NFC deal falls in line with Fox's strategic objective of expanding its audience. Fox executives expect football to draw older viewers, expanding Fox's typical demographic from males aged 18-34 to males aged 18-45. Fox has already demonstrated that young viewers comprise a profitable niche, but, Salhany admitted, the network's goal has always been to capture the audience of 18- to 49-year-olds. "Our average viewer is a 28-year-old male," Salhany revealed. "We want to take that up to a 30-year-old and get more women in there. We just don't want so much dependence on a very fickle audience, young teens."[53]

Football also makes Fox more appealing to a host of new advertisers, particularly since seven of the nine Fox-owned stations fall in NFC markets. "The stations will be able to tap sports advertisers for the first time," noted Jessica Reif, an analyst with Oppenheimer and Co.[54] Moreover, the expanded demographic will make many potential advertisers, such as mass-market retailers and auto makers, more interested in the station that they have traditionally ignored. Of the top twenty prime-time advertisers, six spent less than 5 percent of their budgets on Fox in 1993. NFC football will help to change that. "What Fox is doing is creating more valuable inventory than they previously had," said Dixon.[55]

Fox has certainly come a long way since it was launched in 1987. Network revenue for 1993 reached a gross figure near $650 million with operating profit estimated at $76 million for the year ending in June. "They've successfully created market, but that success makes them look more and more like the other networks," said analyst Dennis McAlpine of Josephthal Lyons and Ross.[56] "They've become a player," added a former Fox executive, "but now they have something to lose."[57]

In the end, says Murdoch, buying the NFC rights provided a cheap way to buy a network. "It's a plan for the future," Salhany explained. "It takes the network to another level. It's good for the network, our stations, and our affiliates."[58]

## CASE QUESTIONS

1. Was Murdoch's decision to buy the NFC rights a programmed or nonprogrammed decision? What elements did he weigh in negotiating for the rights? What other factors should he have considered?

2. What opportunities did Murdoch create through his decision to buy NFC rights? What opportunities did he ignore?

3. Using the rational model of decision making, discuss how Murdoch repositioned Fox.

## CHAPTER 10

# PLANNING AND STRATEGIC MANAGEMENT

**Upon completing this chapter, you should be able to:**

1. Describe the usefulness of goals at an organization.

2. Distinguish between strategic and operational plans.

3. Understand a strategy as an attempt to place an organization in its environment.

4. Trace why the strategic management process has evolved.

5. Express a strategy as a substantive statement about where an organization is headed.

6. Discuss the opportunities and constraints on collaborative approaches to strategy.

# PLANNING FOR THE FUTURE AT FEDERAL EXPRESS[1]

he managers of Federal Express were concerned. They had transformed the company from a small package-delivery service into the major force in overnight delivery. However, they needed to decide on directions for the future. Competition was closing in from several sides, and Federal Express managers felt the need to move quickly if it was to continue to grow and thrive.

Federal Express managers did not consider the company simply a package-delivery service. They saw it as part of a larger, more complex industry that should be thought of in terms of "information delivery." Although they competed with traditional rivals—other overnight carriers like United Parcel Service and the U.S. Postal Service—they also worried about information carriers such as MCI, AT&T, and other telecommunication companies. Therefore, it was important for company managers to speculate on the future directions of all these companies.

Federal Express had a reputation for being at the forefront of trends, and its managers wanted to keep both its position and its reputation. The company had started long before anyone realized overnight-delivery service would become such an important part of doing business.

*For important documents, businesses now think in terms of hours instead of days.*

Although it had taken more than three years for the concept to catch on and make the company profitable, Federal Express was now the leader in the industry. The technology and the attitude of innovation that made it possible to go from handling 40 packages a night to 1.7 million were important assets. Now, managers needed to plan how to use these assets to meet the information-delivery needs of the future.

The postal service was obviously impinging on Federal Express's overnight-delivery business. The "Express Mail" package was a direct and serious challenge. However, the Post Office was somewhat limited as to future directions. It could challenge in terms of price and service, but would probably continue to specialize in the same type of product. United Parcel Service (UPS) was also a direct challenger—one that priced its service considerably below Federal's and was noticeably improving that service. Where would UPS go in the years to come?

Despite the obvious challenges from competing package-delivery services, Federal Express was far more concerned about competition from organizations offering other methods of information transfer. MCI, for example, had recently introduced its MCI Mail System, which transferred documents from one computer to another in far fewer hours than Federal Express could promise. Was this what businesses wanted in the information age? If so, how should Federal react?

Since 1979, the processes of doing business have changed drastically. It is no longer acceptable for a business letter to take a week to move from one coast to the other. For important documents, businesses now think in terms of hours instead of days. The development of a truly global marketplace has also affected the document-delivery business. As international business becomes more common, information-transfer systems have to keep pace.

To assure survival, the people at Federal Express knew the company had to move forward. Federal Express had to be ready to meet the needs of *tomorrow's* businesses, and to do this, they had to anticipate those needs today. Which needs were going to be the most important? What could they do to get ready now?

PLANNING IS A particular kind of decision making that addresses the specific future that managers desire for their organizations. We listed planning in Chapter 1 as the first of the four major activities in the management process—planning, organizing, leading, and controlling. We might think of planning as the locomotive that drives a train of organizing, leading, and controlling activities. Or we can envision planning as the taproot of a magnificent oak tree, from which grow the branches of organizing, leading, and controlling. Planning is *that* crucial for managers.

Planning is not a single event, with a clear beginning and end. It is an ongoing process that reflects and adapts to changes in the environment surrounding each organization. We can see this in the case of Federal Express, which entered the 1980s facing not only stiff competition and the rising expectations of customers, but also evolving technology. Federal Express managers had to reevaluate their plans and plot a new course into the future. They had to watch relationships with their key customers, with competitors such as UPS and the postal service, and with potential marketplace rivals such as MCI, all at the same time. Deciding on actions—and responses to others' actions—is the continual planning challenge for these managers.

In this chapter, we will take a close look at planning and the way plans are created at various levels within organizations. You will learn that one of the most important results of the planning process is a *strategy* for the organization. And you will learn about *strategic management,* a particular kind of planning that has emerged over the past several decades. Strategic management is an ongoing practice of establishing a broad program of organizational goals and the means to achieve them.

## PLANNING: AN OVERVIEW

We all have dreams of finding fame and fortune and winning the respect and admiration of others. To make our dreams come true, we need to set specific, measurable goals with realistic, achievable deadlines. The same is true at organizations. Goals* are important for at least four reasons.

1. **GOALS PROVIDE A SENSE OF DIRECTION.** Without a goal, individuals and their organizations tend to muddle along, reacting to environmental changes without a clear sense of what they really want to achieve. By setting goals, people and their organizations bolster their motivation and gain a source of inspiration that helps them overcome the inevitable obstacles they encounter.

2. **GOALS FOCUS OUR EFFORTS.** Every person and every organization has limited resources and a wide range of possible ways to use them. In selecting a single goal or a set of related goals, we establish priorities and make a commitment about the way we will use our scarce resources. This is especially important at an organization, where managers must coordinate the actions of many individuals.

3. **GOALS GUIDE OUR PLANS AND DECISIONS.** Do you want to become a chess champion? Or a champion gymnast? The answers to such questions will shape both your short-term and your long-term plans and help you make many key decisions. People at organizations face similar decisions, which are clarified by asking, What is our goal? Will this action move us toward or away from our organizational goal?

4. **GOALS HELP US EVALUATE OUR PROGRESS.** A clearly stated, measurable goal with a specific deadline becomes a standard of performance that lets individuals and managers alike evaluate their progress. Thus, goals are an essential part of *control-*

---

* We do not distinguish, as some authors do, between goals and objectives.

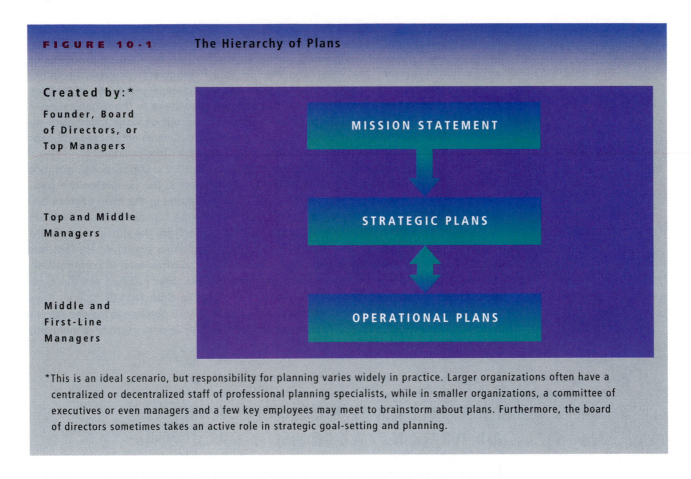

**FIGURE 10-1**     The Hierarchy of Plans

**Created by:***

**Founder, Board of Directors, or Top Managers**

MISSION STATEMENT

**Top and Middle Managers**

STRATEGIC PLANS

**Middle and First-Line Managers**

OPERATIONAL PLANS

*This is an ideal scenario, but responsibility for planning varies widely in practice. Larger organizations often have a centralized or decentralized staff of professional planning specialists, while in smaller organizations, a committee of executives or even managers and a few key employees may meet to brainstorm about plans. Furthermore, the board of directors sometimes takes an active role in strategic goal-setting and planning.

vate members of the organization. Consider the visionary mission described by a former chairman of AT&T some 80 years ago: "The dream of good, cheap, fast, worldwide telephone service . . . is not a speculation. It is a perfectly clear statement that you're going to do something."[5] Of course, since the company's divestiture of local telephone operations in 1984, AT&T managers have altered this mission. The company is now poised to be a "major factor in the worldwide movement and management of information."[6] You can see how the way a mission statement is articulated makes it a driving force for strategic and operational goals and for the actions people will take at an organization.

## HOW STRATEGIC AND OPERATIONAL PLANS DIFFER

Strategic and operational plans differ in three major ways:[7]

**TIME HORIZONS.** Strategic plans tend to look ahead several years or even decades. For operational plans, a year is often the relevant time period. At Federal Express, a strategic plan for new information delivery services could cover, say, five years of actions. A good example of an operational plan, on the other hand, is Wal-Mart's "cross-docking" technique for inventory replenishment, which addresses what happens today and tomorrow and next week. In cross-docking, goods are continuously delivered to Wal-Mart warehouses where they are selected, repacked and sent to individual stores, all within 48 hours. This operational plan allows Wal-Mart employees to achieve economies of scale for large purchases without suffering the usual higher inventory carrying costs. Cross-docking reduces Wal-Mart's cost of sales 2 to 3 percent and allows the company to offer consistently low prices.[8]

**SCOPE.** Strategic plans affect a wide range of organizational activities, whereas operational plans have a narrow and more limited scope. The number of relationships involved is the key difference. For this reason, some management writers distinguish between strategic *goals* and operational *objectives*. At Federal Express, a strategic plan would address the company's presence in selected global marketplaces, its financial goals, and the necessary size of the work force. At a small pizzeria, an operational plan would cover the kinds and amounts of ingredients that go into each pizza.

**DEGREE OF DETAIL.** Often strategic goals are stated in terms that look simplistic and generic. But this breadth is necessary to direct people at organizations to think of the whole of their organization's operations. On the other hand, operational plans, as derivatives of strategic plans, are stated in relatively finer detail. This difference is clear in the case of Federal Express. "Information delivery" is the level of generality we might expect in a strategic plan. "Move *x* packages per hour" is the kind of detail we might expect in an operational plan.

## THE EVOLUTION OF THE CONCEPT OF STRATEGY

**strategy:**
The broad program for defining and achieving an organization's objectives; the organization's response to its environment over time.

**A** strategic plan embodies and revolves around the statement of a **strategy** for an organization. Strategic planning is a process for producing this strategy and updating it as necessary.

### STRATEGY AS THE GRAND PLAN

The concept of strategy is ancient. The word itself comes from the Greek *strategeia,* which means the art or science of being a general. Effective Greek generals needed to lead an army, win and hold territory, protect cities from invasion, wipe out the enemy, and so forth. Each kind of objective required a different deployment of resources. Likewise, an army's strategy could be defined as the pattern of actual *actions* that it took in response to the enemy.

The Greeks knew that strategy was more than fighting battles. Effective generals had to determine the right lines of supply, decide when to fight and when not to fight, and manage the army's relationships with citizens, politicians, and diplomats. Effective generals not only had to plan but had to *act* as well. As far back as the ancient Greeks, then, the concept of strategy had both a *planning* component and a decision-making or *action* component.[9] Taken together, these two concepts form the basis for the "grand" strategy plan.

In the 1920s, Sears, Roebuck and Co. was a giant mail-order house whose president, General Robert E. Wood, recognized the importance of strategy. Wood realized that the growing popularity of the automobile would give increasing numbers of people access to urban areas. A population no longer confined to the countryside, he reasoned, would abandon the mail-order catalog in favor of the retail store. So Sears embarked on the long-range strategy of converting to a retail chain. According to Wood, the company "made every mistake in the book" at first, but its carefully laid plans eventually brought huge success. "Business is like war in one respect," the general wrote. "If its grand strategy is correct, any number of tactical errors can be made and yet the enterprise proves successful."[10]

### THE RISE OF STRATEGIC MANAGEMENT

The connection that managers today make between business and strategy is a relatively recent one. Only since World War II has the idea emerged that strategic

**A STRATEGIC PLAN.** "Leaps and Bounds" play centers were developed by McDonald's as part of a strategic plan to diversify outside the food industry. This type of broad, "grand plan" is then implemented through increasingly detailed operational plans.

**strategic management:**
The management process that involves an organization's engaging in strategic planning and then acting on those plans.

planning and acting on those plans constitute a separate management process—the process we call **strategic management.** This comprehensive approach to developing strategy did not appear overnight. It evolved over time.[11]

In 1962, business historian Alfred D. Chandler proposed that "strategy" be defined as

> the determination of the basic long-term goals and objectives of an enterprise, and the adoption of courses of action and the allocation of resources necessary for carrying out these goals.[12]

Chandler stressed three key elements: (a) courses of *action* for attaining objectives; (b) the process of *seeking* key ideas (rather than routinely implementing existing policy); and (c) *how* strategy is formulated, not just *what* that strategy turns out to be. Chandler abandoned the conventional notion that the relationship between a business and its environment was more or less stable and predictable. He developed his ideas using historical methods and by analyzing the growth and development of such companies as DuPont, General Motors, Standard Oil, and Sears, Roebuck.

As Chandler's concept evolved, two factors soon became evident: (1) *strategic planning* paid off in the world of real business activity, but (2) the role of the manager in the implementation of strategic planning had not yet been clarified (see Chapter 11 for a more complete discussion of strategy implementation). Still to be determined was how top management could deal with the two major problems faced by modern organizations: rapid changes in the interrelationship between the organization and its environment and the rapid growth in size and complexity of modern business organizations. In an effort to address this problem, the strategic management approach began to take shape.

**THE STRATEGIC MANAGEMENT APPROACH.** In 1978, Dan Schendel and Charles Hofer created a composite definition of strategic management. This was based on the principle that the overall design of an organization can be described only if the *attainment of objectives* is added to *policy* and *strategy* as key factors in the strategic management process.[13]

In their synthesis, Hofer and Schendel focused on four key aspects of strategic management. The first is *goal setting.* The next step is *strategy formulation* based

# RESPONDING TO THE CHANGING WORLD OF INFORMATION DELIVERY

Federal Express managers have always had a clear sense of where the company is going: They want to be the leader in the information-delivery business. Yet, as the business grows more complex and diverse, being the best has become more difficult. Take Federal Express's ZapMail facsimile service, which was intended to compete with MCI's Mail System. Zapmail seemed a well-timed innovation and a way to stay ahead of the competition, but Federal Express managers didn't anticipate the number of businesses that would buy their own FAX machines, effectively undermining the new service. They discontinued ZapMail in 1986.

The ZapMail effort was just one example of CEO Fred Smith's responsiveness to the rapidly changing world of information delivery. Having concluded that to stay on top, Federal Express had to become a global player, Smith and his top managers concentrated on foreign markets and acquisitions. However, these efforts were frustrated on several fronts. Difficulties in gaining access to specific foreign delivery routes and government restrictions favoring domestic services, coupled with the high cost of flying small packages in large planes, created a spotty network of service running at high cost.

These problems did not faze Smith. To demonstrate his commitment to global information services, Smith made two key moves. First, he acquired Tiger International, the world's largest cargo hauler. This gave Federal Express access to the vast network of routes Tiger had won over the previous 40 years. These routes gave Federal Express a direct competitive advantage in such nations as Australia, Malaysia, and the Philippines, where landing rights were extremely difficult to come by. Furthermore, it allowed Smith to mix in Federal Express's small parcels with Tiger's larger cargo, providing a more efficient use of space. As another bonus, acquiring Tiger's squadron of long-haul aircraft allowed Federal Express to move its fleet of DC-10s back to the higher-volume parcel routes in the United States.

Second, Federal Express built a new facility in Anchorage, Alaska. This location is in the center of a transportation triad, putting Federal Express within seven hours of key markets in Asia, Europe, and the United States. This move caught the competition off guard, forcing rivals to scramble to follow Smith's lead. One expert claimed these two moves make Federal Express the "undisputed leader" in information delivery. →

**A STRATEGIC POSITION.** Because it is within seven hours of key markets in Asia, Europe, and the United States, the Federal Express facility in Anchorage, Alaska, is an important routing point in the Federal Express system.

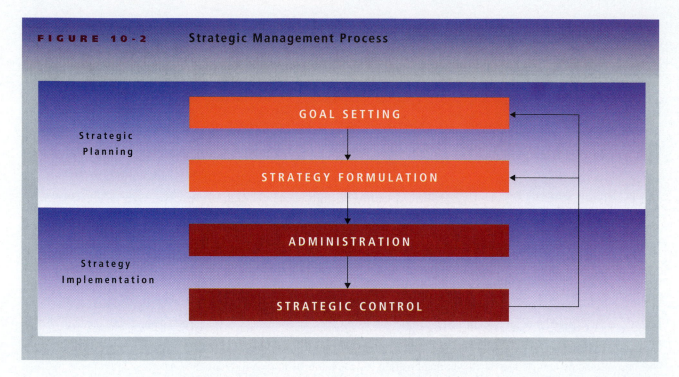

**FIGURE 10-2**     Strategic Management Process

on those goals.[14] Then, to implement the strategy, there is a shift from analysis to *administration*—the task of achieving predetermined goals.[15] Key factors at this stage are the organization's internal "political" processes and individual reactions, which can force the revision of strategy. The final task, *strategic control,* gives managers feedback on their progress. Negative feedback, of course, can touch off a new cycle of strategic planning. The Illustrative Case on Federal Express offers a picture of the strategic management process.

## THE STRATEGIC MANAGEMENT PROCESS

Strategic management provides a disciplined way for managers to make sense of the environment in which their organization operates, and then to act. In broad terms, two phases are involved:

- *Strategic planning* is the name we customarily give to the sense-making activity. This includes both the goal-setting and the strategy-formulation processes that Hofer and Schendel distinguished.
- *Strategy implementation* is the name we customarily give to actions based on that kind of planning. This stage includes Hofer and Schendel's administration and strategic control stages.

We can identify examples of each stage at Federal Express:

- "Global Market leadership in information delivery" is an example of what can emerge from goal setting.
- The Tiger acquisition and Anchorage facility are the products of strategy formulation; that is, particular ways to pursue the goals Smith had set.
- Merging the two disparate ways of running companies at Tiger and at Federal Express was an administration problem.
- The discontinuation of Zapmail is a case in point of strategic control.

The logical flow of this systematic attempt to create a future out of a past of experiences and a present of resources is depicted in Figure 10-2. The two return arrows indicate that this process is ongoing as circumstances change. Ask yourself what circumstances might lead Smith to rethink his goals, for example.

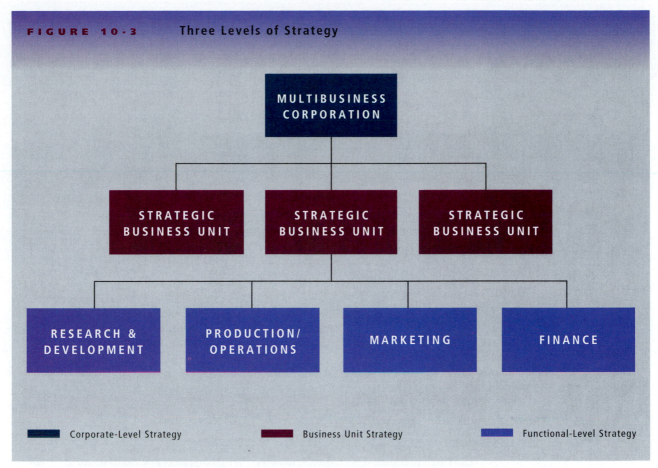

**FIGURE 10-3** Three Levels of Strategy

MULTIBUSINESS CORPORATION

STRATEGIC BUSINESS UNIT

STRATEGIC BUSINESS UNIT

STRATEGIC BUSINESS UNIT

RESEARCH & DEVELOPMENT

PRODUCTION/ OPERATIONS

MARKETING

FINANCE

■ Corporate-Level Strategy   ■ Business Unit Strategy   ■ Functional-Level Strategy

*Source:* Adapted from Rober H. Hayes and Steven C. Wheelwright, *Restoring Our Competitive Edge: Competing Through Manufacturing,* p. 28. Coypright 1984, reprinted by permission of John Wiley & Sons, Inc.

# LEVELS OF STRATEGY: SOME KEY DISTINCTIONS

In discussing strategy, it is useful to distinguish three levels of strategy: corporate-level, business-unit level, and functional-level (see Figure 10-3).[16]

## CORPORATE-LEVEL STRATEGY

**corporate-level strategy:** Strategy formulated by top management to oversee the interests and operations of multiline corporations.

**Corporate-level strategy** is formulated by top management to oversee the interests and operations of organizations made up of *more than one line* of business. The major questions at this level are these: What kinds of businesses should the company be engaged in? What are the goals and expectations for each business? How should resources be allocated to reach these goals?

Top managers at Minnesota Mining and Manufacturing Co. (3M), have been remarkably successful in putting together a number of small, diverse businesses that share the strengths and vision of the total organization, especially the strong emphasis on innovation. For instance, six different units exist under 3M's medical products unit, which is one of three life sciences units. Infusing the activities of so many business units with a company-wide sense of direction is what corporate-level strategists must do.[17]

## BUSINESS-UNIT STRATEGY

**business-unit strategy:** Strategy formulated to meet the goals of a particular business; also called *line-of-business strategy.*

**Business-unit strategy** (also called *line-of-business strategy*) is concerned with managing the interests and operations of a particular line of business. It deals with questions such as these: How will the business compete within its market?

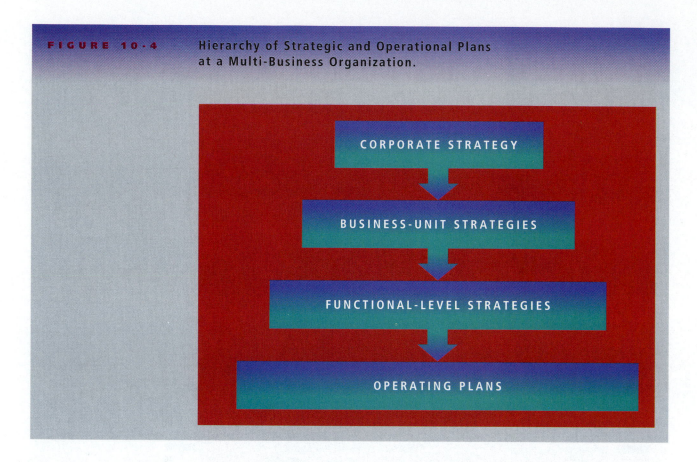

**FIGURE 10·4**     Hierarchy of Strategic and Operational Plans at a Multi-Business Organization.

What products/services should it offer? Which customers does it seek to serve? How will resources be distributed within the business? Business-unit strategy attempts to determine what approach to its market the business should take, and how it should conduct itself, given its resources and the conditions of the market.

Many corporations have extensive interests in different businesses, and top managers have difficulty organizing these corporations' complex and varied activities. One approach to dealing with this problem is to create *strategic business units (SBUs).* In this system of organization, various business activities that produce a particular type of product or service are grouped and treated as a single business unit. The corporate level provides a set of guidelines for the SBUs, which develop their own strategies on the business-unit level. The corporate level then reviews the SBU plans and negotiates changes if necessary.

An example of a corporation with multiple SBUs is the advertising agency Chiat/Day. Chiat/Day's top-ranking managers have formed strategic business units that look after big accounts or bundles of small ones. The idea is that the  agency's most creative people will be more likely to stick around if they are allowed to run their own "agency within the agency." Clients also benefit from having easier access to admakers with the power to make decisions and from having the same admaker on their account even if the person is promoted. As this example shows, SBUs can be a valuable means of forging closer business relationships.[18]

## FUNCTIONAL-LEVEL STRATEGY

**functional-level strategy:** Strategy formulated by a specific functional area in an effort to carry out business-unit strategy.

**Functional-level** strategies create a framework for managers in each function—such as marketing or production—to carry out business-unit strategies and corporate strategies. Thus functional-level strategies complete the hierarchy of strategies. Operational plans, mentioned earlier in this chapter, follow from functional-level strategies, as depicted in Figure 10-4.

# THE CONTENT OF A CORPORATE STRATEGY

**corporate strategy:**
The idea about how people at an organization will interact with people at other organizations over time.

**W**ith a corporate strategy, managers stake a claim for their organization's place in the future. You can think of a **corporate strategy** as an *idea* about how people at an organization will interact with people at other organizations over time. So it is very important to understand that a corporate strategy says *something of substance* that guides people in their day-to-day work *over an extended period of time*. In this section, we will give you a sense of different things that a corporate strategy can "say." Such statements, of course, will vary from organization to organization, because each organization is different.

← Ch. 8, p. 211

← Ch. 6, p. 170

## QUALITY AS PART OF CORPORATE STRATEGY

Quality has become a unifying theme for many organizations, from Xerox to GE. Important to the success of total quality management, however, is linking the quality program to a few clear strategic goals. As *Fortune* magazine points out, "obsessing about quality is no replacement for a well-thought-out corporate strategy."

At Johnson & Johnson, the quality program was redesigned with three targets in mind: boosting customer satisfaction, cutting costs, and reducing product introduction time. At J&J, a very intrapreneurial company where individual units are run like small businesses, each of the 168 units develops its own training program in keeping with these three unifying strategic goals.

At Motorola, the quality program has two targets: defect prevention (with a goal of two defects per billion by the year 2000) and cycle time reduction—decreasing the amount of time it takes to complete a job. This quality goal does not just apply to manufacturing, but to departments such as finance as well. For instance, in 1988 it took Motorola 11 days to close its books each month, but by 1993 it took two days. This time difference translates to a considerable cost savings.

Quality efforts should be clearly focused. In deciding how to tie quality to strategic plans, companies may want to listen to the advice of Motorola vice president Paul Noakes: "Identify three or four critical issues. You can't work on two dozen."[19]

## THE CORPORATE PORTFOLIO APPROACH

In this approach, top management evaluates each of the corporation's various business units with respect to the marketplace and the corporation's internal makeup. When all business units have been evaluated, an appropriate strategic role is developed for each unit with the goal of improving the overall performance of the organization. The corporate portfolio approach is rational and analytical, is guided primarily by market opportunities, and tends to be initiated and controlled by top management only.

**portfolio framework:**
An approach to corporate-level strategy advocated by the Boston Consulting Group; also known as the BCG matrix.

One of the best-known examples of the corporate portfolio approach is the **portfolio framework** advocated by the Boston Consulting Group. This framework is also known as the *BCG Matrix*.[20]

The BCG approach to analyzing a corporate portfolio of businesses focuses on three aspects of each particular business unit: its sales, the growth of its market, and whether it *absorbs* or *produces* cash in its operations. Its goal is to develop a balance among business units that use up cash and those that supply cash.

**FIGURE 10-5**    The BCG Matrix

MARKET GROWTH RATE

HIGH    ★ STAR Modest + or – cash flow    QUESTION MARK Large negative cash flow ?

LOW    CASH COW Large positive cash flow $    DOG Modest + or – cash flow 🐕

HIGH                                          LOW

RELATIVE MARKET SHARE

*Source:* Reprinted by permission of Arnoldo C. Hax and Nicolas S. Majluf, "The Use of the Growth-Share Matrix in Strategic Planning," *Interfaces* 13, no. 1 (February 1983). Copyright ©1983, The Institute of Management Sciences.

Figure 10-5 shows a four-square BCG matrix in which business units can be plotted according to the rate of growth of their market segment and their relative market share. A business unit in the *question mark* category—a business with a relatively small market share in a rapidly growing market—can be an uncertain and expensive venture. The rapid growth of the market may force it to invest heavily simply to maintain its low share, even though that low market share is yielding low or perhaps negative profits and cash flow. Increasing the question mark's share of the market relative to the market leader would require still larger investments. Yet the rapid growth of the market segment offers exciting opportunities if the proper business strategy—and the funds to implement it—can be found.

A business in the *star* category—high relative market share in a rapidly growing market—should be quite profitable. However, the need to go on investing in order to keep up with the market's rapid growth may consume more cash than is currently being earned. The *cash cow*—high relative market share in a slowly growing market—is both profitable and a source of excess cash. The slow growth of the market does not require large investments to maintain market position. Finally, the *dog*—a business with low relative market share in a slowly growing or stagnant market-is seen as a moderate user or supplier of cash.

A *success sequence* in the BCG matrix involves investing cash from *cash cows* and the more successful *dogs* in selected *question marks* to enable them to become *stars* by increasing their relative market shares. Over time, when the rate of market growth slows, the *stars* will become *cash cows,* generating excess cash to invest in the next generation of promising *question marks*.

## "FIVE FORCES" CORPORATE STRATEGY

Another well-known approach to corporate strategy is Michael Porter's "five forces" model.[21] In Porter's view, an organization's ability to compete in a given market is determined by that organization's technical and economic resources, as well as by five environmental "forces," each of which threatens the organization's venture into a new market. The strategic manager, says Porter, must analyze these forces and propose a program for influencing or defending against them. The aim is to find a lucrative and defensible niche for the organization.

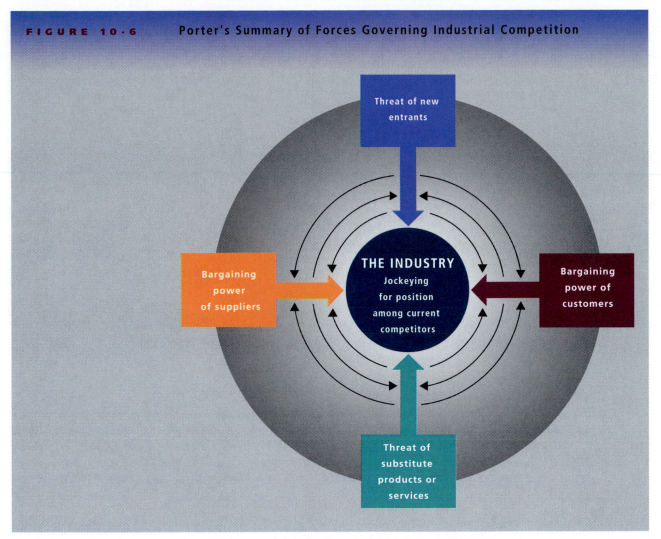

**FIGURE 10·6**    Porter's Summary of Forces Governing Industrial Competition

*Source:* Michael E., Porter, *Competitive Strategy: Techniques for Analyzing Industries and Competitors* (New York: Free Press, 1980), p. 4.

Porter's five forces, shown in Figure 10-6, are all relationships between the managers at a given organization and people acting at other organizations. Here, it is clear that business relationships are "two-way streets." In the following list of the five forces we use Federal Express as an example, suggesting how each force could influence corporate strategy and what kind of guidance managers would find:

1. *Threat of new entrants.* Keep an eye on what American Airlines and United Airlines might do to expand their cargo services into new markets.
2. *Bargaining power of buyers (customers).* Keep prices within *x* percent of UPS and the U.S. Postal Service for similar services. Seek new variations on delivery services; "next day" might not suit everyone's budget.
3. *Bargaining power of suppliers.* Discuss operating plans for acquiring new jet aircraft with manufacturers such as Boeing, to get favorable aircraft delivery slots.
4. *Threat of substitute products.* Watch out for MCI and AT&T, with their global telecommunications presences and newly enhanced network capacities.
5. *Rivalry among competitors.* Watch UPS advertising campaigns and monitor postal service labor contracts.

**RIVALRY AMONG COMPETITORS.** As a major competitor in the package-delivery business, United Parcel Service is a company Federal Express must watch closely. Which of the "five forces" are affected by such competition?

## CORPORATE ENTERPRISE STRATEGY

Peter Drucker and other management consultants and theorists used to argue that the most important question for managers to ask was: What's your business? The emphasis on clearly defining *what* business an organization was in captured the creative and intellectual imagination of an entire generation of management thinkers. The literature of the field is filled with stories about consultants who made a fortune by offering insights such as, "You aren't in the tin can business, you are in the *packaging* business."

But another question lurks at the heart of strategic management decisions: What do you *stand* for? This question calls for a statement of values and principles, for an answer to questions about *why* a company does what it does. The critic who asks, "Why did AT&T agree to divest the Bell operating companies?" may want to know *what* options were available to AT&T, but it is even more likely that the critic wants to know what values and principles lay behind AT&T's decision. Drucker and others call such a statement of values and principles **enterprise strategy** (*E-Strategy* for short).

At least seven different enterprise strategies have been identified:

1. *Stockholder E-Strategy*: The corporation should maximize the interests of stockholders.
2. *Managerial Prerogative E-Strategy:* The corporation should maximize the interests of management.
3. *Restricted Stakeholder E-Strategy:* The corporation should maximize the interests of a narrow set of stakeholders, such as customers, employees, and stockholders.
4. *Unrestricted Stakeholder E-Strategy*: The corporation should maximize the interest of all stakeholders.
5. *Social Harmony E-Strategy:* The corporation should maximize social harmony.
6. *Rawlsian E-Strategy:* The corporation should promote inequality among stakeholders only if inequality results in raising the level of the worst-off stakeholder.

**enterprise strategy (E-strategy):**

A statement of values and principles that explains why an organization does what it does.

**TOM'S OF MAINE.** What is likely to be the E-Strategy of Tom's of Maine, known for its commitment to ethics? (Recall that Tom's, marketer of a line of natural personal-care products, is the subject of the Management 2000 and Beyond feature in Chapter 4.)

7. *Personal Projects E-Strategy:* The corporation should maximize its ability to enable corporate members to carry out their personal projects.

Although these brief statements become immensely more complicated when any organization attempts to put them into practice, the trend toward looking at the ethical foundations of strategy is likely to continue—especially given the uncertain environment of today's organizations and the increasingly critical eye with which its decisions are being examined.[22]

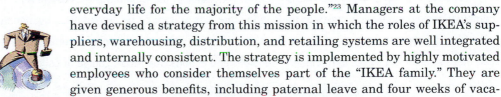

**E-STRATEGY IN PRACTICE.** IKEA managers have established an entire business around the mission of the company's founder, Ingvar Kamprad, to "create a better everyday life for the majority of the people."[23] Managers at the company have devised a strategy from this mission in which the roles of IKEA's suppliers, warehousing, distribution, and retailing systems are well integrated and internally consistent. The strategy is implemented by highly motivated employees who consider themselves part of the "IKEA family." They are given generous benefits, including paternal leave and four weeks of vacation after five years with the company. At the same time, company executives fly coach and stay in lower-priced hotels. So, the E-Strategy at IKEA combines elements of improving people's lives and relating as family members.

Managers at KinderCare Learning Centers, Inc. have recognized the opportunities offered by the increase in women in the workforce. KinderCare operates education-oriented child-care centers. As more women enter the workforce, managers at a variety of organizations have seen the value of offering on-site or subsidized child care as a benefit. It is an excellent enticement and morale-builder for their employees. KinderCare is expanding to meet such corporate needs. It is opening new centers at a rate of more than two a month near mass transit stations and at work sites.[24] So, the "E-Strategy" here appears to combine elements of pre-school education and strong assurances that child care will be conveniently available. Think about the "E-Strategy" that seems to be followed at MTV. Then compare that to an "E-strategy" that managers appear to follow at CNN.

**MANAGEMENT 2000 AND BEYOND**

# COLLECTIVE STRATEGY

There is a trend in strategic management toward more collaborative efforts between people at different organizations. One variation on this theme is called *collective strategy*,[25] which occurs when people at different organizations with common concerns collaborate to determine how they will approach certain issues. The idea here is that strategic managers have reason to worry not only about their own company strategy but also a sense of direction for *some collection* of companies that have common concerns.

Managers at WordPerfect Corporation have developed a new strategy of *strategic partnering* with an array of hardware manufacturers and software developers to encourage high-quality integration with WordPerfect products. Managers at the company believe that such partnerships will combine a partner's technology with in-house development, which will lead to better product solutions and, hence, better products for Wordperfect's customers.[26] If strategic managers at these other companies plan with the same ideas in mind, then a collective strategy can informally (or tacitly) emerge among the companies.

Collective strategies can also be explicit agreements. A vivid example involves the seven Regional Bell Holding Companies created at the 1984 AT&T divestiture—NYNEX, Bell Atlantic, Bell South, Ameritech, Southwestern Bell, US West, and Pacific Telesis. Managers at all of these companies have a common interest in ensuring that the quality and pace of improvements in the nationwide telecommunications network be comparable across the United States. To meet this common need, Bellcore was formed as a vehicle for conducting research and development in the area of telecommunications technologies. Results can be used in each of the seven regions covered by these companies' networks.[27]

Collective strategy-making has one significant constraint in the United States. Federal antitrust laws prohibit price-fixing, combinations among rivals to restrain trade, and other acts that might be agreed upon by managers at a collective of companies. Here is one more example of how webs of relationships, and potential spillover effects from a given business relationship, can make a major difference in managers' decisions and actions. The future course of collective strategy is an open question.

# NEW BUSINESS SERVICES AT FEDERAL EXPRESS

Recently Federal Express managers have been able to employ the company's worldwide distribution advantages along with its information management and technology strengths to enter another market: logistics planning for global companies. Logistics involves managing the movement and storage of materials, parts, and finished goods from suppliers, through the firm, to the customer. Federal Express' new Business Logistics Services unit offers customers an array of business services such as purchase ordering, receipt of goods, order entry and warehousing, inventory accounting, shipping, accounts receivable, and invoice reporting.

For instance, National Semiconductor management recently awarded Federal Express its finished goods delivery business from Southeast Asia to customers worldwide. Federal Express guarantees 2-day delivery, a reduction from the manufacturer's previous 5-18 day cycles. Under the new contract, Federal Express will use its own Singapore warehouse to store finished goods from National Semiconductor's Southeast Asia assembly points, ship the goods, clear them through customs, and deliver them to customers. National Semiconductor will enter orders directly into Federal Express's database and will be able to track them as they are moved from inventory, packed, shipped, and signed for by the customer.

This new service is a culminating example of how strategic planning and strategy implementation—the components of strategic management—are not only the products of what managers envision for a given company such as Federal Express but also a product of converging pursuits. Strategic management is moving into a *hopeful future with others*.

## SUMMARY

1. **Describe the usefulness of goals at an organization.**

   Planning at an organization involves setting goals and choosing the means for people to carry out those goals for the organization. Goals are important because (1) they provide a sense of direction, (2) they focus our efforts, (3) they guide our plans and decisions, and (4) they help us evaluate our progress. Although planning is normally shown as just one of the four management functions, it is more appropriate to think of planning as a locomotive that drives a train of organizing, leading, and controlling activities.

2. **Distinguish between strategic and operational plans.**

   Managers at organizations use two main types of plans. Strategic plans are designed to meet the organization's broad goals, while operational plans show how strategic plans will be implemented in day-to-day endeavors. Strategic plans and operational plans are linked to the organization's mission statement, the broad goal that justifies the organization's existence. Mission statements are based on planning premises, basic assumptions about the organization's place in the world. Strategic plans and operational plans differ in their time horizons, their scope, and their degree of detail.

3. **Understand a strategy as an attempt to place an organization in its environment.**

   A very important output of the planning process is a strategy for an organization. The term *strategy* refers to what managers want the organization to accomplish. A strategy positions the organization in a particular place in the organization's environment.

**4. Trace why the strategic management process has evolved.**

Since World War II, the practice of planning an organization's strategy has become a specialized kind of planning called strategic management. A four-step strategic management process is commonly used by managers to decide on the organization's strategy and then get people to act on—or implement—that strategy. The four steps are goal setting, strategy formulation, administration, and strategic control. Strategic decision-making occurs at the corporate level, the business-unit level, and the functional-level of an organization. At the end of this progression are the operational plans for carrying out the strategy. This makes strategic management all the more specialized.

**5. Express a strategy as a substantive statement about where an organization is headed.**

A strategy gives guidance to managers about the organization's future. Three ways of expressing that guidance in a corporate strategy are a Corporate Portfolio approach, a "Five Forces" approach, and an Enterprise Strategy approach.

**6. Discuss the opportunities and constraints on collaborative approaches to strategy.**

More collaborative approaches to corporate strategy have appeared in recent years. One example is collective strategy. A collaborative approach grows out of the recognition that managers at different organizations can have coinciding interests. Still, antitrust laws and enforcement set limits on what degree of collaboration is feasible.

## REVIEW QUESTIONS

1. Explain the four reasons goals are important to planning.
2. What are the two types of plans and how are they related? Different?
3. Explain the two ways the term *strategy* is used, with examples from organizations you know.
4. How did our current concept of strategy develop?
5. What are the three levels of strategy and how are they different?
6. What do you interpret as the portfolio corporate strategy at your college or university?
7. What do you interpret as the "five forces" strategy that can be effective for your college or university?
8. Under what kind of Enterprise Strategy would you like some day to work?
9. What examples of collaborative strategy do you observe in your daily life?

## KEY TERMS

| | |
|---|---|
| Strategic plans | Business-unit strategy |
| Operational plans | Functional-level strategy |
| Mission statement | Corporate strategy |
| Strategy | Portfolio framework |
| Strategic management | Enterprise strategy |
| Corporate-level strategy | |

## FROM BASIC SPORTSWEAR TO HIGH FASHION: LIZ CLAIBORNE[28]

While entrepreneurs around the world in every industry thrive by taking the consumer by surprise and turning dreams into realities, one company has held its own by doing just the opposite. Liz Claiborne, the largest women's apparel manufacturer in the world, brings women in touch with *themselves,* not their dreams. According to the program for a Liz Claiborne spring 1992 fashion show, Claiborne designs are "[s]imple, straightforward fashion that's designed for women who have more important things to think about than what to wear. No gimmicks. No surprises."[29]

Although Chairman Jerome Chazen understands the ingredients in Claiborne's success, he cannot help but consider whether the strategy will continue to remain effective. Panicky competitors have become entrenched in a pattern of discounting merchandise. Consumers are becoming increasingly averse to paying full price for anything. But Liz Claiborne takes pride in being able to sell more than 55 percent of its clothes at full price. In addition, although Liz Claiborne still holds the lion's share of the market, companies like the Gap and the Limited still present strong competition. Can the company adhere to its traditional conservatism and customer-driven planning and survive?

Liz Claiborne, founded in the 1980s, grew from a basic sportswear business to become a multifaceted fashion house. In 1986, it became one of only two companies started by a woman to be named a member of the Fortune 500. During the past decade, sales have grown at a rate of about 36 percent annually, to nearly $2 billion—almost twice that of the nearest competitor. In addition, profits have increased 42 percent annually, to an impressive $205 million. This has all taken place in spite of the deepest retailing slump since the Depression. Liz Claiborne has become not only the fashion industry leader but also one of the most successful companies in the United States today.

Integral to the company's success is its customer-driven planning. A sophisticated computer system, known as System Updated Retail Feedback (SURF), keeps the company in touch with what is selling and what is not, around the country, around the clock. A $10 million system of IBM computers is used to crunch information and produce bound volumes at the end of each week. Division heads then determine

**LISTENING TO CUSTOMERS.** Liz Claiborne specialists visit shops throughout the United States to talk with customers and solicit feedback.

both short- and long-term planning needs according to customer reactions to particular sales, styles, sizes, and colors.

SURF also enables Liz Claiborne to reach the customer in her favorite store. The same store in different geographic locations often serves different niches. For example, career clothes may move quickly at Bloomingdales in Tyson's Corner, Virginia, whereas casual clothes may sell more easily at Bloomingdales at White Flint Mall in Bethesda, Maryland. Similarly, Macy's at Tyson's Corner might sell more sportswear. SURF allows Liz Claiborne to adjust the merchandise sold in particular outlets according to the niche being served.

Technology can supplement, but does not replace, personal endeavors. Thus Liz Claiborne also monitors customer perceptions through personal interaction with customers and retailers. About 150 specialists around the country have responsibility for talking to customers as they shop to solicit feedback. The company also has about 18 stand-alone stores that serve as testing grounds for new ideas.

Liz Claiborne keeps in close contact with retailers, both to make sure they are handling merchandise properly and to field questions and concerns. The company maintains consistency in the presentation of its merchandise through a group of about 21 consultants who are responsible for visiting department stores to ensure that clothes and displays are arranged uniformly according to "Lizmap" diagrams. The company also has about 95 customer-service telephone operators, most of whom are assigned to respond to retailer questions and concerns.

In effect, the customer does the planning for Liz Claiborne. "This company truly believes it was built by the customer," said Wendy Banks, senior vice president of marketing. "Now every company in America has decided that's what they need—to take care of customers. We've been doing it since the day we started."[30] Jay Margolis, vice chairman of the board and president of the women's sportswear division, echoes the sentiment. "Remember who we listen to: our customer," he noted. "She votes on us every day of the week."[31]

While recognizing the tradition of Liz Claiborne, Chazen must still consider changing industry dynamics. Can the company continue listening to the customer and still remain strong?

### CASE QUESTIONS

1. What actions by others in the industry might be of greatest concern to Chazen?
2. Comment on the internal consistency of what is done strategically at Liz Claiborne. Do goals, strategies, administration, and strategic control seem to be in harmony?
3. What collective strategy opportunities might exist for Chazen to consider?

---

## VIDEO CASE STUDY

### PLANNING FOR A MIRACLE ON 34TH STREET[32]

"There's absolutely no reason for any reasonable person to worry about our financial obligations."[33] These were the confident words of R. H. Macy's CEO Edward S. Finkelstein in 1991. By April 1992, however, the $6.3 billion retailer had filed for Chapter 11 and Finkelstein was no longer CEO. Mounting debt, a lack of new equity, and an antiquated operating system proved to be more imposing obstacles than initially expected.

Macy's, "The World's Largest Store," was not yet ready to give in to defeat, however. Embracing a rather unorthodox idea, the directors placed the company's fate in the hands of two disparate co-CEOs: Myron "Mike" Ullman III, a financial whiz and a relative newcomer to both Macy's and the retail industry, and Mark Handler, Finkelstein's protégé and a career-long Macy's merchandising executive. They were gambling on Ullman's ability to fix the numbers and Handler's skill in maintaining the company's image and revamping its product line.

Almost everything at Macy's was in need of repair: customer service, cost controls, computer systems, even the type and price of its merchandise. Compounding the problem was the fact that almost all of Macy's competitors enjoyed substantial leads in all these areas. To make matters even worse, retailers everywhere were feeling the effects of penny-pinching consumers, and Macy's was no exception. A difficult road lay ahead for Ullman and Handler.

In November 1992, the duo released a five-year plan that would carry Macy's out of the red and back into the black. "We're not predicting 10 percent sales growth and margins improving two points," said Ullman in his no-nonsense manner. "Our plan is realistic."[34] In fact, the plan predicted slow sales for 1993 and did not project a return to previous cash flow levels until 1998. Macy's creditors were impressed by the down-to-earth plan and decided to lighten Macy's covenants and allow the company some breathing room.

Wasting no time, Ullman and Handler decided to shift the company's focus away from the high-priced, glitzy product line for which it had become famous to a new, more moderately priced line to appeal to the new wave of cost-conscious consumers. While some people claimed that such downscaling would cost Macy's its reputation as a fashion authority, the CEOs disagreed. "Moderate is a price point, not a fashion statement," Ullman asserted. "We can sell well-made, stylish clothes that don't cost a fortune."[35]

For example, Macy's began carrying Levi Strauss products again, after having dropped the brand in 1983 when Levi began to sell to competitors such as J. C. Penney's and Sears. At the time, Macy's had considered such retailers inferior, and did not want to carry the same merchandise.

A change of heart came with the change in times. As Ullman explained, managers realized that "customers don't criticize us because they don't like the merchandise we carry"; rather, "We get criticized when we don't have what they want to buy when they come in to buy it."[36] In order to remedy this problem, the CEOs implemented a new system referred to as Buyer-Planner-Store, or BPS for short. "The buyer is the person who is going to shop the market and shop the competition," pointed out Jane Sanford, corporate senior vice president for BPS and MIS. "The buyer will get the best merchandise, the best price, and the best delivery. The planner will influence the quantities of the buys by the buyer and will track variations in customer response store by store. The store manager will pick up nuances in the store that we may miss—after all, this is the person walking the building."[37] Such a system enables Macy's to plan for the customer.

While this represents a quantum leap from Macy's old system, the BPS is not a new idea. Specialty chains such as the Limited and the Gap have been using similar systems for years. Nevertheless, implementation of the system does demonstrate that Macy's is finally waking up to the need for change. "When you had a buyer who was buying for eight or ten stores, back in the good old days," commented Handler, "he or she could make the distributions and still shop the market, and still do the advertising. But now that we expect a buyer to deal with as many as 60 locations, the whole structure needs to be changed."[38]

Attempting to improve customer service and store layout, Ullman and Handler installed a new satellite network to connect suppliers with salespeople, similar to the systems already in place in companies such as Home Depot and Dayton Hudson. Fashion designer Donna Karan, for instance, can inform people how best to coordinate her clothing and accessories for store display. Moreover, the satellite linkup permits Macy's executives to talk directly to their employees about issues or concerns.

In addition, Macy's has taken a step ahead of the competition in what may prove to be the most profitable and successful portion of the CEOs' plan: TV Macy's. Slated to begin in the fall of 1994, TV Macy's is a 24-hour cable channel selling Macy's own private-label apparel, housewares, and other items in addition to national brand products. While rivals such as Saks Fifth Avenue have experimented with one- or two-hour spots on QVC or Home Shopping Network (HSN), TV Macy's will be the first channel devoted entirely to a single retailer. The channel, which will compete directly with HSN and QVC, hopes to tap into the rapidly expanding $2.25 billion home shopping market. In addition, it will serve to familiarize home viewers with Macy's products and provide access to those products to people not located near a Macy's store. Retail consult Isaac Lagando estimates that the channel could generate upwards of $250 million in sales by its fourth year.

While Macy's is far from out of the woods, it appears that under the new direction of its co-CEOs, the 137-year-old retailing chain is at least on the right path. "This has been a very painful exercise," admits Ullman. "We've trailed the industry. But we're trying to return to a leadership position."[39] Considering that Macy's headquarters store is on 34th Street in New York, anything is possible.

## CASE QUESTIONS

1. What steps have the CEOs taken to set realistic goals?
2. Analyze the CEOs' strategy according to the Porter framework.
3. What kind of planning and strategy techniques could Finkelstein have used to prevent the situation that the CEOs confronted when they took over?
4. What planning and strategic measures would you recommend?
5. How does TV Macy's fit in to the company's overall strategy for survival?

## CHAPTER 11

# STRATEGY IMPLEMENTATION

**Upon completing this chapter, you should be able to:**

1. Explain the key aspects of strategy implementation and its relationship to strategic planning.

2. Describe Chandler's thesis concerning the growth and development of an organization's strategy and structure.

3. List the seven factors in the Seven-S model and explain how they interact in strategy implementation.

4. Explain the concept of institutionalizing strategy.

5. Distinguish between the two basic types of operational plans.

6. Explain the concept of management by objectives and describe its essential elements.

# Sonic scores Sega success[1]

In 1990 when Sega Enterprises entered the video game market in the United States, Nintendo held between 80 percent and 90 percent of the $3.5 billion industry. By November 1993, however, Nintendo found itself locked in "mortal combat" with Sega for market dominance, with every point counting. How was it that an upstart company such as Sega came to threaten the dominance of such a clear market leader?

Sonic the Hedgehog.

What Sonic brought to Sega was a hook something to link the customer with the technology through the company. Nintendo had Mario; Sega needed a mascot. So in June 1991, Sega began packaging the new "Sonic the Hedgehog" game with its Genesis system. The character attracted an immediate following and transformed Sega into a serious competitor virtually overnight. By Christmas of that year Sonic had become so popular that Sega was not able to meet the demand for its new Genesis systems. During the next three years Sonic's popularity continued to soar. A 1993 Q-Study by Marketing Evaluation, Inc., placed Sonic the Hedgehog in close competition with Arnold Schwarzenegger and Michael Jordan as the favorite personality of boys aged six to eleven. That same study credited Sonic as the most popular video game character; Tails, Sonic's partner in "Sonic the Hedgehog II," came in second in the study. Mario lagged behind in 24th place.

As obvious as it may seem in retrospect, the need for a company icon was not initially recognized. Indeed, Sega made several unsuccessful attempts at gaining market share before hitting upon a winning solution. Unlike later efforts that recognized the importance of image and brand recognition, early efforts were centered around technological advances. In 1986, Sega introduced its Master System, which offered superior graphics to Nintendo's own Nintendo Entertainment System (NES), but failed to gain more than a toehold in the U.S. market. In 1989, Sega developed the Genesis system, armed with a more powerful microprocessor chip that allowed for far superior graphics and more sophisticated sound; nevertheless, Nintendo was still able to hold on to 85 percent of the market with its technologically-inferior system. It was not until the introduction of Sonic that Sega was finally able to taste success.

Sega's success was not due to Sonic's popularity alone, however. Also working in Sega's favor was its decentralized organizational structure. Nintendo experienced trouble responding to the market as a result of its intricate company bureaucracy. While Nintendo was notorious for requiring Hiroshi Yamauchi, president of Nintendo of America, to spend countless hours in telephone conversations with his superiors in Japan in order to make strategic decisions regarding the U.S. market, Thomas

*Nintendo found itself locked in "mortal combat" with Sega....*

**Sonic the Hedgehog.** Sega's creative mascot, Sonic the Hedgehog, turned Sega's Genesis system into a contender overnight.

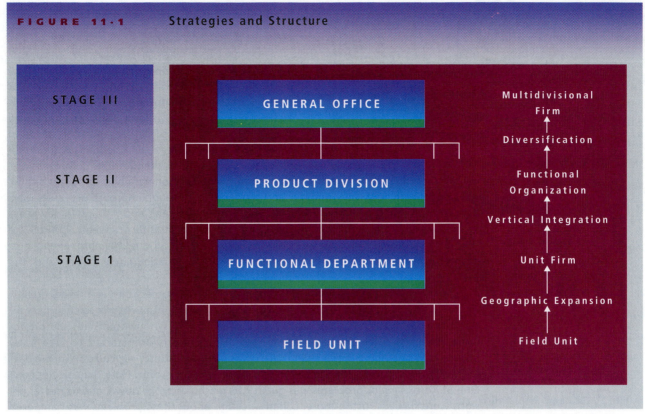

**FIGURE 11-1**     Strategies and Structure

STAGE III

STAGE II

STAGE 1

GENERAL OFFICE

PRODUCT DIVISION

FUNCTIONAL DEPARTMENT

FIELD UNIT

Multidivisional Firm

↑

Diversification

↑

Functional Organization

↑

Vertical Integration

↑

Unit Firm

↑

Geographic Expansion

↑

Field Unit

zation. Not surprisingly, the chances that an organization's strategy will succeed are far greater when its structure matches its strategy. By the same token, as its basic strategy changes over time, so must its structure.[5]

## CHANDLER'S THESIS

In his ground-breaking study of the history of large corporations, Alfred Chandler examined the growth and development of 70 of the largest businesses in the United States, including Du Pont, General Motors, Standard Oil, and Sears, Roebuck.[6] He observed a common pattern in their development. Although the organizations changed their growth strategies to suit technological, economic, and demographic changes, new strategies created administrative problems and economic inefficiencies. Structural changes were needed to solve those problems and to maximize economic performance. Thus, Chandler concluded that organizational structure followed and reflected the growth strategy of the firm.

← Ch. 6, p. 159

According to Chandler, organizations pass through three stages of development, moving from a unit structure, to a functional structure, and then to a multidivisional structure (see Figure 11-1). At first, organizations are small. There is usually a single location, a single product, and a single entrepreneurial decision maker. For example, when Bill Hewlett and Dave Packard founded a company to build an audio oscillator in 1939, they were personally responsible for its design, manufacture, testing, and marketing.[7]

As an organization grows, however, increased volume and additional locations eventually create new challenges. The organization then becomes a unit firm, with several field units and an administrative office to handle coordination, specialization, and standardization among the units.

**VERTICAL INTEGRATION.** The steel companies, pioneers of vertical integration, moved into mining to have more control over their supply of raw material. This mining operation, for instance, is part of Cleveland Heights, a mining company partially owned by Bethlehem Steel.

**Vertical integration:**
Broadening the scope of an organization's operations by buying a supplier or distributor that will contribute to efficient production of primary product or service offerings.

**functional organization:**
A form of departmentalization in which everyone engaged in one functional activity, such as marketing or finance, is grouped into one unit.

**multidivisional firm:**
An organization that has expanded into different industries and diversified its products.

The next step is **vertical integration.** The organization keeps the original product but broadens its scope and strives for economies of scale by acquiring a supplier of raw materials and components or a distributor of finished goods. For example, the pioneers of vertical integration, the steel companies, eventually moved into mining. A manufacturer might naturally move into warehousing and wholesaling. However, vertical integration creates new problems in moving goods and materials through the organization's various functions. Therefore, the organization evolves into a **functional organization,** with finance, marketing, production, and other subdivisions and formalized budgeting and planning systems. Thus, as Hewlett-Packard's production of test equipment expanded, *functional* managers took over operating decisions.

In the third stage, an organization expands into different industries and diversifies its products. This phenomenon poses a significant new challenge: selecting products and industries in which to invest the organization's capital. The result is the **multidivisional firm,** which operates almost as a collection of smaller businesses. Semiautonomous product divisions take responsibility for short-term operating decisions, with the central office remaining responsible for strategic decisions with a longer time horizon. For instance, Sega was organized to give operating units a great deal of autonomy.

Chandler observed that the transition from one structure to another was often both delayed and painful. He concluded that organizations do not readily change structure because their entrepreneurial founders excel at strategy but are generally neither interested in nor knowledgeable about organizational structure. Indeed, when the organization is finally restructured, the entrepreneur often leaves. This has happened frequently in recent years in rapidly growing, technology-oriented firms like Apple Computer.[8] At Railtex Service Co., a freight-car opuse job assignment policies to actively foster the development of new managers. Similarly, new hires are given jobs in the mainstream of the organization, whether that be marketing or new-product innovation. Talented individuals are assigned mentors, put into fast-track programs, exposed to top management, and rapidly moved into positions of real responsibility.

**SKILLS.** The term *skills* refers to those activities organizations do best and for which they are known. For example, Du Pont is known for research, Procter & Gamble for product management, ITT for financial controls, and Hewlett-Packard for innovation and quality. Strategic changes may require organizations to add one or more new skills. Strategic initiatives that require the dismantling or revising of an old skill pose even more difficult implementation problems.

**SUPERORDINATE GOALS.** This refers to guiding concepts, values, and aspirations that unite an organization in some common purpose. Superordinate goals are often captured in a mission statement, but they can also be phrased as a simple slogan, such as "new products" at 3M. Superordinate goals have deep meaning within the organization. They provide a sense of purpose and a certain stability as other, more superficial characteristics of the organization change. In the case continuation, we will see how some of these Seven-S's work at Sega.

# INSTITUTIONALIZING STRATEGY

To emphasize systems, style, staff, skills, and superordinate goals, we need to look at how strategy is institutionalized. An *institution* is a collection of values, norms, roles, and groups that develops to accomplish a certain goal. The institution of education, for example, developed to prepare children to be productive members of society. To *institutionalize* a business strategy, business leaders must also develop a system of values, norms, roles, and groups that will support the accomplishment of strategic goals. So, strategy is institutionalized if it is connected to the culture, the quality system, and the other driving forces in the organization.

We have seen that the drive toward TQM can be institutionalized. Another aspect of organizational life that is also undergoing increasing institutionalization is an emphasis on ethics development. Both shift organizational attention from detection and control to coordination and strategic impact. The ultimate outcome of this shift in focus is an enhanced quality of work environment for employees and increased quality of products and services for customers.[22]

## THE ROLE OF THE CEO

Because chief executive officers (CEOs) spend most of their time developing and guiding strategy, their personal goals and values inevitably shape organizational strategy. For example, Walt Disney valued family entertainment and conceived the idea of a "magical little park" that would amuse and educate both children and their parents. His vision resulted in Disneyland, which opened in 1955. Although Disney died in 1966, his values and vision have continued to shape his company, as evidenced by the completion of his plans for Disney World (opened in 1971) and Epcot Center (opened in 1982). Usually, however, a change in CEO is associated with a change in strategy. Although current Disney CEO Michael Eisner has continued to develop the theme parks, he has moved away from Walt Disney's strategy of offering mainly G-rated films for children to create Touchstone Pictures, which offers PG and PG-13 films that appeal to wider audiences.

# THE SEVEN S'S OF SEGA'S SUCCESS

According to George Harrison, Nintendo's marketing director, Sega's strategy entails beating competitors to the market. "They will be first at all costs," said Harrison.[12] By targeting a broader market than Nintendo—going after the MTV audience of teenagers and adults, not just the younger Playskool audience—Sega has become the market leader. But Sega views its competition as more than merely Nintendo and the other video-game manufacturers. "We have to make our games more fun than watching a half hour of prime-time TV, a basketball game, or the Disney Channel. That's the competition," asserted Kalinske. "The biggest challenge in this business is to maintain our momentum and continually improve the entertainment experience."[13]

Sega's strategy can be characterized as "angle-based." Quite literally, this means that the company approaches the customer from every angle. According to *Marketing* writer Jonathan Durden, "[Sega is] always there, and I half expect to be ambushed from any angle. I think Sega uses all the tools at its disposal and appears to be quite discerning in their implementation."[14] In less than a year, Sega united with Time Warner and TCI to create the Sega Channel scheduled to debut in 1994, joined with AT&T in the creation of Edge 16, which aims at allowing clients to play computer games over telephone lines, introduced games linked to blockbuster movies such as *Jurassic Park* and *Aladdin,* and teamed up with Circus Circus, Inc. to create an elaborate amusement center in Las Vegas—just to name a handful of Sega's exploits. In addition, Sega launched a giant Sonic balloon in the 1993 Macy's Parade. "Sonic the Hedgehog is clearly breathing down the neck of [Nintendo's] Super Mario," said analyst David Leibowitz, senior vice president of Republic New York Securities.[15] In addition, through a cooperative promotion with The Lifesaver Co., purchasers of "lucky packs" of Lifesavers candy can win Sega games or Genesis machines. And don't forget that Sonic the Hedgehog is starring in both a network and syndicated television program. "A year and a half ago we were knocking on doors asking corporations to tie in with us," recalled Edward Volkwein, senior vice president of Sega's marketing. "Today we carefully answer phone calls from companies we think best fit our image."[16] Incidentally, all of this has been accomplished on a marketing budget one-third the size of Nintendo's.

*Sega uses all the tools at its disposal...*

Nintendo's virtual monopoly of the video-game market forced Sega marketing managers to develop skill in doing more with less in terms of spending. Only through intense, innovative marketing exploits has Sega been able to capture the lead. "Sega is having to approach marketing with a shot-gun approach while Nintendo has a 2-ton gorilla at its disposal," said Lee Isgur, an analyst with Volpe, Welty & Co. in San Francisco.

Integral to the success of Sega's strategy in the United States has been its decentralized organizational structure. As previously noted, Kalinske's virtually unchecked authority has enabled him to make the decisions necessary to propel Sega forward. In turn, Kalinske has provided Sega staff with a large degree of freedom and flexibility. "Our average age is about 28, and we try to keep the atmosphere fun and relaxed by letting people work flexible hours," said Kalinske. "It's no secret that our 500 employees are the largest users of pizza and Coca-Cola in the San Mateo community."[17] In addition, Sega draws from a pool of approximately 1,500 freelancers—programmers, writers, musicians and artists—who participate in the process of game creation while working out of their homes. Why has the company adapted its structure to accommodate the needs of a nontraditional workforce? Sega recognizes that the trick to surviving and succeeding in the video-game industry lies in software, and it is willing to do whatever is necessary to support creativity.

Sega achieves its strategic objectives through systems in place that support company efforts without overpowering them. Communication systems are important particularly since staff is geographically scattered. While the majority of Sega's American employees work in the San Francisco Bay area, another 30 work in Los Angeles and 30 more in Chicago. "We need to do a lot of project management work that requires information to be shared by people who are not necessarily located in the same office and (geographic) location," noted William Downs, Sega's director of MIS and telecommunication.[18] Besides the U.S. staff, the company maintains communications with the company's other locations around the world.

Perhaps most important of the systems at Sega are those relating to the company's research and development and marketing efforts. Sega conducts extensive market research in order to continually release leading-edge, exciting software that keeps up the adrenaline of Sega game players. "Kids' No. 1 desire is to be up on new stuff all the time and know things that their parents don't know," said Volkwein.[19] By conducting focus groups two to three times each week and becoming familiar with their target audience to the point of hanging out in their bedrooms and shopping with them in the malls, Sega keeps in touch with its customers.

Through all of the company's endeavors, including the initial decision to enter the video-game market, Sega's style involves taking risks. "Failure's part of the business too," said Kalinske. "The point is that you should not be afraid to take a risk."[20] Sega released a 16-bit system first, while Nintendo delayed the release of a similar machine, because it believed that the 8-bit market was still active. Then in the early 1990s Nintendo decided the market was not ready for a CD system, but Sega, wanting to be first, to make a big splash, to make some noise, plunged ahead and developed Sega CD. Regardless of whether the market was ready, the initial installment of Sega CD sold out within 48 hours. By the end of 1993, Sega CD combined software and hardware sales were estimated to have reached $365 million, about 12 percent of the company's overall expected sales.

Guiding Sega through it all has been the company's superordinate goal, explained best through its advertising campaign, "Welcome to the Next Level." Sega's overriding goal is to lead the way to the most sophisticated, most exciting, most technologically advanced software and hardware, even if it means dragging video-game players along. Sega has discovered that video-game players will buy what's new simply because it is new, even if what's new is not necessarily what's best. Fast-paced, hard-hitting, in-your-face marketing has carried the message to the public that Sega is what's new, what's hot, what's in. "The [public] perception is that Sega *is* the platform of growth, not Nintendo any more," said Isgur.[21] Essentially, Sega took everything that Nintendo was doing right, and added a new image: younger, sleeker, faster, better—the next level. →

Their role in strategy formulation makes CEOs especially important to strategy implementation. First, they *interpret* strategy, acting as final judges when managers disagree on implementation. Second, CEOs *enact*—through their words and actions—the seriousness of an organization's commitment to a strategy. Third, CEOs *motivate,* providing intangible incentives beyond pay or bonuses. By appealing to members' values, beliefs, and loyalties, CEOs can mobilize support for a strategy.

### JIM HENSON AND THE MAGIC OF THE MUPPETS

Because the head of an organization can be central to its direction and culture, an unexpected death—such as that of Muppet-creator Jim Henson—can challenge the survival of an organization. In August 1989, Walt Disney Co. had announced plans to buy the licensing and publishing businesses of Jim Henson Productions and give Muppet creator Jim Henson an exclusive 15-year production arrangement. While affectionate speculations abounded concerning a possible love triangle between Mickey Mouse, the amorous Miss Piggy, and an ever-elusive Kermit, negotiations continued, with Disney offering a reported $150 million to $200 million.

Anticipation turned to confusion on May 16, 1990, when Jim Henson died suddenly of pneumonia. Shock waves were felt throughout the world, as millions of parents—many of whom had themselves grown up with the Muppets—prepared to explain that the voices of Kermit, Ernie, Rowlf, and other characters might never again be heard.

Such fears proved unfounded, however. Henson's 115-person staff was initially devastated. To them Henson was a father figure and they were a family united by his creativity. "We shared the same heart," recalled Muppeteer Richard Hunt.

Less than six weeks later, Brian Henson, Jim's son, was named president of Jim Henson Productions, and Cheryl Henson, Jim's daughter, was named vice president for creative affairs. "My father had wonderful goals and wonderful dreams," Brian noted. "And I saw that in virtually everyone in the company. So I think, in some ways, he's still there in everyone. We've lost our focus temporarily, but we'll get that back right away. He's still there."[23]

Brian recognized the important role his father played as the provider of the company's creative inspiration. He therefore endeavored to protect his father's vision, while, at the same time, building the company. "It's not one man's vision," asserted Brian. "We are a company with a creative team at the top. My father built a company around him; I'm spreading that."[24]

The greatest challenge for Jim Henson Productions lay in figuring out how to be creative without Jim Henson. According to screenwriter Jerry Juhl, this translated into "getting back to center."[25] "You could deal with it corporately—figure out offices and things like that," he explained. "But when it came down to, 'What are we going to do when we put characters on the screen again?' That was hard."[26]

But Jim Henson Productions was able to get back on track. Although the deal with Disney fell through, several joint projects continued, including a 3-D Muppet film and live stage show for the Disney theme parks, and Disney's video arm introduced the Jim Henson Video label of Muppet programs on video cassette. In addition, in December 1992, the company released "The Muppet Christmas Carol," its first feature film project since Jim's death.

Future plans for Jim Henson productions remain uncertain. This does not indicate failure. "We still don't know where we're going to be three years from now. But that was always how my father operated," said Brian. "He constantly wanted to see what felt fresh, what new ideas came along. And then he'd have the courage to try and see if the new idea worked."[27] In this way, Brian has carried on the tradition of his father. ▬▬

## CULTURE AND STRATEGY

In Chapter 7 we saw the importance of organizational culture in understanding today's organizations. Nowhere is this concept more important than in institutionalizing strategy. When an organization's culture is consistent with its strategy, the implementation of strategy is eased considerably. Kotter and Hesketh's concept of "adaptable cultures" is an attempt to build organizational culture on a foundation of paying attention to key stakeholders such as employees, customers, and stockholders, thus ensuring that the culture can change when the organization's strategy must change.

← Ch. 7, p. 188
← Ch. 3, p. 63

It is impossible to successfully implement a strategy that contradicts the organization's culture. Thus, AT&T's traditional belief in the importance of universal telephone service, which dates from the days of its monopoly, has been a major stumbling block in the implementation of its new market-oriented strategy that distinguishes between customers who need different services. It is only recently, with the explicit culture change program introduced by Robert Allen, that AT&T

has begun to be more responsive to its customers and to act quickly when necessary. That AT&T managers are acquiring the ability to move very quickly was evident in their decision to acquire McCaw Cellular, a large, nationwide provider of cellular telephone service.

# OPERATIONALIZING STRATEGY

**operational plan:**
Plan that provides the details needed to incorporate strategy into day-to-day operations.

**I**f strategies set the general goal and course of action for organizations, **operational plans** provide the details needed to incorporate strategic plans into the organization's day-to-day *operations*. Operational plans fall into two general classes. Single-use plans are designed to be dissolved once they have achieved specific, nonrecurring goals. Standing plans, in contrast, are standardized approaches to handling recurrent and predictable situations (see Figure 11-3).[28]

## SINGLE-USE PLANS

**single-use plan:**
A detailed course of action used once or only occasionally to solve a problem that does not occur repeatedly.

**program:**
A single-use plan that covers a relatively large set of organizational activities and specifies major steps, their order and timing, and the unit responsible for each step.

**project:**
The smaller and separate portions of the programs.

**budgets:**
Formal quantitative statements of the resources allocated to specific programs or projects for a given period.

**standing plan:**
An established set of decisions used by managers to deal with recurring or organizational activities; major types are policies, procedures, and rules.

**policy:**
A standing plan that establishes general guidelines for decision making.

**rules:**
Standing plans that detail specific actions to be taken in a given situation.

**procedure:**
A standing plan that contains detailed guidelines for handling organizational actions that occur regularly.

**Single-use plans** are detailed courses of action that probably will not be repeated in the same form in the future. For example, a rapidly expanding firm, such as Fresh Fields natural grocery stores, that is planning to set up a new warehouse will need a specific single-use plan for that project. Even though the company may have established a number of warehouses in the past, the new warehouse presents unique requirements of location, construction costs, labor availability, zoning restrictions, and so forth.

A **program** is a single-use plan that covers a relatively large set of activities. It outlines (1) the major steps required to reach an objective, (2) the organization unit or member responsible for each step, and (3) the order and timing of each step. **Projects** are smaller, separate portions of programs; they are limited in scope and contain distinct directives concerning assignments and time. If the program is to transfer inventory from one warehouse to another, one related project might be to evaluate floor space at the proposed installation. **Budgets** are statements of financial resources set aside for specific activities in a given period of time; they are primarily devices to control an organization's activities, and thus are important components of programs and projects.

## STANDING PLANS

Whenever organizational activities occur repeatedly, a **standing plan**—a preestablished single decision or set of decisions—can effectively guide those activities. Once established, such standing plans help managers conserve time because similar situations are handled in a predetermined, consistent manner. Standing plans consist of policies, rules, and more detailed procedures.

A **policy** is a general guideline for decision making. It sets up boundaries around decisions, telling managers which decisions can be made and which cannot. In this way it channels the thinking of organization members so that it is consistent with organizational objectives. Your university has a number of policies, such as those that dictate the relative importance of athletics and extracurricular activities vis-a-vis academic learning and performance. Sega recently adopted a policy to label the content of its video games, to warn parents of material that may be inappropriate for some audiences. Some policies have **rules** built into them—statements of specific actions to be taken in a given situation. For instance, it may be a rule that an athlete with a grade point average below 2.0 cannot be a member of a varsity team. Most policies are accompanied by detailed **procedures,** called standard operating procedures or standard methods, which are just a de-

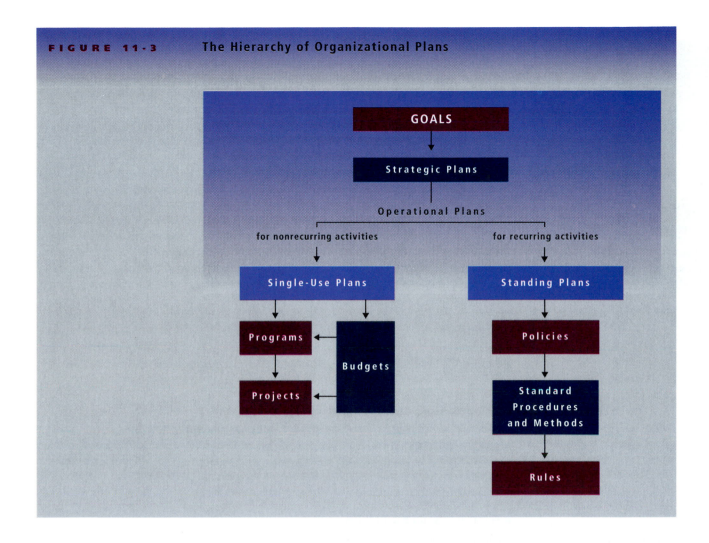

**FIGURE 11-3**     The Hierarchy of Organizational Plans

tailed set of instructions for performing a sequence of actions that occurs often or regularly.

Most organizations have some form of policies, rules, and procedures that help in implementing strategy in cases where routine action is required. At the Limited, a specialty clothing store, standard procedure ensures that customers get an offer of assistance within the first few seconds of entering the store. At Wal-Mart, a discount merchandiser, store procedure requires that one person greet all customers and smile at them.

### THE CHALLENGER DISASTER: PROCEDURES AND POLICIES DON'T ALWAYS WORK

Sometimes the existence of procedures and policies is not enough to prevent disasters. Such was the case with the *Challenger* Space Shuttle disaster. On January 28, 1986, the shuttle lifted off into a clear blue sky. In just 73 seconds, after a flawless liftoff, the *Challenger* erupted in a ball of flame, broke into seg-

**MANAGEMENT 2000 AND BEYOND**

# RETHINKING REWARDS

Today many companies depend on their reward systems to help them implement strategy. From the multimillions awarded to some senior managers in stock options to vacations at resorts for winning salespeople, rewards and incentives are a dominant part of organizational life. Rewards and incentives play an equally important role in the broader society. Teachers use gold stars and demerits for schoolchildren. Religious organizations reward perfect attendance and contributions. Political parties, have complex systems of rewards and incentives.

Imagine what your classes would be like if there were no rewards and punishments. What would motivate students to learn? Would classes be better or worse? More fun or less? What would take the place of rewards and punishments such as grades?

The basic idea is that people engage in behavior because it will lead to rewards. And as the concept of strategy implementation has evolved, many have argued that it is necessary to tie the achievement and implementation of strategic goals and plans to a specific system of rewards. To implement some long range strategic plans managers receive rewards years after the implementation actually took place. While a more thorough study of motivation awaits us in Chapter 16, at least one management writer has questioned the very idea of rewards and incentives.

Alfie Kohn, in *Punished by Rewards: The Trouble with Gold Stars, Incentive Plans, A's, Praise, and Other Bribes,* has argued that "any approach that offers a reward for better performance is destined to be ineffective."[40] He gives four reasons why rewards are a bad idea. First of all, rewards are a form of punishment. When you don't get a reward it's like being punished, and when you do get one, you can easily come to resent the control that it represents. The person giving the reward exerts power and control over you by giving you the reward. Where there is a carrot, a reward, there is also a stick, a punishment. One management theorist, Harry Levinson, says that the only thing people can imagine between a carrot and a stick is a jackass or a donkey. Using rewards and punishment is therefore treating people as equivalent to donkeys on this view.

Second, rewards can destroy relationships. Real cooperation and sharing is necessary for quality products and services (see Chapter 8). If someone is judging you in order to reward or punish you, your actions will be to seek approval or avoid disapproval, rather than to do the tasks that are necessary.

Third, rewards focus on outcomes and can ignore reasons. By rewarding the outcomes we can easily ignore the causes and the bigger system that produces the outcomes. Kohn offers a good example of a worker whose performance has deteriorated and so gets no rewards. But such a program ignores the cause of the decline in performance. He says, "Turning the workplace into a game show ('Tell our employees about the fabulous prizes we have for them if their productivity improves...') does exactly nothing to solve these underlying problems and bring about meaningful change."[41]

Finally, rewards can discourage risk taking. By focusing on the reward, managers can ignore changes in strategy that need to be made as a matter of mid-course correction, and they will not make decisions that may have higher payoffs but have more risk. Again Kohn tells us, "If you have been promised a reward, you come to see the task as something that stands between you and it. The easier that job is, the faster you can be done with it and pick up your prize."[42]

If Kohn's analysis has some validity, managers in the future will have to take a new approach to strategy implementation. They will have to design organizations and work to fit the needs and aspirations of the people doing the work. They will have to formulate strategies that clearly set forth a vision of life that employees want to realize. At least part of what we have called dynamic engagement depends heavily on understanding organizations and work in terms of values that motivate employees and other stakeholders rather than focusing on behavioral rewards.

# "WELCOME TO THE NEXT LEVEL"

The differences between the rivals were clear. While Nintendo chose to target an audience comprised of pre-teens and families, Sega has targeted a more sophisticated audience of older teens and adults. "Sega leaves in all the gory stuff, while Nintendo often softens the violence," said Ed Semrad, editor of *Electronic Gaming Monthly,* the No. 1 videogame users magazine. "Kids know the difference. They want blood."

In mid-1993, a complication arose in this formerly two-player game—new competitors. While Sega and Nintendo continued to dominate, companies such as Atari, Commodore, and Panasonic raised the stakes by introducing even more powerful 32-bit and 64-bit machines with even more exciting software. (Imagine bits as the width of the highway along which data travels; more bits allow game systems to drive increasingly powerful games at greater speeds.) With these companies bringing out the 32-bit and 64-bit systems, it was just a matter of time before Sega's and Nintendo's 16-bit systems became obsolete. The next generation was coming.

In order to buy time for the development of its 64-bit system, the Saturn system, Sega threw everything behind the 13 million 16-bit Genesis systems already installed in U.S. households as of November 1993. Sega bombarded the market with new support gadgets, presumably to keep Genesis owners from straying towards the new higher-bit systems and, of course, the SNES. For example, a full body controller was released, followed by a virtual reality headset. In addition, through an alliance with AT&T, Sega planned to enable people to play each other by modem through "The Edge." Also, the Sega Channel, through an alliance with Time Warner Entertainment and Tele-Communications Inc.

*"Sega's got the hot new technology from CD-ROM to virtual reality..."*

(TCI), to be tested in January of 1994 and available through all cable systems by early 1994, promised to add a new dimension to gameplaying. The Sega Channel would enable players to gain access to a wide range of games, including previews of new releases, for a set monthly fee, expected to end up in the neighborhood of $12 per month. According to Mark Hess, director of TCI new-product deployment, "Sega Channel will begin the process of cable TV delivery of interactive media, and it will be what segues us into the future of true, two-way interactivity." The Sega Channel promised to prove popular, considering that as of 1993, 70 percent of Sega Genesis owners subscribed to cable.

Sega then began vigorously pursuing the development of its Saturn system, knowing all the while that Nintendo was doing the same with Project Reality, its 64-bit system. The players are facing off. "Nintendo and

**KIDS LOVE SONIC.** Sonic was the most popular video game character in 1993, rivaling Arnold Schwarzenegger and Michael Jordan as the favorite personality of young boys.

Sega are dead even in terms of market share, but kids know that Sega's got the hot new technology from CD-ROM to virtual reality," remarked Semrad, who felt Sega would win-out, "and that's what they're watching now." On the other hand, "No one can do what they're all trying to do better than Silicon Graphics," said David Sheff, whose book, *Game Over,* chronicled Nintendo's history. "Just when everybody's written off Nintendo, they can come in and trump everyone." In the final analysis, how Nintendo and Sega implement these ideas for new products will determine their success.

# ORGANIZING

# INTERSECTION

## 1

Part IV of this book is devoted to the process of organizing. These four chapters address how managers shape relationships into organizational structures, and thereby lead employees into the organization's future. Chapter 12 addresses organizational design and structure. Each of the next three chapters then deals with an aspect of making organizational design effective in light of organizational goals. Chapter 13 addresses basic rules by which people operate within an organizational structure. Those rules deal with authority and power. In Chapter 14, we look at the process of preparing people to work effectively and efficiently within organizational structures. This process is called human resource management. Then, in Chapter 15, we consider the managerial challenge of keeping an organizational structure both enduring and sufficiently vibrant to produce new products and services. That is the challenge of managing organizational change and innovation.

## CHAPTER 12

# ORGANIZATIONAL DESIGN AND ORGANIZATIONAL STRUCTURE

**Upon completing this chapter, you should be able to:**

1. Explain the purpose of decisions about organizational design.

2. Describe the logical relationships between division of work, departmentalization, hierarchy, and coordination.

3. Trace the evolution of thinking about what organizational designers must factor into their decisions.

4. Define downsizing in terms of the four building blocks of organizational design.

5. Explain the general benefits of organizational structures, and the benefits and costs of each particular kind of structure.

6. Discuss the reasons why informal organizations exist.

7. Identify the key assumptions that make the virtual corporation different from traditional structures.

# HEWLETT-PACKARD AND THE DIGITAL REVOLUTION[1]

Hewlett-Packard Co. (HP), like many of the leading computer companies, began the 1990s with a changing of the guard. The company announced in July 1992 that Lewis E. Platt would be taking over for longtime chief executive John A. Young. Unlike IBM and Digital Equipment Corp. (DEC), however, HP was an organization that was not in need of reconstruction. In fact, in terms of profits, HP was excelling against nearly all of its competitors, including IBM and DEC. While its computer rivals continued to struggle with weak sales and high overheads, HP's orders and profits remained strong. It seemed as if all Platt had to do was sit back and maintain course. But, during the 26 years he had spent with the company, Platt had learned that success should not give way to complacency. "A company has continually to re-invent itself," he asserted. "The difficult part is making changes while you are doing well. You have got to start before the downhill trends are obvious." [2]

While serving as head of HP's Computer Systems Organization, Platt had witnessed the beginnings of a revolution—a *digital* revolution. As computers, communications, and consumer electronics began to merge, Platt saw that all types of media were being converted into digital form. Everything from television programs to telephone calls was being translated into binary computer code so that it could be transmitted anywhere in the world that a digital network reached. The future of the industry, as Platt saw it, lay in the multibillion-dollar markets that were promising to open through the digitization of business and entertainment, such as interactive games, video-on-demand, home shopping, and personal communication.

> *"The difficult part is making changes while you are doing well."*

The problem was that, while HP continued to outpace its competitors traditional computer industry, the company's place in the new computer industry was less clear. HP was absent from the merger and joint-venture deal-making that was taking place. While IBM, U S West, and Apple were being approached by the likes of Sony and Time-Warner, HP found itself unattached. Platt knew that if HP was not able to hop on to the digital bandwagon, its role in the new digital arena would be severely limited. Despite outward appearances, HP was in some difficulty.

Platt decided that HP was going to need an entirely new line of products and consumers. By marshalling HP's numerous technologies and cross-breeding them, Platt began to drive HP full-speed ahead into a new technological era. Co-founders William Hewlett and David Packard had built HP around precision products for use in testing and measurement, so the problem was not with the quality of the products. Platt therefore brought in a reengineering team, primarily to spruce up the products and restructure the 53-year-old company. In particular, he emphasized

**LEWIS E. PLATT.** As chairman, president, and chief executive officer of Hewlett-Packard Co., Platt provides the vision for changes at HP.

the telecommunications industry and began developing equipment for the fast-paced industry. "We jumped in with both feet," he recalled. "That sector of the business grew 30 percent last year [in 1992]." [3]

By reinventing and rejuvenating what already works, Platt has moved to secure HP a future in the coming digital revolution. Not being one to stop just because things are looking up, Platt set three primary objectives for 1993 and beyond. First, Platt promised aggressive restructuring in an attempt to improve HP's profitability even further. Second, he encouraged customer satisfaction. The company had the reputation of being difficult to deal with, and Platt wants to rectify this. Finally, Platt intends to increase HP's emphasis on enlightened management in the company's culture. "HP's going to be an almost totally different company 10 years from now," predicts Joel S. Birnbaum, HP Laboratories Director.[4] With all of the changes taking place at HP, coupled with Platt's ongoing why-wait-till-tomorrow attitude, the only safe prediction seems that more change will occur. →

HEWLETT-PACKARD'S PLATT sees an opportunity to draw on strengths HP developed in its history: (a) knowledge about customers who use measurement devices; (b) knowledge about making and marketing a family of computer products; and (c) knowledge about making and marketing computers that "talk" in networks. From these strengths will come a redefined Hewlett-Packard strategy, requiring a new structure to support it.

Along with developing a new strategy, Platt must lead a decision-making process to determine how to organize the company for implementing the strategy. It is likely that collaboration among existing parts of the Hewlett-Packard organization, where the knowledge strengths reside, will be necessary. And it is possible that Hewlett-Packard managers and employees will need to cultivate relationships with new "outsiders" to develop some of the new products. According to Platt, "Not one of these new products can be carried out by a single Hewlett-Packard organization."[5]

## ORGANIZATIONAL DESIGN AND ORGANIZATIONAL STRUCTURE

An organization is a pattern of relationships—many interwoven, simultaneous relationships—through which people, under the direction of managers, pursue their common goals. These goals are the products of the decision-making processes that we introduced to you as *planning* (Part III). The goals that managers develop through planning are typically ambitious, far-reaching, and open-ended. Managers want to ensure that their organizations can endure for a long time. Members of an organization need a stable, understandable framework within which they can work together toward organizational goals. The managerial process of *organizing* involves making decisions about creating this kind of framework so that organizations can last from the present well into the future.

← ch. 10, p. 265

At Hewlett-Packard, Lewis Platt must decide on a pattern of working relationships that will enable Hewlett-Packard employees to capitalize on what they know and what they have learned in their past work. Platt does not start from zero. He walked into a preexisting plan of organization. People were accustomed to relating to one another in certain ways. So Platt's organizing challenge is to build on this base as he develops a structure that will take HP into the future.

Managers must take into account two kinds of factors when they organize. First, they must outline their goals for the organization, their strategic plans for pursuing those goals (Chapter 10), and the capabilities at their organizations for carrying out those strategic plans (Chapter 11). These planning tasks filled Platt's agenda from his first day as CEO at HP.

**organizational design:**
The determination of the organizational structure that is most appropriate for the strategy, people, technology, and tasks of the organization.

**organizational structure:**
The way in which an organization's activities are divided, organized, and coordinated.

Simultaneously, managers must consider what is going on now, and what is likely to happen in the future, in the organizational environment (Chapters 3, 4, and 5). At the intersection of these two sets of factors—plans and environments—managers make decisions that match goals, strategic plans, and capabilities with environmental factors. This crucial first step in organizing, which logically follows from planning, is the process of **organizational design.** The specific pattern of relationships that managers create in this process is called the **organizational structure.** Organizational structure is a framework that managers devise for dividing and coordinating the activities of members of an organization. Because strategies and environmental circumstances differ from one organization to the next, there are a variety of possible organizational structures. Making decision about organizational design structure is the focal point of this chapter.

## F OUR BUILDING BLOCKS

← ch. 1, p. 9

**O**rganizing is an ongoing managerial process. Strategies can change, organizational environments can change, and the effectiveness and efficiency of organizational activity does not always measure up to what managers would like. Whether forming a new organization, tinkering with an ongoing organization, or radically altering the pattern of relationships at an organization, managers take four fundamental steps when they begin to make decisions about organizing:[6]

1. Divide the total workload into tasks that can logically and comfortably be performed by individuals or groups. This is referred to as the *division of work*.
2. Combine tasks in a logical and efficient manner. The grouping of employees and tasks is generally referred to as *departmentalization*.
3. Specify who reports to whom in the organization. This linking of departments results in an organizational *hierarchy*.
4. Set up mechanisms for integrating departmental activities into a coherent whole and monitoring the effectiveness of that integration. This process is called *coordination*.

We can think of these four aspects of organizing work as the four "building blocks" of organization. They are apparent even at your favorite fast-food restaurant:

- Work is *divided* between those who cook burgers and those who make fries, for example.
- The crew members who serve customers may be thought of as working in one *department,* while those who cook may be in another department.
- Some people report to other people and take orders and advice from other people. Servers who are in training are lower in the *hierarchy* than are assistant managers, for example.
- Cooks and servers at the drive-up window *coordinate* orders by means of computer printouts and two-way radios.

Let's look at each of these building blocks in greater detail.

### DIVISION OF WORK

Adam Smith's *Wealth of Nations* opens with a famous passage on the specialization of labor in the manufacture of pins. Describing the work in a pin factory, Smith wrote, "One man draws the wire, another straightens it, a third cuts it, a fourth points it, a fifth grinds it at the top for receiving the head." Ten men work-

**BUREAUCRACY.** Massive, impersonal office buildings such as the Arco Center may convey an impression (accurate or not) of bureaucracy. Some companies today are building more campus-like facilities to encourage a different approach.

experience rather than favoritism or whim. He also admired the bureaucracy's clear specification of authority and responsibility, which he believed made it easier to evaluate and reward performance. He and other classical writers, along with their contemporaries in management, lived in a time when this approach to organizational design had precedent in government civil services. The term *bureaucracy* has not always carried the modern negative connotation—a framework for slow, inefficient, unimaginative organizational activity![30]

## THE TASK-TECHNOLOGY APPROACH

A different set of variables internal to the organization are prominent in the *task-technology* approach to organizational design that emerged in the 1960s. "Task technology" refers to the different kinds of production technology involved in making different kinds of products. Classical studies conducted in the mid-1960s by Joan Woodward and her colleagues found that an organization's task technology affected both its structure and its success.[31] Woodward's team divided about 100 British manufacturing firms into three groups according to their respective task technologies: (1) unit and small-batch production, (2) large-batch and mass production, and (3) process production.

*Unit production* refers to the production of individual items tailored to a customer's specifications—custom-made clothes, for example. The technology used in unit production is the least complex because the items are produced largely by individual craftspeople. *Small-batch production* refers to products made in small quantities in separate stages, such as machine parts that are later assembled. *Large-batch* and *mass production* refer to the manufacture of large quantities of products, sometimes on an assembly line (such as computer chips). *Process production* refers to the production of materials that are sold by weight or volume, such as chemicals or drugs. These materials are usually produced with highly complex equipment that operates in a continuous flow.

Woodward's studies led to three general conclusions. First, the more complex the technology—ranging from unit to process production—the greater the number of managers and managerial levels. In other words, complex technologies lead to tall organizational structures and require more supervision and coordination (see Figure 12-3).

Second, the span of management for first-level managers increases as we move from unit to mass production, but decreases when we move from mass to process production. Because lower-level employees in both unit and process production firms usually do highly skilled work, they tend to form small work groups, making a narrow span inevitable. In contrast, a large number of assembly-line workers who perform similar tasks can be supervised by one manager.

Third, as a firm's technological complexity increases, its clerical and administrative staffs become larger because managers need help with paperwork and non-production-related work so they can concentrate on specialized tasks. Also, complex equipment requires more maintenance and scheduling, both of which generate additional paperwork.

Woodward's studies provided evidence of the influence of technology on organizational structure. Other research has suggested that the impact of technology on structure is strongest in small firms (which the firms studied by Woodward tended to be). For large firms, the impact of technology seems to be felt mainly at the lowest levels of the organization.[32]

## THE ENVIRONMENTAL APPROACH

Around the time when Woodward was conducting her studies, Tom Burns and G.M. Stalker were developing an approach to organizational design that incorporates the organizational environment into design considerations. Burns and

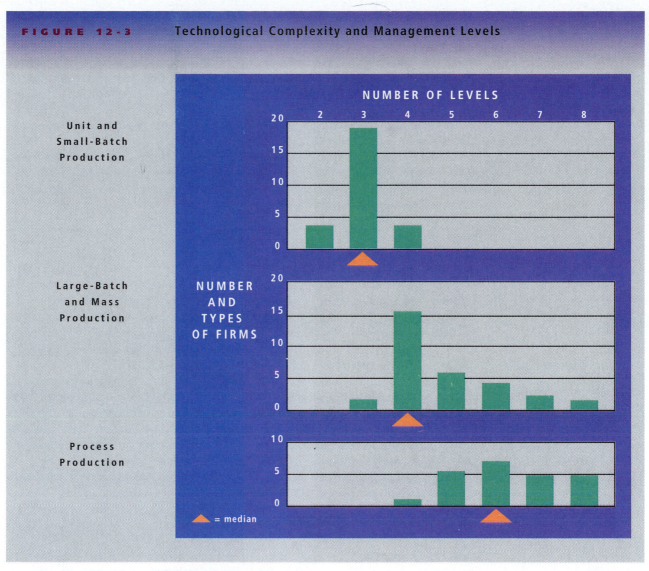

**FIGURE 12-3**  Technological Complexity and Management Levels

Source: Joan Woodward, *Industrial Organization.* Copyright 1965. By permission of Oxford University Press.

**mechanistic system:**

According to Burns and Stalker, one characterized by a bureaucratic organization.

**organic system:**

According to Burns and Stalker, one characterized by informality, working in groups, and open communication.

Stalker distinguished between two organizational systems: mechanistic and organic.[33] In a **mechanistic system,** the activities of the organization are broken down into separate, specialized tasks. Objectives for each individual and unit are precisely defined by higher-level managers following the classical bureaucratic chain of command. In an **organic system,** individuals are more likely to work in a group setting than alone. There is less emphasis on taking orders from a manager or giving orders to employees. Instead members communicate across all levels of the organization to obtain information and advice.

After studying a variety of companies, Burns and Stalker concluded that the mechanistic system was best suited to a stable environment, whereas organic systems were best suited to a turbulent one. Organizations in changing environments would probably use some combination of the two systems.

In a stable environment, each organization member is likely to continue performing the same task. Thus, skill specialization is appropriate. In a turbulent environment, however, jobs must constantly be redefined to cope with the ever-changing world. Organization members must therefore be skilled at solving a variety of problems, not at repetitively performing a set of specialized activities. In addition, the creative problem solving and decision making required in turbulent environments are best carried out in groups in which members can communicate openly. Thus, for turbulent environments, an organic system is appropriate.

An organic system benefits the Ritz-Carlton Hotel Chain, where every department has an idea team in which all employees participate. The teams meet on a formal basis and employ a five-step problem-solving process from brainstorming to implementing a proposed solution. In a recent year one of the hotels in the chain produced 1200 suggestions for improvement and 42 percent of the suggestions were adopted.[34]

At HP, John Young led a decision-making process that moved HP from one version of an organic system to another version. Volatility in many of HP's major markets was a key factor in the two-division organizational structure designed in 1990. Platt's challenge now is to consider whether a newer version of this new version is needed. HP thus appears to be an evolving organic system, in terms of the Burns and Stalker model.

## DOWNSIZING

**downsizing:**

A version of organizational restructuring which results in decreasing the size of the organization and often results in a flatter organizational structure; one way organizations convert to leaner, more flexible structures that can respond more readily to the pace of change in global markets.

In recent years, managers at numerous U.S.-based organizations have practiced a kind of organizational design process that gives significant emphasis to conditions in their organizational environments. This kind of decision making is known generally as restructuring. Today, restructuring usually involves *shrinking* the organization or, more descriptively, **downsizing**.[35]

Managers at many American companies adopted bureaucratic organizational structures when times were more stable, when companies dominated their respective environments, and when assumptions about continued economic growth were regularly borne out. Thus, such companies as Xerox, Exxon, IBM, and GM developed multilayered bureaucracies that eventually became too cumbersome when quick responses to rapidly changing times became necessary.

Waves of mergers, divestitures, and acquisitions; the deregulation of some industries; and an increasing number of new, entrepreneurial firms greatly intensified global competition (Chapters 1, 3, 5, and 6). Far-reaching technological advances further compelled managers at highly bureaucratic companies to adopt less hierarchical structures in order to become more adaptive to their environments. The important concepts today are efficiency, productivity, and quality, with organizations converting to leaner, more flexible structures that can respond more readily to the pace of change in global markets. *Downsizing* refers to this agenda of organizational design changes.

Downsizing has imposed a significant cost on millions who have lost their jobs. As of 1993, it appeared to be the African-Americans who were suffering the most. While other groups—Hispanics (60,404), Asians (55,104), Whites (71,144)—experienced net gains in employment, Blacks experienced a net loss of 59,479 jobs.[36] Another group feeling the sting of downsizing is older Americans (defined as age 40 and over as covered under the protection of the Age Discrimination Act of 1967 and subsequent amendments). In fact, some employees are suing corporations in class action suits based on age. For example, 150 former employees of Nynex have joined in a class action suit alleging that the company selected them for dismissal because of their age.[37]

Recent studies have shown that the victims of downsizing and restructuring bear costs that go beyond lost salary—and often lower salaries when new employment is found—to include such problems as loss of self-esteem, alcoholism and divorce, and permanently lowered standards of living. Katharine Newman observes a phenomenon that she calls *downward mobility*. The term refers to the situation of many middle-level and upper-level managers—a "middle class" American group long believed safe from losing their jobs—whose jobs and departments and divisions have been eliminated.[38] These people join the many non-managers whose jobs have disappeared due to restructuring.

**THE EFFECT OF DOWNSIZING.** As an increasing number of companies seek to remain competitive by cutting costs and reducing their workforces, more and more people are finding themselves out of their old jobs and in line for new ones.

## MINIMIZING THE PAIN OF DOWNSIZING

A dilemma faced not only by large bureaucracies but by any organization that downsizes is how to be as fair as possible to employees whose jobs are being eliminated. A related issue is how to retain the loyalty of the remaining workforce and restore their sense of security. With downsizing seen as a competitive imperative by many organizations, it is an ethical challenge for the 1990s.

Health One demonstrated that companies do not have to abandon their employees when they downsize, that they can even profit from looking out for their employees. When this organization closed a subsidiary, Metropolitan-Mount Sinai Medical Center (MMS), it successfully placed 90 percent of MMS's 1,200 former employees in new jobs. Health One relocated about 30 percent of them in positions elsewhere in the organization, and another 30 percent in positions with affiliated or competitor organizations. It assisted the rest through career transition training, job fairs, and retraining. At the same time, Health One was able to save millions of dollars. Although the company invested $500,000 in a full-service placement center, it saved the money that would have been spent in unemployment and severance expenses, which could have reached as much as $18 million. "Saving money was the short-term advantage," pointed out Tom McLaughlin, vice president of human resources at Health One's Unit Hospital and former vice president of human resources at MMS. "In the long run, we developed trust and respect with a significant number of our employees. I think they know we will do our best for them."[39]

**FIGURE 12-4** Functional Organization Chart for a Manufacturing Company

Note: Each vice president is in charge of a major organizational function.

## TYPES OF ORGANIZATIONAL STRUCTURES

*Organizational structure* refers to the way in which an organization's activities are divided, grouped, and coordinated into relationships between managers and employees, managers and managers, and employees and employees. An organization's departments can be formally structured in three major ways: by function, by product/market, or in matrix form.

## FUNCTIONAL ORGANIZATION

← ch. 1, p. 17

Organization by function brings together in one department everyone engaged in one activity or several related activities that are called <u>functions</u>. For example, an organization divided by function might have separate manufacturing, marketing, and sales departments. A sales manager in such an organization would be responsible for the sale of *all* products manufactured by the firm.

During the early 1990s, Fleet Financial Group found itself entangled in a mess that appeared to result from poor communication between its holding company and its scattered operations. In March 1993, chairman Terrence Murray therefore reorganized Fleet along functional lines. Four senior executives were given corporate-wide responsibility over commercial banking, consumer banking, trust and investment products, and financial operations. "Our slimmed-down management structure...prepares Fleet to take advantage of full national interstate branch banking," Murray asserted, "which we believe will soon be a reality."[40]

**functional organization:**

A form of departmentalization in which individuals engaged in one functional activity, such as marketing or finance, are grouped into one unit.

**Functional organization** is perhaps the most logical and basic form of departmentalization (see Figure 12-4). It is used mainly by smaller firms that offer a limited line of products because it makes efficient use of specialized resources. Another major advantage of a functional structure is that it makes supervision easier, since each manager must be expert in only a narrow range of skills. In addition, a functional structure makes it easier to mobilize specialized skills and bring them to bear where they are most needed.

As an organization grows, either by expanding geographically or by broadening its product line, some of the disadvantages of the functional structure begin to surface. Because functional managers have to report to central headquarters, it can be difficult to get quick decisions. It is often harder to determine accountability

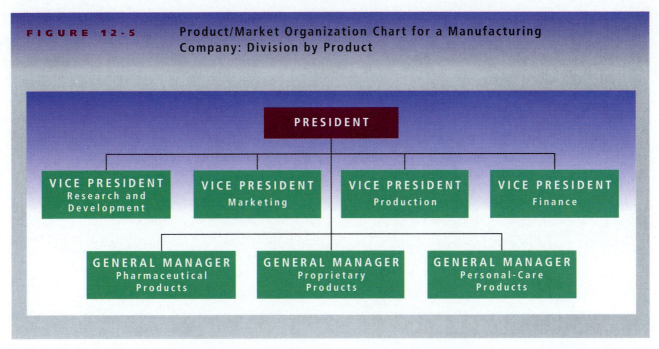

**FIGURE 12-5** Product/Market Organization Chart for a Manufacturing Company: Division by Product

Note: Each general manager is in charge of a major category of products, and the vice presidents of the functional areas provide support services to the general managers.

and judge performance in a functional structure. If a new product fails, who is to blame—research and development, production, or marketing? Finally, coordinating the functions of members of the entire organization may become a problem for top managers. Because members of each department may feel isolated from (or superior to) those in other departments, they may have difficulty working with others in a unified way to achieve the organization's goals. For example, the manufacturing department may concentrate on meeting cost standards and delivery dates and neglect quality control (see Chapter 8). As a result, the service department may be flooded with complaints. In short, a functional structure can be a difficult setting in which managers must coordinate employees' activities.

## PRODUCT/MARKET ORGANIZATION

**product organization:**
The organization of a company into divisions that bring together those involved with a certain type of product.

**market organization:**
The organization of a company into divisions that bring together those involved with a certain type of market.

**division:**
Large organization department that resembles a separate business; may be devoted to making and selling specific products or serving a specific market.

**Product** or **market organization,** often referred to as organization by *division,* brings together in one work unit all those involved in the production and marketing of a product or a related group of products, all those in a certain geographic area, or all those dealing with a certain type of customer. In the 1990 Hewlett-Packard reorganization, John Young replaced one kind of product organization with another kind of product organization.

Most large, multiproduct companies, such as General Motors, have a product or market organization structure. At some point in an organization's existence, sheer size and diversity of products make functional departments too unwieldy. When a company's departmentalization becomes too complex for coordinating the functional structure, top management will generally create semiautonomous **divisions.** In each division, managers and employees design, produce, and market their own products.

Unlike a functional department, a division resembles a separate business. The division head focuses primarily on the operations of his or her division, is accountable for profit or loss, and may even compete with other units of the same firm. But a division is unlike a separate business in one crucial aspect: the division manager must still report to central headquarters.

A product/market organization can follow one of three patterns. Most obvious is *division by product,* shown in Figure 12-5. The Hewlett-Packard organization structure through the 1980s and the early 1990s was this type.

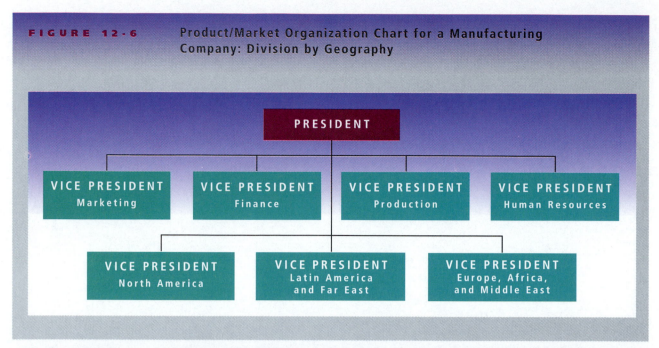

**FIGURE 12-6**    Product/Market Organization Chart for a Manufacturing Company: Division by Geography

Note: Each area vice president is in charge of the company's business in one geographic area. The functional presidents provide support services and coordination assistance for their areas of responsibility.

**FIGURE 12-7**    Functional Organization Chart for a Manufacturing Company: Division by Customer

Note: Each vice president is in charge of a set of products grouped according to the type of customer to whom they will be marketed.

*Division by geography* is generally used by service, financial, and other nonmanufacturing firms, as well as by mining and oil-producing companies (see Figure 12-6). Geographic organization is logical when a plant must be located as close as possible to sources of raw materials, to major markets, or to specialized personnel.

In *division by customer,* the organization is divided according to the different ways customers use products (see Figure 12-7). At Hewlett-Packard, Platt and Birnbaum hint that this might be the product/market focus of the future in the digital telecommunications marketplace.

Organization by division has several advantages. Because all the activities, skills, and expertise required to produce and market particular products are grouped in one place under a single head, a whole job can more easily be coordinated and high work performance maintained. In addition, both the quality and the speed of decision making are enhanced because decisions made at the divisional level are closer to the scene of action. At the same time, the burden on central management is eased because divisional managers have greater latitude to

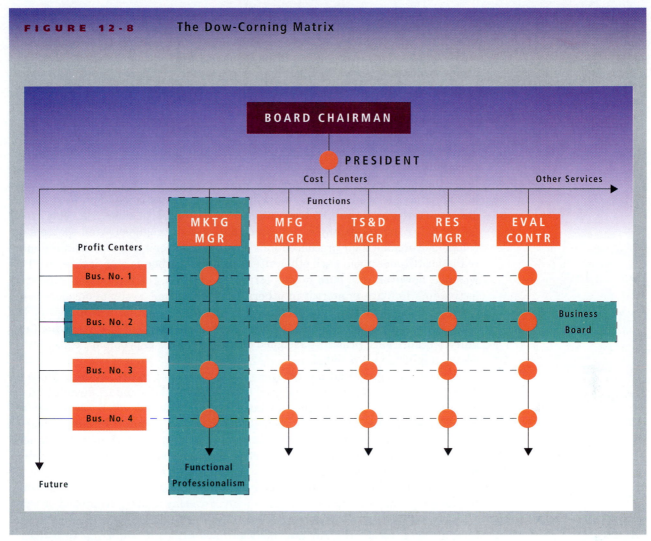

**FIGURE 12-8**   The Dow-Corning Matrix

**matrix structure:**

An organizational structure in which each employee reports to both a functional or division manager and to a project or group manager.

act. Perhaps most important, accountability is clear. The performance of divisional management can be measured in terms of the division's profit or loss.

The divisional structure does have some disadvantages, however. The interests of the division may be placed ahead of the goals for the total organization. For example, because they are vulnerable to profit-and-loss performance reviews, division heads may take short-term gains at the expense of long-range profitability. In addition, administrative expenses increase because each division has its own staff members and specialists, leading to costly duplication of skills.

## MATRIX ORGANIZATION

The **matrix structure,** sometimes referred to as a "multiple command system," is a hybrid that attempts to combine the benefits of both types of designs while avoiding their drawbacks.[41] An organization with a matrix structure has two types of structure existing simultaneously. Employees have in effect two bosses—that is, they work in two chains of command. One chain of command is functional or divisional, the type diagrammed vertically in the preceding charts. The second is a horizontal overlay that combines people from various divisions or functional departments into a project or business team led by a project or group manager who is an expert in the team's assigned area of specialization (see Figure 12-8, which depicts the multidimensional matrix structure of Dow-Corning in the 1970s).

As organizations have become more global, many use a type of matrix form in their international operations. There may be product or division managers, as in a divisionalized firm, as well as national managers for each country in which the company does business. Thus, a division employee would report to the divisional manager on product-related issues and to the national manager on political issues or those involving international relations.

Although matrix organizational structures are necessarily complex, they have advantages.[42] Often the matrix structure is an efficient means for bringing together the diverse specialized skills required to solve a complex problem. Problems of coordination—which plague most functional designs—are minimized here because the most important personnel for a project work together as a group. This in itself produces a side benefit: By working together, people come to understand the demands faced by those who have different areas of responsibility. A report from AT&T Bell Labs, for example, indicated that systems engineers and systems developers overcame their preconceptions about each other's jobs and acquired more realistic attitudes about each other after working together as a project team. (This was not, however, in a pure matrix structure.) Indeed, the interaction was so effective in stimulating interest in others' work that some systems developers decided to move into full-time systems engineering.[43] Another advantage of the matrix structure is that it gives the organization a great deal of cost-saving flexibility: Because each project is assigned only the number of people it needs, unnecessary duplication is avoided.

A disadvantage is that not everyone adapts well to a matrix system. To be effective, team members must have good interpersonal skills and be flexible and cooperative. In addition, morale can be adversely affected when personnel are rearranged once projects are completed and new ones begun.[44] Finally, if hierarchies are not firmly established and effectively communicated, there is the danger, according to some analysts, that conflicting directives and ill-defined responsibilities will tie managers' hands.[45]

To overcome these obstacles, special training in new job skills or interpersonal relationships may be necessary when a matrix overlay is first introduced or when a temporary overlay becomes permanent. To protect individuals who function well in traditional structures but are likely to have difficulty adjusting to a matrix structure, many companies either make special efforts to retrain personnel before assigning them to project teams or select only volunteers for the teams.

## THE FORMAL AND INFORMAL ORGANIZATIONAL STRUCTURE

Organization charts are useful for showing the formal organizational structure and who is responsible for certain tasks. In reality, though, the organization chart cannot begin to capture the interpersonal relationships that make up the **informal organizational structure.** Herbert A. Simon has described this as "the interpersonal relationships in the organization that affect decisions within it but either are omitted from the formal scheme or are not consistent with it."[46] For example, during a busy period, one employee may turn to another for help rather than going through a manager. Or an employee in sales may establish a working relationship with an employee in production, who can provide information about product availability faster than the formal reporting system. And anyone who has worked in an organization knows the importance of secretaries and executive assistants, which never shows on an organization chart. One of the first scholars to recognize the importance of informal structures was Chester Barnard. He noted that informal relationships help organization members satisfy their social needs *and* get things done.

**informal organizational structure:**

The undocumented and officially unrecognized relationships between members of an organization that inevitably emerge out of the personal and group needs of employees.

← ch. 2, p. 39

**MANAGEMENT 2000 AND BEYOND**

# ORGANIZATION AND DISORGANIZATION

Three decades ago, the business historian Alfred Chandler proposed a way of thinking that has been widely adopted in American business (and that this text has presented): an organizational structure logically follows from, and facilitates, an organizational strategy. Over the years, as managers have tried to make structure fit strategy, this approach has resulted in managers building larger and larger "semi-permanent" structures for their organizations. Those structures logically followed strategies designed to make companies bigger and more dominant in the marketplace. Today, many managers are experimenting with very different looking organizational structures because they are experimenting—and succeeding—with a radically different kind of organizational strategy. James Brian Quinn calls these organizations *intelligent enterprises* because their most important product is *knowledge,* packaged as valuable *services.*[47] And once you see your organization as in the "service business," Quinn and Tom Peters say, you'll never organize like you once did.

Three innovative kinds of organizational structures have evolved from this new approach to organizational strategy: (1) what Peters calls "necessary disorganization," (2) the so-called virtual corporation, and (3) what Quinn calls "disaggregated" organizations.

**Necessary Disorganization.** Tom Peters, a powerful voice for business change for more than a decade, is a leader in the charge against traditional organizational designs and structures. Indeed, in his latest book, he argues that *disorganization* is *necessary* in what he calls today's "bonkers" organizational environment: "How do you deal with a bonkers world other than with bonkers organizations peopled with bonkers folks? My answer, in short: You can't!"[48]

Peters advocates organizational design processes that result in flexible and short-lived arrangements of work activities; he predicts, "Tomorrow's effective 'organization' [deliberately in quotes] will be conjured up anew each day."[49]

What Peters asks managers to do is pay much less attention to organizational structures and much more attention to working through problems jointly with people who bring different talents to the task, and who may even come from different organizations to work on that task. In this way, Peters claims, managers and non-managers can work much more creatively to deliver prompt service to their customers.

You can already see examples of the kind of temporary organizational arrangements that Peters describes and promotes. Take the construction of a new house, for example.[50] A general contractor, in addition to overseeing the entire project for the customer, might do the framing, siding, and windows work. The contractor might then arrange for plumbers, electricians, and painters to do their specialized parts of the job. Together, all these people form a kind of temporary, "ad hoc" organization. Once the house is built, the temporary organization disbands—unless construction flaws appear—and these people go their separate ways, probably to be part of other such ad hoc organizations. What is novel and potentially revolutionary about what Peters describes and promotes is its application in the *mainstream* corporate world, in the United States and beyond.

**Virtual Corporations.** According to a recent *Business Week* survey of the *virtual corporation* approach,

> the virtual corporation is a temporary network of independent companies—suppliers, customers, even erstwhile rivals—linked by information technology to share skills, costs, and access to one another's

**TABLE 12-1**    Characteristics of a New Corporate Model

**The Virtual Corporation**

Today's joint ventures and strategic alliances may be an early glimpse of the business organization of the future: The Virtual Corporation. It's a temporary network of companies that come together quickly to exploit fast-changing opportunities. In a Virtual Corporation, companies can share costs, skills, and access to global markets, with each partner contributing what it's best at. Here are the key attributes of such an organization.

| | |
|---|---|
| **Technology** | Informational networks will help far-flung companies and entrepreneurs link up and work together from start to finish. The partnerships will be based on electronic contracts to keep the lawyers away and speed the linkups. |
| **Opportunism** | Partnerships will be less permanent, less formal, and more opportunistic. Companies will band together to meet a specific market opportunity and, more often than not, fall apart once the need evaporates. |
| **Excellence** | Because each partner brings its "core competence" to the effort, it may be possible to create a "best-of-everything" organization. Every function and process could be world-class—something that no single company could achieve. |
| **Trust** | These relationships make companies far more reliant on each other and require far more trust than ever before. They'll share a sense of "co-destiny," meaning that the fate of each partner is dependent on the other. |
| **No Borders** | This new corporate model redefines the traditional boundaries of the company. More cooperation among competitors, suppliers, and customers makes it harder to determine where one company ends and another begins. |

*Source:* Reprinted with permission from "The Virtual Corporation," *Business Week,* February 8, 1993, pp. 98-99.

markets. It will have neither central office nor organization chart. It will have no hierarchy, no vertical integration.[51]

The key ingredients of a virtual corporation are shown in Table 12-1.

Managers at MCI use a kind of virtual corporation when bidding for contracts to provide (and then providing) telecommunications services to large corporations. MCI has never been a manufacturer of equipment.[52] The forte of MCI's employees has been providing services on networks that consist of other suppliers' equipment, such as fiber-optic cables. Says MCI President Daniel Akerson: "If we had to do it on our own, it would cost us at least $300 million to $500 million a year in extra expenses."[53] So, to sell services to Holiday Inns, for example, MCI salespersons might create a virtual corporation in conjunction with salespersons from organizations selling telephones, computers, and software.

**Disaggregated Organizations.** Quinn observes more and more managers trying out seemingly radical organizational structures as means for implementing "intellectual and service" strategies: "Services and service technologies have opened a wide variety of new organizational options for managing intellect on a much more disaggregated basis."[54]

One example of disaggregation is the practice of "outsourcing" production tasks to other organizations. In another era, outsourcing was an admission of weakness; the people at an organization were admitting that they were not up to the task. Now, Quinn argues, outsourcing can be a key part of running an "intelligent enterprise." He observes that Nike managers seek and enter into outsourcing agreements with three kinds of "production partners":[55]

# LEARNING NEW LESSONS

How much Hewlett-Packard people can do themselves in enacting a strategy for the digital era is a question Platt faces. Increasingly, partnerships and virtual organizations are part of the organizing process at the company. In 1992, HP formed a partnership with AT&T and Citizen Watch Co. of Japan to accelerate a project on disk drives. Says Platt, "We know we can't do it all ourselves."[57]

Still, there are skeptics watching the organizational design process at Hewlett-Packard. John B. Jones, Jr., an analyst at Solomon Brothers Inc., says: "The most critical issue is relationships. I haven't seen enough announcements to see that they're assured of success. They're clearly not a shoo-in." [58]

Hewlett-Packard managers are learning an important, but not new, lesson: When it comes to organizational design, you make it up as you go.

> "*The most critical issue is relationships.*"

*Developed partners* produce Nike's latest and most expensive "statement products," which can absorb higher production costs.

*Volume producers* are above-average in size (making 70,000-85,000 units a day, as against 20,000-25,000 units for developed partners).

*Developing sources* … produce exclusively for Nike, which has a strong "tutelage" program to develop them into Nike's higher-level suppliers.

None of these partners is part of the Nike organizational structure per se. But their efforts are crucial to Nike—just as Nike people's efforts are crucial to the partners. By disaggregrating in this way, Quinn notes, "Nike acts primarily in a service role: as design center, production coordinator, and market interface for its system."[56] This is intelligent management, Quinn argues, because each party in the resulting network contributes the knowledge (intelligence) advantage that he or she has to offer.

Disorganization, the virtual corporation, and intelligent disaggregation all share the spirit of reengineering that we introduced in Chapter 6. Reengineering involves thinking first and foremost about the processes by which services are delivered to customers. Organizational design logically follows the reengineering analysis; it is "the cart behind the horse." Peters and Quinn, along with more and more managers, are redefining just what the horse and cart can do!

## SUMMARY

1. **Explain the purpose of decisions about organizational design.**

   Members of an organization need a stable, understandable framework within which they can work together toward organizational goals. Organizational design is the process of deciding on the appropriate way to divide and to coordinate organizational activity in view of the goals and strategic plan of an organization and the environmental circumstances in which that plan is carried out.

## DISNEY'S DESIGN[59]

The Walt Disney Company is heralded as the world's largest entertainment company. It has earned this astounding reputation through tight control over the entire operation: control over the open-ended brainstorming that takes place 24 hours a day; control over the engineers who construct the fabulous theme-park rides; control over the animators who create and design beloved characters and adventurous scenarios; and control over the talent that brings the many concepts and characters to life. Although control pervades the company, it is not too strong a grip. Employees in each department are well aware of their objectives and the parameters established to meet those objectives. But in conjunction with the pre-determined responsibilities, managers at Disney encourage independent and innovative thinking.

People at the company have adopted the phrase "Dream as a Team" as a reminder that whimsical thoughts, adventurous ideas, and all-out dreaming are at the core of the company philosophy. The overall control over each department is tempered by this concept. Disney managers strive to empower their employees by leaving room for their creative juices to flow. In fact, managers at Disney do more than encourage innovation. They demand it. Projects assigned to the staff "imagineers" seem impossible at first glance. At Disney, doing the seemingly impossible is part of what innovation means. Teams of imagineers gather together in a brainstorming session known as the "Blue Sky" phase. Under the "Blue Sky," an uninhibited exchange of wild, ludicrous, outrageous ideas, both "good" and "bad," continues until solutions are found and the impossible is done. By demanding so much of their employees, Disney managers effectively *drive* their employees to be creative.

Current Disney leader Michael Eisner has established the "Dream as a Team" concept. Eisner realized that managers at Disney needed to let their employees brainstorm and create with support. As Disney president Frank Wells says, "If a good idea is there, you know it, you feel it, you do it, no matter where it comes from."

### CASE QUESTIONS

1. What environmental factors influenced management style at Disney?
2. What kind(s) of organizational structure seem to be consistent with "Dream as a Team"?
3. How and where might the informal organization be a real asset at Disney?

---

### VIDEO CASE STUDY

## MGM GRAND: A STRUCTURE FOR SUCCESS[60]

An 88-foot tall, stucco-maned lion with laser beam eyes greets guests to the MGM Grand Hotel, Casino & Theme Park in Las Vegas, Nevada. It symbolizes the grandeur of the huge organization, which manages 5,005 rooms located in four 30-story, emerald green towers, a 171,500-square-foot casino with 3,500 slot machines, a 15,200-seat special events arena, and a 33-acre indoor theme park. Too much? Apparently not: Only two months after it opened on December 18, 1993, the MGM Grand was regularly renting out 4,000 rooms, serving 20,000 meals, and grossing somewhere in the neighborhood of $1.6 million per day.

At the helm of this "city within a city" sits Larry Woolf, chairman, president, and CEO. Woolf, who grew up on a small farm in Idaho and whose high school graduation class consisted of 36 students, appears to revel in the sheer enormity of MGM Grand. According to Woolf, the only difference between managing a hotel the size of the Grand and a small hotel of maybe 150 rooms is scale. All things considered, he says, "I would rather run one 5,000-room hotel than five 500-room hotels."[61] In fact, Woolf claims that the Grand, as an organization, is actually not that complicated.

Operating the Grand, though, is a complicated

process. Outside, on the 15-lane entrance driveway, 86 parking attendants handle the steady stream of visitors and guests. The phone reservation room, with 62 desks, is a constant flurry of activity as the operators field thousands of calls about booking rooms or show tickets. The entrance has a reception area with 38 windows and clerks who handle 16,000 pieces of luggage each day. The 740 guest-room attendants are deployed in pairs; each pair is responsible for cleaning 16 rooms, from top to bottom, in an eight-hour shift. The eight in-house restaurants expect to prepare 32,000 meals daily once the organization is fully underway. A computerized storage system draws from a reserve of 60,000 garments to uniform more than 6,000 employees.

At the Grand, size has not come at the expense of quality. Woolf has aimed for high-quality service from the start. In selecting its 8,000 employees, the Grand carefully screened 100,000 job applicants and required that each employee test drug-free before being hired. In addition, Woolf set the pay at a high rate to encourage high performance and keep the union out.

The structure Woolf put in place distinguishes the Grand from other Las Vegas organizations. The theory X autocratic management style is still firmly entrenched in the Las Vegas gambling industry. The structures of many of the Grand's neighbors have been built upon a very strong sense of distrust. Personnel activities remain under almost constant surveillance and video cameras are located throughout casinos.

Woolf took steps to prevent tension at the Grand, introducing practices to enhance relations between managers and their employees. For one thing, he instituted "cross-training," wherein managers are required to perform the work of their employees periodically to gain insight into what it takes. Woolf explained, "I've had so many jobs in the casino business that by the time I became a manager, I knew most of the departments. If there was a keno problem, I knew something about it. If there was a restaurant problem, I knew something about it."[62] Cross-training enables managers without such experience to gain it on the job.

As evidence of the value of cross-training, Woolf recounts an experience he had as president of Caesars Lake Tahoe:

One day I was working the telephones and one of our purchasing agents called asking to be connected to another in-house number. "Why don't you just dial it direct?" I asked him. I gave him the number, but he still insisted on being connected. He didn't know he was talking to the president, and I knew that if he had ever had to work the phones, he would understand why I then changed the policy to ask everyone to use their phone lists instead of making the operators do it.[63]

The efficiency of the company's switchboard improved as a result of Woolf's cross-training. "No one can convince you by memo why it's important to dial your own phone number," Woolf remarked, "but if you have to experience the problem yourself, you'll have a different feel for it."[64]

Another important aspect of the Grand's organizational structure is the Quality Assurance (QA) program. Developed under the auspices of the American Hotel and Motel Management Association, the QA program focuses on "Japanese-style" participative management. At Grand, management is at the bottom of the structure to support the front-line workers who interact with customers. The QA program is based on four core assumptions: the person who does the job is in the best position to know how to do it; people at the lowest possible levels should be responsible for problem solving and decision making; people are the organization's greatest resource; and empowered employees consistently perform at high levels.

In addition, the Grand is streamlining its bureaucracy through the addition of an integrated system called MultiPlan that will keep track of employees' pension, dental, and health plans. The new system will allow employees to perform calculations on loans, withdrawals, and account transfers for all their benefit packages through central hotel kiosks.

Through a variety of innovative management techniques, Woolf has thus provided the Grand with what it will need to enjoy success.

## CASE QUESTIONS

1. How would you characterize the Grand's organizational structure?
2. What are the factors that lead to the Grand's success as an organization?
3. How is the Grand suited or not suited to its environment?
4. What would you have done differently?

## CHAPTER 13

# POWER AND THE DISTRIBUTION OF AUTHORITY

**Upon completing this chapter, you should be able to:**

1. Distinguish between authority and power.

2. Explain how use of power is related to the history of a people's culture.

3. List and explain the five sources of power.

4. Discuss the two major views of authority.

5. Compare and contrast line, staff, and functional authority.

6. Discuss the advantages of delegation, why managers hesitate to delegate, and the guidelines that can help them delegate effectively.

7. Compare major approaches to job design and the part that authority plays in those approaches.

8. Discuss how authority sometimes can impede strategy implementation and customer service.

# EMPLOYMENT THE NORDSTROM WAY[1]

The customer pointed out to the Nordstrom salesperson that she had bought a pair of shoes at Bloomingdale's (a competitor) that were too small for her. She liked the style, but Bloomingdale's didn't have her size. After being fitted with the same shoe of the proper size, the customer started to pay for the shoes. The salesperson instead suggested that she merely take the too-small shoes in exchange for the new purchase. When the customer reminded the salesperson that she hadn't bought the first pair at Nordstrom, the salesperson said to her, "If I take these shoes for you, you won't have any reason to return to Bloomingdale's."[2]

Such stories abound when people talk about Nordstrom. A *Sixty Minutes* segment recounted an occasion where a salesperson even changed the tire on a customer's car. Such anecdotes underscore the value of *empowerment* in the corporate arena. Empowerment involves granting employees the freedom and responsibility to do their jobs as they think best, without constantly having to appeal to higher authorities for permission. It enables them to make on-the-spot decisions without getting caught up in bureaucratic red tape. At Nordstrom, empowerment is integral to success in serving customers. Nordstrom is renowned for its empowerment of employees.

*At Nordstrom, empowerment is integral to success in serving customers.*

Since being founded in 1901 as a shoe store in Seattle, Washington, Nordstrom has developed into one of the country's leading fashion specialty retailers. As of 1992, Nordstrom operated 52 stores scattered through Washington, Oregon, California, Utah, Alaska, Virginia, Maryland, New Jersey, Illinois and Minnesota. During the preceding decade, net sales climbed from $769 million to $3.4 billion.

Nordstrom management's policy toward employees has made such growth and financial success possible. One way that Nordstrom managers have enfranchised their employees is by using the term "associate" instead of "employee." While on the surface this may seem merely a cosmetic change, the Nordstrom terminology underscores managers' commitment to their people. The company management emphasizes *customer satisfaction* as the single overriding goal.

As a corollary, Nordstrom associates are encouraged to pay more attention to their customers' needs than to their bosses' needs. This means that salespeople are free to do whatever they think necessary to serve their customers' needs best. Some salespeople choose to keep a log of their customers' purchases. This is an individual choice, not a company policy. The salesperson also determines how much of his or her pay comes from salary or commission. Again, choice is vested in the associate. →

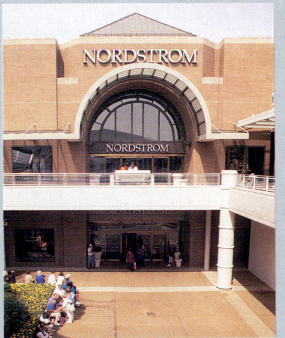

**NORDSTROM.** Nordstrom stores are well-known for exceptional customer service.

ORGANIZATIONAL STRUCTURE provides a stable, logical, and clear-cut pattern of relationships within which managers and employees can work toward organizational goals. But this is only a framework. It does not "run" by itself. People interacting through an organizational structure need rules by which they can make that structure work effectively. By analogy, the United States government *structure* includes the Executive Branch (the Presidency and various agencies), the Legislative Branch (Congress), and the judicial system (the federal courts), and this structure is operated according to the *rules* set forth in the United States Constitution.

Managers set and apply the rules for people acting in an organizational structure by virtue of their *authority* and *power*. Formal authority, a type of power, is what we usually associate with organizational structure and management. But the two terms are intertwined. How effectively managers can use their authority depends in part on how they understand and use power, which, at its core, is the ability to exert *influence* on other people.

How to distribute formal authority throughout the organizational structure is a key organizing decision. Managers clearly cannot do everything that must be done to carry out the strategic plan for an organization. Hence, they must decide how much authority to *delegate* to lower-ranking managers or non-managers. Delegation involves the sharing of power with others. This chapter deals with managerial decisions about distributing authority in organizational structures. It also discusses how people derive their authority and power in organizations, and explores attitudes toward power. Before we look at various aspects of distributing authority, let us consider the broader idea of power.

## P OWER

**power:**
The ability to exert influence; that is, the ability to change the attitudes or behavior of individuals or groups.

← ch. 3, p. 63

← ch. 2, p. 47

**reward power:**
Power derived from the fact that one person, known as an influencer, has the ability to reward another person, known as an influencee, for carrying out orders, which may be expressed or implied.

**coercive power:**
The negative side of reward power, based on the influencer's ability to punish the influencee.

**legitimate power:**
Power that exists when a subordinate or influencee acknowledges that the influencer has a "right" or is lawfully entitled to exert influence—within certain bounds; also called formal authority.

**Power** is the ability to exert influence on other people. Power can be present in any relationship. In organizations, managers exert power. After all, we defined management in Chapter 1 as the process of shaping—that is, influencing—what people do at organizations.

Still, managers are not the only people who can exert influence at organizations. Employees say and do things to influence managers. And, as we saw in Chapter 3, there are many kinds of <u>stakeholders</u> outside the organization that can influence managers and employees. So any organization—like any relationship—is an open <u>system</u> when it comes to power. At Nordstrom, associates and their managers exert influence on each other, and associates take very seriously the influence exerted by customers. In fact, the extent to which managers give power to associates and customers is a distinctive feature of Nordstrom as an organization.

### THE SOURCES OF POWER

Power does not derive simply from an individual's level in the organizational hierarchy. John French and Bertram Raven have identified five sources or bases of power.[3] These aspects of power may be present in a variety of human relationships. In an organization, each may occur at all levels.

**Reward power** is based on one person (the influencer) having the ability to reward another person (the influencee) for carrying out orders or meeting performance requirements. One example is the power of a supervisor to assign work tasks to employees.[4]

**Coercive power,** based on the influencer's ability to punish the influencee for not meeting requirements, is the negative side of reward power. Punishment may range from a reprimand to loss of a job.

**Legitimate power** (formal authority) exists when an employee or influencee acknowledges that the influencer is entitled to exert influence—within certain

**expert power:**
Power based on the belief or understanding that the influencer has specific knowledge or relevant expertise that the influencee does not.

**referent power:**
Power based on the desire of the influencee to be like or identify with the influencer.

bounds. It is also implied that the influencee has an obligation to accept this power. The right of a manager to establish reasonable work schedules is an example of "downward" legitimate power. A plant guard may have the "upward" authority to require even the company president to present an identification card before being allowed onto the premises.

**Expert power** is based on the perception or belief that the influencer has some relevant expertise or special knowledge that the influencee does not. When we do what our doctors tell us, we are acknowledging their expert power.

**Referent power,** which may be held by a person or a group, is based on the influencee's desire to identify with or imitate the influencer. For example, popular, conscientious managers will have referent power if employees are motivated to emulate their work habits. Referent power also functions at the peer level—charismatic colleagues may sway us to their viewpoints in department meetings.

These are *potential* sources of power only. They are the ways in which one person *can* influence another person. Possession of some or all of them does not guarantee the ability to influence particular individuals in specific ways. For example, a manager may have employees' respect and admiration as an expert in his or her field, but still may be unable to influence them to be more creative on the job or even to get to work on time. Thus, the role of the influencee in accepting or rejecting the attempted influence is a key one.

A manager has the potential to operate from all five power bases. Some of them are inherent in the position. A specific degree of legitimate power always accompanies a manager's job. In fact, it shapes the hierarchical relationships within which the other forms of power occur. Along with legitimate power, managers usually have reward and coercive power; they can reward employees with money, privileges, or promotions and punish them by withholding or removing these rewards. Unlike the first three types, expert and referent power cannot be "given" to man-

**REWARD POWER.** Graduation is the ultimate reward for college students. Besides reward power, what other types of power do college professors wield?

agers along with the job title. However, managers are generally assumed to possess some degree of expertise (at least until they prove otherwise). Referent power, which depends on an individual's style and personality, is least likely to be an expected part of a manager's position. It is not unusual, however. When employees try to model themselves after executives they admire, referent power is at work.

## CULTURAL ASPECTS OF POWER

The concept of power involves how people want to view their relationships to one another. Around the globe, you can expect to find diverse experiences, traditions, and practices regarding power in human relationships. In some countries, for example, the culture supports a belief that power in organizations should be unequally distributed. Italy, France, Japan, India, and Brazil are among the nations where power holders are considered superiors by other people; because superiors are thought of as different kinds of people, the belief is that those in power should look as powerful as possible.[5] In the United States, power has long been a subject of considerable interest—and even ambivalence. In understanding a particular culture's attitude toward power, it helps to understand the historical circumstances in which that culture has evolved. Thus, here is one place where an understanding of cultural diversity (Chapter 7) goes hand in hand with an understanding of organizations and management.

### AMERICAN AMBIVALENCE ABOUT POWER

The concept of power and the concept of individual liberty are difficult for Americans to reconcile, perhaps because the United States was founded in opposition to an authoritarian regime and has been populated by successive waves of immigrants fleeing oppressive governments throughout the world. A distrust of excessive power is reflected in the United States Constitution, which both establishes and limits the powers of the federal government. In addition, the Constitution's system of checks and balances was designed to keep each of the three branches of government—legislative, executive, and judicial—from accumulating too much power. Furthermore, the Bill of Rights and subsequent amendments were enacted to protect individuals' rights against government power.

Some Americans, then, have ambivalent feelings about power, both admiring and resenting it in others. They may covet power, but are reluctant to admit it openly, since both history and scientific research have shown how easy it is to misuse and abuse power, with tragic and often horrifying consequences. A related danger is that people may respond to authority blindly, not considering themselves responsible for actions they take at the behest of an authority figure. Consider the outcome of the following well-known scientific experiment.

### THE YALE EXPERIMENTS

In 1960, Stanley Milgram conducted experiments that probed the conflict between personal conscience and obedience to an outside authority figure. He found that when people were ordered to act against their consciences some entered an "agentic state." That is, they viewed themselves as merely instruments (agents) of the authority figure and felt no responsibility for their actions.[6]

In what has become known as the "Yale experiments," Milgram asked a random sample of New Haven residents—excluding students—to participate in an experiment. They were told he was testing whether people learn best by negative or by positive reinforcement. He asked the subjects to serve as "teachers," telling them another subject would be the "learner." The teacher was to read a series of word pairs to the learner and then prompt the learner with the first word of one of the pairs.

If the learner responded correctly with the second word in the pair, the teacher would go on to another series. If, however, the learner answered incorrectly, the teacher was told to give the learner an electric shock. The strength of the shock increased with each wrong answer. A researcher (serving as an authority figure) stayed in the room with the teacher while the teacher read the word pairs and "punished" the learner.

In fact, no electric shocks were being given. The learner was really an *actor* who, as time went on, *pretended* to be in extreme pain and asked to withdraw from the experiment.

Milgram wanted to know how many subjects would complete the experiment and administer up to 450 volts of "electricity" to a stranger. In the basic experiment, depending on the proximity of the teacher to the learner, 30 to 65 percent of the subjects obeyed the experimenter to the end of the test.

In variations on the experiment, Milgram tested to see how peer pressure, the gender of the subject, the clarity of the experimenter's commands, the affiliation of the experimenter to the university, the health condition of the learner, and the physical presence of the experimenter (the authority figure) would affect its outcome. The only factor that tended to cause the teacher to stop the experiment was the absence of the authority figure. ▪

## BALANCING VIEWS ON POWER

Our uneasiness about power perhaps explains the fact that U.S. management writers long neglected the subject. In recent years, that has changed.[7] David McClelland, for example, has described "two faces of power"—a negative face and a positive one.[8] The negative face is usually expressed in terms of dominance-submission: If I win, you lose. In this sense, to have power implies having power over someone else, who is less well off for it. Management based on the negative face of power regards people as little more than pawns to be used or sacrificed as the need arises. This is self-defeating to the power wielder, because people who feel they are pawns tend either to resist authority or to accept it too passively. In either case, their value to the manager is severely limited.

The positive face of power is best characterized by a concern for group goals—for helping to formulate and achieve them. It involves exerting influence *on behalf of*, rather than *over*, others. Managers who exercise their power positively encourage group members to develop the strength and competence they need to succeed as individuals and as members of the organization. Jim Mullen focuses on the positive use of power: "Managers aren't in the managing business at all—they're really in the *teaching* business. Every philosophy, attitude, and business practice used by a company in dealing with its employees will be recycled by the employees with that company's customers." Mullen, president and founder of Mullen, an $85-million advertising and public relations agency in Wenham, Massachusetts, continues:

> When you come to terms with the fact that your employees know more than you do, it's one short step to accepting that, in their areas of expertise, they're quite likely to make better decisions than you will. The secret is to let them get on with their jobs. Management's number-one function, therefore, is to find the most talented, motivated, caring people available, then get the hell out of their way.[9]

---

**EXHIBIT 13-1**    **Kotter's Key Characteristics of Successfully Handled Power**

Kotter maintains that managers who handle power successfully:

1. *Are sensitive to the source of their power.* They keep their actions consistent with people's expectations. For example, they do not try to apply expert power in one field to another field.
2. *Recognize the different costs, risks, and benefits of the five bases of power.* They draw on whichever power base is appropriate to a particular situation or person.
3. *Appreciate that each of the five power bases has merit.* They try to develop their skills and credibility so they can use whichever method is best.
4. *Possess career goals that allow them to develop and use power.* They seek jobs that will build their skills, make people feel dependent on them, and employ a type of power with which they are comfortable.
5. *Act maturely and exercise self-control.* They avoid impulsive and egotistical displays of their power, and they try not to be unnecessarily harsh on others around them.
6. *Understand that power is necessary to get things done.* They feel comfortable using power.

*Sources:* John P. Kotter, "Power, Dependence, and Effective Management," *Harvard Business Review* 54, no. 2 (March-April 1976):100-110; *Power in Management* (New York:AMACOM, 1979); and *Power and Influence* (New York, Free Press, 1983). Reprinted with permission.

McClelland and David H. Burnham report that successful managers have a need to influence others more for the benefit of people at the organization than for self-aggrandizement.[10] Managers who use their power with self-control will be more effective than those who wield power to satisfy a need to dominate others *or* those who refuse to use their power out of a strong need to be liked. When a manager continually eases rules and changes procedures to accommodate employees, employees will see that manager not as flexible, but as weak and indecisive. McClelland concluded that good managers exercise power with restraint on behalf of others. Such managers encourage team spirit, support employees, and reward their achievements, thereby raising morale.

John P. Kotter and Rosabeth Moss Kanter are other prominent writers whose analyses can broaden our understanding of the promise of wielding power. Kotter has argued that the external environment of organizations has contributed to the growing need for power skills among managers.[11] Some of his key characteristics of successful power skills are listed in Exhibit 13.1.

Kanter has argued that power can easily become institutionalized. Those whom others *believe* to possess power seem to find it easier to influence the people around them—and thus to garner even more genuine power. By the same token, "powerlessness" is a difficult condition to overcome. Kanter claims, for example, that many of the problems experienced by women and minorities can be traced to their lack of power rather than to gender or race.[12] Kanter proposes a number of ways an organizational member can acquire power. These are categorized in Exhibit 13-2.

Power is not limited to managers. All members of an organization can have a great deal of power because of their knowledge, their skills, or the resources they control. At Nordstrom, sales associates have power because they are the people in a position to satisfy customers. In a hospital, experienced nurses may gain influence over new doctors when they "show them the ropes." Even copy machine attendants have some power, because they can impede or improve a manager's work flow. As people rely more and more on computers, employees with computer skills can exercise increasing influence over an organization's day-to-day activities.

| EXHIBIT 13-2 | Kanter's Key Means to Organizational Power |
|---|---|

1. *Extraordinary activities.* Making changes, being the first person to occupy a position, or being successful upon taking exceptional risks can lead to greater power.
2. *Visibility.* Being noticed, gaining "exposure" in the eyes of those in power, and even making certain activities appear to be riskier than they actually are can also increase power—a fact that has led Kanter to speculate that public appearance may be a more influential factor than genuine substance.
3. *Relevance.* Solving an authentic organizational problem can be a source of power and may well lend credence to the factors of extraordinary activity and visibility.
4. *Sponsors.* Having a sponsor or mentor—someone who advises you on how to succeed in the organization—can be an informal source of power, especially if the sponsor enjoys a good deal of power. Kanter claims that sponsors are especially important for women who are inexperienced in organizational power politics.

*Source:* Rosabeth Moss Kanter, *Men and Women of the Corporation* (New York: Basic Books, 1977), p. 165-205.

Knowledge, combined with hands-on input into daily activities, is tantamount to power, and those members of an organization who possess key skills are in a position to secure themselves a base of practical power.

Power, then, is an important fact of organizational life. Managers must not only accept and understand it as an integral part of their jobs, but must also learn how to use it (without abusing it) to further their own and organizational goals.[13]

# AUTHORITY

**authority:**
A form of power, often used more broadly to refer to a people's ability to wield power as a result of qualities such as knowledge or titles such as judge.

**A**uthority is a form of power. Specifically, formal authority is legitimate power. But we often use the term more broadly in speaking of other kinds of power as well. When we say that someone is "an authority" in a certain field, we mean that he or she knows a great deal about the subject—and thus has expert power. When we hear that a suspected criminal has been apprehended by "the authorities," we think of those holding the legitimate power of the government to maintain civil order. If the criminal is convicted, the judge has the "authority" or coercive power to mete out punishment.

*Formal authority* is the type of power that we associate with organizational structure and management. It is based on the recognition of the legitimacy of managers' attempts to exert influence. Individuals or groups attempting to exert influence are perceived as having the right to do so within recognized boundaries. This is a right that arises from their formal position in an organization. The basis for formal authority has been a continuing subject for debate in American society. And it *should* be scrutinized, in view of what could go wrong with the use of authority.

## THE BASIS OF FORMAL AUTHORITY: TWO VIEWS

"What gives you the right to tell me what to do?" This familiar, blunt question implies that before we comply with an instruction, we must be satisfied that the person issuing it has the right to do so. Where do managers get the right to direct

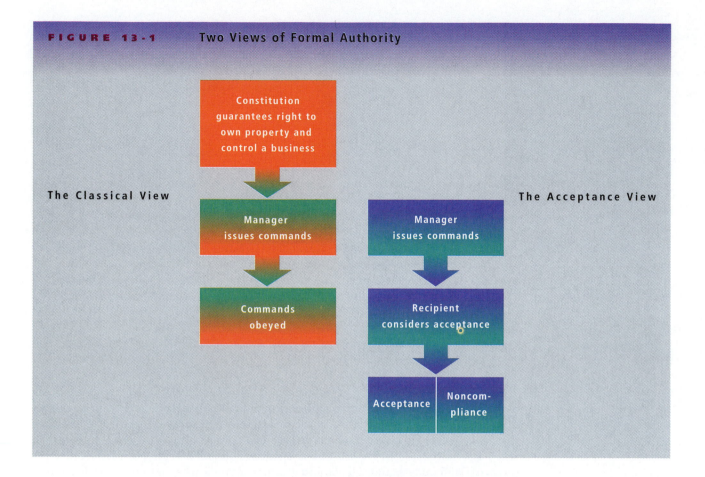

**FIGURE 13-1**     Two Views of Formal Authority

The Classical View

Constitution guarantees right to own property and control a business

Manager issues commands

Commands obeyed

The Acceptance View

Manager issues commands

Recipient considers acceptance

Acceptance | Noncompliance

employees' activities? There are two major competing views on formal authority in organizations: a classical view and the acceptance view (see Figure 13-1).

**A CLASSICAL VIEW.** A classical view of authority is that authority originates at some very high level, and then is lawfully passed down from level to level. At the top of this hierarchy may be God, the state (in the form of king, dictator, or elected president), or the collective will of the people.[14] The military has long operated on this classical view.

According to the classical view of formal authority in American organizations, management has a right to give lawful orders and employees have an obligation to obey. This obligation is, in effect, self-imposed. Members of our society, in agreeing to abide by the Constitution, accept the rights of others to own private property and therefore to own and control businesses. By entering and remaining in an organization, employees in the United States accept the authority of owners and their agents—that is, managers—and therefore have a duty to obey lawful directives.

You might be interested to note that, in most states in the United States, a centuries-old common-law legal doctrine known as *at-will employment* reinforces this classical view of authority. At-will employment is based on an age-old distinction between a "master" of a business—that is, owners and managers—and "servants" of a business—that is, employees.[15] When you accept a job working for a company you do not own, your employment is generally "at will."

**THE ACCEPTANCE VIEW.** The second perspective on the origin of formal authority, the *acceptance view,* finds the basis of authority in the *influencee* rather than in the *in-*

**THE ACCEPTANCE VIEW OF AUTHORITY.** Most management policies, such as wearing uniforms and following assembly-line procedures in preparing food and serving customers, fall within the "area of acceptance" for employees at Wendy's.

*fluencer.* This view starts with the observation that not all legitimate laws or commands are obeyed in all circumstances. Some are accepted by the receiver of the orders, and some are not. The key point is that the *receiver* decides whether or not to comply. For example, if a supervisor storms along an assembly line shouting at everyone to work harder, the employees might not question the supervisor's right to do so, but through anger or indifference, might choose not to comply with the order. The authority of the order will then be nullified because they do not accept the supervisor's message.

This view should not suggest that insubordination and chaos are the norm in organizations. Most formal authority is, in fact, accepted by organization members. Chester I. Barnard, a strong proponent of the acceptance view, has defined the conditions under which a person will comply with higher authority:

> A person can and will accept a communication as authoritative only when four conditions simultaneously occur: (a) he can and does understand the communication; (b) *at the time of his decision* he believes that it is not inconsistent with the purpose of the organization; (c) *at the time of his decision* he believes it to be compatible with his personal interest as a whole; and (d) he is able mentally and physically to comply with it.[16]

Barnard depicts organizations as made up of complex relationships between two equally complex human beings (see Figure 13-2). The wide latitude given to Nordstrom associates by managers suggests an acceptance view in use at that organization.

Barnard and Herbert Simon added to this transactional perspective on formal authority when they proposed that individuals accept orders—and, hence, give the sender authority—within a range of acceptable conditions. Barnard calls this a person's *zone of indifference.*[17] Simon calls it a person's *area of acceptance.*[18] This idea is depicted is Figure 13-3.

FIGURE 13-2          Barnard's View of the Acceptance View of Formal Authority

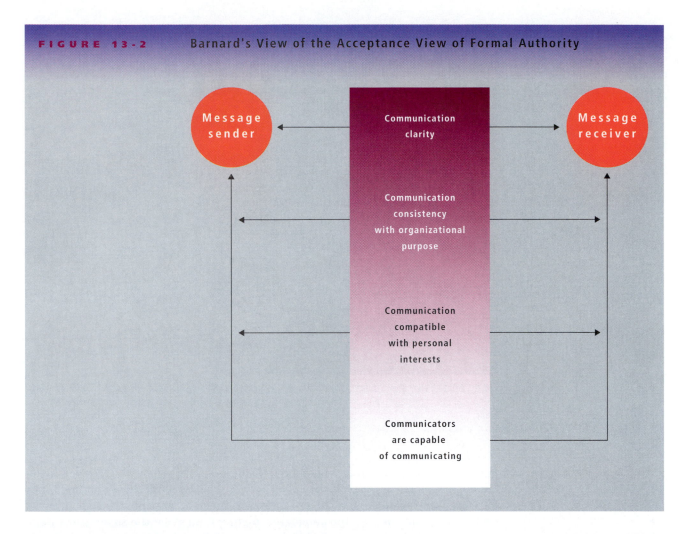

FIGURE 13-3          Range of Acceptable Authority

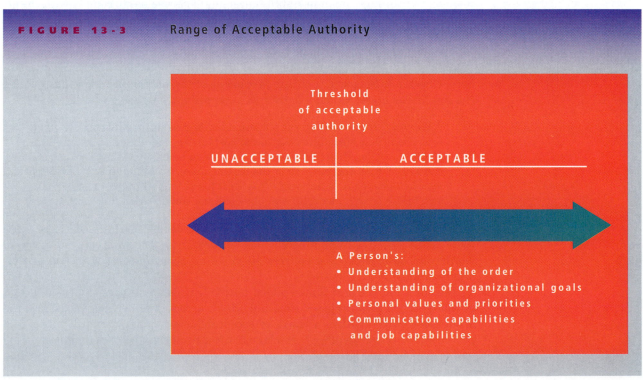

## LINE AND STAFF AUTHORITY

In many organizations, managers use authority by dividing it into *line authority, staff authority,* and *functional authority.*[19] These kinds of authority differ according to the kinds of power on which they are based.

### LINE AUTHORITY

**line authority:**
The authority of those managers directly responsible, throughout the organization's chain of command, for achieving organizational goals.

Managers with **line authority** are those people in the organization who are directly responsible for achieving organizational goals. Line authority is represented by the standard chain of command, starting with the board of directors and extending down through the various levels in the hierarchy to the point where the basic activities of the organization are carried out. Line authority is based primarily on legitimate power.

Since line activities are identified in terms of the company's goals, the activities classified as line will differ in each organization. For example, managers at a manufacturing company may limit line functions to production and sales, while managers at a department store, in which buying is a key element, will consider the purchasing department as well as the sales department as line activities. When an organization is small, all positions may be line roles. At Nordstrom, associates are given considerable line authority.

### STAFF AUTHORITY

**staff authority:**
The authority of those groups of individuals who provide line managers with advice and services.

**Staff authority** belongs to those individuals or groups in an organization who provide services and advice to line managers. The concept of staff includes all elements of the organization that are not classified as line. Advisory staffs have been used by decision makers from emperors and kings to dictators and parliaments over the course of recorded history.[20]

Staff provides managers with varied types of expert help and advice. Staff authority is based primarily on expert power. Staff can offer line managers planning advice through research, analysis, and options development. Staff can also assist in policy implementation, monitoring, and control; in legal and financial matters; and in the design and operation of data-processing systems.[21]

As managers expand organizations over time, staff roles are often added to supplement line activities.[22] For example, partners at many law firms are adding staff members to run the "business side" of the firm. The presence of these specialists frees lawyers to practice law, their line function.

Figure 13-4 depicts a hypothetical mix of line authority and staff authority at an organization.

### FUNCTIONAL AUTHORITY

**functional authority:**
The authority of members of staff departments to control the activities of other departments as they relate to specific staff responsibilities.

The role of staff members—to provide advice and service to line members—implies that staff lacks independent, formal authority. In reality, staff departments, especially those responsible for audit functions, may have formal authority over line members within the limits of their function. The right to control activities of other departments as they relate to specific staff responsibilities is known as **functional authority.** In Figure 13-5, the finance manager of Division A reports through the chain of command to the general manager of Division A, but is also responsible to the vice president for finance at the corporate level. This "dotted-line" relationship indicates the functional authority of specialized staff in relation to line managers.

Functional authority is common in organizations. It is necessary in carrying out many organizational activities, both to provide for a degree of uniformity and

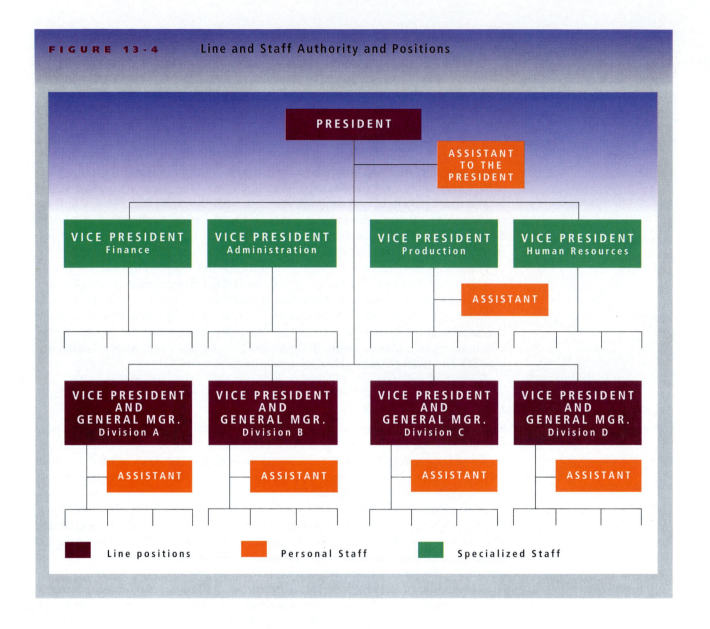

**FIGURE 13-4**    Line and Staff Authority and Positions

← ch. 12, p. 335

to allow unhindered application of expertise. Thus, it is based on both legitimate and expert power. The skills required to manage functional authority relationships and the problems arising from those relationships are similar to the skills required to manage dual-boss relationships in matrix organizations.

Functional authority might be common in modern organizations, but it can be difficult to practice. Take the case of Laura Kozol at the General Electric plant in Lynn, Massachusetts, where jet engines are manufactured for small aircraft.[23] As a design engineer, Kozol has a position traditionally associated with staff authority. When Kozol joined the plant staff, she found that engineers designed engines (staff authority) without consulting those who actually produced the parts (line authority). Partly out of frustration, and partly because downsizing at the plant cut out layers of management, Kozol organized an ongoing collaborative process between engineers and production employees.[24] She now exercises functional authority as she works with production employees.

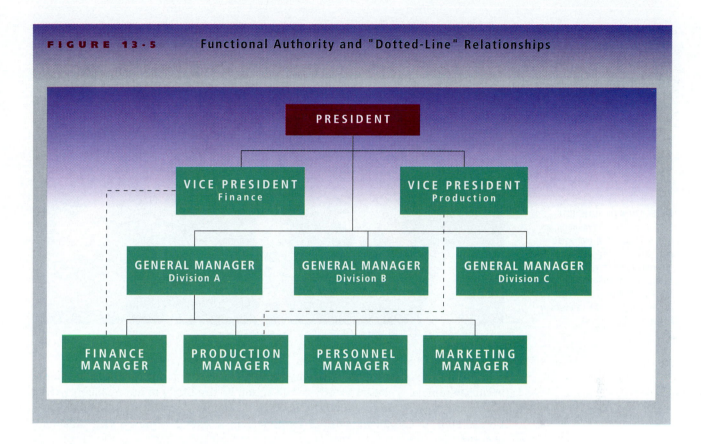

**FIGURE 13-5**  Functional Authority and "Dotted-Line" Relationships

# D ELEGATION

**delegation:**
The act of assigning formal
authority and responsibility
for completion of specific activities to a subordinate.

**H**ow to distribute formal authority throughout the organizational structure is a key organizing decision. **Delegation** is the assignment to another person of formal authority (legitimate power) and accountability for carrying out specific activities. The delegation of authority by managers to employees is necessary for the efficient functioning of any organization, because no manager can personally accomplish or completely supervise all of what happens at an organization.

## THE ADVANTAGES OF DELEGATION

When used properly, delegation has several important advantages. The first and most obvious is that the more tasks managers are able to delegate, the more opportunities they have to seek and accept increased responsibilities from higher-level managers. Thus managers will try to delegate not only routine matters but also tasks requiring thought and initiative, so that they will be free to function with maximum effectiveness for their organizations. In addition, delegation causes employees to accept accountability and exercise judgment. This not only helps train them—an important advantage of delegation—but also improves their self-confidence and willingness to take initiative.

 At Phelps County Bank in Rolla, Missouri, a loan processor researched, proposed, and helped to implement a system of upward evaluations, that is, employee reviews of supervisors. At Intuit, a software company in Palo Alto, California, a technical support supervisor organized a group of experts to assist in answering customer questions in highly specialized areas.

Both of these small businesses encourage employees to suggest and implement ideas for improving operations.[25]

**DELEGATION OF AUTHORITY.**
Efficient functioning of an organization requires that managers must delegate responsibility and authority to employees. Delegating maximizes the effectiveness of employees, speeds up decision making, and can lead to better decisions.

Another advantage of delegation is that it frequently leads to better decisions, because employees closest to "where the action is" are likely to have a clearer view of the facts. For example, a West Coast sales manager would be in a better position to allocate California sales territories than a New York-based vice president of sales.

Effective delegation also speeds up decision making. Valuable time can be lost when employees must check with their managers (who then may have to check with *their* managers) before making a decision. This delay is eliminated when employees are authorized to make the necessary decision on the spot. At Nordstrom, associates are empowered to make many decisions on their own.

The Police Department in South Lake Tahoe, California, has discovered the value of delegating authority. When the former chief of police resigned in 1991, city  manager Kerry Miller used it as an opportunity to change the department's organizational dynamics and move toward more cooperative management. Outside consultants had recently recommended the setting up of a committee to address organizational problems. Miller began by allowing this committee, which now called itself the participative-management team (PMT), to be involved in the selection of the new police chief. This proved an integral step. "With choosing the chief, the process finally went beyond just people airing their differences," recalled patrol officer Rich Hogbin. "We realized we finally were going to be part of the decision-making process. When we did that, we realized the sky was the limit."[26] The PMT does not exercise the authority that should belong to the police chief; rather, when an issue arises, the committee's first decision is whether it even has the authority to deal with the issue. In some ways decisions take more time to make because they are researched and discussed more thoroughly, but the overall response has been favorable.

## BARRIERS TO DELEGATION

Despite these advantages, managers can be reluctant to delegate authority. Managers often have a number of excuses for not delegating: "I can do it better myself"; "My employees just aren't capable enough"; "It takes too much time to explain what I want done." The real reason may be the manager is simply too disorganized or inflexible to delegate work effectively.

**BARRIER TO DELEGATION.** Some managers are simply too disorganized to delegate work effectively, even though they would clearly benefit from doing so.

## LETTING GO: AN ENTREPRENEUR STRUGGLES TO DELEGATE

During her 15 years as president and chief executive officer of Westhaven Services, an institutional pharmacy based in Perrysburg, Ohio, Mary Lou Fox found that her creative, entrepreneurial spirit erected a barrier to delegation. As much as she wanted to develop a management team to succeed her, she failed on at least four separate occasions. "But Mary Lou hasn't been sticking her head in the sand about the whole thing," commented Rolf Schrader, who left in April 1991, after serving as executive vice president, "She's really tried."[27]

Prior to taking over Westhaven, Fox lacked significant business experience. Although she built the company into an $18 million enterprise, she claims that the growth resulted primarily from "dumb marketing" and customer service. "There comes a point when you've got to let go of the reins," asserted Lawrence Cryan, who served as controller during most of 1990. "I don't think she's been trained to do that. She hasn't been exposed to mentors to see how they've done it."[28] After failing on four separate occasions to make the transition to a new management team to succeed her, though, Fox has decided that there is one obstacle left that she can confront: herself. "I will change things," she declared. "I know that the only thing I really have control over is me."[29]

With this in mind, she immediately began delegating authority to her managers in order to start the process of disengaging herself from the company. "She's giving them authority," noted Suzanne Neuber, a consultant pharmacist. "She no longer looks at them as her little children."[30] By challenging the obstacles that lay ahead of her, Fox prevented herself from remaining an obstacle to delegation. ■

Other barriers to delegation are insecurity and confusion about who is ultimately responsible for a specific task—the manager or the employee. Managers cannot sidestep their responsibility to higher-ups simply by delegating difficult or unpleasant tasks. They are always accountable for the actions of their employees—a fact that makes some managers reluctant to take a chance on delegating. Others fear that delegating authority reduces their own authority. Still others feel threatened if their employee does "too good" a job. Some employees, on the other hand, want to avoid responsibility and risk. They prefer that their managers make all the decisions. These barriers can be overcome if managers follow certain guidelines for effective delegation.

## GUIDELINES FOR EFFECTIVE DELEGATION

The practice of delegation challenges managers and employees alike to pay close attention to the terms of their working relationships. Delegation will have a better chance of succeeding, for all parties concerned, if they work to build trust in each other. Here is one more situation where ethics comes to bear in day-to-day organizational activities.

**PREREQUISITES.** The most basic prerequisite to effective delegation remains the manager's willingness to give employees freedom to accomplish delegated tasks. This means letting them choose methods and solutions different from the ones the manager would have chosen. It also means giving them the freedom to make mistakes and to learn from their mistakes. Mistakes are not an excuse to stop delegating, but rather an opportunity to offer training and support.

A second prerequisite for delegation is open communication between managers and employees. Managers who know the capabilities of their employees can more realistically decide which tasks can be delegated to whom. In turn, employees who are encouraged to use their abilities and who feel their managers will back them up are more likely to accept responsibility.[31] The third prerequisite for delegation is the manager's ability to analyze such factors as the organization's goals, the task's requirements, and the employee's capabilities.[32]

**TASKS OF EFFECTIVE DELEGATION.** The prerequisites just discussed are all important to carrying out the following tasks of effective delegation:

1. *Decide which tasks can be delegated.* Many items can and should be delegated. Some of these are minor decisions and recurring chores. However, unusually demanding and challenging assignments may often be delegated to employees and will do much to develop them. Nordstrom managers clearly organize this way.

2. *Decide who should get the assignment.* Who has available time? Does the job require special competence? For whom would it be an appropriate and useful developmental experience? Managers ask these questions when deciding which of their people should get the assignment.

3. *Provide sufficient resources for carrying out the delegated task.* All the delegated authority in the world will not help the recipient, if he or she cannot have the financial, staff, or time resources necessary to do the job.

4. *Delegate the assignment.* In delegating the assignment, effective managers provide all relevant information on the task. As far as possible they specify the results expected, not the methods to be used. Further, they cultivate a climate of free and open communication between themselves and the person to whom they have delegated the task.

5. *Be prepared to run interference, if necessary.* Delegated tasks can get bogged down if resources are insufficient or if the person delegated to do the task runs up against resistance from others. Sometimes this happens because other kinds of power are at work. We can readily imagine a case where a transfer of reward power causes some third party to complain or try to "go around" the person who was delegated the task.

6. *Establish a feedback system.* Delegating managers establish a system of checkpoints and feedback so they will remain advised of progress and can

# THE INVERTED PYRAMID

As an alternative to the traditional command-and-control hierarchy, a structure narrow at the top and wide at the base, Nordstrom has adopted an organizational structure that is an inverted pyramid. According to Working Woman writer Nancy K. Austin, "This pacesetting, service-obsessed specialty retailer literally turned the traditional organizational structure upside down to keep its fortunes right side up."[33]

Nordstrom's inverted pyramid is a relatively flat structure; it includes few levels of management. The salespeople and sales support staff sit on top as the key decision makers, with their only charge being to follow their own best judgment at all times. →

offer advice or "mid-course adjustments" if necessary. They select the feedback system carefully, bearing in mind that the tighter their controls, the less actual delegation is taking place.

## DECENTRALIZATION AND CENTRALIZATION

Managers make decisions about delegation continually. It is an ongoing part of the organizing process. At the same time, top managers make broad decisions about how much delegation they want to practice as a general rule throughout the organizational structure. These decisions are, in effect, *planning* decisions about *organizing* practices.

The degree to which formal authority is delegated by managers throughout the organization runs along a continuum from *decentralization* to *centralization*. In a relatively decentralized organization, considerable authority and accountability are passed down the organizational hierarchy. In a relatively centralized organization, considerable authority and accountability remain at the top of the hierarchy. Nordstrom is a significantly decentralized organization, as is the college or university you attend.

### ADVANTAGES AND DISADVANTAGES

Decentralization has the same advantages as delegation: unburdening of top managers; decision making that is frequently better because decisions are made closer to the scene of action; better training, morale, and initiative at lower levels; and more flexibility and faster decision making in rapidly changing environments. These advantages are so compelling that it is tempting to think of decentralization as "good" and centralization as "bad."

But total decentralization, with no coordination and leadership from the top, would clearly be undesirable. The very purpose of organization—efficient integration of subunits for the pursuit of organizational goals through the strategic plan—would be defeated without some centralized control.

**CENTRALIZATION.** The amount of authority and autonomy given to a multinational divisional manager is a reflection of the relative centralization or decentralization of the organization.

Al Winick, president of Norwest Financial Information Services Group, and Robert Major, president and CEO of Chrysler First, have studied the advantages of both decentralization and centralization in the customer finance market. Winick reports that decentralization is, in the opinion of many, "the best way to develop and retain a close relationship with the customer." He lists the following benefits of decentralization:[34]

- *Proximity to the Market.* Having the same person procure accounts, receive payments, and handle collections and renewals provides the customer with a more personalized level of service.
- *Local Knowledge.* An employee's knowledge of the community can prove critical in the decision to grant a loan.
- *Customer Acceptance and Knowledge.* Local employees are also possessed of a better understanding of a customer's needs due to local economic trends.
- *Dealer's Comfort.* Dealers also feel more comfortable doing business with the person who will be servicing the dealer's customers.

On the other hand, centralization offers a variety of strengths well suited to today's customer finance market, Major finds. He lists the following as reasons for centralizing:[35]

- Specialized skills, talent, and technology are sometimes neither affordable nor practical in multiple locations.
- Decentralized locations usually mean an increase in overhead and staff. Coordination of products, money, and control also add to the cost of decentralized locations.
- Recent improvements in communication technology facilitate the movement of money, credit information, transportation, and data processing from a central location.

As managers in many organizations consider greater decentralization, the important question is not *whether* an organization should be decentralized, but *to what extent* it should be decentralized.

## CHALLENGES OF DECENTRALIZATION

The shift towards decentralization does not come without challenges. More individual authority at the store level requires more thorough manager training. At

Fred Meyer Inc., for example, employees receive classroom-style training from company executives, company training staff, and college professors at the Fred Meyer Institute in order to improve their decision-making abilities.

Decentralization usually entails bringing in additional staff. Fred Meyer Inc. managers decided to replace their centralized Honeywell mainframe management information system with one that uses individual IBM computers at every store. This change required the hiring of a professional staff to put the new system into place and design the software required to run it.[36]

During the late 1980s, Eastman Kodak reorganized itself and developed a framework for thinking about human resource planning which was dubbed "HR Planning in '3D.'" The three dimensions were diversity, dynamism, and decentralization. Decentralization was particularly important in that it enabled decision making to take place at appropriate levels in the organization.[37]

## FACTORS INFLUENCING DECENTRALIZATION

Decentralization has value only to the extent that it helps organization members achieve their objectives. In determining the amount of decentralization appropriate for an organization, the following factors are usually considered:

1. Environmental influences, such as market characteristics, competitive pressures, and availability of materials
2. The organization's size and growth rate
3. Other characteristics of the organization, such as costliness of given decisions, top management preferences, the organization's culture, and abilities of lower-level managers.[38]

**STRATEGY AND THE ORGANIZATIONAL ENVIRONMENT.** A strategic plan will influence the types of markets, technological environment, and competition with which the organization must contend. These factors will, in turn, influence the degree of decentralization that the firm finds appropriate. Alfred Chandler found that managers at firms that developed new products through a strategy of research and development leading to product diversification, such as Westinghouse and General Electric, chose a decentralized structure. Other managers, operating in industries in which markets were more predictable, production processes were less dynamic, and competitive relationships were more stable, tended to choose centralized authority.

For example, several years ago, Nobuhiko Kawamoto, president of Honda Motor Company, acted on his concern about sales prospects for the best-selling Honda Accord by taking a direct role in managing Honda's auto division (the company has several product divisions).[39] Kawamoto's move, designed to improve implementation of Honda's Honda auto strategy, increased decision-making centralization at the company.

Executives at AT&T, on the other hand, have decentralized decision making at the AT&T Universal Card Services division, which faces vigorous competition in the credit card marketplace. AT&T Universal Card Services is structured like a wagon wheel, with a hub, a series of spokes, and an outer rim. The customer is the hub (and actually appears on the organization chart). The business functions (finance, marketing, engineering) and teams (new-product development, customer satisfaction, suppliers) are the spokes. The outer rim, which holds it all together, includes the chief executive and the board, who make sure each employee has the resources at hand to serve the customers. Within such a structure, managers serve as advocates and coaches. This decentralization seems an appropriate way to respond to change in the credit card market.[40]

**SIZE AND RATE OF GROWTH.** As an organization grows in size and complexity, decentralization tends to increase. The faster the rate of growth, the more likely it is that upper management, bearing the weight of an ever-increasing work load, will be forced to accelerate the delegation of authority to lower levels.

**NEW-PRODUCT STRATEGY.**
Rubbermaid's strong record of product diversification makes it more likely to choose a decentralized structure. The company has expanded beyond its traditional kitchen and laundry accessories to make mailboxes, hardware cabinets, garden sheds, window boxes, and many more products.

← ch. 7, p. 182

Nordstrom managers appear to have anticipated such pressures and decentralized accordingly.

**OTHER CHARACTERISTICS OF THE ORGANIZATION.** The extent to which decision-making authority is centralized is also likely to be influenced by internal characteristics of the company, such as the following:

1. *The cost and risk associated with the decision.* Managers may be wary of delegating authority for decisions that could have a heavy impact on the performance of their own subunits or the organization as a whole. This caution reflects consideration for both the company's welfare and their own, since the delegator retains responsibility for the results.

2. *An individual manager's preference and confidence in employees.* Some managers pride themselves on their detailed knowledge of everything that happens within their area of responsibility ("the good manager runs a tight ship" approach). Others take pride in confidently delegating everything possible to their employees.

3. *The organizational culture.* The shared norms, values, and understandings (culture) of members of some organizations support tight control at the top. The culture of other organizations supports the opposite. The history of an organization helps to create its current culture. A firm that has had slow growth under a strong-willed leader may have a very centralized structure. In contrast, managers at a firm that has grown rapidly through acquisitions will have learned to live with the greater independence of the acquired companies.

4. *The abilities of lower-level managers.* This dimension can be circular. If authority is not delegated because managers lack faith in the talent below, the talent will not have much opportunity to develop. In addition, the lack of internal training will make finding and holding talented and ambitious people more difficult, which, in turn, will make it more difficult to decentralize.

One organization that started out with a decentralized structure is Saturn Corporation, which was formed by General Motors executives in the 1980s as an innovative approach to making and selling automobiles.[41] Right from the start, Saturn managers and employees at the lone Saturn plant in Spring Hill, Tennessee, operated with little direction from General Motors headquarters. Saturn's organization is described as "a collection of small, self-directed business units.... Each team manages everything from its own budget and inventory control to hiring, with direct

**DESIGN FOR EFFICIENCY.** At Westinghouse's Baldrige-winning Commercial Nuclear Fuel Division, the Tube Process Optimization Team increased yields, reduced cycle times, and improved productivity by re-designing the pilgering process to reduce the number of "passes" from four to three.

oversight from top management."[42] Saturn managers and employees were hired based on their potential and preference for this very kind of decentralized operation.

# JOB DESIGN

**job design:**
The division of an organization's work among its employees.

**M**anagers translate their preferences for, and decisions about, decentralization into the decisions they make about **job design.** Job design is a vehicle for systematically implementing the degree of decentralization that managers want and believe is necessary for pursuing organizational goals in view of the circumstances that we just discussed. Job design is thus a way for managers to communicate to employees the opportunities that employees will have for exercising power and authority.

The pursuit of quality improvements has encouraged job redesign in many organizations. At Clark-Schwebel Fiber Glass, a producer of the glass-fiber fabric used in computer circuit boards, plants in Georgia, North Carolina, and South Carolina were redesigned to encourage and enable the transformation to total quality and the total involvement of all employees. The assumption is that expert workers, with training and guidance, can then redesign their work and organization to maximize productivity and quality. The result has been increased employee involvement, in addition to improved quality and cycle times and reduced costs.[43]

## APPROACHES TO JOB DESIGN

Experts have been thinking about job design for many years. Indeed, early management practices often concentrated on this aspect of organization. Over the years, three different ways of viewing the subject of job design have emerged: the mechanistic, motivational, and biological approaches.

**MECHANISTIC JOB DESIGN.** Consider the jobs of factory workers on an assembly line. Each worker is required to do only one or two simple things, over and over again. Most of these jobs are fairly easy to learn and to do. Such jobs are suited

← ch. 2, p. 34

to the mechanistic approach to job design, inspired by the turn-of-the-century researcher Frederick W. Taylor who systematically attempted to make jobs simple and efficient. Jobs like these still exist. It is an open question, however, whether they serve anyone's interests well. Very little authority is invested in such jobs as sweeping out a stadium after a concert or game and cutting lawns on a college campus. What authority is present in these cases is a degree of expert power.

**MOTIVATIONAL JOB DESIGN.** As the limits of the mechanistic approach became clear, researchers began to seek out ways of making jobs more varied and challenging. J. Richard Hackman and others identified five core job dimensions: skills variety, task identity, task significance, autonomy, and feedback.[44] Table 13-1 describes these dimensions and gives examples of each.

Hackman argues that employees who have responsible jobs that they understand are more motivated and satisfied with their positions.[45] People whose jobs involve high levels of skill variety, task identity, and task significance experience work as very meaningful. A high level of autonomy makes workers more responsible and accountable for their acts. Feedback gives them a useful understanding of their specific roles and functions. The closer a job comes to having all five characteristics, the more likely it is that the person who holds it will be highly motivated and satisfied.

The Medical University of South Carolina Medical Center in Charleston attempted to enhance the care environment as perceived by patients and their families by redesigning jobs and empowering workers. This was a project that included the creation of patient-care associates, which entailed the collapsing of several work roles into one. The new patient-care associate has 10 to 14 skills and handles a diverse array of tasks. "The worker gets to see more of the fruits of his [or her] contribution," noted Thomas P. Keating, director of general services and co-director of the patient-focused care project. During its first year, the project appeared to satisfy expectations.[46]

Much effort in recent years has gone into making routine jobs more rewarding by redefining such jobs to include greater legitimate and expert authority. The term *empowerment*, as practiced at Nordstrom and in numerous other companies we have profiled, clearly indicates what managers are trying to do in these job redesign decisions. Job enlargement and job enrichment are two empowering ways to redesign jobs.

**Job enlargement** stems from the thinking of industrial engineers. The idea is to break up the monotony of a limited routine and work cycle by increasing a job's *scope*. Work functions from a horizontal slice of an organizational unit are combined, thereby giving each employee more operations to perform. For example, the work from two or more positions may be combined to restore some sense of the wholeness of the job. In the Nordstrom inverted pyramid, associates' tasks are clearly "larger" than those generally assigned to salespeople at other retail stores.

Another basic strategy was inspired by motivational theory. **Job enrichment** tries to deal with dissatisfied workers by increasing the *depth* of their jobs. Work activities from a vertical slice of the organizational unit are combined into one position to give employees more autonomy on the job. The idea is to develop a stronger sense of accountability by allowing workers to set their own work pace, correct their own errors, and decide the best way to perform various tasks. They may also be asked to help make decisions that affect their own subunits. As the work becomes more challenging and worker responsibility increases, motivation and enthusiasm should increase as well.[47] At Nordstrom, job enrichment is the norm.

Workers may also be shifted routinely from job to job within the same company so they can develop a variety of skills. *Job rotation* of this sort motivates workers by challenging them and enabling them to learn new skills. Job rotation may be combined with job enlargement and job enrichment.

← ch. 8, p. 227

**job enlargement:**
The combining of various operations at a similar level into one job to provide more variety for workers and thus increase their motivation and satisfaction; represents an increase in job scope.

**job enrichment:**
The combining of several activities from a vertical cross section of the organization into one job to provide the worker with more autonomy and responsibility; represents an increase in job depth.

**TABLE 13-1** **Task Characteristics in Motivational Job Design**

| Characteristic | Description | High Degree | Low Degree |
|---|---|---|---|
| *Skill variety*-the extent to which a variety of skills and talents are required to complete assigned tasks. | Perform different tasks that challenge the intellect and develop skills in coordination. | Dress designer | Messenger |
| *Task identity*-the extent to which the job involves completion of an identifiable unit, project, or other piece of work | Handle an entire job function from start to finish and be able to show a tangible piece of work as the outcome. | Software designer | Assembly-line worker |
| *Task significance*-the extent to which the task affects the work or lives of others, inside or outside the organization. | Be involved in a job function that is important for the well-being, safety, and perhaps survival of others. | Air traffic controller | House painter |
| *Autonomy*-the extent of the individual's freedom on the job and discretion to schedule tasks and determine procedures for carrying them out. | Be responsible for the success or failure of a job function and be able to plan work schedule, control quality, etc. | Project manager | Cashier in a department store |
| *Feedback*- the extent to which the individual receives specific information (praise, blame,etc.) about the effectiveness with which his or her tasks are performed. | Learn about the effectiveness of one's job performance through clear and direct evaluation from a supervisor or colleagues or the results of the work itself. | Professional athlete | Security guard |

Recent changes at the General Electric plant in Lynn, Massachusetts are examples of job enlargement and job enrichment. Peter Boglioni used to operate one kind of lathe equipment. Now, as a byproduct of downsizing at the plant, he has been trained to operate numerous machines so that he can "make aircraft engine parts from start to finish."[48] This is an example of job enlargement. Another result of downsizing decisions is that Boglioni and his fellow machinists work together in "cells" or units that have no formal supervisors; "the workers manage the job and

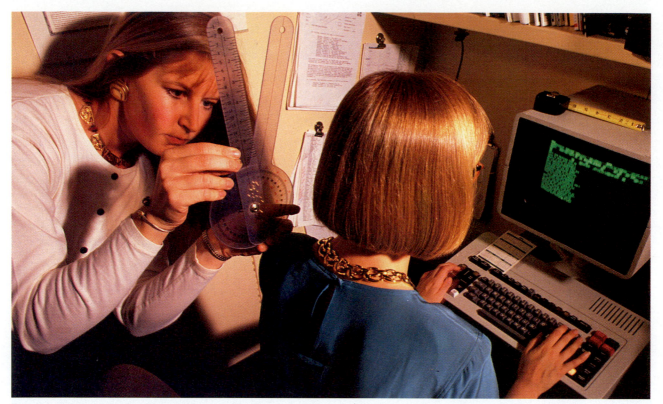

**BIOLOGICAL JOB DESIGN.** Ergonomics consultant Lori Monson uses a goniometer to measure the angle of Business Week writer Suzanne Woolley's neck, an important factor in easing back and neck pain caused by working long hours at a terminal.

call in help only when problems arise."[49] This is job enrichment on top of job enlargement. Boglioni and his associates have been given greater line authority that enriches and enlarges what they do.

**BIOLOGICAL JOB DESIGN.** A whole new approach to job design is a biological approach called *ergonomics,* which is a systematic attempt to make work as safe as possible. One example of the importance of ergonomics comes from Hardee's restaurants.

Some of the employees at Hardee's Food boning department began complaining of aching wrists after working long days.[50] Medical examinations revealed that the employees suffered from carpal tunnel syndrome, a condition similar to arthritis that results from repetitive wrist motions. Carpal tunnel syndrome can cause excruciating pain. It is, however, preventable. Managers at Hardee's quickly undertook an ergonomic study of the affected employees' work conditions. The study revealed a number of steps they could take to reduce the incidence of carpal tunnel syndrome. Best of all, the adjustments suggested were simple, cheap, and effective. "We began a formal knife-sharpening program to make certain our employees exerted a minimum of effort in slicing or carving product. Individual work stations were adjusted to conform to the employees' physical size," says Susan Werner, director of risk management at Hardee's.[51]

Carpal tunnel syndrome often afflicts office workers as well, especially those whose work involves large amounts of keyboard manipulation. Minor adjustments, such as raising or lowering the keyboard, supplying a more suitable chair, or requiring employees to take periodic breaks can often prevent the problem altogether. Besides the financial and productivity considerations in ergonomics issues, there is also an ethical component to take into account as employers wrestle with how soon and how aggressively to address workstation issues that affect employee health and well-being.

In late 1992, Quill Corp., an international distributor of office products based in Lincolnshire, Illinois, launched a campaign that emphasized ergonomics to

increase worker productivity. The organization hired Nancy Huber-Osterman, a specialist in exercise science, to develop an ergonomics plan and she suggested the development of an ergonomics team. Not all employees were supportive of her efforts, however. "Some supervisors were concerned that we would be opening floodgates if we asked for complaints," Osterman noted. "In reality, workers were very reluctant to say they were uncomfortable. They're more likely to take a 'this is a part of my job' attitude."[52] Once changes started taking place and workstations were altered, employees became much more accepting. "Overall, people have been really enthusiastic," reported Cindy Fultz, who trains new employees and customer relations representatives. "There's been a halo effect. Everyone's happy that someone is looking out for them."[53] While the changes are not free, Osterman indicated that about 80 percent of them cost less than $250 per employee—an insignificant cost for a significant increase in productivity and morale.

Ergonomics applications are more and more popular, especially in regard to company compliance with statutes such as the Americans with Disabilities Act. This law requires managers to make reasonable accommodations to allow disabled people to enter their workforce. The increased emphasis on health management and medical cost containment in companies has also increased the popularity of ergonomics.

**MANAGEMENT 2000 AND BEYOND**

# RULES AND SELF-CRITICAL MANAGEMENT

"Tom Peters Ruined My Life" was the attention-grabbing title of a recent *Wall Street Journal* article by Mary Baechler.[54] After attending one of Peters' talks about excellent customer service, Baechler, president of a company that makes strollers, began to reexamine the service she received as a customer and the service she and her employees gave to their customers. She liked less and less of what she saw, and she began to shop and to manage differently. In time, her accustomed patterns were, in her words, "gone, all ruined"; her comfortable methods were replaced by more effective ways of operating.[55]

Baechler joins Peters and more and more managers and commentators in challenging organization members first to rethink how they relate to their customers and then to make this rethinking a regular part of their organizational practices. It is nothing short of passionate management-by-self-criticism that they are advocating.[56]

Baechler and Peters call our attention to a traditional view of customer relations whereby sellers act as if they had authority over their buyers. There are telltale signs of this attitude. If someone throws "It's company policy" in your face, as a salesperson did to Baechler, you are experiencing such a grab for power over you. If someone responds to your unusual request with "If we did it for you, we'd have to do it for everybody (and we wouldn't do *that*, would we?)," you are witnessing authority and rules being used as ends in themselves. As Baechler and Peters point out, these kinds of responses are roadblocks to mutually beneficial transactions between buyers and sellers. Authority used in this way interferes with promising transactions.

An alternative approach is for managers and employees to ask themselves, "*What if* we did things differently for this person, and the next person, and the next?" In this way, managers and employees can critique their own rules as they proceed. It is tantamount to asking, "Why do we operate by these rules?" Certainly, all organizations must operate according to rules and procedures. What Baechler and Peters propose is that managers and employees think carefully about the effects of the rules they use for dealing with customers. If they do that routinely, chances are that their accustomed habits will be "ruined," too.

Baechler reports that the new kind of partnerships that she and her employees have created with customers have been accompanied by a new distribution of legitimate and expert power throughout the organization:

> What does my business do differently now from what we did before Tom's inspiration? Anyone in our company can stop production if he thinks there's a flaw. Any employee can send a stroller that's on order Fed Ex (at $87 a pop) if he feels we have not met our delivery commitments. Beyond our lifetime guarantee for frames and one-year guarantee on the wheels, our customer service people can do whatever it takes, up to $300 per customer, to make things right for the customer (we track costs religiously, so that we can keep this up).[57]

Baechler and her colleagues are sharing power in their kind of "intelligent enterprise," as James Brian Quinn describes organizations that have a fundamental "service" focus. Quinn links new "intelligent enterprises" with a rethinking of authority and power:

> All require a breaking away from traditional thinking about lines of command, one person–one boss structures, the center as a directing force, and lower levels as mere tools for the delivery of wisdom from above.[58]

Keep an eye out for the kinds of customer service you receive, or give. Your life might just be "ruined" for the better!

# Summary

1. **Distinguish between authority and power.**

   Managers and employees alike need rules for interacting in the organizational structures that managers design. In modern management practice, power—and power translated into formal authority—serve as the basis for such rules. Organizational structures do not "run themselves." Rather, people use power to govern their relationships and get things accomplished at organizations.

2. **Explain how use of power is related to the history of a people's culture.**

   Power is much more than an organizational phenomenon. The use and abuse of power, now and in the past, is an important aspect in any culture. In the United States, our central political institutions were designed to prevent abuses of governmental power and continue to be operated on that principle.

3. **List and explain the five sources of power.**

   Power can come in many varieties. Among the more common kinds of power are reward, coercive, legitimate, expert, and referent power. In exercising their power, managers can take a dominance-submission approach toward employees, or they can use a more positive style based on concern for group goals and the encouragement and support of employees. Reward power is based on the influencer having the ability to reward the influencee for carrying out orders or meeting performance requirements. Coercive power is based on the influencer's ability to punish the influencee for not meeting requirements. Legitimate power exists when an influencee acknowledges that the influencer is entitled to exert influence. Expert power is based on the perception or belief that the influencer has some relevant expertise or special knowledge that the influencee does not. Referent power is based on the influencee's desire to identify with or imitate the influencer.

# MANAGEMENT BY COMMITTEE

At Nordstrom, the management structure revolves around a team, not a single decision maker. Nordstrom is actually run by a committee of co-presidents, with the title of president rotating among them. "They continually defy the model of what we in the management field say to do," said Jeffrey Sonnenfeld, an Emory University professor who specializes in management succession and structure. "And yet they make it work."[59]

Until a couple of years ago, Nordstrom was run by three of the founder's grandsons—Bruce A., John N., and James F. Nordstrom. Then they, along with cousin John A. McMillan, became co-chairmen, and four non-family members became co-presidents. This structure invites questions. "Having co-CEOs has to be somewhere between difficult and impossible," said Chuck Griffin, former president of the Sanger Harris chain and now a partner at Ginnie Johansen Designs in Dallas.[60] Additional skepticism has been expressed by Harry Bernard, publisher of the *Colton Bernard Newsletter,* which tracks the retail industry. "Somebody has to take responsibility for ultimate decisions," he says.[61] Nevertheless, Nordstrom management is not alone in the industry in adopting such a form of management. Managers at Dayton Hudson, Dillard and Macy's also manage at least part of their businesses by committee.

At Nordstrom, a strength of the committee lies perhaps in the diversity of the co-presidents. Raymond A. Johnson, raised on a farm, began at Nordstrom in personnel. Darrel J. Hume started his career selling shirts and ties while he was still in college. Galen Jefferson is a skier who worked her way up from Nordstrom's mail-order department through women's fashions. John J. Whitacre is a former college football star who began in the shoe department at Nordstrom's. While this young (mostly early 40s) team reflects diversity, they speak with a single voice. This is imperative, considering the management structure they have chosen.

> *"They continually defy the model of what we in the management field say to do."*

Nordstrom's highly decentralized organizational structure supports this unusual style of decision making. The Nordstrom tradition of empowering employees to make decisions for themselves reduces the number of decisions left to be made by the committee of co-presidents. "The beauty is, we don't have a bottleneck at the top," said Johnson.[62] What this means for the associates is that many work as hard as if the company were their own.

The family co-chairmen are supportive of the committee, according to Hume. "They've made it very clear to us that they don't want to stifle our efforts," he said. "It's the foundation of our culture to allow entrepreneurship.[63]"

4. **Discuss the two major views of authority.**

   Formal authority is a type of power used by certain people at an organization. The justification for a person's having this kind of power has been the subject of considerable debate. From a classical viewpoint, formal authority is a legitimate managerial right that employees are obligated to recognize. From an "acceptance" viewpoint, formal authority is legitimized, or not, by employees.

5. **Compare and contrast line, staff, and functional authority.**

   Authority is distributed at organizations in line, staff, and functional forms. *Line positions* can be defined as those directly responsible for achieving organizational goals. *Staff positions* provide expert advice and service to the line. *Functional* authority is a kind of staff authority that in certain cases is combined with line authority.

6. **Discuss the advantages of delegation, why managers hesitate to delegate, and the guidelines that can help them delegate effectively.**

Authority is distributed at organizations through a managerial decision process known as delegation, necessary for the efficient functioning of any organization. Delegation frees managers to accept other responsibilities, gives growth opportunities to employees, and may lead to better and faster decisions.

Delegation planning results in relative decentralization of top-management authority or relative centralization of that authority. Tendencies toward decentralization or centralization depend on what is happening in the organizational environment, managers' preferences for control, and what people at the organization are capable of doing.

To effectively delegate, managers must decide which tasks can be delegated and who should get the assignment; delegate the task, providing resources and running interference if necessary; and provide feedback.

7. **Compare major approaches to job design and the part that authority plays in those approaches.**

Authority is a consideration that goes into job design for every position in an organizational structure. In recent years, the trend has been toward expanding employees' authority through job enlargement and job enrichment. The idea is that empowering workers taps a great organizational resource. Over the years, three approaches to job design have emerged: the mechanistic, motivational, and biological approaches.

8. **Discuss how authority sometimes can impede strategy implementation and customer service.**

Rules are essential understandings that people use to act and interact at organizations. But rules can become rigid, getting in the way of strategic plans and customer service. New and emerging approaches to management stress greater self-criticism by managers about the rules they make and follow. These new approaches stress the effects of following organizational rules, rather than the number, breadth and familiarity of rules.

## REVIEW QUESTIONS

1. What are the five bases of power described by French and Raven? Give one example of a manager's exercise of each type of power.
2. What are the "two faces of power" described by David McClelland?
3. What are the two major views of authority? How do you think each view would affect a manager's attitude and behavior toward employees?
4. What is the "zone of indifference"?
5. What is the difference between line positions and staff positions?
6. What does *functional staff authority* mean?
7. What are the advantages of delegation? Describe the key guidelines for effective delegation.
8. How are decentralization and delegation related?

9. What factors influence the extent to which an organization is decentralized?

10. What is the purpose of job enlargement and job enrichment?

## KEY TERMS

| | |
|---|---|
| Power | Reward power |
| Coercive power | Legitimate power |
| Expert power | Referent power |
| Authority | Line authority |
| Staff authority | Functional authority |
| Delegation | Job design |
| Job enlargement | Job enrichment |

## CASE STUDY

### BIRKENSTOCK AIMS HIGH[64]

Since 1990, Margo Fraser, founder and CEO of Birkenstock Footwear Inc., has watched her company experience growth nothing short of explosive. Revenue for 1992, at about $50 million, was up 50 percent from 1991, which was up 40 percent from 1990. While the American health-conscious craze of the 1990s, which has brought mainstream acceptance to formerly counterculture values, accounts for some of the company's soaring success, Birkenstock's empowerment of employees cannot be ignored.

The company, based in Novato, California, is the exclusive importer of the "Birkenstock" sandals from Germany. "Birkenstocks" are actually clunky-looking sandals with cork innersoles that cradle the feet. These shoes—sometimes dubbed "shoes for lazy feet," since the wearer just slips them on, with nothing to tie or button—now come in a range of styles and colors. In Germany, the Birkenstock family had been making gesundheitschuhe—health shoes—for roughly two centuries when Fraser stumbled upon them in the mid-1960s. Today, with the baby boomers increasingly interested in comfort, the sandals are not just for Berkeley-types. Whoopi Goldberg and Madonna are among celebrities who have been seen wearing them.

Birkenstock shows respect for its employees. "Because we take a great deal of time out of our employees' lives, we want to provide for more than just their critical needs, such as major medical in-surance," said Pischke. "Employees contribute a lot of themselves to our organization; we should contribute to the quality of their lives."[65] Benefits have therefore been expanded to include stress-management courses, a comprehensive Employee Assistance Program and financial counseling.

At the same time, the company management not only involves employees but actively engages them. This is empowerment. In January 1993, Birkenstock hired a professional trainer to organize employees into teams and teach them how to make the most of those teams. Then, in March, managers created a training advisory council aimed at locating specific areas that still needed improvement. Teams now operate within and across many departments.

Empowerment is not a new concept in Birkenstock. Back in 1989, an in-house marketing manager encouraged the creation of a 12-member "eco task force" with across-the-board departmental representation. This happened after a member of the department approached the manager with her belief that Birkenstock could do more in the area of environmental conscientiousness. The company had already embraced a wide variety of such practices. But the task force did more. An in-house environmental library was developed. A guide to nontoxic resources was compiled. A newsletter on relevant internal activities was produced. And monthly meetings with neighboring businesses were organized to promote the sharing of ideas on environmental products and concerns.

Birkenstock management supports such endeavors because they enable employees to pursue their own concerns, while, at the same time, helping the company. The "eco task force" enabled Birkenstock to cut energy costs at the same time that motivation and loyalty were being reinforced. Today, Birkenstock is noted for its highly productive workforce and low turnover. "We recognize that people have a need to contribute and to feel enthusiastic about what they are doing," said Birkenstock's vice president Mary Jones. "I'm really here to help out."[66]

Fraser's personal values underlie Birkenstock's employee empowerment. "It's a good thing to aim high," she said. "The business can only grow as much as you can as a person. You must grow with it."[67]

## CASE QUESTIONS

1. Discuss the kind(s) of power Birkenstock employees appear to have?
2. What might limit the way Birkenstock managers share power and authority?
3. Based on this case, what kind of organizational structures might be appropriate for Birkenstock?
4. If you were to enlarge jobs at Birkenstock, what might the "new" jobs look like?

## VIDEO CASE STUDY

## "THAT'S NOT MY JOB": LEARNING DELEGATION AT CIN-MADE[68]

When Robert Frey purchased Cin-Made in 1984, the company was near ruin. The Cincinnati, Ohio-based manufacturer of paper packaging had not altered its product line in 20 years. Labor costs had hit the ceiling, while profits were falling through the floor. A solid quarter of the company's shipments were late and absenteeism was high. Management and workers were at each other's throats.

Ten years later, Cin-Made is producing a new assortment of highly differentiated composite cans, and pre-tax profits have increased more than five times. The Cin-Made workforce is both flexible and deeply committed to the success of the company. On-time delivery of products has reached 98 percent, and absenteeism has virtually disappeared. There are even plans to form two spin-off companies to be owned and operated by Cin-Made employees. In fact, at the one-day "Future of the American Workforce" conference held in July 1993, Cin-Made was recognized by President Clinton as one of the best-run companies in the United States.

"How did we achieve this startling turnaround?" mused Frey. "Employee empowerment is one part of the answer. Profit sharing is another."[69]

In the late spring of 1986, relations between management and labor had reached rock bottom. Having recently suffered a pay cut, employees at Cin-Made came to work each day, performed the duties required of their particular positions, and returned home—nothing more. Frey could see that his company was suffering. "To survive we needed to stop being worthy adversaries and start being worthy partners," he realized.[70] Toward this end, Frey decided to call a meeting with the union. He offered to restore worker pay to its previous level by the end of the year. On top of that, he offered something no one expected: a 15 percent share of Cin-Made's pre-tax profits. "I do not choose to own a company that has an adversarial relationship with its employees," Frey proclaimed at the meeting.[71] He therefore proposed a new arrangement that would encourage a collaborative employee–management relationship.

"Employee participation will play an essential role in management."[72]

Managers within the company were among the first people to oppose Frey's new idea of employee involvement. "My three managers felt they were paid to be worthy adversaries of the unions," Frey recalled. "It's what they'd been trained for. It's what made them good managers. Moreover, they were not used to participation in any form, certainly not in decision making."[73] The workers also resisted the idea of extending themselves beyond the written requirements of their jobs. "[Employees] wanted generous wages and benefits, of course, but they did not want to take responsibility for anything more than doing their own jobs the way they had always done them," Frey noted.[74] Employees were therefore skeptical of Frey's overtures toward "employee participation." "We thought he was trying to rip us off and shaft us," explained Ocelia Williams, one of many Cin-Made employees who distrusted Frey's plans.[75]

Frey, however, did not give up, and he eventually convinced the union to agree to his terms. "I wouldn't take no for an answer," he asserted. "Once I had made my two grand pronouncements, I was determined to press ahead and make them come true."[76] But still ahead lay the considerable challenge of convincing employees to take charge:

I made people meet with me, then instead of telling them what to do, I asked them. They resisted.

"How can we cut the waste on this run?" I'd say, or "How are we going to allocate the overtime on this order?"

"That's not my job," they'd say.

"But I need your input," I'd say. "How in the world can we have participative management if you won't participate?"

"I don't know," they'd say. "Because that's not my job either. That's your job."[77]

Gradually, Frey made progress. Managers began sharing more information with employees. Frey was able slowly to expand the responsibilities workers would carry. Managers who were unable to work with employees left, and union relations began to improve. Empowerment began to happen. By 1993, Cin-Made employees were taking responsibility for numerous tasks. Williams, for example, used to operate a tin-slitting machine on the company's factory floor. She still runs that same machine, but now is also responsible for ordering almost $100,000 in supplies.

Williams is just one example of how job roles and duties have been redefined throughout Cin-Made. Joyce Bell, president of the local union, still runs the punch press she always has, but now also serves as Cin-Made's corporate safety director. The company's scheduling team, composed of one manager and five lead workers from various plant areas, is charged with setting hours, designating layoffs, and deciding when temporary help is needed. The hiring review team, staffed by three hourly employees and two managers, is responsible for interviewing applicants and deciding whom to hire. An employee committee performs both short- and long-term planning of labor, materials, equipment, production runs, packing, and delivery. Employees even meet daily in order to set their own production schedules. "We empower employees to make decisions, not just have input," Frey remarked. "I just coach."[78]

Under Frey's new management regime, company secrets have virtually disappeared. All Cin-Made employees, from entry-level employees all the way to the top, take part in running the company. In fact, Frey has delegated so much of the company's operations to its workers that he now feels a little in the dark. "I now know very little about what's going on, on a day-to-day basis," he confessed.[79]

At Cin-Made, empowerment and delegation are more than mere buzzwords; they are the way of doing business—good business. "We, as workers, have a lot of opportunities," said Williams. "If we want to take leadership, it's offered to us."[80]

## CASE QUESTIONS

1. How were principles of delegation and decentralization incorporated into Cin-Made operations?
2. What are the sources and uses of power at Cin-Made?
3. What were some of the barriers to delegation and empowerment at Cin-Made?
4. What lessons about management in a rapidly changing marketplace can be learned from the experience of Cin-Made?

## CHAPTER 14

# HUMAN RESOURCE

# MANAGEMENT

**Upon completing this chapter, you should be able to:**

1. Present an overview of the HRM process.

2. List and describe the various methods of recruitment.

3. Discuss the various legal considerations involved in human relations.

4. Explain the seven-step hiring sequence.

5. Distinguish between training and development programs and give examples of each.

6. Discuss the important issues involved in making promotion, transfer, demotion, and separation decisions.

7. Explain how HRM interacts with organization strategy.

# HUMAN RELATIONS AT SONY[1]

Akio Morita, founder of Sony Corporation, says there is no "magic" in the success of Japanese companies in general and Sony in particular. The secret of their success is simply the way they treat their employees. In his biography, *Made in Japan,* Morita says:

> The most important mission for a Japanese manager is to develop a healthy relationship with his employees, to create a family-like feeling within the corporation, a feeling that employees and managers share the same fate. Those companies that are most successful in Japan are those that have managed to create a shared sense of fate among all employees, what Americans call labor and management, and the shareholders.[2]

When Morita was chairman of Sony, he stressed to new employees that each employee had to seek happiness in his or her work and to decide personally whether to spend the rest of his or her working life at Sony.

At Sony, there are few noticeable differences between management and labor. Although management writers sometimes paint a too-rosy picture of Japanese management-labor relations, Sony's management philosophy is that employees should be treated as colleagues and helpers, not merely as means to profits. Investors are important, Morita acknowledges, but they establish only a *temporary* relationship with the company. Employees are *more* important because they are a *permanent* part of the company, just as much as top management.

*The secret of their success is simply the way they treat their employees.*

In return for showing loyalty to employees, Morita expected loyalty from his employees. But he urged them not only to use their best efforts on the company's behalf, but also to question management views. Ironically, Morita's emphasis on loyalty was partly inspired by his experience with American managers and employees. In its early days, Sony hired many employees in the United States in an effort to keep pace with the remarkable demand for its products. Morita was stunned by an American colleague's blunt advice about a problem employee: "Fire him." Morita was equally surprised when an American employee walked into his office one day and announced he was quitting to take a job with a competitor who had offered him double his salary.

Under Morita, the whole process of recruiting, selecting, training, and appraising employees was built on the premise that employees are the most valuable part of the company. Granted, Morita's policies—especially the idea of lifetime job security—are not as typical of Japanese companies as Americans were once led to believe. In fact, a recent study conducted by the Japanese government showed that only 29 percent of all 20- to 29-year-old Japanese workers planned to stay with the same employer for their entire career. But this does not mean that American management cannot learn a great deal from Morita's philosophy.

**AKIO MORITA.** Sony founder Akio Morita says a key to success is creating a sense of shared fate among all employees.

Indeed, Morita's ideas are the basis for what management writer Tom Peters proposes as a new, more realistic pact between employer and employee: Employees will commit themselves to doing their best to help the company meet its goals, and in return, the company will give employees an opportunity to develop and hone their skills. Of course, they are free to leave and sell these skills to another employer, but ideally, the opportunity to keep learning and to do good work will keep them with the company and increase both their loyalty and their productivity.

This philosophy has been passed on to many Sony executives. For example, Norio Ohga, Sony's current president and CEO, has proven that he shares Morita's commitment to employees. Michael P. Schulhof, head of Sony's entertainment subsidiary and the company's highest ranking non-Japanese executive, appreciatively recounts Morita and Ohga's nurturing role in his development: "For whatever reason, they saw something in me 20 years ago. They took the time and the care to teach me their philosophy. They spent time making sure I understood why they made certain decisions."[3] →

**SONY'S SUCCESS** demonstrates Akio Morita's view that an organization's most important resources are the people who supply the work, talent, creativity, and drive to the organization. It seems logical, then, that among a manager's most critical tasks are the selection, training, and development of people who will best help the organization meet its goals.

In this chapter, we will look at **human resource management (HRM),** the management function through which managers recruit, select, train, and develop organization members. We will begin by discussing the traditional view of human resource management and pointing out how HRM can assure the organization of an adequate and constant supply of skilled employees. We will then show how environmental pressures require the coordination of HRM and strategy.

**human resource management (HRM):**

The management function that deals with recruitment, placement, training, and development of organization members.

# THE HRM PROCESS: A TRADITIONAL VIEW

← ch. 13, p. 354

**H**RM is a staff function. HRM managers advise line managers throughout the organization. Furthermore, the company may need more or fewer employees and managers from time to time. The HRM process is an ongoing procedure that tries to keep the organization supplied with the right people in the right positions, when they are needed. The HRM function is especially important given the current trend toward downsizing.

The HRM process, shown in Figure 14-1, includes seven basic activities:

1. *Human resource planning* is designed to ensure that personnel needs will be constantly and appropriately met. It is accomplished through analysis of (a) internal factors, such as current and expected skill needs, vacancies, and departmental expansions and reductions, and (b) factors in the environment, such as the labor market. The use of computers to build and maintain information about all employees has enabled organizations to be much more efficient in their planning of human resources.

2. *Recruitment* is concerned with developing a pool of job candidates in line with the human resource plan. Candidates are usually located through newspaper and professional journal advertisements, employment agencies, word of mouth, and visits to college and university campuses.

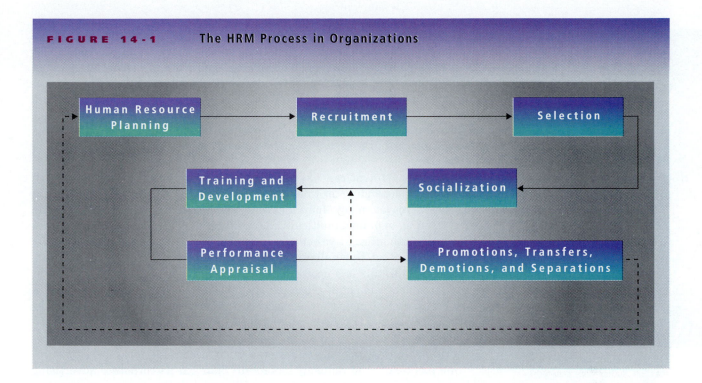

**FIGURE 14-1** The HRM Process in Organizations

3. *Selection* involves using application forms, resumes, interviews, employment and skills tests, and reference checks to evaluate and screen job candidates for the managers who will ultimately select and hire a candidate.

4. *Socialization* (orientation) is designed to help the selected individuals fit smoothly into the organization. Newcomers are introduced to their colleagues, acquainted with their responsibilities, and informed about the organization's culture, policies, and expectations regarding employee behavior.

5. *Training and development* both aim to increase employees' abilities to contribute to organizational effectiveness. Training is designed to improve skills in the present job; development programs are designed to prepare employees for promotion.

6. *Performance appraisal* compares an individual's job performance to standards or objectives developed for the individual's position. Low performance may prompt corrective action, such as additional training, a demotion, or separation, while high performance may merit a reward, such as raise, bonus, or promotion. Although an employee's immediate supervisor performs the appraisal, the HRM department is responsible for working with upper management to establish the policies that guide all performance appraisals.

7. *Promotions, transfers, demotions, and separations* reflect an employee's value to the organization. High performers may be promoted or transferred to help them develop their skills, while low performers may be demoted, transferred to less important positions, or even separated. Any of these options will, in turn, affect human resource planning.

**human resource planning:**

Planning for the future personnel needs of an organization, taking into account both internal activities and factors in the external environment.

## HUMAN RESOURCE PLANNING

The need for **human resource planning** may not be readily apparent. However, an organization that does not do planning for human resources may find that it is not meeting either its personnel requirements or its overall goals effectively. For example, a manufacturing company may hope to increase productivity with new

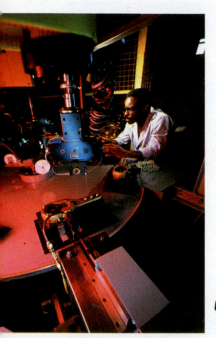

**TRAINED EMPLOYEES NEEDED.**
The introduction of high-tech equipment such as robotics requires human resource planning. Even before such equipment is installed, people must be hired and trained to operate it.

automated equipment, but if the company does not start to hire and train people to operate the equipment *before* installation, the equipment may remain idle for weeks or even months. Similarly, an all-male, all-white organization that does not plan to add women and minority group members to its staff may well have trouble maintaining high performance and is also likely to become the defendant in a civil rights lawsuit. Planning for human resources is a challenging task today, given the increasingly competitive environment, projected labor shortages, changing demographics, and pressure from government to protect both employees and the environment.[4]

The HRM department can have a significant effect on an organization in a number of ways, depending on what goals a company chooses to focus on. For instance, Sun Microsystems in Mountain View, California, has actively used human resource planning to build a multicultural workforce. "Traditionally, companies involved in good faith affirmative action advertising buy banquet tickets at minority functions," pointed out Deborah Yarborough, diversity program manager at Sun. "But we don't think this is a good policy because the money goes into paying for the banquets and not in getting minorities into the work force."[5] Sun has instead created focus groups consisting of minorities, women, homosexuals, and disabled people who are encouraged to coordinate with friends and outside support organizations and take a proactive role in bringing multicultural applicants to hiring managers. Among the numerous other measures Sun has taken, the company has totally changed its corporate advertising campaign, which now conveys the message: "Diversity at Sun is not a destination, but a journey."[6] If anything, though, Sun's efforts are understated. "I wish they would let more people know what they're doing," asserted Rigo Chacon, South Bay bureau chief, KGO Television News, San Francisco. "It's too much of a well-kept secret. I think if they could get themselves better recognized corporately, they would do themselves good."[7]

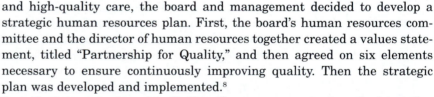

Improving quality was the goal of a human resources effort at Finley Hospital in Dubuque, Iowa. Recognizing the relationship between high-quality employees and high-quality care, the board and management decided to develop a strategic human resources plan. First, the board's human resources committee and the director of human resources together created a values statement, titled "Partnership for Quality," and then agreed on six elements necessary to ensure continuously improving quality. Then the strategic plan was developed and implemented.[8]

At Texas Instruments, based in Dallas, Texas, management worked to tailor human resources policies to the needs of the individual business units by including operations managers in the development and implementation process. In this way they overcame a "we/they" mindset, a perception among operations managers that HR policies somehow weren't a mainstream item. Explained Chuck Nielson, vice president of human resources, "The fact is, the only thing that differentiates us from our competition is our people. The equipment, the building—they're all the same. It's the people who make the difference. Effective management of HR becomes an issue for everyone."[9]

## PLANNING PROCEDURES

Human resource planning has four basic aspects: (1) *planning for future needs* by deciding how many people with what skills the organization will need, (2) *planning for future balance* by comparing the number of needed employees to the number of present employees who can be expected to stay with the organization, which leads to (3) *planning for recruiting or laying off employees* and (4) *planning for the development of employees,* to be sure the organization has a steady supply of experienced and capable personnel.[10] This is an important part of planning, because, as we will discuss later, internal recruitment has a number of advantages.

To be effective, the managers of a human resource program must consider two major factors. The primary factor is the organization's human resource needs. For example, a strategy of internal growth means that additional employees must be hired. Acquisitions or mergers, on the other hand, probably mean the organization will need to plan for layoffs, since mergers tend to create duplicate or overlapping positions that can be handled more efficiently with fewer employees.

The second factor to consider is the economic environment of the future. A booming economy might encourage expansion, which would increase the demand for employees. However, the same booming economy would result in low unemployment, making it harder and more expensive to attract qualified employees. Organizations that want to expand overseas confront similar problems.

More and more companies today are going through downsizing or restructuring and reengineering. Managers at many companies faced with laying off employees have taken extraordinary measures to help their former employees find new jobs. AT&T took out ads in newspapers advertising their excess employees and their skills to other businesses.

## RECRUITMENT

The purpose of **recruitment** is to provide a group of candidates that is large enough to let managers select the qualified employees they need.[11] Sony is constantly looking for the very best engineering talent in general, and it seeks people to fill specific openings in the organization as well.

### JOB AND POSITION DESCRIPTIONS

Before employees can be recruited, recruiters must have some clear ideas regarding the activities and responsibilities required in the job being filled. Job analysis is therefore an early step in the recruitment process. Once a specific job has been analyzed, a written statement of its content and location is incorporated into the organization chart. This statement is called either a **job description** or a **position description.** Each box on the organization chart is linked to a description that lists the title, duties, and responsibilities for that position. For example, a brief position description might read as follows: "Sales Manager: Duties include hiring, training, and supervising small sales staff and administration of sales department; responsible for performance of department; reports to Division Manager."

Once the position description has been determined, an accompanying hiring or job specification is developed. The **hiring specification** defines the education, experience, and skills an individual must have in order to perform effectively in the position. The hiring specification for sales manager might read: "Position requires BBA degree; five years' experience in sales and two years' supervisory experience; energetic, motivated individual with well-developed interpersonal skills."

### SOURCES FOR RECRUITMENT

Recruitment takes place within a *labor market*—that is, the pool of available people who have the skills to fill open positions. The labor market changes over time in response to environmental factors. As Sony became a more global company it had to learn to recruit in many different labor markets.

Sources for recruitment depend on the availability of the right kinds of people in the local labor pool as well as on the nature of the positions to be filled. An or-

---

**recruitment:**
The development of a pool of job candidates in accordance with a human resource plan.

**job description:**
A written description of a non-management job, covering title, duties, and responsibilities, and including its location on the organization chart.

**position description:**
A written description of a management position, covering title, duties, and responsibilities, and including its location on the organization chart.

**hiring specification:**
A written description of the education, experience, and skills needed to perform a job or fill a position effectively.

**PEER RECRUITING PAYS OFF.**
Federal Express often uses peer recruiters in its hiring process. When the people who actually do a job are involved in the recruitment of new employees, both sides benefit, and there are fewer surprises once people are on the job.

ganization's ability to recruit employees often hinges as much on the organization's reputation and the attractiveness of its location as on the attractiveness of the specific job offer. If people with the appropriate skills are not available within the organization or in the local labor pool, they may have to be recruited from some distance away or perhaps from competing organizations.

Federal Express has 25 recruitment centers around the country where candidates are screened. Often a *peer recruiter* is used—someone with actual experience in the type of work for which applicants are being recruited. This system offers dual benefits: the recruit sees firsthand the type of person who would be suited for the position, and, at the same time, the recruiter can offer an experience-based, realistic image of what the position is like.

When telecommunications firm Mercury Communications needed to recruit 1,000 customer-service assistants for its new site in Wythenshawe, near Manchester, England, it set up assessment centers where candidates were asked  to participate in simulated tasks and exercises. "We could just do a 40-minute interview and we would get people far more quickly," admitted Lynne Eccleston, Mercury's personnel and operations manager at Wythenshawe. "But it wouldn't show us how somebody would perform a job or provide people to the standard we require."[12] The goal is to find people with integral behavior skills, not merely qualifications. "Our staff need to have active listening skills, customer sensitivity, and the ability to cope in a pressurised environment."[13]

**OUTSIDE RECRUITMENT FOR MANAGERS AND PROFESSIONALS.** Large companies use various outside recruitment sources to fill vacancies at different levels of management. For many large companies, college and graduate school campuses are a major source of entry-level and new managerial help. Campus recruiting, however, has some disadvantages: The recruitment process can be quite expensive, and it is not uncommon for hired graduates to leave an organization after two or three years. When recruiting to fill middle-management and top-level positions, many large companies resort to even costlier and more competitive hiring strategies.

**EXECUTIVE RECRUITING.** Executive search firms identify and screen highly-qualified prospects for top-level positions.

When top-quality ability is in short supply, middle-management recruitment often requires the services of placement agencies or the purchase of expensive ads in newspapers and national publications. And when recruiting is done to fill top-level positions, many corporate managements turn to executive search firms. These firms generally locate three or four carefully considered prospects who not only are highly qualified but also can be enticed from their present positions by the right offer. Recently Louis Gerstner was recruited from RJR to take over IBM, and George Fisher was recruited from Motorola to take over Eastman Kodak. Such high-level moves are increasingly common, as companies seek different perspectives to meet the challenges of dynamic engagement we discussed in Part II.

### GETTING THE RIGHT PEOPLE THE FIRST TIME

Small businesses such as Gordon Bailey and Associates, Inc., an advertising and marketing agency based in Atlanta, have found traditional methods of recruitment to be inadequate in the presence of the shrinking labor pool and increased competition. "All of a sudden, we were faced with having to terminate several of our new hires in our account services area," recalled Jeri Christopher, vice president of human resources. "It wasn't good for our credibility with clients.... Plus, our training costs skyrocketed. It seemed we were always reinventing the wheel."[14]

The human resources difficulty was the source of problems within the company, so managers examined their procedures. "We had not been doing the kind of hiring job we should have," admitted Gordon Bailey, president of the company. "In small businesses, sometimes your 'need' horse gets ahead of your 'good judgment' horse. We were hiring people too quickly, and they just weren't working out."[15] Bailey therefore took a new approach to hiring, one that recognized that the process is inherently lengthy. "You need to get all the information you possibly can," counsels Ed Ryan, president of MPR Consulting, a Chicago-based human resource firm. "Interview them. Take them to dinner, take them to lunch. Take their spouse to lunch. And check references."[16] There are no shortcuts.

After recognizing this, Gordon Bailey implemented a successful hiring program. "It's a solid program," asserted Christopher. "But you can't cut corners. In the initial stages, we had an urgent need to fill a couple of positions.... So we ignored the warning signs, went on pure instincts, and made two very bad hiring mistakes.... We ended up terminating both employees. After that, we became firm believers in this system and practice it extensively. Today, we literally don't have any turnover. We aren't making wrong hiring decisions anymore."[17]

**RECRUITMENT FROM WITHIN.** Many firms still have a policy of recruiting or promoting from within except in very exceptional circumstances. This policy has three major advantages. First, individuals recruited from within are already familiar with the organization and its members, and this knowledge increases the likelihood they will succeed. Second, a promotion-from-within policy fosters loyalty and inspires greater effort among organization members. Finally, it is usually less expensive to recruit or promote from within than to hire from outside the organization. There are some disadvantages to internal recruitment, however. Obviously, it limits the pool of available talent. In addition, it reduces the chance that fresh viewpoints will enter the organization, and it may encourage complacency among employees who assume seniority ensures promotion.

## LEGAL CONSIDERATIONS

In the early 1960s, the growing civil rights and women's movements called national attention to the discriminatory impact of existing human resource practices. The Equal Pay Act of 1963 and the Civil Rights Act of 1964 were early attempts to rectify the situation. These efforts were later expanded by the courts and most state legislatures as well as through various federal amendments and executive orders. The implications of such legislation for human resource policies and practices are still evolving and being clarified through court decisions and administrative interpretations. Although the median annual earnings of women at work have increased significantly in the past quarter century, the ratio of women's to men's wages varies widely from one occupation to another. Moreover, although there has been a dramatic increase in the number of women in some of the higher-status, higher-paid occupations, the proportion of women in those occupations is still low (See Table 14-1). "For example," as Janet L. Norwood, U.S. Commissioner of Labor Statistics, noted, "the number of women lawyers increased more than fivefold over the last decade, but there are still less than 100,000 in the legal profession, and they make up only 15 percent of the total."[18]

**THE LAWS.** The key legislation is Title VII of the Civil Rights Act of 1964 (amended in 1972 to establish the Equal Employment Opportunity Commission [EEOC] to enforce the provisions of Title VII), which prohibits employment discrimination on the basis of race, sex, age, religion, color, or national origin. These requirements for nondiscriminatory treatment are called *equal employment opportunity (EEO)* requirements. They apply to virtually all private and public organizations.

**TABLE 14-1**  **The Wage Gap Between the Sexes**

| | WOMEN AS PERCENT OF ALL WORKERS | | EARNINGS RATIO FEMALE TO MALE | |
|---|---|---|---|---|
| | 1979 | 1988 | 1979 | 1988 |
| Accounts and auditors | 34% | 45% | 0.60 | .79 |
| Computer programmers | 28 | 40 | 0.80 | 0.81 |
| Computer systems analysts | 20 | 30 | 0.79 | 0.82 |
| Lawyers | 10 | 15 | 0.55 | 0.63 |
| Managers and administrators | 22 | 29 | 0.51 | 0.67 |
| Sales of business services | 28 | 34 | 0.58 | 0.79 |
| Teachers, elementary school | 61 | 82 | 0.82 | 0.96 |

*Note:* Figures are for full-time workers in selected occupations.
*Source:* Census Bureau

Although the original legislation did not apply to people working outside U.S. boundaries, the 1991 Civil Rights Act extended protection to U.S. citizens who are employed in a foreign country by American-owned or -controlled companies.[19] Executive Orders 11246 and 11375 of 1965 and 1968 (amended in 1977) require, in addition, that firms doing business with the federal government make concentrated efforts to recruit, hire, and promote women and members of minority groups. These concentrated efforts define the "affirmative" in *affirmative action (AA)*.[20] The differences between equal employment opportunity and affirmative action are summarized in Table 14-2.

At Tenneco Inc., affirmative action is more than a legal mandate; it is becoming reality. The company has introduced a variety of initiatives aimed at encouraging the advancement of women and minorities. In the early 1980s, the organization recognized the importance of promoting women and minorities in its executive resource review and functional review process. In the late 1980s, the Multicultural Advisory Council and the Women's Advisory Council were developed. In addition, Tenneco links executive incentive bonuses to affirmative action performance, and has developed the Work/Family Support Program to help employees balance their work and family lives.[21]

Women are also making inroads at J. C. Penney. In the late 1980s, William R. Howell, Penney's chairman and CEO, approached Gale Duff-Bloom, then manager of investor relations, and asked her to take an active role in helping women break through the glass ceiling and reach senior management positions. Duff-Bloom therefore established and chaired the Women's Advisory Team. Its goal was to create an environment more sensitive to the needs of female employees. "For the first time," Duff-Bloom recalled, "subjects that were considered taboo were discussed

**TABLE 14-2**    Differences Between EEO Nondiscrimination and AA

|  | EEO | AFFIRMATIVE ACTION |
|---|---|---|
| Who is affected? | Virtually everyone is covered by law | Legally applies only to certain organizations |
| What is required? | Employment neutrality | Systematic plan |
| What are the sanctions? | Legal charges can be filed. Possible court action | Withdrawal of contracts or funds if noncompliant |
| What are some examples of compliance? | Not barring female, minority, or disabled persons from employment Selecting, promoting, and paying people solely on the basis of bona fide job-related qualifications | Actively recruiting and hiring female, veteran, minority, or disabled persons Validating tests; rigorously examining company practices in selection, promotion, and benefits to eliminate non-job-related qualifications that discriminate against protected persons |

Source: *The Management of Affirmative Action* by Francine S. Hall and Maryann H. Albrecht. Copyright 1979 by Scott, Foresman and Company. Reprinted by permission.

openly between management and employees."[22] Duff-Bloom became the executive vice president and director of administration for J. C. Penney in April 1993. "Diversity isn't a numbers game at the Penney Company," she asserted. "We're building our company based on the talent that we already have."[23]

The Equal Pay Act, originally introduced in 1946, prohibits discrimination in which employers pay men more than women for performing jobs requiring substantially equal skill, effort, responsibility, and working conditions. Thus, the Equal Pay Act requires *equal pay—like* pay for *like* jobs.

**comparable worth:**

The principle that jobs requiring comparable skills and knowledge merit equal compensation even if the nature of the work activity is different.

A more recent approach to fairness in pay is known as **comparable worth.** Comparable worth is the principle that different jobs that require *comparable* skills and knowledge deserve comparable pay. This idea evolved from the observation that women tended to be segregated in certain occupations, such as nursing and teaching, that are lower paying than some male-dominated fields, despite similar educational requirements and responsibilities. In fact, some women-dominated fields require more education than better-paying men's jobs. Over and over again, statistics show that women make less than 70 cents for every dollar men earn. Much of this difference is attributed to occupational segregation. By taking into account the actual skills and knowledge needed for jobs, the principle of comparable worth seeks to invalidate patterns of wage and job discrimination that have often established or influenced salary guidelines.[24]

The employment rights of persons 40 and older are protected by the Age Discrimination in Employment Act of 1967 (amended in 1986). The Vocational Rehabilitation Act of 1973 (amended in 1974) added protection for the physically and mentally disabled if they were qualified to perform job tasks with reasonable accommodation by the employer. The Veterans' Readjustment Act of 1974 requires those doing business with the federal government to extend affirmative action programs to veterans of the Vietnam War era and to disabled veterans in general.

The rights of the disabled were further protected in 1990 when Congress passed the Americans with Disabilities Act (ADA).[25] This hotly disputed act promises sweeping changes in the American workplace, which must now accom-

**OPPORTUNITIES EXPANDED.** The Americans with Disabilities Act requires companies to make accommodations to meet the needs of workers with disabilities. Often, only simple changes are needed. This 1990 act promises sweeping changes in the American workplace.

modate workers with physical and mental disabilities, as well as those with chronic illnesses.

The passing of the ADA prompted companies such as the Great Atlantic & Pacific Tea Co. (A&P), based in Montvale, New Jersey, to make changes. "The A&P's policy has always been, and continues to be, to provide a safe shopping environment for customers and a safe working environment for its employees," asserted Carl J. Frey, corporate safety director. "We picked up on what we were doing and upgraded it to comply with the law."[26] Changes at A&P, such as the introduction of an applicant screening program for heavy-lifting jobs, have resulted in cost savings in addition to the benefits to customers and employees. "The payback has been extremely high," said Frey.[27] For example, the number of injuries, particularly back-related, has decreased substantially, resulting in significant cost savings.

At the Embassy Suites Hotel at SeaTac Airport near Seattle, managers learned that more is often necessary than merely following the letter of the law. "You can have the Taj Mahal of accessibility and a manager who can recite every nuance of the law, but if your employees are uncomfortable around persons with disabilities," noted Cheryl Duke, co-creator of Woodford, Virginia-based Opening Doors program, which Embassy uses chain-wide, "it doesn't matter."[28] Embassy used Opening Doors to prepare for the 6th annual meeting of the Society for Disability Studies, which brought 125 guests with disabilities to the hotel for almost a week. According to Sandy Blondino, director of sales at Embassy, the Opening Doors program was integral to staff's ability to serve the guests effectively.

The Disabled Bill of Rights is important because disabled Americans were not covered by the 1964 Civil Rights Act, which banned discrimination on the basis of race, sex, religion, and national origin. The same protections are now guaranteed to the disabled.

The first right the Disabled Bill of Rights protects is the right to employment. Employers are prohibited from discriminating against any job applicant who can perform "essential" job responsibilities; they are obliged to make "reasonable accommodations" as long as they can do so without "undue" hardship. This provision went into effect in 1992 for employers with 25 or more employees, and in 1994 for employers with 15 or more employees.

Many hope the law will open employers' eyes to the fact that disabled workers can perform many tasks using personal computers and "adaptive technology"—devices such as voice-recognition software, Braille keypads, and "sip-and-puff" breath sticks, which allow quadriplegics to use a computer. With this equipment, disabled workers can perform such skilled tasks as drafting, telemarketing, research, accounting, and word processing.

Employers who want proof that this accommodation can work need look no further than the Social Security Administration's Office of Appeal and Adjudication, where word processors input decisions written by the agency's administrative law judges. These word processors are the most productive team in the national organization and their work meets the agency's highest standards—even though six out of the nine word processors are blind. To do their work, they use specially modified PCs, voice-recognition software, and Braille keypads. The cost is about $8,000 per worker versus $3,000 for a standard word processing setup. Meanwhile, IBM and other major computer manufacturers have been training the disabled as computer programmers for nearly ten years.

← ch. 7, p. 193

Title VII prohibits <u>sexual harassment</u>—unwanted sexual requests or advances, or the creation of a sexually harassing environment through sexual jokes and remarks—in hiring or promotion decisions or the work environment.[29] A 1978 amendment to Title VII, the Pregnancy Discrimination Act, prohibits dismissal of women solely because of pregnancy and protects their job security during maternity leaves.[30] Legislation in various states extends these rights to employees of

**AIDS DISCRIMINATION IN THE WORK-PLACE.** In the 1993 movie *Philadelphia,* Tom Hanks starred as an attorney with AIDS who sued his employers for discrimination when they concocted an excuse to fire him.

very small firms and to specific groups not mentioned in federal legislation, such as homosexuals and former prison inmates.[31] While the examples we have given involve U.S. law, the rules may differ, country by country. Companies such as Sony must pay careful attention to the legal environments of the countries in which they operate.

**IMPLICATIONS FOR MANAGERS.** In the recruitment process, the human resources department normally has primary responsibility for ensuring compliance with the mass of legislation and subsequent legal decisions concerning discrimination. Two kinds of discrimination are of concern to managers. *Access discrimination* refers to hiring considerations and practices (e.g., different qualifying tests, lower starting salaries) that are based on the candidate's membership in a particular population subgroup and not related in any way to present or future job performance. *Treatment discrimination* involves practices unrelated to job performance that treat subgroup members differently from others once they are in the workforce (e.g., less favorable work assignments, slower promotion rates).[32]

Ultimately, however, the human resources department must instruct and educate managers in the implications of compliance for their respective departments. Even job titles can be sexist and reflect de facto discrimination. For example, the job titles *foreman* and *salesman* are now outmoded. Many companies have replaced them with *supervisor* and *salesperson,* respectively. Managers do not have completely free choice in recruiting, hiring, training, and promoting people for their organization. Any individual or organization that fails to comply with the law may be reported to the Equal Employment Opportunity Commission (EEOC) for investigation or may become a defendant in a class action or specific lawsuit.

For practical assistance in interpreting and complying with equal employment opportunity legislation, managers can turn to the Uniform Guidelines on Employee Selection Procedures, issued in 1978. Under these guidelines, organization practices or policies that adversely affect employment opportunities for any race, sex, or ethnic group are prohibited unless the restriction is a justifiable job requirement. Thus, courts have found height and weight requirements illegal when they prevented employment of women and people of Hispanic or Asian origin and were not shown to be job-related. There are justifiable instances in which discriminatory hiring requirements are permitted—such as hiring only males to play male roles in theater productions. These are called *bona fide occupation qualifications (BFOQs).* Race and color, however, have never been ruled acceptable BFOQ criteria.

In recent years, a host of social issues are affecting both recruitment and management more and more. For example, a 1987 Supreme Court ruling held that the Vocational Rehabilitation Act of 1973 covers workers with contagious diseases, a rule with wide-ranging implications given the current concern over AIDS.[33] Another controversial and important issue is privacy. The use of drug testing, AIDS testing, computer surveillance, and even genetic screening by many companies has stirred fears among workers and others that employers are delving too far into employees' personal lives.

Drug testing is particularly controversial. Drug use costs U.S. industry about $50 billion a year due to employee turnover and absenteeism, and countless dollars due to less reliable and productive work.[34] Lives have been lost in accidents caused by employees under the influence of alcohol, drugs, or both. This situation has caused some companies to insist on random drug testing of employees. Such mandatory drug testing raises the issue of employee civil rights. Some experts predict that except for a small number of occupations, such as train operators and pilots, American workers will not be randomly tested. However, an increasing number of companies—IBM, American Airlines, Dupont, GE, and Kodak among them—are currently testing all job applicants.[35]

Some companies have addressed the reality of drug and alcohol problems at all levels within the organization in a way that employees perceive as more supportive. Employee Assistance Programs (EAPs) provide confidentiality, appropriate referrals, and other support to employees whose job performance is impaired because of drug dependency.[36]

# SELECTION

**selection:**
The mutual process whereby the organization decides whether or not to make a job offer and the candidate decides whether or not to accept it.

The **selection** process ideally involves mutual decision. The organization decides whether to make a job offer and how attractive the offer should be, and the job candidate decides whether the organization and the job offer fit his or her needs and goals. In reality, the selection process is often more one-sided. In situations when the job market is extremely tight, several candidates will be applying for each position, and managers at the organization will use a series of screening devices to identify the most suitable candidate. On the other hand, when there is a shortage of qualified workers, or when the candidate is a highly qualified executive or professional being courted by several organizations, managers at the organization will have to sweeten the offer and come to a quicker decision.

## STEPS IN THE SELECTION PROCESS

The standard hiring sequence is the seven-step procedure described in Table 14-3.[37] In practice, however, the actual selection process varies with different organizations and between levels in the same organization. For example, the selection interview for lower-level employees may be quite perfunctory. Heavy emphasis may be placed instead on the initial screening interview or on tests. Although written tests designed to define a candidate's interests, aptitudes, and intelligence were long a staple of employment screening, their use has declined over the past 25 years. Many tests have proved to be discriminatory in their design and results, and it has been difficult to establish their job relatedness when they have been subjected to judicial review.

In selecting middle- or upper-level managers, the interviewing may be extensive and there may be little or no formal testing. Instead of initially filling out an application, the candidate may submit a resume. Completion of the formal application may be delayed until after the job offer has been accepted. Some organizations omit the physical examination (Step 6 in Table 14-3) for managers hired at this level.

For many positions, particularly in management, the in-depth interview is an important factor in management's decision to make a job offer and in the individual's decision to accept or decline the offer. The most effective interviews—those that are best able to predict the eventual performance of applicants—are usually planned carefully. Ideally, all candidates for the same position are asked the same questions.[38] Most interviews, however, tend to be far less structured and deliberate.

**realistic job preview (RJP):**
Information on a job provided by the organization to applicants and new employees that gives both the positive and negative aspects of the job.

The reliability of the interview may be affected by the differing objectives of the interviewer and interviewee. The prospective employer wants to sell the organization as a good place to work and may therefore exaggerate its strengths; the prospective employee wants to be hired and may therefore exaggerate his or her qualities. Some managers have attempted to reduce this problem through the **realistic job preview (RJP),** in which candidates are exposed to the unattractive as well as the attractive aspects of the job, and by using structured, focused interviews to acquire a more accurate picture of each interviewee's likely job performance.[39]

**TABLE 14-3**                **Steps in the Selection Process**

| PROCEDURES | PURPOSES | ACTIONS AND TRENDS |
| --- | --- | --- |
| 1. Completed job application | Indicates applicant's desired position; provides information for interviews. | Requests only information the predicts success in the job.* |
| 2. Initial screening interview | Provides a quick evaluation of applicant's suitability. | Asks questions on experience, salary expectation, willingness to relocate, etc. |
| 3. Testing | Measures applicant's job skills and the ability to learn on the job. | May include computer testing software, handwriting analysis, medical and physical ability. |
| 4. Background investigation | Checks truthfulness of applicant's resume or application form. | Calls the applicant's previous supervisor (with permission) and confirms information from applicant. |
| 5. In-depth selection interview | Finds out more about the applicant as an individual. | Conducted by the manager to whom the applicant will report. |
| 6. Physical examination | Ensures effective performance by applicant; protects other employees against diseases; establishes health record on applicant; protects firm against unjust worker's compensation claims. | Often performed by company's medical doctor. |
| 7. Job offer | Fills a job vacancy or position. | Offers a salary plus benefit package. |

*See, for example, Robert Hershey, "The Application Form," *Personnel* 48, no. 1 (January-February 1971):38; and Irwin L. Goldstein, "The Application Blank: How Honest Are the Responses?" *Journal of Applied Psychology* 55, no. 5 (October 1971):491; David Tuller, "What's New in Employment Testing?" *The New York Times,* February 25, 1985, p. F17; Kirk Johnson, "Why References Aren't Available on Request?" *The New York Times,* June 9, 1985, pp. F8-F9.
*Source:* Wendell L. French, *The Personnel Management Process,* 6th ed. Copyright 1987 by Houghton Mifflin Co. Adapted with permission.

Managers at the British Broadcasting Corp. (BBC) have developed a new strategy for job assessment. When the program was introduced, an independent consultant carried out job analyses through structured interviews to determine what each job entails. Now, when a position opens, ads run that invite inquiries. When people inquire, the BBC responds with detailed information about the job and a self-selection guide. The emphasis now is on giving information to the applicant. Before, without much information aside from the initial ad, the applicant would merely complete forms, which were then used to screen applicants for interviews. Now, not only is the list of suitable candidates narrowed down by self-selection, but the interviews themselves are more detailed than in the past, often involving a visit to the workplace, a group exercise, a written expression test, and a panel interview.[40]

## MANAGER SELECTION

Organizations may seek to hire experienced managers for a variety of reasons. A newly created post may require a manager with experience not available within the organization; the talent to fill an established post may not be available within the organization; a key position may suddenly open up before there is time to train a replacement; or a top performer in a competing organization may be sought to improve the organization's own competitive position.

An experienced manager who is up for selection usually goes through several interviews before being hired. The interviewers are almost always higher-level managers who attempt to assess the candidate's suitability and past performance. Interviewers try to determine how well the candidate fits their idea of what a good manager should be and how compatible the candidate's personality, past experience, personal values, and operating style are with the organization and its culture.

Inexperienced managers or trainees with management potential usually enter the organization after graduating from college. Their performance in entry-level positions strongly influences the range of management opportunities that will be available to them.

Most assessments of prospective managers who are recent college graduates begin with a review of college grades. Other aspects of the college record can provide some insights into nonacademic abilities such as interpersonal skills, leadership qualities, and ability to assume responsibility.[41] Finally, like experienced managers, prospective managers may be interviewed extensively to determine whether they have what the interviewers consider an appropriate personal style for a manager.

## ORIENTATION OR SOCIALIZATION

**orientation:**
A program designed to help employees fit smoothly into an organization; also called socialization.

**Orientation** or **socialization** is designed to provide new employees with the information needed to function comfortably and effectively in the organization. Typically, socialization conveys three types of information: (1) general information about the daily work routine; (2) a review of the organization's history, purpose, operations, and products or services, as well as a sense of how the employee's job contributes to the organization's needs; and (3) a detailed presentation (perhaps in a brochure) of the organization's policies, work rules, and employee benefits.

**INTERVIEWING NEW MANAGERS.**
Many companies send recruiters to college campuses around the country to interview young professionals for entry-level positions. At this level, college grades and other aspects of the college record are part of the assessment.

Many studies have shown that employees feel anxious upon entering an organization. They worry about how well they will perform in the job; they feel inadequate compared to more experienced employees; and they are concerned about how well they will get along with their co-workers. Effective socialization programs reduce the anxiety of new employees by giving them information about the job environment and about supervisors, by introducing them to co-workers, and by encouraging them to ask questions.[42]

Early job experiences—when the new employee's expectations and the organization's expectations come together or collide—seem to play a critical role in the individual's career with the organization. If the expectations are not compatible, there will be dissatisfaction; turnover rates are almost always highest among an organization's new employees.[43] An important aspect of job satisfaction—for all workers—is the assurance that employees can work for the company's good without neglecting their personal obligations. One of the most pressing concerns in this area is adequate child care.

Few parents can do their best work when they are worried about their children. Yet this is the plight of millions of working parents who cannot find adequate, affordable day care. Over 50 percent of mothers with infants and toddlers hold jobs outside the home, and the percentage of two-career households continues to rise. Furthermore, young professionals often live far from doting grandparents, who, in any case, are often working themselves.[44] So the need for reliable, affordable day care is an important issue in the workplace.

The supply of day-care centers has not kept pace with demand, and fewer women (historically, the labor pool for this service industry) are available to care  for children in the home. In some areas, the shortage is so acute that good day-care centers have waiting lists of up to two years. And if finding child care for the conventional workday is difficult, finding it for a night shift is all but impossible. Small entrepreneurial companies like Bright Horizons have made a business out of supplying the day-care services needed by corporations.

## TRAINING AND DEVELOPMENT

**training program:**
A process designed to maintain or improve current job performance.

**developmental program:**
A process designed to develop skills necessary for future work activities.

**Training programs** are directed toward maintaining and improving *current* job performance, while **developmental programs** seek to develop skills for *future* jobs. Both managers and nonmanagers may receive help from training and development programs, but the mix of experiences is likely to vary. Nonmanagers are much more likely to be trained in the technical skills required for their current jobs, whereas managers frequently receive assistance in developing the skills required in future jobs—particularly conceptual and human relations skills.

In 1992, Granite Rock received the Malcolm Baldrige National Quality Award in the small business category. According to Val Verutti, director of quality support for Granite Rock, the company spent an average of $1,697—an average of 37  hours—for each employee on training and education during the year. This thrust toward training and education followed on the heels of a program introduced in the late 1980s, the Individual Professional Development Plan (IPDP), which encouraged employees to set personal education and training goals each year. After supervisors meet with their employees to discuss their goals, the supervisors are required to make other supervisors aware of the employees' expectations to minimize the possibility of supervisors "burying" employees for their own benefit and denying them promotions. The results have been positive. "Our earnings per employee are 30 percent higher than the industry average," commented Verutti. "Our market share has increased more than

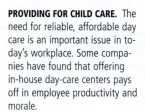

**PROVIDING FOR CHILD CARE.** The need for reliable, affordable day care is an important issue in today's workplace. Some companies have found that offering in-house day-care centers pays off in employee productivity and morale.

ever. And our turnover is way down. People just don't leave this company anymore. And we can get anyone we want to fill a position—mostly from within the company."[45]

## TRAINING PROGRAMS

New employees have to learn new skills, and since their motivation is likely to be high, they can be acquainted relatively easily with the skills and behavior expected in their new position. On the other hand, training experienced employees can be problematic. The training needs of such employees are not always easy to determine, and when they can be, the individuals involved may resent being asked to change their established ways of doing their jobs.

Managers can use four procedures to determine the training needs of individuals in their organization or subunit:

1. *Performance appraisal.* Each employee's work is measured against the performance standards or objectives established for his or her job.
2. *Analysis of job requirements.* The skills or knowledge specified in the appropriate job description are examined, and those employees without necessary skills or knowledge become candidates for a training program.
3. *Organizational analysis.* The effectiveness of the organization and its success in meeting its goals are analyzed to determine where differences exist. For example, members of a department with a high turnover rate or a low performance record might require additional training.
4. *Employee Survey.* Managers as well as nonmanagers are asked to describe what problems they are experiencing in their work and what actions they believe are necessary to solve them.

Once the organization's training needs have been identified, the human resources manager must initiate the appropriate training effort. Managers have available a variety of training approaches. The most common of these are *on-the-job training* methods, including *job rotation,* in which the employee, over a period of time, works on a series of jobs, thereby learning a broad variety of skills; *in-*

*ternship,* in which job training is combined with related classroom instruction; and *apprenticeship,* in which the employee is trained under the guidance of a highly skilled co-worker. Sony uses a variety of these approaches to meet the training needs of its employees.

*Off-the-job training* takes place outside the workplace but attempts to simulate actual working conditions. This type of training includes *vestibule training,* in which employees train on the actual equipment and in a realistic job setting but in a room different from the one in which they will be working. The object is to avoid the on-the-job pressures that might interfere with the learning process. In *behaviorally experienced training,* activities such as simulation exercises, business games, and problem-centered cases are employed so that the trainee can learn the behavior appropriate for the job through *role playing.* Off-the-job training may focus on the *classroom,* with seminars, lectures, and films, or it may involve **computer-assisted instruction (CAI),** which can both reduce the time needed for training and provide more help for individual trainees.[46]

**computer-assisted instruction (CAI):**

A training technique in which computers are used to lessen the time necessary for training by instructors and to provide additional help to individual trainees.

## MANAGEMENT DEVELOPMENT PROGRAMS

Management development is designed to improve the overall effectiveness of managers in their present positions and to prepare them for greater responsibility when they are promoted. Management development programs have become more prevalent in recent years because of the increasingly complex demands on managers and because training managers through experience alone is a time-consuming and unreliable process. The investment for many companies in management development is quite large. For example, for years, IBM has required a minimum of 40 hours of human resource management training for all new managers.[47]

Similar levels of training continue after this initial involvement. Some companies, however, do not rely on costly formal training approaches. Managers at Exxon, for example, prefer to nurture new talent by providing practical job experience. Thus executives at all levels are dispatched to key positions around the world to broaden their outlook and hone their judgment.

**ON-THE-JOB METHODS.** On-the-job methods are usually preferred in management development programs. The training is far more likely than off-the-job training to be tailored to the individual, to be job-related, and to be conveniently located.

There are four major formal on-the-job development methods:

1. *Coaching*—the training of an employee by his or her immediate supervisor—is by far the most effective management development technique. Unfortunately, many managers are either unable or unwilling to coach those they supervise. To be meaningful, on-the-job coaching must be tempered with considerable restraint—employees cannot develop unless they are allowed to work out problems in their own way. Managers too often feel compelled to tell their employees exactly what to do, thereby negating the effectiveness of coaching. In addition, some managers feel threatened when asked to coach an employee, fearing they are creating a rival. Actually, the manager has much to gain from coaching, since a manager frequently will not be promoted unless there is a successor available to take his or her place. Many companies have even replaced manager titles with coach titles. At AT&T, Jere Stead is the "head coach" of the Global Information Solution division.

Many firms make a point of training their managers in the fine art of coaching. Conscientious managers often keep a "development file" for each of their employees, indicating the training they are receiving, the skills they are acquiring, and how well they are performing. A record of *critical incidents*—situations in which an employee displayed desirable or undesirable behavior—may be included. In discussing these incidents with the employee, managers can reinforce good habits

**ON THE MOVE.** Key to moving up for young managers in many companies is accepting transfers to new locations. Companies nurture talented managers by moving them from one assignment to another, providing a broad range of experiences.

("You really handled that customer's complaint well"), gently point out bad habits ("Do you think you should be firmer with the supplier?"), and identify areas in which the employee needs further development.

2. *Job rotation* involves shifting managers from position to position so they can broaden their experience and familiarize themselves with various aspects of the firm's operations.

3. *Training positions* are a third method of developing managers. Trainees are given staff posts immediately under a manager, often with the title of "assistant to." Such assignments give trainees a chance to work with and model themselves after outstanding managers who might otherwise have little contact with them.

4. Finally, *planned work activities* involve giving trainees important work assignments to develop their experience and ability. Trainees may be asked to head a task force or participate in an important committee meeting. Such experiences help them gain insight into how organizations operate and also improve their human relations skills.

**OFF-THE-JOB METHODS.** Off-the-job development techniques remove individuals from the stresses and ongoing demands of the workplace, enabling them to focus fully on the learning experience. In addition, they provide opportunities for meeting people from other departments or organizations. Thus, employees are exposed to useful new ideas and experiences while they make potentially useful contacts. The most common off-the-job development methods are in-house classroom instruction and management development programs sponsored by universities and organizations such as the American Management Association.

Almost every management development program includes some form of *classroom instruction* in which specialists from inside or outside the organization teach trainees a particular subject. Classroom instruction is often supplemented with case studies, role playing, and business games or simulations. For example, managers may be asked to play roles on both sides in a simulated labor-management dispute.

Some organizations send selected employees to *university-sponsored management development programs*. Many major universities have such programs, which range in length from a week to three months or more. Some universities also have

**TRAINING EXPERIENCED EMPLOY-EES.** Even experienced employees may benefit from training, but determining their training needs is not always easy.

one-year full-time study programs for middle-level managers. Usually, these managers have been slated for promotion. Their organizations send them to university programs to broaden their perspectives and prepare them for movement into general (as opposed to functional) management. University programs often combine classroom instruction with case studies, role playing, and simulation.

Increasingly, large corporations are assuming many of the functions of universities with regard to advanced off-the-job training of employees. Many corporations and industry associations offer advanced, accredited academic degrees. Xerox, RCA, Arthur Anderson, GE, and Holiday Inns have each acquired educational facilities that closely resemble university campuses.[48]

The Disney organization has a strong training program on several levels. Thousands of professionals attend Walt Disney Productions' management seminars to learn how to train and motivate employees.[49] In addition, the "Traditions I" employee orientation class presents the elements of the Disney culture, which all employees, management and hourly, must embrace. This class teaches the Disney language and aspects—safety, courtesy, show, and efficiency—and the components—past, present, and future. Orientation on policies and procedures takes place in a program offered by the division in which the employee will work. After completing the classroom orientation, employees must work with a trainer until they are ready to work alone. Once employees begin to work without supervision, they can participate in cross training. Teaching the Traditions I class is one opportunity for cross training. Using experienced Disney employees to teach the orientation class helps both the employees and the company. New employees learn from those who have experienced the Disney culture, and experienced employees learn presentation skills, earn recognition, and add variety to the job. Disney is both saving money and promoting employee development. Only 30 percent of Disney employees are hired from the outside; most positions are filled through promotions from within the company.

# PERFORMANCE APPRAISAL AND COMPENSATION

**A**lthough helping others improve their performance is one of the manager's most important tasks, most managers freely admit performance appraisal and improvement coaching gives them difficulty. Judging an employee's performance accurately is not always easy. Often it is even harder to convey that judgment to the employee in a constructive and painless manner and to translate feedback on past performance into future improvement. Determining appropriate compensation is a related task of great importance.

### A MODEL EVALUATION PROGRAM

At Prudential Property & Casualty Insurance, Priscilla Smith, vice president of human resources, initiated a human resources program that, among other things, invites employees to learn more about the insurance business to add value to the company. To ensure that performance expectations are clear, new hires receive a blank copy of the evaluation form that will be completed the following year. An employee who fails to measure up goes through a performance improvement process that begins with

# PEOPLE AS RESOURCES

Sony has long been a leader in human resources management in Japan. The company has adopted such American concepts as the five-day, 40-hour work week, even though Japanese law still sanctions a maximum of 48 hours, and the average in Japanese manufacturing remains 43 hours per week. Moreover, Sony was one of the first Japanese firms to close its factories for one week every summer to allow all its employees to be off work at the same time.

In addition, the Japanese system enforces a different view of recruits. Morita urges managers to see recruits as rough stones and the managerial job as the task of building a strong and sturdy wall out of these rough stones. The Japanese ideal is to shape and smooth managerial recruits so that they become a cohesive part of the company.

Japanese companies, at least the large ones, also have a humane attitude toward dealing with employees in declining industries. Most companies offer retraining—and most workers eagerly accept it. At Sony, workers are retrained when their particular jobs become obsolete.

*Sony develops among its workers a sense of commitment to the overall goals of the firm.*

Clearly, Akio Morita's human resource policies accommodate Sony's overall strategy. By focusing on the shared fate of management and employees, Sony develops among its workers a sense of commitment to the overall goals of the firm. Partly because of this employee commitment, Sony has been able to stay competitive in terms of wages and benefits and to motivate highly competent people to continue to innovate.

By focusing on people as resources rather than as costs, companies like Sony are writing the book on future management theory and practice. →

his or her own development of an action plan. If this does not work, then the employee takes a day off to decide to resign or commit to change. So far, more than 60 percent of the employees who have gone through the performance improvement process have shown improvement. "Supervisors are thrilled with it," Smith explained, "and associates are more aware of their own performance."[50] In addition, employees are recognized for outstanding performance with compensation awards, for which 15 percent of management staff already qualifies regularly. Turnover at Prudential dropped three percent between 1991 and 1992, and, in the first six months alone, Smith reported $97,000 in savings from process improvements in areas including communication, training, and benefits—three times the company's year-end goal of $30,000. This success has attracted the attention of companies such as AT&T who are currently looking toward Prudential as a model or benchmark. ■

← ch. 8, p. 225

## INFORMAL APPRAISALS

We will use the term **informal performance appraisal** to mean the continual process of feeding back to employees information about how well they are doing their work for the organization. Informal appraisal can be conducted on a day-to-day basis. The manager spontaneously mentions that a particular piece of work

**informal performance appraisal:**
The process of continually feeding back to subordinates information regarding their work performance.

was performed well or poorly, or the employee stops by the manager's office to find out how a particular piece of work was received. Because of the close connection between the behavior and the feedback on it, informal appraisal is an excellent way to encourage desirable performance and discourage undesirable performance before it becomes ingrained. An organization's employees must perceive informal appraisal not merely as a casual occurrence but as an important activity, an integral part of the organization's culture.[51]

## FORMAL SYSTEMATIC APPRAISALS

**Formal systematic appraisal** usually occurs semiannually or annually. Formal appraisal has four major purposes: (1) to let employees know formally how their current performance is being rated; (2) to identify employees who deserve merit raises; (3) to locate employees who need additional training; and (4) to identify candidates for promotion.

It is important for managers to differentiate between the current performance and the promotability (potential performance) of employees. Managers in many organizations fail to make this distinction because they assume that a person with the skills and ability to perform well in one job will automatically perform well in a different or more responsible position. This is why people are often promoted to positions in which they cannot perform adequately.[52]

Who is responsible for formal performance appraisals? In answer to this question, four basic appraisal approaches have evolved in organizations. The first approach, *a manager's rating of an employee,* is by far the most common. However, other approaches are becoming more popular and can be a valuable supplement to appraisal by a single person.

A *group of managers rating an employee* is the second most frequently used appraisal approach. Employees are rated by a managerial committee or by a series of managers who fill out separate rating forms. Because it relies on a number of views, this approach is often more effective than appraisal by a single manager. However, it is time-consuming and often dilutes employees' feelings of accountability to their immediate supervisor.

**formal systematic appraisal:**
A formalized appraisal process for rating work performance, identifying those deserving raises or promotions, and identifying those in need of further training.

The third appraisal approach is *a group of peers rating a colleague.* The individual is rated separately and on paper by co-workers on the same organizational level.

The fourth approach is *employees' rating of bosses.* This approach is used in some colleges, where faculty are asked to evaluate their dean on a number of performance measures. But it is increasingly used at businesses that are responding to the furor of dynamic engagement. At AT&T and other companies, many employees rate their bosses in what is called "360° Feedback." Even the chairman gets a review from his direct subordinates.

## COMPENSATION[53]

Compensation has traditionally been linked to a particular job or job description. The general idea is that the more responsibility a manager has, the more compensation he or she should earn. Oftentimes jobs are rated by a job evaluation system which measures such variables as the number of subordinates, level in the organizational hierarchy, and the complexity and importance of the job function. In such a traditional or bureaucratic approach, senior organizational executives tend to be paid very well. Lower-level employees may be well paid, especially in the United States and Europe, but they have been increasingly underutilized. When competition from other countries with lower pay scales emerges, companies find they are no longer competitive. Compensation systems that make organizations more productive must therefore be devised.

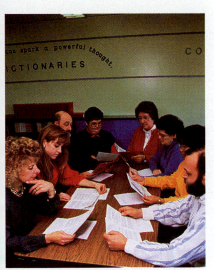

**EMPLOYEES RATING BOSSES.** One approach to performance appraisal involves asking employees to evaluate their bosses. Although this approach has a longer history in schools and colleges, it is increasingly being used in businesses as well.

**new pay approach:**
An approach toward compensation that links it to the process of setting and achieving organizational objectives.

In Chapter 11 we discussed how compensation should be linked to the process of setting and achieving organizational objectives. Many organizations have adopted a new approach to compensation that avoids the sometimes bureaucratic and hierarchical linkage to job descriptions and spans of control. Edward Lawler has dubbed this new approach "the new pay," or, as it is sometimes called, "strategic pay." The **new pay approach** is based on responses to the world of dynamic engagement that organizations face. New global competition and a changing labor force spell the need for creative human resources strategies, especially with regard to compensation.

The new pay consists of a strategic approach to total compensation. Total compensation involves base pay, variable pay (often called "incentive pay"), and indirect pay (often called "benefits"). Organizations attempt to match base pay with labor market conditions in order to have competitively priced labor forces at their disposal. Incentive or variable pay is used to reward performance improvements. In addition, it gives management and employees the idea that they are partners in the competitive success of their organizations. Indirect pay or benefits have changed dramatically during the last few years as many organizations have moved toward flexible benefits packages that allow employees to tailor packages to their particular situations. On issues such as health care benefits, many organizations are experimenting with cost management and cost sharing techniques.

By linking base pay to the labor market and variable pay to the success of the organization, managers can use the compensation system to foster teamwork and other organizational goals. At Johnsonville Sausage, for example, hourly workers have a base pay rate determined by the labor market. Since the goals of Johnsonville Sausage include the self-improvement of its employees and the encouragement of teamwork, the company has linked an increase in the base pay rate with the education and skill training of the employees and an annual bonus with overall organizational performance. Many consulting firms and investment banks adopt strategic pay. They compensate people at a base rate necessary to hire and keep the best people, and they offer bonuses based on firm or work-group performance.

# PROMOTIONS, TRANSFERS, DEMOTIONS, AND SEPARATIONS

The movement of personnel within an organization—their promotion, transfer, demotion, and separation—is a major aspect of human resource management. The actual decisions about whom to promote and whom to fire can also be among the most difficult, and important, a manager has to make.

## PROMOTIONS

The possibility of advancement often serves as a major incentive for superior managerial performance, and promotions are the most significant way to recognize superior performance. Therefore, it is extremely important that promotions be fair—based on merit and untainted by favoritism. Still, even fair and appropriate promotions can create a number of problems. One major problem is that frequently organization members who are bypassed for promotion feel resentful, which may affect their morale and productivity. Another major problem is discrimination. Most people accept the need, or at least the legal obligation, to avoid racial, sexual, or age discrimination in the *hiring* process. Less attention has been paid to discrimination against women, older employees, and minority groups in *promotion* decisions. Consequently, affirmative action programs have been introduced to assure that potential victims of discrimination are groomed for advancement.

### TRANSFERS

Transfers serve a number of purposes. They are used to give people broader job experiences as part of their development and to fill vacancies as they occur. Transfers are also used to keep promotion ladders open and to keep individuals interested in the work. For example, many middle managers reach a plateau simply because there is no room for all of them at the top. Such managers may be shifted to other positions to keep their job motivation and interest high. Finally, inadequately performing employees may be transferred to other jobs simply because a higher-level manager is reluctant to demote or fire them. Increasingly, however, some employees are refusing transfers because they do not want to move their families or jeopardize a spouse's career.

### DISCIPLINE, DEMOTIONS, AND SEPARATIONS

*Discipline* is generally administered when an employee violates company policy or falls short of work expectations, and managers must act to remedy the situation. Discipline usually progresses through a series of steps—warning, reprimand, probation, suspension, disciplinary transfer, demotion, and discharge—until the problem is solved or eliminated.[54] Some ineffective managers may be asked to go for retraining or development, others may be "promoted" to a position with a more impressive title but less responsibility.

If demotion or transfer is not feasible, separation is usually better than letting a poor performer stay on the job. No matter how agonizing the separation decision may be, the logic of human resource planning frequently requires that it be made. (Interestingly, a surprising number of poor performers at one firm become solid successes at another.)

Union Carbide has approached discipline in an alternative fashion through what is called "positive discipline." When problems arise at work, the supervisor confronts the employee. Although subsequent incidents are met with increasing severity, punishment is not the initial response. The first time an incident occurs, for example, an employee may be required to take a day's leave (with pay) to think about what happened. At the same time, positive discipline encourages recognition of good performance by employees.[55]

As we have already discussed, the accelerated trend toward restructuring in today's turbulent environment of increased competition has contributed to a growing rate of separations. As a result, some companies provide *outplacement services* to help separated employees find new positions.

Duracell, for example, worked closely with outplacement consultants Pauline Hyde Associates (PHA) when it closed its factory in Crawley, England. Even before the announcement of the closing, PHA quietly contacted 5,000 companies about  job opportunities, resulting in the posting of 100 unadvertised vacancies potentially available for Duracell workers. Then, immediately after the news of the closing was delivered, PHA counselors began meeting with employees on-site. Of the 300 workers, 150 were out of a job immediately with three months' severance pay. Employees registered at the job shop, which was available to them whenever they needed it. The job shop had a firm orientation toward achievement, with an average placement rate of two people a day. News about job successes was posted on bulletin boards to generate optimism among the employees still working. In the end, 92 percent of those laid off found new positions through the outplacement effort.[56]

**OUTPLACEMENT.** Some companies that downsize provide outplacement services to help separated employees find new positions.

Rhino Foods, a $5-million specialty-dessert maker in Burlington, Vermont, chose to avoid layoffs altogether by contracting out idle workers temporarily to other local businesses. Employees collected the salary the other company normally paid for the same work or, if the other company normally paid less than what the worker earned at Rhino, Rhino paid the difference. The costs that Rhino incurred were not insignificant, but Rhino management believed they amounted to less than layoffs would have cost. In addition, many employees acquired new ideas from the temporary employers, such as one worker who returned from Ben and Jerry's with a suggestion for rotating breaks for production-line employees.[57]

It has become increasingly important for managers to establish—and follow to the letter—a policy on termination. For many years, it was accepted doctrine that managers could fire at their own discretion. Through legislative and judicial action, however, employees have won an increasing number of complex rights. As a result, more and more companies are finding themselves answering charges of "wrongful termination" in courts that seem to view jobs as a form of legal contract or property, with roughly comparable rights. Judgments of wrongful termination challenge the doctrine of "at-will" employment used in many jurisdictions.

To handle disputes about discipline and document their resolution, formal complaint procedures are common. At Federal Express, the discipline procedure includes a formal grievance review process called the Federal Express Guaranteed Fair Treatment Procedure (GFTP). It provides for up to three levels of review: management review, officer review, and executive review. Employees not satisfied with the results of review at one level may resubmit the complaint to the next level. At each stage, both the complaint and the response must be timely and in writing.

# HRM AND STRATEGY

As Table 14-4 shows, environmental changes require a number of reactions by organizations trying to meet their strategic goals. Because so many of these reactions involve human resources, HRM is feeling the pressure.[58] In the rest of this section, we will see how HRM can analyze environmental pressures and then evaluate its effectiveness in meeting these pressures.

## HRM AND ENVIRONMENTAL PRESSURES

Researchers at the Harvard Business School have proposed a broad way of understanding human resources management that takes HRM beyond the narrow connotation of planning, selecting, training, and appraising. Figure 14-2 indicates how external stakeholder interests, such as union interests, and situational factors, such as the local labor market, can influence HRM policies. These policies naturally have consequences for the organization itself—consequences that, in turn, affect both the environment and the organization.

← ch. 3, p. 63

For example, many people are forecasting a labor shortage in the United States for the late 1990s. If this proves true, then business strategies must take this fact into account. Some labor-intensive activities may have to be transferred to other countries, or, alternatively, executives may have to lobby for a liberalization of immigration laws. Additionally, industries will be affected differently by a labor shortage. Companies may have to adopt a variety of new reward systems and even new ways of dividing and sharing work.

**TABLE 14-4**     Reactions of an Organization to Changes in Its Environment

| ACTIONS | REACTIONS |
|---|---|
| Situational/Stakeholder Pressures Influencing Effectiveness | Countervailing Measures by HRM to Retain Effectiveness |
| Increasing international competition | Improve human productivity |
| | Increase employee commitment |
| | Ensure long-term supply of competent people |
| Increasing complexity and size of organizations | Reduce levels of bureaucratization |
| | Improve HRM in diverse societies |
| Slower growth and declining markets | Reevaluate advancement opportunities to high potential employees |
| | Reevaluate employment security to long-service employees |
| Greater government involvement | Reexamine HRM policies and practices |
| | Develop new HRM policies and practices |
| Increasing education of the work force | Reexamine employee competency |
| Changing values of the work force | Reexamine employee autonomy |
| More concern with career and life satisfaction | Reexamine employee career paths, lifestyle needs, and work schedules |
| Changes in work force demography | Reexamine all policies, practices, and managerial values affecting minorities |

Source: Adapted with permission of The Free Press, a Division of Macmillan, Inc., from *Human Resource Management* by Michael Beer, Bert A. Spector, Paul R. Lawrence, and Richard E. Walton. Copyright 1985 by The Free Press.

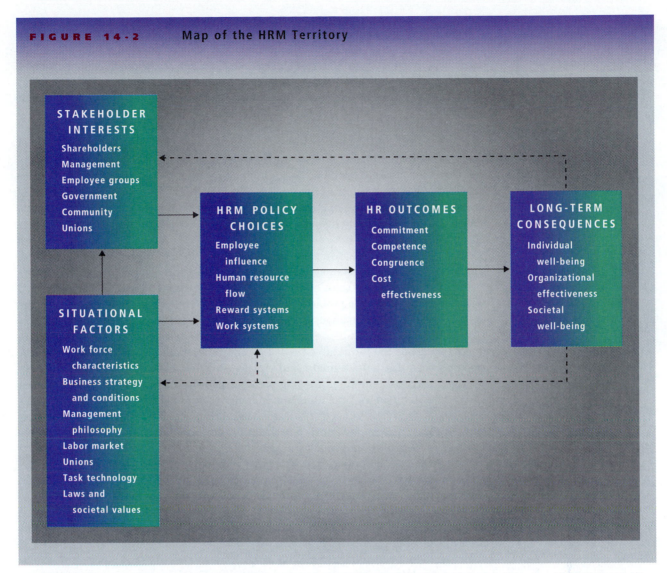

**FIGURE 14-2** Map of the HRM Territory

*Source:* Reprinted with permission of The Free Press, a Division of Simon & Schuster Inc., from *Human Resource Management* by Michael Beer, Bert A. Spector, Paul R. Lawrence, and Richard E. Walton. Copyright © 1984 by The Free Press.

Such considerations provide clear evidence that the HRM process cannot be divorced from strategy—the overall direction of the firm. The most important point to remember, however, is that unless HRM policies are influenced by all stakeholders, the organization will fail to meet the needs of the stakeholders in the long run and will fail as an organization.

## THE FOUR C'S MODEL FOR EVALUATING HUMAN RESOURCES

To evaluate the effectiveness of the HRM process within an organization, the Harvard researchers have proposed a "four C's" model: competence, commitment, congruence, and cost effectiveness. Examples of questions related to each of the four C's, and some methods for measuring them, are given in the following list.[59]

1. *Competence.* How competent are employees in their work? Do they need additional training? Performance evaluations by managers can help a company determine what talent it has available. To what extent do HRM policies attract, keep, and develop employees with skills and knowledge needed now and in the future?

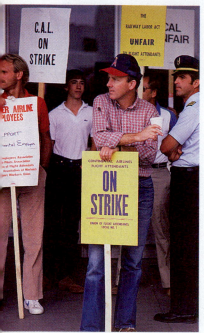

**STRIKES AND THE "FOUR C'S" MODEL.** A strike, or a pattern of frequent strikes, may undermine the cost-effectiveness of HRM policies and indicate a lack of congruence between employees and their company.

2. *Commitment.* How committed are employees to their work and organization? Surveys can be conducted through interviews and questionnaires to find answers to this question. Additional information can be gained from personnel records about voluntary separation, absenteeism, and grievances. To what extent do HRM policies enhance the commitment of employees to their work and organization?

3. *Congruence.* Is there congruence, or agreement, between the basic philosophy and goals of the company and its employees? Is there trust and common purpose between managers and employees? Incongruence can be detected in the frequency of strikes, conflicts between managers and subordinates, and grievances. A low level of congruence results in low levels of trust and common purpose; tension and stress between employees and managers may increase. What levels of congruence between management and employees do HRM policies and practices enhance or retain?

4. *Cost effectiveness.* Are HRM policies cost-effective in terms of wages, benefits, turnover, absenteeism, strikes, and similar factors?

Even more difficult than addressing and measuring the extent of the four C's within a company is the problem of assessing HRM *outcomes.* In other words, how do you make judgments about the long-term consequences of HRM policies on employee and societal well-being and organizational effectiveness? How, for example, do you go about the formidable task of assigning a value to employee commitment or to an organizational climate and culture that encourages motivation and employee growth? In the final analysis, managers need the participation of a broad range of stakeholders (including management, unions, and governmental agencies) to obtain the data needed to evaluate the impact of HRM practices and policies. At Sony, it is important to pay attention to the impact of HRM practices if it is to be successful in its worldwide approach.

By shaping HRM policies to enhance commitment, competence, congruence, and cost effectiveness, an organization increases its capacity to adapt to changes in its environment.[60] *High commitment,* for example, means better communication between employees and managers. Mutual trust is enhanced, and all stakeholders are responsive to one another's needs and concerns whenever changes in environmental demands occur. *High competence* means that employees are versatile in their skills and can take on new roles and jobs as needed. They are better able to respond to changes in environmental demands. *Cost effectiveness* means that human resource costs, such as wages, benefits, and strikes, are kept equal to or less than those of competitors. Finally, *higher congruence* means that all stakeholders share a common purpose and collaborate in solving problems brought about by changes in environmental demands. This capacity to collaborate is crucial in an ever-changing environment.

**MANAGEMENT 2000 AND BEYOND**

# JOB DESCRIPTIONS: WHAT'S NEXT?

As forward-looking CEOs restructure their organizations with flatter hierarchies and empower employees to make decisions in a less encumbered organizational setting, new approaches to describing the work of the organization need to be developed. Traditionally, job descriptions have been functional and narrow, discretely detailing the scope and depth of a job and fitting the person to the job rather than the other way around. But the new environment of information-driven work and changing technology dictates that "decisions must be made at the drop of a fax." To maintain productivity and flexibility, managers depend increasingly on utilizing the complex skills of the people they manage; they cannot afford to have them "boxed in" by narrow job descriptions.

One organization that is grappling with this situation is the Exploration Division of British Petroleum (BPX), with locations all over the globe. The third-largest oil company in the world, BPX was typical of large-scale organizations in that it had accumulated layers of bureaucracy. Career advancement was based on time-in-grade, and career success was equated with management titles. So, to advance to the top levels of the company technical people such as engineers had to move over into management. Expectations of growth were built into the system.

Senior management decided that a radical change was needed. What they envisioned was a strategic shift to a more dynamic system that would challenge employees to gain and apply new skills demanded by the changes to the business. But if they abandoned the old job descriptions, what would take their place? Without formal job descriptions, how would people know what their responsibilities were? The answer at BPX was to develop a new framework, a set of skill matrices.

"Each skill matrix describes steps in the career ladder—from the lowest level to the highest—along the vertical axis, and describes the skills and competencies that are required for each step across the horizontal axis." Two types of skill matrices were developed: One type guides the career development of people in management and the other type is for more technical people whose talents and expertise lie in individual contributions rather than management. This dual-track system was developed by a multidisciplinary team of BPX staff from its many locations around the world. They developed descriptions for skills and levels of performance for job families rather than specific jobs, and they made the paths common on a global level (for example, the career path for drilling managers would be the same in Aberdeen as in Alaska). While the management matrix is common across all job families, the individual contributor path is unique for each of the job families.

Existing management tracks were rethought; both of the new track systems were developed after much thought was given to how it ought to be done. In addition, generic skills such as problem solving, analysis, decision making, and communication were applied to all jobs. The matrices are so detailed that an employee can identify what skills are needed to be successful in the future. Therefore employees can take responsibility for and plan their own career development.

The system has many advantages:

- It saves time because the people in the current role revise the job and develop themselves without waiting for the HR department.
- The dual career path system enables people to grow and advance in areas of their greatest strength, whether these are technical or business. That is, technical people can climb the career ladder without crossing over to a management track; continuing promotion and increasing rewards can be achieved on the technical track as well.
- Managers know what to expect of their employees and employees know what the company expects from them.
- Both employees and managers are challenged continually.
- Because the roles are not fixed or static, they are more adaptable to the unpredictabilities of today's business conditions.

A turbulent, rapidly changing, and highly competitive business environment will likely continue to be a fact of life in the twenty-first century. Thus organizations must adapt to new ways of doing HRM. Traditional job descriptions are well-suited to the pyramidal bureaucracy but ill-suited to the flexible, flat organizations needed now and in the future.[61]

# ON-SITE DINING FOR THE SONY FAMILY

Sometimes human resource management can involve something as seemingly unrelated as providing an on-site corporate dining facility. As more and more companies consolidate their urban offices into single, low-rent, suburban developments, the benefits of on-site dining are becoming increasingly apparent.

At Sony, on-site dining is perceived as more than merely a pleasant eating experience. "When employees eat in, they tend to exchange work ideas," explained Sony's Gordon Casanova, director of facilities management, corporate services. "They continue the workday on a different level."[62] On-site dining has allowed Sony to confine lunch breaks to 45 minutes, since it eliminates the need for commuting to lunch. Moreover, added Casanova, "[o]n-site dining sharply curtails lunch-hour abuses."[63]

In addition, on-site dining brings employees together in a more relaxed setting, outside the work environment, so that they can have the opportunity to bond socially. This, in turn, can ease work relationships and enhance productivity. Also, the on-site dining encourages intra-company networking by bringing together people of different positions from different departments. Such networking can ultimately facilitate internal communication by giving people faces to attach to the names with whom they work.

*On-site dining also helps to break down barriers between management and staff.*

At Sony, on-site dining also helps to break down barriers between management and staff. "I have always made it a point to know our employees, to visit every facility of our company, and to try to meet and know every single employee," said Morita. "This became more and more difficult as we grew, and it is impossible to really know the more than forty thousand people who work for us today, but I try. I encourage all of our managers to know everybody and not to sit behind a desk in the office all day."[64] The dining facility thus helps to strengthen work-related relationships. According to Morita, a company is a sort of family. When CEO, he considered socializing with employees an integral part of his day. "It was not just part of my job; I like those people. They are family."[65]

By providing in-house dining, Sony was able to increase employee productivity and morale and promote its familial culture. "We have a policy that wherever we are in the world we deal with our employees as members of the Sony family, as valued colleagues," explained Morita. "[W]e brought management people, including engineers, to Tokyo and let them work with us and trained them and treated them just like members of our family, all of whom wear the same jackets and eat in our one-class cafeteria. This way they got to understand that people should not be treated differently.... We urged the management staff to sit down with their office people and share the facilities."[66] For Morita, it is not human resource management; it is respect for one's family.

# SUMMARY

1. **Present an overview of the HRM process.**

   The HRM process includes (1) human resource planning; (2) recruitment; (3) selection; (4) socialization; (5) training and development; (6) performance appraisal; (7) promotions, transfers, demotions, and separations. Human resources planning includes planning for the future personnel needs of the organization, planning what the future balance of the organization's personnel will be, planning a recruitment-selection or layoff program, and planning a development program. Human resource plans are based on forecasting and on the human resource audit, in which the skills and performance of organization members are appraised. To be meaningful, human resource plans must consider both the strategic plan and the external environment of the organization.

2. **List and describe the various methods of recruitment.**

   General and specialized recruitment are designed to supply the organization with a sufficiently large pool of job candidates. Before recruitment can take place, a job analysis, consisting of the position description and job specification, must be made. Job recruits can be drawn from within or outside the organization.

3. **Discuss the various legal considerations involved in human relations.**

   Successive federal and state legislation, executive orders, and legal decisions since the early 1960s have mandated equal employment opportunity (EEO) regardless of race, sex, age, color, religion, or ethnic group membership. EEO legislation also covers Vietnam era and disabled veterans and the physically and mentally handicapped. Nondiscriminatory procedures must provide equal access to jobs, training, and promotion and equal treatment in the workplace. Firms doing business with the federal government are subject to affirmative action (AA) programs to add and develop women and minority group members.

4. **Explain the seven-step hiring sequence.**

   The selection process follows a seven-step procedure: completed job application, initial screening interview, testing, background investigation, in-depth selection interview, physical examination, and job offer. For managerial positions, the in-depth interview is probably the most important step. Ideally, it should be realistic and factually based. Socialization helps the new employee and the organization adapt to each other. Giving new employees challenging assignments correlates with future success.

5. **Distinguish between training and development programs and give examples of each.**

   Training programs seek to maintain and improve current job performance, while development programs are designed to impart skills needed in future jobs. The need for training may be determined through performance appraisal, job requirements, organizational analysis, and human resource surveys. Both training and development methods can be classified as on-the-job or off-the-job. Coaching is the most important formal on-the-job development method. Other development methods include job rotation and classroom teaching. Both training and development should be reinforced in the work situation.

**6. Discuss the important issues involved in making promotion, transfer, demotion, and separation decisions.**

Performance appraisal may be informal or formal. To improve performance, appraisal should be based on goals jointly set by managers and subordinates. To be useful as employee incentives, promotions must be fair. Discrimination in promotion, though illegal, has not disappeared. Transfers are used to broaden a manager's experience, to fill vacant positions, and to relocate employees whom the organization does not want to demote, promote, or fire. Demotion is an infrequently used option in dealing with ineffective managers. Separations, though painful, are more widely used and frequently prove beneficial to the individual as well as to the organization.

**7. Explain how HRM interacts with organization strategy.**

New trends call for linking HRM more closely with an organization's strategy. The four C's— competence, commitment, congruence, and cost effectiveness—provide a useful model for evaluating how effectively an organization's human resource policy is supporting its business strategy.

## REVIEW QUESTIONS

1. What are the steps in the HRM process? Are managers likely to be engaged in more than one step at a time? Why or why not?
2. Why is human resource planning necessary? Name the four steps in human resource planning. What factors must managers of a human resource planning program consider?
3. What methods of recruitment can managers use? What are the advantages and disadvantages of recruitment from within?
4. What changes have occurred in EEO and Affirmative Action in recent years? What are the implications for managers?
5. What is the standard seven-step hiring sequence? Is this sequence the same under all conditions? Why or why not?
6. What are the defects of in-depth interviews? How can they be minimized?
7. What information is socialization designed to provide?
8. What is the difference between training and development?
9. What development approaches and methods can managers use? Which method is most effective?
10. What are the basic differences between systematic and informal appraisal? What are the four basic appraisal approaches? How may formal appraisals be made more effective in improving performance? What appraisal pitfalls do managers need to avoid?
11. What are the problems associated with promotions? How may these problems be overcome?
12. When are transfers used in organizations?
13. Explain how the four C's criteria may be used to evaluate the effectiveness of a human resource management policy.

## KEY TERMS

Human resource management (HRM)
Human resource planning
Recruitment
Job description
Position description
Hiring specification
Comparable worth
Selection
Realistic job preview (RJP)

Orientation
Socialization
Training program
Developmental program
Computer-assisted instruction (CAI)
Informal performance appraisal
Formal systematic appraisal
New pay approach

## CASE STUDY

## HERSHEY GONE HEALTHY[67]

The 1990s have witnessed the skyrocketing of health care costs which for several years grew at an annual rate greater than 15 percent. Companies have shouldered a great deal of this burden through benefits packages offered to employees. Although many companies have explored a variety of cost-reduction strategies during the past decade, corporate health care costs continue to climb. What is a company to do? The answer for Hershey Foods Corporation lay in a wellness incentive program.

Hershey made the decision to focus on employee health in 1991, after an outside consulting firm attributed 25 to 35 percent of Hershey's health care costs to employee lifestyles. Hershey set about creating incentives to encourage employee "wellness."

In April 1991, Hershey launched a pilot wellness incentive program for 624 of its salaried employees at its Pennsylvania headquarters. The program was designed to reduce modifiable health risk factors such as smoking and high blood pressure, intended to decrease the company's health care expenditures, and, in line with Hershey's "strong people orientation and care for every employee" philosophy, increase employee health and morale.[68] "We've had a commitment to well employees and employees' well-being for years," noted Rick Dreyfuss, director of executive compensation and employee benefits at Hershey. "Now, we've taken it one step further by linking employee wellness to annual health care costs."[69]

Under the experimental program, which, if successful, was to be expanded to all 11,000 of Hershey's employees, people received debits or credits according to how they ranked on certain risk factors. For example, employees who did not smoke in 1993 earned $48 that could be taken as cash or applied to out-of-pocket costs for their benefit program. Employees who did smoke, however, were charged as much as $444 for the year. Other categories included blood pressure, regularity of aerobic exercise, weight, and cholesterol level. Employees under a doctor's care for any of the categories were considered "cost neutral" and were neither rewarded nor penalized. While weight, blood pressure, and cholesterol level were measured confidentially by the company's medical department, Hershey relied on an honor system to determine if employees smoked or regularly exercised. "We entrust our employees with the responsibility to play fair," said Dreyfuss. "Do we get 100 percent accuracy? I'm sure the answer is no."[70] Nevertheless, Hershey decided to stick with the honor system out of respect for its employees.

The incentive-based program did show impressive first-year results for Hershey employees, particularly in light of the limited success enjoyed by previous wellness programs and cost-shifting strategies. A survey of the first-year program participants revealed that half had altered their lifestyles in some way. Nearly 30 percent of the respondents reported that they had begun exercising more regularly and had lowered their cholesterol levels.

However, the program has also met with considerable resistance. "Some employees thought this was the best thing we've ever done," said Dreyfuss. "Others thought the company was more involved in their personal lives than it needed to be."[71] One such person was Earl Light, business manager for Local 464 of the Bakery, Confectionery, and Tobacco Worker's Union, which represents 2,800 Hershey factory employees. "I feel uncomfortable about any program that dictates lifestyle," he explained. "I don't have a problem with programs that offer incentives to be healthy, but I don't think you should penalize people who don't meet company standards. There's no way our union is going to agree to this program, and I believe I speak for all unions."[72] Despite union objections, however, Hershey has kept the program in place. "We don't see this as dictating lifestyle or an invasion of privacy," asserted Dreyfuss. "We simply believe employees need to be financially accountable to the health care system."[73]

## CASE QUESTIONS

1. Has Hershey gone too far? Why or why not?
2. How does such a program influence recruitment?
3. To what degree should a company's human resource management department be able to influence employees' lifestyles?
4. What stakeholders does such a program affect?
5. Evaluate the program according to the Four C's model.

---

## VIDEO CASE STUDY

### THE UNITED WAY OF COMPENSATING EXECUTIVES[74]

On February 27, 1992, William Aramony's tenure as president of United Way of America (UWA) came to an abrupt halt. In response to growing dissension at local United Way chapters across the country, coupled with donor and media calls for his withdrawal, Aramony resigned from his position as head of the largest charity organization in the United States. "I do this because media attention is overshadowing the importance of the work of the United Way," wrote Aramony in a letter to LaSalle Leffall, Jr., chairperson of UWA Board of Governors executive committee.[75]

The "media attention" to which Aramony referred consisted of allegations of misuse of funding and excessive compensation. In addition to a $463,000 annual compensation package and a $4.4 million retirement package, Aramony allegedly enjoyed a "first-class only" travel budget and annually spent about $40,000 for trans-Atlantic Concorde flights and nearly $100,000 for limousine services.[76]

Many people balked at these numbers and questioned how an executive of a non-profit charity organization could possibly rationalize such "outrageous" expenses and compensation. "We're hearing from people that they're very concerned that any money they're giving to charity is being wasted," noted Geoffrey Edwards, president of the United Way of the National Capital Area. "We're really concerned that we might suffer from the adverse publicity."[77]

Although preliminary investigations during December 1991 did not find any wrongdoing by Aramony, he nevertheless submitted his resignation. He left in an attempt to minimize negative fallout on the organization. "It hurts me to see and hear unfair criticism of a system that has done so much for this country," Aramony explained. "I've never been through something like this in my life."[78] Many people, such as Walter Annenburg, who donated $450,000 to the United Way in 1991, believed that Aramony had to leave to prevent negative repercussions for the UWA organization and its affiliates. "It's definitely the right thing to do given the circumstances, pressure and questions that United Way has to deal with," agreed Kenneth Albrecht, president of National Charities Information. "People will remember these charges for several years down the road."[79]

UWA definitely felt the blow of the Aramony scandal. "This kind of stuff leaves you grief stricken," remarked Albrecht. "It doesn't just affect the United Way of America, it affects local United Ways, it could affect local senior-citizen and day-care centers. It affects every single one of us who [is] involved in the charitable field in this country. We are all diminished, and the public trust has been diminished."[80] During 1992, contributions to United Way chapters dropped for the first time since 1946. It was estimated that the United Way network as a whole raised $66 million dollars less in pledges in 1992 that it did in 1991—a 2.5% decline. "The scandal has tarred and feathered the United Way's motherhood-and-apple-pie image," said Robert O. Bothwell, executive director of the National Committee for Responsive Philanthropy.[81] For the first time, UWA was under scrutiny.

Recovering from the scandal presented an imposing challenge for the company, but one that the organization faced head-on. In response to public concern, the UWA conducted an investigation and published a report that detailed numerous financial abuses by its management during the prior five years. In addition, the UWA board suspended Aramony's $4.4 million retirement package. Aramony appeared on ABC's "Nightline" and attempted to speak up in his own behalf. During his tenure he increased UWA fundraising to $3.1 billion and established a powerful marketing alliance with the National Football League through which the UWA received millions of dollars worth of free advertising. But, in the end, even Aramony realized he had made at least one mistake. "I did not pay enough attention to detail or to the way some of my actions... and my personal style could have been perceived by certain people," Aramony conceded.[82]

Since the Aramony experience, many changes have taken place at UWA. Managers are now held responsible for their budgets and are monitored monthly by senior vice-presidents. Coach travel is mandated for all business trips (including the president's), and a daily meal allowance has been set. Perhaps most important, individuals can now pledge directly to the charity of their choice through the UWA. "It's going to be a rough couple of years," stated UWA President Elaine L. Chao, shortly after taking control of the organization. "The old way of doing things has got to change—the old-boy network and the whole culture."[83]

What happened at UWA reflects a concern that has affected corporate America as a whole, not just nonprofit organizations. The UWA experience serves as a lesson for all companies, as the 1990s bear witness to a general public outcry against lavish executive compensation packages. While many people argue that executives must receive compensation commensurate with the responsibilities they carry, others contend that discretion must still be used. As Aramony learned, perceptions are extremely important.

## CASE QUESTIONS

1. What concerns must an organization balance in determining how much to compensate its executives?
2. What sort of impact could the changes taking place, such as the more frequent monitoring, have on UWA employees?
3. How does such a scandal influence recruitment?
4. What sort of executive compensation is appropriate in an organization?
5. What else can the UWA do now to help raise morale, such as through training?
6. What else can the UWA do now to help recover from the bad publicity?

## CHAPTER 15

# Managing Organizational Change and Innovation

**Upon completing this chapter, you should be able to:**

1. Define the term *planned change* and identify situations in which it is appropriate.

2. List and discuss the concepts of Kurt Lewin's force-field theory.

3. List the three types of planned change and give an example of each.

4. Define the term *organizational development* and explain how it differs from other approaches to planned change.

5. Describe the most widely used OD techniques.

6. Distinguish between innovation and creativity and explain how organizations can encourage both.

# ORGANIZATIONAL TRAUMA AND TRIUMPH AT AT&T[1]

In perhaps the most celebrated case in business history, AT&T agreed in 1982 to a consent decree with the Department of Justice to divest itself of three-quarters of its $150 billion in assets. Until that time AT&T and the associated Bell Telephone Companies were widely and highly regarded as among the most consistently profitable and best-managed companies in the world. The changes that resulted from divestiture were enormous. Each of the resulting multibillion-dollar companies had to establish new ways of planning and organizing, and AT&T itself was plunged into a brand-new competitive world.

Prior to 1984, AT&T was the largest private employer in the United States. It was well known for rewarding loyalty, perseverance, and hard work with responsibility and job security. The tradition of serving the public interest was deeply ingrained in AT&T employees. Under the stress of change, however, many of the company's traditions collapsed. As part of its cost-cutting efforts, AT&T eliminated 75,000 jobs, some via retirement but many more through layoffs.

James E. Olson, then AT&T's chairman, began a move to unify the company and heal its wounds. He outlined broad new goals: to protect AT&T's core telecommunications business, drive its sagging computer business out of the red, and increase AT&T's overseas revenues. Part of his strategy was to do away with the multiple payroll procedures, phone systems, and ID badges that had characterized the old divisions of the company and to forge a single new corporate culture.

*The last few years have seen AT&T reap the rewards of the changes of the previous decade.*

Olson began implementing this strategy during a special meeting of his 27 top executives. After five days of hard-fought battles over the new shape of AT&T, each of the executives had to stand and publicly affirm his commitment to the plan when asked, "Are you with me?"

Still troubled by the morale problem, Olson took to the road, touring seven cities, and spoke to over 40,000 AT&T workers in an effort to explain the company's problems and his proposed solutions. Unfortunately, he died of cancer early in 1988. His successor, Robert Allen, faced a difficult job in continuing the task of organizational change.

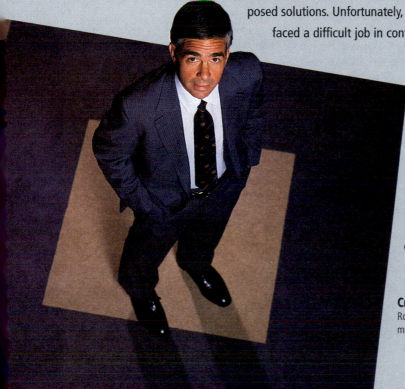

The last few years have seen AT&T reap the rewards of the changes of the previous decade. Allen has been lauded for his leadership. Fresh from a stunning success in implementing a credit card product, the Universal Card, AT&T managers are able to act more quickly to changes in the marketplace. Under Allen's tutelage AT&T has bought a computer company, NCR, a cellular phone company, McCaw, and a number of small high-tech companies such as EOS, to position itself as a leader in the changing telecommunications industry. →

**CHARTING A COURSE FOR THE FUTURE.** Under the tutelage of current CEO Robert E. Allen, AT&T is positioning itself as a leader in the changing communications industry.

**A**T&T IS ONLY one of many organizations undergoing the tumultuous and potentially rewarding process of *planned change*. Simply, planned change is the systematic attempt to redesign an organization in a way that will help it adapt to significant changes in the environment and to achieve new goals. In this chapter, we will look at the reasons organizations embark on a course of planned change, a model of the change process, and the aspects of the organization that can be changed. Then we will end the chapter by looking at *organizational development,* one of the major approaches to changing the culture and people within an organization, with special emphasis on how managers can encourage creativity and innovation.

# WHY PLANNED CHANGE IS NEEDED

← ch. 3, p. 63

**E**very organization makes minor structural adjustments in reaction to changes in its <u>direct-action and indirect-action environments</u>, of course. A sales form is revised to eliminate customer confusion. Or, the human resources department may create a training program on OSHA-mandated safety programs. What distinguishes planned change from these routine changes is its scope and magnitude. Planned change aims to prepare the *entire* organization, or a major part of it, to adapt to significant changes in the organization's goals and direction. A detailed definition of **planned change** is "the deliberate design and implementation of a structural innovation, a new policy or goal, or a change in operating philosophy, climate or style."[2]

**planned change:**
The systematic attempt to redesign an organization in a way that will help it adapt to changes in the external environment or to achieve new goals.

Change programs are necessary today precisely because of the shift in time and relationships that we have seen throughout the organizational world. The sophistication of information processing technology, together with the increase in the globalization of organizations, means that managers are bombarded with more new ideas, new products, new challenges than ever before (see Figure 15-1). To handle such an increase in information, accompanied by a decrease in the decision-making time managers can afford to take, managers must improve their ability to manage change. Many large organizations have explicit *change management programs* to increase the ability of people throughout the organization to anticipate and learn from the changes that are occurring.

Some of the largest, most successful, and most venerable firms are victims of their own success. Over the years they have built up highly stable, bureaucratic, and tall organizational structures that are very efficient at achieving certain goals in a given environment. Decision making, though, is methodical, even sluggish, and new ideas and opportunities for <u>competitive advantages</u> tend to get strangled by red tape. Many organizations are experimenting with flatter organizational structures that encourage teamwork and faster communication. The idea is that these "leaner" organizations will be more flexible, creative, and innovative in reacting to environmental changes of every type. At AT&T, business unit managers are encouraged to adopt these approaches.

← ch. 5, p. 139

Recession and new European business opportunities have prompted Asea Brown Boveri (ABB), the Swedish-Swiss electrical engineering company, to reorganize. In the first big shake-up since the merger that created the company in 1988, ABB underwent a major restructuring effort. While the goal is to maintain the matrix structure, the company's executive committee was reduced by a third. According to CEO Percy Barnevik, this slimmed-down executive committee clarifies responsibility and expedites transnational decision making. "The purpose of the reorganisation is to facilitate integrated system thinking, encourage teamwork by eliminating borderlines, and thus concentrate more effectively on the needs of customers and markets,"

FIGURE 15.1    The Impact of Globalization and Information Technology

**PRIMARY FORCES AT WORK**
Globalization

**RESULTS**

**OVERALL IMPACT**

**IMPACT AT COMPANY PERSONAL LEVEL**

Recovered Dominant Economies
- Japan
- Germany

Newly Industrialized Countries
- Korea
- Taiwan
- Singapore
- Spain

Shift Toward Market Economies
- Eastern Europe
- Russia
- China

New Power Blocks
- EEC 1992
- "Yen Block"

Information Technology

- End of U.S company dominance
- "Value-added" competition among high-wage nations

- Low-cost, high-quality commodities
- Move toward "value-added"

- More sources of goods
- Enriched global network
- Wild card

- End of U.S. policy domination

- "Age of intangibles"
- Micromarkets
- "Real-Time" global/ local linkages
- All products obsolete/ every product redefined
- Entrepreneurial explosion All company relationships redefined
- Economics of production and distribution scale challenged
- Mixed-scale alliances
- Markets over hierarchies

"Global Village" Realized

Economic Volatility
- Oil
- Currency
- Trade Flows

Lack of Cohesive Global Economic Leadership

Old Industry Restructuring
- LBOs
- Mergers and Breakups

New Industry Emergence

Service Sector Dominant/"Service Added" in Manufacturing Brain-Based Everything

New Organizational Forms
- No hierarchy

New Combinations of Organizations
- Networks

Perpetual Change

Careers Redefined
- Flexibility

Education Redefined
- Lifelong
- Creativity

Everyone (Person/Firm) a "Global Player"

Entrepreneurs Taking on Any Task

New Winners and New Losers
- Jobs
- People
- Firms
- Industries

Search for New Bases for Competitive Advantage
- Speed/Time
- Flexibility
- Quality/design
- Information technology
- Alliances/networks
- Fast innovation improvement
- Skill upgrading
- "Service added"
- "Small within big"
- Subcontracting
- Globalization

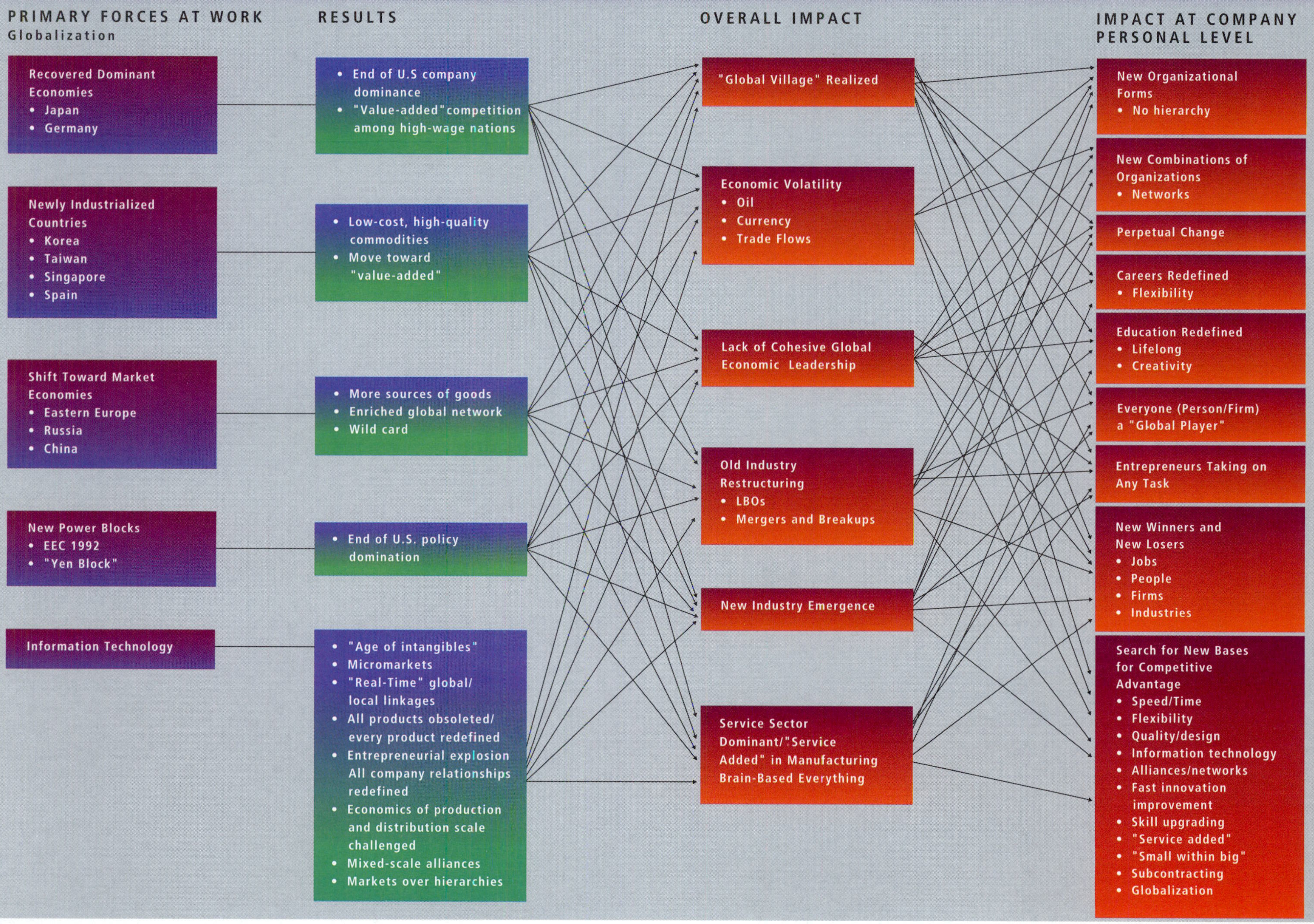

Barnevik explained. "However, with our reinforced product segments and new regional structure, we will become more effective in dealing with the challenges of the 1990s. The new organization will strengthen the operating advantages of our matrix and enable us to react even faster to market developments."[3]

### COOKING UP CHANGE AT CAMPBELL SOUP

When David Johnson took over as CEO of Campbell Soup, simple restructuring wasn't enough. By the time he arrived, crisis had set in. "Crisis was inevitable," Johnson pointed out. "There were too many inefficiencies. There were decisions that were overdue. That's an opportunity for the new man coming in. But you've got to be bold. You've got to believe that fortune rewards the bold."[4] And bold he was. Indeed, he set about the task of rebuilding the American institution, piece by piece. At times this entailed departing from what the company had become to answer the question, "Who are we?"[5]

Johnson left no stone unturned. He questioned every budget and forced employees to rethink their spending. He looked for areas where employees had become sloppy as a result of too much comfort. For example, he discovered that soup executives were wasting 10 percent of the marketing budget on an annual tomato soup promotion timed to coincide with the tomato harvest. This would have made sense, except that years ago Campbell had stopped using fresh tomatoes in soup.

In addition, Johnson introduced an incentive plan that bases 20 percent of a manager's bonus on overall corporate performance, instead of only on operating unit results. And Johnson has also initiated a comprehensive appraisal system to let each employee know how much he or she is valued within the organization. Quality has improved significantly as a result of Johnson's efforts. "He really turned this place on," remarked Fred George, regional vice president of manufacturing, referring particularly to the plant in Maxton, North Carolina.[6] Work teams, statistical process control, and total quality had been introduced at Maxton under the former CEO, but under Johnson they took effect. The plant's operating efficiency soared, and manufacturing costs were driven below 50 percent of the retail price of products. ■

## A MODEL OF THE CHANGE PROCESS

**A**lthough organizations are beset by many forces for change, it is important to recognize that opposing forces act to keep an organization in a state of equilibrium. These opposing forces, then, support stability or the status quo. To understand how this works, let's take a look at a model of the change process that is based on the work of Kurt Lewin.

### FORCE-FIELD ANALYSIS

According to the *force-field theory* of Kurt Lewin, every behavior is the result of an equilibrium between *driving* and *restraining* forces.[7] The driving forces push one way; the restraining forces push the other. The performance that emerges is a reconciliation of the two sets of forces. An increase in the driving forces might increase performance, but it might also increase the restraining forces.

Lewin's model (see Figure 15-2) reminds us to look for multiple causes of behavior rather than a single cause. Programs of planned change based on Lewin's

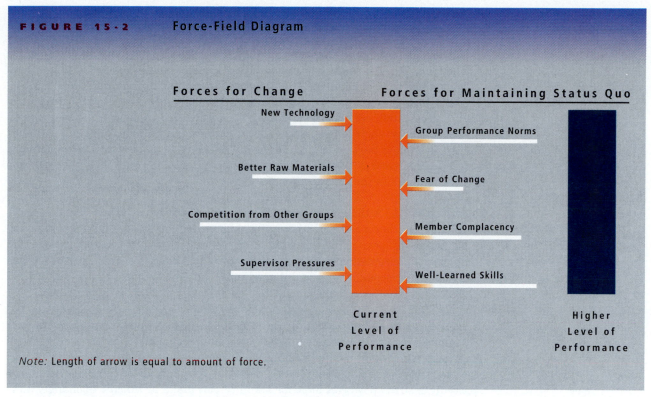

**FIGURE 15-2**    Force-Field Diagram

Forces for Change — Forces for Maintaining Status Quo

New Technology
Better Raw Materials
Competition from Other Groups
Supervisor Pressures

Group Performance Norms
Fear of Change
Member Complacency
Well-Learned Skills

Current Level of Performance

Higher Level of Performance

*Note:* Length of arrow is equal to amount of force.

*Source:* Adapted by permission from *Organization Development and Change,* 3rd ed. by Edgar F. Huse and Thomas G. Cummings, p. 73. Copyright ©1985 by West Publishing Company. All rights reserved.

ideas are directed first toward removing or weakening the restraining forces and then on creating or strengthening the driving forces that exist in organizations.

## SOURCES OF RESISTANCE

The restraining forces—the ones that keep an organization stable—are of special interest, since they represent potential sources of resistance to planned change. If managers can change these forces or *address their underlying concerns,* they have a much better chance of accomplishing any planned change. For convenience, we will group these sources of resistance into three broad classes: the organizational culture, individual self-interests, and individual perceptions of organizational goals and strategies.

← ch. 7, p. 182

**ORGANIZATIONAL CULTURE.** Of the three forces, culture may be the most important in shaping and maintaining an organization's identity. As we saw in Chapter 7, culture is a primary force in guiding employees' behavior. As a general rule, employees stay with an organization because the work helps them meet their life goals and because their personalities, attitudes, and beliefs fit into the organizational culture. Indeed, many employees identify with their organization and take its gains and losses personally. As a result, they may feel threatened by efforts to make radical changes in the organization's culture and "the way we do things."

Rapid growth at Waste Management, a $6 billion company that began less than 25 years ago, has necessitated changes in the organizational culture to accommodate its size. "People understand that we cannot operate like a small business [anymore]," explained Don O'Toole, manager of marketing and advertising. "We are obviously a high-profile company with environmentalists....We have a vice president-environmental policy and ethical standards who watches this critical area full-time."[8] Increased size has not made the company sluggish, however. "Rapid growth is still part of our culture," O'Toole asserted. "This is still a very exciting culture. We are not structure bound."[9]

Changing demographics in the workplace has created anxiety for some members of the "old order." In fact, as they hire and promote minorities and women,  some companies have experienced backlash by some white males who feel frustrated, resentful and most of all, afraid. This has been the case particularly at such companies as AT&T, DuPont, and Motorola, where diversity is a major part of the organizational mission. To address this issue, DuPont established a "Men's Forum" to help individuals come to terms with the changes in the organization.[10]

**SELF-INTERESTS.** Although employees can and do identify with their organizations, they are also concerned with themselves. In return for doing a good job, they expect adequate pay, satisfactory working conditions, job security, and certain amounts of appreciation, power, and prestige. When change occurs, employees face a potentially uncomfortable period of adjustment as they settle into a new organizational structure or a redesigned job.

**PERCEPTIONS OF ORGANIZATIONAL GOALS AND STRATEGIES.** Goals and strategies are extremely powerful for organizing and coordinating the efforts of any organization. Indeed, mission statements (such as Nordstrom's "give the customer the best service possible") can guide employee actions in the absence of formal policies and procedures. This powerful force for stability can make it difficult to change, however. Sometimes employees do not understand the need for a new goal because they do not have the same information their managers have. Or they may long for the "good old days." AT&T's long history of success and public service have proven to be substantial barriers to change.

## THE PROCESS OF CHANGE

Lewin also studied the process of bringing about effective change. Most efforts at change fail for two reasons, he thought. First, people are unwilling (or unable) to alter long-established *attitudes* and *behavior*. Tell a manager he or she must learn a new analytic technique and that manager will probably accept the suggestion. Tell the same manager he or she is too aggressive and abrasive in dealing with others, and he or she may be resentful and resistant to change.

Lewin believed that after a brief period of trying to do things differently, individuals left on their own tend to return to their habitual patterns of behavior. To overcome obstacles of this sort, Lewin developed a three-step sequential model of the change process. The model, later elaborated by Edgar H. Schein and others, is equally applicable to individuals, groups, and entire organizations.[11] It involves "unfreezing" the present behavior pattern, "changing" or developing a new behavior pattern, and then "refreezing" or reinforcing the new behavior.

1. **Unfreezing** involves making the need for change so obvious that the individual, group, or organization can readily see and accept it.
2. **Changing** involves discovering and adopting new attitudes, values, and behaviors. A trained **change agent** leads individuals, groups, or the entire organization through the process. During this process, the change agent will foster new values, attitudes, and behavior through the processes of *identification* and *internalization*. Organization members will identify with the change agent's values, attitudes, and behavior, internalizing them, once they perceive their effectiveness in performance.
3. **Refreezing** means locking the new behavior pattern into place by means of supporting or reinforcing mechanisms, so that it becomes the new norm.

**unfreezing:**
Making the need for change so obvious that the individual, group, or organization can readily see and accept that change must occur.

**changing:**
Discovering and adopting new attitudes, values, and behaviors with the help of a trained change agent, who leads individuals, groups, or the entire organization through the process. Organization members will identify with the change agent's values, attitudes, and behavior, internalizing them, once they perceive their effectiveness in performance.

**change agent:**
The individual leading or guiding the process of change in an organizational situation.

**refreezing:**
Transforming a new behavioral pattern into the norm through reinforcement and support mechanisms.

Change agents can be members of the organization or consultants brought in from the outside. For complex and lengthy change programs, hiring an outside consultant has many advantages. First, the outside consultant typically offers specialized expertise and skills. Second, the consultant will not be distracted by day-to-day operating responsibilities. Third, as an outsider, the consultant may have more prestige and influence than an insider. Fourth, because the consultant has no vested interest in the organization, he or she may be more objective than an insider and find it easier to win the confidence of employees.[12]

Table 15-1 describes some common methods for dealing with resistance to change.

# TYPES OF PLANNED CHANGE

**A**n organization can be changed by altering its structure, its technology, its people, or some combination of these features.[13] (See Figure 15-3.)

## APPROACHES TO STRUCTURAL CHANGE

Changing an organization's structure involves rearranging its internal systems, such as the lines of communication, work flow, or management hierarchy. If you recall the aspects of structure discussed in Chapter 12, you will recognize that these are the changes that can be made:

← ch. 12, p. 184

**ORGANIZATIONAL DESIGN.** Classical <u>organizational design</u> focuses on carefully defining job responsibilities and on creating appropriate divisions of labor and lines of performance. As we have noted frequently, one of the most significant structural trends is toward the flat, lean organization, in which middle layers of management are eliminated to streamline the interaction of top managers with non-management employees, who are given more responsibilities. Wal-Mart, recently named the United States's leading retailer, has a flat structure.[14]

**TIP OF THE ICEBERG.** A recent facelift for the familiar Campbell's soup label may be the only sign of change visible to the general public, but major changes have been taking place within the organization, led by CEO David Johnson.

**TABLE 15-1**        **Methods for Dealing with Resistance to Change**

| APPROACH | INVOLVES | COMMONLY USED WHEN | ADVANTAGES | DISADVAN-TAGES |
|---|---|---|---|---|
| 1. Education + communication | Explaining the need for and logic of change to individuals, groups, and even entire organizations. | There is a lack of information or inaccurate information and analysis. | Once persuaded, people will often help implement the change. | Can be very time-consuming if many people are involved. |
| 2. Participation + involvement | Asking members of organization to help design the change. | The initiators do not have all the information they need to design the change, and others have considerable power to resist. | People who participate will be committed to implementing change, and any relevant information they have will be integrated into the change plan. | Can be very time-consuming if participators design an inappropriate change. |
| 3. Facilitation + support | Offering retraining programs, time off, emotional support, and understanding to people affected by the change. | People are resisting because of adjustment problems. | No other approach works as well with adjustment problems. | Can be time-consuming, expensive, and still fail. |
| 4. Negotiation + agreement | Negotiating with potential resisters; even soliciting written letters of understanding. | Some person or group with considerable power to resist will clearly lose out in a change. | Sometimes it is a relatively easy way to avoid major resistance. | Can be too expensive if it alerts others to negotiate for compliance. |
| 5. Manipulation + cooptation | Giving key persons a desirable role in designing or implementing change process. | Other tactics will not work or are too expensive. | It can be a relatively quick and inexpensive solution to resistance problems. | Can lead to future problems if people feel manipulated. |
| 6. Explicit + implicit coercion | Threatening job loss or transfer, lack of promotion, etc. | Speed is essential, and the change initiators possess considerable power. | It is speedy and can overcome any kind of resistance. | Can be risky if it leaves people angry with the initiators. |

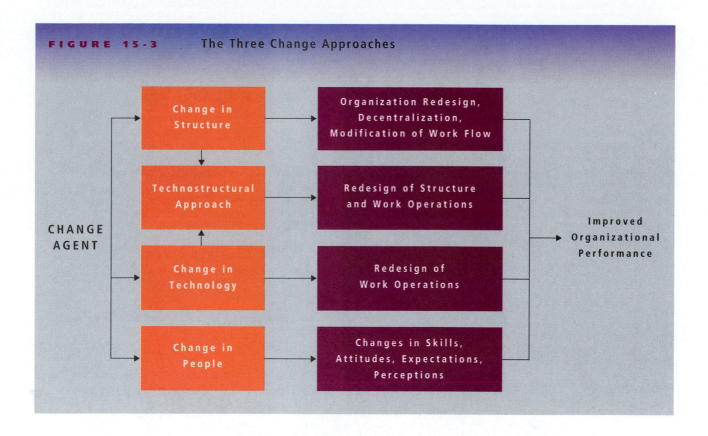

**FIGURE 15-3**    The Three Change Approaches

← ch. 13, p. 359

**DECENTRALIZATION.** One approach to decentralization involves creating smaller, self-contained organizational units that are meant to increase the motivation and performance of unit members and to focus their attention on high-priority activities. Decentralization also encourages each unit to adapt its structure and technology to its particular tasks and to its environment. Cray Research's decision to let founder Seymour Cray pursue his own research interests in a new company, Cray Computer, is a good example. Another is Disney's decision to create Touchstone Pictures, which offers more sophisticated films than the traditional Disney fare.

**MODIFIED WORK FLOW.** Modification of the work flow and careful grouping of specialties may also lead to an improvement in productivity and morale. One expression of this trend is the amount of money employees can spend without getting authorization. The consulting firm of A.T. Kearney found that the best-performing companies in the Fortune 200 let division managers spend as much as $20 million on their own signature.[15] On a smaller scale, the WIX division of the Dana Corporation lets any employee spend $100 on a process innovation without going through a slow and potentially painful and humiliating process of getting authorization. Another expression of this idea is management writer Tom Peter's suggestion that managers speed product development by "jamming people from disparate functions together in the same room or workspace or cubby hole...."[16]

## APPROACHES TO TECHNOLOGICAL CHANGE

Changing an organization's technology involves altering its equipment, engineering processes, research techniques, or production methods. This approach goes back to the scientific management theory of Frederick W. Taylor.

← ch. 2, p. 34

As we saw in Chapter 12, production technology often has a major effect on organizational structure. For that reason, *technostructural* or *sociotechnical* ap-

**A TECHNOSTRUCTURAL APPROACH.** Milliken & Co., a 1989 Baldrige Award winner, builds in opportunities for job enlargement and job enrichment through its cross training program. Employees have an opportunity to move from job to job and learn a variety of skills.

← ch. 13, p. 366

proaches attempt to improve performance by simultaneously changing aspects of an organization's structure and its technology. Job enlargement and job enrichment are examples of technostructural approaches to change.

### APPROACHES TO CHANGING PEOPLE

Both the technical and the structural approaches try to improve organizational performance by changing the work situation. The people approaches, on the other hand, try to change employee behavior by focusing on their skills, attitudes, perceptions, and expectations. We will explore an extension of this approach to change now when we discuss organizational development.

# ORGANIZATIONAL DEVELOPMENT

**organizational development (OD):**

A long-range effort supported by top management to increase an organization's problem-solving and renewal processes through effective management of organizational culture.

**M**any of the approaches to planned change are appropriate for solving immediate and specific problems. **Organizational development (OD),** in contrast, is a longer-term, more encompassing, more complex, and more costly approach to change that aims to move the entire organization to a higher level of functioning while greatly improving its members' performance and satisfaction. Although OD frequently includes structural and technological changes, its primary focus is on changing people and the nature and quality of their working relationships.

Formally, OD has been defined as

> a top-management-supported, long-range effort to improve an organization's problem-solving and renewal process, particularly through a more effective and collaborative diagnosis and management of organization culture—with special emphasis on formal work team, temporary team, and intergroup culture—with the assistance of a consultant-facilitator and the use of the theory and technology of applied behavioral science, including action research.[17]

This definition includes a number of important phrases. *Problem-solving process* refers to the organization's methods of dealing with the threats and op-

# AT&T'S "COMMON BOND"

The managers at AT&T could no doubt identify with all of the concepts discussed in this chapter. Both organizational and environmental forces for change clearly existed. Even before the divestiture, AT&T had undertaken programs designed to make changes; for example, the company had already negotiated a union agreement with the Communications Workers of America that included a new quality-of-work-life program to improve management-labor communications and cooperation.

Because AT&T was so huge before the divestiture, overcoming inertia took constant effort. Once the layoffs started, resistance to change increased among some employees in proportion to the company's own uncertainty, but it lessened in others—those who were eager for something, almost anything, to happen.

*Overcoming the sheer inertia of an organization comprising over one million employees…required constant vigilance.*

Recently CEO Robert Allen has implemented a change program at AT&T aimed at shifting the culture of the giant to be more responsible and more flexible. Built around a set of values called "Our Common Bond," this planned change program is aimed at developing a foundation of ethical and business values which AT&T can build upon in all of its businesses. At its Universal Card subsidiary, which won the prestigious Malcolm Baldrige National Quality Award, a set of values like Our Common Bond was instrumental in developing a "can-do" employee attitude. →

portunities in its environment, while *renewal process* refers to the way managers adapt their problem-solving processes to the environment. One aim of OD is to improve an organization's self-renewal process so that managers can quickly adapt their management style to new problems and opportunities.

For Allan Willett, chairman and sole proprietor of Willett International, organizational development involved bringing in outside help. In ten years he built the company into a significant contender in the fast-paced product marking and coding business with an annual turnover near £50 million and a workforce of 600 employees around the world. He then recognized that the company had become more than he could handle alone. He therefore hired a group manager and organized a team of experienced professionals. "I had to let them be managers," he admitted. "To do that I had physically to depart from the scene."[18] Now he spends nine months of the year visiting overseas subsidiaries and distributors and concentrates on "the vision thing." The company nevertheless continues to thrive, and expanding the product base is an option currently under consideration.

Another aim of OD is the sharing of management power with employees, a goal indicated by the phrase *collaborative management*. **Collaborative management** means that managers put aside the hierarchial authority structure and let employees play a greater role in decision making. To carry out this change, managers must consciously change the organizational culture—the members' shared attitudes, beliefs, and activities.

**collaborative management:**
Management through power sharing and subordinate participation; the opposite of hierarchical imposition of authority.

421

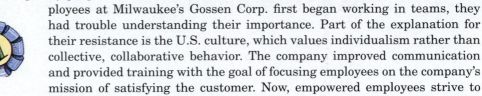

The development of teams and the empowerment of employees, both elements of quality programs, often result in a more collaborative approach. But when employees at Milwaukee's Gossen Corp. first began working in teams, they had trouble understanding their importance. Part of the explanation for their resistance is the U.S. culture, which values individualism rather than collective, collaborative behavior. The company improved communication and provided training with the goal of focusing employees on the company's mission of satisfying the customer. Now, empowered employees strive to identify customer requirements and develop processes that will fill those requirements. Rather than worrying about pleasing their boss, employees can focus entirely on the customer.[19]

A final key phrase, **action research,** refers to the way OD change agents go about learning what aspects of the organization need to be improved and how the organization can be helped to make these improvements. Briefly, action research involves (1) a preliminary diagnosis of the problem by OD change agents, (2) data gathering to support (or disprove) the diagnosis, (3) feedback of the data to organization members, (4) exploration of the data by organization members, (5) planning of appropriate action, and (6) taking appropriate action.

## TYPES OF OD ACTIVITIES

Change agents have many techniques and intervention approaches available to them, not all of which will be used in a given change program. One useful way of classifying these techniques is in terms of the target groups with which they might be employed. The techniques can be used to improve the effectiveness of individuals, the working relationship between two or three individuals, the functioning of groups, the relationship between groups, or the effectiveness of the total organization.[20]

**OD FOR THE INDIVIDUAL.** **Sensitivity training** was an early and fairly widespread OD technique. In "T" (training) groups, about ten participants are guided by a trained leader to increase their sensitivity to and skills in handling interpersonal relationships. Sensitivity training is less frequently used by organizations nowa-

**action research:**
The method through which organizational-development change agents learn what improvements are needed and how the organization can best be aided in making those improvements.

**sensitivity training:**
An early personal growth technique, at one time fairly widespread in organizational development efforts, that emphasizes increased sensitivity in interpersonal relationships.

**MEMBERS' SHARED ATTITUDES.** A commitment to quality is part of the organizational culture at Baldrige-winning Marlow Industries. In addition to "living" that commitment in their work, employees put their commitment in writing by signing Marlow's "Quality Pledge."

| TABLE 15-2 | Team Building Activities | |
|---|---|---|
| ACTIVITY | FAMILY GROUPS | SPECIAL GROUPS |
| Diagnosis | Diagnostic meetings: "How are we doing?" | Diagnostic meetings: "Where would we like to go?" |
| Task accomplishment | Problem solving, decision making, role clarification, goal setting, etc. | Special problems, role and goal clarification, resource utilization, etc. |
| Building and maintaining relationships | Focus on effective interpersonal relationships, including boss-subordinate and peer | Focus on interpersonal or interunit conflict and underutilization of other team members as resources |
| Management of group processes | Focus on understanding group processes and group culture | Focus on communication, decision making, and task allocations |
| Role analysis and role negotiation | Techniques used for role clarification and definition | Techniques used for role clarification and definition |

*Source:* Adapted from Wendell L. French and Cecil H. Bell, Jr., *Organization Development: Behavioral Science Interventions for Organization Improvement*, p. 104. Used by permission of Prentice Hall, Englewood Cliffs, N.J.

days, and participants are usually screened to make sure they can withstand the anxiety raised by a T group. Precautions are also taken to ensure that attendance is truly voluntary.[21]

**OD FOR TWO OR THREE PEOPLE.** **Transaction analysis (TA)** concentrates on styles and content of communication (transactions or messages) between people. It teaches people to send messages that are clear and responsible and to give responses that are natural and reasonable. Transactional analysis attempts to reduce destructive communication habits or "games" in which the intent or full meaning of messages is obscured.[22]

Pioneered by Eric Berne, TA encourages people to recognize the context of their communications. For example, sometimes the words of a boss's message to an employee sound pleasant, such as "Please have the report on Friday," but if the boss doesn't think Friday is a realistic deadline, the context of the message is "Now I've gotcha!" TA encourages people to be more open and honest and to address the contexts of their messages.

**OD FOR TEAMS OR GROUPS.** In **process consultation,** a consultant works with organization members to help them understand the dynamics of their working relationships in group or team situations. The consultant helps the group members to change the ways they work together and to develop the diagnostic and problem-solving skills they need for more effective problem solving.[23]

**Team building,** a related approach, analyzes the activities, resource allocations, and relationships of a group or team to improve its effectiveness. This technique can be used, for example, to develop a sense of unity among members of a new committee.[24] Team building can be directed at two different types of teams or working groups: an existing or permanent team made up of a manager and his or her employees, often called a *family group*; or a new group that either has been formed to solve a specific problem or has been created through a merger or other structural change in the organization, which we will call a *special group*.

For both kinds of groups, team-building activities aim at diagnosing barriers to effective team performance, improving task accomplishment, improving relationships between team members, and improving processes operative in the team, such as communication and task assignment. Table 15-2 summarizes these activities for both family and special groups.

**transaction analysis (TA):**
An approach to improving interpersonal effectiveness, sometimes used in organizational development efforts, that concentrates on the styles and content of communication.

**process consultation:**
A technique by which consultants help organization members understand and change the ways they work together.

**team building:**
A method of improving organizational effectiveness at the team level by diagnosing barriers to team performance and improving interteam relationships and task accomplishments.

Many management writers define *creativity* as the generation of a new idea and *innovation* as the translation of a new idea into a new company (Apple Computer), a new product (the Sony Walkman), a new service (Federal Express's overnight delivery), a new process (one waiting line for multiple services at a bank or amusement park), or a new method of production (computer-aided design and manufacturing).

Economic historian Joseph Schumpeter viewed innovation as the source of success in the market economy, a view that is reinforced by today's changing and competitive environment. The organization that is not creative and innovative may not survive. Thus, managers at more and more organizations are looking for ways to encourage and foster creativity and innovation on both the individual and the organizational level.[28]

Once known primarily for their ability to replicate and improve on the products of others (particularly U.S. products), the Japanese are demonstrating how to create cultures that nurture innovation. A 1991 study of 14 top U.S. and Japanese companies found that "the Japanese were more consistent across the board in their innovation practices. They plan like demons, execute brilliantly, and yet are constantly asking how they can do better.[29]

**A CREATIVE INDIVIDUAL.** Steve Wosniak, co-founder of Apple Computer, has a high degree of individual creativity. Typical qualities of creative people, such as a tendency to stick to their guns when their ideas are challenged, question authority, and work long and hard on something that intrigues them, are often crucial to getting new ideas off the ground.

## INDIVIDUAL CREATIVITY

Individuals differ in their ability to be creative. If asked to suggest possible uses for automobile tires, noncreative people might say "buoys" and "tree swings." Creative people might suggest such things as "eyeglass frames for an elephant" or "halos for big robots." Creative people also tend to be more flexible than noncreative people. They are able and willing to shift from one approach to another when tackling a problem. They prefer complexity to simplicity and tend to be more independent than less creative people, sticking to their guns stubbornly when their ideas are challenged. Creative people also question authority quite readily and are apt to disobey orders that make no sense to them. For this reason they may be somewhat difficult to manage in most organizations. Motivated more by an interesting problem than by material reward, they will work long and hard on something that intrigues them.

## ORGANIZATIONAL CREATIVITY AND INNOVATION

Just as individuals differ in their ability to translate their creative talents into results, organizations differ in their ability to translate the talents of their members into new products, processes, or services. To enable their organizations to use creativity most effectively, managers need to be aware of this process of innovation in organizations and to take steps to encourage this process. The creative process in organizations involves three steps: idea generation, problem solving or idea development, and implementation.[30]

**GENERATION OF IDEAS.** The generation of ideas in an organization depends first and foremost on the flow of people and information between the firm and its environment. For example, the vast majority of technological innovations have been made in response to conditions in the marketplace. If organization managers are unaware that there is potential demand for a new product or that there is dissatisfaction with already existing products, they are not likely to seek innovations.

Outside consultants and experts are important sources of information for managers, because they are frequently aware of new products, processes, or service developments in their field. New employees may have knowledge of alternative approaches or technologies used by suppliers and competitors. Among the organization's regular members, those who are constantly exposed to information outside

**INNOVATIVE SWISS WATCH.** For the Swiss watch industry, long famous for tradition and individual craftsmanship, the decision to compete in the lower-end watch market with colorful, trendy, inexpensive wristwatches was a creative and successful idea.

their immediate work setting are valuable sources of new ideas. These people, called "technological gatekeepers" by Thomas Allen, can play a particularly important role in stimulating creativity and innovation in research and development labs.[31]

According to Rosabeth Moss Kanter, the generation of ideas is more likely to promote innovation when those ideas issue from the grass-roots level of the organization. She argues that empowering people on the lower levels of organizations to initiate new ideas within the context of a supportive environment is a valuable means of implementing successful innovations.[32] In addition, although many new ideas challenge a company's cultural traditions, such innovative companies as Hewlett-Packard and Toyota nevertheless routinely encourage their employees to generate new ideas.[33]

**IDEA DEVELOPMENT.** Unlike idea generation, which is greatly stimulated by external contacts, idea development is dependent on the organizational culture and processes within the organization. Organizational characteristics, values, and processes can support or inhibit the development and use of creative ideas. Commitment to the rational problem-solving approaches discussed in Chapter 9 increases the likelihood that high-quality, creative ideas will be recognized and developed fully.

The organizational structure also plays an important role. Rigid organizational structures that inhibit communication between departments will often keep potentially helpful people from even knowing that a problem exists. By creating barriers to communication, rigidly structured organizations may also prevent problem solutions from reaching managers who need them. Management information systems (MIS), decision support systems (DDS), and expert systems store and retrieve generated ideas and aid managers in idea development.[34] Recent advances in the networking of such systems are especially helpful for integrative problem solving.

**IMPLEMENTATION.** The implementation stage of the creative process in organizations consists of those steps that bring a solution or invention to the marketplace. For manufactured goods, these steps include engineering, tooling, manufacturing, test marketing, and promotion. While a high rate of innovation often reduces short-term profitability, it is crucial for long-term growth. For example, the Swiss watch industry, which operates by traditional practices and old-fashioned individual craftsmanship, has been in decline since the mid-1970s, when more innovative competitors introduced new products such as digital watches into the market. When Swiss watchmakers recently introduced new products such as the popular, inexpensive Swiss wristwatch, they were able to regain part of a market that had appeared to be lost to them.

For innovation to be successful, a high degree of integration is required among the various units of the organization. Technical specialists, responsible for the engineering side of a new product, must work with administrative and financial specialists responsible for keeping the cost of innovation within practical limits. Production managers, helping to refine the specifications of the new product, must work with marketing managers, who are responsible for test marketing, advertising, and promoting it. Proper integration of all these groups is necessary for a quality innovation to be produced on time, on budget, and for a viable market. Managers at organizations that are too rigidly structured may have a difficult time integrating such activities. In contrast, frequent and informal communication across an organization has been shown to have positive effects on innovation.[35] For this reason, task forces (to be discussed in Chapter 18) and matrix-type organizational structures, which encourage interdepartmental communication and integration, are particularly suited for generating, developing, and implementing creative ideas and approaches.

EXHIBIT 15-1

**KANTER'S "TEN RULES FOR STIFLING INNOVATION"**

1. Regard any new idea from below with suspicion - because it's new, and because it's from below.
2. Insist that people who need your approval to act first go through several other levels of management to get their signatures.
3. Ask departments or individuals to challenge and criticize each other's proposals. (That saves you the job of deciding; you just pick the survivor.)
4. Express your criticisms freely, and withhold your praise. (That keeps people on their toes.) Let them know they can be fired at any time.
5. Treat identification of problems as signs of failure, to discourage people from letting you know when something in their area isn't working.
6. Control everything carefully. Make sure people count anything that can be counted, frequently.
7. Make decisions to reorganize or change policies in secret, and spring them on people unexpectedly. (That also keeps people on their toes.)
8. Make sure that requests for information are fully justified, and make sure that it is not given out to managers freely. (You don't want data to fall into the wrong hands.)
9. Assign to lower-level managers, in the name of delegation and participation, responsibility for figuring out how to cut back, lay off, move people around, or otherwise implement threatening decisions you have made. And get them to do it quickly.
10. And above all, never forget that you, the higher-ups, already know everything important about this business.

*Source:* Rosabeth Moss Kanter, *The Change Masters* (New York: Simon & Schuster, 1983), p. 101.

## ESTABLISHING A CLIMATE FOR ORGANIZATIONAL CREATIVITY AND INNOVATION

As we have seen, creativity is best nurtured in a permissive climate, one that encourages the exploration of new ideas and new ways of doing things. Many managers find it difficult to accept such a climate. They may be uncomfortable with a continuing process of change, which is the essential accompaniment of creativity. They may also be concerned that a permissive atmosphere encourages the breakdown of discipline or cost control.

### PROMOTING CREATIVITY THROUGH CULTURE AT XEROX

At Xerox's Palo Alto Research Center (PARC), organizational culture posed a potential obstacle to creativity. When Xerox chief scientist John Seely Brown, Ph.D., took over PARC in 1988 he found that the existing culture did not support continued radical innovation. Together with Elise Walton, Director at Delta Consulting Group, he has worked toward building a more appropriate cultural architecture. The starting point was a plan called Xerox 2000, which provided a strategic view of where the organization would be in the year 2000. Anthropologists were hired to study the organization. They uncovered many interesting discrepancies. For example, Xerox came face-to-face with what Brown calls the "notion of a double-bind—a self-cancelling, self-sealing set of beliefs." Xerox articulates

| EXHIBIT 15-2 | SOME PRESCRIPTIONS FOR FOSTERING ORGANIZATIONAL CREATIVITY |
|---|---|

1. *Develop an acceptance of change.* Organization members must believe that change will benefit them and the organization. This belief is more likely to arise if members participate with their managers in making decisions and if issues like job security are carefully handled when changes are planned and implemented (see our discussion on overcoming resistance to change earlier in this chapter).

2. *Encourage new ideas.* Organization managers, from the top to the lowest-level supervisors, must make it clear in word and deed that they welcome new approaches. To encourage creativity, managers must be willing to listen to subordinates' suggestions and to implement promising ones or convey them to higher-level managers.

3. *Permit more interaction.* A permissive, creative climate, is fostered by giving individuals the opportunity to interact with members of their own and other work groups. Such interaction encourages the exchange of useful information, the free flow of ideas, and fresh perspectives on problems.

4. *Tolerate failure.* Many new ideas prove impractical or useless. Effective managers accept and allow for the fact that time and resources will be invested in experimenting with new ideas that do not work out.

5. *Provide clear objectives and the freedom to achieve them.* Organization members must have a purpose and direction for their creativity. Supplying guidelines and reasonable constraints will also give managers some control over the amount of time and money invested in creative behavior.

6. *Offer recognition.* Creative individuals are motivated to work hard on tasks that interest them. But, like all individuals, they enjoy being rewarded for a task well done. By offering recognition in such tangible forms as bonus and salary increases, managers demonstrate that creative behavior is valued in their organizations.

commitment to teamwork, as evidenced by part of the company's logo, "Team Xerox," yet hero-worshipping is deeply embedded in the corporate culture. These inherently opposite cultural tenets caused dysfunctional behavior that worked against creativity. Management aimed therefore at adjusting the organizational "hardware"—structure, rewards, incentives, and so on—and launched the new organization through a program dubbed "Good Start." "The key challenge is a dichotomy," asserted Brown. "Keep the restructuring as simple as possible, but realize that the details matter."[36] The result is an organization comprising many new employees and many old employees in brand-new positions, but united by a common culture developed to be more supportive of rapid innovation. ▪

After studying attitudes and policies regarding innovation and creativity in a number of large organizations, Rosabeth Moss Kanter was able to describe the means by which some managers regularly stifled innovation and prevented employees from generating new ideas. She developed a list of ten managerial attitudes—contrasted with the appropriately counterproductive behavior—that she believes ensure the stifling of innovative efforts. Chapter 3 of her book, *The Change Masters*, addresses these ten "rules for stifling innovation," which are presented in Exhibit 15-1.

But what is the other side of the coin? How can managers accommodate their concerns about the effects of change and innovation to the increasing need to foster a climate that encourages creative participation by employees at various levels of the organization? Some positive steps—some possible answers to these questions—are listed in Exhibit 15-2.

one tradition I am happy to be without," she asserted. "This magazine is sort of a mare's-nest of strong hierarchies, yet it's non-hierarchical. Once you do a masthead you put one over another who never saw himself as over or under another. It's too complex, too weird. It would be a nightmare. It would only encourage the management to halve the staff, so I prefer not to do it."[53]

The overall effect of Brown's changes appears to have been positive for *The New Yorker*. According to Eric Utne, a writer for *Columbia Journalism Review,* "She has given it a face lift without changing it beyond recognition."[54] She has revitalized the staff and reinvigorated readers. "What's interesting is that some of the earlier writers who seemed burned out have come back to life," Gould remarked.[55] Part of her success perhaps has resulted from the free reign she's been given by Florio. "She's far and away the best editor I've ever worked with," he praised. "A big part of my job is to encourage her and then stand back and watch her test the envelope."[56]

Though Brown may aim for perfection, it is not what she expects. "Any new administration is going to make mistakes," she admitted. "The alternative is to not be alive. The alternative is to just be safe, to treat the magazine like a stuffed owl of which I'm the curator."[57] But that is not Brown's style. "I don't intend to be a curator," she stated. "I intend to be an editor."[58]

### CASE QUESTIONS

1. Was planned change needed at *The New Yorker*?
2. Describe the organizational culture at *The New Yorker,* before and after Brown took over.
3. How has Brown influenced the magazine's creativity?
4. What could Brown have done differently?

## VIDEO CASE STUDY

### UNITED'S NEW OWNERS: UNITED[59]

The early 1990s witnessed a startling new trend among businesses: mass layoffs. Numerous headlines told of once great companies such as IBM that were having to institute tremendous labor cuts to become more competitive. More and more companies decided to downsize. Widespread layoffs, however, resulted in decreased worker productivity and poorer job performance. Fear of job loss caused employees to take less initiative and offer fewer suggests. In the meantime, employee-ownership emerged as an alternative to massive corporate downsizing. It enables companies to reduce costs and increase productivity without having to resort to layoffs. Between 1979 and 1994, the number of employee-owned companies skyrocketed from less than 1,000 to more than 11,000.

United Airlines was one company that chose employee ownership. In December 1993, United Airlines chairman Stephen M. Wolf struck a deal with union leaders to sell control of the $14 billion airline to its employees in exchange for more than $5 billion in wage and benefit reductions and work concessions. According to the agreement, almost all of United's 80,000 employees would experience a wage reduction and would accept longer work hours and an unpaid lunch break. In return, employees were to receive job security and stock worth between $40,000 and $72,434 (depending upon United's fate in the stock market) per member. Most importantly, however, the employees would collectively own 53 percent of United's common stock. In effect, they would control the company. Assuming the details could be worked out, United would become the largest and most complex employee-owned company.

A variety of factors led to this agreement. Between 1991 and 1993, United lost $1.3 billion, even though the airline was carrying more people to more places than ever before. United's market share was climbing and the number of empty seats was falling, but the company's profitability was nevertheless suffering. United's future seemed bleak if it could not find a way to reduce costs drastically. "We slashed and burned and did everything we could," said J. C. Pope, president of United. "It wasn't enough."[60]

Actually, United was suffering from the same problems that almost all major carriers had been dealing with since the 1978 deregulation of the airline industry, which permitted competition between the large, established carriers and the low-cost, budget airlines. "There is a secular change in our society," Wolf commented. "The American consumer wants safe, reliable transportation, but they want low fares. There is a certain prudence in the American consumer, whether you are wealthy or not so wealthy. That is, I just want to go somewhere. … Why do I want to spend a lot of money just getting from here to there?"[61] In fact, in the 15 years following deregulation, no airline had been able to reduce labor costs without resorting to threats of downsizing or bankruptcy protection. In some cases, the costs did not go down until the threats turned into reality. Wolf did not want that to happen at United.

In addition, severe labor-management relation problems had been dogging the airline. During the mid-1980s, United's pilots instituted a massive strike that ultimately resulted in Richard Ferris being ousted as chairman of UAL Corp., United's parent company. In December 1993, immediately prior to the agreement to transfer company ownership to United's employees, mechanics at the San Francisco airport carried a coffin with Wolf's name on it across the tarmac. In fact, the union had decided that Wolf was going to have to go. "The principal reason I feel Mr. Wolf should not be CEO is that in talking to him,

I just don't think his mind-set fits into employee ownership," explained Roger Hall, head of the United pilots' union. "Wolf is someone who is in control and wants to direct. He doesn't seem so interested in input from the employees."[62]

In light of this, Wolf made a decision. The only way to gain union support of his cost reduction plan was to offer employee ownership to United's workers, and the only way to achieve employee ownership was for him to leave. He realized that the changes necessary for United's survival would not come about if he remained as CEO. He thus left the company in order to save it. "Would I like to sit here and ride that stagecoach?" Wolf mused. "Of course. But that's just not in the cards."[63] The only way for Wolf to succeed as a manager was to leave. He had the insight, but it was up to others to carry out his plans.

Wolf placed great confidence in the idea of employee ownership and the concept of empowerment. When employees have a vested interest in the company, they work harder, smarter, and enjoy work more. "The associated benefits [of employee ownership] are truly significant," Wolf remarked. "it takes away labor animus. You are now owners of the company. You understand the reality of stock going up and what it means for yourself."[64]

## CASE QUESTIONS

1. What external environmental conditions are having an impact on United?
2. What internal conditions are having an impact on United?
3. How would you describe the type of change that is taking place?
4. Has Wolf done the right thing?
5. What other changes could he have made?

# Leading

# INTERSECTION 5

The challenge of envisioning a desired future for an organization and moving the organization into that future is a central task of management. This is the challenge of *planning* (Part III) and *organizing* (Part IV). Still, it is not by any means a forgone conclusion that a sensible strategic plan and a sensible organizational structure will result in the fulfillment of organizational goals. To translate these decisions into actions and sustain them, managers must be prepared to encourage and support the people who carry out the plans and work within the structures. This managerial effort to keep people focused on the goals for an organization is the process of *leading.* Leading, the subject of Part V, is about the *human skills* of management.

Because strategic plans take time to implement, Motivation (Chapter 16) is important for keeping people focused on goals, and Leadership (Chapter 17) is essential for keeping group members working in union. And because strategic plans are carried out by people working in a world of complex relationships that can change over time, groups are not automatically cohesive units, and the flow of vital information can at times be impeded. We address these concerns with Teams and Teamwork (Chapter 18) and Communication and Negotiation (Chapter 19).

## CHAPTER 16

# MOTIVATION

**Upon completing this chapter, you should be able to:**

1. Explain why managers and researchers have been so interested in motivation.

2. Define motivation and motivating.

3. Explain the basic assumptions of motivation processes in organizations.

4. Identify five contemporary motivation theories and trace their origins.

5. Differentiate among five contemporary motivation theories.

6. Discuss current challenges to managers' motivating practices.

# WAL-MART: A MODEL IN MOTIVATION[1]

Sam [Walton, CEO of Wal-Mart] whips out his primary tool of empowerment, his tape recorder. "I'm here in Memphis at store 950, and Georgie has done a real fine thing with this endcap display of Equate Baby Oil. I'd like to try this everywhere." Georgie blushes with pride.

A manager rushes up with an associate in tow.

"Mr. Walton, I want you to meet Renee. She runs one of the top ten pet departments in the country."

"Well, Renee, bless your heart. What percentage of the store (sales) are you doing?"

"Last year it was 3.1 percent," Renee says, "but this year I'm trying for 3.3 percent."[2]

This situation, as recalled by *Fortune* reporter John Huey, typifies the management style of Sam Walton, founder of and inspiration behind Wal-Mart. For many years, such situations were commonplace as Walton and his tape recorder visited stores around the country. Until the organization became too big, he visited every Wal-Mart store at least once a year.

"Right now there are probably about 30 stores I've never been to and a bunch of others I haven't seen in more than a little while," said Walton in the fall of 1991. "I've got to get to 'em soon."[3] From one store in 1962, he developed his organization into a $40 billion enterprise by the time of his death 30 years later. Walton never lost the personal touch. He was adored by his employees and took every step necessary, including buying airplanes for the Wal-Mart "air force," to remain close with the people he claimed were responsible for his company's success.

> *Walton never lost the personal touch. He was adored by his employees....*

Visiting stores was as important to Walton as it was to the workers, who received a personal connection to management. "This is still the most important thing I do, going around to the stores, and I'd rather do it than anything I know of. I know I'm helping our folks when I get out to the stores. I learn a lot about who's doing good things in the office, and I also see things that need fixing, and I help fix them. Any good management person in retail has got to do what I do in order to keep his finger on what's going on. You've got to have the right chemistry and the right attitude on the part of the folks who deal with the customers."[4]

Walton's tape recorder—his "tool of empowerment"—was a constant reminder that Walton and Wal-Mart cared and listened. His taping of impromptu conversations with people at various stores not only served to refresh Walton's recollection later and remind him of things that needed to be done, but also immediately demonstrated that he was listening to what his colleagues had to say. Perhaps most important about these taped conversations, however, is that he later acted upon what he found out. If employees expressed dissatisfaction with their supervisors, Walton would often good-naturedly assure them, "Don't worry, I'll kick his butt."[5] In addition, Walton treated people with

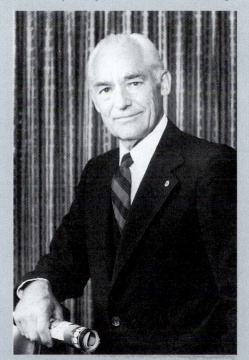

**WAL-MART'S GREAT MOTIVATOR.** Wal-mart founder Sam Walton's ability to motivate his workforce was legendary.

respect. To start with, workers are called "associates," not employees. This indicates that these men and women have a substantial stake in the company.

"What sets us apart is that we train people to be merchants," said Walton. "We let them see all the numbers so they know exactly how they're doing within the store and within the company; they know their costs, their mark-up, their overhead, and their profit. It's a big responsibility and a big opportunity. You give a pet department to someone like Renee, and she gets at it. She learns that what's important is buying stuff four gross at a time and then selling four gross. Nobody gets anything out of just standing there going through the motions."[6]

Walton realized that all the cheerleading in the world could not feed an associate's family; therefore, he included financial incentives to keep associates happy. Profit-sharing, incentive bonus, and stock purchase plans linked associates to Wal-Mart's financial success. "I know your backs are sore, and your feet hurt, but this is one of the very best Wal-Mart stores in the U.S., and no other stores have this much fun. Has sharing the profits with you made the difference? [A deafening YES! here.] A lot of companies would have shared them with the stockholders, but as you know, we don't pay much dividend."[7]

Walton will always be remembered for the level of motivation he achieved from his Wal-Mart workforce. Indeed, Wal-Mart stands as a model that many strive to emulate. "Because of what he has done, virtually every consumer in this country is better off," said retail analyst Kurt Barnard. "Giant corporations in the world of industry send their key executives to Bentonville, Arkansas, to learn how it is done."[8] →

# THE CHALLENGE OF MOTIVATION

**motivation:**

The factors that cause, channel, and sustain an individual's behavior.

**M**anagers and management researchers have long believed that organizational goals are unattainable without the enduring commitment of members of the organization. **Motivation** is a human psychological characteristic that contributes to a person's degree of commitment. It includes the factors that cause, channel, and sustain human behavior in a particular committed direction. *Motivating* is the management process of influencing people's behavior based on this knowledge of "what makes people tick." Motivation and motivating both deal with the range of conscious human behavior somewhere between two extremes: (1) reflex actions, such as a sneeze or flutter of the eyelids; and (2) learned habits, such as brushing one's teeth or handwriting style.[9] This range of behavior is shown in Figure 16-1.

## BASIC ASSUMPTIONS ABOUT MOTIVATION AND MOTIVATING

You need to understand several basic assumptions as we delve into theories of motivation and motivational practices by managers.

First, *motivation is commonly assumed to be a good thing.* Do you ever hear people praised for being *un*motivated? We are taught in a variety of settings (including school, church, family, work, and organized sports) that you can't feel very good about yourself if you are unmotivated. Wal-Mart puts this assumption about motivation into daily practice.

Second, *motivation is one of several factors that goes into a person's performance.* Important, too, are such factors as ability, resources, and conditions under which one performs. You can be highly motivated to pursue a career helping peo-

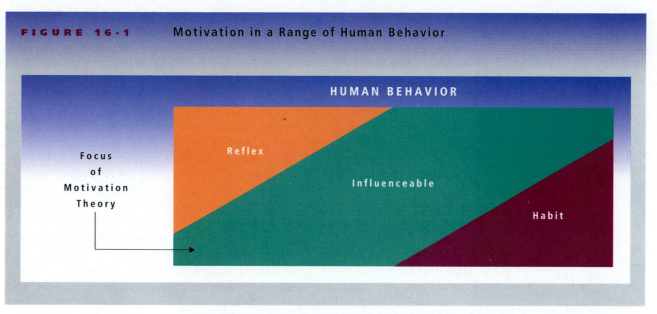

**FIGURE 16-1**     Motivation in a Range of Human Behavior

HUMAN BEHAVIOR

Focus of Motivation Theory

Reflex

Influenceable

Habit

*Source:* This figure draws on ideas presented in F. Landy and W. Becker, "Motivational Theory Reconsidered." In L. Cummings and B. Staw (eds.), *Research in Organizational Behavior,* Volume 9 (Greenwich, CT: JAI Press, 1987): 1–38.

ple as a medical professional. But to that motivation must be added your scientific ability, learning resources at your college (such as up-to-date laboratories), and such conditions as regular access to your professors. Wal-Mart associates get latitude to act—a kind of resource—in addition to receiving motivational messages from their supervisors.

Third, managers and researchers alike assume that *motivation is in short supply and in need of periodic replenishment.* Motivation is like the heat in a house during winter months in Northern climates. Because heat gradually escapes, the furnace must cycle on frequently to maintain the warmth of the house. Motivation theory and motivational practices deal with processes that never really end, based on the assumption that motivation can "escape" over time. Sam Walton tried to replenish employee motivation frequently.

Fourth, *motivation is a tool with which managers can arrange job relationships in organizations.* If managers know what drives the people working for them, they can tailor job assignments and rewards to what makes these people "tick." Thus, knowledge about motivation joins strategic plans (Chapter 10) as inputs into the process of designing relationships at organizations (Chapter 12) and distributing power in those work relationships (Chapter 13). The Wal-Mart store visits and the responsibility given to associates are two cases in point.

All these assumptions run deep in the discussion about the evolution of motivation theory that follows the example below. At the same time, these assumptions are not necessarily timeless. Current challenges to them are the subject of the "Management 2000 and Beyond" discussion with which we close this chapter.

## OWNERSHIP IS MOTIVATING AT SPRINGFIELD REMANUFACTURING CORP.

At Springfield Remanufacturing Corp. (SRC), survival was a key motivating force. Once a part of International Harvester, Springfield was cut loose by the financially troubled parent. Harvester offered to sell the company to the former employees, who accepted the challenge, even though they would have a large debt load. The 119 new owners—managers, supervisors, and workers—set out to enter what they termed the "great game of business."

Two slogans guided their actions and motivated them: "You get what you give" and "It's easy to stop one guy, but pretty hard to stop 119." To play the game successfully, they felt, they needed to think in untraditional ways about how a company should be run. Their idea was that at the heart of the game of business is the simple proposition that "the best, most efficient, most profitable way to operate a business is to give everyone in the company a voice in saying how the company is run and a stake in the financial outcome, good or bad." The rewards of the game are continuous improvement in the life and livelihood of everyone involved.

SRC remanufactures engines and engine components, a noisy, dirty business. The key to the success and growth was educating all the employees about the business and sharing knowledge so that everyone could do his or her job as well as possible. New recruits to the company are told that only 70 percent of the job is disassembly or other tasks; the other 30 percent is learning. All receive basic financial training on understanding and making money. The training is reinforced at meetings designed to promote team spirit and help everyone make sense of the business.

The employees are motivated by four rules of the game:

1. *We want to live up to our end of the employment bargain.*
2. *We want to do away with jobs.* The idea is for people not to get caught up psychologically in a do-the-same-job routine but to seek challenge by thinking about where they want to go in their work and what they want to do with their lives.
3. *We want to get rid of the "employee" mentality.* Each person thinks and acts like an owner.
4. *We want to create and distribute wealth.* Productivity will improve as the Springfield team works to create an organization that continuously improves and where people do more to help one another.

Springfield Remanufacturing owners take a traditional factory with most processes based on Taylor's scientific management and gives it new life with a new focus. Springfield owners know what motivates them: They strive to succeed for themselves, their team, their company, and their society.[10]  ▬

## THEORIES OF MOTIVATION: AN OVERVIEW

**T**here are many motivation theories.[11] Each motivation theory attempts to describe what human beings are and what human beings can become. For this reason, it is customary to say that a motivation theory has *content* in the form of a particular view about people. The content of a motivation theory helps us understand the world of *dynamic engagement* in which organizations operate by depicting managers and employees *engaging* in organizations every day. Since motivation theories deal with people's development, the content of a motivation theory also helps managers and employees wrestle with the *dynamics* of organizational life.

← ch. 2, p. 49

Frank Landy and Wendy Becker observe that motivation research is still a vigorous contest for finding "one best way" to think about motivation.[12] Thus, one of the major themes in this chapter is that you will encounter different motivational practices in your life. We encourage you to think of this chapter as a sampler of ideas about what motivation involves.[13]

**ACKNOWLEDGING SOCIAL NEEDS.** At Baldrige-winning Marlow Industries, family picnics with activities for all ages help to build camaraderie among employees.

## EARLY VIEWS OF MOTIVATION

← ch. 2, p. 34

Motivation was one of the earliest concepts with which managers and management researchers wrestled. A so-called *traditional model* is often associated with Frederick Taylor and scientific management. Managers determined the most efficient way to perform repetitive tasks and then motivated workers with a system of wage incentives—the more workers produced, the more they earned. The underlying assumption was that managers understood the work better than workers, who were essentially lazy and could be motivated only by money. A legacy of this model is the practice of paying salespersons on a commission basis.

← ch. 2, p. 42

A so-called *human relations model* is often associated with Elton Mayo and his contemporaries. Mayo and other human relations researchers found that the boredom and repetitiveness of many tasks actually reduced motivation, while social contacts helped create and sustain motivation. The conclusion is that managers could motivate employees by acknowledging their social needs and by making them feel useful and important. Modern-day legacies of this model include suggestion boxes, company uniforms, organization newsletters, and employee input in the performance evaluation process. We see this at Wal-Mart.

Under the traditional model, workers had been expected to accept management's authority in return for high wages. Under the human relations model, workers were expected to accept management's authority because supervisors treated them with consideration and allowed them to influence the work situation. Note that the intent of managers remained the same: to get workers to accept the work situation as established by managers.

A so-called *human resources model* is often associated with Douglas McGregor. McGregor and other theorists criticized the human relations model as simply a more sophisticated approach to the manipulation of employees. They also charged that, like the traditional model, the human relations model oversimplified motivation by focusing on just one factor, such as money or social relations.

**TABLE 16-1**     **Early Views of Motivation**

| TRADITIONAL MODEL | HUMAN RELATIONS MODEL | HUMAN RESOURCES MODEL |
|---|---|---|
| **Assumptions** | | |
| 1. Work is inherently distasteful to most people. | 1. People want to feel useful and important. | 1. Work is not inherently distasteful. People want to contribute to meaningful goals that they have helped establish. |
| 2. What they do is less important than what they earn for doing it. | 2. People want to belong and to be recognized as individuals. | 2. Most people can exercise far more creativity, self-direction, and self-control than their present jobs demand. |
| 3. Few want or can handle work that requires creativity, self-direction, or self-control. | 3. These needs are more important than money in motivating people to work. | |
| **Policies** | | |
| 1. The manager should closely supervise and control subordinates. | 1. The manager should make each worker feel useful and important. | 1. The manager should make use of underutilized human resources. |
| 2. He or she must break down tasks into simple, repetitive, easily learned operations. | 2. He or she should keep subordinates informed and listen to their objections to his or her plans. | 2. He or she must create an environment in which all members may contribute to the limits of their ability. |
| 3. He or she must establish detailed work routines and procedures, and enforce these fairly but firmly. | 3. The manager should allow subordinates to exercise some self-direction and self-control on routine matters. | 3. He or she must encourage full participation in important matters, continually broadening subordinate self-direction and self-control. |
| **Expectations** | | |
| 1. People can tolerate work if the pay is decent and the boss is fair. | 1. Sharing information with subordinates and involving them in routine decisions will satisfy their basic needs to belong and to feel important. | 1. Expanding subordinate influence, self-direction, and self-control will lead to direct improvements in operating efficiency. |
| 2. If tasks are simple enough and people are closely controlled, they will produce up to standard. | 2. Satisfying these needs will improve morale and reduce resistance to formal authority—subordinates will "willingly cooperate." | 2. Work satisfaction may improve as a "by-product" of subordinates' making full use of their resources. |

Source: Adapted from Richard M. Steers and Lyman W. Porter, eds., *Motivation and Work Behavior*, 3rd ed. (New York: McGraw-Hill, 1983), p. 14. Copyright 1983 by McGraw-Hill, Inc., publisher of the English edition. Reproduced by permission.

← ch. 2, p. 44

As discussed in Chapter 2, McGregor identified two different sets of assumptions about employees. The traditional view, known as Theory X, holds that people have an inherent dislike of work. Although workers may view it as a necessity, they will avoid it whenever possible. In this view, most people prefer to be directed and to avoid responsibility. As a result, the work is of secondary importance, and managers must push employees to work.

Theory Y is more optimistic. It assumes that work is as natural as play or rest. In Theory Y, people want to work and can derive a great deal of satisfaction from work. In this view, people have the capacity to accept—even seek—responsibility and to apply imagination, ingenuity, and creativity to organizational problems.[14]

The problem, according to Theory Y, is that modern industrial life does not fully tap the potential of human beings. To take advantage of their employees' innate willingness and ability to work, managers using Theory Y should provide a climate that gives employees scope for personal improvement. *Participative management* is one way to do this.

These three earlier views of motivation are summarized in Table 16-1.

## CONTEMPORARY VIEWS OF MOTIVATION

Landy and Becker have sorted the many modern approaches to motivation theory and practice into five categories: need theory, reinforcement theory, equity theory, expectancy theory, and goal-setting theory.[15] This is the sampler we present in this chapter.

Each of these views enables managers and their employees to fill in the following statement in a different way: "A person is motivated when he or she _____." What is *common* to all of these five views, nonetheless, is the crucial role of a person's awareness of what is important to him or her and the circumstances in which he or she works.[16] Throughout this chapter we invite you to try using each model to describe your life as a student.

### NEED THEORY

**need theory:**
Theory of motivation that addresses what people need or require to live fulfilling lives, particularly with regard to work.

**Need theory** has a long-standing tradition in motivation research and practice. As the term suggests, need theory focuses on what people require to live fulfilling lives. In practice, need theory deals with the part work plays in meeting such needs.

According to need theory, a person is motivated *when he or she has not yet attained certain levels of satisfaction* with his or her life. A satisfied need is not a motivator. There are various need theories, which differ regarding what those levels are and when satisfaction is actually reached. The basic logic of any need theory is depicted in Figure 16-2.

**Maslow's hierarchy of needs:**
Theory of motivation that people are motivated to meet five types of needs, which can be ranked in a hierarchy.

**MASLOW'S HIERARCHY OF NEEDS. Maslow's hierarchy of needs,** developed by Abraham Maslow, has probably received more attention from managers than any other theory of motivation. Maslow viewed human motivation as a hierarchy of five needs, ranging from the most basic physiological needs to the highest needs for self-actualization (see Figure 16-3).[17] According to Maslow, individuals will be motivated to fulfill whichever need is *prepotent*, or most powerful, for them at a given time. The prepotency of a need depends on the individual's current situation and recent experiences. Starting with the physical needs, which are most basic,

**FIGURE 16-2**     A Need Theory of Motivation

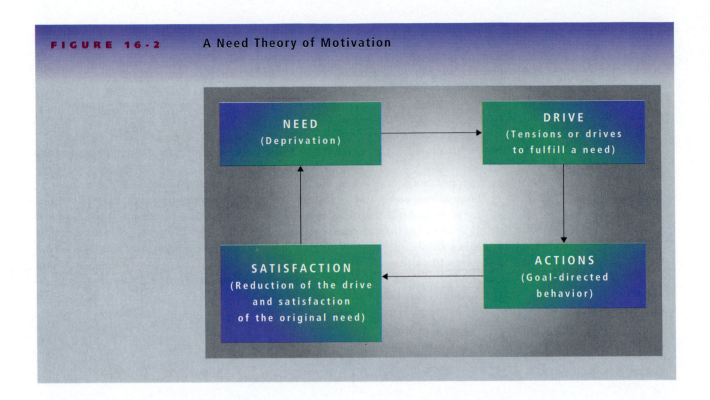

**FIGURE 16-3**     Pyramid Representing Maslow's Hierarchy of Needs

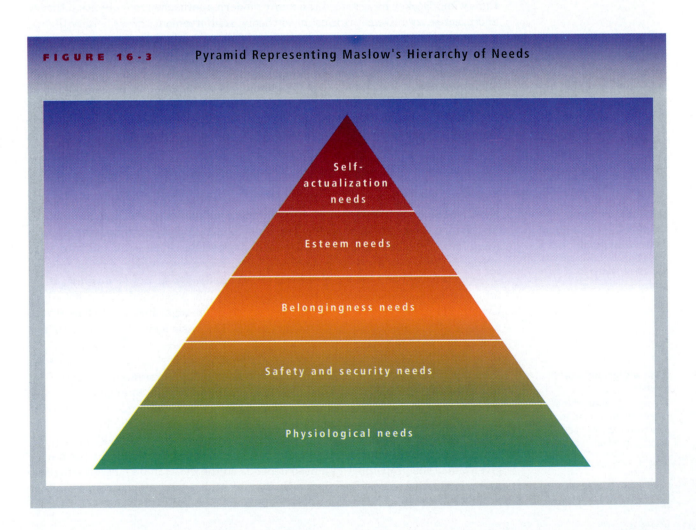

each need must be satisfied before the individual desires to satisfy a need at the next higher level.

## MEETING THE NEEDS OF THE HOMELESS

In our society, we have long assumed that almost everyone can meet his or her most basic needs. In recent times, however, as the number of homeless men, women, and children has grown, this can no longer be assumed. At two organizations, managers have attempted in novel ways to assist people fulfill their most basic needs. Both programs involve hiring homeless persons.[18] In both cases, the idea is to help people get in on the "ground floor" of Maslow's hierarchy.

The first well-publicized organization to hire the homeless was *Street News*, a monthly newspaper based in Manhattan. Launched in November 1989 by Hutchinson Persons, a former rock musician, as a nonprofit, charitable venture, all of the paper's resources and office space were donated by Manhattan businesses. *Street News*, usually a 28-page tabloid, featured a mix of news stories and celebrity interviews.

Homeless vendors received 50 cents from each 75-cent paper they sold and deposited 5 cents per paper in a mandatory apartment savings plan. Within four months, 200 homeless people had saved enough money to move into their own rooms and apartments.

Days Inn of America is another organization that has a work program for what it calls "special-sector people"—the homeless, the elderly, and the disabled. The program, which employs these workers as reservation sales clerks, has been growing since 1985. Most of the homeless employees are drawn from shelters for battered women. Because most of these women don't have job skills or previous experience in an office situation, Days Inns provides classroom instruction and on-the-job training. ▪▬

An obvious conclusion of Maslow's theory is that employees first need a wage sufficient to feed, shelter, and protect them and their families satisfactorily, as well as a safe working environment. Then their security needs must be met—job security, freedom from coercion or arbitrary treatment, and clearly defined regulations. Then managers can offer incentives designed to provide employees with esteem, feelings of belonging, or opportunities to grow.

According to Maslow, when all other needs have been adequately met, employees will become motivated by the need for *self-actualization*. They will look for meaning and personal growth in their work and will actively seek out new responsibilities. Maslow stresses that individual differences are greatest at this level. For some individuals, producing work of high quality is a means for self-actualization, while for others, developing creative, useful ideas serves the same need. By being aware of the different self-actualization needs of their employees, managers can use a variety of approaches to enable employees to achieve personal as well as organizational goals.[19]

Need theory is a challenge for managers to practice for two reasons. First, any manager works in a complex web of relationships with people whose needs probably differ widely. These differences are all the more pronounced in an era of global business conducted across cultural "borders." Geert Hofstede, whose 1973 study of the differences in motivation and business practices in various cultures was introduced in Chapter 5, concluded that Maslow's hierarchy of needs does not describe a universal human motiva-

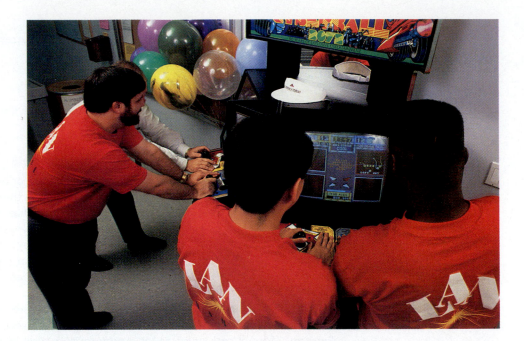

**BELONGINGNESS NEEDS.** Workplace amenities such as a game room can contribute to employees' social needs and feelings of belonging. According to Maslow, this type of motivator can be effective once more basic physical and security needs have been met.

tional process. Rather, it is the description of a specific value system—namely, that of the American middle class.[20] Thus people in cultures that have other value systems may be concerned about social or self-esteem needs before security needs become a major focus of their activities.

Second, any one person's needs can change over time. Although Maslow thought in terms of people progressing *up* his hierarchy, sometimes circumstances dictate moving *down* the hierarchy. A recent *Wall Street Journal* report gives an example of this among "survivors" of corporate downsizing. These people's esteem, belonging, and even security needs can quickly become unsatisfied, even though they retain their jobs.[21] You can have very meaningful work but still, as you see your co-workers fired, worry "am I next to go?" That's a question about your basic security needs.

**ERG theory:**
Theory of motivation that says people strive to meet a hierarchy of existence, relatedness, and growth needs; if efforts to reach one level of needs are frustrated, individuals will regress to a lower level.

**ERG THEORY.** Clayton Alderfer agreed with Maslow that worker motivation could be gauged according to a hierarchy of needs. However, his **ERG theory** differs from Maslow's theory in two basic ways.[22]

First, Alderfer broke needs down into just three categories: *Existence* needs (Maslow's fundamental needs), *relatedness* needs (needs for interpersonal relations), and *growth* needs (needs for personal creativity or productive influence). The first letters of each category form the acronym ERG. Some research indicates that workers themselves tend to categorize their needs much as Alderfer does.[23]

Second, and more important, Alderfer stressed that when higher needs are frustrated, lower needs will return, even though they were already satisfied. Maslow, in contrast, felt that a need, once met, lost its power to motivate behavior. Where Maslow saw people moving steadily up the hierarchy of needs, Alderfer saw people moving up and down the hierarchy of needs from time to time and from situation to situation. This, again, is a phenomenon that is all too familiar to people affected by corporate downsizing in recent years.

**THREE NEEDS.** John W. Atkinson has proposed three basic drives in motivated persons: the need for achievement, the need for power, and the need for affiliation, or close association with others. The balance between these drives varies from person to person. For example, one person might have a strong need for affiliation, while another might have a strong need for achievement.[24]

**MEASURING NEED FOR ACHIEVEMENT.** In the test McClelland used to measure achievement needs, individuals are shown ambiguous pictures and then make up stories about the pictures. McClelland and his associates then analyze the stories to assess the degree of achievement they project.

David C. McClelland's research has indicated that a strong need for achievement—the drive to succeed or excel—is related to how well individuals are motivated to perform their work tasks. People with a high need for achievement like to take responsibility for solving problems; they tend to set moderately difficult goals for themselves and take calculated risks to meet those goals; and they greatly value feedback on how well they are doing.[25] Thus, those with *high achievement needs (nAch)* tend to be highly motivated by challenging and competitive work situations; people with low achievement needs tend to perform poorly in the same sort of situations.[26]

There is considerable evidence of the correlation between high achievement needs and high performance. McClelland found, for example, that people who succeeded in competitive occupations were well above average in achievement motivation. Successful managers, who presumably operated in one of the most competitive of all environments, had a higher achievement need than other professionals.[27] McClelland's work indicates that need for achievement resides in managers and non-managers alike.

The need for affiliation—*nAff*, in McClelland's scheme—has been a concern of managers since Elton Mayo and his colleagues were involved in the famous Hawthorne experiments. The need for affiliation has been cited as a reason why "telecommuting"—working from one's home via telecommunications lines to the office—has not become as widespread in urban areas as once predicted. Many people, not surprisingly, *want* to be around their co-workers![28]

The need for power—*nPow*, in McClelland's scheme—deals with the degree of control a person desires over his or her situation. This need can be related to how people deal with failure and success. *Fear of failure*, and an erosion of one's power, can be a strong motivator for some people.[29] Conversely, for some people, *fear of success* can be a motivating factor.[30] We have all read stories about celebrities such as musicians, actresses, or professional athletes who, once they have achieved certain levels of fame and fortune, bemoan the intrusions in their lives—which reduce their sense of power or control.

For managers, this work by McClelland and others highlights the importance of matching the individual and the job. Employees with high achievement needs thrive on work that is challenging, satisfying, stimulating, and complex. They welcome autonomy, variety, and frequent feedback from supervisors. Employees with low achievement needs prefer situations of stability, security, and predictability. They respond better to consideration than to impersonal, high-pressure supervision, and they look to the workplace and co-workers for social satisfaction.

**ENCOURAGING A HIGH ACHIEVER.** John Allegretti (center) convinced Hyatt Vice President Don DePorter (left) to let him head a recycling project. It worked out so well that Hyatt let Allegretti develop and run a new waste-consulting company for Hyatt, called ReCycleCo Inc. Hyatt President Thomas J. Pritzker (right) encourages such staff suggestions.

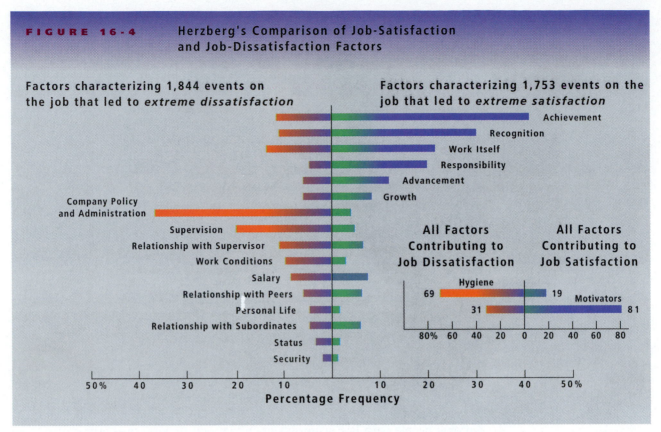

**FIGURE 16-4**   Herzberg's Comparison of Job-Satisfaction and Job-Dissatisfaction Factors

McClelland's research also suggests that managers can, to some extent, raise the achievement need level of employees by creating the proper work environment. Managers can do this by permitting employees a measure of independence, increasing responsibility and autonomy, gradually making tasks more challenging, and praising and rewarding high performance.[31]

**THE TWO-FACTOR THEORY OF MOTIVATION.** In the late 1950s, Frederick Herzberg and his associates conducted a study of the job attitudes of 200 engineers and accountants. As Figure 16-4 shows, Herzberg placed responses in one of 16 categories: the factors on the right side of the figure were consistently related to *job satisfaction*; those on the left side to *job dissatisfaction*. From this research, Herzberg concluded that job dissatisfaction and job satisfaction arose from two separate sets of factors. This theory was termed the **two-factor theory.**[32]

*Dissatisfiers* (which he called "hygiene" factors) included salary, working conditions, and company policy—all of which affected the *context* in which work was conducted. The most important of these factors is company policy, which many individuals judge to be a major cause of inefficiency and ineffectiveness. Positive ratings for these factors did not lead to job satisfaction but merely to the absence of dissatisfaction.

*Satisfiers* (motivating factors) include achievement, recognition, responsibility, and advancement—all related to the job *content* and the rewards of work performance.

Herzberg's work was influential in the growth of job enrichment programs. This more complicated model of needs—whereby both satisfiers and dissatisfiers can be present for a person—underscores how important it is that managers understand differences between human beings when designing motivational approaches. For evidence of how needs vary among people and over time, talk to your

**two-factory theory:**
Herzberg's theory that work dissatisfaction and satisfaction arise from two different sets of factors.

← ch. 13, p. 366

classmates, friends, colleagues at work, and professors about satisfiers and dis-satisfiers in their lives—and then do it again a year from now.

**SUMMARY OF NEED THEORY.** Each of the need theories we have summarized em-phasizes the satisfaction of some important personal needs that people have ac-quired over time. Each theory also emphasizes that people decide on their degree of satisfaction by consciously comparing their circumstances with their needs. Finally, each theory leaves room for considerable variation from person to person, and "within" a person over time.

Wal-Mart managers consistently act as if they have studied these various ver-sions of need theory. Giving associates responsibility in their store areas is re-sponsive to self-actualization needs. Some Wal-Mart policies seemed to be aimed at potential job dissatisfiers. Achievement, affiliation, and power needs can all be met by Wal-Mart policies. "Lower" needs, such as financial security, are part of the motivation equation at Wal-Mart, too.

← ch. 8, p. 211

## TQM AND NEEDS THEORY

An effective quality program depends on motivated employees. Fortunately, when we think about needs theory we can see how elements of a TQM program itself might build that motivation. Such a program engages everyone in the organization in the quality effort and seeks to reward people on a number of levels. For employees, developing creative ap-proaches to once-routine work, having your ideas respected and implemented, con-tributing to a high-quality product, and being valued as an expert in your field are all factors that can meet needs and build motivation. Add financial incentives to that mix, and a dedicated, motivated employee group can develop.

When Fort Sanders Health System, based in Knoxville, Tennessee, decided to estab-lish a quality program, an 11-week pilot program was developed to get people in-volved once the organization had sense of how and where quality improvements were needed. A "team alliance" program was established to test how the employees felt about the potential changes in the organization. Voluntary teams were established throughout the organization, and a procedure was defined for the teams to follow when creating and submitting ideas on improving patient care and increasing savings and revenues. If a suggestion was implemented, the team members received cash awards. Fully 90 percent of the company's 2800 employees participated in the program, generating $3.2 million worth of ideas.

The program had several other benefits. First, it became clear to managers that employees *wanted* to share their ideas. The program also pinpointed important areas where training was needed, including training of managers who were not sup-porting the quality effort. Indeed, the company spent ten months working with unen-thusiastic managers and developing training programs to support their quality efforts. The quality approach at Fort Sanders Health Systems was devised to enhance the needs of the organization members and to reach quality goals through motivation directed at quality.[33]  ▪▬

**equity theory:**
A theory of job motivation that emphasizes the role played by an individual's be-lief in the equity or fairness of rewards and punishments in determining his or her per-formance and satisfaction.

## EQUITY THEORY

**Equity theory** is based on the assumption that a major factor in job motivation is the individual's evaluation of the equity or fairness of the reward received. *Equity* can be defined as a *ratio* between the individual's job inputs (such as effort or skill) and job rewards (such as pay or promotion). According to equity theory, in-

**RECOGNIZING SUPERIOR EFFORT.** At Marlow Industries, employees know their efforts will be appreciated and recognized. This group is being honored for exceeding their production quota in an effort that gained Marlow the Abbott Lab Certified Supplier Award.

dividuals are motivated when they experience satisfaction with what they receive from an effort *in proportion to the effort they apply*. People judge the equity of their rewards by comparing them either to the rewards others are receiving for similar input or to some other effort/reward ratio that occurs to them.[34] An example will demonstrate the difference.

Suppose that you and a co-worker are both assigned projects that involve developing a pricing strategy on a product. "Your" product is a new part of the organization's product line and faces a complex competitive situation. Your co-worker's product has been sold for ten years and has a track record regarding the relationship between sales and price levels. Your effort will probably need to be much greater than your co-worker's, given the relatively greater uncertainties that you'll face in completing the task.

According to equity theory, you will factor in this difference in job inputs between the two of you in deciding if your reward is equitable. This is the first kind of equity comparison—a comparison *between people's situations*. On the other hand, if you have in mind that working sixty-hour weeks on projects like this should earn you compensating "time off," you are making the second kind of equity comparison—judging against some standard you prefer. In either case, equity theory joins need theory as another view of what satisfies or dissatisfies people.

Most discussion and research on equity theory focuses on money as the most significant reward in the workplace. People compare what they are being paid for their efforts with what others in similar situations receive for theirs. When they feel inequity exists, a state of tension develops within them, which they try to resolve by appropriately adjusting their behavior. A worker who perceives that he or she is being underpaid, for example, may try to reduce the inequity by exerting less effort.

Recent studies have shown that an individual's reaction to an inequity is dependent on that person's *history of inequity*. This is how time enters into motivation

# GLASS TAKES OVER WHERE "MR. SAM" LEFT OFF

Sam Walton had charisma. His people loved "Mr. Sam," as he was known throughout the organization. Wal-Mart's associates were motivated not only by the company's treatment of employees, but by Mr. Sam himself. When Walton died, the Wal-Mart style could have faltered. But it did not.

In 1988, four years before Walton's death, David D. Glass was named CEO of Wal-Mart. A Fall 1992 *Fortune* survey named him the most admired CEO. After picking up the reins at Wal-Mart, he has demonstrated that the culture instilled by Walton can be carried on without its creator.

Like Walton, Glass recognizes the value of the front-line associates—those who interact with the customers daily. A shopper, recognizing Glass as the CEO, walked up to him and said, "So you're the big man." Without missing a beat Glass responded, "Nah,… I just front this deal."[35]

Carrying a notebook in lieu of Mr. Sam's tape-recorder, Glass continues the practice of visiting stores. On one occasion, when an employee complained that the store was not using environmentally responsible trash bags, Glass responded, "No? Well, the buyer's up here today. Just go and hang him."[36]

Glass's interaction with associates entails more than seeking them out in the stores. He is available to his associates at all hours, wherever he is. He has even been known to receive phone calls at motels where he was staying while out-of-town. One warehouse worker in Texas, who felt he was unjustly fired, tracked Glass down at 11:00 p.m. at his motel room. The worker had called Glass's home in Bentonville, Arkansas, where Mrs. Glass freely gave the worker the number where her husband could be reached.

The result is that Wal-Mart associates aim high. "Our people are relentless," said Glass.[37] And a large part of their drive stems from the goals and expectations Glass sets. "There's no question that his expectation is 110 percent," noted one senior executive. "I mean, he never has to tell you. You know what it is before you ever talk to him."[38] →

theory. Richard A. Cosier and Dan R. Dalton point out that work relationships are not static and that inequities are not usually isolated or one-time events.[39] They suggest that there is a threshold up to which an individual will tolerate a series of unfair events, but that one too many incidents can push him or her over the edge. That is, a relatively minor injustice—"the straw that breaks the camel's back"—pushes the individual beyond his or her limit of tolerance, and an extreme and seemingly inappropriate reaction will result. For example, an outstanding worker who is denied an afternoon off for no compelling reason may suddenly become enraged if he or she has experienced a string of similar petty decisions in the past.

People use different methods to reduce inequity. Some will rationalize that their efforts were greater or less than they originally perceived them to be, or that the rewards are more or less valuable. For example, one person failing to receive a promotion may "decide" that the previously desired job actually involved too much responsibility. Others may try to make the co-workers with whom they are comparing themselves change their behavior. Work team members receiving the same pay but exerting less effort may be persuaded to work harder. High-performing workers

## WILL-BURT: EDUCATION EVERY STEP OF THE WAY[74]

In October 1985, the Will-Burt Company found itself on the verge of liquidation. A small, family-owned manufacturing firm based in Orrville, Ohio, Will-Burt had just had its insurance coverage canceled following a liability suit in which the company lost $6 million. With additional suits pending, any one of which could have finished Will-Burt, the owners gave CEO Harry Featherstone until December 31 to find a buyer. Without a new owner, the company would permanently close its doors in January.

Featherstone, who had just taken charge as CEO in October, found himself at the helm of what appeared to be a doomed company. Will-Burt had $20 million in sales, but profits had not topped 5 percent in recent years. Product quality was so poor that workers were spending nearly 25,000 hours a year remaking faulty parts. Workers were earning $2 less than the area's average, and employee turnover had reached a staggering 30 percent. Employee morale was also exceptionally low. "Because of the lawsuits, people didn't know if we were going to stay in business or not," explained Terry Wheeler, account salesman for Will-Burt. "People didn't see any future."[75]

Featherstone, however, did see a future for Will-Burt and he was determined to make the company work at whatever cost. First, he reviewed his limited options. "We could have liquidated, but I didn't want to tell 350 people and their families that the business was closing," he recalled. "We thought of merging, but who wants a company burdened with all that litigation?"[76] Featherstone's lawyer finally arrived at a solution: a leveraged buyout by Featherstone followed by the institution of an employee stock ownership plan (ESOP).

This plan saved the company from liquidation and served as a preemptive strike against further lawsuits. "My attorney told me that if we got ourselves highly leveraged, we wouldn't make much money, but neither would we be a deep-pocket target for some liability lawyer," Featherstone commented. "Lawyers love rich companies, and we wouldn't be one."[77] Moreover, he hoped that employees would become more committed to Will-Burt's success if they were to own a piece of the company.

With Will-Burt temporarily saved from extinction, Featherstone then set about turning the company around. His first task lay in making his employees understand that, through the ESOP, they owned the company. "We all heard the word ESOP, but nobody knew what it was all about," explained Cecil Martin, an assembler for Will-Burt at that time. "We all said, ESOP? What's an ESOP? They got some pamphlets out to us and said we'd all own a piece of the place. But a lot of people had trouble grasping the concept."[78] "They hated it," stated Featherstone bluntly.[79] "After all, I had forced them into an equity ownership that they didn't understand," he remarked. "And what you don't understand, you're often afraid of."[80]

So Featherstone decided to help the new owners of Will-Burt understand. Although ESOP law did not require him to open the company's books to the employees, he wanted them to have access to the numbers. In 1986, Featherstone therefore began handing out profit-and-loss statements to all employees. Unfortunately, this did not work. "People told me they couldn't read the thing, that it made no sense to them," he recalled.[81] He therefore simplified the handouts to a few lines: this is what sales were, here is what it cost us, here is what we made. Finally the employees understood that they had a direct stake in the welfare of the company. And the workers realized, perhaps for the first time, that they held the power to determine whether or not Will-Burt would succeed.

Featherstone then turned his attention to profitability. Will-Burt had $2.5 million in debt more than the company was worth on its books. In addition, the company owed $1 million to the bank in 1986, with the first payment of $250,000 due in only a few months. Will-Burt had never in its corporate history earned $1 million in a year, but this year it had to do so. After months of analyzing and re-analyzing the company's books, Featherstone found an answer: quality.[82] Will-Burt was spending $700,000 a year reworking defective parts. By making the parts properly the first time, the company would not only save money but also attract new customers.

Then Featherstone made the decision that would ultimately save his company: As an essential step in improving quality he decided to educate his workforce. With assistance from the University of Akron, he developed a program to train employees in the basic skills necessary for them to perform their jobs. Work-based classes in math, blueprint reading, geometry, and statistics were designed and made mandatory for all employees. Featherstone invested in the teachers and materials, and, in addition, paid employees at their normal hourly wage rate for their time spent in class. He hoped that this would emphasize the importance of the education to the employees and the company.

The program worked. "Out of 100 people," noted Featherstone, "perhaps 10 to 20 didn't like having to learn. But the other 80 wanted more education. They understood that they could improve their lives."[83] By the end of 1988, Will-Burt's annual rework expenses had dropped almost 75 percent to $180,000, and the time devoted to remaking parts fell from 2,000 hours per month to only 400 hours per month. This, coupled with a new pay system that resulted in a raise for nearly everyone in the company, caused employee morale to soar. Absenteeism fell to 2 percent and workers' compensation costs dropped from $160,000 in 1985 to a meager $662 in 1992.

Riding on the wave of employee enthusiasm, Featherstone and the University of Akron began adding more courses, including advanced blueprint reading, geometric tolerancing, and statistical process control. Featherstone also initiated a "mini MBA" program to help employees, by this time referred to as "associates," understand better the basics of owning and running a business. "I found that education creates involvement," commented Featherstone, "and involvement creates knowledge, and knowledge says I want more education so I can get more involved."[84] A new emphasis on quality and innovation spread quickly throughout the company.

Camaraderie and pride replaced apathy. According to Featherstone, "We have formed a team, a solidarity—from our janitor to our salesperson to our clerk—when it comes to our customers."[85]

## CASE QUESTIONS

1. What assumptions underlie the employer-employee relationship at Will-Burt prior to 1985? What assumptions now drive the relationship?

2. What obstacles did Featherstone confront in motivating his employees?

3. How else could Featherstone have addressed Will-Burt's employee-related financial difficulties? What would you have done?

4. What was the impact of educating employees on Will-Burt's performance?

5. To what do you attribute Will-Burt's success?

## CHAPTER 17

# LEADERSHIP

**Upon completing this chapter, you should be able to:**

1. Define leadership and explain how it is similar to and different from management.

2. Explain the key ideas of the trait approach to leadership.

3. Discuss and evaluate the behavior approach to leadership.

4. List and explain the major contingency approaches to leadership.

5. Explain the concept of transformational or charismatic leadership and give examples.

6. Discuss some recent challenges to leadership theory.

# NEW LEADERSHIP POLICIES AT GE[1]

**J**ack Welch took over as chairman of General Electric in 1981 after an extensive and well-publicized competition. Welch, with a doctorate in chemical engineering, became GE's eighth and youngest chief executive officer. He quickly made sweeping changes in almost every aspect of the company, shifting its business mix and corporate culture. His stated goal was to make GE number one or number two in market share in every business in which it competes. He has confronted this challenge with single-minded determination.

A competitor from his youth in boyhood sports to his career in business, Welch has been with GE his entire career. In his initial success with the company, he increased the revenues of the plastics division from a small part to a major portion of GE's sales and profits. From his early days at GE, Welch had been frustrated by the company's bureaucracy, and he spent a lot of time trying to find new ways to get things done by working around the system. He had found that the key ingredients for accomplishing things were initiative, managerial freedom, and an intolerance for managers who did not produce.

From his years of GE experience, Welch was convinced that the company was too bureaucratic—so fat with layer upon layer of management that it was not capable of making quick decisions, let alone implementing them. By eliminating several layers of management, he was able to delegate authority to the lower levels of management, where problems were first encountered and solutions were most readily available. In 1981, each of GE's business units included between nine and eleven layers of bureaucracy. By 1991,

*Welch brought to the company a passion for change and a vision of how to compete.*

Welch had cut management layers in half, to between four and six. He had reduced the corporate staff from 1,700 to under 1,000 and made cuts in all parts of the company. Since 1981, GE has trimmed over 180,000 employees and sold $12 billion worth of businesses.

**AN ACTIVE LEADER.** As chairman of General Electric, Jack F. Welch has made sweeping changes throughout the company.

The sailing has not been totally smooth. Selling major business units and cutting 50 percent of the workforce in the 1980s had severe effects on morale. Employees became polarized. They reportedly either admired or detested Jack Welch. Organized labor has been an outspoken opponent of Welch's methods. "GE has a disease—Welch-ese," said Joseph F. Egan, chairman of International Union of Electronic Workers. "It is caused by corporate greed, arrogance, and contempt for its employees."[2]

But Welch's admirers believe he is doing an outstanding job. They claim that his vision and the often difficult changes he has made at GE are exactly what the company needed. Before Welch's arrival, a GE vice chairman noted that the company was "as smooth and predictable as the digestive system, and just about as exciting."[3] Welch brought to the company a passion for change and a vision of how to compete in the demanding global marketplace of the future. →

Is Jack Welch an effective leader? How does he compare to such world-famous leaders as Abraham Lincoln, Martin Luther King, and Nelson Mandela?

Although managers are seldom called on to be leaders in the heroic mold of a Lincoln or a Mandela, their leadership abilities and skills play a major role in their organizations' success or failure. For this reason, thousands of scholars have studied leadership. They have used three major approaches—the study of *traits*, the study of leadership *behaviors*, and the study of *contingencies*, or the situations in which leaders act.

In this chapter, we will see what each of these approaches has contributed to our understanding of leadership, concluding with some current trends in our thinking about leadership. Before we do this, though, let's take a closer look at the meaning of *leadership*.

## DEFINING LEADERSHIP

In his survey of leadership theories and research, Ralph M. Stogdill pointed out that "there are almost as many different definitions of leadership as there are persons who have attempted to define the concept."[4] We will define managerial **leadership** as the process of directing and influencing the task-related activities of group members. There are four important implications of our definition.

First, leadership involves *other people*—employees or followers. By their willingness to accept directions from the leader, group members help define the leader's status and make the leadership process possible; without people to lead, all the leadership qualities of a manager would be irrelevant.

Second, leadership involves an unequal distribution of **power** between leaders and group members. Group members are not powerless; they can and do shape group activities in a number of ways. Still, the leader will usually have more power.

Where does a manager's power come from? We answered this question in Chapter 13 when we discussed the five bases of a manager's power: *reward power, coercive power, legitimate power, referent power, and expert power.*[5] The greater the number of these power sources available to the manager, the greater his or her potential for effective leadership. Yet it is a commonly observed fact of organization life that managers at the same level—with the same amount of legitimate power—differ widely in their ability to use reward, coercive, referent, and expert power.

Thus, a third aspect of leadership is the ability to use the different forms of power to **influence** followers' behaviors in a number of ways. Indeed, leaders have influenced soldiers to kill and leaders have influenced employees to make personal sacrifices for the good of the company. The power of influence brings us to the fourth aspect of leadership.

This fourth aspect combines the first three and acknowledges that leadership is about *values*. James McGregor Burns argues that the leader who ignores the moral components of leadership may well go down in history as a scoundrel, or worse. Moral leadership concerns values and requires that followers be given enough knowledge of alternatives to make intelligent choices when it comes time to respond to a leader's proposal to lead.[6] As noted ethicist Michael Josephson has argued, "We don't learn ethics from people who sermonize or moralize or try to preach to us about ethics; we learn ethics from the people whom we admire and respect, who have power over us. They're the real teachers of ethics....It's important to reinforce ideals, if they're sincere. It is very important for leaders and role models, whether they be sports figures or politicians, to make positive statements of ethics, if they're not hypocritical."[7]

It is worth noting that although leadership is highly related to and important to management, leadership and management are not the same concepts. To dra-

---

**leadership:**
The process of directing and influencing the task-related activities of group members.

← ch. 13, p. 345

**power:**
The ability to exert influence—that is, to change the attitudes or behavior of individuals or groups.

**influence:**
Any actions or examples of behavior that cause a change in attitude or behavior of another person or group.

**LEADERS MOTIVATE.** Raymond Marlow, CEO of Baldrige-winning Marlow Industries, seemingly is everywhere in his ongoing motivational strategies. Each month he delivers Marlow's "Clean Act Award" to the department with the highest housekeeping standards.

matize the difference, leadership writer Warren Bennis has said that most organizations arc *overmanaged* and *underled*.[8] A person can serve as an effective manager—a good planner and a fair, organized administrator—but lack the motivational skills of a leader. Others can serve as effective leaders—skilled at inspiring enthusiasm and devotion—but lack the managerial skills to channel the energy they arouse in others. Given the challenges of <u>dynamic engagement</u> in today's organizational world, many organizations are putting a premium on managers who also possess leadership skills.

← ch. 2, p. 49

## THE TRAIT APPROACH TO LEADERSHIP

The first systematic effort by psychologists and other researchers to understand leadership was the attempt to identify the personal characteristics of leaders. This approach assumed that leaders share certain inborn personality traits. This view—that leaders are born, not made—is still popular among laypersons, though not among professional researchers.

In searching for measurable leadership traits, researchers have taken two approaches: (1) comparing the traits of those who have emerged as leaders with the traits of those who have not; and (2) comparing the traits of effective leaders with those of ineffective leaders.

### LEADERS AND NONLEADERS

Most studies on leadership traits have fallen into the first category. However, they have largely failed to uncover any traits that clearly and consistently distinguish leaders from followers.[9] It is true that leaders as a group have been found to be brighter, more extroverted, and more self-confident than nonleaders. They also tend to be taller. But although millions of people have these traits, most of them will never attain leadership positions. And many indisputable leaders have not had these traits—Abraham Lincoln, for example, was moody and introverted, and Napoleon was rather short. It is also possible that individuals become more assertive and self-confident once they occupy a leadership position, so some of the traits identified may be the *results* of leadership experience rather than the *causes* of leadership ability. Although personality measurements may one day become exact enough to isolate leadership traits, the evidence thus far suggests that people who emerge as leaders possess no single constellation of traits that clearly distinguishes them from nonleaders.

 The issue is also clouded by the question of cultural bias. For example, tallness has long been associated with American leaders. Does this mean that tallness is a leadership trait? Or does it just reflect our culture's inclination to seek its leaders from among the ranks of Caucasian males? Our assumptions about leadership traits may well change as increasing numbers of women, minorities, gays, and disabled people assume leadership positions.

## EFFECTIVE AND INEFFECTIVE LEADERS

Attempts to compare the characteristics of effective and ineffective leaders—the second category of leadership trait studies—are more recent and fewer in number, but they, too, have generally failed to isolate traits strongly associated with successful leadership. One study did find that intelligence, initiative, and self-assurance were associated with high managerial levels and performance.[10] However, this study also found that the single most important factor related to managerial level and performance was the manager's supervisory ability—that is, his or her skill in using supervisory methods appropriate to the particular situation. Most other studies in this area also have found that effective leadership does not depend on a particular set of traits, but rather on how well the leader's traits match the requirements of the situation.[11]

← ch. 7, p. 194

Some researchers have also found that although women are still less likely than men to emerge as leaders, they are just as effective when they do. Even though an increasing number of people believe in equality of ability and opportunity, persistent, often unconscious, sexual stereotyping continues to hamper the recognition of women as potential leaders. Women who do become leaders, however, not only perform as well as male leaders according to objective measures, but also are generally perceived as equally effective by their employees.[12]

← ch. 4, p. 97

Anita Roddick of The Body Shop (see Chapter 7) is one example of a woman who is a successful leader. Susie Tompkins of Esprit is another. Like Roddick, Tompkins believes in corporate social responsibility. "We can be a company that inspires its employees, that tries to do more in the community, that tries to make a more conscientious product," Tompkins noted. "The wave of the '90s is to do good things….The '80s were all about style and lifestyle. The '90s are about soul-searching."[13] Such a philosophy led to the announcement that ran in the Esprit catalog during the late 1980s with detailed information about how to avoid contracting AIDS. Tompkins was pleased by the positive response Esprit received to the announcement. "It was the first time I could see the difference between a letter congratulating me for making a difference and one congratulating me for creating a nice, cute collection."[14]

As a leader, Tompkins has made a difference. Esprit initiatives have also included attention to the environment. The company now uses more enzymes and fewer chemical pollutants in its manufacturing. "In the '80s we gave our employees French lessons….Now we're giving them character-building opportunities."[15]

Racial stereotyping, of course, is another problem when attempting to identify the connections between traits and leadership qualities, because leadership qualities may go unrecognized and untapped. Although the number of African Americans in managerial ranks has been growing, very few have made it to the highest echelons in organizational hierarchies. However, such organizations as GM, AM International, Xerox, Avon, Godfather's Pizza, IBM, and Procter &

**EFFECTIVE LEADERSHIP.**
Although intelligence, initiative, and self-assurance are associated with high managerial performance, the single most important factor may be the manager's supervisory ability. Though fewer women than men have leadership positions, those who do are generally perceived as being equally effective by their employees.

Gamble have initiated programs to enhance the placement of black men and women in leadership positions.[16]

Members of minorities are doing what they can to gain a foothold in the business world. Outside networking across corporations is one way that black businesspeople are helping build economic growth for African Americans. An informal, but powerful, system of contacts and relationships, called "the network," is creating strong beachheads in a variety of fields ranging from communications and entertainment to consumer goods. By working together they are forming pools of capital and new opportunities that are helping to overcome the traditional barriers to success.[17]

Many minority group members are finding a degree of success in small businesses endeavors, although they remain particularly vulnerable to economic conditions. Edward Owens, for example, is struggling to hold on to H. F. Owens Movers, the moving company that his father began. During the 1980s, Owens prospered as

Owens Cos. ventured into construction, real estate, and warehousing as well. "I had to be a star," he confessed. "I wanted to show Boston that a black man could be successful."[18] And he was, that is, until the New England economy collapsed in late 1987. Since then, he has struggled to keep from going under. "I walk around my office, look at the pictures of some of the activities I've been involved in in the past years—my business, my family, my life," Owens explained. "I look around and see how fortunate I've been. I just want to hold on to my business, hold on to my house, and educate my kids. Those sound like very basic values, but I feel that if I can do that, it will be a big contribution."[19]

## THE BEHAVIORAL APPROACH TO LEADERSHIP

When it became evident that effective leaders did not seem to have a particular set of distinguishing traits, researchers tried to isolate the *behaviors* characteristic of effective leaders. In other words, rather than try to figure out who effective leaders *are,* researchers tried to determine what effective leaders *do*—how they delegate tasks, how they communicate with and try to motivate their followers or employees, how they carry out their tasks, and so on. Behaviors, unlike traits, can be *learned,* so it followed that individuals trained in appropriate leadership behaviors would be able to lead more effectively. These researchers have focused on two aspects of leadership behavior: leadership functions and leadership styles.

**leadership functions:**
The group-maintenance and task-related activities that must be performed by the leader, or someone else, for a group to perform effectively.

## LEADERSHIP FUNCTIONS

Researchers exploring **leadership functions** came to the conclusion that to operate effectively groups need *someone* to perform two major functions: *task-related* or problem-solving functions and *group-maintenance* or social functions. Group-maintenance functions include such actions as mediating disputes and ensuring that individuals feel valued by the group.

An individual who is able to perform *both* roles successfully would be an especially effective leader. In practice, however, a leader may have the skill or temperament or time to play only one role. This does not mean that the group is doomed, though. Studies have found that most effective groups have some form of *shared* leadership: one person (usually the manager or formal leader) performs the task function, while another member performs the social function.[20]

## LEADERSHIP STYLES

**leadership styles:**
The various patterns of behavior favored by leaders during the process of directing and influencing workers.

The two leadership functions—task-related and group-maintenance—tend to be expressed in two different **leadership styles.** Managers who have a *task-oriented style* closely supervise employees to be sure the task is performed satisfactorily. Getting the job done is given more emphasis than employees' growth or personal satisfaction. Managers with an *employee-oriented style* put more emphasis on motivating rather than controlling subordinates. They seek friendly, trusting, and respectful relationships with employees, who are often allowed to participate in decisions that affect them. Most managers use at least a little of each style, but put more emphasis on either tasks or employees.

Prue Leith is an example of manager with a strong task focus. She owns the successful UK-based Leith Group, which includes a restaurant, catering business, and the School of Food and Wine. The group boasts annual sales of £9 million. She employs a staff of 350 full-time workers and retains complete control over all business operations. She personally reviews all new business proposals and requests for tenders and is the one who decides what jobs are accepted.[21]

Wayne Yetter and Rob Cohen are managers with a strong employee focus. At the Astra/Merck Group, a pharmaceuticals company in Wayne, Pennsylvania, where Yetter is company president and Cohen is chief information officer (CIO), they encourage managers to delegate work and empower teams. They consider this the best way for the company to do the amount of work to be done within the limited time available. As a result, the employees have been able to create their own corporate culture.[22]

Robert Tannenbaum and Warren H. Schmidt were among the first theorists to describe the various factors thought to influence a manager's choice of leadership style.[23] While they personally favored the employee-centered style, they suggested that a manager consider three sets of "forces" before choosing a leadership style: forces in the manager, forces in employees (whom they call subordinates), and forces in the situation.

How a manager leads will undoubtedly be primarily influenced by his or her background, knowledge, values, and experience *(forces in the manager).* For example, a manager who believes that the needs of the individual must come second

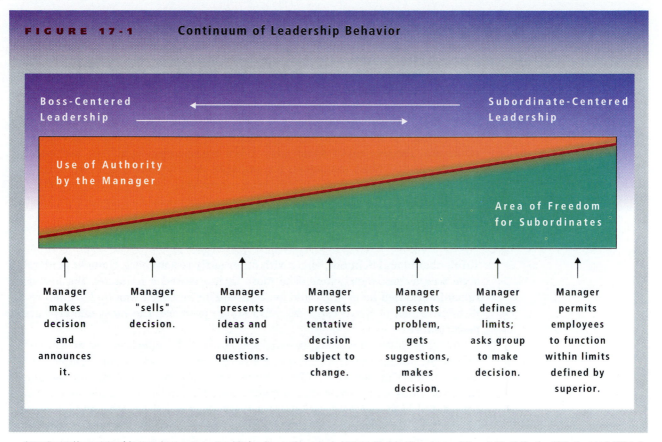

**FIGURE 17-1** Continuum of Leadership Behavior

Boss-Centered Leadership

Subordinate-Centered Leadership

Use of Authority by the Manager

Area of Freedom for Subordinates

| Manager makes decision and announces it. | Manager "sells" decision. | Manager presents ideas and invites questions. | Manager presents tentative decision subject to change. | Manager presents problem, gets suggestions, makes decision. | Manager defines limits; asks group to make decision. | Manager permits employees to function within limits defined by superior. |

*Source:* Reprinted by permission of the *Harvard Business Review.* An exhibit from "How to Choose a Leadership Pattern" by Robert Tannenbaum and Warren H. Schmidt (May–June 1973). Copyright © 1973 by the President and Fellows of Harvard College. All rights reserved.

to the needs of the organization is likely to take a very directive role in employees' activities (see Figure 17-1).

Through experience, Steve Braccini learned not to take an overly directive role in employees' activities. As founder and CEO of Pro Fasteners Inc., an industrial-parts distributor based in San Jose, California, Braccini confronted the challenge of increasing the quality of the company's products. Pro had become accustomed to accepting mistakes. Since customers rarely became particularly upset, the company did not feel compelled to reach for higher standards. Then, in the early 1990s, Braccini noticed tremendous market opportunities, but realized that Pro would have to decrease errors to only a few per million parts shipped in order to be eligible for the lucrative long-term contracts that were becoming available. He first attempted the directive approach. "I suppose I followed a lot of my peers in thinking that my job was to control anything and everything about this company," Braccini confessed.[24] He soon realized, though, that he alone could not improve quality; the employees had to take ownership of their work. "I began selling the employees on the idea that this was *their* company," he explained, "that they needed to run this company."[25] And it was through this—by taking a less directive approach—that Pro was able to reach the desired quality standards.

But *characteristics of subordinates* must also be considered before managers can choose an appropriate leadership style. According to Tannenbaum and Schmidt, a manager can allow greater participation and freedom when employees crave independence and freedom of action, want to have decision-making responsibility, identify with the organization's goals, are knowledgeable and experienced enough to deal with a problem efficiently, and have experiences that lead them to expect *participative management*. Where these conditions are absent, managers might need initially to adopt a more authoritarian style. They can, however, modify their leadership behavior as employees gain in self-confidence, skill, and organizational commitment.

Finally, a manager's choice of leadership style must address such *situational forces* as the organization's preferred style, the size and cohesiveness of a specific work group, the nature of the group's tasks, the pressures of time, and even environmental factors—all of which may affect organization members' attitudes toward authority. Most managers, for example, lean toward the leadership style favored by the organization's top ranking executives.

## THE OHIO STATE AND UNIVERSITY OF MICHIGAN STUDIES

Tannenbaum and Schmidt, along with other early researchers, thought leadership style was a "zero-sum" game: The more task-oriented a manager, the less relationship-oriented he or she could be. Subsequent research was undertaken to determine which of these two leadership styles produces the most effective group performance.

At Ohio State University, researchers studied the effectiveness of what they called "initiating structure" (task-oriented) and "consideration" (employee-oriented) leadership behaviors. They found, as might be expected, that employee turnover rates were lowest and employee satisfaction highest under leaders who were rated high in consideration. Conversely, leaders who were rated low in consideration and high in initiating structure had high grievance and turnover rates among their employees. Figure 17-2 diagrams the leadership styles studied at Ohio State. Interestingly, the researchers also found that employees' ratings of their leaders' effectiveness depended not so much on the particular *style* of the leader as on the *situation* in which the style was used. For example, Air Force commanders who rated high on consideration were rated as less effective than task-oriented commanders. It is possible that the more authoritarian environment of the military, coupled with the air crews' belief that quick, hard decisions are essential in combat situations, caused people-oriented leaders to be rated less effective. On the other hand, nonproduction supervisors and managers in large companies were rated more effective if they ranked high in consideration.

Leadership expectations differ globally as well, even in the military. In 1956 the Egyptian army was routed by the much smaller Israeli army, even though the Egyptians were better equipped and far better positioned geographically. An analysis of the confrontation revealed that the Israeli army was built on what might be called Theory Y values: Soldiers were treated and taught to treat others humanely, hierarchy played a greatly reduced role, cross-communications flourished, coordination was high, and intra-organizational rivalries were at a minimum. Because all were working for the end goals, the job of the high command was leadership, not direction.[26]

← ch. 2, p. 44

Researchers at the University of Michigan found a different result. They distinguished between production-centered and employee-centered managers. Production-centered managers set rigid work standards, organized tasks down to the last detail, prescribed work methods to be followed, and closely supervised employees' work. Employee-centered managers encouraged employee participation in goal setting and other work decisions and helped ensure high performance by inspiring trust and respect. The Michigan studies found that the most productive work groups tended to have leaders who were employee-centered rather than production-centered. They also found that the most effective leaders had supportive relationships with their employees, tended to depend on group rather than indi-

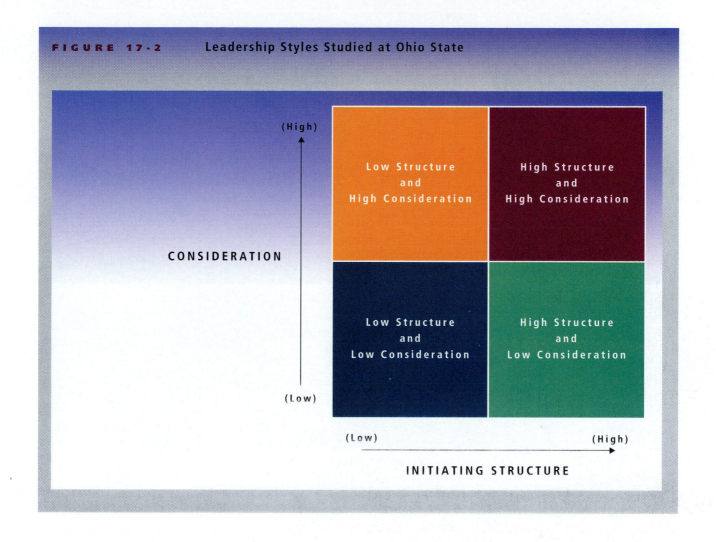

**FIGURE 17-2** Leadership Styles Studied at Ohio State

CONSIDERATION

(High)

| Low Structure and High Consideration | High Structure and High Consideration |
| Low Structure and Low Consideration | High Structure and Low Consideration |

(Low)

(Low) (High)

**INITIATING STRUCTURE**

vidual decision making, and encouraged employees to set and achieve high performance goals.[27]

← ch. 8, p. 211

## EMPLOYEE-CENTERED LEADERSHIP AND TQM

Some aspects of the movement toward quality are in concert with the employee-centered leadership style. For example, under TQM managers' priorities are reordered: Their decision-making and control functions contract while their roles as coaches expand. As the distinction between "those who think" and "those that do" is blurred, the job itself becomes less specialized both horizontally and vertically. For instance, shop-floor teams become involved with teams from other departments and units in communication and coordination of work.

Researchers have found that even the best quality programs are bound to fail if employees are not involved. At Associated Company Inc., a Wichita, Kansas-based supplier of machine parts to aviation companies, management knows the value of employee involvement. In 1987 the company instituted a Work Smart quality program designed to

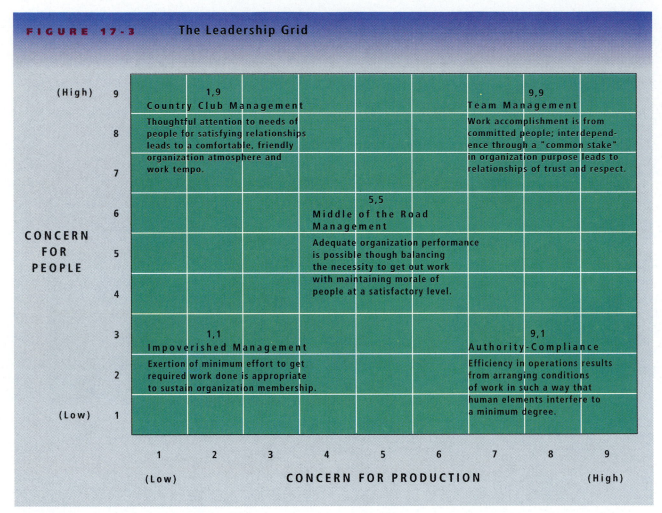

**FIGURE 17-3**     The Leadership Grid

← ch. 8, p.214, p. 211

reduce the high costs created by high scrap and rework rates and product failures experienced by customers. The plan established an attainable quality goal: a 0.5 percent defect rate. Based on the teachings of Juran and Deming, the plan encouraged the employees to be innovative and take risks.

Though there was a period of trial-and-error in establishing employee commitment, the scrap and rework rates declined quickly to 0.25 percent, and employee turnover decreased sharply. Specific goals were set, rewards such as dinners, movie tickets, and savings bonds were used to reinforce behavior, and continuous feedback on group progress was provided so that corrections could be made. Eventually the groups became committed to quality. Management attitude was important, too: The company treated its people as human resources to be valued rather than merely as a source of labor costs to be minimized. A high level of commitment and motivation led to overall increased quality and the ability to stay on course for long-term goals.[28]

## THE MANAGERIAL GRID

**Managerial Grid:**

Diagram developed by Blake and Mouton to measure a manager's relative concern for people and production.

One conclusion from the Ohio State and Michigan studies is that leadership style might not be unidimensional. *Both* task orientation and employee orientation are not only possible, but could be crucial to superior performance. The **Managerial Grid,** developed by Robert Blake and Jane Mouton to help measure a

# TEAM MANAGEMENT: MEANS FOR SUCCESS

In the 1980s, much of the controversy at GE focused on Welch's intense leadership style. Welch devoted a great deal of time and energy to trying to get managers at GE to confront one another, to be more open about solving conflicts. One story goes that after a bitter argument in which Welch ripped apart one manager's ideas, Welch hugged the man for openly engaging in debate and creative conflict.

Welch pushes his values and corporate vision on every level of the organization. All employees are evaluated according to a "360° Leadership Assessment" form that Jack Welch calls a "values sheet." The report assigns the employee a rating of 1 to 5, with 5 being outstanding, on a number of performance and value-oriented criteria. Welch stresses that the values sheet enables him to target individual personnel problems. "So, when I go into what we call a Session C in each business, we'll target Mr. Y or Miss X. And we'll look at the values sheet. People are removed for having the wrong values. Integrity violations clearly are the worst ones. We don't talk about what the numbers are."[29]

Welch wants people to focus on tasks, to bring a higher level of intensity to their jobs. He believes that such intensity is one of the keys to being a successful competitor—to achieving his goal of making GE number one and number two in every industry segment in which the company is engaged. But he also knows that managing relationships is equally important—that managers accomplish tasks through people. In short, he has made team management the means for GE's future success.

Welch believes that GE needed drastic changes to survive in the global marketplace. "Incremental change doesn't work very well in the type of transformation GE has gone through. If your change isn't big enough, revolutionary enough, the bureaucracy can beat you. When you get leaders who confuse popularity with leadership, who just nibble away at things, nothing changes."[30] →

manager's relative concern for people and tasks, reflects this bidimensional nature of leadership.[31]

The Managerial Grid (republished as the Leadership Grid figure in 1991 by Robert R. Blake and Anne Adams McCanse) identifies a range of management behaviors based on the various ways that task-oriented and employee-oriented styles (each expressed as a continuum on a scale of 1 to 9) can interact with each other (see Figure 17-3). Thus, Style 1,1 management, at the lower left-hand corner of the grid, is *impoverished management*—low concern for people and low concern for tasks or production. This style is sometimes called *laissez-faire management* because the leader does not take a leadership role. Welch at GE could never be accused of this.

Style 1,9 management is *country club management*—high concern for employees but low concern for production. Its opposite, Style 9,1 management, is *task* or *authoritarian management*—high concern for production and efficiency but low concern for employees. Style 5,5 is *middle-of-the-road management*—an intermediate amount of concern for both production and employee satisfaction.

Style 9,9 is called *team* or *democratic management*—a high concern for both production and employee morale and satisfaction. The presence of this category contrasts with the earlier assumption that leaders had to have one orientation or the other. Blake and Mouton argue strongly that Style 9,9 is the most effective management style. They believe this leadership approach will, in almost all situations, result in improved performance, low absenteeism and turnover, and high employee satisfaction. The Blake and Mouton Managerial Grid is widely used as a training device for managers.

# CONTINGENCY APPROACHES TO LEADERSHIP

**R**esearchers using the trait and behavioral approaches showed that effective leadership depended on many variables, such as organizational culture and the nature of tasks. No *one* trait was common to all effective leaders. No *one* style was effective in all situations.

Researchers therefore began trying to identify those factors in each *situation* that influenced the effectiveness of a particular leadership style.[32] Taken together, the theories resulting from this research constitute the **contingency approach** to leadership. These theories focus on the following factors:

**contingency approach:**
The view that the management technique that best contributes to the attainment of organizational goals might vary in different types of situations or circumstances.

- Task requirements
- Peers' expectations and behavior
- Employees' characteristics, expectations, and behavior
- Organizational culture and policies

In the sections that follow, we will review four of the more recent and well-known contingency models of leadership.

### HERSEY AND BLANCHARD'S SITUATIONAL LEADERSHIP® MODEL

**situational leadership model:**
An approach to leadership developed by Hersey and Blanchard that describes how leaders should adjust their leadership style in response to their subordinates' evolving desire for achievement, experience, ability, and willingness to accept responsibility.

One of the major contingency approaches to leadership is Paul Hersey and Kenneth H. Blanchard's **situational leadership model,**[33] which holds that the most effective leadership style varies with the "readiness" of employees. Hersey and Blanchard define readiness as desire for achievement, willingness to accept responsibility, and task-related ability, skill, and experience. The goals and knowledge of followers are important variables in determining effective leadership style.

Hersey and Blanchard believe that the relationship between a manager and follower moves through four phases as employees develop, and managers need to vary their leadership style (see Figure 17-4). In the initial phase of readiness high amounts of task behavior by the manager is most appropriate. Employees must be instructed in their tasks and familiarized with the organization's rules and procedures. A  nondirective manager would cause anxiety and confusion in new followers. A participatory, high relationship behavior approach would also be inappropriate at this stage because the follower requires structure.

As followers begin to learn their tasks, task-behavior remains essential because they are not yet able to function without the structure. However, the leader's trust in and support of employees increases as the leader becomes familiar with them and wishes to encourage further efforts on their part. Thus, the leader needs to increase relationship behavior.

In the third phase, employees have more ability and achievement motivation begins to surface and they actively begin to seek greater responsibility. The leader will no longer need to be as directive (indeed, close direction might be resented).

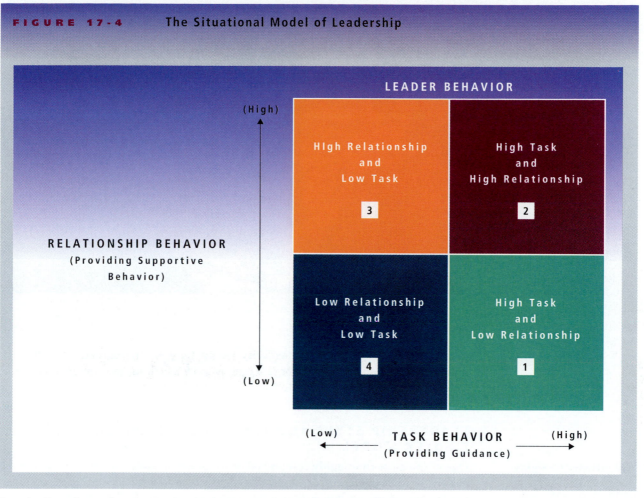

**FIGURE 17-4**     The Situational Model of Leadership

*Source:* Adapted from Paul Hersey and Kenneth H. Blanchard, *Management of Organizational Behavior: Utilizing Human Resources,* 5th ed., p. 173. Copyright © 1988. Reprinted by permission of Leadership Studies, Inc.

However, the leader will still have to be supportive and considerate in order to strengthen the followers' resolve for greater responsibility.

As followers gradually become more confident, self-directing, and experienced, the leader can reduce the amount of support and encouragement. In this fourth phase, followers no longer need or expect direction from their manager. They are increasingly on their own.

The situational leadership model has generated interest because it recommends a leadership type that is dynamic and flexible rather than static. The motivation, ability, and experience of followers must constantly be assessed to determine which style combination is most appropriate under flexible and changing conditions. If the style is appropriate, according to Hersey and Blanchard, it will not only motivate employees but will also help them develop professionally. Thus, the leader who wants to develop followers, increase their confidence, and help them learn their work will have to shift style constantly.[34]

Yet a practical question remains: To what extent are managers actually able to choose among leadership styles in different situations? This issue is important because it affects management selection, placement, and promotion. If managers are flexible in leadership style, or if they can be trained to vary their style, presumably they will be effective in a variety of leadership situations. If, on the other hand, managers are relatively inflexible in leadership style, they will operate effectively only in those situations that best match their style or that can be adjusted

**MATCHING THE MANAGER TO THE SITUATION.** Kenneth I. Chenault, president of American Express Consumer Card Group, USA, excels at task-related functions, such as analyzing competitive information and devising innovative techniques for achieving strategic goals. Just as importantly, Chenault is seen as "the quarterback" of American Express, a team builder who is confident, approachable, diplomatic, and motivating.

to match their style. Such inflexibility would hamper the careers of individual managers and complicate the organization's task of filling its management positions effectively. This leads us to the next contingency model.

### LEADERSHIP STYLE AND THE WORK SITUATION: THE FIEDLER MODEL

**least preferred co-worker (LPC):**

Fiedler's measuring instrument for locating a manager on the leadership-style continuum.

One of the most thoroughly researched contingency models was developed by Fred E. Fiedler. Fiedler's basic assumption is that it is quite difficult for managers to alter the management styles that made them successful. In fact, Fiedler believes, most managers are not very flexible, and trying to change a manager's style to fit unpredictable or fluctuating situations is inefficient or useless. Since styles are relatively inflexible, and since no one style is appropriate for every situation, effective group performance can only be achieved by matching the manager to the situation or by changing the situation to fit the manager. For example, a comparatively authoritarian manager can be selected to fill a post that requires a directive leader, or a job can be changed to give an authoritarian manager more formal authority over employees.

The leadership styles that Fiedler contrasts are similar to the employee-centered and task-oriented styles we discussed earlier. What differentiates his model from the others is the measuring instrument he used. Fiedler measured leadership style on a scale that indicated "the degree to which a man described favorably or unfavorably his **least preferred co-worker (LPC)**"—the employee with whom the person could work least well.[35] This measure locates an individual on the leadership-style continuum. According to Fiedler's findings, "a person who describes his least preferred co-worker in a relatively favorable manner tends to be permissive, human relations-oriented, and considerate of the feelings of his men. But a person who describes his least preferred co-worker in an unfavorable manner— who has what we have come to call a low LPC rating—tends to be managing, task-controlling, and less concerned with the human relations aspects of the job."[36]

According to Fiedler, then, high-LPC managers want to have warm personal relations with their co-workers and will regard close ties with employees as important to their overall effectiveness. Low-LPC managers, on the other hand, want to get the job done. The reactions of employees to their leadership style is of far lower priority than the need to maintain production. Low-LPC managers who feel that a harsh style is necessary to maintain production will not hesitate to use it.

Fiedler has identified three "leadership situations" or variables that help determine which leadership style will be effective: leader-member relations, the task structure, and the leader's position power. (Fiedler's studies did not include such other situational variables as employee motivation and the values and experiences of leaders and group members.)

The quality of **leader-member relations** is the most important influence on the manager's power and effectiveness. If the manager gets along well with the rest of the group, if group members respect the manager for reasons of personality, character, or ability, then the manager might not have to rely on formal rank or authority. On the other hand, a manager who is disliked or distrusted may be less able to lead informally and could have to rely on directives to accomplish group tasks.

**Task structure** is the second most important variable in the leadership situation. A highly structured task is one for which step-by-step procedures or instructions are available. Group members therefore have a very clear idea of what they are expected to do. But when tasks are unstructured, as in committee meetings and many research and development tasks, group member roles are more ambiguous.

The leader's **position power** is the final situational variable identified by Fiedler. Some positions, such as the presidency of a firm, carry a great deal of power and authority. The chairperson of a fund-raising drive, on the other hand, has little power over volunteer workers. Thus, high-position power simplifies the leader's task of influencing others, while low-position power makes the leader's task more difficult.

Fiedler then went on to specify eight possible combinations of these three variables in the leadership situation: Leader-member relations can be good or poor, tasks may be structured or unstructured, and position power may be strong or weak (see Figure 17-5).

Using these eight categories of leadership situations and his two types of leaders—high-LPC and low-LPC—Fiedler reviewed studies of over 800 groups to see which type of leader was most effective in each situation. Among the groups he studied were basketball teams, executive training workshops, and Air Force and tank combat crews. A well-liked leader of a bomber crew, for example, would be in category 1 of Figure 17-5, while a disliked temporary committee chairperson would be in category 8. He found that low-LPC leaders—those who were task-oriented or authoritarian—were most effective in extreme situations: situations in which the leader either had a great deal of power and influence or had very little power and influence. High-LPC leaders—those who were employee-oriented—were most effective in situations where the leader had moderate power and influence.

Fiedler's model, then, suggests that an appropriate match of the leader's style (as measured by the LPC score) to the situation (as determined by the interaction of these three variables) leads to effective managerial performance. His model has been used with some success as the basis of a training program in which managers are shown how to alter the situational variables to match their leadership styles rather than their styles to fit the situation.[37]

## A PATH-GOAL APPROACH TO LEADERSHIP

Like other contingency approaches, the **path-goal model** of leadership tries to help us understand and predict leadership effectiveness in different situations. The model was formulated by Martin G. Evans[38] and Robert J. House.[39]

---

**leader-member relations:**

The quality of the interaction between a leader and his or her employees; according to Fiedler, the most important influence on the manager's power.

**task structure:**

A work situation variable that, according to Fiedler, helps determine a manager's power. In structured tasks, managers automatically have high power; in unstructured tasks, their power is diminished.

**position power:**

The power, according to Fiedler, that is inherent in the formal position the leader holds. This power may be great or small, depending on the specific position.

**path-goal model:**

A leadership theory emphasizing the leader's role in clarifying for subordinates how they can achieve high performance and its associated rewards.

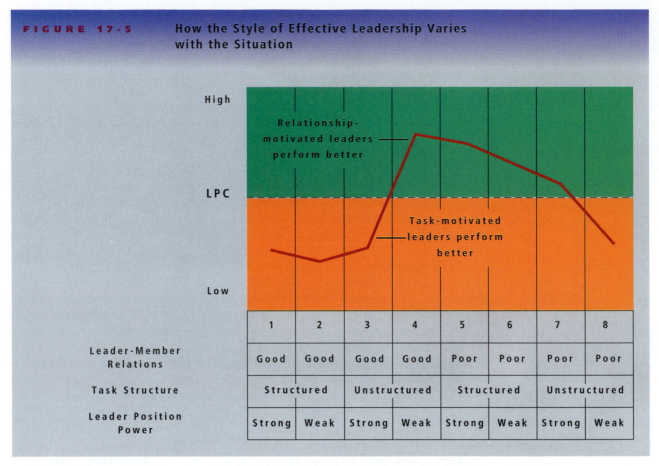

**FIGURE 17-5**    How the Style of Effective Leadership Varies with the Situation

|  | 1 | 2 | 3 | 4 | 5 | 6 | 7 | 8 |
|---|---|---|---|---|---|---|---|---|
| **Leader-Member Relations** | Good | Good | Good | Good | Poor | Poor | Poor | Poor |
| **Task Structure** | Structured | | Unstructured | | Structured | | Unstructured | |
| **Leader Position Power** | Strong | Weak | Strong | Weak | Strong | Weak | Strong | Weak |

*Source:* Fred E. Fiedler and Martin M. Chemers, *Leadership and Effective Management* (Glenview, Ill.: Scott, Foresman, 1974), p. 80. Reprinted by permission of Fred E. Fiedler.

← ch. 16, p. 456

The path-goal approach is based on the expectancy model of motivation, which states that an individual's motivation depends on his or her expectation of reward and the *valence,* or attractiveness of the reward. Although managers have a number of ways to influence employees, Evans notes, the most important is their ability to provide rewards and to specify what employees must do to earn them. Thus, managers determine the availability of "goals" (rewards) and the "paths" that will earn them.

Evans suggests that a manager's leadership style influences the rewards available to employees, as well as employees' perceptions of the path to those rewards. An employee-centered manager, for example, will offer not only pay and promotion, but also support, encouragement, security, and respect. That type of manager will also be sensitive to differences between employees and will tailor rewards to the individual. A task-oriented manager, on the other hand, will offer a narrower, less individualized set of rewards, but will usually be much better at linking employee performance to rewards than an employee-centered manager. Employees of a task-oriented manager will know exactly what productivity or performance level they must attain to get bonuses, salary increases, or promotions. Evans believes that the leadership style most effective in motivating employees depends on the types of rewards they most desire.

House and his colleagues have tried to expand the path-goal theory by identifying two variables that help determine the most effective leadership style: the *personal characteristics of employees* and the *environmental pressures and demands in the workplace* with which employees must cope.

**LEADERSHIP STYLE AND EMPLOYEE SKILL.** Employees who are skilled and capable, like these electronics workers, may prefer a low-supervisory manager who will give them the freedom to do their jobs without unnecessary supervision.

# PERSONAL CHARACTERISTICS OF EMPLOYEES

The leadership style employees prefer will be, according to House, partially determined by their personal characteristics. He cites studies suggesting that individuals who believe their behavior affects the environment favor a participatory leadership style, while those who believe events occur because of luck or fate tend to find an authoritarian style more congenial.

Employees' evaluations of their own ability will also influence their style preference. Those who feel highly skilled and capable may resent an overly supervisory manager, whose directives will be seen as counterproductive rather than helpful. On the other hand, employees who feel less skilled may prefer a more directive manager, who will be seen as enabling them to carry out their tasks properly and earn organizational rewards.

## ENVIRONMENTAL PRESSURES AND WORKPLACE DEMANDS

Environmental factors also affect the leadership styles preferred by employees. One such factor is the nature of the employees' tasks. For example, an overly directive style may seem redundant and even insulting for a highly structured task. If a task is unpleasant, however, a manager's consideration may add to the employee's satisfaction and motivation. Another factor is the organization's formal authority system, which clarifies which actions are likely to be met with approval (coming in *under* budget, say) and which with disapproval (coming in *over* budget). A third environmental factor is the employees' work group. Groups that are not very cohesive, for example, usually benefit from a supportive, understanding style. As a general rule, a leader's style will motivate employees to the extent that it compensates them for what they see as deficiencies in the task, authority system, or work group.

At New Hope Communications, a publishing company based in Boulder, Colorado, CEO Doug Greene faced a problem attracting the types of leaders his company needed. He observed, "We knew we needed better thinking and leadership, but couldn't afford it."[40] Greene dealt with the problem by introducing a flexible employment approach he called "part-time" leadership. Part-time leadership allows smaller, growing companies to attract the kind of talent often associated with larger, more-established companies. Drawing talent from other geographic regions, it enables employees to contribute to the company without having to relocate. For example, Ron Moyer, former circulation director for *Institutional Investor,* is now responsible for New Hope's circulation strategy and planning—part-time. Though he does not live in Colorado, he and Greene are in constant communication through e-mail. "By being involved in separate entities, these people can bring more to the table…. They are leaders," Greene asserted, "with the kind of involvement that goes with it."[41]

## DECIDING WHEN TO INVOLVE SUBORDINATES: THE VROOM-YETTON AND VROOM-JAGO MODELS

In their 1988 book, Victor Vroom and Arthur Jago criticize the path-goal theory because it fails to take into account the situation within which managers decide to involve employees. As a solution, they extend the classic Vroom-Yetton model of situational leadership to include a concern for both the quality and the acceptance of decisions.[42]

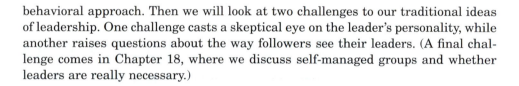

EXHIBIT 17-2     **FUNDAMENTAL PRACTICES AND BEHAVIORS OF EXCEPTIONAL LEADERS**

**CHALLENGING THE PROCESS**
  1. Search for Opportunities
  2. Experiment and Take Risks
**INSPIRING A SHARED VISION**
  3. Envision the Future
  4. Enlist Others
**ENABLING OTHERS TO ACT**
  5. Foster Collaboration
  6. Strengthen Others
**MODELING THE WAY**
  7. Set the Example
  8. Plan Small Wins
**ENCOURAGE THE HEART**
  9. Recognize Individual Contribution
  10. Celebrate Accomplishments

*Source:* James M. Kouzes and Barry Z. Posner, *The Leadership Challenge: How to Get Extraordinary Things Done in Organizations.* (San Francisco: Jossey-Bass, 1987).

**transactional leaders:**

Leaders who determine what subordinates need to do to achieve objectives, classify those requirements, and help subordinates become confident they can reach their objectives.

**transformational leaders:**

Leaders who, through their personal vision and energy, inspire followers and have a major impact on their organizations; also called *charismatic leaders.*

**A CHARISMATIC LEADER.**
Occasionally a leader emerges whose high visibility and personal charisma catches the public consciousness. Now-retired auto-industry executive Lee Iacocca, who led Chrysler Corporation back from the edge of bankruptcy, engendered considerable public recognition and support.

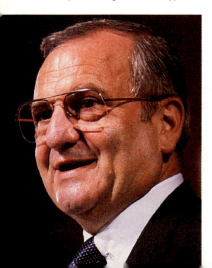

behavioral approach. Then we will look at two challenges to our traditional ideas of leadership. One challenge casts a skeptical eye on the leader's personality, while another raises questions about the way followers see their leaders. (A final challenge comes in Chapter 18, where we discuss self-managed groups and whether leaders are really necessary.)

## TRANSFORMATIONAL OR CHARISMATIC LEADERSHIP

One area of growing interest is the study of individuals who have an exceptional impact on their organizations. These individuals may be called *charismatic*[47] or *transformational*[48] leaders. The recent interest in such transformational leaders stems from at least two sources. First, many large companies—including such giants as AT&T, IBM, and GM[49]—have embarked on organizational "transformations," programs of extensive changes that must be accomplished in short periods of time. Such transformations, it has been argued, require transformational leaders.[50] Second, many feel that by concentrating on traits, behaviors, and situations, leadership theory has lost sight of the *leader.* The visibility of a business leader like Lee Iacocca or a military figure like General Norman Schwartzkopf reminds us that some leaders seem to have personal characteristics that do make a difference—but are not accounted for by existing theories.

**BASS'S THEORY OF TRANSFORMATIONAL LEADERSHIP.** In his explorations of the concept of transformational leadership, Bernard M. Bass has contrasted two types of leadership behaviors: *transactional* and *transformational.* **Transactional leaders** determine what employees need to do to achieve their own and organizational objectives, classify those requirements, and help employees become confident they can reach their objectives by expending the necessary efforts. In contrast, **transformational leaders** "motivate us to do more than we originally expected to do" by raising our sense of the importance and value of our tasks, by "getting us to transcend our own self-interests for the sake of the team, organization, or larger policy," and by raising our need level to the higher-order needs, such as self-actualization.[51]

Much of the leadership theory that we have discussed in this chapter fits Bass's transactional category reasonably well, and Bass argues that such theory is useful and helpful, as far as it goes. However, to be fully effective—and to have a major impact on their organizations—leaders need to use their personal vision and energy to inspire their followers.

← ch. 2, p. 37

**HOUSE'S THEORY OF CHARISMATIC LEADERSHIP.** Although the transformational leadership concept dates back at least to Max Weber's discussion of charismatic leaders in the first decades of the century,[52] the concept received relatively little research attention until recently. One of the notable early contributions to systematic analysis of the subject is Robert J. House's theory of charismatic leadership.[53]

← ch. 13, p. 345

House's theory suggests that charismatic leaders have very high levels of referent power and that some of that power comes from their need to influence others. The charismatic leader has "extremely high levels of self-confidence, dominance, and a strong conviction in the moral righteousness of his/her beliefs"— or at least the ability to convince followers that he or she possesses such confidence and conviction.[54] House suggests that charismatic leaders communicate a *vision* or higher-level ("transcendent") goal that captures the commitment and energy of followers. They are careful to create an image of success and competence and to exemplify in their own behavior the values they espouse. They also communicate high expectations for followers and confidence that followers will perform up to those expectations.

One aspect of House's theory that is likely to receive careful attention is the *type* of vision transformational leaders and their followers pursue. Though the names and deeds of Winston Churchill, Mahatma Gandhi, and Martin Luther King are stirring, House and others are well aware that the ability to inspire great commitment, sacrifice, and energy is no guarantee that the cause or vision is a worthwhile one. Adolf Hitler was also known for his charisma—and for the tragedies his leadership brought to his followers and others. Transformational leaders may possess great potential for revitalizing declining institutions and helping individuals find meaning and excitement in their work lives, but they can pose great dangers if their goals and values are opposed to the basic tenets of civilized society.

## CHALLENGES TO LEADERSHIP THEORY

The example of Hitler has led some people to suggest that we question all leaders' motives. In a series of studies, theorist Manfred Kets de Vries has concluded that leadership theories are based on an oversimplified model of human nature.[55]

**A PSYCHOANALYTIC APPROACH TO LEADERSHIP.** To understand why some people become leaders, Kets de Vries argues, we need to take a *psychoanalytic view*. This view, originated by Sigmund Freud, holds that much of human behavior is shaped by unconscious efforts to satisfy unfulfilled needs and drives. In other words, we may not know why we do what we do. Indeed, much human behavior can be traced to early childhood experiences, which are difficult to recall.

Take House's concept of the charismatic leader rallying people to a heroic vision. In reality, Kets de Vries suggests, the adult leader may be acting out a three-year-old's need to control his or her environment. The fact that this misplaced drama has positive social consequences may be of secondary importance to the leader, who is unconsciously trying to ease a personal frustration.

Kets de Vries holds that appearances can be deceiving, and that we need to return to a more basic theory of human nature if we are to understand the complex dynamics of leadership.

**THE ROMANCE OF LEADERSHIP.** A second challenge to traditional theories of leadership focuses on the followers—the people who look to leaders for guidance. In this view, followers have developed *romanticized,* or idealized, views of what leaders do, what they can accomplish, and how they can affect followers' lives. These romantic views have evolved because most of us find it hard to understand the workings of the large, complex systems within our society, so we turn to leaders to simplify our lives. Thus, romantic views of leadership and leaders say as much about followers as they do about leaders. It may be that people need a romanticized view of leaders to help them focus on and meet organizational needs. If this is so, a leader will be able to motivate and influence only so long as the followers retain confidence in that leader. Once that confidence is lost, the leader's effectiveness will be diminished, no matter what he or she may do.[56] The romance of leadership suggests that leadership is not really necessary, a challenge taken up by the concept of "self-managed" teams and groups (see Chapter 18).

**MANAGEMENT 2000 AND BEYOND**

# Max depree and leadership jazz[57]

In two recent books, *Leadership Jazz* and *Leadership Is An Art,* Max DePree, Chairman of Herman Miller Inc., has suggested that many of the scientific studies that attempt to define leadership miss the most important part: the art form. He says that "Leadership is constructive, the right actions taken in the context of clear and well-considered thinking," where the leader is able to find an authentic voice and touch that moves followers to art. Leadership is learned through practice and by paying attention to followers. DePree suggests that we look to roving leaders as models, people who anticipate needs and respond, outside any formal position and hierarchy. He says eloquently:

> The condition of our hearts, the openness of our attitudes, the quality of our competence, the fidelity of our experience—these give vitality to the work experience and meaning to life. These are what it takes to make roving leadership possible. And roving leadership, freely and openly practiced together, is the vehicle we can use to reach our potential.[58]

# Summary

**1. Define leadership and explain how it is similar to and different from management.**

Leadership is an important subject for managers because of the critical role leaders play in group and organizational effectiveness. Leadership may be defined as the process of influencing and directing the task-related activities of group members. Motivational skills are a critical component of leading, whereas the focus of management is planning and administration.

**2. Explain the key ideas of the trait approach to leadership.**

Three approaches to the study of leadership have been identified: the trait, behavior, and contingency approaches. The trait approach has not proved useful, since no one combination of traits consistently distinguishes leaders from nonleaders or effective leaders from ineffective leaders.

# A DIFFERENT BRAND OF LEADER

As GE's environment changed from one characterized by tight government regulation and high inflation in the 1970s to one of intense global competition in the 1980s, GE needed a different brand of leader. The company chose Jack Welch to lead that change.

Leaders can also change. In GE's 1991 annual report, Jack Welch proclaimed, "We cannot afford management styles that suppress and intimidate."[59] Signaling a kinder and gentler leadership approach, Welch urged his managers to have "the self-confidence to empower others and behave in a boundaryless fashion."[60] Welch has shifted his managerial focus from one of cost cutting and streamlining to the realm of humanistic values. Welch claims that his shift in focus was not possible before he streamlined his organization. "If you've got a fat organization, soft values won't get you very far," Welch noted.[61]

The GE training facility in Crotonville, New York, instituted a program called "Work-Out," designed to eliminate unnecessary work, empower employees, and push GE corporate values to the core of the organization. The program, a humanist approach to Welch's old policy of creative conflict, appears to be working. Welch reports that hourly-paid employees in the company's Schenectady, New York, plant "now run, without supervision, $20 million of new milling machines that they specified, tested, and approved."[62]

Other corporate leaders apparently believe in Jack Welch's leadership successes. He was selected by a committee of his peers as the 1993 Chief Executive of the Year.

3. **Discuss and evaluate the behavior approach to leadership.**

The behavior approach has focused on leadership functions and styles. Studies have found that both task-related functions and group-maintenance functions have to be performed by one or more group members if a group is to function effectively. Studies of leadership styles have distinguished between a task-oriented, authoritarian, or initiating structure on the one hand and an employee-centered, democratic, or participative style on the other. Some studies suggest that the effectiveness of a particular style depends on the circumstances in which it is used. Tannenbaum and Schmidt, for example, maintain that a manager's choice of leadership style should be influenced by various forces in the manager, in subordinates, and in the work situation.

4. **List and explain the major contingency approaches to leadership.**

The contingency approach to leadership attempts to identify which of these situational factors is most important and to predict which leadership style will be more effective in a given situation. The Hersey-Blanchard situational theory of leadership suggests that leadership style should vary with the maturity of subordinates. The manager-subordinate relationship moves through four phases as subordinates develop greater skill, knowledge of their work, and self-confidence; a different leadership style is appropriate for each phase. According to the Fiedler model, leader-member relations, task structure, and the leader's position power are the most important situational variables; this model predicts which types of leaders (high-LPC or low-LPC) will be most effective in the eight possible combinations of these variables.

**5. Explain the concept of transformational or charismatic leadership and give examples.**

A more recent focus of leadership is the transformational or charismatic leader, one who has the ability to lead a company through a major transformation.

**6. Discuss some recent challenges to leadership theory.**

Recent challenges to traditional leadership theory include the psychoanalytic approach, which questions the leader's unconscious motives, and the romantic approach, which focuses on followers' romanticized or idealized views of what the leader can accomplish and how he or she can affect their lives.

## REVIEW QUESTIONS

1. How is leadership defined in this chapter? Discuss three implications of this definition.
2. How does leadership differ from management?
3. What are three approaches to the study of leadership?
4. Why was the trait approach a logical attempt to understand leadership? What did trait studies reveal about leadership?
5. Describe the two basic leadership functions needed for effective group performance. Must one leader perform both these functions?
6. Outline the basic idea of the Tannenbaum and Schmidt model. What factors should influence a manager's style, according to this model? What are some of the practical considerations the model suggests managers must take into account in selecting a style?
7. What are the two basic leadership styles identified by the Ohio State and University of Michigan studies? Which style was thought to be more effective?
8. Outline the basic theory of the Managerial Grid. Which leadership style in the grid do Blake and Mouton believe is most effective?
9. What basic assumptions underlie the Fiedler model? What is the LPC scale? What are the basic elements in the work situation that determine which leadership style will be most effective? In what situations is a high-LPC leader effective? In what situation is a low-LPC leader effective?
10. Describe the path-goal model. On what theory of motivation is the model based? According to this model, how do managers with different leadership styles differ in their ability to influence or reward subordinates? What variables, according to this theory, help determine the most effective leadership style? Why?
11. What are the five styles of managerial decision making suggested by Vroom and Yetton? What are the most important modifications made by Vroom and Jago to the Vroom-Yetton model of leadership?
12. Why are charismatic leaders sometimes dangerous?
13. How does the psychoanalytic approach challenge traditional theories of leadership?
14. Why does the romantic approach say we follow leaders?

## KEY TERMS

Leadership

Power

Influence

Leadership functions

Leadership styles

Managerial Grid

Contingency approach

Situational leadership theory

Least preferred co-worker (LPC)

Leader-member relations

Task structure

Position power

Path-goal model

Transactional leaders

Transformational leaders

## CASE STUDY

### DAVE THOMAS: WENDY'S "DAD"[63]

R. David Thomas, founder and senior chairman of Wendy's International, Inc., has been called many things in his day. His franchisees, citing his barnstorming market tours as a source of inspiration, call him the "Great Communicator." Most of America knows him as the funny, folksy character on Wendy's renowned television commercials. Some may even recognize him as the lonely boy from his autobiography, *Dave's Way*. But Jim Near, Wendy's chairman and CEO, sees him as "Wendy's Dad." According to Near, "No other chain has an active founder like him leading the way."[64]

Indeed, few companies can boast a founder as well-known and well-liked as Dave Thomas. Ironically, however, such stardom was not among Thomas' goals. In fact, after years of virtually non-stop work building the Wendy's name, Thomas retired from day-to-day management in the early 1980s. "I left the company to people smarter than me to run," he explained.[65] His charming modesty proved to be a liability, however, for, shortly after his departure, franchise problems arose on the heels of the celebrated "Where's the Beef?" television spot that boosted Wendy's up the fast-food charts. "Funny things happen when people start to make money," Near noted. "It's easy to take your mind off what's important."[66] Many of Wendy's original franchise owners had sold their stores to owners who were not interested in Thomas' standards of excellence, which had become integral to the restaurant chain. Other owners, assuming the business could run itself, simply left their franchises stranded. Some franchisees

even decided to go public. Very quickly Wendy's began to lose its customer-oriented focus and the chain suffered.

Aware that something had to be done, but reluctant to relinquish his hard-earned retirement, Thomas attempted to leave the situation to Near, who had been drafted in 1986 to become president and COO of the company. Thomas hoped he had found his savior in Near, a board member since 1981 and one of Wendy's most successful franchise owners, but Near was less enthusiastic. "This was the last place I wanted to be," he recalled. "Franchisees had just given management a vote of no confidence. They weren't even giving them a chance."[67] But Thomas persisted and eventually Near agreed to take over. As a condition of accepting the position, though, Near insisted that Thomas become an active Wendy's spokesperson and ambassador. Thomas consented and so was born "Dave."

Although Thomas may have been initially reluctant, he has thrown himself wholeheartedly into the role of Wendy's figurehead. Maintaining an office next to Near's, Thomas tours the country regularly for market visits, promotional appearances, and television spots. Thomas' spots have scored consistently high in audience recognition and he has become a favorite of critics. "Wait till you see the latest creative," praised Near. "We had no idea that Dave would be so good on TV."[68]

The "Wendy's Wildest Tie Contest," which began in April 1994, illustrates how well Thomas has learned to play his audience. Prior to the contest, a television spot for Wendy's "Spicy Chicken" sandwich featured Thomas sporting what he considered the "wildest tie around." Always the showman, however, Thomas decided to hold a contest to see if anyone could top his exotic neckwear. "If you got an old tie that's looking wilder every year, then send it on in," he said. "If I think it tops mine, I'll give you an entire collection of new designer ties."[69] The winner received a choice of either a $1,500 neckwear wardrobe, featuring ties by designers such as Armani, Hermes, Nicole Miller, or the cash equivalent. Two runner-ups received a $500 collection or the cash equivalent.

Such visibility has not only made Thomas a well-known figure, but it has also helped to shoot Wendy's profitability and popularity back up and make it one of Wall Street's favorite restaurants. In 1988, Wendy's posted an unprecedented $5 million loss. By 1994, with the help of "Dave," Wendy's claimed 4,200 restaurants worldwide and annual sales near $4 billion. Many people attribute Wendy's astonishing comeback to the enthusiasm and energy emanated by their appointed leader. For Thomas himself, however, the success of Wendy's belongs to those people who helped bring it about: his employees. "[I'm] nobody really," Thomas confessed. "I just make hamburgers for a living."[70]

### CASE QUESTIONS

1. Is Thomas an effective leader? If so, what makes him effective? If not, why not?
2. Who does Thomas lead?
3. Do you consider Thomas charismatic? Why?
4. Are there types of businesses in which Thomas' style might be less effective? More effective?

## VIDEO CASE STUDY

### BLOOMBERG: WANTED DEAD OR ALIVE[71]

Everyone is out to get Michael Bloomberg. Dow Jones, the 110-year-old publisher of business news, had marked him: "You tell that fella I'm gonna get him," said Henry Becher, a Dow Jones executive vice president.[72] Reuters, the British-based international news service, has released a product. And EJV, a consortium of Wall Street's heaviest hitters, has singled him out as their No. 1 competitor.

So why is Michael "most-wanted" Bloomberg smiling? Perhaps because his company, Bloomberg Limited Partners, parent company to Bloomberg Business News (BBN), is the fastest-growing provider of financial data, analysis, and news. "The competition focuses on us," Bloomberg said wryly, "while we focus on our customers."[73]

For Bloomberg, drawing attention to himself has become a way of doing business. Fresh out of Harvard Business School, he took a modest position with Salomon Brothers as a clerk processing trades. But he didn't plan to stay low on the totem pole for long. "I used to get in at 7 A.M.," he recalled. "I was the only one in the trading room other than Billy Salomon, and so we chitchatted. Then I would stay till 7 at night, and after 6 the only other person in the room was John Gutfreund, and he'd give me a ride uptown. So the managing partner and the heir apparent became my friends when I was just starting as a clerk."[74] Through initiative and what many would call an unhealthy obsession for work, Bloomberg quickly climbed the ranks to the position of head of equity and sales.

But Bloomberg had greater ambition: He wanted to run Salomon. "I kept telling Gutfreund I could run the goddamn company better," Bloomberg asserted.[75] But such abrasive cockiness eventually led instead to a demotion. Rather than quitting immediately, though, Bloomberg stuck it out, staying with the company long enough to collect a $10 million consolation prize when Salomon went public in a merger with Phibro in 1981. Armed with the idea that investment bankers and traders needed a single terminal loaded with research and up-to-the-minute corporate data, Bloomberg used this money to begin his own company. Outfinanced and underexperienced, Bloomberg nevertheless took on the giants of the electronic financial information industry.

Relying on a shrewd low-pricing strategy, in-house technology, and persistence, Bloomberg began his battle. In 1982, he approached Merrill Lynch with a pitch for a system for pricing U.S. government bonds. Merrill's computer specialists told him they would need at least six months to consider the viability of his proposal. Bloomberg pounced. "I'll deliver a finished product in six months," he responded confidently, "and if you don't like it you don't have to pay for it."[76] And six months later Bloomberg delivered a system, which Merrill purchased, that could perform complex calculations on government bonds as well as keep track of Merrill's inventory.

Bolstered by his initial success with Merrill, Bloomberg set about the task of turning the financial information industry upside down. Bloomberg Financial Markets broke Dow Jones Telerate's stranglehold on government bond pricing, snatched away the prestigious Bank of England as a client from Reuters, and ended Quotron's monopoly over stock-quoting. Very quickly, people began to view Bloomberg as a force with which to be reckoned.

"Whenever you see a business that's done the same thing for a long time,…a new guy can come in and do it better," explained Bloomberg. "I guarantee it."[77] Bloomberg brought his customers a new level of information services. Bloomberg's machines, dubbed "Bloombergs," enable traders to obtain a comprehensive view of a company through a single source, whereas they previously would have had to consult a variety of sources. "Nobody comes close to Bloomberg in terms of the breadth of information," noted Nancy Freund-Heller, director of private placements at TIAA/CREF, which has been replacing its old Telerate screens with Bloombergs.[78]

Almost singlehandedly, Bloomberg led his industry to new heights in technology and service. "Bloomberg jumps higher and faster than anyone else in this business," observed Eric Philo, a media analyst at Goldman Sachs. "He sees the technology's there, and he says, 'Let's do it,' and it gets done, while his stodgier competitors sit around and discuss it."[79]

As Bloomberg's much larger competitors fight to catch up in terms of information supply and technology, Bloomberg continues to lead the way into the future. "The future belongs to multimedia, not one-product companies," he predicts. "I'm going to make sure that we're one of those New Age compa-

nies."[80] Toward this end, Bloomberg's name has begun appearing in numerous formats. Thanks to BBN, the Bloomberg name makes regular appearances in newspapers that use the news service, such as *The New York Times*. In September 1993, Bloomberg began broadcasting on WNEW-AM, quickly renamed Bloomberg Business Radio and changed to an all-business news format. And then there's *Bloomberg Magazine,* an advertiser-supported monthly magazine distributed to all Bloomberg terminal users. Also, there's "Bloomberg Forum," a series of video interviews with leading business executives aired on USA Network and CNBC. Finally, a joint effort between BBN and Maryland Public Television (MPT) has resulted in a daily 15-minute show distributed to MPT and to all Bloomberg Financial Markets' 30,000 multimedia computer terminals in 135 countries worldwide.

Bloomberg disagrees with those who perceive diversification as a potential drawback. "People said to me, 'What the hell are you in radio for?' But it fits in," Bloomberg pointed out. "It generates audio for our terminals, enhancing the product that keeps this company successful. Like the news service. It's all integrated, all the parts feed into each other."[81]

In the end, publicity may serve as Bloomberg's strongest asset. Whereas Dow Jones and Reuters are essentially faceless corporations, Bloomberg is a household name in business circles—all his products bear his name. Moreover, his aggressive and sometimes overly straightforward manner has made him something of a media figure. But even Bloomberg admits that he has at least one worry. "What frightens me," he confesses, "is the little guy in the garage I don't even know about right now." In other words, what Bloomberg fears is another Bloomberg: another leader.

## CASE QUESTIONS

1. What forces have helped to shape Bloomberg's leadership style?
2. Would you characterize Bloomberg as a charismatic leader?
3. What traits make Bloomberg an effective leader?
4. What traits hinder Bloomberg's leadership ability?
5. As a competitor, what could you learn from him?

## CHAPTER 18

# TEAMS AND

# TEAMWORK

**Upon completing this chapter, you should be able to:**

1. Distinguish between the major types of teams found in organizations.

2. Outline characteristics of superteams and self-managed teams.

3. Discuss guidelines for increasing team cohesiveness.

4. Provide guidelines for making teams more effective.

5. Explain how managers can deal with conflicts within teams.

# PARTNERING FOR SUCCESS AT SATURN[1]

n 1991, for the first time in 15 years, an American car manufacturer sold more cars per dealer than any other manufacturer, including Honda. And the performance was repeated the following year. The company? Saturn Corporation.

The inspiration for Saturn came out of the early 1980s, as domestic U.S. car manufacturers, confronting fierce competition from Japanese manufacturers such as Toyota and Honda, had been steadily losing ground since the late 1970s. Roger Smith, then chairman of General Motors, set his sights on developing a world-class economy car that could beat the Japanese imports. And so was born Saturn, GM's $3.5 billion subsidiary, staffed by fiercely loyal people who are working hard to keep up with customer demand for their quality cars.

In launching Saturn, GM departed from traditional industry and company norms. Smith determined that if Saturn were to produce a different caliber of cars, it had to be a different type of company. So Saturn was set up as an independent subsidiary, not a division, to allow the company to "break the rules" by which U.S. auto manufacturers have traditionally been managed.

Instead of accepting labor/management antagonism as inevitable, GM based Saturn on principles of participative management. The result was a partnership between traditional rivals, GM management and the United Auto Workers (UAW), through a contract signed in 1985. "The system is designed so that decisions are made in partnership between the UAW employees and management," noted Chuck Stridde, a people systems advisor at Saturn, "which gives the employees a sense of empowerment."[2]

*If Saturn were to produce a different caliber of cars, it had to be a different type of company.*

Saturn set up shop in Tennessee. As of June 1992, 6,885 people worked there. "I came to Saturn because of its vision about how it was going to operate, what it was intending to do," recalled Gary Wilson, a maintenance coordinator in the body shop area. "It's hard to see what's going on, not only in the auto industry but in U.S. business in general, and not feel angry about the deterioration. There's got to be a better way [to run a business], and I want to be part of that. We are on a mission to make this [partnership between management and labor] successful, so that we as a country, GM, and I personally can survive."[3]

But the partnership between GM and the UAW was not an automatic success. Key to the success of this revolutionary new concept of cooperative management was executive support. In addition, it took preparation. "It's not an easy proposition to get existing organizations to turn in place and get where we have here—to create a new culture from an existing one," said Stridde. "I believe one reason for our success is the trust we've built with the union and the way we can work together. But that trust wasn't built overnight; it took a lot of planning."[4]

The management/labor partnership has actually enhanced Saturn's employment flexibility. Because of the partnership, work classifications have been reduced. There is only one classification for production workers and five for skilled trades. Everyone is on salary—the partnership did away with the hourly wage for production workers. In addition, every team member knows the other members' jobs and receives the same salary. Team members

**SATURN.** The popularity of Saturn cars is a source of pride to the many team-oriented workers who contribute their best efforts to producing quality automobiles.

rotate jobs regularly to prevent employees from having to perform the same task for too long a period of time. "The teams, or work units, are charged with making a lot of decisions about their jobs," said Stridde. "And they're not only responsible for direct work, but also for work that is indirect."[5]

"The biggest difference between Saturn and other auto plants is that there are no management prerogatives for decision-making," asserted Michael Bennett, president of Union Local 1853. "Decisions at Saturn are made by all stakeholders, with the UAW sharing fully in that process....The fact that the decision-making process at Saturn is fully integrated, with union members at all levels, is unique in the United States, and even goes far beyond what progressive European countries have legislated concerning union involvement."[6]

All Saturn employees participate in at least one team. Employees work in self-managed teams of 5 to 15 people on the production floor and determine for themselves everything from budgeting to scheduling, hiring, and training. Consensus building is the guiding principle. Team members do not vote. If the entire team does not feel comfortable enough with a decision to support it, that decision will not be made.

The teams are self-monitoring. Instead of having nonmembers do the checking, the members themselves do it. "We've broadened the scope of their responsibility so they have a better and bigger picture of what it takes to run the business," said Joseph D. Rypkowski, a vice president of the UAW and business team advisor for Saturn's people systems. "Even though their piece of running the business may be relatively small, they gain a better appreciation for what the organization has to do and what it costs in dollars."[7] Team members receive monthly reports on budgeted expenses and actual expenditures for their team, for example.

Disagreements can arise. "There is conflict, but it's managed differently," Bennett pointed out. "It's not adversarial. It's more advocacy in terms of finding a better solution or better options."[8] An example occurred during the fall of 1991, when the original management/labor contract was reopened for further talks. During that time, GM chairman Robert Stempel arrived to find a demonstration with union people wearing black-and-orange armbands to protest a plan to increase production quickly to 700 cars a day—a plan which they believed would compromise quality. The workers were afraid that adding teams to the line too quickly would hamper efforts to work out the already-existing problems. In response to the demonstration, Saturn decided to increase production more slowly.

According to Robert Boruff, Saturn vice president of manufacturing operations, this incident underscored the rarity of what Saturn represents. "Think about an organization where you've got people coming from 136 [GM] locations, all of whom have been raised with a bias that the numbers are first and quality is second. They aren't protesting line speedups. They're not protesting health and safety issues. They just want to ensure the quality of the product. That's not a problem, that's a gift from God."[9] →

As Saturn illustrates, much organizational work is done in teams. Indeed, to meet the challenges of the business environment today (see Part II) more and more organizations are replacing old hierarchies and formal systems with teams and teamwork. Many organizations are finding that the best way to make individual employees productive is to pay attention to the way work groups and teams are managed. In this chapter, we will describe work groups and teams and explain how they can be managed effectively.*

---

*Note that we will use the terms "groups" and "teams" interchangeably to reflect a reality in modern organizations. Some might see groups as lacking the common vision of a team.

# TYPES OF TEAMS

**A team** is defined as two or more people who interact and influence each other toward a common purpose.[10] Traditionally, two types of teams have existed in organizations: formal and informal. Today, however, teams exist that have the characteristics of both.

## FORMAL AND INFORMAL TEAMS

Formal teams or groups are created deliberately by managers and charged with carrying out specific tasks to help the organization achieve its goals. The most prevalent type of formal group is the **command team,** which includes a manager and all employees who report to that manager. In some organizations that want to de-emphasize hierarchy, the titles may change. For instance, at NCR, the managers of command teams are called "coaches," and the team members are called "associates."

Another type of formal team is the **committee,** which generally lasts a long time and deals with recurrent problems and decisions. For instance, your university or college probably has a committee for student affairs to deal with recurring issues that involve students' lives. While members of this committee may come and go, the committee remains in place over time.

A quality circle is a kind of team. At Reynolds Metal Company's McCook Sheet & Plate Plant, based in McCook, Illinois, quality circles have been a significant component of a quality program that has dramatically improved productivity and quality since 1981. In a program called Cooperative Hourly and Management Problem Solving (CHAMPS), quality circle teams meet for an hour weekly to discuss work-related problems, investigate the causes, recommend solutions, and take corrective action. When a team has completed its investigation and identified a solution, it makes a formal presentation to the plant management and staff. Of the almost 475 solutions offered in the first four years of the program, almost 400 were approved. The total savings from the ideas has been eight times their cost, a significant amount in a major manufacturing facility where cost control is very important. Over a three-year period, McCook was able to double the pounds of aluminum per employee that it shipped and deliver more than 2,000 items to a specific customer without a single rejection.[11]

Some formal teams are temporary. They may be called **task forces** or **project teams.** These teams are created to deal with a specific problem and are usually disbanded when the task is completed or the problem is solved. For instance, President Clinton formed a project team, headed by Hillary Rodham Clinton, to formulate a proposal for a national health care plan.

Informal teams or groups emerge whenever people come together and interact regularly. Such groups develop within the formal organizational structure. Members of informal teams tend to subordinate some of their individual needs to those of the team as a whole. In return, the team supports and protects them. The activities of informal teams may further the interests of the organization—Saturday morning softball games, for example, may strengthen the players' ties to each other. Or a women's group may meet to discuss various actions that can make the organization a better place for women to work.

The following example is a case in point. In 1990, female employees at the telephone giant, NYNEX Corporation, formed mentoring circles to assist women in moving up the corporate advancement ladder.[12] NYNEX women created these informal groups independently and outside management auspices. The groups encourage, recognize, and strengthen the bonds of women at all levels of the company. The NYNEX employees turned to the group format because there was a shortage of female upper-level managers to serve as mentors. However, participants believe the

**team:**
Two or more people who interact with and influence each other toward a common purpose.

← ch. 8, p. 214

**command team:**
A team composed of a manager and the employees that report to that manager.

**committee:**
A formal organizational team, usually relatively long-lived, created to carry out specific organizational tasks.

**task force or project team:**
A temporary team formed to address a specific problem.

**INFORMAL TEAMS.** Company softball games are just one way in which informal teams get together, strengthening their ties to the organization. A softball game at a company picnic is a good opportunity for employees of Marlow Industries to interact.

group process is actually better than one-on-one mentoring. In the circles, which have a minimum of eight participants and a maximum of twelve, the mentored women have an increased exposure to different ideas and an increased network.

**norms:**

Assumptions and expectations about how members of a group will behave.

**FUNCTIONS OF INFORMAL GROUPS.** Informal groups serve four major functions.[13] First, they maintain and strengthen the **norms** (expected behavior) and values their members hold in common. Second, they give members feelings of social satisfaction, status, and security. In large corporations, where many people feel that their employers hardly know them, informal groups enable employees to share jokes and complaints, eat together, and socialize after work. Informal groups thus satisfy the human needs for friendship, support, and security.

Third, informal groups help their members communicate. Members of informal groups learn about matters that affect them by developing their own informal channels of communication to supplement more formal channels. In fact, managers often use informal networks to convey information "unofficially."

Fourth, informal groups help solve problems. They might aid a sick or tired employee or devise activities to deal with boredom. Quite often, such group problem solving helps the organization—for example, when co-workers tell nonproductive employees to "shape up." But these groups can also *reduce* an organization's effectiveness—for example, when they pressure new employees to reduce their efforts so the group's normal standards will not be called into question.

Beyond these four functions, informal groups may act as **reference groups**— groups that we identify with and compare ourselves to (thus, they have referent power). A middle manager's reference group, for example, might be higher-level managers. Because people tend to model themselves after their reference groups, these groups have an important influence on organizational life.

## HIGH PERFORMANCE TEAMS OR SUPERTEAMS

Some groups today have characteristics of both formal and informal teams. **Superteams** or **high-performance teams**—groups of 3 to 30 workers drawn

**reference group:**
A group with whom individuals identify and compare themselves.

**superteams or high-performance teams:**
Groups of 3 to 30 workers drawn from different areas of a corporation who get together to solve the problems that workers deal with daily.

**A SUPERTEAM'S SUPER EFFORT.**
To enter an industry competition, Whirlpool put together a superteam to develop a high-energy, no-CFC refrigerator on a tight timeline. The team not only came through on schedule, their product won the contest and a $30 million prize.

from different areas of a corporation—are an example. Initially called "self-managed work teams," "cross-functional teams," or "high-performance teams," these kinds of teams were dubbed *superteams* by *Fortune* magazine in May 1990, and the name has stuck.[14]

At Federal Express, superteams figured out how to solve a billing problem and wound up saving the company $2.1 million a year. At one of General Mills' cereal plants in California, superteams run the factory during the night shift—without the help of a manager.

Superteams are also becoming important to small businesses such as advertising agencies. At one time, it was technology that distinguished advertisers. According to Bill Westbrook, a judge for the One Show advertising awards, the advertising industry is now moving away from technology toward strategy. With the expansion of the entertainment and communications network to 500 channels, Lee Garfinkel of Lowe and Partners explains that advertising is becoming a more appealing industry. Some agencies are therefore adopting strategies that include the creation of superteams comprised of top directors, copywriters, and art directors.[15]

What sets superteams apart from other formal teams is that they ignore the traditional "chimney hierarchy"—a strict up-and-down arrangement with workers at the bottom and managers at the top—that is often too cumbersome to solve problems workers deal with every day. Well-run superteams *manage themselves*, arrange their work schedules, set their productivity quotas, order their own equipment and supplies, improve product quality, and interact with customers and other superteams.

Large corporations such as Corning, DEC, General Mills, and Federal Express all use superteams. Superteams seem to work as well in the service and finance sectors as they do in manufacturing. They can be created to work on a specific project or problems, or they can become a permanent part of the company's work force. The superteam concept is central to the organization at Saturn where all employees participate in at least one self-managed, self-monitored team that makes decisions regarding everything from budgeting to scheduling, hiring, and training.

According to General Mills, productivity is up by 40 percent in plants that use superteams. And at Johnsonville Foods in Wisconsin, superteams of blue-collar workers helped CEO Ralph Stayer decide to proceed with a plant expansion. They also told Stayer they would be able to increase sausage production faster than he thought reasonable to ask. Between 1986 and 1990, productivity at Johnsonville rose 50 percent.

Superteams are not all "roses and rainbows," however. For simple problems, such as those encountered in assembly-line production, the superteam may be too much. Superteams make the most sense when there is a complex problem to solve or layers of progress-delaying management to cut through; the key concept here is cross-functionalism. And superteams are not the right choice for every company culture. Middle managers can feel threatened by superteams because they leave fewer rungs on the corporate ladder to move up.

Organizing a corporation into superteams is a long, complex process that may take years. A Harvard Business School study found that it is easier to start a new plant with superteams (as GM did at Saturn) than it is to convert an existing plant into superteams. Still, some experts think that superteams may turn out to be the most productive business innovation of the 1990s.

## SELF-MANAGED TEAMS

Superteams that manage themselves without any formal supervision are called **self-managed teams** or **self-managed work groups.** These teams usually have the following characteristics:[16]

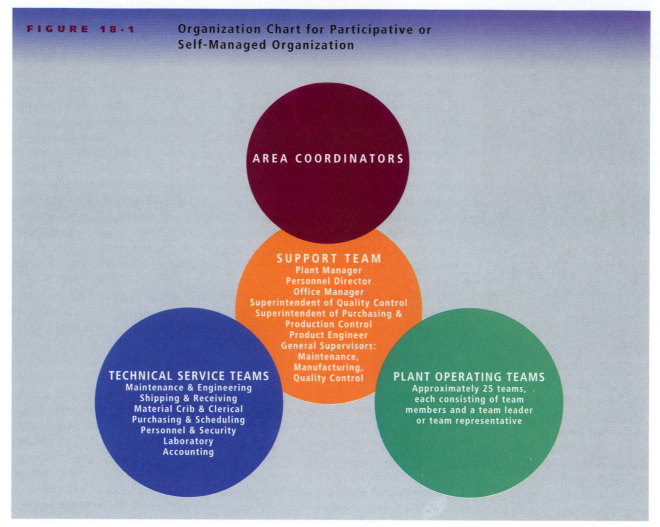

**FIGURE 18-1** Organization Chart for Participative or Self-Managed Organization

**AREA COORDINATORS**

**SUPPORT TEAM**
Plant Manager
Personnel Director
Office Manager
Superintendent of Quality Control
Superintendent of Purchasing &
Production Control
Product Engineer
General Supervisors:
Maintenance,
Manufacturing,
Quality Control

**TECHNICAL SERVICE TEAMS**
Maintenance & Engineering
Shipping & Receiving
Material Crib & Clerical
Purchasing & Scheduling
Personnel & Security
Laboratory
Accounting

**PLANT OPERATING TEAMS**
Approximately 25 teams,
each consisting of team
members and a team leader
or team representative

*Source:* From *Thriving on Chaos: Handbook for Management Revolution,* by Tom Peters. Copyright © 1987 by Excel, a California Limited Partnership. Reprinted by permission of Alfred A. Knopf, Inc.

**self-managed team or self-managed work group:**

Teams that manage themselves without any formal supervision.

- The team has responsibility for a "relatively whole task."
- Team members each possess a variety of task-related skills.
- The team has the power to determine such things as work methods, scheduling, and assignment of members to different tasks.
- The performance of the group as a whole is the basis for compensation and feedback.

The presence of such groups in industry means individual strategies for completing tasks are replaced by group methods for job accomplishment.

As with superteams in general, this participative approach is seen in both manufacturing and nonmanufacturing organizations within the United States. For example, in Worthington Industries and Chaparral Steel, it is routine for security guards to enter orders and run ambulances, for supervisors to hire and train their own staffs, and for supervisors to determine operating procedures for new equipment. Similarly, at the GM Delco-Remy plant in Fitzgerald, Georgia, workers generally handle all quality control, track their own time, and rotate as work-team leaders. Chaparral's steel is of superb quality, and the GM Delco-Remy plant has an exceptionally good record on absenteeism, quality, and productivity. (A simplified schematic of the Delco-Remy plant organization is presented in Figure 18-1.)[17]

## SELF-MANAGED TEAMS AT XEL COMMUNICATIONS

Another company that has had much success with self-managed teams is XEL Communications Inc., a spin-off from GTE Corporation. XEL competes with giants like AT&T and Northern Telecom in the manufacture of telecommunications equipment, such as customized circuit boards.[18] In the mid-1980s, company managers developed self-managed teams to cope with high costs and slow responses to customer needs. The teams were organized as cellular production groups that build whole families of circuit boards. The team concept is working. XEL recorded sales of approximately $25 million in 1993, up from $17 million in 1992.

To support the team process, banners are hung in the manufacturing facilities to mark each team's work area. The company displays team performance on wall charts that track attendance, on-time deliveries, and other variables. Teams meet daily, without a supervisor, to plan their work to meet production requirements. The teams meet with management once a quarter to make a formal presentation on group accomplishments and setbacks.

XEL has found some difficulties in the team approach, however. The team process has made staffing and hiring decisions very difficult. Managers must consider not only whether the job candidate has the requisite skills, but whether he or she can perform within a particular team. The company tried to hire temporaries, but the "temps" could not fit into the team process.

Determining compensation is also more difficult than in a traditional compensation system that rewards individual performance. Here, the compensation system must support the group. XEL uses a three-part compensation system. Part one sets an hourly wage based on the skills the employee has mastered. Part two includes merit increases based on team performance and peer reviews. Part three is profit sharing based on company performance. ▪

One organization with an effective approach to individual performance evaluation of employees who are part of self-managed teams is Digital Equipment Corporation's Eastern Massachusetts Financial Management Center. In January 1992, the General Accounting Group, which had been reorganized into three teams, introduced a peer performance review process. They developed a form, the first portion of which was to be completed by the team member being reviewed. The team member was to summarize his or her role and note accomplishments before passing the form on to the other team members, who jointly answered the remaining questions concerning the team member's performance. The questions solicited feedback on qualities such as initiative, leadership, creativity, and sensitivity. After completing the form, the team members forwarded it to Barbara Cofsky, head of the group and the original promoter of the team structure, who included key points in the team member's performance appraisal. In addition, Cofsky met with each team member one-on-one to deliver the reviews. "Already we have seen some benefits to the approach we are using in terms of increased awareness, sensitivity, and mutual support," noted Cofsky.... "We are trying to be careful in how we use these peer reviews so we don't use them with the traditional management mind set of control and power, but, instead, we use them to support each other, build trust and openness, and learn how to use each other's strengths and tap into each other's interests and motivations."[19]

# THE MISSION OF SUCCESS

If "different" is what Saturn aimed for, Saturn has definitely succeeded. "It's as different as it has ever been," said R. Timothy Epps, vice president of people systems at Saturn. "We're committed to an entirely different set of beliefs. One is to have UAW involvement in all aspects of the business. The other crucial principle is that we believe that those people affected by a decision should be involved in the decision."[20]

One factor at the heart of Saturn's success is its explicit mission statement:

> The mission of Saturn is to market vehicles developed and manufactured in the United States that are world leaders in quality, cost and customer satisfaction through the integration of people, technology and business systems, and to transfer knowledge, technology and experience throughout General Motors.[21]

This statement is more than mere words on paper at Saturn. "Most people have it committed to memory," commented Jack O'Toole, UAW Local 1853 vice president of people systems. "Everyone knows the mission…. We explain it from the time we start recruiting them. The mission tells us what we exist for—and what would not happen if we didn't exist."[22]

The three primary concerns underscored in the mission statement involve the people, technology, and business of the company. Saturn's goal is to achieve a balance among the three. "If you make a decision that is just good for people, but impacts the other two, you've got a contented workforce, but you go out of business," O'Toole pointed out. "If you make a great business decision that alienates the workforce, you go out of business. If you decide to use a technology that isn't compatible with your people, you go out of business."[23]

At Saturn, what this means is that assignments are not made. Rather, options are proposed. In 1991, car sales climbed, necessitating that, in order to meet demand, the workforce put in 10-hour days four out of five days per week. In planning how to meet 1992 demand, Saturn managers did not simply schedule five 10-hour days. According to O'Toole, Saturn instead let workers decide what to do: "Here's the scenario. Working four 10-hour days and an occasional Friday, here's the production we'll get. Working five 10-hour days, here's what we'll get. It's your company, what do you want to do?"[24] And the employees made their choices. In the end, 90 percent of the people did opt for the longer workweek, but Saturn's involving them in the decision-making and empowering them to decide is the essence of the company's management style.

Empowerment has resulted in increased feelings of accountability among employees. While absenteeism averages 10 percent to 14 percent at most GM plants, it hovers nearer to 2.5 percent at Saturn. The emphasis on teamwork breeds team loyalty—in addition to company loyalty—and discourages team members from skipping out on work, because it would mean that other team members would have to pick up the slack.

"There's a level of excitement, dedication and commitment at Saturn that I don't recall seeing at any other [GM] division," noted Stridde. "And I think it's because of the way we've approached how people fit into the organization and what they can contribute."[25] →

# CHARACTERISTICS OF TEAMS

The first step in learning to manage teams effectively is to become aware of their characteristics—that is, the way they develop leadership roles, norms, and cohesiveness.

## LEADERSHIP ROLES

The formal leader of a team is usually appointed or elected. Informal leaders, on the other hand, tend to emerge gradually as group members interact. The man or woman who speaks up more than the others, who offers more and better suggestions than anyone else, or who gives direction to the group's activities usually becomes the informal leader. This occurs not just in informal groups, but even in formal groups, where such a self-confident, assertive individual may develop into a rival of the formally chosen leader, thereby weakening the leader's hold on team members.[26]

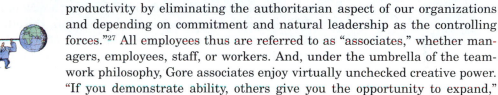

At W. L. Gore and Associates, the value of team leadership is emphasized, but not at the expense of individual employee freedom. "We, as leaders," asserted founder Wilbert L. Gore, "can unleash much more of this inherent creativity and productivity by eliminating the authoritarian aspect of our organizations and depending on commitment and natural leadership as the controlling forces."[27] All employees thus are referred to as "associates," whether managers, employees, staff, or workers. And, under the umbrella of the teamwork philosophy, Gore associates enjoy virtually unchecked creative power.

"If you demonstrate ability, others give you the opportunity to expand," noted Arthur Punchard, the UK fabric plant's leader, "and you can change roles quite dramatically across disciplines."[28] Such flexibility and teamwork have enabled the company to achieve worldwide sales in the neighborhood of $950 million.

## STAGES OF TEAM DEVELOPMENT[29]

More than two decades ago, B. W. Tuckman suggested that small groups move through five stages as they develop: Forming, Storming, Norming, Performing, Adjourning.

**FORMING.** During the initial stage, the group *forms* and learns what sort of behavior is acceptable to the group. By exploring what does and does not work, the group sets implicit and explicit ground rules that cover the completion of specific tasks as well as general group dynamics. By and large, this stage is a period of both orientation and acclimation.

**STORMING.** As group members become more comfortable with one another, they may oppose the formation of a group structure as they begin to assert their individual personalities. Members often become hostile and even fight ground rules set during the forming stage.

**NORMING.** At this time, the conflicts that arose in the previous stage are addressed and hopefully resolved. Group unity emerges as members establish common goals, norms, and ground rules. The group as a whole participates, not merely a few vocal members. Members begin to voice personal opinions and develop close relationships.

**PERFORMING.** Now that structural issues have been resolved, the group begins to operate as a unit. The structure of the group now supports and eases group dynamics and performance. The structure becomes a tool for the group's use instead

When cooperation is especially vital—for instance, in meeting strategic goals—managers have four ways to improve cohesiveness: introduce competition, increase interpersonal attraction, increase interaction, and create common goals and common fates for employees.

**INTRODUCE COMPETITION.** Conflict with outside individuals or other teams increases group cohesiveness. With this factor in mind, GE has developed a new program to train managers in creating and leading competitive work teams.[37] Competition is also used at Nintendo, the company that brought us Super Mario Brothers, where creative director Shiegeru Miyamoto often encourages creativity by dividing his 200 designers into opposing teams.[38]

**INCREASE INTERPERSONAL ATTRACTION.** People tend to join teams whose members they identify with or admire. Thus, an organization may want to begin by trying to attract employees who share certain key values. Managers at Rosenbluth Travel, winner of a Tom Peters award as Service Company of 1990, use carefully worded advertisements and unique interviewing techniques (such as an impromptu baseball game) to discover associates who share a concern for consideration and service. More importantly, Rosenbluth follows through with training, seminars, and policies that foster pride in meeting the common organizational goal of providing outstanding service.[39]

**INCREASE INTERACTION.** Although it is not often possible for people to like everyone they work with, increased interaction can improve camaraderie and communication. Corporations such as Tandem Computers and Genentech, a biotechnology firm, hold regular beer parties to which all employees are invited. At Merle Norman Cosmetics, managers sponsor Saturday night movies and serve ice cream at a 1920s-style movie emporium.[40] In Huntsville, Alabama, Goldstar of America, Inc., occasionally closes down its plant early for volleyball games in which employees can meet one another in a spirit of camaraderie as well as good-natured competition. This subsidiary of the South Korean firm Lucky-Goldstar is noted for its success in encouraging parallel production teams to compete against one another. Here we see the interaction of two techniques for increasing cohesiveness (competition and interaction).[41]

**task interdependence:**
The extent to which a group's work requires its members to interact with one another.

**sense of potency:**
Collective belief of a group that it can be effective.

← ch. 10, p. 265

**outcome interdependence:**
The degree to which the work of a group has consequences felt by all its members.

**CREATE COMMON GOALS AND COMMON FATES.** Gregory Shea and Richard Guzzo have proposed that a group's effectiveness is a function of three variables: task interdependence, potency, and outcome interdependence (see Figure 18-3).[42] **Task interdependence** is the extent to which a group's work requires its members to interact with one another. A high level of task interdependence increases the group's **sense of potency,** which is the shared belief of a group that it can be effective. **Outcome interdependence** is the degree to which the consequences of the group's work are felt by all the group's members.

Shea and Guzzo further explain how astute managers can create successful teams. Managers must first give each group a *charter*—a clear and achievable set of objectives. A strategic planning group, for example, might be chartered to devise a five-year company plan. Because groups should be given flexibility in arranging their own affairs, the manager should "concentrate on getting the charter right and not on details of how a group organizes itself." The members of the group should decide how much task interdependence their work requires. However, the members must believe the organization has given them sufficient resources—skills, money, flexibility—to fulfill the charter.

In addition, managers must strive to create a sense of outcome interdependence. If the members of a group do not share some common fate, they will have

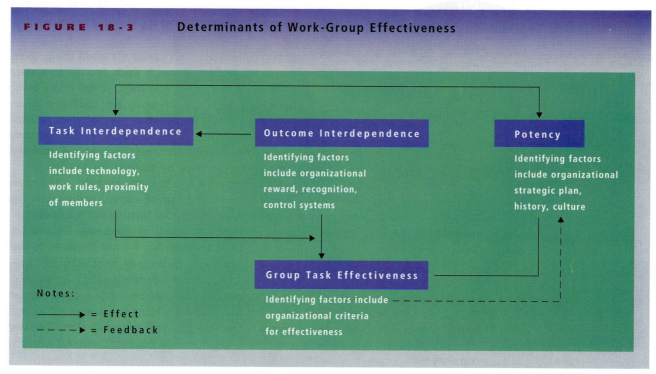

**FIGURE 18-3**    **Determinants of Work-Group Effectiveness**

**Task Interdependence**

Identifying factors include technology, work rules, proximity of members

**Outcome Interdependence**

Identifying factors include organizational reward, recognition, control systems

**Potency**

Identifying factors include organizational strategic plan, history, culture

**Group Task Effectiveness**

Identifying factors include organizational criteria for effectiveness

Notes:

⟶ = Effect

---▶ = Feedback

*Source:* Gregory P. Shea and Richard A. Guzzo, "Group Effectiveness: What Really Matters?" *Sloan Management Review* 27 (Spring 1987): 26. Copyright © 1987 by the Sloan Management Review Association. All rights reserved.

little sense of belonging. Group bonuses or peer evaluation can help create this sense of common fate. Rewards do not have to take the form of money. In fact, recognition can be as strong or stronger than money. For example, a group of managers at Honeywell won a $100 million contract. Their reward? Their manager bought them all ice cream cones. Unusual, perhaps, but many engineers still have the photo taken that day.[43]

It is important to remember that the effectiveness of teams is affected by the national culture. As Geerte Hofstede found, not all countries look at teams in the same way. Japan and the Scandinavian countries are noted for their teamwork. In fact, companies such as Sweden's Volvo, discussed later in the chapter, have built much of their culture around work teams. Japan is known as a collectivist nation where identity is based on "belonging" and there is a strong belief in group decisions. In the United States, on the other hand, the culture has primarily been structured around individualism, where identity is based on the individual and there is a strong belief in individual decisions. Thus, although working in groups has proved effective in U.S. organizations, it is not without some alteration in our values and views.[44] Another perspective comes from China, where entrepreneurs have been part of a long, rich history, and historically teamwork is not as highly prized as in other Asian nations. While some factories try to use teams, they may come up against the viewpoint about the value of group efforts expressed by the following comment from a senior manager: "One worker can carry two buckets of water (using a shoulder pole); two workers can carry one bucket; and three workers probably would end up not carrying any water at all."[45]

**A CLEAR CHARTER.** Vince Anderson and Bob Ho, pictured here, led the team responsible for the development of the Whirlpool super-efficient refrigerator in record time.

**FORMAL PROCEDURES.**  Several formal procedures are useful in helping committees operate effectively.[52]

- The committee's goals should be clearly defined, preferably in writing. This will focus the committee's activities and focus discussion of what the committee is supposed to do.
- The committee's authority should be specified. Is the committee merely to investigate, advise, and recommend, or is it authorized to implement decisions?
- The optimum size of the committee should be determined. With fewer than 5 members, the advantages of teamwork may be diminished. Potential group resources increase as group size increases. Size will vary according to circumstances, but for many tasks the ideal number of committee members ranges from 5 to 10. With more than 10 to 15 members, a committee usually becomes unwieldy, so that it is difficult for each member to influence the work.
- A chairperson should be selected on the basis of his or her ability to run an efficient meeting—that is, to encourage the participation of all committee members, to keep meetings from getting bogged down in irrelevancies, and to see that the necessary paperwork gets done. (Appointing a permanent secretary to handle communications is often useful.)
- The agenda and all supporting material for the meeting should be distributed to members before the meeting to permit them to prepare in advance. This makes it more likely they will be ready with informed contributions and will stick to the point.
- Meetings should start and end on time. The time when they will end should be announced at the outset.

**EFFECTIVE MEETINGS.**
Ineffective meetings are notorious time-wasters. An effective chairperson should keep the members focused on a clear agenda, avoid bogging down in irrelevancies, encourage participation from all members, and see that results are recorded.

## PARTICIPATIVE MANAGEMENT IN SCANDINAVIAN COUNTRIES

One of the challenges in making formal groups effective is ensuring that everyone has a chance to contribute and participate. After all, no one can predict who will offer the best ideas. People in the Scandinavian countries, especially Sweden, have a long history with systematic procedures for **participative management.**[53] In these countries, worker

**participative management:** A management style that supports employees in taking on enhanced, empowered roles.

participation is not a temporary experiment or an ad hoc measure. In fact, corporate accomplishments are regarded as the results of the combined creative and decision-making talents of all participants. There is a basic respect for individual dignity and contribution, and companies tend to ensure tangible rewards for individual contributions to the effectiveness of the group. Some analysts suggest that this orientation is a significant factor in the ability of such companies as Scandinavian Airline System (SAS) and Volvo to maintain strong competitive positions in international competition.

Both SAS and Volvo are models of participatory management. The central theme of SAS's management approach is a strong belief in the ability and integrity of front-line personnel, who are entrusted with a great deal of responsibility in servicing the needs of customers. The role of management is not to dictate top-level policy but to assist the front-line people who are directly in charge of day-to-day customer relations. Volvo, which during the 1960s and early 1970s shared with its American counterparts problems of employee dissatisfaction and alienation on the assembly line, has worked for years to develop a system to replace the assembly-line technique dating back to Henry Ford with small teams of workers who rotate assignments and perform their jobs with considerable autonomy. Through this participatory approach, management and the company's unions have come closer together in their basic values and in their ideas about how to improve overall corporate effectiveness. ▬▬▬

Certainly, some American companies are reorienting themselves and successfully managing according to such models; Saturn is evidence of that. Analysts suggest that one key is adopting the premise that, by and large, the work force consists of intelligent people who want to do a good job. Without an acceptance of this underlying premise, they argue, experiments in participatory management will, at best, produce mixed results.

## FOCUSING TEAMS ON PERFORMANCE

In an important study of teams in today's organizations, Jon Katzenbach and Douglas Smith developed a commonsense understanding of what makes teams work.[54] They suggest that, first and foremost, performance challenges are the best way to create teams, and that "team basics includ[ing] size, purpose, goals, skills, approach, and accountability" are often overlooked.[55] Figure 18-4 depicts the basic building blocks of teams: the skills of the team members, accountability of the team, and commitment of the team members. Katzenbach and Smith also found that it is most difficult to create teams at the very top of an organization, primarily due to many mistaken assumptions about how teams work.

Katzenbach and Smith also found some very surprising—"uncommonsense"—things about teams. Table 18-1 summarizes their findings.

Finally, they claim that a few simple rules can greatly enhance team performance, especially when applied to teams at the top of an organization. First, team work assignments need to address specific, concrete issues rather than broad generalizations. Second, work has to be broken down and assigned to subgroups and individuals. Teams are not the same as "meetings." Third, team membership must be based on what each member can achieve and the skills that each has, rather than on the formal authority or organizational position of the person. Fourth, each team

**MANAGEMENT 2000 AND BEYOND**

# TEAMWORK: THE NEW ORGANIZATIONAL PARADIGM[58]

The old paradigm or model of organizational structure was based on the assumptions of hierarchy—that top leadership knows all the answers and is in charge of the goals and work processes for the organization. The emerging team paradigm, on the other hand, is constructed on new assumptions—that knowledge, and therefore insight and answers, are found throughout the organization in the abilities and know-how of all organizational members when brought together in teams. In this model, goals are mutually determined and work processes are built around teams of experts.

For example, to prepare for the twenty-first century, CEO Jack Welch is trying to build a boundaryless organization at GE. He is working to eliminate barriers within the business, such as those created by the functional groups most hierarchies are constructed around—such as marketing, production, human resources, and engineering. To bring creativity, work processes, and knowledge together, GE has introduced cross-functional teams, project teams, and partnerships. GE is also breaking down the barriers between the company and its environment by creating alliances with others and building teams with customers and suppliers.

With the organizational environment likely to remain unstable and turbulent, the flexibility and adaptability created by teams is a significant advantage. In fact, Tom Peters and many others predict that teamwork will replace hierarchy as the dominant form of organization in the twenty-first century. According to *Fortune* magazine, Peters futurists such as Alvin Toffler and CEOs like Allied Signal's Lawrence Bossidy all agree that "the demise of the old authoritarian hierarchies, from the USSR to General Motors, is a global, historical phenomenon that none can evade. Like it or not, everyone who works for a living is helping create a new relationship between individual and corporation, and a new sense of employer and employee."[59]

As envisioned by Peters, businesses of the future will be organized somewhat like a movie production company. Teams of specialists will come together for a specific project and then move on into other teams in the same or other organizations. Key to the success of this approach is the understanding that managers must share both power and responsibility with teams of people who were once disempowered by the rigid bureaucratic lines of authority.

The downsizing of many corporations, creating flatter organizations with fewer middle managers available to manage in the traditional hierarchical manner, has forced organizations to more fully empower organization members into true teams. According to C. K. Prahalad of the University of Michigan, the emphasis will be on people skills. Even those managers designated leaders will need to learn how to follow the team: "A team is not like a pack of sledge dogs, with one dog the leader....It's more like a flight of wild geese: The leader always changes, but they fly in a flock."[60]

The team phenomenon is particularly suited to the era of information technology and globalization. Information highways and networks connect teams from all over the continent and the globe, facilitating the exchange of information and creative ideas. Global alliances create new opportunities to use multinational teams to develop cooperation and creative exchange. Global alliances will seem like "standard operating procedure" in the next century as multinational teams create new ventures for an exciting future.

# TRAINING SATURN WORKERS FOR SUCCESS

One key to the success of employee empowerment at Saturn is that employees are trained to take on responsibility. Employees spend 5 percent of their time—about 92 hours a year—in training, compared to 2 percent to 3 percent for the best of the competitors. "Since our goal is to leapfrog the competition,…we figured we'd probably have to double [the amount of time they dedicate to training]," said O'Toole.[61] However, at Saturn, training is not about learning and re-learning how to build a car. Rather, it is about enabling employees to understand the concerns of people, technology, and business systems, in addition to the concerns of quality, cost, and customer satisfaction. According to O'Toole, even when companies spend more than enough money on knowledge and skills, they often neglect the "why." "That's where the mission and philosophy come in [at Saturn]," said O'Toole.[62]

Training has played an integral role in the development of Saturn. "Doing the right training in the right way at the right time really does leverage our ability to build more cars and increase our salary levels," said Epps.[63]

Through both centralized and decentralized efforts, Saturn emphasizes training. There are thirty people in the company's training and organization development department who are responsible for guiding the strategic focus of Saturn's training. They prepare and administer the company courses taken by most employees.

In addition, each of the three main Saturn plant buildings has a team of about five training coordinators who are responsible for handling daily training needs. For example, if a production team finds that a process does not work effectively, a new process and equipment may be put in place, and the on-site coordinators help train workers to use the new process.

It is each team's training champion, however, who is responsible for determining the members' needs and scheduling their training. In addition, team members informally cross-train other members to handle administrative duties as well as to perform assembly-line tasks.

Training is actually linked to Saturn's "risk-and-reward" compensation system. "Employees earn a base salary set below the industry average," explained Bennett. "They can earn additional compensation to meet or exceed industry parity by meeting or exceeding goals in quality, productivity and training."[64] In general, the risk-and-reward compensation system places a certain portion of employees' base wages at risk. This means that in order for employees to receive that portion, everyone must meet certain goals. If employees exceed their goals, then they'll qualify for bonuses.

Training is grouped in the "risk" portion of employees' salaries. Saturn guarantees employees 95 percent of their base wages, but does not pay the remaining 5 percent unless all employees meet their training goal. In the first quarter of 1992, the goal was 155,687 hours; more than 300,000 hours were actually recorded. Employees thus received bonuses for that quarter.

Success at Saturn is something that is shared. "I'm very proud," said Patrick. "I'm proud when people from home tell me they see [the cars] on the road. I'm proud when people tell me they bought one because it's a quality car. My doctor bought one because it's a quality car. I can go to this doctor and be proud about what I do. Since I came from GM, I heard it all the time about how raggedy the cars were and I was kind of ashamed to be associated with the car industry. Now I can hold my head up and my chest out and say, 'Yeah, that's me. I'm Saturn.'"[65]

## Summary

1. **Distinguish between the major types of teams found in organizations.**

   Organizations have both formal and informal groups. Formal groups are created deliberately by managers and charged with carrying out specific tasks. The most prevalent types of formal groups are command groups, committees, and task forces. Informal groups develop whenever people come into contact regularly—with or without management's encouragement. Informal groups perform four functions: they (1) maintain and strengthen group norms and values—which may differ from management's; (2) provide members with social satisfaction and security; (3) help members communicate; and (4) help members solve problems.

2. **Outline characteristics of superteams and self-managed teams.**

   Superteams are groups of workers that have characteristics of both formal and informal teams. Superteams are distinguished by their non-traditional structure that enables workers to solve the problems that they deal with daily. Well-run superteams manage themselves, arrange their work schedules, set their productivity quotas, order their own equipment and supplies, improve product quality, and interact with customers and other superteams. Self-managed teams are superteams that manage themselves without any formal supervision. Self-managed teams usually are responsible for entire tasks, include members who have a variety of task-related skills, have the power to determine such things as work methods, scheduling, and assignment of members to different tasks, and are compensated and given feedback according to the performance of the group as a whole.

3. **Discuss guidelines for increasing team cohesiveness.**

   All groups share some common characteristics. They all have group norms and pressure members to conform to those norms. In addition, they have some degree of cohesiveness, which can be enhanced by introducing competition, increasing interpersonal attraction, expanding the opportunities for interaction, and creating common goals and fates for all group members.

4. **Provide guidelines for making teams more effective.**

   Managerial skill in guiding, but not dominating, group activities is an important factor in achieving success in group work. Suggestions for effective results include formal procedures for meetings and guidelines for group leaders and members.

5. **Explain how managers can deal with conflicts within teams.**

   Although conflicts sometimes disrupt groups, Smith and Berg suggest that conflict is normal and natural when different people attempt to act in an integrated way. Groups that understand this process can use their conflicts creatively.

## REVIEW QUESTIONS

1. What are the major types of teams found in organizations?
2. What are superteams?
3. What are self-managed teams?
4. What do all groups have in common?
5. How can team cohesiveness be increased?
6. How can teams be made more effective?
7. How can managers deal with conflicts within teams?

## KEY TERMS

| | |
|---|---|
| Team | High-performance teams |
| Command team | Self-managed teams |
| Committee | Self-managed work groups |
| Task force | Cohesiveness |
| Project team | Task interdependence |
| Norms | Sense of potency |
| Reference group | Outcome interdependence |
| Superteams | Participative management |

## CASE STUDY

## THE NEW-PRODUCTS TEAM[66]

Karen Smith looked at her calendar for the day. It was Thursday, and the report she had been working on was due tomorrow. That meant the group would have to meet today to hammer out its recommendations and presentation. She was not looking forward to an afternoon spent devoted to this task.

The team had been formed to design the market introduction of the company's newest product. Since the company had never before marketed a retail product, no one was quite sure what to expect. Karen and her group were charged with producing recommendations for advertising and promotion, product distribution and rollout, and for anything else they thought important. After the plan was approved, implementation would probably fall to Karen, although it could be given to another member of the Marketing Department. It was a large undertaking, and Karen and four other people had given it most of their time for the last few months.

Right from the start, the team had not worked well together. This had not surprised Karen: The personalities were strong all around, and she knew at the outset that there would be some personality conflicts. All four group members were on the same level in the company, and no one had been designated the leader. Therefore, the early meetings were mostly a struggle for leadership.

Karen realized very early that Ben had a deep-seated belief that women had no place in business—and certainly were not capable of leading men. Even though other women had warned her, the venom in some of his comments had come as a surprise. Ben clearly thought he was the only one capable of leading the group: After all, had he not just finished four years in the Navy? James was only slightly more open-minded than Ben. The two of them often formed a team, and once they had come to a joint decision, it was impossible to get them to consider anyone else's recommendations. Charles was more willing to listen to others, but, he had a tendency to show up armed with so much data that the group often spent all of its time trying to understand how the data had been derived rather than making decisions. All in all, Karen was quite frustrated at both the group's slow progress and the tense atmosphere that pervaded their meetings.

They were nowhere near finished with their plan, but they would have to present their recommendations tomorrow morning. She knew that senior management was expecting a full report, and she was not very confident that she could deliver one. How would the group members manage to work together well enough at today's meeting to agree on a set of recommendations? The atmosphere at past meetings had been so poor that Karen shuddered to think what would happen when the stress of a deadline was added. She wondered if she could control the show of tempers that usually marked their gatherings, the last of which had dissolved into a shouting match between herself and Ben when she had tried, as tact-

fully as possible, to suggest that one of his ideas for a promotional campaign was impractical. He had quickly dropped the discussion and moved to a more personal level: accusing her of undermining his authority by trying to imply that she, a mere woman, knew more than he did. He had even said she could not be a true Christian, since any Christian woman would be at home raising children. Her faith was important to her, but she never considered it related to her job performance. It certainly wasn't something she was willing to discuss in the group.

She sighed. It was going to be a very long day. Should she call the other group members to set the time, or should she let one of them call her? How should she act toward Ben? What could she do to keep things on track in preparation for tomorrow's presentation? All she really wanted to do was tell her boss she was sick and go home.

### CASE QUESTIONS

1. Why is Karen's group having problems?
2. Can you use the Shea-Guzzo model to give Karen a better idea of why the group is dysfunctional?
3. What should Karen do now?

---

## SQUARE D ADDRESSES THE NEED FOR MANAGEMENT TEAMS[67]

Teams are becoming increasingly pervasive among modern organizations. They are being used for an endless variety of purposes. For example, at Square D, an electrical-equipment manufacturer, teams are employed in areas ranging from manufacturing to international research and development financing. As new challenges emerge, companies are turning to team-management approaches to overcome them.

Sadly, the challenge Square D recently confronted was one of work-related violence. According to field

experts, the number of violent work-related altercations is on the rise. A 1994 American Management Association (AMA) survey revealed that of the 589 companies polled, more than half had experienced either threats or actual acts of violence during the past four years. A 1993 symposium on workplace violence indicated even more disturbing facts. "Murder has become the third-leading cause of death on the job and the No. 1 cause of death for working women," commented Postmaster General Marvin Runyon at the symposium. "Some 750 people were murdered on the job last year, and experts estimate that more than 110,000 acts of workplace violence occur annually."[68] In fact, 10 percent of the men and 40 percent of the women killed on the job in the United States are murdered. And, in 1992, workplace violence cost American businesses $4.2 billion.

At Square D, the problem of workplace violence arose when John Ebeling, vice president of purchasing for the company, was stabbed to death in his Schaumburg, Illinois, apartment. The man accused of killing him was Neal Allen, manager of international corporate purchasing. Ebeling was his supervisor.

According to police records, the stabbing was classified as workplace violence because the dispute apparently originated over paperwork. "It was a dispute over paperwork and who was supposed to be responsible for it," said Sgt. Ron Dutner of the Schaumburg Police Department. "Unfortunately, we don't know exactly what the involvement was with the paperwork, what the intensity was that was involved."[69] Allen, the accused, claimed that Ebeling had attacked him and he had been forced to kill him in self-defense. "The defendant said the victim produced a knife," said Schaumburg Police Detective Michael Egan. "His statement was he stabbed the victim numerous times."[70]

Of the firms in the AMA study that had experienced violence, 54 percent had no risk management programs in place at the time of the incident. At Square D, managers had actually sought help from an outside agency prior to Ebeling's murder. In December 1993, the company contacted Joseph Kinney, a consultant and executive director of the National Safe Workplace Institute in Chicago. "They talked to me about problems they were having," said Kinney. "They talked about a workshop on violence reduction and prevention."[71] Unfortunately that workshop never took place.

In light of such cases as the one experienced by Square D, many companies are beginning to increase the use of psychological testing of employees as well as more intensive personal screening. "Companies are paying more attention to it…they are beginning to take precautions," said Francine Scott, urban affairs director at the Chicagoland Chamber of Commerce. Ira Lipman, president of Guardsmark Inc., one of the largest security firms in the country, pointed out that there are some simple measures businesses can take to reduce the risk of workplace violence, such as rigorous screening of job applicants.

Lipman also recommends that companies form threat management teams. A threat management team typically consists of a counselor, an attorney, and a security officer. The team can serve as a forum for employees to report threats or actual acts of workplace violence. Moreover, the counselors and attorneys can provide either advice or merely a source of relief by allowing employees to vent their anger. These teams are invaluable in assessing the seriousness of potential conflicts as well as in reducing tension between employees. "In all cases we studied, rarely was there a case where there weren't recognizable threats. Sometimes, co-workers knew there were problems, but they didn't know who to report them to," said Dr. Dennis Johnson. Johnson studied 125 cases of job-related violence between 1989 and 1993; the cases involved 390 deaths. "Employers must create an atmosphere where workers are encouraged to report threats," Johnson explained. "Too often, employers have ignored threats and violence has occurred, frequently with fatal results."[72]

Many companies unfortunately wait until job-related violence has actually occurred before they institute precautionary measures such as the threat management team. "There are uncanny parallels to the violence issue and the whole sexual harassment issue," Kinney observed. "Ten years ago, most corporations did not have a sexual harassment policy, and to the extent it existed, people were embarrassed to talk about it. The same is true of verbal abuse and even physical assault. Now people are talking about this more."[73]

## CASE QUESTIONS

1. How would you go about introducing threat management teams?
2. How are threat management teams distinguished from other types of teams?
3. Would you introduce threat management teams in your organization? Why or why not?

## CHAPTER 19

# COMMUNICATION AND NEGOTIATION

**Upon completing this chapter, you should be able to:**

1. Link communications processes to the management processes of planning, organizing, leading, and controlling.

2. Discuss the key elements in interpersonal communication processes.

3. Explain challenges in interpersonal and organizational communications processes.

4. Distinguish various communication networks.

5. Discuss the differences between integrative and distributive negotiation processes.

6. Explain the effects of new communication technologies on organizational decision making.

# THE "HUMAN FACTOR" AT HALLMARK[1]

Every day Hallmark Cards Inc., the world's largest greeting card company, produces 11 million greeting cards, in addition to 1.5 million other personal communications products. Top managers at Hallmark recognize that the continued effort, insight, and creativity of Hallmark employees are key to maintaining that success. "The only sustainable edge for a corporation is the energy and cleverness of its people," said Irvine O. Hockaday, Jr., president and CEO of Hallmark Cards. "To tap that, a chief executive must craft a vision, empower employees, encourage teamwork, and kindle the competitive fires."[2] Hockaday has found that successful communication is essential to tapping the talent at Hallmark.

In late 1991, however, Hockaday confronted a situation he found unacceptable: It was taking 18 to 20 months for a card to go from concept to store, when it should have been taking only four to six months. At that time, Hallmark Cards was creating greeting cards through a step-by-step process reminiscent of Henry Ford's assembly line for cars. Employees such as artists and writers worked in different departments and rarely communicated with one another. In fact, the employees who designed the decorative lettering actually worked in a separate building, located a quarter-mile away. According to Carol Kobza, who designs cards for Hallmark's Ambassador line, "I never knew what went on in the next department."[3]

*"The only sustainable edge for a corporation is the energy and cleverness of its people."*

Hallmark managers thus decided to reengineer—radically redesign—the card-creation process. First and foremost, this involved taking steps to enable employees to communicate with one another. Employees were relocated within the buildings so that they could communicate and share ideas during the creative process. Now, groups of employees from virtually every department are located in the same room. And employees serve on teams that take charge of particular Hallmark holidays.

In addition, these teams are empowered to make decisions, instead of having to ask permission from managers. "I don't like the term 'reengineering' because it sounds so cold and anatomical," said Hockaday. "Empowerment is ultimately what makes it work."[4]

Now, when Kobza has a question for an artist or photographer, she simply has to walk a few steps to find the person. This enables quick changes to be made, as when she decided to trim the ears on the Easter bunny by $1/8$-inch to reduce scrap. In the reengineered organization, employees such as Kobza are able to consult with people quickly and are empowered to make decisions on the spot. "The work is more satisfying…and I have a lot more control over what happens," noted Kobza.[5]

**A HALLMARK SHOP.** The continuing creativity of Hallmark employees is needed to keep the racks of Hallmark shops and other card outlets filled with new cards for every occasion.

The result has been that since 1991 Hallmark has cut in half—to less than a year—the time it takes to get a card to market. Easing communication between employees has had other positive results as well. "This wasn't a cost-cutting exercise," pointed out Buddy Jones, a Hallmark vice president, "but it did save us a lot of money."[6] →

**DECODING.** In this discussion of an important workplace issue, does the man look like he is listening carefully? Does he appear to understand, or is he confused? What else can you infer about the communication?

Since noise can interfere with understanding, managers should attempt to restrict it to a level that permits effective communication. It can be very tiring to listen to employees who speak softly on a noisy assembly line or to try to conduct a conversation over telephone static.[14] Physical discomfort such as hunger, pain, or exhaustion can also be considered a form of noise and can interfere with effective communication. The problems are made worse, of course, by a message that is excessively complex or unclear to begin with. On the other hand, a clear message expressed in a straightforward fashion ("Turn off that radio!") can be conveyed even in an extremely "noisy" environment.

# IMPROVING COMMUNICATIONS PROCESSES

The difference between effective and ineffective communication can be traced to how well the communicating parties deal with four aspects of the communications process: perception differences, emotions, inconsistencies between verbal and non-verbal communications, and prior trust (or distrust) between the parties.[15]

## DIFFERING PERCEPTIONS

This is one of the most common communication barriers. People who have different backgrounds of knowledge and experience often perceive the same phenomenon from different perspectives. Suppose that a new supervisor compliments an assembly-line worker for his or her efficiency and high-quality work. The supervisor genuinely appreciates the worker's efforts and at the same time wants to encourage the other employees to emulate his or her example. Others on the assembly line, however, may regard the worker's being singled out for praise as a sign that he or she has been "buttering up the boss." They may react by teasing or being openly hostile. Individual perceptions of the same communication thus differ radically.

Language differences are often closely related to differences in individual perceptions. For a message to be properly communicated, the words used must mean the same thing to sender and receiver. Suppose that different departments of a company receive a memo stating that a new product is to be developed in "a short time." To people in research and development, "a short time" might mean two or three years. To people in the finance department, "a short time" might be three to six months, whereas the sales department might think of "a short time" as a few weeks. Since many different meanings can be assigned to some words (the 500 most common English words have an average of 28 definitions each)[16] great care must be taken that the receiver gets the message the sender intended.

Perceptual differences can arise due to gender differences. The communications differences and styles between genders has been the topic of much recent research. In the last decade research has shown that women and men in our culture  use distinctive styles of speech and tend to play different roles when speaking to each other. These differences can lead to miscommunication and conflict. For instance, Linguist Robin Lakoff of the University of California has noted that women who speak directly and assertively may be ostracized as "unfeminine" by both men and women. On the other hand, women who adopt a more "traditional" women's style and role—that is, expressing their thoughts more tentatively and working harder to get someone's attention—may be dismissed as someone of dim intelligence or not to be taken seriously. Gender communication as well as crosscultural communication will continue to be important areas of organizational understanding.[17]

## OVERCOMING DIFFERING PERCEPTIONS

To overcome differing perceptions and languages, the message should be explained so that it can be understood by receivers with different views and experiences. Whenever possible, we should learn about the background of those with whom we will be communicating. Empathizing—seeing the situation from the other person's point of view—and delaying reactions until the relevant information is weighed will help to reduce ambiguity. When the subject is unclear, asking questions is critical.[18]

To overcome language differences, it is particularly helpful to ask the receiver to confirm or restate the main points of the message. When all members of an organization or group are going to be dealing with a new terminology, it may be worthwhile to develop a training course of instruction to acquaint them with the new topic. Receivers can be encouraged to ask questions and to seek clarification of points that are unclear.[19]

Solectron Corporation, a contract manufacturing company based in Milpitas, California, recognized the need to overcome language barriers among employees  when it introduced a new 401(k) program in 1992. So HR professionals at the company created *SolectLine,* a toll-free phone line through which employees and their families can receive enrollment details, facts on how the plan works, and descriptions of investment choices in any of four languages: English, Spanish, Chinese, or Vietnamese. In the United States, Solectron's workforce is comprised of 3,500 employees who together speak 18 languages or dialects. "It's one of our basic beliefs that in respecting every individual who works for the enterprise," said Bill Webb, vice president of corporate human resources, "we communicate effectively with them."[20] This multi-  lingual-communications effort is indicative of the company's ongoing commitment to the welfare and interests of its employees. Solectron's attitude of concern for employees and commitment to effective communication with all stakeholders was a factor in qualifying Solectron for the Baldrige award, which it earned in 1991.

and guests to scan up-to-date information about the company, its clients, and the industry, and to hear from the company's legendary founder, David Ogilvy. "He's a passionate man and it's wonderful to hear the words coming out of his mouth," remarked VP-assistant media director Suzan Nanfeldt. "One month he's doing something on direct marketing, another month he's in India....His perspective is what started it all. We make an effort to maintain what he started in terms of the Ogilvy culture....He has particular views on every aspect of communication [and on conducting] business in a gentlemanly manner. Getting some of him on film is very meaningful....It's a great way to keep in touch with the client stories."[40]

**PROBLEMS OF VERTICAL COMMUNICATION.** Downward communication is likely to be filtered, modified, or halted at each level as managers decide what should be passed down to their employees. Upward communication is likely to be filtered, condensed, or altered by middle managers who see it as part of their job to protect upper management from nonessential data originating at the lower levels.[41] In addition, middle managers may keep information that would reflect unfavorably on them from reaching their managers. Thus, vertical communication is often at least partially inaccurate or incomplete.

The importance to an organization of vertical communication was emphasized by Lyman W. Porter and Karlene H. Roberts, whose survey of research reported that two-thirds of a manager's communications take place with higher-ranking and lower-ranking people in the organization.[42] The studies reviewed by Porter and Roberts also found that the accuracy of vertical communication was aided by similarities in thinking between higher-ranking and lower-ranking people. But accuracy was limited by status and power differences between manager and employee, by an employee's desire for upward mobility, and by a lack of trust between manager and employee.

Problems in downward communication exist when managers do not provide employees with the information they need to carry out their tasks effectively. Managers are often overly optimistic about the accuracy and completeness of their downward communication. In fact, they can fail to pass on important information (such as a higher-level change in policy) or to instruct employees adequately on how to perform their duties. This lack of communication is sometimes deliberate, as when managers withhold information to keep employees dependent on them. The net effect of incomplete downward communication is that employees can feel confused, uninformed, or powerless and might fail to carry out their tasks properly.

The auto-repair service of Sears, Roebuck & Company provides one example of downward vertical communication going awry—with ethical implications. In 1992 Sears was inundated with complaints that consumers had been misled about needed automotive repairs. What appears to have created the situation is the communication of increased work quotas and the introduction of productivity incentives for mechanics. At the time, Sears was facing declining revenues and looking for a means to spur performance. Unfortunately, some employees' judgment suffered, and management failed to clarify the line between unnecessary service and legitimate preventive maintenance. This situation, coupled with customer ignorance, created a vast gray area subject to a wide range of interpretation.[43]

Becton Dickinson (BD), a $2.5 billion medical technology company, used a Strategic Human Resource Management (SHRM) process to improve its internal vertical communication. The maker of disposable medical devices, such as syringes, needles, and scalpels, realized that the lower levels of the company were unaware of strategic business objectives. Through the SHRM process, BD implemented more formal and frequent communications with employees. Lower organization levels now feed information up to senior executives. BD executives believe that it is more important to have a healthy, functioning process than to deal only with specific issues. "If the process works," asserted James R. Wessel, BD's vice-president of human resources, "we will be able to successfully deal with the issues. Otherwise, we will not."[44]

## LATERAL AND INFORMAL COMMUNICATION

**lateral communication:**
Communication between departments of an organization that generally follows the work flow rather than the chain of command, and thus provides a direct channel for coordination and problem solving.

**Lateral communication** usually follows the pattern of work flow in an organization, occurring between members of work groups, between one work group and another, between members of different departments, and between line and staff employees. The main purpose of lateral communication is to provide a direct channel for organizational coordination and problem solving. In this way, it avoids the much slower procedure of directing communications through the chain of command.[45] An added benefit of lateral communication is that it enables organization members to form relationships with their peers. As we have seen, these relationships are an important part of employee satisfaction.[46]

The large amount of lateral communication that takes place outside the chain of command often occurs with the knowledge, approval, and encouragement of managers who understand that lateral communication may help relieve their communication burden and also reduces inaccuracy by putting relevant people in direct contact with each other.[47]

**informal communication:**
Communication within an organization that is not officially sanctioned.

One type of **informal communication,** not officially sanctioned, is the grapevine. The grapevine within organizations is made up of several informal communication networks that overlap and intersect at a number of points—that is, some well-informed individuals are likely to belong to more than one informal network. Grapevines circumvent rank or authority and can link organization members in any combination of directions—horizontal, vertical, and diagonal. As Keith Davis puts it, the grapevine "flows around water coolers, down hallways, through lunch rooms, and wherever people get together in groups."[48]

In addition to its social and informal communication functions, the grapevine has several work-related functions. For example, although the grapevine is hard to control, it often operates much faster than formal communication channels. Managers may use it to distribute information through planned "leaks" or judiciously placed "just-between-you-and-me" remarks.

**grapevine chains:**
The various paths through which informal communication is passed through an organization; the four types are the *single strand, gossip, probability,* and *cluster chains.*

Davis has identified four possible types of **grapevine chains** (see Figure 19-2).[49] In the *single-strand chain,* person A tells something to person B, who tells it to person C, and so on down the line. This chain is least accurate at passing on information. In the *gossip chain,* one person seeks out and tells everyone the information he or she has obtained. This chain is often used when information of an interesting but non-job-related nature is being conveyed. In the *probability chain,* individuals are indifferent about whom they offer information to. They tell people at random, and those people in turn tell others at random. This chain is likely to be used when the information is mildly interesting but insignificant. In the *cluster chain,* person A conveys the information to a few selected individuals, some of whom then inform a few selected others.

Davis believes that the cluster chain is the dominant grapevine pattern in organizations. Usually, only a few individuals, called "liaison individuals," pass on the information they have obtained, and they are likely to do so only to people they trust or from whom they would like favors. They are most likely to pass on information that is interesting to them, job-related, and, above all, timely.

## COMMUNICATION BY ORGANIZATIONS

**O**rganizations also pay attention to the messages they send to external stakeholders, such as customers. The Italian Chemical Company, EniChem Polimeri,

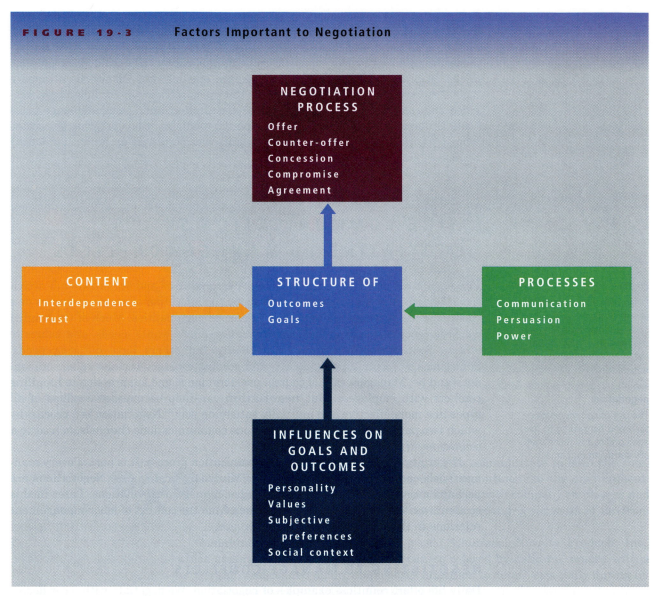

**FIGURE 19-3**    Factors Important to Negotiation

**NEGOTIATION PROCESS**
Offer
Counter-offer
Concession
Compromise
Agreement

**CONTENT**
Interdependence
Trust

**STRUCTURE OF**
Outcomes
Goals

**PROCESSES**
Communication
Persuasion
Power

**INFLUENCES ON GOALS AND OUTCOMES**
Personality
Values
Subjective preferences
Social context

Source: Roy Lewicki and Joseph Litterer, *Negotiation and Negotiator: Readings, Exercises, and Cases* (Homewood, Ill.: Irwin, 1985), p. 44. Copyright © 1985 by Richard D. Irwin, Inc. Reprinted by permission.

their interests as depending on each other (regardless of whether they actually do or not); (2) the extent of trust or distrust between the parties; (3) each party's ability to communicate clearly and to persuade or coerce the other party to accept its point of view; (4) the personalities and idiosyncrasies of the actual people involved; and (5) the goals and interests of the parties.

Negotiation is a complex communication process, all the more so when one round of negotiations is just an episode in a longer-term relationship. Such is often the case in labor-management relations. Preparation is a key concern for the negotiator. That preparation should include a review of the history of previous negotiating sessions and previous negotiated outcomes. The negotiator risks a great deal if he or she acts as if history is unimportant to the other party. This entanglement of relationships and time in the negotiating process is clear in the guidelines offered by Reed Richardson for conducting negotiations (see Exhibit 19-2).

Note, too, how often the value of planning (Chapter 10) is implied in the list of guidelines. <u>Organizational strategies</u> and functional plans serve as standards and thresholds that set limits on what a negotiator should and should not do.

← ch. 10, p. 267

**EXHIBIT 19-2**

**GUIDELINES FOR CONDUCTING NEGOTIATIONS**

- Have set, clear objectives on every bargaining item and understand the context within which the objectives are established.
- *Do not hurry.*
- When in doubt, *caucus.*
- Be *well prepared* with firm data support for clearly defined objectives.
- Maintain *flexibility* in your position.
- *Find out the motivations* for what the other party wants.
- Do *not get bogged down.* If there is no progress on a certain item, move on to another and come back to it later. Build the momentum for agreement.
- Respect the importance of *face-saving* for the other party.
- Be a good *listener.*
- Build a reputation for being *fair* but *firm.*
- Control your *emotions.*
- Be sure as you make each bargaining move that you know its *relationship* to all other moves.
- *Measure each move* against your objectives.
- Pay close attention to the *wording* of each clause negotiated.
- Remember that negotiating is by its nature a *compromise* process.
- Learn to *understand* people—it may pay off during negotiations.
- Consider the *impact of present negotiations on future ones.*

*Source:* Adapted from Reed C. Richardson, *Collective Bargaining by Objectives: A Positive Approach* (Englewood Cliffs, N.J.: Prentice Hall, 1985), pp. 168-169.

# STABILITY OF NEGOTIATIONS OUTCOMES

It is clear that when two parties interact, through negotiation, to resolve a conflict, both parties have an idea about what they want to gain from the conflict. Just as clearly, capable negotiators are interested in the stability of the outcome that they jointly shape. If either party, or both, settles on a negotiated outcome that they have reason to regret or resent, they have the incentive to reopen the negotiations, often in a hostile way. If, however, a negotiated outcome endures over time, it is a *stable outcome.* Stability is not the only feature of successful negotiations, but it is a necessary one.

**integrative process:**
Negotiation process in which the prospects for both parties' gains are encouraging; also known as a win-win situation.

Linda Putman has distinguished two generic kinds of negotiation processes that differ in their relative prospects for stability.[56] An **integrative process** is one in which the prospects for both parties' gains are encouraging. This is often known as a *win-win situation.* Such integrative processes—that is, those in which the parties attempt to reconcile their stakes—are characterized by open, empathetic communications.[57]

Medicis Pharmaceutical Corporation is a small company whose negotiations with much larger companies often result in win-win situations. The current trend is for large manufacturers to focus on core products and services. They typically sell off non-core product lines—usually to other larger manufacturers. Low-volume castoffs, though, tend to fall into the hands of smaller companies, such as Medicis, who, through close attention, enable these product lines to be successful. This is exactly what has happened with the increasingly successful Esoterica line of skin-care products, for which Medicis acquired U.S. and Canadian marketing rights from SmithKline Beecham PLC.[58]

**distributive process:**

Negotiation process in which each of the parties tends to seek maximum gains and wants to impose maximum losses on the other; also known as a *win-lose situation* or *zero sum.*

A **distributive process** is one in which each of the parties tends to seek maximum gains and wants to impose maximum losses on the other.[59] This is often known as a *win-lose situation.* Another description is *zero sum*—that is, one party's gain and the other party's loss counterbalance, and sum to zero. Such distributive processes, Putnam shows, are contentious and unstable processes that can become self-perpetuating.

Putnam claims that both integrative and distributive processes are at work in every negotiation. So, rather than two negotiators choosing one kind of process over the other, negotiations involve a tension between the two. Putnam says this is healthy because it enables each negotiator to communicate in a way that protects his or her own interests.[60] The trick, of course, is not to destabilize the entire process.

There are times when a negotiator has reason to take an integrative approach by sharing information voluntarily and encouraging the other party to do the same. The past history of a relationship between the parties often has a bearing on this. If the negotiators have built trust through revealing information that each has held in confidence, and if past negotiations have resulted in outcomes satisfactory to both parties, then we might expect them to be more and more forthcoming with information in future negotiations. International diplomacy is one arena where this can happen. Slowly but surely, as relations between the United States and the former Soviet Union improved over the years, arms reduction talks moved forward partly because the parties were telling each other more about their respective positions, concerns, and needs.[61]

Events in other relationships surrounding the negotiations in question can also encourage negotiators to reveal more and more information and work integratively. The break-up of American Telephone & Telegraph (AT&T) in the early 1980s is an example. Although many in the media reported—and still report—that the federal government broke up AT&T, there is considerable evidence from diverse sources that then-AT&T chairman Charles Brown broke the logjam between AT&T and the Department of Justice by voluntarily offering a divestiture plan. In the neighborhood of Brown's negotiations with Justice Department officials were several situations that made the time right for Brown's integrative move. The Reagan Cabinet was deadlocked on the issue. New competitors were gaining in markets long dominated by AT&T. Factions within AT&T were pressing for the company to compete differently.[62] Likewise, Justice Department officials reportedly wanted to improve their standing in the Reagan administration.[63] An integrative process was appropriate for the times.

Sometimes, however, a negotiator has reason to take a distributive approach and be selective about revealing information to the other party. Uncertain future prospects for a relationship can be one reason for doing this. Again, international diplomacy is a context where this can happen. Anytime there is a significant change in the government in one nation, officials of other governments temporarily have reason to be wary and guard information accordingly. In 1993, after many years out of power, the Liberal Party took control of the Canadian Parliament. Liberal Party leader and new Prime Minister Jean Chretien began to make noises about official Canadian opposition to the North American Free Trade Agreement (NAFTA). This was a significant change of policy from that endorsed by Chretien's two Conservative Party predecessors.[64] Accordingly, officials in the Clinton administration had reason to ponder how much of a mandate Chretien had in taking this position, how long he would likely remain in power, and what other areas of difference between the United States and Canada might now be widened or narrowed. There were, in short, temptations for the Clinton administration to take a distributive approach in this situation, even with an ally as loyal as Canada. In Putnam's model, integrative and distributive negotiating processes are simultaneously at work here.

**CHRYSLER IN MEXICO.** The possibilities for numerous other U.S. businesses to open factories in Mexico can affect labor negotiations in the U.S.

## RELATIONS BETWEEN LABOR AND MANAGEMENT

Stability in negotiations processes is a major concern of union leaders and their management counterparts because their relationship is one that they usually anticipate will continue into the future indefinitely. It is also a concern because, generally speaking across industries in the United States and over many decades, stability has been elusive in labor-management relations. Four contemporary cases of ongoing labor-management relationships can give you a flavor of the communication difficulties—such as working through different perceptions and values—and the communications opportunities that attend a negotiations process.

**NEGOTIATIONS AT XEROX.** Joseph W. Laymon, Xerox's director of corporate industrial relations, introduced an alternative bargaining approach he learned at the University of Wisconsin while he was earning a master's degree in economics and doing the course work for a master's degree in labor relations. The previous approach at Xerox tended to involve four months of sessions every 3 years with 40 representatives from each side "dueling it out."[65]

Shortly after the 1989 round, Laymon approached the union leadership with a plan for smaller negotiating teams, training courses for both management and union negotiators, benchmarking best practices, ending position bargaining, and discussing and implementing focused factories. Representatives of both labor and management spent nine months in training on statistics, interpersonal skills, negotiation methods, quality measures, employee involvement and problem solving.

The result was that the 1992 negotiations took only five weeks, without long weekend hours. In addition, 4,000 Amalgamated Clothing & Textile Workers Union (ACTWU) members approved the contract overwhelmingly. Instead of 75 to

**A FAILURE OF NEGOTIATIONS.**
Good negotiating strategies can reduce or eliminate the problems that result from breakdowns in communication, such as strikes.

200 demands being presented by the two sides, this time, the company presented 7 and the union only 12. This eliminated endless hours wasted in determining the legitimate needs of both sides.

**NEGOTIATIONS AT CHEVRON.** In 1990, when Chevron's Salt Lake Refinery management attempted negotiations with the Oil, Chemical & Atomic Workers' Union (OCAW), the company attempted to use a take-it-or-leave-it approach to implement a random drug-testing program. Because of the bitterness that resulted, Jim Edmisson, operations superintendent and the chief management negotiator in 1990, pursued a better process. "There has to be a better mechanism for resolving issues than we used in 1990. We got a signed contract, but we've paid for it in many ways since then," he pointed out.[66]

Julie Holzer, OCAW international representative for District 2, described a new process called mutual-gains bargaining in a monthly union-management communications meeting. Wayne Murakami, chairman of the Workers' Committee, added his support, and the company began developing its own mutual-gains strategy. For three months, 40 employees, broken into seven teams, discussed 56 issues identified to be problems for either management or labor (though they were not designated as to which). Finally, recommendations were finalized, 24 days before the contract expired, and a near-unanimous union ratification vote followed, finalizing the agreement.[67]

**NEGOTIATIONS AT GM.** In the summer of 1993, the negotiation process between GM management and its workers was of particular importance, because GM simply could not afford a strike at that time. Thus successful negotiations between the United Auto Workers union (UAW) leaders and GM management were critical. "Our biggest concern," said GM Executive Vice President William E. Hoglund, "is to get a contract that gives us the opportunity to continue the improvement in our process and productivity."[68]

The issues at the forefront involved the level of staffing, work rules, and total labor costs in the assembly plants and factories responsible for 60 percent of components used in completed vehicles. "On the economic issues that affect individuals, the union understands the issues well," remarked Hoglund. "Of course, the attitude of workers is, don't take anything out of my paycheck."[69]

The problem was that GM executives doubted whether GM products could remain competitive with the current wage rates. GM employees earned $42.21 an hour (including fringe benefits). This was almost twice what employees of many competitive outside parts suppliers earned. The UAW negotiators would not agree to lowering wage rates. According to UAW President Owen Bieber, "We don't see lower wages as the solution to the problem....That's not a wise thing for an upward-moving society."[70]

GM management and UAW leaders also disagreed with regard to staffing levels. The UAW sought guarantees for continued employment (even so far as the guarantee of filling positions of retired employees with new employees), while GM managers felt the need—particularly as the company faces the increasingly competitive global environment—to decrease the payroll. They wanted to cut the hourly workforce of 272,000 by about a third. What was happening was that GM management was trying to improve its manufacturing process and decrease the labor time needed, but this worked against employees' interests; if the time was decreased, it would mean that less labor was needed (i.e., more staff reductions).[71]

**NEGOTIATIONS AT FORD.** Contrary to what has happened at other large companies faced with downsizing, managers at Ford quickly called in the UAW to talk about strategy. Together they created a joint employee retraining program to enable as many Ford employees as possible to reenter the work force as quickly as possible.

"We approached that trauma with one thing in mind," explained Ken Dickinson, Ford's executive director of the Ford-UAW Training Center, "What could be done by a union and a company that had never been done before to help employees upgrade their skills and get into other fields of employment?"[72]

Ford management set up comprehensive reeducation centers at plants and started programs to train employees in skills anticipated to be sought by potential employers, such as English language fluency, high school equivalency, and diverse technical skills including welding, basic computer programming, and cable-TV installation. In addition, the company allowed employers to interview Ford employees at the factory site. The result was that 80 percent of the displaced workers had found new jobs through the Ford-UAW partnership within two years.

These four cases are examples of the communication process that we introduced in this chapter. They are also a sampling of the possibilities that can arise when parties with long histories of less-than-warm relationships can keep working toward harmonious, stable outcomes through their expertise at communication—and their willingness to communicate.

**MANAGEMENT 2000 AND BEYOND**

# TECHNOLOGY AND NEW COMMUNICATIONS PRACTICES

There is good reason why this chapter about communication and negotiation is situated where it is in this book— that is, at the end of the planning, organizing, and leading processes and at the doorstep of controlling processes. Managers and management researchers alike have long believed that information is a primary source of power and that communications processes are ways to maintain control over what happens at organizations ("informal organizations" notwithstanding). As long as the important information at an organization was stored in a central computing system managed by the staff functions of accounting and finance, such information control through communications seemed plausible. Several generations of middle managers were trained to support this kind of management practice.

Modern technology can challenge all that. Through managers' conscious choices at many organizations, information technology has changed how people communicate. This has altered, accordingly, the way many organizations are managed. One of the vanguard elements of this challenge was the personal computer, which Richard Lanham calls "a device of radical democratization."[73] The personal computer broke the firm grip of the organization's central computer system (and related staff functions) on the flow of information at organizations. One consequence of such decentralization of information was the end of the related firm grip of middle management on corporate communications. This change in organizational power structures became painfully apparent to many middle managers who—when many organizations were being buffeted by global competitive pressures, too—lost their jobs in corporate restructuring and downsizing. Greater still has been the technological effect of computer networking on organizational communications. The personal computer put greater power on more people's desks. But those people frequently worked in isolation from other personal computer users.[74] Now, however, a whole new array of products—software capabilities known generally as *groupware*—has begun to challenge that practice and has begun to change organizational communication patterns.[75] As Linda Applegate says: "Instead of managing data, computers are being used, in effect, to manage networks of relationships between people."[76] (By this point in this text, her reference to relationships should look familiar!)

Electronic mail (or E-mail) is one kind of new technological capability. E-mail users send messages between each other's computers. But E-mail is a relatively private communication channel compared to groupware networks, which serve as combinations of bulletin boards and conferences that many managers and employees can tap into at an organization. According to a *Fortune* report, more than 300 groupware products were on the market in 1993.[77]

- At a prominent New York City bank, an executive used a groupware network to solicit questions about rumored layoffs. Assured of their anonymity, many message senders responded, enabling the executive to assure people, quickly and widely, that the rumors were unfounded.[78]

- At MTV networks, a groupware system linking members of the sales force enabled those people to share seemingly isolated tidbits of information about a competitor's moves. "Suddenly it clicked; we figured out their game," says one network participant.[79] Without such a system, these people would have had more difficulty discerning a pattern in the competitor's strategy.

- A Price Waterhouse office staff was able to respond under significant time pressures and win a consulting contract using a groupware system to create a proposal.[80] The proposal was written in one weekend by four executives located in three states. Their computers were linked by a groupware product. Other executives reviewed the proposal-in-making by joining what a Fortune writer called a "dialogue on-screen."[81]

The organizational challenge posed by groupware should not be underestimated. For one thing, there is still much to be gained by communicating with other people face-to-face. Important nonverbal cues and voice inflections, discussed in this chapter, are "cleansed" if the message is sent electronically.[82] Another consideration is that information is still power to many people. For groupware to be effective, useful information must be available across a network.

Also, groupware can challenge organizational chains of command. The military is a case in point. At Wright-Patterson Air Force Base in Fairborn, Ohio, one kind of groupware has this effect, according to an officer:[83]

> Rank doesn't really matter when you're on line. An enlisted man could send a message to a colonel. [Before this groupware system] there wouldn't have been an easy way for a sergeant to share an idea with a colonel short of making a formal appointment to go see him in his office.

On the other hand, a person's greater visibility on a groupware network can give him or her a previously unavailable opportunity to "stand out."[84]

Groupware, just like personal computers, is one more example of a point made in Chapter 1 of this book. Managers move in a world in which many things are technologically possible. Their task is to translate those possibilities into actions that are meaningful to human beings at organizations.

## SUMMARY

1. **Link communications processes to the management processes of planning, organizing, leading, and controlling.**

   Communication may be defined as the process by which people attempt to share meanings through symbolic messages. The process of communication is important to managers because it

# MEETING THE CHALLENGE OF EFFECTIVE AND PRODUCTIVE COMMUNICATION

Formal communications opportunities take numerous forms at Hallmark. In addition to those discussed earlier in this chapter, two practices go to the heart of the Hallmark way of doing things. First, according to Robert Levering and Milton Moskowitz, who observed operations at Hallmark:

> Twenty-fifth anniversary celebrations remain a big deal here. An employee can invite all of his or her friends throughout the company to share the anniversary cake and coffee. Once a year the quarter-century club members are invited to a big dinner in their honor. Nearly a quarter of the firm's work force—2,668 members—were invited to the 1992 banquet.

Second, creative retreats and workshops give members of Hallmark's creative staff—which numbers nearly 700 people—the chance to talk with other creators and to share creative insights. These artists return from retreats with samples of their ideas that are posted on office walls. Whenever someone other than the artist stops to look at those walls, another opportunity for conversation arises.

Still, effective and productive communication is always a challenging process at any company. In early 1990, according to what Levering and Moskowitz found, several minority employees at Hallmark received anonymous hate mail at work. Responding swiftly to this threatening use of a formal communications channel, CEO Hockaday condemned the act in a statement published in Noon News. Hockaday announced that the sender would be dismissed from the company. The sender was never found. Communication channels, of course, are conduits for all sorts of messages. That is a risk, but it is also an opportunity for managers and employees to keep working to strengthen their ties at work.

enables them to carry on the management functions of planning, organizing, leading, and controlling. The activity of communication, particularly oral communication, takes up a large portion of a manager's work time.

2. **Discuss the key elements in interpersonal communication processes.**

   The major elements of interpersonal communication are the sender, encoding, message, channel, receiver, decoding, and noise. Encoding is the process by which the sender converts the information to be transmitted into the appropriate symbols or gestures. Decoding is the process by which the receiver interprets the message. If the decoding matches the sender's encoding, the communication has been effective. Noise is whatever interferes with the communication.

3. **Explain challenges in interpersonal and organizational communications processes.**

   Barriers to communication include such factors as differing perceptions, language differences, emotionality, inconsistent verbal and nonverbal communications, and distrust. Many of these barriers can be overcome by using simple, direct language, attempting to empathize with the receiver, avoiding distractions, being aware of one's own emotionality and nonverbal behavior, and being honest and trustworthy. Encouraging feedback and repeating one's message may also be helpful.

4. **Distinguish various communication networks.**

Vertical communication is communication that moves up and down the organization's chain of command. Lateral communication improves coordination and problem solving and fosters employee satisfaction. Informal communication occurs outside the organization's formal channels. The grapevine is a particularly quick and pervasive type of informal communication.

5. **Discuss the differences between integrative and distributive negotiation processes.**

All of a manager's communication skills come to bear in negotiations, a bargaining process that can be used to manage conflicts over the allocation of scarce resources or clashes in goals or values. Three elements of the negotiation situation are a conflict of interest, a lack of fixed or established rules for resolving the conflict, and a willingness to search for an agreement rather than fight or break off communication. Thus, negotiation requires a certain amount of trust and a desire to communicate.

Negotiations can proceed through integrative processes toward mutual-gain resolutions, or through distributive processes toward individual gains. Usually, both processes are at work simultaneously in negotiations, because negotiating parties can have legitimate incentives both to reveal and to withhold information.

6. **Explain the effects of new communication technologies on organizational decision making.**

New communication technologies, categorized commonly as groupware, have improved the accuracy and timeliness of organizational communications, and hence organizational action, and have been challenging traditional lines of authority.

## REVIEW QUESTIONS

1. Why is effective communication important to the manager?
2. List and connect the major elements in the expanded communication model.
3. What are some of the considerations involved in choosing the correct channel for one's message?
4. What is "noise" in a communication system?
5. Describe the common barriers to effective interpersonal communication. How may these barriers be overcome?
6. What four factors influence the effectiveness of organizational communication? How do they exert this influence?
7. What are the functions of vertical communication? How is accurate and complete vertical communication hindered?
8. What is the function of the grapevine? Why do managers sometimes use the grapevine to convey information? What are some possible grapevine chains? Which chain is most likely to be used in organizations?

9. How might the barriers to organizational communication be overcome?

10. What are the key elements in the negotiation situation? How can negotiation be used to manage conflicts?

11. Why do negotiators have good reason to withhold and share information in the course of their bargaining processes?

12. What contemporary situations seem to be examples of stable negotiating outcomes and unstable negotiating outcomes? What makes these situations stable or unstable?

13. Why might groupware products be slow to win widespread adoption in organizations?

14. How might groupware products change the ways individuals work together in organizations?

15. How might groupware improve your life as a college student?

## KEY TERMS

| | |
|---|---|
| Communication | Job specialization |
| Message | Information ownership |
| Sender | Vertical communication |
| Receiver | Lateral communication |
| Encoding | Informal communication |
| Decoding | Grapevine chains |
| Noise | Conflict |
| Channel | Negotiation |
| Formal channel of communication | Integrative process |
| Authority structure | Distributive process |

## THE SOUND OF NEGOTIATIONS[85]

What are companies to do when irate parents attack? Can managers ignore parental uproar, or must they simply give in? Or is there the possibility of negotiations? These are the questions that the music industry initially confronted during the mid-1980s. By 1985, the music industry had become a powerful force in American society with $4.4 billion in annual sales. Twenty-six percent, or $1.14 billion, of this $4.4 billion was being generated by the ever-controversial style of music traditionally known as "rock-'n'roll." Of course, the surge of rock'n'roll's popularity brought with it mounting concern over the message this brand of music was carrying. At issue were the provocative, sexually explicit lyrics and videos of artists such as Led Zepplin, Black Sabbath, Deep Purple, Kiss, Twisted Sister, and Motley Crue. The record industry had to decide how to handle the charges levied by irate parents that the content of many rock'n'roll songs was unfit for the teenage audiences that the songs were attracting.

Parents were reacting in particular to the allegedly obscene rock'n'roll lyrics and videos that were becoming popular among teenagers. Rock musicians, on the other hand, felt that their music was simply a reflection of what their fans wanted. Nikki Sixx, bass player for Motley Crue, for example, described bands such as his as representatives of "the American youth." According to Sixx, "[Y]outh is about sex, drugs, pizza, and more sex. We're intellectually on the crotch level."[86] Moreover, rock'n'roll was popular among youths because, as *The Economist* pointed out, of the "teenage trinity" of sex, drugs, and rock'n'roll, only rock'n'roll was freely available.

Initially, the rock'n'roll industry, represented by the Recording Industry of America Association (RIAA), whose member companies marketed approximately 85 percent of recordings nationwide, attempted to respond to the issues raised by parents. When the National Parent Teachers Association (PTA) recommended setting standards to guide companies in determining whether or not to apply warning labels to new releases, Stan Gortikov, president of RIAA, acknowledged the need for such standards. But he was not able to draw industry support as the RIAA had no direct control over the musicians it marketed. The PTA, however, did not see it this way. They felt they "were being stonewalled by the industry."[87]

In the wake of the failed PTA-RIAA negotiations, the Parents' Music Resource Center (PMRC) took over. The PMRC was formed by several women, in-

cluding Tipper Gore who became outraged when she heard Prince's album *Purple Rain,* which she had purchased for her 11-year-old daughter. When she and her daughter heard "Darling Nikki," the rock industry made another enemy. "The vulgar lyrics embarrassed both of us," said Gore. "At first, I was stunned—then I got mad! Millions of Americans were buying *Purple Rain* with no idea of what to expect."[88] The message the PMRC sent out was one of warning—a warning to parents about the kind of music their kids were listening to, and a warning to rock musicians that they had better clean up their "art."

Negotiations between parents and the music industry began anew during the summer of 1985. On behalf of the PMRC, Gore met with Gortikov and requested the development of guidelines or a rating system similar to the movie industry's rating system. In addition, Gore also requested that the lyrics of rock'n'roll songs be printed on the outside of album jackets so that parents could inspect them for potentially harmful references.

Gortikov ultimately refused all of Gore's requests. But he did offer an explanation. According to Gortikov, it would have been impossible to label every song due to sheer volume. Whereas at that time only 325 movies were made each year, 25,000 new songs were released. Furthermore, 95 percent of music purchasers were adults. Therefore, the expense of a rating system did not seem justified for merely 5 percent of the buying audience. In addition, printing lyrics on the album jackets did not seem possible since the record companies seldom owned the rights to the lyrics, and did not have the funds to purchase them.

As a compromise, Gortikov offered to recommend the use of a generic warning label that read, "Parental Guidance: Explicit Material," that would be used whenever an individual company felt it necessary. In fact, 19 RIAA member companies, representing 80 percent of U.S. record and tape sales, had already agreed to use such a label. This was not acceptable to the PMRC, though, and negotiations came to a dead end.

As the negotiators were unable to reconcile their differences, the Committee on Commerce, Science and Transportation held a hearing on the issue of record labeling. The purpose of the meeting was not to pass any legislation, but to "air out" the issue. Several musicians attended the hearing in support of the rock'n'roll industry. "Many musicians write and perform their own material and stand by it as their art, whether you like it or not," asserted the late Frank Zappa. "An imposed rating system will stigmatize them as individuals. How long before composers and performers wear festive little armbands with their scarlet letter on it?"[89] In addition, Zappa pointed out that the concerns of "parents" were not inherently different from the concerns of musicians. "I am a parent," said Zappa. "I have four children. Two of them are here. I want them to grow up in a country where they can think what they want to think, be what they want to be and not what somebody's wife or Government makes them be."[90] Zappa concluded his testimony with a defense of the right of all artists, rock musicians included, "to conduct their business without trade-restraining legislation whipped up like instant pudding by the Wives of Big Brother."[91]

The situation remained unresolved. Even as parents were up in arms regarding the allegedly provocative content of rock'n'roll songs, people in the industry were equally disturbed. "This is censorship," asserted Gary Stevens, president of Doubleday Broadcasting Company. "Many of us have been careful not to play pornographic records, but a few well-connected people have imposed their views of good taste on the masses. The record industry has caved in, and the broadcasters are bearing the brunt of it."[92] In addition, according to Gortikov, only 9 percent of purchases of rock'n'roll music are made by children under 14. People over 20 are responsible for 69 percent of the purchases.

The dispute continued into the 1990s. "As bad as things are going lately [in 1990]," said Lee Ballinger, West Coast editor of *Rock and Roll Confidential,* an industry newsletter, "I doubt if Prince will even be able to play his song '1999' by the time 1999 rolls around."[93]

In the spring of 1990, top managers at the country's major record companies agreed to create uniform warning labels. This step was taken primarily to discourage state legislatures from requiring such labeling by law. According to Sue Henseler, State Representative in Rhode Island, "There are two rea-

sons why bills get introduced....One is that you see a need for them, and secondly, you raise the consciousness of a lot of people so that things get done voluntarily."[94] Once the record companies agreed to take voluntary action, she agreed to withdraw her bill.

This does not mean that everyone was pleased with the outcome. In Boston, Greg Wallis, general manager of Tower Records, was far from content. "The legislatures are forcing the record industry to do the parenting for kids," he said. "It's not like these type of lyrics and suggestions haven't been in recorded music since recorded music has been in existence. It's too bad that it's come to this. But this should be sufficient enough to do what the parents want."[95]

The following June, a U.S. District Judge in Ft. Lauderdale, Florida, ruled for the first time that some rock'n'roll could be considered obscene. In this case, Judge Jose Gonzalez held that the lyrics in 2 Live Crew's "As Nasty as They Wanna Be" album were obscene. This meant that retailers could be arrested for selling the albums and the same could happen to broadcasters for airing them. Retailers were now on the spot. "Whenever a judge in court finds some expression of speech obscene, all speech is chilled. We hope this is an isolated situation," said Mark Siegal, executive vice president of the Los Angeles-based Shamrock Holdings, Inc., parent company to Show Industries and the 137-store Sound Warehouse chain. "Instead, we favor labeling products and restricting labeled products to...adults."[96]

## CASE QUESTIONS

1. Explain the negotiations statements in terms of difficulties that the parties have in encoding and decoding one another's messages.
2. What should the PMRC leaders do next and why, if they want to keep the process going?
3. What might a stable, integrative process solution to this dispute look like?

## CHAPTER 20

# EFFECTIVE

# CONTROL

**Upon completing this chapter, you should be able to:**

1. Explain why managers believe they need control.

2. Describe the steps in the control process.

3. Discuss the importance of key performance areas and strategic control points to the design of effective control systems.

4. Explain why financial controls are important to managers.

5. List some of the reasons budgets are used so widely.

6. Explain the main types of responsibility centers and the budget considerations associated with each.

7. Describe the budgeting process.

8. Explain the uses of external and internal auditing.

# CONTROLLING STABILITY AT DEERE & CO.[1]

In the 1860s, John Deere, a blacksmith in Vermont, invented a plow that was able to turn the thick, rich soil of the vast and fertile midwestern U.S. prairies. Then in 1868, Deere formed a company to distribute his plows and stressed a philosophy of quality products and customer service. By 1911, that company had evolved into a full-time manufacturer of farm equipment. In 1918, through its purchase of a Waterloo, Iowa-based gasoline engine, Deere became instrumental in the conversion of American agriculture from animal to machine power. Through diversification Deere has remained a viable concern, and today Deere stands as the largest producer of farm equipment in the world. In addition, Deere is a major supplier of construction machinery. Managers emphasize the globalization of Deere enterprises (including facilities in Mexico, Canada, Spain, France, Australia, and elsewhere) and stable leadership. Deere has had only four CEOs since 1928.

Although Deere has worked with GM on diesel engines and with NASA on developing metal alloys, agricultural equipment remains its core business. As of 1994, Deere held 35 percent of the farm tractor market and approximately half of the self-propelled combine market.

During recent years, however, American agriculture has experienced ups and downs. In the United States, for instance, many farmers accrued overwhelming debt burdens in the late 1980s that compelled them to part with land that had belonged to their families for generations. Some of the land was consolidated into larger farms. Much of it was sold to housing developers.

Even when the industry began to pick up in the early 1990s, few farmers rushed to buy new tractors, combines, or farming equipment. In fact, an article in the *Wall Street Journal* in 1992 reported that the average tractor in the United States was 19 years old. This could be due, at least in part, to the expense of Deere products. Even a modest piece of farm equipment manufactured by Deere can cost as much as a luxury automobile, while the latest, most sophisticated tractors retail for as much as $80,000. Deere's fortunes therefore tend to rise and fall with those of the farmers. In 1990, for example, Deere posted earnings of $411 million—the best in the company's history. In 1991, however, the company suffered a loss of $37 million. Then, the industry began to recover in 1992 and 1993, and Deere reported 1993 earnings of $184 million. Given such volatility, how does Deere keep going?

*Today Deere stands as the largest producer of farm equipment in the world.*

**JOHN DEERE.** John Deere tractors are a familiar sight in America's farmland.

One of Deere's strategies involves helping dealers offer incentives, such as price cuts, sales promotions, and low-interest financing through Deere's credit subsidiary. Dealers, hoping to compensate for lost profit through future parts and service business, often end up selling equipment at near cost.

Price incentives and promotional campaigns help Deere create regular demand for its goods. Under ordinary circumstances, farm equipment sales are seasonal—high in the spring and summer but low during the rest of the year. If Deere were to ignore

Another useful consideration is the identification of places where change occurs in a productive process. For example, in an organization's system for filling customer orders, a change occurs when the purchase order becomes an invoice, when an inventory item becomes an item to be shipped, or when the item to be shipped becomes part of a truckload. Since errors are more likely to be made when such changes occur, monitoring change points is usually a highly effective way to control an operation.

## DAMAGE CONTROL AT STERLING COURIER

Sterling Courier Systems based in Hendon, Virginia is a provider of same-day-delivery services. Although Sterling may do everything right to meet its delivery commitments, it relies on commercial airlines to transport its parcels—and occasionally fails to make its deadlines. Sterling relies on commercial airlines to transport its parcels. Delays are usually a result of packages being misplaced in airlines' tracking systems. Such incidents are beyond Sterling's control. But from the customer's vantage point, the failure is Sterling's problem.

To control the damage created by such delays, Sterling had to take some corrective measures. For example, for several months in late 1990 and early 1991 several Sterling deliveries disappeared in transit. The packages turned up later, but the customers had already suffered financial losses. Yet because the packages were eventually recovered, neither insurance nor the airlines was liable. The decision for president Glenn Smoak was whether to compensate the customers for their losses or simply not to charge them for the shipments. Smoak concluded that not charging for the shipment was an inadequate response, given the suffered downtime. But paying the $30,000 in losses would push the then-five-year-old $5 million company into a loss for the quarter. Smoak's decision was to pay out the $30,000 in gratis service, the customers stayed, and Sterling continues to grow.[11]

**BOARD CONTROL.** Boards of directors are charged with a duty to "manage the affairs" of the organization in the interests of stockholders and perhaps other stakeholders. Because directors do not directly manage the organization, their primary role is one of control—ensuring that actual decisions get made in the correct interest.

# EFFICIENT BY DESIGN . . .

Deere's ability to show profits or losses on its financial statements often depends upon the ability of managers to control costs and increase the efficiency of its operations. To improve profitability, Deere undertook a four-year reconfiguration of plant operations during the early 1990s. This initiative has enabled Deere to increase its farm tractor production by 22 percent without making it necessary to add costly floor space. In addition, Deere now relies on 15 percent fewer line and staff workers. While Deere's sales are expected to increase more than 15% during 1994 and 1995, the company should not need to increase production capacity. "Sales per employee will be at post-war highs," said Barry Banister, analyst with S. G. Warburg & Co.[12]

Deere's increased employee efficiency has resulted at least in part from the company's implementation of cellular manufacturing. Cellular manufacturing involves the physical grouping of the supplies and machinery necessary for building a specific product. This approach enables Deere to break its manufacturing processes down into more manageable and autonomous "subfactories." As a result, the company is able to cut manufacturing time and storage costs. Between 1984 and 1994, the cellular manufacturing approach enabled Deere to increase output per employee by more than 60 percent.

Through its innovative approach to manufacturing, Deere has reduced its company-wide break-even point to a mere 40 percent of capacity—20 percent below the industry average. Moreover, throughout all of the industry turbulence and restructuring, Deere has maintained a high level of research and development. By turning out new products quickly and efficiently, Deere hopes to increase its market share and squeeze higher margins out of its sales. Deere's new line of "no-till" tractors, for example, will allow farmers to abide by new federal erosion rules and should thus prove quite popular.

According to Forbes's Steve Weiner, Deere & Co. has one extremely valuable asset that will never show up on any financial statement—a loyal group of customers who would not consider buying a tractor or combine that was not painted "Deere green." →

# FINANCIAL CONTROLS

Managers use a series of control methods and systems to deal with the differing problems and elements of their organizations. The methods and systems can take many forms and can be intended for various groups. However, financial controls have a special prominence, since money is easy to measure and tally. In this section of the chapter, we will begin by discussing financial statements, which provide insight into an organization's performance and long-term prospects. Next we will look at budgetary control methods, which help managers control an organization's financial resources. We will end the section with a discussion of auditing, which compares an organization's performance to its budgets.

## FINANCIAL STATEMENTS

**Financial statements** are used to track the monetary value of goods and services into and out of the organization. They provide a means for monitoring three major financial conditions of an organization:

1. *Liquidity:* the ability to convert assets into cash in order to meet current financial needs and obligations.

## BEN & JERRY'S SUPER AUDIT CRUNCH[26]

**O**rganizations' annual reports typically consist of a combination of SEC filings and glossy photographs. Numbers, audits, footnotes, and portraits of smiling executives all come together to produce an organization's "best side," then presented to stockholders as the actual status of the company. Failures, financial or otherwise, are often sugar-coated or ignored altogether. Promises of growth and improvements abound with little attention to troubles the company may be experiencing. Moreover, annual reports tend to focus on only one aspect of an organization's well-being: the financials. "One of the problems is that annual reports only tell part of the story and they only talk to one audience—the financial community," noted Robert Rosen, president of Health Companies, a not-for-profit, Washington D.C.—based group that strives to redefine how businesses are organized and run. "Companies do not report how well they are doing in terms of managing the human capital side of the business or whether they are building a health company."[27]

Then there is Ben & Jerry's Homemade, Inc., the Waterbury, Vermont-based, super-premium ice cream maker renowned for its innovative and exceptionally tasty flavors, such as "Chocolate Chip Cookie Dough" and "Cherry Garcia" (named after Jerry Garcia of the Grateful Dead). Ben & Jerry's annual reports fall somewhere outside the norm. Since 1988, Ben & Jerry's has published two types of bottom lines in its annual report: one financial, the other social.

At Ben & Jerry's, management believes that a company should be evaluated not only on its financial performance but on its social performance as well. "[T]o be profitable for its shareholders and to be socially responsible, inside and outside the organization" is an assertion boldly made in the company's mission statement. "We decided that we wanted to measure our success by changing the definition of our bottom line," explained co-founder Jerry Greenfield. "For most businesses, their bottom line is just their profits, how much money is left over at the end of the year. We said we're going to have a two-part bottom line. We'll measure our success both by how we do financially and how we do with our social mission."[28]

The Ben & Jerry's social audit rates the company in areas such as employee benefits, plant safety, ecology, community involvement, and customer service. In order to make sure that no stone is left unturned, the auditor, an outside expert not employed with Ben & Jerry's, is given access to all employee and corporate documents during the conducting of the review.

"It's all in keeping with our two-part bottom line," noted Mitch Curren, P.R. Info Queen at Ben & Jerry's (yes, that is her real title).[29] The findings of the audit, positive or negative, are then published, unedited, so as to guarantee complete candor.

As a result, Ben & Jerry's annual reports tend toward brutal honesty. The 1992 social audit, for example, openly criticized the company for poor plant safety. At two plants, the number of injuries suffered had increased from 52 in 1991 to 75 in 1992. According to Paul Hawken, noted author and speaker on social responsibility and conductor of the 1992 audit, the number of days lost as a result of injuries or accidents during this period showed an 87% increase, far in excess of increased sales and production. Hawken also examined Ben & Jerry's unique "7:1(RATIO)" salary ratio, which prevented the highest-paid employee from making more than 7 times the salary of the lowest-paid employee. While Hawken admired the willingness of Ben & Jerry's board of directors to set such a cap on executive salaries ($100,000 as of 1992), he pointed out that the policy left a number of key positions vacant since many qualified applicants were able to find much higher salaries elsewhere. All of these criticisms found their way into Ben & Jerry's annual report, intact and unedited.

Even Ben & Jerry's charitable efforts have been attacked in the social audits. "One of the year's [1991] unmitigated flops was the 'Save the Family Farm' campaign," said Milton Moskowitz, author of the social audit in Ben & Jerry's 1991 annual report.[30] Originally designed to rally support for independent farmers, Moskowitz criticized the campaign's vague directives such as "write your Senators and Representatives to tell them to support a dairy program that provides farmers with a decent living." Moskowitz likened the "Save the Family Farm" effort to "a drive for motherhood: everyone's for it but what do you do about it?"[31] While this review was somewhat chafing, it did alert all of Ben & Jerry's stakeholders to the presence of a problem in need of correction—a problem, like plant safety and the salary cap, that might have remained unnoticed and neglected had it not been for the published social audit. "One reason business is so good at making money is because that is what they measure," commented Greenfield. "We said, if we're ever going to get our social mission to be an important thing to the company, we have to be able to measure it."[32]

While many people might criticize the practice of publishing corporate failures for the world to see, Curren argues that accountability is important, particularly in a business context. "We try to be up-front, to show whether we've 'walked the talk,'" Curren asserted.[33] According to Dixie Watterson, executive vice president of The Investors Relations Company in Northbrook, Illinois, publicly acknowledging its own shortcomings also serves to enhance Ben & Jerry's credibility. Investors may perceive such openness as something that sets the company apart from the pack, and a company that does not cover up its problems is apt to be admired by stockholders and consumers alike.

Still, inclusion of an uncensored social audit in an annual report is still a rare practice. "It's difficult for a company to allow that kind of criticism," commented Moskowitz.[34] In his opinion, even Ben & Jerry's has not yet demonstrated that it is fully committed to public scrutiny. "The real test would come if Ben & Jerry's had a bad year, if sales were down or they had to significantly reduce their workforce," Moskowitz speculated. "It's a different game then."[35]

## CASE QUESTIONS

1. Discuss what types of control process seems to be a part of the Ben & Jerry's way of doing business?

2. What are the benefits of Ben & Jerry's method of control?

3. What are its drawbacks?

4. In what other types of companies would Ben & Jerry's system work well?

5. In what types of companies would Ben & Jerry's system not work well?

## CHAPTER 21

# OPERATIONS MANAGEMENT

**Upon completing this chapter, you should be able to:**

1. Describe operations as a system in both production and service organizations.

2. Discuss the relationship between operations management, productivity efficiency, and customers' competitive priorities.

3. Describe operations system design issues.

4. Explain the job-design issues that are important to operations management.

5. Discuss the importance and challenge of inventory management.

6. Explain the proposition that all operations, including production, are services.

# A HIGH RETURN FROM "HOTELING"[1]

In the wake of corporate mergers, managers inevitably confront numerous challenges. Although the coming together of two companies often holds the promise of substantial benefits, managers must look at several areas to avoid duplication and waste. In particular, operations systems must be revised to meet new needs.

In October 1989, partners (or senior managers) at Ernst & Young confronted such challenges when the Ernst & Whinney accounting firm merged with the Arthur Young accounting firm. At that time, Ernst & Young abandoned three separate Chicago locations in order to consolidate its operations on seven floors of the Sears Tower. Noted Mike Thompson, operations and facilities director for Ernst & Young in Chicago, "Management's goal was to consolidate three offices without increasing space costs, as well as to present a unified and positive image of the firm to our clients and the business community." But how?

At Ernst & Young, the answer was found in a revolutionary new workplace alternative: "hoteling." The root word, of course, is *hotel,* a place where people stay only briefly. Hoteling is a space allocation process that enables companies to support employees who spend most of their time away from the office, without providing them with permanent office space. Instead, through hoteling, such employees share office space by reserving space only for the times they need to spend at their home base.

Hoteling has paved the way for dramatic space savings and greater utilization of corporate assets. Since pioneering the hoteling system in its Chicago office, Ernst & Young has been able to decrease space usage by approximately 150 feet per person—from 250 feet to 100 feet. When Ernst & Young's 1,350 employees moved into the Sears Tower in June 1992, about 500 audit and consulting professionals began using office space on an "as needed" basis. "Conceptually, the goal was to make the workplace both comfortable and efficient and as economical as we could," said Brian Casey, the Ernst & Young partner responsible for the move. "People who are out of the office a great deal of time do not get a permanent office. But they can have a fully furnished, technologically equipped office when they are here. When they know they will be in, they just have to call in."[2]

The hoteling system seems straightforward now, but it did not reach this point without careful planning. "Privacy, adequate work space, and the ability to get telephone calls had to be built in. A huge issue was the ability to take advantage of all of the technologies that were out there," Thompson pointed out.[3]

> *When the visiting employee arrives...even family pictures are on the desk.*

**GETTING SITUATED.** Users of hotel-type office space at Ernst & Young find their names on the door, as well as other information to orient them to their location.

The Ernst & Young hoteling system operates very much like that of a Hyatt or Hilton Hotel. Ernst & Young has a certain number of temporary offices available, scattered across the seven floors the company occupies in the Sears Tower, and employees without permanent office space—known as "visiting employees"—can call and reserve times to use those work areas as their offices.

Employees reserve space by telephoning the hotel coordinator, sometimes called the "concierge," and requesting space. At Ernst & Young, the employee can call as late as 4:30 P.M. to request an office for 9:00 A.M. the following day or 9:00 A.M. to request an office for 12:00 P.M. that same day.

Through a sophisticated computer-aided facilities management system, the hotel coordinator has immediate access to employees' company profiles, including their job descriptions and required supplies. With this information, the hotel coordinator scans available space to determine the most appropriate temporary locations for visiting employees, aiming to locate them in work stations as close as possible to their colleagues. Each visiting employee is given a space commensurate with his or her level, from a private office to a cubicle.

Visiting employees have their work materials—files, auditor's papers, and personal items—stored in assigned permanent lockers. Once a temporary workspace assignment is made, the contents of the employee's permanent locker are moved to the workspace along with any requested supplies. When the visiting employee arrives, his or her name is on the door, files are in the office, even family pictures are on the desk. In addition, the employees have their own phone numbers, which follow them to whatever workstation they are assigned. The visiting employee thus has access to all tangible materials, as well as to personal telephone and computer services, as if the temporary workstation were his or her own permanent office. →

**operations:**
The transformation activities of an organization.

*OPERATIONS* REFERS TO the way that members of an organization transform inputs—labor, money, supplies, equipment, and so on—into outputs—goods or services.[4] The practice of **operations** is complex. It takes in all the nitty-gritty, day-to-day activities by which the members of an organization strive to reach their goals. Managers at Ernst & Young take seriously the "nitty gritty" operations matter of making office space useful.

So, too, must the many managers and employees at Chicago's O'Hare International Airport. Each year, these people work to ensure that *hundreds of thousands* of takeoffs and landings are timely, safe, and comfortable.[5] O'Hare is the world's busiest airport, covering 7,700 acres over which thousands of vehicles, from baggage carts to jumbo jets, move in organized patterns.[6] O'Hare is but one example of how operations is an all-encompassing process that shapes the quality of work life as well as the organization's efficiency and effectiveness. To see how all this works, we will first look at operations as a system. We will then look at some of the similarities and differences between production and service organizations. Throughout this chapter, we will stress how operations is a *common thread* that links the managerial processes of planning, organizing, leading, and controlling. For an organization, operations is where it all comes together, or falls apart.

## THE OPERATIONS SYSTEM: A MODEL

← ch. 2, p. 46

**A**s we saw in Chapter 2, any organization can be viewed as a *system*, a set of related and interacting subsystems that perform functions directed at reaching a common goal. These subsystems can, in turn, be viewed as separate systems. This idea is the basis for Figure 21-1.

As the diagram shows, inputs include human labor, capital (money needed to acquire land, equipment, and so on), technology, and information. These are the resources that will be transformed into outputs that reflect the organization's goals.

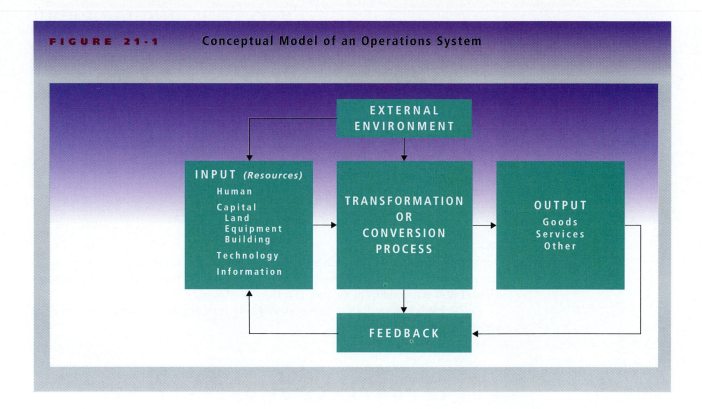

**FIGURE 21-1    Conceptual Model of an Operations System**

For Ford Motor Co., desired outputs are cars, trucks, and parts of a certain quality. For the Red Cross, desired outputs are safe supplies of blood and emergency aid to disaster victims. For a hospital, desired outputs would be patient care and preventive health care. At Ernst & Young, accounting services are a primary output. Outputs may include both positive and negative byproducts, such as new jobs and air pollution. Outputs can also affect other subsystems in the organization. If the people running the human resources subsystem declare a six-month moratorium on hiring, people in the operations subsystem will certainly feel the effects when workers who leave are not replaced.

The transformation process from input to output varies from organization to organization. *Physical transformations* of raw materials into finished goods occur mainly in production organizations, although service organizations also transform materials (i.e., forms and writing equipment) into finished goods (i.e., completed tax forms). Transportation involves *locational transformations,* while retailing involves *exchange transformations* (i.e., money for goods). In legal and accounting firms, there is usually an *information transformation* in which information is transformed from one form into another.

The feedback loop in Figure 21-1 represents the information gained by people at an organization during the entire process. This information makes it possible for them to monitor the system's performance and decide whether corrective changes are needed. As we emphasized in the previous chapter, this feedback loop is a key piece of the control function.

A **production organization** produces physical goods, such as cars, computers, plastic bottles, or paint. These goods can be stored in a warehouse and consumed over time. Some customizing is available, of course—customers can order extra-cost options on cars or request special tinting of paint, for example—but the overall emphasis is on making uniform, mass-produced goods. As a result, there is little customer contact or participation in the production of individual products.

A **service organization,** in contrast, produces largely intangible goods that cannot be stored. Doctors, lawyers, accountants, and barbers, for example, produce customized labor in the form of advice and services that reflect the needs of

**production organization:**
Organization that produces tangible goods that can be mass-produced and stored for later consumption.

**service organization:**
Organization that produces intangible goods that require consumer participation and cannot be stored.

---

**EXHIBIT 21-1**    **Characteristics of Products and Services**

|                        | **PRODUCT**              | **SERVICE**              |
|------------------------|--------------------------|--------------------------|
| Output                 | Tangible                 | Intangible               |
| Output consumption     | Over time; can be stored | Immediate; cannot be stored |
| Nature of work         | Producer intensive       | Labor intensive          |
| Customer contact       | Minimal, indirect        | Direct                   |
| Customer participation | Little or none           | Essential                |

*Source:* Adapted from Everett E. Adam, Jr., and Ronald J. Ebert, *Production and Operations Management,* 4th ed. (Englewood Cliffs, N.J.: Prentice Hall, 1989), p.7.

---

individual consumers. A telephone company provides communication services. An airline provides transportation. Services cannot be performed without customer contact and participation; neither can they be stored.

These basic differences between production operations and service operations are shown in Exhibit 21-1.

# THE IMPORTANCE OF OPERATIONS MANAGEMENT

**operations management:**
Complex management activity that includes planning production, organizing resources, directing operations and personnel, and monitoring system performance.

**O**perations management refers to the complex set of management activities involved in planning, organizing, leading, and controlling an organization's operations. At one time, operations management was considered the backwater of management activities—a dirty, drab necessity. This view has changed in recent years, as more and more managers realize how operations can be a "beehive" of activity with major financial consequences for any organization. For instance, to support the work of Johns Hopkins University Hospital in Baltimore, the facilities department *each year* handles more than 40,000 work orders, oversees hundreds of construction projects, and manages an annual capital budget nearing $200 million.[7] Operations management also includes something seemingly as mundane as mailing. Many, many companies spend millions annually on mailing costs. With rising Postal Service rates and widening global business operations, managers pay very close attention to mailing costs and alternatives.[8] Indeed, a whole new industry has emerged in competition with the Postal Service as managers take mailing operations seriously. Later in this chapter we will talk more about the prominent "players" in that industry—United Parcel Service (UPS) and Federal Express.

Operations management is important to an organization's managers for at least two reasons. First, it can improve *productivity,* which improves an organization's financial health. Second, it can help organizations meet customers' *competitive priorities.*

## TO IMPROVE PRODUCTIVITY: A MEASURE OF EFFICIENCY

**productivity:**
Measure of how well an operations system functions and indicator of the efficiency and competitiveness of a single firm or department.

**Productivity,** the ratio of output to input, is a measure of a manager's or an employee's efficiency in using the organization's scarce resources to produce goods and services. The higher the numerical value of this ratio, the greater the efficiency. Ernst & Young managers use "hoteling" to affect both parts of this ratio. They seek to cut inputs (space costs) and to boost the output of traveling accountants.

## A TOTAL-QUALITY APPROACH TO OPERATIONS IMPROVEMENT

The quality movement, with such approaches as small-scale continuous improvement processes and the large-scale radical redesign of processes, is directly affecting productivity and measures of efficiency. Take, for example, the Dutch telecommunications company, Philips Business Communication Systems (PBCS). PBCS was long sheltered by import barriers and captive government contracts. Recently it has found itself in a competitive global economy and a deregulated, privatized network where customers shop around for services. When David Kynaston became managing director of the company in 1990 he found much in need of change: Poor service had damaged sales, and profits had declined to the point where the parent company, Philips Electronics, could no longer support the company.

Assisted by a team of London-based consultants from Coopers & Lybrand, PBCS strove to cut costs while improving services. The focus was on the supply chain, partly because that was where a great amount of working capital was being wasted and partly because it provided the catalyst for reviewing all components of the operation. Calculations showed that logistics improvements—changes in how material and goods are procured, transported, and stored—could reduce stocks by 30 percent and raise the speed and quality of service by more than 20 percent. Improvement has advanced primarily through more efficient order processing. Goods are now ordered centrally and shipped directly to clients from the company's three factories in Europe. The financial health of the company has improved dramatically. Changes arising from increased employee involvement are anticipated to deliver another 10—15 percent savings in working capital. Kynaston and the team also believe that reengineering approaches will yield additional savings from increased efficiency and other improvements.[9] ▬

← ch. 20, p. 563

To understand the connection between productivity and efficiency, look back at Figure 21-1 and try to visualize it as a series of <u>strategic control</u> points. This concept refers to junctures at which a major change occurs. In filling a customer order, for example, strategic control points would occur when the purchase order becomes an invoice, when an inventory item becomes an item to be shipped, and when an item to be shipped becomes part of a truckload of goods to be delivered. Any of these strategic control points is a potential source of confusion and inefficiency, as work is passed from one set of workers to another. An unclear form or a confusing policy— say, for handling out-of-stock items—creates the risk that orders will be lost or mishandled, wasting valuable time, money, or energy. From this vantage point, the operations system looks like a sieve that can leak valuable resources unless it is managed efficiently. Productivity offers one measure of this efficiency.

For example, assume that a legal clinic with eight lawyers (the input) produces output consisting of 100 client consultations per day. Productivity would equal 100/8 or 12.50. Assume that a second legal clinic next door has 15 lawyers handling 125 consultations per day. The productivity ratio would be 125/15 or 8.33. The smaller clinic has a higher productivity ratio on a *quantitative basis*, which may or may not reflect anything about the *quality* of its output, of course.

**TYPES OF PRODUCTIVITY RATIOS.** There are two basic types of productivity ratios. The first, *total productivity*, relates the value of all output to the value of all input, using the ratio total output/total input. The second, *partial productivity*, relates the value of all output to the value of major categories of input, using the ratio total output/partial input.

**REEVALUATING PRODUCTIVITY RATIOS.** In an effort to increase productivity, Federal Express began electronically monitoring its 2,500 customer service agents. Holding each call to 140 seconds counted for 50 percent of an agent's evaluation. Two years later, faced with mounting complaints about stress and having to cut customers off, Fed Ex adopted a new system. Agents like Paula Biffle (left) are monitored only twice a year, and follow-up talks with manager Tish Montesi (right) focus on quality. As a result, service improved and the average call dropped to 135 seconds.

The legal clinic is an example of a partial productivity ratio, called a *labor productivity index* or output per work-hour ratio. Most productivity measures quoted by economists and business executives are, in fact, labor productivity indexes, since labor is one of the greatest ongoing costs for most organizations. Other partial productivity ratios measure the amount of scrap (wasted materials); the number of units that have to be reworked or fixed before they meet quality standards; cycle time, the length of time to perform an operation; and downtime, the unproductive time spent retooling a production line or waiting for customers. Any of these measures gives an indication of whether resources are being used to good advantage or wasted.

**USES OF PRODUCTIVITY RATIOS.** Productivity ratios can be calculated for a specific time period, which measures the efficiency of operations at that time, or they can be compared with other ratios over time, as a measure of gains or losses in productivity. For example, between 1988 and 1992, Mexican manufacturing employees recorded an approximate 6.5 percent average annual productivity increase, compared to 3 percent average annual gain over the same period by U.S.-based manufacturing employees.[10]

In recent years, U.S. manufacturers have tried to boost productivity by closing plants, downsizing, laying off production workers, and selling off failing or unwanted businesses. Still, as an economic system, the United States lags behind Japan, South Korea, Great Britain, Norway, Sweden, France, and other countries in productivity *growth*. Many government officials and executives are searching for solutions to this problem.

Many experts say the problem is the emphasis on productivity itself. They charge that, in trying to improve "the numbers"—quantitative measures of productivity—too many U.S. managers have focused on capital investment in automation as a way to reduce labor costs. This short-term focus has caused them to overlook the benefits of investing in the organization's **human capital**—employees and their skills—and improving quality.

This emphasis is changing as managers at more organizations concentrate on finding the right mix of capital investment and human investment. One of the

**human capital:**
An organization's investment in the training and development of its members.

**workforce literacy:**
Knowledge and skills directly related to job performance.

← ch. 18, p. 501

most important trends in operations management today is the focus on increasing **workforce literacy,** knowledge and skills that relate directly to job performance. Another is the trend toward <u>participative management</u> and the use of <u>self-managed work teams</u> to improve productivity and quality simultaneously.

Corning Inc.'s experience at its Blacksburg, Virginia, plant illustrates both these trends. Rather than force workers to do repetitive, restricted jobs, plant managers decided to use a combination of automation and a multiskilled, team-based production force to challenge employees. Out of 8,000 people who applied for jobs, Corning selected the 150 who performed the best on tests of problem-solving skills and showed a willingness to work in a team setting. In the first year of production, 25 percent of work hours were devoted to extensive training in technical and interpersonal skills, at a cost of $750,000.

The rewards were well worth the expense. A Blacksburg team can retool a line in just 10 minutes, six times faster than the norm in traditionally managed plants. As a result, the Blacksburg plant earned $2 million in profits during an 8-month start-up period, although it had been projected to lose $2.3 million. As an additional bonus, morale is high. Productivity, product quality, and Corning profits have all increased. Buoyed by this success, managers at Corning are planning to convert 27 other plants to a team-managed approach, using on-the-job training to improve worker skills.[11]

Investment in human capital is increasingly important not only to manufacturing but to the service and knowledge-oriented economy. As millions of people are displaced by technology, the downsizing of corporations, and competition from around the globe, issues of social responsibility of companies toward their employees become more crucial. According to Peter F. Drucker, raising the productivity of service work is management's first social responsibility. He argues that we must work *smarter*. This involves making sure that continuous learning accompanies productivity gains and recognizing that knowledge workers and service workers learn most when they teach.[12]

### TO MEET CUSTOMERS' COMPETITIVE PRIORITIES

Most companies develop competitive problems when managers lose sight of operations' primary reason for being: to produce quality products and services that *consumers want* at prices that seem reasonable. This relates back to measures of organizational effectiveness: the ability to set the "right" goals, ones that build on organizational strengths *and* meet the needs and wants of potential consumers. Of course, individual needs and wants vary widely, as do price perceptions. Rather than try to be all things to all consumers, effective managers make strategic decisions about how their organizations can best meet their customers' **competitive priorities,** and then adjust their operations accordingly. After all, customers use an organization's products and services in their own competitive contexts. The four major competitive priorities for operations management are pricing, quality level, quality reliability, and flexibility.

**competitive priorities:**
Four major criteria, including pricing, quality level, quality reliability, and flexibility, on which products and services are evaluated.

**PRICING.** For many consumers, price is a major consideration, either because their funds are limited or because the differences between a higher-priced item and a lower-priced item do not seem justified. One task of the operations manager is to keep costs down so that the organization can offer "good" prices and still make a profit. At Ernst & Young, hoteling is one way to do this.

Earl Scheib, Inc., of Beverly Hills, which operates a nationwide chain of discount car-repair shops offering low-priced paint jobs, is an example of an organization that has built high sales volume through low prices. Scheib's low prices have resulted in annual sales increases of 15 percent and earnings increases of almost 50 percent. At the same time, Scheib protects its profit margins by careful

**KEEPING CUSTOMERS SATISFIED.** Municipalities and other non-profit organizations, like for-profits, have to keep costs in control while providing services for their "customers." Many communities have added curbside recycling programs to satisfy residents and reduce the rate of landfill.

cost accounting. Cost accounting is also important in retail stores, since a name-brand good offers the same quality and warranty whether it is bought in a luxurious department store or a discount warehouse.

Although pricing considerations are usually associated with for-profit organizations, they are also a concern of nonprofit organizations (such as charities and professional associations) and government agencies, which charge "prices" in the form of dues, donations, taxes, and user fees. To increase consumer satisfaction and avoid complaints, these organizations need to use operations management to keep prices down while still providing high-quality service.

**QUALITY LEVEL.** Quality level has two components: high-performance design and fast delivery time. Characteristics of high-performance design are superior features, close tolerances, and greater durability of the product or service. An example is Maytag washers and dryers. In an industry marked by highly competitive products and prices, Maytag has been able to charge premium prices because customers believe in the superior capability and the expected longer life of its washers and dryers. Customers also expect efficient repair schedules if anything does go wrong with a Maytag product. Quality level is also exemplified by Pizza Hut employees, who offer quick-service guarantees during the weekday lunch hour.

**QUALITY RELIABILITY.** Quality reliability means consistent quality and on-time delivery. Consistent quality measures the frequency with which the design specifications are met. McDonald's restaurants are world-renowned for uniformly achieving their design specifications. You can expect the same quality standards whether you eat at a McDonald's in Charlotte, New York, or Paris. Toyota's small cars are not noted for the ability to compete with Cadillacs on quality *level* (consequently, Toyota's price is much lower), but they are world-renowned for their quality *reliability*—they are highly consistent in quality from one car to another. In general, the "lean production" system pioneered by Toyota and other companies has stressed the organizational and managerial aspects of production, including reduction of inventories and process times, just-in-time inventory, continuous improvement, and a skilled labor force. This model has worked extremely efficiently under the conditions of a totally cooperative environment and an absolute dedication to work of all employees.[13]

**FLEXIBILITY.** Flexibility refers to both product and volume flexibility. *Product flexibility* means that product designs can be changed quickly and that managers emphasize making such changes to please customers—they customize products to

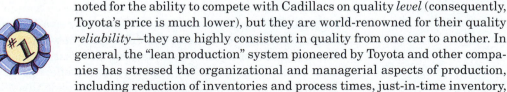

**MEETING MULTIPLE PRIORITIES.** At Southwest Airlines, flexible work rules and multi-skill training allow high productivity per employee, contributing to low prices without jeopardizing customer service.

individual preference. In this case, the level of output for an individual product is necessarily low because the firm competes primarily on its ability to produce difficult, one-of-a-kind products. This is the exact opposite of mass production, where standardization of the product has occurred and the producer makes large quantities of one item.

*Volume flexibility* is the ability to make quick changes in the rate of production as the demand for a firm's product changes. McDonald's is a good example; managers increase or decrease their workforce from hour to hour to meet anticipated changes in customer demands. McDonald's managers use a certain number of employees for an 8-hour shift and supplement them by adding part-time employees at noon and 6 P.M. These part-time employees can include retired people supplementing their Social Security benefits by working a few hours each week.

**MEETING MULTIPLE PRIORITIES.** All four of these competitive priorities—pricing, quality level, quality reliability, and flexibility—involve doing something with customers' preferences in mind. The primary problem with trying to meet competitive priorities is that they often conflict. Consumers want reasonable prices, but they also want high quality levels, reliability, and flexible, feature-laden products and services. At one time, meeting all these expectations would have been impossible, since high-quality, customized goods have traditionally been expensive to produce. In recent years, though, creative operations managers have shown that organizations can offer high quality and flexible goods and services at competitive prices.

A contemporary case in point is Southwest Airlines, based in Dallas, Texas.[14] The airline has carved out a distinct short-haul market niche. Herbert Kelleher, Southwest's founder, chairman, president, and chief executive officer, directs an operational strategy aimed at keeping fares low. Southwest's low fares are intended to compete not only with other airlines, but also with driving.

Southwest is unique more for what it does not do than for what it does. It has no airport hubs and does not seek long-haul traffic. The carrier does not subscribe to any major computer reservation system and does not accept interline traffic. The airline does not reserve specific seats or serve in-flight meals.

People at Southwest address customers' competitive priorities through the following four-point service strategy:[15]

1. Low fares, averaging 60 to 70 percent below competing airlines (pricing)
2. Maintaining high productivity per employee through flexible work rules and multi-skill training, allowing rapid turnarounds of airplanes (quality level)
3. Direct, non-stop flights, supporting on-time departures and arrivals (quality reliability)
4. Regularly-spaced, frequent flights throughout the day (flexibility)

# DESIGNING OPERATIONS SYSTEMS

← Ch. 10, p. 269

**B**ecoming aware of competitive priorities is just one way that managers can match operational plans to strategic plans. These operational plans, in turn, affect the design of operations systems. Designing an operations system involves making decisions about *what* and *how many* products or services will be produced, *how* and *where* they will be produced, and *who* will produce them.

## WHAT TO PRODUCE

Computer technology assists the manager in product design.

**design for manufacture (DFM):**

Technique that involves streamlining the design of products to simplify assembly.

**DESIGN FOR MANUFACTURE (DFM).** One of the most promising trends in this area is **design for manufacture (DFM),** which streamlines design to simplify assembly. Bell Labs successfully used this technique to design a new digital loop carrier, a device that transmits phone signals through fiber-optic cable. Instead of ironing out production problems on the factory floor, design engineers and production engineers worked together to select plastics that could stand up to the heat of manufacture and to identify and eliminate potentially costly engineering mistakes before production began.[16] This technique is also used at Boeing Corporation, where cross-functional "design-build" teams bring together people from design, engineering, and manufacturing long before an aircraft goes into production.[17]

**CAD (computer-aided design):**

Design and drafting performed interactively on a computer.

**CAD.** At one time, product design was a time-consuming multistep process that involved the creation and testing of prototypes, or working models. Today this process is faster and cheaper thanks to **computer-aided design (CAD),** which allows product design, drafting, and simulated testing to be performed interactively on a computer.

Because much of a product's cost is determined by its design, most manufacturers are turning to simultaneous or concurrent engineering, where design and manufacturing engineers work together to simplify a design. General Motors now uses CAD to design the metal-stamping dies for its new cars. Car bodies are made from sheet metal that is stamped in large presses that use different dies, or stamping forms, to bend the metal into hoods, fenders, and so on. These dies must be carefully designed to prevent wrinkling or tearing the sheet metal during the process. With CAD, GM designers can create and test computer models of proposed dies early in the design process. Before CAD, it took about 27 months to create the tooling for new car models. With CAD, GM officials estimated, the time has been cut by up to 7 months.[18]

**bill of materials:**

Listing of the type and number of parts needed to produce a given product.

The benefits of CAD do not stop there. Because the design is stored in the computer system, it can be "exploded" to create a **bill of materials,** a listing of the

| EXHIBIT 21-2 | The Complex Process of Capacity Planning |
| --- | --- |

- Forecast future demand, including, insofar as possible, the likely impact of technology, competition, and other events.
- Translate these forecasts into actual physical capacity requirements.
- Generate alternative capacity plans to meet the requirements.
- Analyze and compare the economic effects of the alternative plans.
- Identify and compare the risks and strategic effects of the alternative plans.

*Sources:* Everett E. Adams, Jr., and Ronald J. Ebert, *Production and Operations Management: Concepts, Models, and Behavior*, 5th ed. (Englewood Cliffs, N.J.: Prentice Hall, 1986); E.S. Buffa, *Modern Production/Operations Management*, 6th ed. (New York: Wiley, 1980).

types and number of parts needed to make each unit. As we will see later, this information is crucial for ensuring that the organization has adequate supplies of the right materials on hand when needed.

## HOW MANY TO PRODUCE

**capacity planning:**
Operations decision concerned with the quantity of goods or services to be produced.

The second decision in designing the operations system is *how many* products—or *how much* service—will be produced. This is called **capacity planning,** a process of forecasting demand and then deciding what resources will be needed to meet that demand. This process is summed up in Exhibit 21-2.

Long-range technological forecasting—which can extend five or ten years into the future—may be needed to anticipate or forecast future capacity demands. Unforeseeable events—new technological discoveries, wars, recessions, embargoes, and the effects of an unknown inflation rate—cannot always be factored into forecasting equations.

Capacity planning at Boeing is an excellent example. In the commercial aviation marketplace, passenger airline executives place orders for aircraft to be delivered well into the future—say, 5 years.[19] As a consequence, manufacturers such as Boeing build what is known as an *order backlog.* Boeing's order backlog totalled nearly $100 billion in future revenues![20] But backlog orders are not always firm. Passenger airlines have suffered major financial setbacks in recent years, causing some to cancel some, or all, of their aircraft orders.[21] So, long-range forecasting at Boeing must address, among other factors, backlog "stability."

Completed forecasts must be translated into capacity requirements. This implies that existing capacity must be measured. In some cases, measuring capacity is easy enough. For example, gauging the number of tons of steel produced by a steel mill is not difficult. For a system with a diverse and less readily classified product or service, such as a legal office, measuring capacity is less straightforward. Input measures are generally used for such systems; that is, capacity may be defined as the number of lawyers in the legal office. Ernst & Young managers deal with a kind of capacity issue when they arrange hoteling. After all, Ernst & Young revenues come from fees charged to clients. Hoteling is a way to increase the public accounting firm's capacity by intense use of the available "production facilities" by Ernst & Young accountants. At Boeing, executives like order backlogs, because they are then able to maintain steady capacity and production levels. You can now see why they do not like "erosion" in the backlog!

The forecasted physical capacity requirements could compel managers to change the operations system to meet future demand. Capacity changes might be brought about by either short-run or long-run modifications, or both. *Short-run capacity changes* include scheduling overtime work, shifting existing personnel, subcontracting, and using inventories or back orders. Ernst & Young "hoteling" deals with short-run capacity. *Long-run capacity changes* involve adding or removing

**CONTINUOUS PROCESS PRODUCTION.** Dealing with high heat and molten metal, steel mills keep their production operations going 24 hours a day to avoid expensive start-ups and shutdowns.

capacity by physical facility expansion (more press hammers, more lawyers) or contraction (fewer press hammers, fewer lawyers). Long-run capacity changes can be very expensive for Boeing, because producing aircraft is quite complex.

Alternative capacity plans, each of which fits the required demand but through different means (more press hammers, subcontracting) can be analyzed. The costs of each and all of their strategic effects can be weighed and compared. The alternative with the lowest cost could turn out to result in lost sales and lost market share, which might (or might not) be inconsistent with organizational strategy. (A subcontracting slowdown might cause delays in delivery and thus loss of market to a competitor.) Costs, risks, and strategic effects must be thoroughly weighed by managers.

## HOW TO PRODUCE

Process selection, which determines *how* the product or service will be produced, involves four phases of technological decisions:

**1. MAJOR TECHNOLOGICAL CHOICE.** Does technology exist to produce the product? Are there competing technologies among which to choose? Should innovations be licensed from elsewhere, such as foreign countries, or should an internal effort be made to develop the needed technology? The importance of the major technological choice phase is highlighted by such recent developments as microchips and gene splicing. Although the major technological choice is largely the province of engineers, chemists, biogeneticists, and other technical specialists, top managers should comprehend as fully as possible the technology, its likely evolution, and the alternatives.

**2. MINOR TECHNOLOGICAL CHOICE.** Once the major technological choice is made, there may be a number of minor technological *process alternatives* available. The operations manager is involved in evaluating alternative transformation processes for costs and for consistency with the desired product and capacity plans. Should the process be continuous? A continuous process, which is carried out 24 hours a day to avoid expensive start-ups and shutdowns, is used by the steel and chemical industries, among others. An assembly-line process follows the same series of steps to mass-produce each item, but need not run 24 hours a day. Examples are the automobile and ready-to-wear clothing industries. Job-shop processes produce items in small lots, perhaps custom-made for a given market or customer. Examples are lumberyards and aircraft manufacturers.

**3. SPECIFIC-COMPONENT CHOICE.** What type of equipment (and degree of automation) should be used? Should the equipment be dedicated (tied to a specific purpose) or general purpose (leaving open the possibility of using it to make other products)? To what degree should machines replace people in performing and controlling the work? Increasingly, human workers are being used to program and monitor automated equipment, rather than doing the work themselves.

This trend began in the early 1960s, when numerically controlled (NC) lathes, milling machines, and drill presses began to show up on the shop floor. These were *dedicated machines,* meaning they performed a specific task according to instructions contained in a program written on plastic mylar tape. (There was no memory, as in a computer.) The strength of NC machines is that they perform operations with a consistency and reliability that far exceeds those of the normal machinist. Their weakness is the downtime and expense involved in changing their setup—the task they are ready to perform.

This barrier was overcome, to some extent, when newly developed microcomputer chips were used to create computerized numerical control (CNC) machines. These machines are easier to reprogram and set up for another task, but they cost anywhere from $50,000 to $500,000, depending on their size and the complexity of the operations they can perform. Obviously, such a capital investment cannot be taken lightly. It requires good planning and operations management. The same is true of flexible manufacturing systems (FMS), which combine CNC machines in flexible systems of production that can be easily and efficiently set up to produce batches of different products.

**CAD/CAM (computer-aided design and computer-automated manufacturing)**
is an integrated approach in which the computer software that is used to design a product can be used to translate the design into a computer program that will operate the NC or CNC machine. Typically, only companies that have high-volume production can afford to invest in such a system.

**CIM (computer-integrated manufacturing)** is an even more integrated approach that incorporates CAD/CAM, robots, and materials-requirement planning (MRP)—a computerized approach to managing inventory.

Most industrial robots are basically computer-controlled mechanical arms that can be equipped with grippers, vacuum cups, painting guns, welding torches, or other tools. As such, they are good choices for moving and handling hazardous materials (hot ingots, radioactive rods) or for performing tasks that require precision under hazardous conditions (spray painting and welding). Robots, for example, can paint for hours and never suffer ill effects from breathing the fumes. In the future, more sophisticated robots will be equipped with video imaging systems, allowing them to "see" their work, and onboard computers, allowing them to perform certain tasks independently.

**4. PROCESS-FLOW CHOICE.** How should the product or service flow through the operations system? This final process-selection step determines how materials and products will move through the system. Assembly drawings, assembly charts, route sheets, and process flow charts are used to analyze process flow. Analysis may lead to resequencing, combining, or eliminating operations to reduce materials-handling and storage costs. In general, the less storage and delay involved in the process, the better.

**CAD/CAM (computer-aided design and computer-automated manufacturing:**
Integrated approach in which the software used in designing products is also used to write a computer program to control the machinery.

**CIM (computer-integrated manufacturing):**
Integrated approach that combines *CAD/CAM* with the use of robots and computerized inventory management techniques.

**THE FUTURE OF ROBOTICS.** Robot engineers around the world are working to design field robots, such as this Aqua Robot, which inspects undersea building sites for Japan's Transport Ministry. Unlike factory robots, field robots are equipped with wheels, tracks, legs, and even wings that let them move about outside the structured environment of the factory, as well as artificial vision (to prevent robotic pratfalls), and expert-systems software to make fairly quick and independent decisions about inspections, cleaning up nuclear waste sites, fighting fires, and other hazardous tasks.

In recent years, greater use has been made of automated guided vehicle systems (AGVS), which employ driverless battery-operated vehicles to move back and forth between pickup and delivery points. Currently, this is achieved by placing a wire guide path in the floor that can be sensed by the vehicle's antennas. Research is now in process to do away with the wire and to combine AGVS with robotics to create mobile robots.[22] Some managers have extended this approach to automate their warehouse and loading facilities.

Greater use of computer networking is another recent development that has enabled manufacturers to work more closely with people at other organizations who supply components for the organization's product. In fact, General Motors management now requires suppliers to link up to a GM network.[23] Not only is product quality improved through greater communication about component specifications and design, but administrative efficiency is gained, too. Far fewer paper transactions mean lower input costs for GM *and* the suppliers.

In service systems, process selection depends on the nature of the system. Service systems with low customer contact, such as the check-clearing operation of a bank, can carry out process selection by following the four phases outlined above. In systems with high customer contact, such as retail establishments, the processes or procedures for interacting with the customer must also be selected. For a standardized service, these processes can be specific and allow for little variability—for example, the cash-dispensing function of an automated teller machine (ATM) at a bank. For customized services, variable procedures must be designed— for example, the evaluation of a personal loan application at the same bank. There are specialized computer systems designed to assist bank, department store, and other service industry managers in performing customized evaluations.[24]

For commuter airlines such as City Flyer Express in the United Kingdom, "how to produce" becomes in part a question of how to coordinate route schedules with British Airways.[25] City Flyer is a "code-sharing" partner of British Airways. This means that City Flyer flights into and out of

**LAYOUT PLANNING VIA COMPUTER.** Alan B. Pritsker displays some of the animated simulation software Pritsker & Association Inc. created to help managers plan a layout and see how it will function at various levels of capacity.

London's Gatwick Airport are listed on British Airways' reservation system. This enables passengers of both carriers to make easier connections on British Airways' trans-Atlantic flights. Operations at City Flyer always depend, in part, on operations at British Airways and on communications between people at both organizations.

**FACILITY-LOCATION PLANNING.** Choosing where to locate the production facility is one of the most important design decisions. The objective of location planning is to position the capacity of the system in a way that minimizes total production and distribution costs. For every new or additional facility, *fixed capital costs* for construction, land, and equipment, as well as *variable operations costs* (such as wages, taxes, energy and materials acquisition, and distribution) are incurred. The location decision requires balancing all of these costs, effects on potential revenues, and qualitative factors such as labor availability, quality of life, and community attitudes. Clearly, Ernst & Young managers were trying to minimize the disruptions of the merger when they implemented hoteling in Chicago.

Facility-location planning is affected, and sometimes complicated, by the efforts of local government officials to woo managers into locating in that government's jurisdiction. This happens continually, it seems, with owners of professional sports franchises. Among typical enticements offered by government officials are tax reduction or waivers and such infrastructure improvements as new access roads and railroad connections.[26]

**LAYOUT PLANNING.** Layout planning involves decisions about *how* to arrange space in the physical facilities. In layout planning, process and equipment decisions are translated into physical arrangements for production.

Space must be provided for:

- *Productive facilities,* such as work stations and materials-handling equipment.
- *Nonproductive facilities,* such as storage areas and maintenance facilities.
- *Support facilities,* such as offices, restrooms, waiting rooms, cafeterias, and parking lots.

Space must also be provided for materials and additional capacity. Any location-related requirements, such as docking facilities or heating units, must also be planned. A good layout minimizes materials handling, maximizes worker and equipment efficiency, and satisfies a host of other factors, such as minimizing worker exposure to hazardous fumes.

## WHO WILL DO THE WORK

The final decision in designing the operations system concerns the structure of individual jobs—*how* the work will be done and *who* will do it, a process discussed in Chapter 13. Because job design is reflected in labor expenses, any inefficiencies or mistakes here will ultimately affect operating costs. In recent years, three issues have become important for job design: (1) the level of skills employees bring to the workplace; (2) workplace safety; and (3) workplace cooperation.

**WORKER SKILLS.** Employers have always expected to provide some on-the-job training for new employees. The problem today is that many U.S. job applicants lack basic reading and math skills. One international fastener manufacturer in the United States has found it necessary to have applicants fill out application forms in person to be sure they know how to read and write. This "skills shortage" is expected to get worse as computers and other sophisticated technology become more commonplace. As a consequence, many corporate executives have committed their organizations to take preemptive action by contributing time and money and talent to the improvement of American public schools.[27] This, they reason, will help *future* workers move into job designs necessary in today's and tomorrow's global markets.

**WORKER SAFETY.** Job design must also take into account health and safety requirements set forth in the Occupational Safety and Health Act of 1970 (OSHA) and subsequent federal, state, and local regulations.

One of the most serious issues is repetitive motion injuries—potentially crippling tendinitis or nerve damage in the hands and wrists that results from performing the same motions over and over again. Such injuries are most common among production workers, who often perform the same task thousands of times on an 8-hour shift, but white-collar workers who type at computers for long periods of time are also vulnerable.

← Ch. 13, p. 366

*Ergonomics*, the biological design of jobs to reduce such hazards, is receiving new respect. OSHA officials recently prepared guidelines to prevent repetitive motion injuries. It led Ford Motor Co. managers to institute company-wide programs to cut down on such injuries, sometimes by simply repositioning materials.[28] Tendonitis was also a hazard at a zipper company, where workers tested zippers by hand. At first, managers introduced job rotation to minimize the risk. Eventually they decided to turn the testing over to robots.

**WORKPLACE COLLABORATION.** One theme running throughout this book is the growing practice of workplace collaboration, slowly replacing the worker—manager tensions of the early days of industrial management. One of the operations implications of this shift, or "sea change" as some see it, involves who does what work.

For more than 20 years, the people of Moosewood Restaurant of Ithaca, New York, have performed their culinary wizardry out of a 10-foot by 25-foot kitchen that includes dishwashing and prep space.[29] The restaurant seats 54 patrons and averages two and a half table turns at dinner. During warmer weather, the restaurant serves an additional 35 outside. Moosewood changes its menu twice each day. The dinner menu offers three main dishes and two soups. Moosewood is not incorporated. Instead, the restaurant op-

# COMFORT FOR THE WORKSTATION DWELLERS

Consistency is an important driver of the hoteling system at Ernst & Young. The layout of work areas is the same on every floor to facilitate wiring and design and to make the transient workstation dwellers feel as at home and comfortable with the surroundings as possible. "As hoteling developed…we quickly learned that people would need a sense of place," recalled Maureen Durack, network manager of the facility.[30] "When they walk onto one of our floors, regardless of what office they have, they know that there is a printer here, and here, and here; they know its name and what kind of paper it has in it. It really simplifies our approach to know that everything is exactly the same on every floor."[31]

The goal, according to the managers of Sverdrup Interiors, the firm that designed the project, was an international, universal, crisp professional image. Instead of the coveted "corner offices," there are corner conference rooms, available for all to use.

In addition, etched glass in walls and partitions helps to bring in light. Wood accents are confined to public areas where the greatest number of people can enjoy them.

"Technology is the driving force behind this office," said Durack. "Management had the determination to make this an office-wide technology plan. We have been very focused in making sure that technology supports the goal of cohesion throughout the office."[32]. →

**DIRECTORY ASSISTANCE.** Visitors use the touch-screen computer terminal in the Ernst & Young lobby to determine the current office location of any "hoteling" employee.

erates as a collective with 18 members. A different collective member serves as the menu planner each week. The menu planner purchases food, selects presentations, and directs the cooks.

Changes in an organization's structures can also affect collaborative efforts. The National Labor Relations Board (NLRB) has ruled that companies cannot require worker participation in quality circles and similar groups unless they allow workers to choose their representatives and give the groups a genuine voice in decision making.[33] Many experts believe the decision clouds the future of labor-management workplace cooperation. The NLRB was concerned that many of the workplace groups were operating as employer-controlled unions, a practice with an unhappy past in American industry.

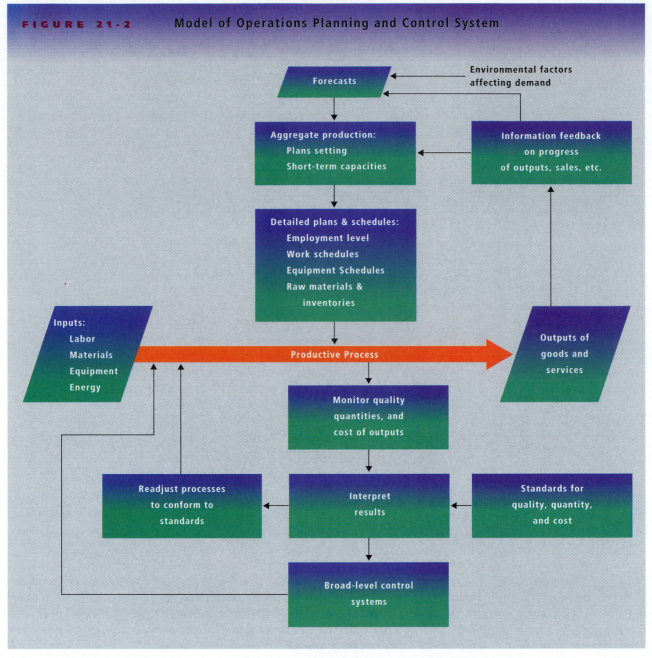

**FIGURE 21-2**     Model of Operations Planning and Control System

Source: Adapted from Elwood S. Buffa, *Modern Production/Operations Management*, 6th ed., p. 159. Copyright © 1980 by John Wiley & Sons. Used by permission.

# OPERATIONAL PLANNING AND CONTROL DECISIONS

Even after the operations system has been successfully designed and placed into actual use, considerable managerial discretion remains. This is because decisions must be made on a shorter-term basis—month to month, day to day, even hour to hour—as to how the system will be operated and controlled. As Figure 21-2 illustrates, operational planning and control decisions involve scheduling and control of labor, materials, and capital input to produce the desired quantity and quality of output most efficiently.

**"THE TIGHTEST SHIP"** At United Parcel Service, time-and-motion studies were used to develop tight standards for the details of package delivery, while high-tech computer systems track the location of every package at any time.

Operational planning and control are based on forecasts of future demand for the output of the system. But even with the best possible forecasting and the most finely tuned operations system, demand cannot always be met with existing system capacity in a given time period. Unexpected market trends, new-product developments, or competitors' actions can throw the forecasts off, and problems in the operations system can reduce capacity. At these times, shorter-term managerial decisions must be made to allocate system capacity to meet demand. This is what the hoteling system at Ernst & Young makes possible. At these times, as well, managers must also think about the longer-term implications of the changes in demand and capacity needs. United Parcel Service (UPS) and Federal Express are two organizations where long-term trends in package volumes are the ever-present concerns of managers.

### SHIPPERS DELIVER EXCELLENCE THROUGH OPERATIONS PLANNING AND CONTROL

Privately-owned United Parcel Service held a virtual monopoly on small-package deliveries until Federal Express arrived on the scene in 1973.[34] By 1986, Federal Express was earning four times the profit of UPS on approximately one-eighth of UPS's daily package and letter volume. Its technological edge permitted Federal Express to operate with one-third the number of UPS employees.

In 1986, UPS management embarked on a ten-year, $4.7 billion information systems transformation to narrow the technology gap with its competitors. UPS's information services department has grown from 100 employees in 1986 to 2,000 people working in a new $100 million data and telecommunications center. UPS's new computer system "tells" delivery centers how many packages to expect and to which zip codes the packages are going. High-volume customers are provided with a PC-based on-site system interface that permits clients to exercise control within the entire distribution system.

Other high-tech productivity advances involve UPS's fleet of 428 aircraft. To improve the operations of one of the world's largest airlines, the UPS information technology system manages flight scheduling, FAA real-time air tracking, incident alerts, maintenance checks, and weather advisories. UPS delivered 2.9 billion packages in 1991.

UPS managers' concerns with planning and controlling operations "nitty gritty" reaches to each delivery person in the familiar brown uniform and brown truck.[35] To improve productivity, UPS management has reportedly conducted a series of time-motion studies on its 62,000 driver-deliverers. The studies dictate such minutiae as how fast delivery people should walk (three feet per second), which finger should be used to hold their keys (the middle one) and how they should fold their money (face up, sequentially ordered). Drivers precisely arrange packages in their skylighted trucks to see the labels easily. Every clockwork action has its purpose; nothing deviates from standard procedure.[36] No wonder then that the UPS slogan for years has been "We run the tightest ship in the shipping business."[37] Operations planning and control makes that statement possible.

Federal Express's PowerShip information technology system allows customers to generate their own billing labels and invoices.[38] The system, available to customers that ship as few as six packages or generate at least $75 in shipments each business day, allows customers to track their own packages through FedEx's massive delivery network. More than 25,000 Federal Express customer sites have been equipped with a PowerShip personal computer and software package. Federal Express information system personnel and sales representatives collaborated on the system to meet both internal company needs and external customer service objectives.

To assist in the processing of 14 million daily on-line transactions, Federal Express management undertook a 3.5-year, 100-person effort called Cosmos2.[39] Printers inside every FedEx van issue bar-coded tracking labels that help route and sort packages. The system includes 60,000 Supertrackers that scan packages every time a shipment changes hands.[40] The strategic information system, Cosmos2, won the 1990 Computerworld Smithsonian Award in the transportation category. ▬

## INVENTORY MANAGEMENT

**Inventory** is the supply of raw materials, partially finished goods—called **work in progress**—and finished goods an organization maintains to meet its operational needs. As such, it represents a sizeable investment and a potential source of waste that needs to be carefully controlled. If managers keep too much inventory on hand, they will waste money storing it and lose money if inventories are damaged or stolen. On the other hand, managers who run out of inventory may have to stop production until the necessary materials are supplied, wasting time and labor. To minimize these costs and maintain inventories at optimum levels, numerous mathematical and computer-based inventory models have been developed to help operations managers decide when and how much inventory to order. Three important methods are materials-requirements planning (MRP), materials-resource planning (MRP II), and just-in-time inventory (JIT).

**MATERIALS-REQUIREMENTS PLANNING AND MATERIALS-RESOURCE PLANNING**
**Materials-requirements planning (MRP)** was a first attempt to look at a product and, by working backward, determine all the materials, labor, and other resources required to produce it. This method helps managers see the impact of late deliveries, low-quality raw materials, and so forth on the production system. This degree of control would not be possible without computer systems able to process the massive amounts of information needed to describe typically complex products and production systems.

**Materials-resource planning (MRPII)** goes beyond MRP to include input from the finance and marketing departments. Whereas MRP focuses on planning

---

**inventory:**

Supply of raw materials, *work in progress,* and finished goods an organization maintains to meet its operational needs.

**work in progress:**

Partially finished goods.

**materials-requirements planning (MRP):**

Operational planning system in which end products are analyzed to determine the materials needed to produce them.

**materials-resource planning (MRPII):**

Operational planning system that extends MRP by comparing needs to known resources and calculates unit costs; can also be used with other computer programs to handle order entry, invoicing, and other operations tasks.

**JUST-IN-TIME.** To increase their competitiveness, U.S. automobile manufacturers have adopted just-in-time inventory systems. The parts needed in each phase of production are not stored in a warehouse, but are produced and delivered as needed, "just in time" to be used.

requirements, MRP II also focuses on available resources. Labor hours and other costs can be integrated into the decision making as per-unit costs. MRP II programs can also interface with other programs in the computer system, such as order entry, invoicing, billing, purchasing, capacity planning, and warehouse management. As such, MRP II provides better and more comprehensive control over materials than MRP.

**just-in-time (JIT) inventory system:**

Inventory system in which production quantities are ideally equal to delivery quantities, with materials purchased and finished goods delivered *just in time* to be used; also known as *kanban.*

**JUST-IN-TIME INVENTORY.** Traditionally, operations managers set inventory levels by using formulas that balance the average fixed costs of buying raw materials with the variable costs of storing them. In the mid-1970s, though, the world took notice of the Japanese *kanban,* or **just-in-time (JIT) inventory system.** *Kanban* strives toward an ideal state in which production quantities are equal to delivery quantities. This minimizes carrying costs, the expense of storing and moving inventories from storage to the production floor. Materials are bought more frequently and in smaller amounts, "just in time" to be used, and finished goods are produced and delivered "just in time" to be sold. At one time, an automaker would order a truckload of spark plugs to be delivered within a two- or three-day window. Now that same firm will order a one-quarter load to be delivered within a 2- to 3-*hour* window. The Nissan plant in Smyrna, Tennessee, allows trucks a 1-hour window for delivery. In place of a warehouse, it uses a few trailers across the street from the plant for temporary storage. Trucks are loaded in order of need, with a forklift coming directly from the assembly line to pick up the parts.

JIT savings can be impressive. But the system requires clockwork timing and coordination within the operations system and between the organization and suppliers to be effective. Even this requirement is seen as a benefit, though, because it can reveal problems in the operation system's design whose correction can yield dramatic improvements in both productivity and quality. Just-in-time thinking is at the heart of Ernst & Young's hoteling system, which is far from the factory floor but every bit as much an efficiency opportunity as *Kanban* is.

**MANAGEMENT 2000 AND BEYOND**

# SERVICES AND "THINGS GONE RIGHT"

Tom Peters and James Brian Quinn are at it again. When we last heard from them (in Chapter 13), Peters and Quinn were asking us to rethink time-honored beliefs and methods regarding organizational design and structure. This time, Peters and Quinn have surveyed the management and organizational scene of the 1990s and have projected that operations practices will and must look different in the year 2000.

Peters and Quinn want us to take the traditional view of operations and turn it inside out. Modern thinking about operations and operations management—which we have communicated to you in this chapter—emerged from the factories of the late nineteenth century and Henry Ford's innovations in those factories (Chapter 2). It should not be surprising to you that operations traditionally has been a matter of inputs, transformations, and outputs. That's what happens to steel, automobiles, and, in late years, computers. Nor should it be surprising that this *production* operations emphasis was the platform on which people sooner or later came around to talking about *service* operations. In short, it is no accident that you have an operations course in your curriculum, but probably not a services course.

Peters and Quinn now advocate, in effect, tossing out that legacy and approaching operations from a new angle. Their reasoning is straightforward. Operations is a matter of talented human beings using their heads to deliver value to customers. This applies whether we are talking about building jet aircraft at Boeing or serving clients at the hair stylist's salon.

Managers are recognizing this and running their organizations (and also restructuring their organizations) to tap this talent—which Peters calls brainware/software and Quinn calls intellectual assets.[41] As customers become more sophisticated around the globe, Peters and Quinn continue, the successful operations will be those that serve these intelligent customers with comparably intelligent services. Peters and Quinn conclude that all operations turn on running what Quinn calls an "intelligent enterprise."[42] Peters says, simply yet powerfully, "All firms are becoming professional service firms."[43]

An important consequence of this different and more and more popular view is that the principal criteria of operations effectiveness must also change. Peters says that operations is typically managed on a "Things Gone Wrong" basis.[44] You've seen that in this chapter's discussion of efficiency and productivity: establish a standard and, if operations fall short, you have a "thing gone wrong." Peters says that, in an era when intelligent customers help "run" your business, customers don't care what your "Things Gone Wrong" index reads. They want service that enables them to serve their customers well. In this context, Peters says, operations must be run on a "Things Gone Right" (for the customer) attitude.[45] He cites, as one example, a Toronto, Ontario, hospital executive who strives with his colleagues to make a hospital stay a "great experience."[46] For anyone who has ever stayed in a hospital and thus knows how stressful that can be, "a great experience" is a remarkable operations objective.

# PREPARING FOR THE WORKFORCE OF THE FUTURE

Virtually every manager today is looking for ways to cut costs and improve efficiency. Particularly in the larger cities, there is often no money or space for large reception areas, roomy storage areas, and ornate employee offices. This, coupled with advances in technology, is encouraging managers to be more active in seeking ways to utilize corporate assets more efficiently through employee workplace alternatives such as the hoteling system pioneered by Ernst & Young. According to Jack Staley, managing partner at Ernst & Young's Chicago Office, hoteling will prepare Ernst & Young for the workforce of the future:

> What we've built here will posture us well for the workforce of the future. It's happening very quickly. You'll find individuals working less out of their physical offices and spending more time in client offices on projects, which is where they ought to be in a professional service firm.

> We're going to see a greater use of people resources—people who happen to be in other cities. We're going to see more seasonal people. We're going to see more people who at some time in their careers want to take leave and have a family.

> By using concepts like hoteling, by having networked data that permits personnel to link into the system from off-site locations, to transfer data, to do research in the library, we will benefit our clients and our workforce.

> All of this would be cost-prohibitive if we had the space that we had ten years ago. It would be hard and costly to make this kind of investment in technology in a building that doesn't have the wiring in the walls and the floors.

> Hoteling is a cultural thing. People have to understand it, to get used to it. All of its benefits can't be achieved on day one. Hopefully, we'll be able to continue to grow and to add professionals without having to take any more space.

Planning, organizing, leading, and controlling all come together in this single projection into the future through an operations management perspective.

# SUMMARY

1. **Describe operations as a system in both production and service organizations.**

   The term operations refers to the day-to-day activities an organization uses to transform inputs into outputs. As such, operations can be viewed as a system. Production organizations are primarily concerned with producing physical goods that can be mass-produced and stored for later consumption. Service organizations, in contrast, produce largely intangible goods that require customer participation and cannot be stored.

2. **Discuss the relationship between operations management, productivity efficiency, and customers' competitive priorities.**

   Operations management is important because it is a way to improve efficiency, as measured by productivity, and increase effectiveness, as measured by an organization's ability to meet customers' competitive priorities of pricing, quality level, quality reliability, and flexibility.

3. **Describe operations system design issues.**

   Designing an operations system is a multistep process that deals with what products or services to produce, how many to produce, how and where to produce, and who will do the production work. One of the most significant changes in recent years is the emphasis on design for manufacture, in which operations managers work with design engineers to simplify designs in order to make them easier to produce and more reliable. Another significant change is the use of computer-aided design. Such designs can be used to generate a bill of materials used in managing inventory and to create the instructions that operate computerized production equipment, a process known as CAD/CAM. Computer-integrated manufacturing (CIM) combines CAD/CAM with robots and computerized inventory management.

4. **Explain the job-design issues that are important to operations management.**

   Job design involves who will do the production work and how it will be done. Issues important to job design include worker skills, worker safety, and workplace collaboration.

5. **Discuss the importance and challenge of inventory management.**

   Once the operations system is designed, managers must make operational planning and control decisions. Inventory management is a major element of these decisions. The term inventory refers to the supply of raw materials, work in progress, and finished goods an organization keeps on hand to meet its operational needs. Because it represents an expense, operations managers try to keep inventory levels at optimum levels. Materials-requirements planning (MRP) uses a computerized diagram of products to work backward to determine all materials that will be needed. Materials-resource planning (MRP II) is a refinement of MRP that factors in unit costs for labor and other resources. Most organizations today are striving for kanban or just-in-time (JIT) inventory, which minimizes the expense of storing inactive inventories.

6. **Explain the proposition that all operations, including production, are services.**

   More and more managers, along with management researchers, are rethinking operations management as a thoroughly service-filled activity. This discards the previous production–service distinction. This new approach gives great emphasis to customer satisfaction, and less emphasis on efficiency as a goal.

## REVIEW QUESTIONS

1. What are operations and why can they be considered a system?
2. List some of the major differences between products and services.
3. Why is operations management important to efficiency?
4. How does operations management help organizations meet customers' competitive priorities?
5. What are the key factors in product or service design?
6. What are the major considerations in process selection? In facility-location planning?
7. What is involved in operational planning and control?
8. What are the three types of inventory management and why are they important?
9. In what industries might it be most challenging to think of operations management as a service process?

## KEY TERMS

Operations                          Bill of materials
Production organization             Capacity planning
Service organization                CAD/CAM
Operations management               CIM
Productivity                        Inventory
Human capital                       Work in progress
Workforce literacy                  Materials-requirements planning (MRP)
Competitive priorities              Materials-resource planning (MRPII)
Design for manufacture              Just-in-time (JIT) inventory system

## CASE STUDY

## HIGH-TECH ANSWERS TO DISTRIBUTION PROBLEMS AT ROLLERBLADE[47]

**W**hen a manager finds that demand exceeds inventory, the answer lies in making more goods. When a manager finds that inventory exceeds demand, the answer lies in making fewer goods. But what if a company management finds that they just do not know which situation applies?

This is the situation that recently confronted management at Rollerblade, the popular skate manufacturer based in Minnetonka, Minnesota. Roller-blade has been one of the leading firms in the fast growing high-performance roller skates marketplace. As dozens of manufacturers, including European ski-equipment makers enter the U.S. roller skate marketplace, it matters a great deal for Rollerblade managers whether demand and inventory are in balance, or not.

Rollerblade was in a bind. The product literally could not be shipped out the door. The managers found that workers were not able to ship products because, as a result of poor storage structures, they could not find the products. Once they were found, overcrowded aisles, in addition to other space constraints, still prevented efficient shipping because the workers could barely manage to get the products out the door. "We were out of control because we didn't know how to use space and didn't have enough of it," said Ian Ellis, director for facilities and safety.[48] "Basically, there was no more usable space left in the warehouse, a severe backlog of customer orders, and picking errors were clearly in the unacceptable range," added Ram Krishnan, principal of NRM Systems, based in St. Paul, Minnesota.[49]

The answer for Rollerblade was found in technology. High-tech companies have introduced a collection of computer simulations, ranging in cost roughly from $10,000 to $30,000, that assist managers in generating effective facility designs. With the help of Layout Master IV simulation software, developed by NRM, Rollerblade management was able to imple-

ment a new distribution design. As a result of the distribution improvement, Rollerblade was able to increase the number of customer orders processed daily from 140 to 410 and eliminate order backlog. "Now we have a different business," says Ellis. "The new layout has taken us from being in a crunch, to being able to plan."[50]

### CASE QUESTIONS

1. With retailers as their primary customers, what customer competitive imperatives could be affected by Rollerblade's inventory problems?

2. How appropriate might a just-in-time inventory system be for a product such as roller skates?

3. What opportunities are there for Rollerblade managers to see themselves as selling services, instead of simply roller skates?

## VIDEO CASE STUDY

## VIRTUAL MANUFACTURING AT BOEING[51]

Pacific Rim customers account for approximately 75 percent of Boeing's large aircraft orders. Therefore, when heavy economic activity and growth began to occur in the region, Boeing knew that it was time to build a new mega-liner. "This is big airplane country—the bigger the airplane, the better," declared James F. Chorlton, vice president of international sales for Boeing. "Customers are asking, 'Are you going to make a bigger one? When are you going to make it, and how big will it be?'"[52]

Boeing's answer: *real* big. Boeing's latest accomplishment, the Boeing 777 twin-engine jetliner, boasts an empty manufacturer's weight increase of 57% over its predecessor, the 767. With more than 3 million individual parts, the overall cost of the development and production of the 777 fell somewhere in the neighborhood of $10 to $12 billion. With such a massive financial investment, both Boeing and its customers wanted to be sure that the plane would fly, without the need for modification, right off the assembly line.

Boeing therefore relied extensively on the use of computer-aided design to develop a three-dimensional computerized modeling system. CAD's ability to model in solids allowed Boeing to design everything from the 777's main cabin to the tools that would be used to perform maintenance on the craft. More than 1,700 engineers worked together on the project to produce parts and tools that would work together perfectly their first time out.

Here is how the CAD works. First, a proposed aircraft component is generated by a computer. Then, a digitally-generated "human" tries out the component. In Boeing's case, this virtual test subject is drawn from any of 12 population sets, each of which contains thousands of people measured according to more than 35 dimensions. Utilizing these measures, a wide variety of human body styles can be generated and then used to test the aircraft's ergonomics. For example, the designers of the 777 discovered through this CAD technique that a mechanic would have difficulty reaching the 25-pound chiller fan above the main cabin. Standing on a ladder and reaching through an access hatch, the mechanic would be severely overbalanced and likely to fall. Using the CAD system, the designers were able to reconfigure the access hatch to eliminate the problem. The design, construction, and modification of the hatch all took place on the computer, without the need to change a single screw.

CAD also enables tool designers to receive constantly updated, three-dimensional information from engineers. Before sending tool specifications to the designers, engineers previously had to manually make tracings of the aircraft parts around which tools were to be built. With CAD, the part is represented in three dimensions in the actual location it will occupy on the aircraft. The designer can then create a tool specifically for use on that part. In addition, the designer can even check the tool's size against its allotted storage space.

Since CAD programs can be customized to provide simulations of virtually any aspect of design, production, or use, Boeing decided to employ CAD in areas other than maintenance as well. Computer generated humans also stood in for pilots, flight attendants, and passengers. In the cabin, for instance, factors such as controls, seating, and leg room must be designed. The digital human used to test the specifications could be programmed to simulate someone anywhere from 5 feet, 2 inches, to 6 feet, 4 inches in height. Similarly, lavatory seats were designed using digital humans who simulated an even wider variety of physical measurements.

CAD was also effective in improving the actual construction of the 777. Assembly line workers were able to receive enhanced work instructions that included detailed graphics and explicit instructions as to how to assemble the plane. Graphics generated by computers enjoy the added advantage of being able to be altered easily, in the event that design changes should occur.

Overall, CAD has redefined the very nature of building an aircraft. "In the past, manufacturing was at the end of the pipeline," recalled Dale M. Hougardy, vice president of Boeing's operations. "With this approach, from day one we started with the manufacturing plan. The plan was developed as engineering matured. This is concurrent engineering in action."[53] The ability to incorporate producibility factors as the design matures, instead of only upon completion, resulted in sharply reducing the cost of manufacturing the 777.

Utilizing CAD technology has enabled Boeing designers to save the company both time and money. A reduced need for modification and repair will also improve the 777's overall efficiency and profitability. Moreover, greater customer satisfaction is likely to result from improvements such as the enhanced tool storage and easier maintenance. Through CAD technology, Boeing has developed the 777 in less time and money and with greater quality and safety.

## CASE QUESTIONS

1. What human factors complicated Boeing's previous manufacturing process?
2. What are Boeing customers' competitive priorities?
3. How does use of CAD influence job design?
4. In what other types of companies would you recommend CAD be used?
5. In what instances should CAD not be used to replace actual testing?

# INFORMATION
# SYSTEMS

**Upon completing this chapter, you should be able to:**

1. Explain the relationship between data, information, and control.

2. Describe criteria for usefulness of information.

3. Explain why managers at different levels of the organization have different information needs.

4. Discuss the reasons potential users may resist the implementation of a computer system and give some suggestions for overcoming their resistance.

5. Define the term end-user computing and explain why it has arisen.

6. Describe how decision support systems and expert systems differ from conventional management information systems.

7. Define and discuss the organizational significance of the so-called national "information superhighway."

# YOUR DAYS AS STUDENTS ARE NUMBERED

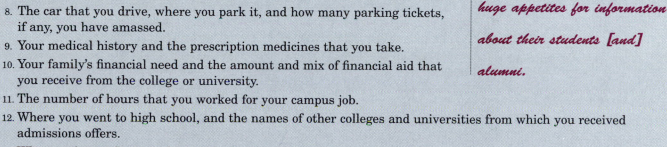

ou might not know it, but professors, administrators, and other professionals at your college or university are watching you. They want to know how you spend your days and nights, and your days and weeks and semesters. Among the tidbits of information that interest these people are some or all of the following:

1. Courses you have taken, your performance in those courses, and patterns in your course selection (some of which are required and some not, of course.)
2. Library materials that you checked out of the library, as well as those you simply removed from shelves for use in the library.
3. The frequency, duration, and times of day of your use of computer facilities on campus.
4. What you buy and how often you buy at the campus bookstore.
5. How often you eat at the dining facilities on campus.
6. The amount of heat and electricity that you use in your residence on campus, and the janitorial attention that must be given to your floor of the building.
7. The recreation facilities that you use.
8. The car that you drive, where you park it, and how many parking tickets, if any, you have amassed.
9. Your medical history and the prescription medicines that you take.
10. Your family's financial need and the amount and mix of financial aid that you receive from the college or university.
11. The number of hours that you worked for your campus job.
12. Where you went to high school, and the names of other colleges and universities from which you received admissions offers.
13. When you're ready to graduate, whether you have met all your curricular and financial obligations.

> *Colleges and universities have huge appetites for information about their students [and] alumni.*

**PROSPECTIVE ALUMNI.** These graduates may be leaving campus, but they won't be forgotten.

If you have ever thought, even worried, that too few people know you on campus, all this interest in you might come as a surprise. People who participate in the operations of colleges and universities have huge appetites for information about their current students as well as their alumni and prospective students. →

ALL THE MANAGERIAL FUNCTIONS—planning, organizing, leading, and controlling—rely on a steady stream of information about what is happening at, and beyond, an organization. Only with accurate and timely information can managers monitor progress toward their goals and turn plans into reality. If managers cannot stay "on track," anticipating potential problems, developing the skills to recognize when corrections are necessary, and then making appropriate corrections or adjustments as they progress, their work may be both fruitless and costly.

Information systems enable managers to control how they do business. If you were to look at a new Toyota in a showroom, you would find the car has a computer-generated sticker attached to the window to display the pricing and Environmental Protection Agency (EPA) information. The Toyota dealer probably has a computerized inventory system to tell you if a car is available with the options you want—perhaps even the color you have dreamed about. Should you need financing, the bank computer can help the salesperson check your credit quickly and close the sale. From the largest corporation to the modest hometown auto dealer, the computer plays a vital part in the control of business operations.

At your college or university, information about who you are and what you do is of interest to many people. Referring back to the opening segment of the illustrative case, the information listed in item 1 (courses you have taken...) is of interest to professors and academic deans; the information in item 2 is of interest to library professionals. Continue down the list as we examine who is interested in each type of information: (3) Professors, financial administrators, and computer center staff; (4) Bookstore managers; (5) Dining service managers; (6) Financial administrators and maintenance managers; (7) Athletics department managers; (8) Campus security officers; (9) Medical center staff; (10) Financial aid administrators; (11) Academic deans and financial aid administrators; (12) Admissions staff and planners; and (13) Academic deans and financial administrators. At this point, you may have noticed a lot of overlap. In fact, we probably haven't listed all the overlaps in appetites for information about you.

Managers at all levels are finding that computer-based information systems provide the information necessary for effective operation. These **management information systems (MIS)** are rapidly becoming indispensable for planning, decision making, and control. How quickly and accurately managers receive information about what is going right and what is going wrong largely determines how effective the control system will be.[1] With information systems playing such an important role in managing organizations, it has become crucial for managers to understand how these systems should be designed, implemented, and managed. With colleges and universities facing economic and enrollment pressures in the 1990s, the importance of management information systems can be seen every day on your college campus, if you look for it.

**management information systems (MIS):**
Computer-based information system for more effective planning, decision making, and control.

## INFORMATION AND CONTROL

To appreciate the central role played by information in making control effective, consider a modest-sized manufacturer of automobile replacement parts with annual sales of $10 million. Every year, the firm's 350 employees service 20,000 customer orders. These orders must be processed, billed, assembled, packed, and shipped—adding up to some 400,000 transactions that must be controlled.

And that is only the beginning. The firm writes 25,000 checks annually. Half of these cover wages. Most of the others pay for the 5,000 purchase orders issued every year. Costs are assembled from 17,000 time cards, 6,000 job orders, and 20,000 materials requisitions. Each year, that small $10 million firm is processing almost a million pieces of information related to its activities—and that figure does not include all the other pieces of information related to inventory and quality control. Nor does it include the market analyses and other information an organization's people collect as part of their <u>strategic planning</u>. Increasingly, information is being seen as a key factor in helping managers respond to the complex and turbulent environment.[2]

← Ch. 10, p. 265

Small wonder, then, that more and more managers view information itself as a valuable asset—one that needs to be carefully managed and protected.[3] To understand this view, we need to take a closer look at the nature of information and the differing types of information.

**data:**

Raw, unanalyzed numbers and facts.

**information:**

Data that have been organized or analyzed in some meaningful way.

## THE NATURE OF INFORMATION

Although we tend to use the terms *data* and *information* interchangeably, there is a distinction between the two concepts. **Data** are raw, unanalyzed numbers and facts about events, such as the number of computer disks produced per week or the inventory of computer disks at a local office supply store. **Information,** in contrast, results when data are organized or analyzed in some meaningful way. Thus, the operations manager at the disk manufacturer might compare one week's output to the previous week's or to production quotas as one way of monitoring and controlling performance. Similarly, managers at the software store could compare their inventory levels of disks to industry standards as one way of assessing their performance. At your college or university, for example, the number of history majors is a point of data. The pattern of courses that they have chosen over the past four years is a piece of information.

Although they have different operations and objectives, the disk manufacturer, the office supply store manager, and college administrators will evaluate the information they receive on four factors: its quality, timeliness, quantity, and relevance to management.

**INFORMATION QUALITY.** The more accurate the information, the higher its quality and the more securely managers can rely on it when making decisions. In general, however, the cost of obtaining information increases as the quality desired becomes higher. If information of a higher quality does not add materially to a manager's decision-making capability, it is not worth the added cost. The Director of Admissions faces this cost-benefit tradeoff when he or she considers the value of knowing not only where you received admissions offers, but also what campuses you visited while looking at colleges.

**INFORMATION TIMELINESS.** For effective control, corrective action must be applied before there has been too great a deviation from the plan or standard. Thus, the information provided by an information system must be available to the right person at the right time for the appropriate action to be taken. Professors acting as advisers cannot do their jobs if your course records are two semesters behind what you have actually completed.

**INFORMATION QUANTITY.** Managers can hardly make accurate and timely decisions without sufficient information. However, managers are often inundated with irrelevant and useless information. If they receive more information than they can

**INFORMATION OVERLOAD.**
Computers generate so much information that the manager can easily be overwhelmed. Reasonable quantities of high-quality, timely, relevant information contribute to productivity instead of reducing it.

productively use, they may overlook information on serious problems. Every student's class attendance records would probably overload the Registrar's records for no good reason.

**INFORMATION RELEVANCE.** Similarly, the information that managers receive must have relevance to their responsibilities and tasks. The personnel manager probably does not need to know inventory levels—and the manager in charge of reordering inventory does not need to know about the status of staff members in other departments. Similarly, the librarian does not need to know how many students apply each year for admission (although he or she might be interested in that information).

## FOCUS ON CUSTOMER SATISFACTION AT BANC ONE

At Banc One, identifying what customers wanted became a prerequisite to effective quality assurance as customer satisfaction became the cornerstone of the business. In 1985 Banc One, based in Columbus, Ohio, began a formal quality improvement effort in its customer service and processing areas. The bank found that the quality of service customers received provided enough of a difference in customer's minds to determine where they bank.

Banc One adopted an eight-step approach to assure quality service to its customers: 1) survey customers about such factors as accuracy of service, completeness of service, timeliness of service, and attitude and behavior of service providers; 2) translate customer requirements into quality measures; 3) implement these measures by having management communicate and explain their importance and the reasons for their existence to ensure employee understanding; 4) motivate and train managers with the goal of having every manager be a customer champion, adhering absolutely to the quality standards and procedures developed from ongoing communications with customers; 5) motivate and train employees; 6) create teams of employees to develop improvement projects; 7) measure results by comparing expectations with actual results and take the necessary steps to assure future performance; and 8) reward performance and recognize employees through such means as "We Care" awards for employees who go above and beyond the call of duty and "Best of the Best" award to the branch with the best service record.

The emphasis on quality had led to more than $6 million in savings and revenue enhancement per year by the program's fourth year, and satisfaction rates among customers ranged from very satisfied to 75-80 percent satisfied.[4] ■

# MANAGEMENT INFORMATION SYSTEMS

We will define an MIS as a formal method of making available to management the accurate and timely information necessary to facilitate the decision-making process and enable the organization's planning, control, and operational functions to be carried out effectively. The system provides information about the past, present, and projected future and about relevant events inside and outside the organization.

Organizations have always had some kind of management information system, even if it was not recognized as such.[5] In the past, these systems were highly informal in setup and utilization. When registrar office staff kept transcripts on handwritten charts, they were using an information system. Not until the advent of computers, with their ability to process and condense large quantities of data, did the design of management information systems become a formal process and a field of study.

## EDP

When computers were first introduced into organizations, they were used mainly to process data for a few organizational functions—usually accounting and billing. This was true at colleges and universities, too. Because of the specialized skills required to operate the expensive, complex, and sometimes temperamental equipment, computers were located in **electronic data-processing (EDP)** departments. As the speed and ease of processing data grew, other data-processing and information-management tasks were computerized. To cope with these new tasks, EDP departments developed standardized reports for the use of operating managers.

**electronic data-processing (EDP):**
Computerized data-processing and information management, including report standardization for operating managers.

## MIS EMERGES

The growth of EDP departments spurred managers to focus more on planning their organizations' information systems. These efforts led to the emergence of the concept of **computer-based information systems (CBIS),** which became better known as computer-based MIS—or simply MIS. As the EDP departments' functions expanded beyond routine processing of masses of standardized data, they began to be called MIS departments.

The U.S. Army has been able to utilize MIS effectively and humanely as an immense aid in the downsizing of the post-Cold War military. In 1992, for example, more than 170,000 people left the Army. As many as one-third of the Desert Storm-era personnel will be affected by force reductions before the downsizing of the Army is complete. To ease the process, the Army has developed the most advanced and comprehensive military outplacement program ever. This program includes the establishment of 55-job-assistance centers worldwide, a qualified group of 286 job counselors, and a computer data base linked to more than 11,000 U.S. national employers. The Job Assistance Center (JAC) a job-bank network, is a state-of-the-art system. The custom-designed, automated

**computer-based information systems (CBIS):**
Information system that goes beyond the mere standardization of data to aid in the planning process.

**Information Requirements by Decision Category**

| CHARACTERISTICS OF INFORMATION | OPERATIONAL CONTROL (FIRST LINE) | MANAGEMENT CONTROL (TOP AND MIDDLE LEVEL) | STRATEGIC PLANNING (TOP LEVEL) |
| --- | --- | --- | --- |
| Source | Largely internal | | Largely external |
| Scope | Well defined, narrow | | Very wide |
| Level of aggregation | Detailed | | Aggregate |
| Time horizon | Historical | | Future |
| Currency | Highly current | | Less current |
| Required accuracy | High | | Low |
| Frequency of use | Very frequent | | Less frequent |

*Source:* Adapted from G. Anthony Gorry and Michael S. Scott Morton, "A Framework for Management Information Systems," *Sloan Management Review* 13, no. 1 (Fall 1971):59. Copyright 1971 by the Sloan Management Review Association. All rights reserved.

system consolidates client services, counseling support, scheduling, and administration. The user-friendly program even has an automated résumé writer designed specifically for Army personnel.[6]

### DSS

A **decision support system** (DSS) is an interactive computer system that is easily accessible to, and operated by, people who are not computer specialists, who use the DSS to help them plan and make decisions. The use of DSSs is expanding, as recent advances in computer hardware and software allow managers and other designated employees to gain "on-line" or "real-time" access to the databases in MIS's. The widespread use of microcomputers has enabled managers to create their own databases and electronically manipulate information as needed rather than waiting for reports to be issued by the EDP/MIS department. While MIS reports are still necessary for monitoring ongoing operations, DSS permits less structured use of databases as special decision needs arise.[7] An academic dean might use a DSS system to analyze grade trends in certain courses, without needing to commission a formal study of the matter by the registrar's office.

**decision support system (DSS):**

Computer system accessible to nonspecialists to assist in planning and decision making.

### DIFFERING INFORMATION FOR DIFFERENT MANAGEMENT LEVELS

G. Anthony Gorry and M. S. Scott Morton have pointed out that an organization's information system must provide information to managers with three levels of responsibilities: operational control, management control, and strategic planning.[8] We can think of these three categories in terms of the activities that take place at first-line, middle, and top levels of the managerial hierarchy. The design of the MIS must take into account the information needs of the various managerial levels, as well as the routine transaction-processing needs of the total organization. For example, as shown in Table 22-1, the information sources for operational control are found largely within the organization, while the information sources for strategic planning tend to be outside the organization.

**OPERATIONAL CONTROL.** An MIS for operational control must provide highly accurate and detailed information on a daily or weekly basis. A production supervisor must know if materials waste is excessive, if costly overruns are about to occur, or if the machine time for a job has expired. The MIS must provide a high volume of timely and detailed information derived from daily operations. The college Food Service manager must track daily usage of certain staples for ordering and cost control purposes.

**MIDDLE MANAGEMENT.** Middle-level managers, such as division heads, are concerned with the current and future performance of their units. They therefore need information on important matters that will affect those units—large-scale problems with suppliers, abrupt sales declines, or increased consumer demand for a particular product line. Thus, the type of information middle-level managers require consists of aggregate (summarized) data from within the organization as well as from sources outside the organization. An example of what a middle-level marketing manager at an airline might need to see is monthly passenger traffic—often called passenger "load factor" information. That information can be presented in comparison to other carriers' load factors.

**TOP MANAGEMENT.** For top managers, the MIS must provide information for strategic planning and management control. For strategic planning, the external sources of information—on economic conditions, technological developments, the actions of competitors—assume paramount importance.[9] Because the supporting data come  from outside the organization, this information is more difficult to gather and computerize than internal information. The college president and director of admissions, for example, are keenly interested in trends in numbers of high school graduates likely to attend college. Strategic and operational plans often hinge on this information and related information about projected future enrollments. The changing demographics of college enrollments, for example, is of ongoing interest. As organizations downsize, increasing numbers of people are going back to school. In general, the shift to the information and knowledge economy has created a great demand for college education for the so-called Generation X, the 79 million Americans born after 1964 (see Chapter 16). In addition, women, minorities, and immigrants are entering colleges and universities in record numbers.[10]

 Having external data on sources of information workers helped Texas Instruments plan its global operations. In the 1980s, unable to find enough software designers in Europe, Texas Instruments found that India was training more than it could use. The company established an impressive software programming operation in Bangalore, a city of four million in the south of India. Recognizing a good idea, over 30 companies, including IBM and Motorola, have since set up software programming offices in the area. Thus competitors' activities are another important source of information.[11]

For the *management* control functions of top managers, the sources of information must be both internal and external. Top managers are typically concerned with the overall financial performance of their organizations. They therefore need information on quarterly sales and profits, on the other relevant indicators of financial performance (such as stock value), on quality levels and customer satisfaction, and on the performance of competitors. Internal control reports for top managers come in at monthly, quarterly, and sometimes even annual intervals. A university president in tight economic times spends a great deal of time studying expense reports, as well as reports about alumni donations to the university.

How can the various needs of different managerial levels be translated into a management information system? One major company designed the manufacturing component of its MIS this way. *Supervisors* receive daily reports on direct and indirect labor, materials usage, scrap, production counts, and machine downtime. *Superintendents* and *department heads* receive weekly departmental cost summaries and product-cost reports. *Plant managers* receive weekly and monthly

**DECISION SUPPORT SYSTEMS.** When DSS users need information, they can immediately consult their own on-line system. DSS applications software can be used to make projections and determine the likely effects of alternative proposals, allowing end-users to make informed decisions without waiting weeks or months for an analysis from an MIS department.

what they want to the EDP/MIS staff.[22] Managers are, therefore, more likely to get the information they need when they need it. In addition, direct manipulation of data has the advantage of greater security for sensitive information.

Another key difference between an MIS and a DSS is that a DSS helps managers make nonroutine decisions in unstructured situations.[23] An MIS, on the other hand, emphasizes standard, periodical reports and cannot respond well to nonroutine, unstructured, or ad hoc situations.[24] MIS departments may be unfamiliar with the decisions made in such situations. Because they often have a tremendous backlog of requests for data, they may be unable to respond quickly to additional special requests. Conversely, some managers who have no difficulty manipulating the data themselves may have difficulty explaining their information requirements to MIS staff.

**USING DSS.** At Pet Foods in St. Louis, the sales-forecasting department performs a large percentage of its own data-processing tasks. Using readily available DSS applications software, users can project sales demand by units per territory and region and translate that information into a financial forecast. Through this process, the department can determine the effects of closing a particular warehouse in a matter of days, where the same task might take the MIS department weeks or months.[25] This is but one example of the successful application of DSS.

## EXPERT SYSTEMS AND ARTIFICIAL INTELLIGENCE

Even as DSSs are being widely adopted, it seems likely that **expert systems (ESs)** will take their place in time as tools for improving organizational decision making and control.[26] Expert systems are built on a framework of known facts and

**expert system:**
A computer-based system using artificial intelligence techniques to diagnose problems, recommend approaches to solving or avoiding them, and provide a rationale for these recommendations.

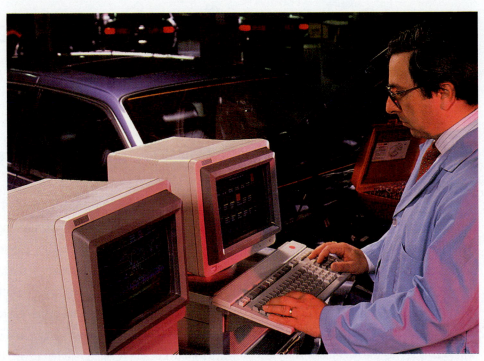

**DIAGNOSING PROBLEMS.** A technician uses a computer to test a car engine. An expert system programmed with the knowledge and reasoning patterns of an expert mechanic could diagnose problems and recommend alternative solutions.

**artificial intelligence (AI):**

Development of computational approaches to simulate intelligent human thought or behavior.

responses to situations. They rely on **artificial intelligence (AI).**[27] Artificial intelligence refers to the use of the computer to simulate characteristics of human thought by developing computational approaches to intelligent behavior.[28] So expert systems use artificial-intelligence techniques to diagnose problems, recommend strategies to avert or solve those problems, and offer a rationale for the recommendations. In effect, the expert system acts like a human "expert" in analyzing unstructured situations.

Expert systems are designed to apply the fruits of AI research to scientific, technological, and business problems by emulating the abilities and judgments of human experts and by making the experts' point of view available to nonexperts. Typically, a human expert has specialized knowledge that he or she uses to solve specific problems. Expert systems perform like human experts: They can diagnose problems, recommend alternative solutions and strategies, offer rationales for their diagnoses and recommendations, and in some instances learn from previous experiences by adding information developed in solving problems to their current base of knowledge.[29] The expert systems developed in the 1980s now function productively in diverse areas, such as medical diagnosis, mineral and oil exploration, and equipment-fault locating.[30]

An expert system guides users through problems by asking them an orderly set of questions about the situation and drawing conclusions based on the answers it has been given. Its problem-solving abilities are guided by a set of programmed rules modeled on the actual reasoning processes of human experts in the field.[31] Expert systems are particularly relevant for unstructured problems and are more tolerant of errors and imperfect knowledge than are conventional programs.[32]

# THE INFORMATION SUPERHIGHWAY UNDER CONSTRUCTION

**MANAGEMENT 2000 AND BEYOND**

In the 1960s and 1970s, the words "Road Under Construction" were familiar and frustrating to any American who traveled across states, much less across the nation, by car. No, it was not an epidemic of potholes. Rather, the United States Federal Government, together with private contractors, embarked on a massive capital project to build America's interstate highway system. The interstate highways brought Americans in general, and American consumers and producers in particular, together like never before. Most of us probably take for granted these highways that parallel the old U.S. route system (e.g., Interstate 80 traces the route of US 6) while providing an unparalleled opportunity to go new places and see new faces (and distant cousins, aunts, and uncles). It is no wonder then that what many see as the next major change in America's infrastructure is being referred to as "the information superhighway."[33]

Just as the interstate highway system paralleled the old US highways, the information superhighway is designed to parallel the nationwide telephone network that we have long taken for granted. Whereas we travel the interstate system by car or van or motorcycle, entry to the information superhighway will be available at home or at work. Our access will be the telephone, the personal computer, the television set, and new hybrids of these familiar devices.

The term "information superhighway" refers to a number of changes in the way Americans can communicate with each other and with people around the world. The superhighway is *increased capacity* in the nation's telecommunications networks. The superhighway is also multiple available *means of communication,* from traditional wired telephones to cellular telephones to satellite delivery to an antenna on your windowsill. The superhighway is also multiple forms of messages sent and received over the *same* network, even simultaneously. Cellular telephone users can send and receive voice and FAX messages. Some homeowners can receive movies over their telephone lines. Some television viewers can receive telephone calls over their cable TV lines. And voice and data messages can be sent together over a single line from one personal computer user to another. All of these possibilities, and more, rely significantly on *fiber-optic cable,* a high-volume, versatile, low-distortion, glass replacement for the copper wiring network that has connected people in the United States over the past century.

The information superhighway is developing into a dizzying array of business relationships between the Federal Government and all sorts of businesses, as well as among telephone companies, movie producers, computer makers, telephone manufacturers, satellite operators, and cable TV franchisees. If this superhighway is to be "paved" across the nation, these suppliers must cooperate on technical matters—such as communications compatibility among their products—and on economic matters–such as who pays for the highway construction. Perhaps the ultimate question yet unanswered is: Will Americans use this "road," or not?

The information superhighway has significant implications for the design, scope, and uses of information systems at any one organization. First, managers must decide—to a greater extent than ever before—what information is and is not necessary for running the organization. The prospects for "information overload" are enormous as managers confront situations equivalent to a homeowner receiving 500 channels on a cable TV system![34] Ultimately, strategic planning is crucial in this decision. Knowing "who you are" sets limits on what you need to know.

Second, following from the first issue, managers face new decisions about investments in equipment and services with which they and their employees can "travel" the information superhighway. For example, must all salespersons have a laptop computer and cellular telephone? Are so-called "voice mail" systems more cost effective than having answering machines or extra secretarial staff? These kinds of questions, once again, can be framed by the results of strategic planning. Otherwise, new technologies can become "playthings" rather than tools for running an organization efficiently and effectively.

Third, managers and their employees can feel a loss of control over information that is key to their business, now that it becomes more and more publicly available over the information superhighway. Information about competitors' products, market growth trends, impending regulations, and global prospects *can* be a source of competitive advantage if your organization has it and others do not.[35] So, possession of information becomes less important than using that information in ways that serve customers distinctively (see "Management 2000 and Beyond" in Chapter 21), in the new information superhighway era.

Fourth, and on the heels of the preceding point, the information superhighway continues the trend *within* organizations of decentralization of information systems management. If end-user computing began to change the role of MIS professionals from remote experts working behind closed doors to advisors and teachers, the information superhighway portends continuation of that shift. With groupware, picturephones, and fiber optic cables, a buyer at one retail organization can simultaneously talk and compare sketches and send data to a supplier of children's clothing, for example. In traveling the information superhighway, such buyers, more and more, become MIS professionals in the regular course of their job. Job redesign for MIS becomes a real possibility.[36]

Fifth, ownership of information becomes more complicated than it already is under copyright laws. If more and more people are acquiring and transforming information on the information superhighway, protection for those who created the information becomes a heightened concern for all. More extensive negotiations and new kinds of property protection will likely emerge.

Sixth, the spread of the information superhighway raises ethical concerns about who knows what about whom. In particular, more information about consumers will become diffused around the nation's network and databases. And those consumers might be testy, if not militant, about how that information is used. Managers must keep in mind that new terms of relationships with customers will probably become necessary. That requires sensitivity to consumers' concerns, not merely assuming that more information makes everyone better off.

The so-called Caller ID (or Automatic Line Identification) is a prime case in point.[37] Available now in many states, Caller ID is a software feature of the telephone network that displays on an inexpensive device or special phone the telephone number of the person making the call to the person receiving the call. Along the information superhighway, in other words, the caller's voice and telephone number are transmitted simultaneously.

To some users, Caller ID can be a big help. People running a "911" center want to know where a call originates in a life-or-death crisis. Some people might want to ignore calls from unfamiliar numbers. Still others might want advance notice of who is calling, even if for only a moment before picking up the receiver, so they can prepare a greeting or other response.

But some people complain that Caller ID can also enable the receiver to act too familiarly.[38] If you call a mail-order organization equipped with, say, Caller ID and state-of-the-art end-user computing capabilities, your call might be answered by a stranger who says, "Hello, (your name). I hope that the shoes you ordered last month are satisfactory" before you can open your mouth.[39] The old distance between caller and receiver has faded. For managers, this can usher in the need to rethink how employees interact with customers.

All in all, the information superhighway will require new kinds of cooperation among the many participants traveling on that "road." The information highway is one more example of a point that has permeated this book: Management is a process of arranging and re-arranging relationships among different parties who hold dear their own interests and whose interests are always subject to change.

2. What four factors determine the value of information?

3. What are the five components of an information system?

4. Compare and contrast the information needs of operational, middle-level, and upper-level managers.

5. Based on your knowledge of a medium-sized business that you patronize, such as a supermarket chain, what different levels of needs are important in designing an MIS? Describe the different reports that might be produced by that MIS.

6. Why do people sometimes resist the implementation of a new computer system? How can their resistance be addressed?

7. Compare and contrast decision support systems, expert systems, and conventional management information systems.

8. What is the significance of the information superhighway for MIS professionals? For top managers?

## KEY TERMS

Management information systems (MIS)

Data

Information

Electronic data-processing (EDP)

Computer-based information systems (CBIS)

Decision support system (DSS)

End-user computing

Expert system (ES)

Artificial intelligence (AI)

## CASE STUDY

## ONE-STOP SHOPPING AT 7-ELEVEN[40]

Management information systems can be important control mechanisms for ensuring efficient operations inside an organization. Operations can be logically arranged, streamlined, and monitored at various points through an organization-wide, computerized MIS. In this sense, MIS serves as a kind of organizational structure that parallels the organization's formal lines of authority. Both structures control what happens *inside* the organization.

At the same time, the MIS is increasingly being used by managers as a means for interacting more intelligently and more quickly with people at other organizations. In other words, MIS can help managers deal more effectively with such "external" players as suppliers and competitors. In this way, MIS becomes as much an accompaniment to strategic planning and operations management as it is to organizational structure.

Management practices at 7-Eleven Japan are a prime example of this "external" use of MIS. A NEC personal computer has been specially designed for these stores to collect and distribute all sorts of information at the "point of sale"—that is, during the check-out process. Among the things that store managers can do with this information and the system's network links are:

- Spot declining inventories and then order new supplies by sending orders electronically to suppliers.
- Monitor which kinds of products sell better than others (and at which times of day) and then enter into agreements with suppliers who make products tailored to these buying patterns.
- Share store information with the headquarters MIS which distributes buying trends and consumer preference information to other store managers.
- Coordinate shipments to each store in order to cut down on delivery time and bottlenecks.

In addition to these new ways of dealing with suppliers, managers at 7-Eleven Japan have added the capability for customers to pay insurance and utility bills at the 7-Eleven store. Such greater one-stop shopping distinguishes the company from other convenience store competitors.

### CASE QUESTIONS

1. What new roles can headquarters MIS professionals assume now that information generation and usage has been decentralized as it has at 7-Eleven Japan?
2. What internal and external factors limit how far store managers can go with this kind of MIS?
3. What kind(s) of organizational structure can support this use of information?

## VIDEO CASE STUDY

### TRAVELERS ON THE GO[41]

It has been nearly a week since John A. Cruz, a 32-year-old account executive at Travelers Insurance, has stepped foot in the office. Strangely, though, his absence has gone virtually unnoticed—there are no backlogs of messages or mail, and his managers do not appear the least bit concerned. Why? Because Cruz is one of the company's telecommuters, which means that he works primarly out of his home. "They do give you an option, if you think you do need to come into the office for any reason, obviously you can come in any time you want," Cruz explained. "But right now the push is toward working out of our homes and being more on the road."[42]

Cruz is just one of the rapidly increasing number of American employees who have moved out of the traditional office environment and into the ever-expanding realm of telecommuting. According to LINK Resources, a New York-based research firm, the number of telecommuters in the United States has climbed at an astounding rate since the early 1990s. Between 1990 and 1991, the number of telecommuters and corporate homeworkers increased 14 percent, rising from 14.1 million in 1990 to more than 16 million in 1991. The firm projected that this number would reach nearly 19 million by 1995. And by the year 2000, roughly 25 percent of the entire American corporate workforce is expected to be telecommuting full- or part-time.

The growth of telecommuting has been especially pronounced in the insurance industry, where pressures to cut costs have led many companies to seek alternative ways of conducting business. The nature of the industry enables insurance companies to provide flexible working conditions for their employees, who can then spend more time on the road with clients. The great strides that have been achieved in telecommunication technology have made it possible for field agents easily and cost-effectively to keep in close touch with their co-workers and managers without actually having to be present in the office. And managers have discovered that the host of telecommunication products—laptops, modems, cellular phones, voice mail, electronic mail, and pagers—actually enable them to keep better track of employees, regardless of where they are.

Insurance agents have also been able to increase their productivity through telecommuting. Cruz's task of evaluating a client's risk/premium profile used to involve 30 separate steps and took about 40 days. But Cruz now has at his disposal software capable of revealing risk/premium discrepancies in no time at all. At the touch of a button, he can now use his portable laptop to access endless information and to accomplish in 24 hours what used to take 40 days to complete. As a result, Travelers is saving in the neighborhood of $6 million a year.

Telecommuting is not limited to insurance salespeople. Most workers not tied to fixed machinery could benefit from telecommuting. Even managers are beginning to explore the notion. "Personally, I have to say that telecommuting has increased my loyalty to The Travelers. It has given me the flexibility to maintain the kind of balance I need in my life, and it has reinforced the trust I have in my employees," noted Diane Bengston, a Travelers human resources director who oversees 38 employees and has 15 direct reports. "Simply put, it works."[43] When Bengston decided to try telecommuting, some people feared that her communication with her employees would suffer and cause the quality of her department's work to drop. But, as it turned out, interdepartmental communication actually improved and Bengston was easier to reach for phone consultations than she had ever been for in-person interviews. Moreover, her department's productivity and quality of work even increased as employees took the initiative to work independently and aggressively in her absence. "Many employees," Bengston remarked, "have been pleasantly surprised to find what they're capable of doing."[44]

Travelers as a company has benefited immensely from the introduction of telecommuting. Aside from monetary savings and enhanced productivity, telecommuting has also reduced absenteeism, improved opportunities for disabled employees, and increased the company's ability to attract and retain talent. "It's an old notion that if you can't see employees, you can't manage them," explained Doug Willet, second vice president of Human Resources at The Travelers Companies in Hartford, Connecticut. "Telecommuting supports our belief in the professional work force—that is, that all employees are professionals who can take individual initiative, target their own goals and work without constant supervision."[45] Telecommuting is not an automatic answer for all companies, however. "You have to be secure in your management skills," Willet suggested, "have faith in your employees and not decrease your expectations."[46]

The introduction of new technology into the workplace almost always is accompanied by new managerial challenges. Telecommuting is not an exception. By recognizing this ahead of time, however, Travelers has been able to take steps to facilitate the transition.

For example, the implementation of a one-day training module, "How to Manage the Telecommuter," helped to prepare managers by giving them guidance in how to set objectives, allocate work, and effectively communicate with both telecommuters and in-office employees. In addition, the module assisted in making managers aware of the impact telecommuting would have on non-telecommuters. "A good part of training is restating the notion that even workers in the office are making a lot of independent decisions," said Willet. "Good managers manage by making clear what needs to get done and then giving employees the freedom and the space to do it. They may have occasional conversations about the progress of their work, but it's not an hourly occurrence. With a telecommuter, it's the same situation, but with a physical separation."[47]

Utilizing telecommuting technology has required adjustments from Travelers employees. "Employees had to get comfortable calling me at home, people had to learn that I wouldn't always be here on the days they wanted to schedule meetings, and I have to make an extra effort to keep in the loop," Bengston pointed out.[48] "We used to have an office feeling," Cruz added. "Now it's really like you're on your own."[49] In the end, however, telecommuting has proved an effective alternative to the traditional office setting, particularly for Travelers, which aims eventually to have 25% of its 28,000 employees engaging in some form of telecommuting. Once again, technology is demonstrating its role as an influential force in both intra-office and inter-office dynamics. Telecommuting may very well become the accepted norm for businesses in the near future, and those companies exploring its potential now will thus have a jump on becoming the industry leaders of tomorrow.

## CASE QUESTIONS

1. How has the technology revolution fueled the growth of telecommuting?
2. How might telecommuting serve as a barrier to effective management?
3. How might telecommuting facilitate effective management?
4. What types of employees are best suited to telecommuting?
5. What sort of safeguards can be put in place to ensure the rights of both workers who telecommute and workers who do not?

# NOTES

**CHAPTER 1**

1 James Campbell Quick, "Crafting an Organizational Culture: Herb's Hand at Southwest Airlines," Organizational Dynamics, Autumn 1992, pp. 45-56.

2 The Random House and Microsoft stories can be found in The New York Times, September 11, 1993, p. 39. The NASA and MTA stories can be found in The New York Times, September 12, 1993, pp. 35, 56.

3 Tom Chappell, The Soul of Business: Managing For Profit & The Common Good (New York: Bantam Books, 1993).

4 For a popular critique of American management practice, see Steve Lohr, "Overhauling America's Business Management," The New York Times Magazine, January 4, 1981, pp. 15ff.

5 For a popular analysis of some of the apparent successes and possible failures of Japanese organizations, see Peter F. Drucker, "Behind Japan's Success," Harvard Business Review 59, no. 1 (January-February 1981):83-90.

6 For a discussion of the complexity of evaluating organizational performance, see Terry Connolly, Edward J. Conlon, and Stuart Jay Deutsch, "Organizational Effectiveness: A Multiple-Constituency Approach," Academy of Management Review 5, no. 2 (April 1980): 211-217.

7 Peter F. Drucker, The Effective Executive (New York: Harper & Row, 1967).

8 Maryann Keller, Rude Awakening: The Rise, Fall, and Struggle For Recovery of General Motors (New York: William Morrow and Company, Inc., 1989).

9 Peter F. Drucker, Managing for Results (New York: Harper & Row, 1964), p. 5. The pressures to focus on efficiency versus effectiveness are great in all organizations. Drucker also observed, in a seminar for federal executives during the Eisenhower administration, that "the greatest temptation is to work on doing better and better what should not be done at all."

10 See also Stephen J. Carroll and Dennis J. Glidden, "The Classical Management Functions: Are They Really Outdated?" Proceedings of the Forty-Fourth Annual Meeting of the American Academy of Management (August 1984): 132-136.

11 Michael H. Mescon, Michael Albert, and Franklin Khedouri, Management: Individual and Organizational Effectiveness, 2nd ed. (New York: Harper & Row, 1985), stress that "resources" should be defined to include not just general economic categories like labor and capital, but information and technology as well.

12 Shari Caudron, "Keys to Starting a TQM Program," Personnel Journal, February 1993, pp. 28-35.

13 W. Edwards Deming, "Improvement of Quality and Productivity Through Action by Management," National Productivity Review 1 (Winter 1981-1982): 12-22.

14 Henry Mintzberg, The Nature of Managerial Work (Englewood Cliffs, New Jersey: Prentice Hall, 1973). Important precursors of Mintzberg's work include Sue Carlson, Executive Behavior: A Study in the Work Load and Working Methods of Managing Directors (Stockholm, Sweden: Stromberg Aktiebolag, 1951); Peter F. Drucker, The Practice of Management (New York: Harper & Row, 1954); and Rosemary Stewart, Managers and Their Jobs: A Study of the Similarities and Differences in the Ways Managers Spend Their Time (London: MacMillan, 1967). More recent studies of the manager's job include Colin P. Hales, "What do Managers Do? A Critical Review of the Evidence," Journal of Management Studies 23 (January 1986): 88-115; and two articles by Hugh C. Willmott, "Images and Ideals of Managerial Work: A Critical Examination of Conceptual and Empirical Accounts," Journal of Management Studies 21 (1984): 349-368 and "Studying Managerial Work: A Critique and a Proposal," Journal of Management Studies 24 (May 1987): 249-270.

15 "The Best Small Companies to Work for in America," INC., November 1992, pp. 89-99.

16 Ibid.

17 This idea is very clearly introduced in H. Igor Ansoff, "Corporate Capability for Managing Change," in R. Lamb, ed., Advance in Strategic Management, Vol. 1 (Greenwich, Connecticut: JAI Press, 1983): 2.

18 Because of their responsibilities for many diverse functions, it is increasingly important for top managers to have broad corporate experience. See W. Walker Lewis, "The CEO and Corporate Strategy in the Eighties: Back to Basics," Interfaces 14, no. 1 (January-February 1984): 3-9.

19 INC., January 1994, p. 28.

20 Maryann Keller, Rude Awakening: The Rise, Fall, and Struggle For Recovery of General Motors; Paul Adler, "Time-and-Motion Regained," Harvard Business Review, January-February 1993, pp. 97-108; and Thomas A. Mahoney and John R. Decktop, "Y'Gotta Believe: Lessons form American-vs.Japanese-Run U. S. Factories," Organizational Dynamics, Spring 1993, pp. 27-38.

21 David Armeke, "Sole Searching: Nike Treads Lightly on the Planet," OMNI, August 1992.

22 Charlene Marmer Solomon, "Managing Today's Immigrants," Personnel Journal, February 1993, pp. 57-65.

23 As quoted in Sheryl Hilliard Tucker and Kevin D. Thompson, "Will Diversity = Opportunity + Advancement for Blacks?" Black Enterprise, November 1990, p. 60.

24 Michelle Litvin, "Extended Family: Accounting Firms Reach out to Keep Employees," Chicago Tribune, May 23, 1993, p. 1.

25 Wilma Randle, "Firms Coming Face-to-Face with Diversity Issues," Chicago Tribune, January 12, 1993, p. 1.

26 As quoted in Robert Reich, "'New Work' is the Way for Labor," Philadelphia Inquirer, September 6, 1993.

27 As listed in Walter Kiechel III, "How We Will Work in The Year 2000," Fortune, May 17, 1993, p. 39. Brian Dumaine calls attention to this future by referring to "non-manager managers" to reflect a major shift from traditional thinking. Brian Dumaine, "The New Non-Manager Manages," Fortune, February 2, 1993, pp. 80-84.

28 From Cases and Problems for Decisions in Management, Saul Gellerman. Copyright 1984 by Saul Gellerman and published by McGraw-Hill, Inc. Reprinted by permission of McGraw-Hill, Inc.

29 This case is based on the following sources: Edna Gundersen, "MTV Ten Years Young: The medium that made music visual," USA Today, July 26, 1991, p. 1D; Jane Hall, "The Channel that Ate the World: For 10 Years, MTV has Survived Ever-Fluctuating Teen Tastes and Meager Ratings to Become a Cable Cornerstone. Now the Music-Video Network is Plugged in as an Ambassador of Pop Culture," Los Angeles Times, July 28, 1991, p. 6; Robert Pittman, "The Man Behind the Monster; It May be Hard to Recall Life before MTV, but Bob Pittman, who Shaped and Sold the Concept, Remembers it Well," Los Angeles Times, July 28, 1991, p. 7; Robert Hilburn, "MTV Led to the Rebirth of Rock in America...Now it's Got to Work to Retain Viewers' Trust," Los Angeles Times, July 28, 1991, p. 9; Mark Landler, "The MTV Tycoon," Business Week, September 21, 1992, pp. 56-62; Scott Donaton, Gary Levin, Christy Fisher and John P. Cortez, "The Media Wakes up to Generation X; Twentysomethings are $125B market," Advertising Age, February 1, 1993, p. 16; "Cultural and gender concerns," USA Today, April 14, 1993, p. 10D; Marco R. della Cava, "MTV's Tabitha Soren stands up to stereotypes," USA Today, April 14, 1993, p. 10D; Matthew Gilbert, "The mighty cool world of MTV: At age 12, the hip machine plugs into movies, politics, even the soaps," The Boston Globe, July 25, 1993, p. B23; Martin Dickson, "The Whole World Wants Its MTV: Music channel reaches 233 million homes in 77 countries," The Financial Post, December 4, 1993, p. 51; Rita Ciolli, "Inside the 'New News': Even the White House is Watching,"

Newsday, December 8, 1993, p. 68; Charlene Marmer Solomon, "When People are the Bottom Line," Black Enterprise, February 1994, p. 131. The video accompanying the case is from Business World, May 3, 1992.

30  Hall, "The Channel that Ate the World," p. 6.

31  Pittman, "The Man Behind the Monster," p. 7.

32  Ibid.

33  Gilbert, "The mighty cool world of MTV," p. B23.

34  "Cultural and gender concerns," p. 10D.

35  Gilbert, "The mighty cool world of MTV," p. B23.

36  Pittman, "The Man Behind the Monster," p. 7.

37  Ciolli, "Inside the 'New News': Even the White House is Watching," p. 68.

38  Ibid.

39  Ibid.

40  Donaton, Levin, Fisher and Cortez, "The Media Wakes up to Generation X," p. 16.

41  Hall, "The Channel that Ate the World," p. 6.


C H A P T E R   2

1  Adaptation compiled from The Reckoning by David Halberstam. Copyright 1986 by David Halberstam. By permission of William Morrow and Company, Inc.

2  Peter Bondanella and Mark Musa, ed. and trans., The Portable Machiavelli (New York: Penguin, 1979).

3  Sun Tzu, The Art of War, Samuel B. Griffith, trans. (London: Oxford University Press, 1963).

4  John Clancy, The Invisible Powers: The Language of Business (Lexington, Massachusetts: Lexington Books, 1989).

5  See Jonathan Clarke, "The Conceptual Poverty of U.S. Foreign Policy," The Atlantic Monthly, September 1993, pp. 54-66.

6  Deborah Stead and Robert Hof, "Math Genius with Lab, Will Work for Food," Business Week, June 14, 1993, pp. 85-86.

7  Alfred P. Sloan, Jr., My Years with General Motors (New York: Doubleday, 1963).

8  Maryann Keller, Rude Awakening: The Rise, Fall and Struggle For Recovery of General Motors (New York: William Morrow and Company, Inc., 1989); David Dyer, Malcolm Salter and Alan Webber, Changing Alliances (Boston: Harvard Business School Press, 1987).

9  For an excellent treatment of the process of change in theories, see Thomas S. Kuhn, The Structure of Scientific Revolutions, 2nd ed., enlarged (Chicago: University of Chicago Press, 1970). See also Richard G. Brandenberg, "The Usefulness of Management Thought for Management," in Joseph W. McGuire, ed., Contemporary Management: Issues and Viewpoints (Englewood Cliffs, New Jersey: Prentice Hall, 1974), pp. 99-112.

   Much of the discussion in this chapter on the evolution of management theory is based on Claude S. George, Jr., The History of Management Thought, 2nd ed. (Englewood Cliffs, New Jersey: Prentice Hall, 1972); and Daniel A. Wren, The Evolution of Management Thought, 2nd ed., (New York: Wiley, 1979).

10  An excellent discussion of this evolutionary process appears in Harold J. Leavitt, "Structure, People, and Information Technology: Some Key Ideas and Where They Come From," Management Psychology, 4th ed. (Chicago: University of Chicago Press, 1978).

11  Charlene Marmer Solomon, "Managing Today's Immigrants," Personnel Journal, February 1993, pp. 57-65.

12  See Frederick W. Taylor, Scientific Management (New York: Harper & Brothers, 1947). For an assessment of Taylor's impact on contemporary management, see Edwin A. Locke, "The Ideas of Frederick W. Taylor: An Evaluation," Academy of Management Review 7, no. 11 (January 1982): 14-24. See also Allen C. Bluedorn, Thomas L. Keon, and Nancy M. Carter, "Management History Research: Is Anyone Out There Listening?" in Richard B. Robinson and John A. Pearch, II, eds., Proceedings of the Academy of Management (Boston, 1985): 130-133.

13  Another important contributor to scientific management was Harrington Emerson. See his book The Twelve Principles of Efficiency, published in 1913.

14  Peter B Peterson, "The Evolution of the Gantt Chart and Its Relevance Today," Journal of Management Issues, Summer 1991, pp. 131-155.

15  Henri Fayol, Industrial and General Administration, J. A. Coubrough, trans. (Geneva: International Management Institute, 1930).

16  Max Weber, The Theory of Social and Economic Organizations, Talcott Parsons, ed., A. M. Henderson and Parsons, trans. (New York: Free Press, 1947).

17  Richard Stillman II, The American Bureaucracy (Chicago: Nelson-Hall, 1987), p. 4; Brian Dumaine, "The Bureaucracy Busters," Fortune, June 14, 1991, pp. 35-50.

18  See Mary P. Follett, The New State (Gloucester, Massachusetts: Peter Smith, 1918); Henry C. Metcalf and Lyndall Urwick, eds., Dynamic Administration (New York: Harper & Brothers, 1941); and L. D. Parker, "Control in Organizational Life: The Contribution of Mary Parker Follett," Academy of Management Review 9, No. 4 (October 1984):736-745.

19  Michael E. McGill and John W. Slocum, Jr., "Unlearning the Organization," Organizational Dynamics, Autumn 1993, pp. 73-74; Tricia Welch, "Best and Worst: Corporate Reputations," Fortune, February 7, 1994, pp. 58-66.

20  See Chester I. Barnard, The Functions of the Executive (Cambridge, Massachussets: Harvard University Press, 1938).

21  Lori Bongiorno, Ann Therese Palmer and Judy Temes, "The Horizontal Corporation," Business Week, December 20, 1993, pp. 76-83.

22  For extensive discussions of Mayo's work, see Elton Mayo, The Human Problems of an Industrial Civilization (New York: Macmillan, 1953); and F. J. Roethlisberger and W. J. Dickson, Management and the Worker (Cambridge, Massachusetts: Harvard University Press, 1939). Also see Roethlisberger's autobiography, The Elusive Phenomena, George F. F. Lombard, ed. (Boston: Division of Research, Graduate School of Business Administration, Harvard University, 1977). Analysis, criticism, and defense of the Hawthorne Studies can be found in George C. Homans, The Human Group (New York: Harcourt, Brace, 1950), pp. 48-155; Alex Carey, "The Hawthorne Studies: A Radical Criticism," American Sociological Review 32, No. 3 (June 1967); Henry A. Landsberger, Hawthorne Revisited (Ithaca, New York: Cornell University Press, 1958); John M. Shepard, "On Carey's Radical Criticism on the Hawthorne Studies," Academy of Management Journal 14, No. 1 (March 1971): 23-32; Dana Bramel and Ronald Friend, "Hawthorne, the Myth of the Docile Worker, and Class Bias in Psychology," American Psychologist 36, No. 8 (August 1981): 867-878.

23  John Schreitmueller, "Employees Drive Reorganization at Sky Chefs," Personnel Journal, September 1993, pp. 144-150.

24  Abraham H. Maslow, Motivation and Personality (New York: Harper & Row, 1964. Douglas McGregor, The Human Side of Enterprise (New York: McGraw-Hill, 1960).

25  James G. March and Herbert A. Simon, Organizations (New York: Wiley, 1958).

26  Geert Hofstede, "Motivation, Leadership and Organizations: Do American Theories Apply Abroad?" Organizational Dynamics, Summer 1980, pp. 54-56.

27  Larry M. Austin and James R. Burns, Management Science (New York: Macmillan, 1985); Robert J. Thierauf, Management Science: A Model Formulation Approach with Computer Applications (Columbus, Ohio: Merrill, 1985); and Kenneth R. Baker and Dean H. Kroop, Management Science: An Introduction to Decision Models (New York: Wiley, 1985).

28  See David Halberstam, The Reckoning (New York: Avon, 1986), pp. 201-221.

29  The management science approach has been applied to other uses besides industrial problem solving. Jay Forrester and his colleagues, for example, have pioneered attempts to stimulate the operations of whole enterprises. He and others have also simulated economic activities of Third World nations and even of the world system as a whole. See Jay W. Forrester, Industrial Dynamics (Cambridge, Massachusetts: MIT Press, 1961), and World Dynamics, 2nd ed. (Cambridge, Massachusetts: MIT Press, 1979); Dennis H. Meadows et al., The Limits to Growth (New York: Universe Books, 1972); Dennis H. Meadows, ed., Alternatives to Growth, Vol. 1: A Search for Sustainable Futures (Cambridge, Massachusetts: Ballinger, 1977); and Mihajlo Mesarovic and Eduard Pestel, Mankind at the Turning Point (New York: Dutton, 1975).

30  See Ludwig von Bertalanffy, Carl G. Hempel, Robert E. Bass, and Hans Jonas, "General System Theory: A New Approach to Unity of Science," I-VI, Human Biology 23, no. 4 (December 1951): 302-361; and Kenneth E. Boulding, "General Systems Theory—The Skeleton of Science," Management Science 2, no. 3 (April 1956): 197-208.

31  See Seymour Tilles, "The Manager's Job—A Systems Approach," Harvard Business Review 41, no. 1 (January-February 1963): 73-81.

32  Marvin Cetron, "An American Renaissance in the Year 2000," The Futurist, March-April 1994, p. 11; Jessica Cohen, "Earth," OMNI, January 1993, p. 24.

33  Fremont E. Kast and James E. Rosenzweig, "General Systems Theory: Applications for Organization and Management," Academy of Management Journal 15, no. 4 (December 1972): 447-465. See also Arkalgud Ramaprasad, "On the Definition of Feedback," Behavioral Science 28, no.1 (January 1983): 4-13.

34  Howard Gleckman, John Carey, Russell Michell, Tim Short, and Chris Rouch, "The Technology Payoff," Business Week, June 14, 1993, pp. 57-68.

35  Michael E. McGill, John W. Slocum, Jr., and David Lei, "Management Practices in Learning Organizations," Organizational Dynamics, Summer 1992, p. 9.

36  Thomas J. Peters and Robert H. Waterman, Jr., In Search of Excellence (New York: Harper & Row, 1982), p. 51.

37  Kenichi Ohmae, The Borderless World: Power and Strategy in the Interlinked Economy (New York: Harper Business, 1990), p. 17.

38  Peters' subtitle is one impetus for the "dynamic engagement" label. Thomas J. Peters, Liberation Management: Necessary Disorganization for the Nanosecond Nineties (New York: Alfred A. Knopf, 1992).

39  John Case, "A Company of Businesspeople," INC., April 1993, p. 79-83.

40  This case has been adapted from John M. Champion and John H. James, Critical Incidents in Management: Decisions and Policy Issues, 5th ed. (Homewood, Illinois: Richard D, Irwin, 1985), pp. 36-37. Copyright 1986 by Richard D. Irwin, Inc.

41  This case is based on the following sources: Jim Dickinson, "Is FDA a Major Failure?" Medical Marketing & Media, (October 1990), pp. 4-8; James G. Dickinson, "An end to Washington gridlock?" Medical Marketing & Media, (July 1993), pp. 82-4; John Carey, "Getting the lead out at the FDA," Business Week, (October 25, 1993), pp. 94-6; Peter Brimelow and Leslie Spencer, "Food and drugs and politics," Forbes, (November 22, 1993), p. 115. In addition, the accompanying video is "American Agenda—Morning-After Pill," ABC World News Tonight, Transcript #4003-7, January 5, 1994.

42  Carey, "Getting the lead out at the FDA," p. 96.

43  Ibid., p. 97.

44  Ibid., pp. 97-8.

45  Dickinson, "An end to Washington gridlock?" p. 82.

46  Brimelow and Spencer, "Food and drugs and politics," p. 115.

47  Carey, "Getting the lead out at the FDA," p. 96.

## C H A P T E R   3

1  This case is based on the following sources: Jackie Prince and Richard D. Denison, "Launching a New Business Ethic: The Environment as a Standard Operating Procedure at McDonald's and at Other Companies," November 1991; Sharon M. Livesay, "McDonald's and the Environment," Harvard Business School Case Study, 1990; Curtis A. Moore, "McTruth: Fast Food for Thought," Washington Post, December 10, 1989; John Holusha, "An Alliance of 6 Big Consumers Vows to Use More Recycled Paper," The New York Times, August 19, 1993, p. 1; Joseph Daniel, "Responsible Publishing," Folio: The Magazine for Magazine Management, vol. 21, no. 10, (1993), pp. 224-226; Joan Oleck, "The Great Clamshell Debate," Restaurant Business Magazine, November 1, 1992, p. 68.

2  Moore, "McTruth: Fast food for thought."

3  Livesay, "McDonald's and the Environment," p. 6, quoting "McDonald's Combines a Dead Man's Advice with Lively Strategy," The Wall Street Journal, December 18, 1987, p. 12.

4  Jaclyn Fierman, "The Fine Art of Niche Picking," Fortune, Autumn/Winter, 1993, pp. 81-82.

5  Joseph M. Juran, "Made in USA: A Renaissance in Quality," Harvard Business Review, June-July, 1993, p. 46.

6  Diane Filipowski, "The Tao of Tandem," Personnel Journal, October 1991, pp. 72-78.

7  Associated Press, "Maker of Marlboro Considers Splitting," Sacramento Bee, April 16, 1994, p.1; News/Trends, Fortune, May 2, 1994.

8  G. Wilson, Interest Groups in the United States, (New York: Oxford University Press, 1981).

9  E. Epstein, "Business Political Activity: Research Approaches and Analytical Issues," in L. Preston, ed., Research in Corporate Responsibility and Social Policy, vol. 2 (Greenwich: JAI Press, 1980).

10  A. Hirschmann, Exit, Voice and Loyalty (Cambridge: Harvard University Press, 1970).

11  See David H. Rosenbloom and Jay M. Shafritz, Essentials of Labor Relations (Reston, Virginia: Reston Publishing, 1985) and Arthur A. Sloane and Fred Witney, Labor Relations, 6th ed. (Englewood Cliffs, New Jersey: Prentice Hall, 1988).

12  Shari Caudron, "How HR Drives TQM," Personnel Journal, August 1993, pp. 48M-48O.

13  See Lyn S. Wilson, "Managing in the Competitive Environment," Long Range Planning 17, no. 1 (February 1983): 59-64.

14  Pete Engardio, "Taiwan: The Arms Deal in the Computer Wars," Business Week, June 28, 1993, pp. 51-54.

15  David Vogel, "Trends in Shareholder Activism: 1970-1982," California Management Review 25, no. 3 (Spring 1983): 68-87.

16  Ralph Nader, Unsafe at Any Speed, (New York: Grossman Publishers, 1972).

17  Richard L. Hudson, "SEC Tightens Annual Meeting Proposal Rules," The Wall Street Journal, August 17, 1983, p. 4.

18  Edward L. Hennessy Jr., "The Raiders Make It Harder to Compete," The New York Times, March 13, 1988, p. F3.

19  Bryan Burrough & John Heylar, Barbarians at the Gate: The Fall of RJR Nabisco (New York: Harper & Row, 1990).

20  Peter F. Drucker, "Reckoning with the Pension Fund Revolution," Harvard Business Review, March 4, 1991, pp. 106-111.

21  Thomas A. Stewart, "The King is Dead," Fortune, January 11, 1993, pp. 34-43.

22  Livesay, "McDonald's and the Environment," p. 14, quoting "The Green Revolution: McDonald's," Advertising Age, January 29, 1991, p. 32.

23  Prince and Denison, "Launching a New Business Ethic."

24  Oleck, "The Great Clamshell Debate," p. 68.

25  W. Graham Astley, "Toward An Appreciation of Collective Strategy," Academy of Management Review 9 (1984): 526-35; W. Graham Astley and Charles J. Fombrun, "Collective Strategy: Social Ecology of Organizational Environments," Academy of Management Review 8 (1983): 576-87.

26  R. Edward Freeman and Daniel R. Gilbert, Jr., "Managing Stakeholder Relationships," in Business and Society: Dimensions of Conflict and Cooperation, S. Prakash Sethi and Cecilia M. Falbe, eds. (Lexington, Massachusetts: Lexington Books, 1987).

27  William M. Evan and R. Edward Freeman, "A Stakeholder Theory of the Modern Corporation: Kantian Capitalism," in Ethical Theory and Business, 3rd ed., Tom L. Beauchamp and Norman E. Bowie, eds. (Englewood Cliffs, New Jersey: Prentice Hall, 1988): 102-3.

28  Our discussion of the indirect-action variables in the following sections is largely drawn from Liam Fahey and V. K. Narayanan, Macroenvironmental Analysis for Strategic Management (St. Paul: West Publishing, 1986).

29  Michele Galen & Therese Palmer, "White, Male, and Worried," Business Week, January 31, 1994, p. 51.

30  Arsenio Oloroso, Jr., "Elder Care Comes of Age," Crain's Chicago Business, July 9, 1990, pp. 17, 19-20.

31  Fahey and Narayanan, Macroenvironmental Analysis, p. 73. The remainder of this section is based on Fahey and Narayanan, pp. 74-8.

32  Marshall Sashkin, "Participative Management is an Ethical Imperative," Organizational Dynamics 12, No. 4 (Spring 1984): 5-22.

33  Kristen S. Wevee & Christopher S. Allen, "Is Germany a Model for Managers?" Harvard Business Review, September 10, 1992, pp. 36-43.

34  Sources for the section include: Roger E. Shamel and Joseph J. Chow, "Biotechnology: On the Rebound and Heading for a Boom," Chemical Week, September 27, 1989, pp. 31-32; Jacob M. Schlesinger, "One High-Tech Race Where U.S. Leads: Personal Computers," The Wall Street Journal, October 21, 1989, pp. A1, A12; Neil Gross, "Japan's Next Battleground: The Medicine Chest," Business Week, March 12, 1990, pp. 68-72; "Strategic Challenges in Commercializing Biotechnology," California Management Review, (Spring 1990): 63-72; Barbara Buell, et al., "A Shopping Spree in the U.S.," Business Week, Innovation 1990 Issue, pp. 86-87.

35  Laura Zinn, "Teens: Here Comes the Biggest Wave Yet," Business Week, April 11, 1994, pp. 76-86.

36  See Rogene A. Buchholz, Alfred A. Marcus, and James E. Post, Managing Environmental Issues: A Casebook (Englewood Cliffs, N.J.: Prentice Hall, 1992).

37  J. Naar, Design for a Livable Planet (New York: Harper and Row, 1990); and Miller, Jr. and G. Tyler, Living in the Environment: An Introduction to Environmental Science, sixth edition (Belmont, Cal.: Wadsworth, 1990).

38  Trends, "Imby Please," Fortune, October 4, 1993, pp. 13-14.

Street Journal, March 8, 1990, p. A11; Kay M. Jones, "Westerners Learn to Read the Tea Leaves," Management Review, (April 1990), pp.46-49; Lora Western, "Hong Kong Deadline Doesn't Curb Deals," Crain's Chicago Business, March 18-24, 1991, p.1.

24  Hal Platkin, "In the China Shop."

25  Louis Kraar, "Top U.S. Companies Move into Russia," Fortune, (July 31, 1989), pp. 165-170.

26  Martha H. Peak, "Revolutions Signal Opportunity for American Business," Management Review, (March 1990), pp. 8-13.

27  Max Messmer, "A U.S. Based Russian Company's Staffing Solution," in Eliza Herman, "Post-Soviet Reform," Personnel Journal, April 1994, p. 47.

28  "NAFTA," Business Week, September 13, 1993, p. 28.

29  Gary Robins, "International Agenda," Stores, (December 1992).

30  Friedland, "Systematic Solution: Itoman's Problems Will Be Spirited Away," p. 86.

31  Helm, "For a Japanese Keiretsu, It's a Family Affair," p. 1.

32  Keith Bradsher, "Side Agreements to Trade Accord Vary in Ambition," The New York Times, September 19, 1993, pp. 1, 38.

33  Russell E. Palmer, "Trends in International Management: Toward Federations of Equals," Business Quarterly 152, no. 1 (Summer 1987): 116-120.

34  Young, "Global Competition: The New Reality," p. 12.

35  Thurow, "Revitalizing American Industry: Managing in a Competitive World Economy," p. 10.

36  New Trends, "Good Morning Vietnam II," Fortune, March 7, 1994, pp. 16-17.

37  This section is based upon William A. Dymsza, "Trends in Multinational Business and Global Environments: A Perspective," Journal of International Business Studies (Winter 184): 25-46. See also Isaiah Frank, "Meeting the Challenges of the 1990s: Trade and Investment Policies for a Changing World Economy," Business in the Contemporary World 5 (Spring 1990): 63-76.

38  Our definition is from Stefan H. Robock and Kenneth Simmonds, International Business and Multinational Enterprises, 3rd ed. (Homewood, Illinois: Irwin, 1983), p. 7. See also Yair Aharoni, "The Issue of Defining Transnational Corporations," in Transnational Corporations in World Development: A Reexamination (New York: United Nations, 1978), pp. 158-161, and "On the Definition of a Multinational Corporation," Quarterly Review of Economics and Business 11, no. 3 (Autumn 1971): 27-37.

39  See, for example, Richard J. Barnet and Ronald E. Muller, Global Reach: The Power of the Multinational Corporations (New York: Simon & Schuster, 1974) for a popular critique of MNEs, widely cited by critics of MNEs in the 1970s. See also Joseph S. Nye, Jr., "Multinationals and Developing Countries: Myths and Realities," Foreign Affairs 53, no. 1 (October 1974): 121-143 (both reprinted in Moyer, International Business).

40  This discussion is based on Christopher M. Korth, International Business, Environment, and Management, 2nd ed., Englewood Cliffs, NJ: Prentice Hall 1985), pp. 277-297, 308-326.

41  Robock and Simmonds, International Business and Multinational Enterprises, p. 233 (originally from "Dollar Diplomacy, 1972 Style," Newsweek, April 10, 1972).

42  Lawrence G. Franko, "Foreign Direct Investment in Less Developed Countries: Impact on Home Countries," Journal of International Business Studies 9, no. 2 (Winter 1978): 55-65, and Robert G. Hawkins and Bertran Finn, "Regulation of Multinational Firms' Foreign Activities: Home Country Policies and Concerns," Journal of Contemporary Business 6, no. 4 (Autumn 1977): 14-30 (both reprinted in Moyer, International Business).

43  Reed Moyer, ed., International Business Issues and Concepts (New York: Wiley, 1984), p. 138. For a discussion of the types of jobs U.S. MNEs might move overseas and the impacts of doing so on the U.S. economy and work force, see Robert A. Reich, The New American Frontier, (New York: Times Books, 1983).

44  Jennifer Laabs, "Training Program Assures Supply of Global Talent," Personnel Journal, January 1993, p.53.

45  Korth, International Business, Environment and Management, 2nd ed., p. 7.

46  "Global Alliances 1993," Fortune, August 23, 1993, p. S11.

47  This section on global strategic partnerships is based upon their article, "Cooperate to Compete Globally," Harvard Business Review 64, (March-April 1986): 136-152.

48  Ibid., p. 137.

49  For an interesting early book that called managers' attention to these kinds of differences, see Edward T. Hall, The Silent Language, (New York: Doubleday, 1959).

50  Perlmutter and Heenan, "Cooperate to Compete Globally," pp. 136-152.

51  This feature is based on the following sources: David Kalesh, "Women Entrepreneurs Helped by World Bank Group," Los Angeles Times, January 15, 1991, p. 8; James E. Austin, "Women's World Banking," 1991 by the President and Fellows of Harvard College, Rev. 3/26/91; Suzanne Wittebort, "Why Women Have a Friend at the World Bank," Institutional Investor, October 1991, p. 105; Abbie Jones, "Seed Money: Alternatives Help Poor Enter Marketplace," Chicago Tribune, September 6, 1992, p. 1; "It's a Team Scene," Banker, August 1993, pp. 27-8; "Bank Specializing in Loans to Poor Women Says Women Are Better Repayment Risks than Men," Business Wire, October 18, 1993; Andrea Larson, Assistant Professor of Business Administration, with the help of Jeanne Mockard, Research Assistant, 1991 by the University of Virginia Darden School Foundation, Rev. 3/93.

52  "Bank Specializing in Loans to Poor Women Says Women Are Better Repayment Risks than Men."

53  Jones, "Seed Money: Alternatives Help Poor Enter Marketplace," p. 1.

54  Geert Hofstede, "The Cultural Relativity of Organizational Practices and Theories," Journal of International Business Studies 14, no. 1 (Fall 1983): 78-85 and Culture's Consequences: International Differences in Work-Related Values (Beverly Hills, Calif.:Sage Publications, 1980). For a rich debate on the applicability of Western management in other cultures, see Geert Hofstede, "Motivation, Leadership, and Organization: Do American Theories Apply Abroad?" Organizational Dynamics 9, no. 1 (Summer 1980):42-63 and "Do American Theories Apply Abroad? A Reply to Goodstein and Hunt," Organizational Dynamics 10, no. 1 (Summer 1981):63-68 and John W. Hunt, "Applying American Behavioral Science: Some Cross-Cultural Problems," Organizational Dynamics 10, no. 1 (Summer 1981):55-62.

55  Geert Hofstede, "The Cultural Relativity of Organizational Practices and Theories," Journal of International Business Studies 14, no. 1 (Fall 1983); Culture's Consequences: International Differences in Work-Related Values.

56  William G. Ouchi, Theory Z: How American Business Can Meet the Japanese Challenge (Reading, Mass.: Addison-Wesley, 1981). Other studies of note are Richard Pascale and Anthony Athos, The Art of Japanese Management (New York: Simon & Schuster, 1981) and N. Hatvany and V. Pucik, "An Integrated Management System: Lessons from the Japanese Experience," Academy of Management Review 6, no. 3 (July 1981): 469-480.

57  Ouchi, Theory Z: How American Business Can Meet the Japanese Challenge, p. 58.

58  These ideas are discussed in James A.F. Stoner and Charles B. Wankel, World Class Managing: Two Pages at a Time, Book I (New York: Fordham Graduate School of Business, 1990); "Teaching the New Global Management Paradigm: Five Years' Experience," Proceedings, Fifty-first Annual Meeting of the Academy of Management (Miami Beach, FL, 1991), 126-130; "Putting Total Quality Management into Contemporary Polish Management Development," The Journal of Management Development 12, no. 3 (1993): 65-72; and James A.F. Stoner and Frank M. Werner, Managing Finance for Quality: Bottom-Line Results from Top-Level Commitment (Milwaukee: Quality Press and the Financial Executives Research Foundation, 1994).

59  This section is based on Quick Studies, "Culture of Urgency," Forbes ASAP: A Technology Supplement, September 13, 1993, pp. S25-S28.

60  This case is based on the following sources: "The Chief Salesman," Success, May 1991, p. 14; Faye Brookman, "Re-Inventing Pier 1," Stores, January 1991, pp. 76-80; Stephanie Anderson Forest, "A Pier 1 in Every Port?" Business Week, May 31, 1993, p. 88; Allyson L. Stewart, "U.S. Puts Pier Pressure on Europe's Retailers," Marketing News, August 2, 1993, pp. 6-7.

61  Forest, "A Pier 1 in Every Port?" p. 88.

62  This case is based on the following sources: Cyndee Miller, "Marketers waiting for South Africa to stabilize before investing there," Marketing News, November 8, 1993, pp. 5-6; Brian Bremner, "Doing the Right Thing in South Africa?" Business Week, April 27, 1992, p. 60, 64; Gillian Findlay, "U.S. Marketers Cautious on S. Africa," Advertising Age, October 26, 1993, p. 96; Henry Harington, "South Africa: On the Threshold of a New Era," Barron's, October 11, 1993, p. 70; Paul Taylor, "Zulus to Vote with Ballots or Bullets," Washington Post, March 28, 1994, pp. A1, A18; W. Joseph Campbell, "South Africa Beckons, but State Companies Remaining Cautious," Hartford Courant, April 17, 1994, p. E1;

"S. Africa Lures U.S. Companies; the Country's Resources and Promise as an Economic Power Can't Be Ignored," Orlando Sentinel, April 28, 1994, p. D11. In addition, the accompanying video is "South Africa Seeking Foreign Investors," Transcript #3250-6, ABC World New Tonight, December 16, 1993.

63 Harington, "South Africa: On the Threshold of a New Era," p. 70.

64 Miller, "Marketers waiting for South Africa to stabilize before investing there," p. 6.

65 Ibid.

66 Findlay, "U.S. Marketers Cautious on S. Africa," p. 96.

67 Miller, "Marketers waiting for South Africa to stabilize before investing there," p. 6.

68 Ibid., p. 5.

69 Ibid., p. 6.

70 Ibid.

71 Campbell, "South Africa Beckons, but State Companies Remaining Cautious," p. E1.

72 Ibid.

## CHAPTER 6

1 This case is based on the following sources: The New York Times, September 2, 1992; Nicholas K. Geranios, "Specialty Coffee Emerges as Hot-Selling Product," Los Angeles Times, December 6, 1992, p. 5; Starbucks 1992 Annual Report; Starbucks 1992 10-K; Matt Rothman, "Into the Black," Inc., (January 1993), pp. 58-65; Ingrid Abramovitch, "Miracles of Marketing," Success, (April 1993), pp. 22-7; Kate Rounds, "Corporate Spotlight: Starbucks Coffee," Incentive, (July 1993), pp. 22-23; Star Tribune, July 9, 1993; Andrew Swerwer, "America's 100 Fastest Growers," Fortune, (August 9, 1993), pp. 40-56; Steve Kaufman, "Seattle Firm is Coffee King, Houston Chronicle, January 4, 1993, p. D14.

2 D. Bruce Merrifield, "Intrapreneurial Corporate Renewal," Journal of Business Venturing, 8 (1993), p. 383.

3 Andrew Serwer, "America's 100 Fastest Growers," Fortune, (August 9, 1993), pp. 40-56.

4 "Tall Order for Small Business," Business Week, (April 19, 1993), pp. 114-118.

5 Brian O'Reilly, "The New Face of Small Business," Fortune, May 2, 1992, p. 82.

6 Sam Walton, with John Huey, Sam Walton: Made in America: My Story, (New York: Doubleday, 1992).

7 Peter Temin, with Louis Golambos, The Fall of the Bell System (Cambridge: Cambridge University Press, 1987).

8 Alfred P. Sloan, Jr., My Years With General Motors (New York: Anchor Books edition, 1972), pp. 19-28.

9 Joseph A. Schumpeter, Capitalism, Socialism and Democracy (New York: Harper & Row, 1975 edition), p. 84.

10 Jules Backman, ed., Entrepreneurship and the Outlook for America (New York: Free Press, 1983), p. 3.

11 Martha E. Mangelsdorf and Alessandra Bianchi, "State of the Art: Contemporary Greetings," INC., January 1994, p. 29.

12 John Case, "Quality with Tears," INC., June 1992, pp. 83-95; John Case, "The Best Small Companies to Work for in America," INC., November 1992, p. 92.

13 Paul H. Wilken, Entrepreneurship: A Comparative and Historical Study (Norwood, N.J.: Ablex Publishing, 1979), p. 60.

14 Peter F. Drucker, Innovation and Entrepreneurship (New York: Harper & Row, 1986), pp. 27-28.

15 Wilken, Entrepreneurship, p. 57.

16 Sloan, My Years With General Motors, pp. 275-285.

17 George Gilder, Wealth and Poverty (New York: Basic Books, 1981).

18 The fourth point comes from Zolton J. Acs, "Small Business Economics: A Global Perspective," Challenge, (November-December, 1992), p. 39.

19 Karl H. Vesper, Entrepreneurship and Public Policy (Pittsburgh: Carnegie-Mellon University, The Graduate School of Industrial Administration, 1983), p. 14.

20 David Birch, "Who Creates Jobs," The Public Interest 65 (Fall 181).

21 David Birch, The Job Creation Process (Cambridge, Mass.: MIT Program on Neighborhood and Regional Change, 1979), referred to in Sue Birley, "The Role of New Firms: Births, Deaths, and Job Generation," Strategic Management Journal 7 (1986):363. See also D. Littler and R.C. Sweeting, "The Management of New Technology-Based Businesses," Omega 18, no. 3 (1990): 231-240.

22 Thomas A. Stewart, "U.S. Productivity: First But Fading," Fortune, October 19, 1992, p. 52.

23 Backman, Entrepreneurship and the Outlook for America, p. 17.

24 Acs, "Small Business Economics," p. 39.

25 Vesper, Entrepreneurship and Public Policy, p. 42.

26 Donna Fenn, "Saudi Arabia: Unveiled Opportunities," INC., January 1994, p. 66.

27 This discussion is drawn from Wilken, Entrepreneurship, p. 20.

28 For example, Thomas Begley and David P. Boyd, "The Relationship of the Jenkins Activity Survey to Type A Behavior Among Business Executives," Journal of Vocational Behavior 27 (1987): 316-328; C. Borland, "Locus of Control, Need for Achievement, and Entrepreneurship," unpublished doctoral dissertation (Austin: University of Texas, 1974); David P. Boyd, "Type A Behavior, Financial Growth, and Organizational Growth in Small Business Firms," Journal of Occupational Psychology 57: 137-140; J.A. Hornaday and J. Abboud, "Characteristics of Successful Entrepreneurs," Personnel Psychology 24: 141-153; P.R. Liles, New Business Ventures and the Entrepreneur (Homewood, Ill.: Richard D. Irwin, 1974); J.A. Timmons, "Characteristics and Role Demands of Entrepreneurship," American Journal of Small Business 3 (1987): 5-17; J.A. Walsh and J.P. White, "Converging Characteristics of Entrepreneurs," in K.H. Vesper, ed., Frontiers of Entrepreneurship Research (Wellesley, Mass.: Babson Center for Entrepreneurial Studies, 1981), pp. 504-515. See also Thomas Begley and David P. Boyd, "Psychological Characteristics Associated with Performance in Entrepreneurial Firms and Smaller Businesses," Journal of Business Venturing 2 (1987): 79-93.

29 Ellen A. Fagenson, "Personal Value Systems of Men and Women Entrepreneurs Versus Managers," Journal of Business Venturing, 8 (1993), p. 422.

30 Ibid., pp. 422-423.

31 Sharon R. King, "Back from the Brink," Black Enterprise, March 1988, pp. 40-43; Nathan McCall, "With M&M Buy, B.M.L. Moves into Hair-Care Business," Black Enterprise, (August 1989), p. 17; Patricia Raybon, "Nuggets Buy Makes History: Will It Crumble Barrier?" Black Enterprise, (September 1989), pp. 17-18; Leah J. Nathans, "What Do Women Want? A Piece of the Muni Business," Business Week, (February 12, 1990), p. 60; Frank Swoboda, "Looking for a Way to Break the 'Glass Ceiling,'" Washington Post, August 28, 1990, p. A15.

32 Susan Chandler and Kate Murphy, "Women Entrepreneurs," Business Week, April 18, 1994, pp. 104-110; Elizabeth Ehrlich, "Welcome to the Woman-Friendly Company," Business Week, August 6, 1990, pp. 48-55.

33 Chandler and Murphy, "Women Entrepreneurs," ibid.

34 Vesper, Entrepreneurship and Public Policy, pp. 59-68.

35 Chandler and Murphy, "Women Entrepreneurs," p. 110.

36 Anne Underwood, "The King of Cream Returns," Newsweek, (November 1, 1993), p. 48.

37 Calvin Trillin, "Competitors," The New Yorker, July 8, 1985, pp. 31-32, 35-38, 41, 43-45; Len Strazewski, "Four Davids Reject Goliath-Like Path," Advertising Age, (October 12, 1987), pp. S3, S4, S6, S8; Keith H. Hammonds, "Is Häagen-Dazs Trying to Freeze Out Ben & Jerry's? Business Week, (December 7, 1987), p. 65; Lawrence Ingrassia, "Ice Cream Makers Rivalry Heating Up," The Wall Street Journal, (December 21, 1988), p. 1; Matha Groves, "Courting Ruling Fails to Melt Double Rainbow's Resolve," Los Angeles Times, March 7, 1990, pp. D2, D14.

38 LII, Jane H., "All Bout/Ice Cream; In the Cut-Throat World of Ice Cream, Flavormania!" The New York Times, August 2, 1992, p. 8.

39 Hwang, Suein L., "While Many Competitors See Sales Melt, Ben & Jerry's Scoops Out Solid Growth," The Wall Street Journal, May 25, 1993, p. 1.

40 Charles Burck, "The Real World of the Entrepreneur," Fortune, (April 5, 1993), p. 62.

41 Ira Kantrow, The Constraints of Corporate Tradition: Doing the Correct Thing, Not Just What the Past Dictates, (New York: Harper & Row, 1987).

42 Peter Senge, "The Leader's New Work: Building Learning Organizations," Sloan Management Review, (Fall 1990): 7-23.

43 Ibid.: 8.

44 James Brian Quinn, The Intelligent Enterprise, (New York: Free Press, 1992).

45 Chris Argyris, "Education for Leading-Learning," Organizational Dynamics, Winter 1993, pp. 5-17.

46 Gifford Pinchot III, Intrapreneuring (New York: Harper & Row, 1985); and Robert A. Burgelman, "Design for Corporate

40  James P. King, "Union Pacific Gets Back On Track With Customers," Training and Development (August 1993).

41  Spechler, Managing Quality in America's Most Admired Companies, pp. 11-2.

42  Neil Gross, "Rails that Run on Software," Business Week, Special Quality Issue, October 25, 1991.

43  Spechler, Managing Quality in America's Most Admired Companies, p. 12.

44  John Templeman, "Grill-To-Grill with Japan," Business Week, Special Quality Edition, October 25, 1991.

45  Robert C. Camp, "A Bible for Benchmarking, by Xerox," Financial Executive (July/April 1993).

46  Frank Rose and Rebecca Lewis, "Now Quality Means Service Too," Fortune, April 22, 1991, p. 97.

47  Robert W. Schrandt, "Quality Service," Executive Excellence, May 1992.

48  Ibid.

49  Ibid.

50  Aaron Bernstein, "Quality is Becoming Job One in the Office Too," Business Week, April 29, 1991, p. 52.

51  Tessa DeCarlo, "The Gospel According to Deming," San Francisco Chronicle, January 6, 1991, p. 9.

52  David A. Garvin, "How the Baldrige Really Works," Harvard Business Review, November-December 1991.

53  K. Krantz, "How Velcro Got Hooked on Quality," Harvard Business Review (September-October 1989): p. 34.

54  Kevin Doyle, "Can Saturn Save GM?" Incentive (December 1992): 30-37.

55  Larry Armstrong and William C. Symonds, "Beyond 'May I Help You?'" Business Week, special Quality issue, October 25, 1991.

56  Hart, "What's Wrong—and Right—with the Baldrige Awards," p. 36.

57  Kindel, "What Backlash?" p. 46.

58  Ibid.

59  J. M. Juran, "The Upcoming Century of Quality," keynote address at the 1994 ASQC Annual Quality Congress, Las Vegas, May 24, 1994.

60  Tom Peters, The Tom Peters Seminar: Crazy Times Call for Crazy Organizations (New York: Vintage Press, 1994).

61  Hughes, "Motorola Nears Quality Benchmark After 12 Year Evolutionary Effort," p. 65.

62  Ibid., p. 263.

63  This case is based on the following sources: "The Ritz-Carlton Hotel Co.," Business America, November 2, 1992; Edwards Watkins, "How Ritz-Carlton Won the Baldrige Award," Lodging Hospitality, November 1992; Shari Caudron, "Keys to Starting a TQM Program," Personnel Journal, February 1993.; John J. Kendrick, "The Ritz-Carlton Hotel Co.," Quality, January 1993.

64  Watkins, "How Ritz-Carlton Won the Baldrige Award," p. 23.

65  This case is based on Bruce McDougall, "The Thinking Man's Assembly Line," Canadian Business, November 1991, pp. 40-41. In addition, the accompanying video case is World News Tonight with Peter Jennings, July 6, 1993.

66  McDougall, "The Thinking Man's Assembly Line," p. 41.

67  Ibid., pp. 42-43.

68  Ibid., p. 43.

69  Ibid.

70  Ibid.

71  Ibid.

72  Ibid., p. 44.

# CHAPTER 9

1  Sources: Ed Graney and Mark Zeigler, "Jordan's Exit Slam-dunks Kids," The Sam Diego Union-Tribune, October 7, 1993, p. A1; William D. Murray, "Jordan's Exit Leaves Void Not Just in Locker Room, but in Boardroom As Well," U.P.I., October 6, 1993; J. Linn Allen, "Nike, Air Jordan High-Flying Act: Pair a Dream Selling Team," Chicago Tribune, October 7, 1993, p.1; Drew Jubera, "The Amazing Grace of Michael Jordan: More Than Any Star, More Than Any Celebrity, His Feats, His Flights Were Simply Superhuman," The Atlanta Constitution, October 7, 1993, p. 1; Jack Friedman, "Gooden, Murphy Go to Bat for Nike's New Line," The Business Journal-Portland, August 12, 1985, p. 3; George Lazarus, "Michael Jordan Shoe Also Having Big Rookie Season," Chicago Tribune, May 14, 1985, p. 6, "Air Jordan Takes Off,"

Newsweek, June 17, 1985, p. 79; Michael Knisley; "Nike Poohbah Is on Top of the World—At Least in Sports," Star Tribune, January 10, 1993, p. 5C; Randy Harvey, "Clear the Dunkway, Michael Jordan is ... Taking to Air; NBA Star Leaps into Profitable Shoe Market," Los Angeles Times, April 26, 1985, p. 1; Donald Katz, "Triumph of the Swoosh," Sports Illustrated, August 16, 1993; Nike (A)(Condensed) and Teaching Note, Rev.1/14/92; Nike (C)(Condensed), Rev.10/87; Jacqueline S. Gold, "Marathon Man?" Financial World, February 16, 1993; Matthew Grim, "Dream II? Nike, Coke Mull Brand Alliances," Brandweek, February 15, 1993; Glenn Rifkin, "All About Basketball Shoes; High Tops: High Style, High Tech, High Cost," The New York Times, January 5, 1992, p. 10; Pat Sloan, "Reebok, Nike Look Beyond Sneakers," Advertising Age, June 28, 1993; Elizabeth Comte, "Art for Shoes' Sake," Forbes, September 28, 1992, pp. 128-30; Genevieve Soter Capowski, "Designing a Corporate Identity," Management Review (June 1993):37-40; Melissa Campanelli, "What Women Want," Incentive (June 1993), pp.57-66; and Kate Bednarski, "Convincing Male Managers to Target Women Customers," Working Woman, June 1993, pp. 23-24, 28.

2  Allen, "Nike, Air Jordan high-flying act," p. 1.

3  Ibid.

4  Ibid.

5  Lazarus, "Michael Jordan Shoe Also Having Big Rookie Season," p. 6.

6  Min Chen, "Chinese and Japanese Negotiating Styles," The International Executive, March-April 1993, p. 148.

7  News/Trends, "Georgia Farmers Go Global," Fortune, May 16, 1994, pp. 16-17.

8  W. E. Pounds, "The Process of Problem Finding," Industrial Management Review (Fall 1969): 1-19. See also Peter F. Drucker, The Practice of Management, New York: Harper & Brothers, 1954, pp. 351-354.

9  Shari Caudron, "Coca-Cola Learns from Its Training Mistakes," Personnel Journal (August 1993): 48H.

10  Marjorie A. Lyles and Ian I. Mitroff, "Organizational Problem Formulation: An Empirical Study," Administrative Science Quarterly 25, no. 1 (March 1980): 102-119. For a discussion of the use of intuition by managers, see Thomas S. Isaack, "Intuition: An Ignored Dimension of Management," Academy of Management Review 3, no. 4 (October 1978): 917-922; W.H. Agor, "Tomorrow's Intuitive Leaders," Futurist, August 1983, pp. 49-53; and W. H. Agor, "The Logic of Intuition: How Top Executives Make Important Decisions," Organizational Dynamics 14 (Winter 1986): 5-18.

11  Sara Kiesler and Lee Sproull, "Managerial Response to Changing Environments," Administrative Science Quarterly 27, No. 4 (December 1982): 548-570.

12  The author uses the phrase, "the Pollyanna theory of management" to describe the belief that every problem has an opportunity embedded in it. Robert J. Graham uses the maxim that "problems are merely opportunities in disguise" in "Problem and Opportunity Identification in Management Science," Interfaces 6, no. 4 (August 1976): 79-82.

13  Personal communication.

14  For a discussion of dialectical inquiry, see Richard A. Cosier, "Approaches to the Experimental Examination of the Dialectic," Strategic Management Journal 4, no. 1 (January-March 1983): 79-84; Lyle Sussman and Richard Herden, "Dialectical Problem Solving," Business Horizons, January-February 1982, pp.66-71; and David M. Schweiger and Phyllis A. Finger, "The Comparative Effectiveness of Dialectical Inquiry and Devil's Advocate: The Impact of Task Biases on Previous Research Findings," Strategic Management Journal 5 (1984): 355-350; and Cosier and Schwenk. "Agreement and thinking alike: Ingredients for poor decisions," Academy of Management Executive (February 1990): 69-74.

15  Peter F. Drucker, Managing for Results (New York: Harper & Row, 1964),p. 5. See also J. Sterling Livingston, "Myth of the Well-Educated Manager," Harvard Business Review 49, no. 1 (January-February 1971): 79-89.

16  News/Trends, "Beer Clubs Make a Splash," Fortune, May 5, 1994, p. 17.

17  See William S. Guth and Tenato Tagiuri, "Personal Values and Corporate Strategy," Harvard Business Review 37, no. 5 (September-October 1965):123-132.

18  Betsy Weisenberger, "Benchmarking in Intelligence Fuels Management Moves," Public Relations Journal, November 1993, pp. 20-22.

19  De Witt C. Dearborn and Herbert A. Simon, "Selective Perception: A Note on the Departmental Identification of Executives," Sociometry 21, no. 2 (June 1958):140-144.

20 Robert J. Graham, "'Give the Kid a Number': An Essay on the Folly and Consequences of Trusting Your Data," Interfaces 12, No. 2 (June 1982):41.

21 See also Herbert A. Simon, The New Science of Management Decision, rev. ed. (Englewood Cliffs, N.J.: Prentice Hall, 1977), pp. 45-49.

22 Allan Halcrow, "Life is Enriched at Lotus Development Corporation," Personnel Journal, January, 1994, p.62.

23 See F. H. Knight, Risk, Uncertainty and Profit (New York: Harper & Brothers, 1920); and Stephen A. Archer, "The Structure of Management Decision Theory," Academy of Management Journal 7, no. 4 (December 1964): 269-287. See also Samuel M. Natale, Charles F. O'Donnell, and William R.C. Osborne, Jr., "Decision Making: Managerial Perspectives," Thought 63, No. 248 (1990): 32-51.

24 Larry Armstrong, "Golden State Warriors," Business Week, February 8, 1993, p. 116.

25 Weiner, "Norwest Corp.: 'The Wal-Mart of Banking,'" Forbes, (March 4, 1992), pp. 62, 65.

26 In this section we will use the terms problem solving and decision making more or less interchangeably because most of our discussion focuses on the decision-making portion of the total process.

27 Francis J. Bridges, Kenneth W. Olm, and J. Allison Barnhill, Management Decisions and Organizational Policy, (Boston: Allyn & Bacon, 1971).

28 The discussion that follows is based on John Dewey, How We Think (Boston: Heath, 1933), pp. 102-118; Drucker, The Practice of Management (New York: Harper & Row, 1954), pp. 354-365; Charles H. Kepner and Benjamin B. Tregoe, The Rational Manager: A Systematic Approach to Problem Solving and Decision Making (New York: McGraw-Hill, 1965); and Ernest R. Archer, "How to Make a Business Decision: An Analysis of Theory and Practice," Management Review 69, no. 2 (February 1980): 43-47. We have adapted and modified Archer's approach for our basic model.

29 Jennifer J. Laabs, "Business Growth Driven by Staff Development," Personnel Journal, April 1993, pp. 120-123.

30 A "corporate devil's advocate" who would specifically search for the flaws in solutions has been suggested by Theodore T. Herbert and Ralph W. Estes in "Improving Executive Decisions by Formalizing Dissent: The Corporate Devil's Advocate," Academy of Management Review 2, no. 4 (October 1977): 662-667.

31 Solo, "J.B. Hunt Transport Services: Every Problem Is an Opportunity," Fortune (November 16, 1992), p. 93.

32 Kepner and Tregoe, The Rational Manager,: A Systematic Approach to Problem Solving and Decision Making, pp. 190-194. See also Morgan W. McCall, Jr., and Robert E. Kaplan, Whatever It Takes: Decision Makers at Work (Englewood Cliffs, N.J.: Prentice Hall, 1985).

33 Comte, "Art for Shoes' Sake," p. 128.

34 Herbert A. Simon, Models of Man: Social and Rational (New York: Wiley, 1957). See also James G. March and Herbert A. Simon, Organizations (New York: Wiley, 1958); Herbert A. Simon, Administrative Behavior, 3rd ed. (New York: Free Press, 1976); Herbert A. Simon, Reason in Human Affairs (Stanford, Calif.: Stanford University Press, 1983), pp. 12-23; Anna Grandori, "A Prescriptive Contingency View of Organizational Decision Making," Administrative Science Quarterly 29, no. 2(June 1984):192-209; and Neil M. Agnew and John L. Brown, "Bounded Rationality: Fallible Decisions in Unbounded Decision Space," Behavioral Science, (July 1986), pp. 148-161.

35 A. Tversky and D. Kahneman, "Judgement under Uncertainty: Heuristics and Biases," Science 18 (1974): 1124-1131.

36 Tversky and Kahneman, "Availability: A Heuristic for Judging Frequency and Probability," Cognitive Psychology 5 (1973): 207-232.

37 E. McDowell, "American Air Cuts Most Fares in Simplification of Rate System," The New York Times, April 10, 1992, pp. A1, D3; J. Greenwald, "Fasten Your Seat Belts for the Fare War," Time (April 27, 1992), pp. 41-42; E. McDowell, "Airlines Tally the Damage From Summer's Fare War," The New York Times, September 12, 1992, pp. 1, 34; B. O'Brien, "AMR's Airline-Industry Fare Structure Heads for That Big Hanger in the Sky," The Wall Street Journal, October 9, 1992, pp. B1, B6; E. McDowell, "Air Fare Plan Fails, American Admits," The New York Times, October 19, 1992, pp. 41-42; J. Hirsch, "Airlines Taking Yet Another Stab at Boosting Fares," The Wall Street Journal, November 27, 1992, p. B2.

38 T. Schelling, Micromotives and Macrobehavior, (New York: W.W. Norton, 1978).

39 S. Oster, Modern Competitive Analysis (New York: Oxford University Press, 1990), pp. 249-268.

40 See W. Poundstone, Prisoner's Dilemma: John von Neumann, Game Theory, and the Puzzle of the Bomb (New York: Doubleday, 1992) and A. Dixit and B. Nalebuff, Thinking Strategic lly: The Competitive Edge in Business, Politics, and Everyday Life (New York: W.W. Norton, 1991).

41 D. Gilbert, Jr., The Twilight of Corporate Strategy: A Comparative Ethical Critique (New York: Oxford University Press, 1992), pp. 126-144, and R. Stavey, Managing the Unknowable: Strategic Boundaries Between Order and Chaos in Organizations (San Francisco: Jossey-Bass, 1992).

42 Ibid., pp. 77-79.

43 Campanelli, "What Women Want," p. 63.

44 Bednarski, "Convincing Male Managers to Target Women Customers," p. 23.

45 Ibid., p. 24.

46 Sources: Gail DeGeorge, Ronald Grover and Richard Brandt, "Wayne's World: Busting Beyond Video," Business Week (November 1, 1993), pp. 122-124; Gail DeGeorge, "They Don't Call It Blockbuster for Nothing," Business Week (October 19, 1993), pp. 113-4; Greg Clarkin, "The Marketing Successes of 1989—Entertainment: Fast Forward," Marketing & Media Decisions (March 1990), pp. 57-9; Leland Montgomery, "Hit Men Nix Pix Wiz," Financial World (August 3, 1993), pp. 44-45.

47 Clarkin, "The Marketing Successes of 1989," p. 57.

48 DeGeorge, Grover, and Brandt, "Wayne's World: Busting Beyond Video," p. 122.

49 This case is based on the following sources: "Act II: Seven Years of Fox," Mediaweek, October 11, 1993, pp. 16-23; Michael Marray, "Fox Goes for Billion Dollar Touchdown," The Independent, January 30, 1994, p. 7; Alan Pergament, "Fox 'Delighted' to Have Madden, but $32 Million?" The Buffalo News, February 5, 1994, p. 2; John Kimelman, "News Corp.: Crazy Like a Fox," Financial World, February 1, 1994, p. 1( "NBC Gets Final N.F.L. Contract While CBS Gets Its Sundays off," The New York Times, December 21, 1993, p. A1; Leonard Shapiro, "Owners Cash In, Carry NFL to New Home," The Washington Post, December 19, 1993, p. D9; Barbara Holsopple, "Fox Shakes Up Networks with its NFC Football Deal," The Phoenix Gazette, January 28, 1994, p. 22; Eric Schmuckler, "Scoring Fox's Football Deal; Fox Broadcasting Network Television Rights to National Football Conference," Mediaweek, January 3, 1994, p. 13; Jon Lafayette and Thomas Tyrer, "Winners and Losers; Fox NFC Buy Shakes Up Station Fortunes," Electronic Media, January 3, 1994, p. 1. In addition, the accompanying video is "Fox Network Outbids CBS for Sunday NFL Football," World News Saturday, Transcript #351-3, December 18, 1993.

50 Holsopple, "Fox Shakes Up Networks," p. 22.

51 Marray, "Fox Goes for Billion Dollar Touchdown," p. 7.

52 Lafayette and Tyrer, "Winners and losers," p. 1.

53 "Act II: Seven Years of Fox," p. 18.

54 Kimelman, "New Corp.: Crazy Like a Fox," p. 16.

55 Marray, "Fox Goes for Billion Dollar Touchdown," p. 7.

56 "Act II: Seven Years of Fox," p. 17.

57 Ibid.

58 Schmuckler, "Scoring Fox's Football Deal," p. 13.

## CHAPTER 10

1 This case is based on the following sources: Larry Reibstein, "Turbulence Ahead: Federal Express Faces Challenges to Its Grip on Overnight Delivery," The Wall Street Journal, January 8, 1988, pp. 1, 10; Arthur M. Lewis, "The Great Electronic Mail Shootout," Fortune, (August 20, 1984), pp. 167-169; Joan M. Feldman, "Federal Express: Big, Bigger and Biggest," Air Transport World, (November 1985), pp. 46-8; John J. Keller with John W. Wilson, "Why Zapmail Finally Got Zapped," Business Week, (October 13, 1986), pp. 48-9; David H. Freedman, "Redefining an Industry Through Integrated Automation," Infosystems, (May 1985), pp. 26-7; Katie Hajner, "Fred Smith: The Entrepreneur Redux," Inc., (June 1984), pp. 38, 40; John Mervin, "Anticipating the Evolution," Forbes, (November 4, 1985), pp. 163-4; Dean Foust et al., "Mr. Smith Goes Global," Business Week, (February 13, 1989), pp. 68-72; Stephen W. Quickel, "Wisely, Fed Ex Opted to Join 'Em," Business Month, (March 1989), pp. 17-18; Eugene Carlson, "Federal Express Wasn't an Overnight Success," The Wall Street Journal, June 6, 1989, p. B2; Peter Waldman, "Federal Express Pilots Upset by Handling of Seniority Issue in Merger with Tiger," The Wall Street Journal, August 4, 1989, p. A6; Glenn Ruffenbach, "Federal Express Earnings Plunge 79% But Firm, Others See Turnaround," The Wall Street Journal, March 20, 1990, p. A3;

Atlantic to Fly out of S.F.," San Francisco Chronicle, March 7, 1994, p. B1; David Campbell, "People Power is Key to Next Millennium," Herald (Glasgow), March 10, 1994, p. 5; Eric Reguly, "Virgin Boss Has Reputation for Stunts but Behind the Headlines Is a Shrewd Entrepreneur," Financial Post, February 19, 1994, p. S10; Everett Potter, "Virgin Atlantic Turns 10," Houston Chronicle, January 9, 1994, p. 2. In addition, the accompanying video is Business World, November 22, 1992.

46  Reguly, "Virgin Boss Has Reputation for Stunts," p. S10.

47  Potter, "Virgin Atlantic Turns 10," p. 2.

48  Reguly, "Virgin boss Has Reputation for Stunts," p. S10.

49  Potter, "Virgin Atlantic Turns 10," p. 2.

50  Potter, "Virgin Atlantic Turns 10," p. 2.

51  Reguly, "Virgin boss Has Reputation for Stunts," p. S10.

52  Ibid.

53  Reguly, "Virgin Boss Has Reputation for Stunts," p. S10.

## CHAPTER 12

1  This case is based on the following sources: John W. Verity, et al., "In Computers, a Shakeout of Seismic Proportions," Business Week, October 15, 1990, pp. 34-6; Barbara Buell et al., "Hewlett-Packard Rethinks Itself," Business Week, April 1, 1991, pp. 76-9; "Can Morton Calm Ruffled Feathers?" Industry Week, August 20, 1984, p. 64; Robert L. Yeager, "Hewlett-Packard: Continuing the Search for Excellence," Business Marketing, November 1985, pp. 74, 76; Kathleen K. Wiegner, "John Young's New Jogging Shoes," Forbes, November 4, 1985, pp. 42-4; John A. Young, "The Quality Focus at Hewlett-Packard," The Journal of Business Strategy 5 (Winter 1985): 6-9; David Finn, "Growing Up with the Founding Fathers," Across the Board 23 (March 1986): 47-55; Weiger, "Making the Short List Again," Forbes, June 15, 1987, pp. 124-26; Jonathan B. Levine, "Mild-Mannered Hewlett-Packard Is Making Like Superman," Business Week, March 7, 1988, pp. 110-11, 114; Jim Carlton, "Hewlett-Packard Tried to Revive Share of Market of Realigning Computer Lines," The Wall Street Journal, October 8, 1990, p. B4; Barbara Buell et al., "Hewlett-Packard Rethinks Itself," Business Week, April 1, 1991, pp. 76-9; Robert D. Hof, "Hewlett-Packard Digs Deep for a Digital Future," Business Week, October 18, 1993, pp. 72-5; Alan Cane, "Hewlett-Packard Reaps the Reward of Rise—The Computer Company's New Chief Executive Finds No Room for Complacency," Financial Times, June 22, 1993, p. 30.

2  Cane, "Hewlett-Packard Reaps the Reward of Rise," p. 30.

3  Ibid.

4  Hof, "Hewlett-Packard Digs Deep for a Digital Future," p. 73.

5  Ibid., pp. 72-75.

6  Ernest Dale, Organization (New York: American Management Association), p. 9. The five-step process described here is an elaboration of Dale's original three-step process.

7  Adam Smith, Wealth of Nations (New York: Modern Library, 1937; orig. pub. 1776), pp. 3-4.

8  Gareth R. Jones, "Task Visibility, Free Riding, and Shirking: Explaining the Effect of Structure and Technology on Employee Behavior," Academy of Management Review, October 1984, pp. 684-95; Dan R. Dalton and Debra J. Mesch, "The Impact of Flexible Scheduling on Employee Attendance and Turnover," Administrative Science Quarterly 35 (June 1990): 370-87; J. Barton Cunningham and Ted Eberle, "A Guide to Job Enrichment and Redesign," Personnel, February 1990, pp. 56-61; Benjamin Schneider and Andrea Marcus Konz, "Strategic Job Analysis," Human Resource Management 28, no. 1 (Spring 1989): 51-63.

9  Robert R. Rehder, "Sayonara, Uddevalla?", Business Horizons, November-December 1992, pp. 8-18.

10  Some early writers did, however, consider situational factors. Early in this century, for instance, F. R. Mason referred to variables that affected the span of management in Business Principles and Organization (Chicago: Cree Publishing, 1909). Considerably later, Lyndall F. Urwick emphasized the interdependence of the work of subordinates, and Luther Gulick mentioned a variety of important factors, such as the type of work and the variety of tasks performed. See Lyndall F. Gulick, "The Manager's Span of Control," Harvard Business Review 34, no. 3 (May-June 1956): 39-47; and Luther Gulick, "Notes on the Theory of Organization," in Luther Gulick and L. Urwick, eds. Papers on the Science of Administration (New York: Institute of Public Administration, Columbia University, 1937), pp. 1-46.

11  Teri Lammers, "The New, Improved Organization Chart," Inc. 14, no. 10 (October 1992): 147.

12  Ibid.

13  Mats Alvesson, "A Flat Pyramid: A Symbolic Processing of Organizational Structure," International Studies of Management and Organization 19, no. 4 (Winter 1989/1990): 5-23.

14  Jana Schilder, "Work Teams Boost Productivity," Personnel Journal, February 1992, pp. 67-71.

15  For subsequent research on span of management, see David Van Fleet and Arthur G. Bedeian, "A History of the Span of Management," Academy of Management Review 2, no. 3 (1977):356-372; and Van Fleet, "Empirically Testing Span of Management Hypotheses," International Journal of management 2, no. 2 (1984):5-10.

16  James Mooney defines coordination as "the orderly arrangement of group effort, to provide unity of action in the pursuit of a common purpose." See The Principles of Organization, rev. ed. (New York: Harper & Brothers, 1947), p. 5.

17  See Joseph L. C. Cheng, "Interdependence and Coordination in Organizations: A Role-System Analysis," Academy of Management Journal 26, no. 1 (March 1983): 156-162.

18  James D. Thompson, Organizations in Action: Social Sciences Bases of Administrative Theory (New York: McGraw-Hill, 1967), pp. 54-60.

19  "US and the Big Three Will Attempt to Create an 82.5 mpg Auto," Philadelphia Inquirer, September 30, 1993, pp. A1, A10.

20  Ibid.

21  Paul R. Lawrence and Jay W. Lorsch, Organization and Environment: Managing Differentiation and Integration (Homewood, Ill.: Irwin, 1967), p. 9.

22  Eliezer Rosenstein, "Cooperativeness and Advancement of Managers: An International Perspective," Human Relations 38, no. 1 (January 1985): 1-21.

23  Our discussion of coordination is based to a large extent on Jay R. Galbraith, "Organization Design: An Information Processing View," Interfaces 4, no. 3 (May 1974): 28-36; Galbraith, Organization Design (Reading, Mass.: Addison-Wesley, 1977); and Michael L. Tushman and David A. Nadler, "Information Processing as an Integrating Concept in Organizational Design," Academy of Management Review 3, no. 3 (July 1978): 613-24.

24  Tom Peters and R. H. Waterman, Jr., In Search of Excellence (New York: Harper & Row, 1982).

25  "Hewlett-Packard Digs Deep For a Digital Future," p. 75.

26  Galbraith, Organization Design, pp. 50-52. Galbraith also offers a third method: managing the organization's relationship with the environment so as to reduce the need for tight coordination. We consider this part of the basic task of relating the organization to the environment through its strategy-making and planning/controlling systems. However, Galbraith's discussion calls attention to the open nature of the organization as a system: It can reduce the need for internal capacity by altering the ways in which it deals with the external environment.

27  See Kenneth E. Marino and David R. Lange, "Measuring Organizational Slack: A Note on the Convergence and Divergence of Alternative Operational Definitions," Journal of Management 9, no. 1 (Fall 1983): 81-92.

28  For the overall perspective in this section, the authors are indebted to Kenneth N. Wexly and Gary A. Yukl, Organizational Behavior and Personnel Psychology, rev. ed. (Homewood, Ill.: Irwin, 1984); Y.K. Shetty and Howard M. Carlisle, "A Contingency Model of Organizational Design," California Management Review 15, no. 1 (Fall 1972): 38-45; and Jay R. Galbraith and Daniel A. Nathanson, "The Role of Organizational Structure and Process in Strategy Implementation," in Dan E. Schendel and Charles W. Hofer, eds., Strategic Management: A New View of Business Policy and Planning (Boston, Mass.: Little, Brown, 1979), pp. 249-283. See also Daniel Robey, Designing Organizations, 2nd ed. (Homewood, Ill.: Irwin, 1986).

29  Max Weber, Economy and Society: An Outline of Interpretative Sociology (New York: Bedminster Press, 1968; orig. pub. 1925), pp. 956-58.

30  Weber addressed this criticism by defining a hypothetical "ideal" organization that incorporated every one of the characteristics of bureaucracy. He believed that the closer an actual institution approached this ideal one, the more fully it would enjoy the benefits of bureaucracy.

31  Joan Woodward, Industrial Organization (London: Oxford University Press, 1965). See also Karl O. Magnusen, "A Comparative Analysis of Organizations," Organizational Dynamics 2, no. 1 (Summer 1973): 16-31; James D. Thompson, Organizations in Action (New York: McGraw-Hill, 1967); Charles Perrow,

Complex Organizations: A Critical Essay, 2nd ed. (Glenview, Ill.: Scott Foresman, 1979); and Paul D. Collins and Frank Hull, "Technology and Span of Control: Woodward Revisited," Journal of Management Studies 23 (1986): 143-164.

32  See, for example, David J. Hickson, D.S. Pugh, and Diana C. Pheysey, "Operations Technology and Organizational Structure: A Clinical Reappraisal," Administrative Science Quarterly 14, no. 3 (September 1969): 378-97.

33  Tom Burns and G. M. Stalker, The Management of Innovation (London: Tavistock, 1961).

34  John A. Bryne, "The Horizontal Organization," Business Week, December 20, 1993, pp. 76-83.

35  Rod Willis, "What's Happening to America's Middle Managers?" Management Review, January 1987, pp. 24-33; "The Downside of Downsizing," Fortune, May 23, 1988, pp. 45-52; Michael J. Mandel, "This Time the Downturn Is Dressed in Pinstripes," Business Week, October 1, 1990, pp. 130-31.

36  Alfred Edmond, Jr., "Gee, Blacks Really Did Lose More Jobs," Black Enterprise 24, no. 5 (December 1993): 20.

37  John A. Byrne, "The Pain of Downsizing," Business Week, May 9, 1994, p. 68.

38  K. Newman, Falling From Grace: The Experience of Downward Mobility in the American Middle Class (New York: Vintage, 1989).

39  Karen Matthes, "The Pink Slip Turns into Something Rosier," Management Review 81, no. 4 (April 1992): 5.

40  Stephen Davis, "Terry Murray, Contender," Institutional Investor 27, no. 8 (August 1993): 52.

41  John F. Mee, "Matrix Organizations," Business Horizons 7, no. 2 (Summer 1964): 70-72; Jay R. Galbraith, "Matrix Organization Designs," Business Horizons 14, no. 1 (February 1971): 29-40; Stanley M. Davis and Paul R. Lawrence, Matrix (Reading, Mass.: Addison-Wesley, 1977); and Harvey F. Kolodny, "Evolution to a Matrix Organization," Academy of Management Review 4, no. 4 (1979): 543-553.

42  For a discussion of the typical evolution of a matrix structure, see Davis and Lawrence, Matrix, pp. 39-45.

43  R. F. Grantges, V. L. Fahrmann, T. A. Gibson, and L. M. Brown, "Central Office Equipment Reports for Stores Program and Control Systems," Bell System Technical Journal 62, no. 7 (September 1983): 2365-395.

44  Christopher A. Bartlett and Sumantra Ghoshal, "Matrix Management: Not a Structure, a Frame of Mind," Harvard Business Review, July-August 1990, pp. 138-145.

45  Ralph Katz and Thomas J. Allen, "Project Performance and the Locus of Influence in the R&D Matrix," Academy of Management Journal, March 1985, pp. 67-87.

46  Herbert A. Simon, Administrative Behavior, 3rd ed. (New York: Macmillan, 1976). For other rich discussion of informal group, see Chester I. Barnard, The Function of the Executive (Cambridge, Mass.: Harvard University Press, 1938); R. J. Roethlisberger and William J. Dickson, Management and the Worker (Cambridge, Mass.: Harvard University Press, 1947); and Charles Perrow, Complex Organizations, 3rd ed. (New York: Random House, 1986).

47  J. B. Quinn, Intelligent Enterprise: A Knowledge And Service Based Paradigm for Industry (New York: Free Press, 1992).

48  Tom Peters, Liberation Management: Necessary Disorganization for the Nanosecond Nineties (New York: Alfred A. Knopf, 1982), p. 8.

49  Ibid., p. 11.

50  "The Virtual Corporation," Business Week, February 8, 1993, p. 100.

51  Ibid., p. 99. See also T. Brown, "Think in Reverse," Industry Week, July 19, 1993, pp. 14-22.

52  See S. Call, The Deal of the Century: The Breakup of AT&T (New York: Atheneum, 1986).

53  "The Virtual Corporation," p. 101.

54  Quinn, Intelligent Enterprise, p. 172.

55  Ibid., pp. 61-62.

56  "Hewlett-Packard Digs Deep For a Digital Future," p. 72.

57  Ibid., p. 73.

58  Ibid., pp. 63.

59  This case is based on Dennis Hightower, "Creativity Is Our Business," Executive Excellence (September 1993): 5-6.

60  This case is based on the following sources: Christopher Reynolds, "Inside the New Las Vegas; In the Belly of the Beast; With 5,0005 Rooms, The MGM Grand is the World's Biggest Hotel. How Do You Run a Behemoth and Keep Everyone Happy?" Los Angeles Times,

February 20, 1994, p. L1; Steve Hemmerick, "Integrated Data Base Keeps Tabs on All Plans," Pensions & Investments, May 17, 1993, p. 97; Michael Adams, "Woolf At the Door," Successful Meetings, April 1993, pp. 103-6; Bernard C. Reimann, "The Newest Game in Vegas is Strategic Management," Planning Review (January/February 1993): 38-9, 49. In addition, the accompanying video is ABC News: World News Tonight, Transcript #351, December 19, 1993.

61  Reynolds, "Inside the New Las Vegas," p. L1.

62  Adams, "Woolf At the Door," p. 106.

63  Ibid.

64  Ibid.

## CHAPTER 13

1  This case is based on the following sources: Leonard A. Schlesinger and James L. Heskett, "Enfranchisement of Service Workers," California Management Review (Summer 1991): 83-100; Nancy K. Austin, "Reorganizing the Organization Chart," Working Woman (September 1993): 23-26; Dori Jones Yang, "Nordstrom's Gang of Four," Business Week, June 15, 1992, pp. 122-3.

2  Schlesinger and Heskett, "Enfranchisement of Service Workers," p. 83.

3  John R. P. French and Bertram Raven, "The Bases of Social Power," in Dorwin Cartwright, ed., Studies in Social Power (Ann Arbor: University of Michigan Press, 1959), pp. 150-167.

4  Gary Yukl and Tom Taber, "The Effective Use of Managerial Power," Personnel 60, no. 2 (March-April 1983): 37-44.

5  Geert Hofstede, "Motivation, Leadership and Organizations: Do American Theories Apply Abroad?" Organizational Dynamics, Summer 1980, pp. 45, 51.

6  Stanley Milgram, Obedience to Authority (London: Tavistock Publications, 1975). c. 1974 by Stanley Milgram. Some researchers responded to Milgram's experiment with outrage because he had misled his subjects about the nature of the experiment and manipulated them in a way that was dangerous from a psychological standpoint. In fact, the American Psychological Association censured Milgram and instituted strict guidelines for the conduct of numerous types of experiments. In Milgram's defense, it must be said that he was in control of his procedure and had established a comprehensive debriefing and follow-up procedure to mitigate any potentially harmful consequences to his subjects.

7  Jeffrey Pfeffer has explored the basis for the contemporary unease about power and politics and has concluded that power processes are often ubiquitous and generally beneficial rather than harmful to organizations and the people who work in them. See Jeffrey Pfeffer, Power in Organizations (Marshfield, Mass.: Pitman, 1981); and Henry Mintzberg, Power in and Around Organizations (Englewood Cliffs, N.J.: Prentice Hall, 1983).

8  David C. McClelland, "The Two Faces of Power," Journal of International Affairs 24, no. 1 (1970): 29-47.

9  Jim Mullen. "Owners Need Not Apply," Inc., August 1990, pp. 76-8.

10  David C. McClelland and David H. Burnham, "Power Is the Great Motivator," Harvard Business Review 54, no. 2 (March-April 1976): 100-110.

11  John Kotter, "Power, Dependence, and Effective Management," Harvard Business Review 54, no. 2 (March-April 1976): 100-10; Kotter, Power in Management (New York: AMACOM, 1979); Kotter, Power and Influence (New York: Free Press, 1983).

12  Rosabeth Moss Kanter, Men and Women of the Corporation (New York: Basic books, 1977), pp. 165-205. See also Kanter, "Men and Women of the Corporation Revisited," Management Review, March 1987, pp. 14-5; Kanter, The Change Masters (New York: Simon & Schuster, 1983), pp. 156-79; Kanter, "Power Failure in Management Circuits," Harvard Business Review 57, no. 4 (July-August 1979): 65-75; and Sharon Nelton, "Meet Your New Work Force," Nation's Business 76, no. 7 (1988): 14-21.

13  A key concern of current research is the integration of the various theories of power into a unified theory. See W. Graham Astley and Paramjit S. Sachdeva, "Structural Sources of Intraorganizational Power: A Theoretical Synthesis," Academy of Management Review 9, no. 1 (January 1984): 104-13; and Anthony T. Cobb, "An Episodic Model of Power: Toward an Integration of Theory and Research," Academy of Management Review 9, no. 3 (July 1984): 482-93.

14  See Max Weber, "The Three Types of Managerial Rule," Berkeley Journal of Sociology 4, (1953; orig. pub. 1925): 1-11; and Cyril O'Donnell, "The Source of Managerial Authority," Political Science Quarterly 67, no. 4 (December 1952): 573-88.

15  Hershberger v. Jersey Shore Steel Co., 575 A.2d 944 (Pa. Super. 1990); K. Decker, "Individual Employment Rights Begin Maturing in Pennsylvania," Pennsylvania Law Journal-Reporter 12, no. 26 (1989): 1, 4-5.

16  Chester I. Barnard, The Functions of the Executive, 30th Anniversary ed. (Cambridge, Mass.: Harvard University Press, 1968), p. 165.

17  Ibid., pp. 167-170.

18  Herbert A. Simon, Administrative Behavior, 3rd ed. (New York: Macmillan, 1976), pp. 12, 18.

19  See, for example, Gerald G. Fisch, "Line-Staff Is Obsolete," Harvard Business Review 39, no. 5 (September-October 1961): 67-79; and Vivian Nossiter, "A New Approach Toward Resolving the Line and Staff Dilemma," Academy of Management Review 4, no. 1 (January 1979): 103-6.

20  Alfred Kieser, "Advisory Staffs for Rulers: Can They Increase Rationality of Decisions?" Unpublished paper delivered at the seminar on "Improvement of Top-Level Decision-Making" at the Institute for Advanced Study, Berlin, February 1983.

21  For an early discussion of ways in which staff members can support line managers, see Louis A. Allen, "The Line-Staff Relationship," Management Record 17, no. 9 (September 1955): 346-349ff.

22  For a discussion of the various ways staff activities are integrated in the organizational structure, see Harold Stieglitz, "On Concepts of Corporate Structure: Economic Determinants of Organization," Conference Board Review, February 1974, pp. 148-150.

23  Peter T. Kilborn, "An American Workplace, After the Deluge," The New York Times, September 5, 1993, sect. 3, pp. 1, 4.

24  Ibid., p. 4.

25  John Case, "The Best Small Companies to Work for in America," INC., November 1992, p. 96.

26  Beverly Geber, "A New Kind of Police Department," Training 30, no. 10 (October 1993): 71.

27  Joshua Hyatt, "No Way Out," Inc. 13, no. 11 (November 1991): 78.

28  Ibid., p. 92.

29  Ibid., p. 90.

30  Ibid., p. 92.

31  See Gerald G. Fisch, "Toward Effective Delegation," CPA Journal 46, no. 7 (July 1976): 67; and William Newman, "Overcoming Obstacles to Effective Delegation," Management Review 45, no. 1 (January 1956): 36-41.

32  See Fisch, "Toward Effective Delegation," pp. 66-67.

33  Austin, "Reorganizing the Organization Chart," p. 24.

34  Barbara E. Van Gorder, "Moving Back to Centralization," Credit (May/June 1990): 12-5.

35  Ibid.

36  "Fred Meyer Overhauls Itself," Discount Merchandiser (July 1990): 44, 46.

37  John W. Boroski, "Putting it Together: HR Planning in '3D' at Eastman Kodak," Human Resource Planning 13, no. 1 (1990): 45-57.

38  See Ernest Dale, Organization (New York: American Management Associations, 1967), pp. 114-130.

39  "A Car is Born," Business Week, September 13, 1993, pp. 64-72.

40  N. Austin, "Recognizing the Organization Chart," Working Woman (September 1993): 23-6.

41  "Saturn," Business Week, August 17, 1992, pp. 86-91.

42  "Where Employees Are Management," Business Week: Reinventing America, 1992, p. 66.

43  Helen F. Uhlfelder, "Redesign for Total Quality," Quality 31, no. 8 (August 1992): Q19-Q20.

44  J. Richard Hackman and Edward E. Lawler, "Employee Reactions to Job Characteristics," Journal of Applied Psychology, Monograph 55 (1971): 269-86; Hackman and Greg R. Oldham, "Development of the Job Diagnostic Survey," Journal of Applied Psychology 60, no. 2 (April 1975): 159-70; and Hackman and J. Lloyd Suttle, eds., Improving Life at Work (Santa Monica, Calif.: Goodyear, 1977), pp. 130-31.

45  J. Richard Hackman, "Work Design," in Hackman and Suttle, eds., Improving Life at Work, pp. 128-30.

46  Fred Bazzoli, "Patient-focused Care Aims to Counter Institutional Culture," Modern Healthcare 23, no. 49 (December 6, 1993): 48-52.

47  Robert N. Ford, "Job Enrichment Lessons from AT&T," Harvard Business Review 51, no. 1 (January-February 1973): 96-106, describes some of the techniques used by AT&T to redesign white-and blue-collar jobs in one of the most extensive job-enrichment programs in American industry.

48  Kilborn, "The Workplace, After the Deluge," p. 1.

49  Ibid., p. 4.

50  Susan M. Werner, "Ask A Risk Manager: It's Become a Buzzword, but Ergonomics Can Be a Valuable Safety Tool," Business Insurance, October 12, 1992, p. 30.

51  Ibid.

52  "Quill Moves Toward Ergonomic Effectiveness," Occupational Hazards 55, no. 9 (September 1993): 205.

53  Ibid.

54  Mary Baechler, "Tom Peters Ruined My Life," Wall Street Journal, October 25, 1993, p. A20.

55  Ibid.

56  Tom Peters and Nancy Austin, A Passion for Excellence (New York: Random House, 1985); Peters, Liberation Management: Necessary Disorganization for the Nanosecond Nineties (New York: Alfred A. Knopf, 1992).

57  Baechler, "Tom Peters Ruined my Life."

58  James Brian Quinn, Intelligent Enterprise: A Knowledge and Service Based Paradigm for Industry (New York: Free Press, 1992), p. 172.

59  Yang, "Nordstrom's Gang of Four," p. 122.

60  Ibid.

61  Ibid.

62  Ibid., p. 123.

63  Ibid.

64  This case is based on the following sources: Howard Rothman, "The Power of Empowerment," Nation's Business (June 1993): 49-52; Rob Brookler, "HR in Growing Companies," Personnel Journal (November 1992): 80A-O; Daniel Akst, "California & Co./Daniel Akst: Birkenstocks set trends all the way to bank," Los Angeles Times, October 6, 1992, p. 1; Barbara De Lollis, "Birkenstock CEO Answers the Call of the Foot-Weary," San Francisco Business Times September 18, 1992, p. 13.

65  Brookler, "HR in Growing Companies," p. 80G.

66  Rothman, "The Power of Empowerment," p. 49.

67  De Lollis, "Birkenstock CEO Answers the Call of the Foot-Weary," p. 13.

68  This case is based on the following sources: Cheryl Powell, "CEO Finds 'Empowerment' Pays: Cin-Made President, Once Barrier to Change, Evangelizes at Work-Force Summit," Cincinnati Enquirer, July 29, 1993, p. B9; Robert Frey, "The Empowered and the Glory: A Firm's Turbulent Turnaround; How Employees and Managers Became Reluctant Saviors," The Washington Post, December 26, 1993, p. H1; Mark Memmott, "Clinton Listens to Firms That Work," USA Today, July 27, 1993, p. 2B. In addition, the accompanying video is World News Tonight with Peter Jennings, July 26, 1993.

69  Frey, "The Empowered and the Glory," p. H1.

70  Memmott, "Clinton Listens to Firms That Work," p. 2B.

71  Frey, "The Empowered and the Glory," p. H1.

72  Ibid.

73  Ibid.

74  Ibid.

75  Memmott, "Clinton Listens to Firms That Work," p. 2B.

76  Frey, "The Empowered and the Glory," p. H1.

77  Ibid.

78  Powell, "CEO Finds 'Empowerment' Pays," p. B9.

79  Memmott, "Clinton Listens to Firms That Work," p. 2B.

80  Powell, "CEO Finds 'Empowerment' Pays," p. B9.

## CHAPTER 14

1  This case is based on the following sources: Akio Morita, Made in Japan (New York: E.P. Dutton, 1986); Joel Kotkin, "Japan's New Face," Inc., October 1990; Tom Peters, "Goal of Employment Security for a Lifetime Is Out of Sync with the Times," Chicago Tribune, October 1, 1990, Sect. 4, p. 6; "Mickey Schulhof: Sony's American Ninja," Forbes, December 7, 1992, pp. 50-51; Paul Helou, "Michael P. Schulhof," Chief Executive (May 1993): 18-20; Joanna Smith Bers, "On-Site Dining Fattens Company Coffers," Facilities Design & Management (October 1992): 50-7.

2  Morita, Made in Japan, p. 130.

3   Helou, "Michael P. Schulhof," p. 20.

4   Cynthia A. Lengnick-Hall and Mark L. Lengnick-Hall, "Strategic Human Resources Management: A Review of the Literature and a Proposed Typology," Academy of Management Review 3, no. 3 (1988): 454-70.

5   Michael J. Major, "Sun Sets Pace in Work Force Diversity," Public Relations Journal 49, no. 6 (June 1993): 12.

6   Ibid., p. 13.

7   Ibid., p. 32.

8   Stephen C. Hanson and Jeffrey D. Fagot, "Developing a Human Resources Plan," Trustee 45, no. 7 (July 1992): 10.

9   Peggy Stuart, "HR and Operations Work Together at Texas Instruments," Personnel Journal 71, no. 4 (April 1992): 64.

10  See Edwin L. Miller; Elmer H. Burack, and Maryann H. Albrecht, Management of Human Resources (Englewood Cliffs, N.J.: Prentice Hall, 1980); and Burckhardt Wenzel, "Planning for Manpower Utilization," Personnel Administrator 15, no. 3 (May-June 1970): 36-40. For an example, see John W. Boroski, "Putting It Together: HR Planning in '3D' at Eastman Kodak," Human Resource Planning 13, no. 1 (1990): 45-57.

11  See John B. Miner and Mary G. Miner, Personnel and Industrial Relations, 3rd ed. (New York: Macmillan, 1977); Richard M. Coffina, "Management Recruitment Is a Two-Way Street," Personnel Journal 58, no. 2 (February 1979): 86-9; and John P. Wanous, Organizational Entry: Recruitment, Selection, and Socialization of Newcomers (Reading, Mass.: Addison-Wesley, 1980).

12  "Front-line' Staff Selected by Assessment Centre," Personnel Management 25, no. 11 (November 1993): 83.

13  Ibid.

14  Tom Owens, "New Approach to Hiring," Small Business Reports 15, no. 10 (October 1990): 39-40.

15  Ibid., p. 40.

16  Ibid., p. 41.

17  Ibid., p. 47.

18  William Serrin, "Experts Say Job Bias Against Women Persists," The New York Times, November 25, 1984, pp. A1, A32; Madeline E. Heilman, Caryn J. Block, Michael Simon, and Richard F. Martell, "Has Anything Changed? Current Characterizations of Men, Women, and Managers," Journal of Applied Psychology 74, no. 6 (1990): 935-42.

19  Patricia Feltez, Robert K. Robinson, and Ross L. Fink, "American Female Expatriates and the Civil Rights Act of 1991: Balancing Legal and Business Interests," Business Horizons, March-April 1993, pp. 82-85.

20  See Ann Weaver Hart, "Intent vs. Effect: Title VII Case Law That Could Affect You (Part I)," Personnel Journal 63, (1984): 31-47; and Hart, "Intent vs. Effect: Title VII Case Law That Could Affect You (Part II)," Personnel Journal 63 (1984): 50-58.

21  Kenneth L. Otto, "Integrated Leadership: Tenneco Breaks the Barriers," Human Resources Professional 4, no. 2 (Winter 1992): 51-4.

22  Diane Filipowski, "Breaking Glass at Penney's," Personnel Journal 72, no. 12 (December 1993): 54.

23  Ibid.

24  See George Ritzer and David Walczak, Working: Conflict and Change, 3rd ed. (Englewood Cliffs, N.J.: Prentice Hall, 1986), pp. 104-106; John B. Golper, "The Current Legal Status of 'Comparable Worth,' in the Federal Sector," Labor Law Journal 34 (1983): 563-580; Golper, Pay Equity and Comparable Worth (Washington, D.C.: Bureau of National Affairs, 1984), pp. 13-34; and Marsha Katz, Helen Laven, and Maura Malloy, "Comparable Worth: Analysis of Cases and Implications for Human Resource Management," Compensation and Benefits Review, May-June 1986, pp. 26-38.

25  Bradford A. McKee, "A Troubling Bill for Business," Nation's Business, May 190, pp. 58-59; Helen Dewar, "Senate Approves Disabled Rights Bill," The Washington Post, July 14, 1990, pp. A1, A7; Len Strazewski, "Pcs Level Field for Disabled," Crain's Chicago Business, June 11, 1990, pp. T1, T2.

26  Meg Fletcher, "ADA Cutting Some Costs," Business Insurance 27, no. 31 (July 26, 1993): 20.

27  Ibid., p. 21.

28  Grace Wagner, "Taking a Lead on ADA," Lodging Hospitality 49, no. 11 (October 1993): 48.

29  Our discussion of equal employment opportunity and affirmative action issues derives from Terry L. Leap, William H. Holley, Jr., and Hubert S. Field, "Equal Employment Opportunity and Its Implications for Personnel Practices in the 1980s," Labor Law Journal 31, no. 11 (November 1980): 669-82; and Francine S. Hall and Maryann H. Albrecht, The Management of Affirmative Action (Santa Monica, Calif.: Goodyear, 1979), pp. 1-23. See also David P. Twomey, A Concise Guide to Employment Law (Cincinnati: South-Western, 1986).

30  Leap, Holley, and Field, "Equal Employment Opportunity," pp. 677-79. See also Bette Ann Stead, Women in Management (Englewood Cliffs, N.J.: Prentice Hall, 1978). Attitudes toward women in an organization might be assessed using the MATWES scale in Peter Dubno, John Costas, Hugh Cannon, Charles Wankel, and Hussein Emin, "An Empirically Keyed Scale for Measuring Managerial Attitudes Toward Women Executives," Psychology of Women Quarterly 3, no. 4 (Summer, 1979): 357-64.

31  Leap, Holley, and Field, "Equal Employment Opportunity," p. 671. See also Richard A. Fear and James F. Ross, Jobs, Dollars, and EEO (New York: McGraw-Hill, 1983).

32  Hall and Albrecht, The Management of Affirmative Action, pp. 9-10. See, for example, David A. Thomas, "Mentoring and Irrationality: The Role of Racial Taboos," Human Resource Management 28, no. 2 (Summer 1989): 279-90.

33  School Board of Nassau County v. Airline, No. 85-1277 (1987).

34  See "Privacy," Business Week, March 28, 1988, pp. 61-8; Craig Mellon, "The Dope on Drug Testing," Human Resource Executive 2, no. 4 (1988): 34-7; and Jeffrey Rothfeder, "Looking for a Job? You May Be Out Before You Go In," Business Week, September 24, 1990, pp. 128, 130.

35  Ibid.

36  Ibid.

37  Wendell L. French, The Personnel Management Process, 5th ed. (Boston: Houghton Mifflin, 1982).

38  See Robert E. Carlson, Donald P. Schwab, and Herbert G. Heneman III, "Agreement Among Selection Interview Styles," Journal of Industrial Psychology 5, no. 1 (March 1970): 8-17.

39  See Wanous, Organizational Entry, and S. L. Premack and Wanous, "A Meta-Analysis of Realistic Job Preview Experiments," Journal of Applied Psychology 70 (1985): 706-19.

40  Philip Schofield, "Improving the Candidate Job-Match," Personnel Management (February 1993): 69.

41  See Frank Malinowski, "Job Selection Using Task Analysis," Personnel Journal 60, no. 4 (April 1981): 288-91.

42  See, for example, Earl R. Gomersall and M. Scott Myers, "Breakthrough in On-the-Job Training," Harvard Business Review 44, no. 4 (July-August 1066): 62-72. See also Gareth R. Jones, "Organizational Socialization as Information Processing Activity: A Life History Analysis," Human Organization 42, no. 4 (1983): 314-20.

43  For studies of the relationship between early job experience and subsequent job performance and career progress, see David E. Berlew and Douglas T. Hall, "The Socialization of Managers," Administrative Science Quarterly 11, no. 2 (September 1966): 207-223; also James A. F. Stoner, John D. Aram, and Irwin M Rubin, "Factors Associated with Effective Performance in Overseas Work Assignments," Personnel Psychology 25, no. 2 (Summer 1972): 303-318. See also Morgan W. McCall, Jr., "Developing Executives Through Work Experiences," Human Resource Planning 11, no. 1 (1988): 1-11.

44  National Research Council, Work and Family: Policies for a Changing Work Force, ed. Marianne A. Ferber and Brigid O'Farrell (Washington, D.C.: National Academy Press, 1991), p. 2.

45  Craig Steinburg, "Taking Training for Granite," Training & Development 47, no. 2 (February 1993): 8.

46  Dennis L. Dossett and Patti R. Hulvershorn, "Increasing Technical Training Efficiency: Peer Training via Computer-Assisted Instruction," Journal of Applied Psychology 68, no. 4 (November 1983): 552-558; Stephen Schwade, "Is It Time to Consider Computer-Based Training?" Personnel Administrator 30, no. 2 (February 1985): 25-8; and William C. Heck, "Computer-Based Training—The Choice Is Yours," Personnel Administrator 30, no. 2 (February 1985): 39-48.

47  George T. Milkovich and William F. Glueck, Personnel: Human Resource Management 4th ed. (Plano, Tex.: Business Publications, 1985), pp. 72-3.

48  Edward B. Fiske, "Blooming Corporate Education Efforts Rival College Programs, Study Says," The New York Times, January 28, 1985, p. A10.

49  Michael Wellin, "Delivering the Goods on Customer Care," Personnel Management, March 1993, pp. 34-7.

50  Jennifer Reingold, "Prudential Insurance," Financial World 162, no. 19 (September 28, 1993): 60.

2   Huey, "America's Most Successful Merchant," p. 50.

3   Ibid., p. 47.

4   Ibid., p. 50.

5   Ibid., p. 54.

6   Ibid.

7   Ibid.

8   Neuborne, "Walton Dies: Built 1 Store into Wal-Mart," p. 1A.

9   F. Landy and W. Becker, "Motivation Theory Reconsidered." In L. Cummings and B. Staw (eds.), Research in Organizational Behavior, vol. 9 (Greenwich, CT: JAI Press, 1987): p. 4.

10  Jack Stack, "The Great Game of Business," INC., June 1992, pp. 52-62.

11  Any discussion of motivation, performance, and satisfaction in the workplace is in fact a discussion of industrial/organizational (I/O) psychology—the general study of organizational behavior with an emphasis on behavior in the workplace. This field of study was introduced by the German psychologist Hugo Münsterberg in 1913, with his book Psychology and Industrial Efficiency. See the following: A. Anastasi, Fields of Applied Psychology, 2nd ed. (New York: McGraw-Hill, 1979); B.M. Staw, "Organizational Behavior: A Review and Reformulation of the Field's Outcome Variables," Annual Review of Psychology 35 (1984): 627-66; B. Schneider, "Organizational Behavior," Annual Review of Psychology 36 (1985): 573-611; Frank H. Landy, Psychology of Work Behavior, 3rd ed. (Homewood, Ill.: Dorsey, 1985); T. Peters and N. Austin, A Passion for Excellence: The Leadership Difference (New York: Random House, 1985). The complex variety of principles established by I/O psychologists informs Thomas J. Peters and Robert H. Waterman's In Search of Excellence (New York: Harper & Row, 1082), pp. 55-7, 80-1. For a major part of our discussion on motivation, we are deeply indebted to Richard M. Steers and Lyman W. Porter, eds., Motivation and Work Behavior, 3rd ed., (New York: McGraw-Hill, 1983); and to Lyman W. Porter and Raymond E. Miles, "Motivation and Management," in Joseph W. McGuird, ed., Contemporary Management: Issues and Viewpoints (Englewood Cliffs, N.J.: Prentice Hall, 1974), pp. 545-70.

12  Landy and Becker, "Motivation Theory Reconsidered," p. 7.

13  Ibid., p. 2.

14  Douglas McGregor, The Human Side of Enterprise (New York: McGraw-Hill, 1960); and The Professional Manager (New York: McGraw-Hill, 1967).

15  Landy and Becker, "Motivation Theory Reconsidered," pp. 1-38.

16  Ibid., pp. 7-8. These processes are commonly called "cognitive processes."

17  See Abraham H. Maslow, Motivation and Personality, 2nd ed. (New York: Harper & Row, 1970), pp. 35-58.

18  This section is based on the following sources: Bill Stack, "Jobs Available: Homeless and Seniors Encouraged to Apply," Management Review 78 (August 1989): 13-6; Leslie Whitaker, "Helping Them Help Themselves," Time, February 26, 1990, p. 56; Fara Chideya, "The Kindness of Strangers," Newsweek, August 12, 1990, p. 48.

19  See Ellen L. Betz, "Two Tests of Maslow's Theory of Need Fulfillment," Journal of Vocational Behavior 24, no. 2 (April 1984): 204-20; and Howard S. Schwartz, "Maslow and the Hierarchical Enactment of Organizational Reality," Human Relations 36, no. 10 (October 1983): 933-56.

20  Geert Hofstede, "Motivation, Leadership, and Organization: Do American Theories Apply Abroad?" Organizational Dynamics, Summer 1980, pp. 42-63; Hofstede and Michael Harris Bond, "The Confucius Connection: From Cultural Norms to Economic Growth," Organizational Dynamics (Spring 1988): 5-21; Joe R. Feagin, Racial and Ethnic Relations, 2nd ed. (Englewood Cliffs, N.J.: Prentice Hall, 1984), Chap. 9.

21  J. Lublin, "Survivors of Layoffs Battle Against Anger, Hurting Productivity," Wall Street Journal, December 6, 1993, pp. A1, A16.

22  C.P. Alderfer, "An Empirical Test of a New Theory of Human Needs," Organizational and Human Needs 4 (1969): 142-75, and Existence, Relatedness, and Growth: Human Needs in Organizational Settings (New York: Free Press, 1972).

23  J. Rauschenberger, N. Schmitt, and J.E. Hunter, "A Test of the Need Hierarchy Concept by a Markov Model of Change in Need Strength," Administrative Science Quarterly 25 (1980): 654-70.

24  John W. Atkinson and David Birth, An Introduction to Motivation, rev. ed. (New York: Van Nostrand Reinhold, 1978), pp. 346-48; and John W. Atkinson, Personality, Motivation, and Action: Selected Papers (New York: Praeger, 1983), pp. 174-88.

25  David C. McClelland, The Achieving Society (Princeton, N.J.: Van Nostrand Reinhold, 1961), and "Business Drive and National Achievement," Harvard Business Review 40, no. 4 (July-August 1962): 99-112. Also see John G. Nicholls, "Achievement Motivation: Conceptions of Ability, Subjective Experience, Task Choice, and Performance," Psychological Review 91, no. 3 (July 1984): 328-46. For a good discussion of achievement motivation in work situations, see Edward E. Lawler III, Motivation in Work Organizations (Monterey, Calif.: Brooks/Cole, 1973), pp. 20-3.

26  Danny Miller, "The Correlates of Entrepreneurship in Three Types of Firms," Management Science 29, no. 7 (July 1983): 770-91.

27  See McClelland, "Business Drive and National Achievement," pp. 99-112; and Michael J. Stahl, "Achievement, Power and Managerial Motivation: Selecting Managerial Talent with the Job Choice Exercise," Personnel Psychology 36, no. 4 (Winter 1983): 775-89.

28  "The Care and Feeding of 'Love Eagles'" Business Week, November 15, 1993, p. 58.

29  See Leonard H. Chusmir, "Personnel Administrators' Perception of Six Differences in Motivation of Managers: Research-Based or Stereotyped?" International Journal of Women's Studies 7, no 1 (January-February 1984): 17-23; and Heinz-Dieter Schmalt, and Klaus Schneider, Achievement Motivation in Perspective (Orlando, Fla.: Academic Press, 1985).

30  Maureen Kearney, "A Comparison of Motivation to Avoid Success in Males and Females," Journal of Clinical Psychology 4, no. 4 (July 1984): 1005-7.

31  David C. McClelland, "Toward a Theory of Motive Acquisition," American Psychologist 20, no. 5 (May 1965): 321-33. Also see the interview with David C. McClelland in "As I See It," Forbes, June 1, 1969, pp. 53-7.

32  Frederick Herzberg, Bernard Mausner, and Barbara Synderman, The Motivation to Work (New York: Wiley, 1959). See also Frederick Herzberg, Work and the Nature of Man (New York: World Publishing, 1966), and "One More Time: How Do You Motivate Employees?" Harvard Business Review 46, no. 1 (January-February 1968): 53-62. For a critique of this and other models, see James A. Lee, The Gold and Garbage in Management Theories (Athens: Ohio University Press, 1980).

33  Shari Caudron, "Keys to Starting a TQM Program," Personnel Journal, February 1993, p. 35.

34  J. Stacey Adams, "Toward an Understanding of Inequity," Journal of Abnormal and Social Psychology 67, no. 5 (November 1963): 422-36. See also Robert P. Vecchio, "Models of Psychological Inequity," Organizational Behavior and Human Performance 34, no. 2 (October 1984): 266-82.

35  Saporito, "David Glass Won't Crack Under Fire," p. 75.

36  Ibid., p. 80

37  Ibid.

38  Ibid.

39  Richard A. Cosier and Dan R. Dalton, "Equity Theory and Time: A Reformulation," Academy of Management Review 8, no. 2 (April 1983): 311-19.

40  Ellen E. Spragens, "Employees as Family," INC., December 1992, p. 31.

41  David A. Nadler and Edward E. Lawler III, "Motivation—a Diagnostic Approach," in J. Richard Hackman, Edward E. Lawler III, and Lyman W. Porter, eds., Perspectives on Behavior in Organizations (New York: McGraw-Hill, 1977), p. 27.

42  We thank an anonymous reviewer of a draft manuscript for sharing this thought with us.

43  Ibid.

44  Nadler and Lawler, "Motivation—A Diagnostic Approach." Here is where a process approach (six steps) follows logically from a content model (expectancy theory) of motivation. This is another example showing that the longstanding "content-process" distinction is optional.

45  Philip M. Podsakoff, William D. Tudor, Richard A. Grover, and Vandra L. Huber, "Situational Moderators of Leader Reward and Punishment Behaviors: Fact or Fiction?" Organizational Behavior and Human Performance 34, no. 1 (August 1984): 21-63.

46  V. Alonzo, "The Wrath of Kohn," Incentive (September, 1993): 100-4.

47  The original formulation of the law of effect was based on years of animal experiments by Edward L. Thorndike and appeared in Animal Intelligence (New York: Macmillan, 1911), p. 244.

48  Landy and Becker, "Motivation Theory Reconsidered," pp. 2, 11-14.

49  See, for example, B.F. Skinner, Beyond Freedom and Dignity (New York: Alfred A. Knopf, 1971).

50 Herbert Lefcourt, Locus of Control: Current Trends in Theory and Research (Hillsdale, N.J.: Erlbaum, 1976); D.C. Glass, B. Rein, and J.E. Singer, "Behavioral Consequences of Adaptation to Controllable and Uncontrollable Noise," Journal of Experimental Social Psychology 7 (1971): 244-57; D.C. Glass, J.E. Singer, and L.N. Friedman, "Psychic Cost of Adaptation to an Environmental Stressor," Journal of Personality and Social Psychology 12 (1969): 200-10; D.C. Glass, J.E. Singer, H.S. Leonard, D. Krantz, S. Cohen, and H. Cummings, "Perceived Control of Aversive Stimulation and the Reduction of Stress Responses," Journal of Personality 41 (1973): 577-95; Tom Peters and Robert Waterman, In Search of Excellence (New York: Harper & Row, 1982).

51 E.A. Locke, K.N. Shaw, L.M. Saari, and G.P. Latham, "Goal Setting and Task Performance, 1969-1980," Psychological Bulletin 90 (1981): 125-52; and Frank J. Landy, Psychology of Work Behavior, 3rd ed. (Homewood, Ill.: Dorsey, 1985).

52 P.C. Earley and C. Shalley, "New Perspectives on Goals and Performance: Merging Motivation and Cognition." In G. Ferris and K. Rowland (eds.), Research in Personnel and Human Resources Management, vol. 9 (Greenwich, Conn.: JAI Press, 1991): pp. 121-26.

53 James C. Naylor and Daniel R. Ilgen, "Goal Setting: A Theoretical Analysis of a Motivational Technique," in Research in Organizational Behavior, vol. 6, B.M. Staw and L.L. Cummings, eds. (Greenwich, Conn.: JAI Press, 1984), pp. 95-140.

54 Miriam Erez, P.C. Earley, and C.L. Hulin, "The Impact of Participation on Goal Acceptance and Performance: A Two-Step Model," Academy of Management Journal 28 (1985): 50-66.

55 W. Safire, Safire's New Political Dictionary: The Definitive Guide to the New Language of Politics, (New York: Random House, 1993), p. 279. Safire traces the term to a 1930 book by Winston Churchill.

56 S. Ratan, "Why Busters Hate Boomers," Fortune, October 4, 1993, pp. 56-70.

57 Ibid., p. 57. See also T. Murphy, "Boomers, Busters, and 50-Plussers: Managing the new Generation Gaps," Working Woman (July 1991): 41-5.

58 S. Ratan, "Why Busters Hate Boomers," pp. 58, 62, 64, 70.

59 T. Murphy, "Boomers, Busters, and 50-Plussers," p. 43. See also M. Nies, "Baby Talk Helps Bridge Generation Gaps," IABC Communications World (December 1991): 27-9.

60 Saporito, "A Week Aboard the Wal-Mart Express," p. 77.

61 Ibid.

62 Ibid., p. 79.

63 Ibid.

64 Ibid., p. 84.

65 Ibid.

66 This case is based on the following sources: Kevin Doyle, "Lean & Mean," Incentive, January 1993, 28-33; "The Salvation Army: Driven by Mission and Service," Incentive, January 1993, p. 33; Gwen Kinkead and Patricia A. Langan, "America's Best-Run Charities," Fortune, November 9, 1987, p. 145; Pam Grout, "Helping the Homeless," Fund Raising Management (August 1991): 41-4.

67 Langan, "America's Best-Run Charities," p. 145.

68 Ibid.

69 Grout, "Helping the Homeless," p. 42.

70 Ibid.

71 "The Salvation Army: Driven by Mission and Service," p. 33.

72 Ibid.

73 Ibid.

74 This case is based on the following sources: Donna Brown Hogarty, "A Little Education Goes a Long Way," Management Review, June 1993, pp. 24-8; Jay Finegan, "The Education of Harry Featherstone," Inc., July 1990, pp. 57-60, 62, 66; Easy Klein, "Training Undereducated Workers," D&B Reports, May/June 1992, pp. 34-7. In addition, the accompanying video is "Look at Company Making Profits After Schooling Workers," ABC News: American Agenda, May 12, 1993.

75 Hogarty, "A Little Education Goes a Long Way," p. 25.

76 Finegan, "The Education of Harry Featherstone," p. 57.

77 Ibid.

78 Ibid, p. 58.

79 Ibid.

80 Hogarty, "A Little Education Goes a Long Way," p. 25.

81 Finegan, "The Education of Harry Featherstone," p. 59.

82 Hogarty, "A Little Education Goes a Long Way," p. 26.

83 Ibid.

84 Ibid., p. 27.

85 Ibid.

CHAPTER 17

1 This case is based on the following sources: Russ Mitchell and Judith H. Dobrzynski, "Jack Welch: How Good a Manager?" Business Week, December 14, 1987, p. 92; "Alfred Sloan, Move Over," Chief Executive, July/August 1993; John Holusha, "A Call for Kinder Managers at GE," New York Times, March 9, 1992; "Jack Welch's Lesson For Success," Fortune, January 25, 1993; Louis Wallis, "Welch's Juice," Across the Board, April 1993.

2 Mitchell and Dobrzynski, "Jack Welch: How Good a Manager?" p. 92.

3 Wallis, "Welch's Juice," p. 57.

4 Bernard M. Bass, Stogdill's Handbook of Leadership: A Survey of Theory and Research, 3rd ed. (New York: Free Press, 1990), p.7. For a thorough review of recent theory, see Gary Yukl, "Managerial Leadership: A Review of Theory and Research," Journal of Management 15, no. 2 (1989): 251-89.

5 John R.P. French and Bertram Raven, "The Bases of Social Power," in Dorwin Cartwright, ed., Studies in Social Power (Ann Arbor: University of Michigan, 1959), pp. 150-67. See also Dennis A. Gioia and Henry P. Sims, Jr., "Perceptions of Managerial Power as a Consequence of Managerial Behavior and Reputation," Journal of Management 9, no. 1 (Fall 1983): 7-26; and Edwin P. Hollander, "Leadership and Power," in Gardner Lindzey and Elliot Aronson, eds., Handbook of Social Psychology, 3rd ed. (New York: Random House, 1985), Chapter 9. For a recent summary of research, see Gary Yukl, Leadership in Organization, 3rd ed., Englewood Cliffs: Prentice Hall, 1994.

6 James McGregor Burns, Leadership (New York: Harper & Row, 1978).

7 Michael Josephson, as interviewed by Bill Moyers in A World of Ideas (New York: Doubleday, 1989), pp. 15-16.

8 Warren Bennis and B. Nane, Leaders: The Strategy for Taking Charge (New York: Harper & Row, 1985).

9 Robert J. House and Mary L. Baetz, "Leadership: Some Empirical Generalizations and New Research Directions," in Barry M. Staw, ed., Research in Organizational Behavior, vol. 1 (Greenwich, Conn.: JAI Press, 1979), pp. 348-54; David A. Kenny and Stephen J. Zaccaro, "An Estimate of Variance Due to Traits in Leadership," Journal of Applied Psychology 68, no. 4 (November 1983): 678-685; Ralph M. Stogdill, "Personal Factors Associated with Leadership: A Survey of the Literature," Journal of Psychology 25, no. 1 (January 1948): 35-71; R.D. Mann, "A Review of the Relationships Between Personality and Performance in Small Groups," Psychological Bulletin 56, no. 4 (July 1959): 241-70; and Howard M. Weiss and Seymour Adler, "Personality and Organizational Behavior," Research in Organizational Behavior 6 (1984): 1-50.

10 See Edwin E. Ghiselli, Explorations in Managerial Talent (Pacific Palisades, Calif.: Goodyear, 1971), pp. 39-56.

11 See Dorwin Cartwright and Alvin Zander, eds., Group Dynamics, 3rd ed. (New York: Harper & Row, 1968).

12 Natalie Porter, Florence Lindauer Geis, and Joyce Jennings, "Are Women Invisible Leaders?" Sex Roles 9, no. 10 (October 1983): 1035-49; Robert W. Rice, Debra Instone, and Jerome Adams, "Leader Sex, Leader Success, and Leadership Process: Two Field Studies," Journal of Applied Psychology 69, no. 1 (February 1984): 12-31; and Susan M. Donnell and Jay Hall, "Men and Women as Managers: A Significant Case of No Significant Difference," Organizational Dynamics 8, no. 4 (Spring 1980): 60-77.

13 Ellie McGrath, "Esprit the Sequel," Working Woman, September 1991, p. 66.

14 Ibid.

15 Ibid.

16 Colin Leinster, "Black Executives: How They're Doing," Fortune, January 18, 1988, pp. 109-20.

17 Elizabeth Lesly and Maria Mallory, "Inside the Black Business Network," Business Week, November 29, 1993, pp. 70-81.

18 Charles Burck, "The real world of the entrepreneur," Fortune, April 5, 1993, p. 76.

19 Ibid.

20 See Robert F. Bales, Interaction Process Analysis (Reading, Mass.: Addison-Wesley, 1951). A more recent study that found contrary evidence is C. Roger Rees and Mady Wechsler Segal, "Role

31 James A. Belasco, "Teaching the Elephant to Dance," Success (July-August 1990): 50-1.

32 James R. Idstein, "Small Company TQM," Management Accounting 75, no. 3 (September 1993): 39.

33 Ibid.

34 Sears, Freedman, and Peplau, Social Psychology, pp. 356-57. See also Robert S. Feldman, Social Psychology: Theories, Research, and Applications (New York: McGraw-Hill, 1985); and Steven Penrod, Social Psychology, 2nd ed. (Englewood Cliffs, N.J.: Prentice Hall, 1986).

35 John C. Whitney and Ruthu A. Smith, "Effects of Group Cohesiveness on Attitude Polarization and the Acquisition of Knowledge in a Strategic Planning Context," Journal of Marketing Research 20, no. 2 (1983): 167-76.

36 Risa B. Hyman, "Creative chaos in high-performance teams: An experience report," Communications of the ACM 36, no. 10 (October 1993): 59.

37 A. Nicholas Komanecky, "Developing New Managers at GE," Training and Development Journal 42, no. 6 (1988): 62-4.

38 Susan Moffat, "Can Nintendo Keep Winning?" Fortune, November 5, 1990, pp. 131-36.

39 "Many Happy Returns," Inc., October 1990, pp. 30-43.

40 David L. Kirp and Douglas C. Rice, "Fast Forward- Styles of California Management," Harvard Business Review 66, no. 1 (1988): 74-83.

41 Henry Easton, "The Corporate Immigrants," Nation's Business (April 1987): 12-9.

42 Gregory P. Shea and Richard A. Guzzo, "Groups as Human Resources," Research in Personnel and Human Resources Management 5 (1987): 323-56; Shea and Guzzo, "Group Effectiveness: What Really Matters," Sloan Management Review 27 (Spring 1987): 25-31. Shea and Guzzo's model is a natural and more modern extension of the classical work of George Homans.

43 Belasco, "Teaching the Elephant to Dance," pp. 50-51.

44 Geert Hofsteede, "Motivation, Leadership, and Organization: Do American Theories Apply Abroad?", Organizational Dynamics, Summer 1980, pp. 45-48.

45 James O'Toole, "The Good Managers of Sichuan," Harvard Business Review, May-June 1981, p. 30.

46 Craig Haney, Philip Zimbardo, and W. Curtis Banks, "Interpersonal Dynamics in a Simulated Prison," International Journal of Criminology and Penology 1 (1973): 69-97; Molly Harrower, "Were Hitler's Henchmen Mad?" Psychology Today (July 1976): 76-80; and Janice T. Gibson and Mika Haritos-Fatouros, "The Education of a Torturer," Psychology Today (November 1986): 50-8.

47 Gibson and Haritos-Fatouros, "The Education of a Torturer," p. 50.

48 Ibid.

49 Harrower, "Were Hitler's Henchmen Mad?"

50 Haney et al, "Interpersonal Dynamics in a Simulated Prison."

51 Rollie Tillman, Jr., "Committees on Trial," Harvard Business Review 48, no. 4 (1960): 6-7ff.

52 Cyril O'Donnell, "Ground Rules for Using Committees," Management Review 50, no. 10 (1961): 63-7. See also Anthony Jay, "How to Run a Meeting."

53 Ron Zemke, "Scandinavian Management-A Look to the Future," Management Review 77, no. 7 (1988): 44-7; Kalmar: Ten Years Later," Via Volvo, vol. 6 (1984): 14-9; Pehr G. Gyllenhammar, People at Work (Reading, Mass.: Addison-Wesley, 1977).

54 Jon R. Katzenbach and Douglas K. Smith, The Wisdom of Teams: Creating the High-Performance Organization (Boston: Harvard Business School Press, 1993).

55 Ibid., p. 3.

56 Ibid., pp. 230-4.

57 Kenwyn K. Smith and David N. Berg, Paradoxes of Group Life (San Francisco: Jossey-Bass, 1987); and Smith and Berg, "A Paradoxical Conception of Group Dynamics," Human Relations 40, no. 10 (1987): 633-58.

58 This feature is based on the following sources: Stratford Sherman, "A Brave New Darwinian Workplace," Fortune, January 25, 1993, pp. 50-56; Noel M. Tichy, "Revolutionize Your Company," Fortune, December 13, 1993, pp. 114-118; Charles Handy, The Age of Paradox (Boston: Harvard Business School Press, 1994), p. 165; Amy Borrus, Joyce Barnathan, Bruce Einhorn, and Stewart Toy, "China's Gates Swing Open," Business Week, June 13, 1994, pp. 52-53; Joan E. Rigdon, "Silicon Graphics Plans to Unveil Pact with NTT," The Wall Street Journal, June 8, 1994, p. B6.

59 Stratford Sherman, "A Brave New Darwinian Workplace," Fortune, January 25, 1993, pp. 50-51.

60 Ibid., p. 52.

61 Lee, "The Vision Thing," p. 31.

62 Ibid.

63 Geber, "Saturn's Grand Experiment," p. 33.

64 Doyle, "Can Saturn Save GM?" p. 32.

65 Geber, "Saturn's Grand Experiment," p. 33.

66 This case was written by Rebecca Villa and R. Edward Freeman and based on actual situations. It was prepared especially for this book.

67 This case is based on the following sources: Sue Ellen Christian, "Companies on Violence Alert; Rise in Work Incidents Rattles Firms Into Prevention," Chicago Tribune, April 14, 1994, p. D1; Julie Irwin and Jahan Hanna, "Executive's Stabbing a Puzzle," Chicago Tribune, April 14, 1994, p. NW1; Julie Irwin, Sue Ellen Christian, and Andrew Martin, "Business Meeting Deadly Affair; Aide Held in Exec's Death at Home," Chicago Tribune, April 13, 1994, p. D1; Diana Kunde, "Defusing Violence in the Workplace; Experts Offer Strategies for Dealing With Growing Problem," The Dallas Morning News, January 19, 1994, p. 1D; Greg Pierce, "Postal Service Looks at Violence on Job," Washington Times, December 17, 1993, p. A13. In addition, the accompanying video is "Assembly Line Teams are Better Trained and More Efficient," ABC News: World News Tonight, February 24, 1993.

68 Pierce, "Postal Service Looks at Violence on Job," p. A13.

69 Irwin, Christian, and Martin, "Business Meeting Deadly Affair," p. D1.

70 Irwin and Hanna, "Executive's Stabbing a Puzzle," p. NW1.

71 Christian, "Companies on Violence Alert," p. D1.

72 Pierce, "Postal Service Looks at Violence on Job," p. A13.

73 Christian, "Companies on Violence Alert," p. D1.

## CHAPTER 19

1 This case is based on the following sources: John Hillkirk, "More Companies Reengineering/ Challenging status quo now in vogue," USA Today, November 9, 1993, p. 18; Irvine O. Hockaday, Jr., "The Lamplighter CEO," Chief Executive (March 1993): 30-3; Karen Matthes, "Greetings from Hallmark," HR Focus (August 1993): 12-3; Jenell Wallace, U.P.I., September 29, 1991; Mary Billard, "The Executive Life; A Hidden Upside In All the Downsizing," New York Times, October 27, 1991, p. 25; R. Levering & M. Moskowitz, "The Ten Best Companies to Work For in America," Business & Society Review (Spring 1993): pp. 26-38; K. Matthes, "Greetings from Hallmark," HRFocus (August 1993): 12-3.

2 Hockaday, "The Lamplighter CEO," p. 31.

3 Hillkirk, "More Companies Reengineering/ Challenging Status Quo," p. 18.

4 Ibid.

5 Ibid.

6 Ibid.

7 Fred Luthans and Janet K. Larsen, "How Managers Really Communicate," Human Relations 39 (1986): 161-78.

8 Rosemary Stewart, Managers and Their Jobs (London: Macmillan, 1967), pp. 72-3.

9 F.E.X. Dance, "The 'Concept' of Communication," Journal of Communication 20, no. 2 (1970): 201-10.

10 Lyman W. Porter and Karlene H. Roberts, "Communication in Organizations," in Marvin D. Dunnett, ed., Handbook of Industrial and Occupational Psychology, 2nd ed. (New York: Wiley, 1983), pp. 1553-589.

11 See Paul R. Timm and Christopher G. Jones, Business Communication: Getting Results (Englewood Cliffs, N.J.: Prentice Hall, 1983), p. 5.

12 Larry R. Smeltzer and John L. Waltman, Managerial Communication: A Strategic Approach (New York: Wiley, 1984), pp. 4, 5, 41.

13 See James L. Gibson, John M. Ivancevich, and James H. Donnelly Jr., Organizations: Behavior, Structure, Processes, 5th ed. (Dallas: Business Publications, 1985), p. 535.

14 Smeltzer and Waltman, Managerial Communication, p. 189.

15 C. Glenn Pearce, Ross Figgins, and Steven P. Golen, Principles of Business Communication: Theory, Application, and Technology (New York: John Wiley, 1984), pp. 516, 538.

16  Ibid., p. 524.

17  Shari Caudron, "Training Ensures Success Overseas," Personnel Journal, December 1991, p. 29.

18  Pearce et al., Principles of Communication, pp. 522-23.

19  Ibid., pp. 522, 524.

20  Dawn Gunsch, "Multilingual Communication Sells 401(k)," Personnel Journal 72, no. 11 (November 1993): 45.

21  "Productivity's Defined at World Book," Modern Office Technology (March 1992): 20.

22  R. Buck, The Communication of Emotion (New York: Guilford Press, 1984). For a discussion of how nonverbal behavior communicates such messages as sympathy, threat, or status, see A.W. Siegman and S. Feldstein, Multichannel Integrations of Nonverbal Behavior (Hillsdale, N.J.: Erlbaum, 1985). Nonverbal cues can also contribute to turn-taking during communication; see C.L. Kleinke, "Gaze and Eye Contact: A Research Review," Psychological Bulletin 100 (1986): 78-100.

23  W. Charles Redding, The Corporate Manager's Guide to Better Communication (Glenview, Ill.: Scott Foresman, 1984), pp. 74-5.

24  H. Simon, Administrative Behavior, (New York: Free Press, 1945).

25  Hockaday, "The Lamplighter CEO," p. 32.

26  Matthes, "Greetings from Hallmark," p. 12.

27  Ibid.

28  Ibid., p. 13.

29  Wallace, UPI.

30  Billard, "The Executive Life."

31  Bill Siwicki, "Communication, Mission Make Methodist One of '100 Best,'" Healthcare Financial Management, June 1993.

32  Yvetta Sunderland, "Communicating through Change; Planning the Launch of Argon Group Real Estate Strategists," Journal of Property Management, vol. 57, no. 5 (September 1992): 28.

33  David R. Altany, "Urban Renewal: More than a Matter of Money," Industry Week, January 4, 1993, pp. 29-30.

34  Joyce E. Santora, "Pacific Bell Primes the Quality Pump," Personnel Journal, October 1991, pp. 63-66.

35  See Raymond V. Lesikar, "A General Semantics Approach to Communication Barriers in Organizations," in Keith Davis, ed., Organizational Behavior: A Book of Readings, 5th ed. (New York: McGraw-Hill, 1977), pp. 336-37.

36  Dawn Gunsch, "Electronic Newspaper Keeps Employees Up-to-Date," Personnel Journal, April 1993.

37  Elizabeth Conlin, "The Vital Signs Assessment," Inc., April 1993.

38  Kenneth N. Wexley and Gary A. Yukl, Organizational Behavior and Personnel Psychology, rev. ed. (Homewood, Ill.: Irwin, 1984), pp. 80-3.

39  Joan E. Rigdon, "Tipsters Telephoning Ethics Hot Lines Can End Up Sabotaging Their Own Jobs," Wall Street Journal, August 27, 1992, p. B1.

40  Chris Slaybaugh, "David's presence enhanced at Ogilvy; Corporate Culture Machine keeps staff current," Advertising Age (August 22, 1988): S-12.

41  Michael J. Glauser, "Upward Information Flow in Organizations: Review and Conceptual Analysis," Human Relations 37, no. 8 (1984): 613-43.

42  Porter and Roberts, "Communication in Organizations," pp. 1573-574. See also Robert A. Snyder and James H. Morris, "Organizational Communication and Performance," Journal of Applied Psychology 69, no. 3 (1984): 461-65.

43  Lynn Sharp Paine, "Managing for Organizational Integrity," Harvard Business Review, March-April 1994, pp. 107-108.

44  James R. Wessel, "The Strategic Human Resource Management Process in Practice," Planning Review, September/October 1993.

45  Wexley and Yukl, Organizational Behavior and Personnel Psychology, pp. 82-3.

46  See also Robert E. Kaplan, "Trade Routes: The Manager's Network of Relationships," Organizational Dynamics 12, no. 4 (1984): 38-52; and Eric M. Eisenbert, Peter R. Monge, and Katherine I. Miller, "Involvement in Communication Networks as a Predictor of Organizational Commitment," Human Communication Research 10, no. 2 (1983): 179-201.

47  See Richard L. Simpson, "Vertical and Horizontal Communication in Formal Organizations," Administrative Science Quarterly 4, no. 2 (1959): 188-96.

48  Keith Davis, "Grapevine Communication Among Lower and Middle Managers," Personnel Journal 48, no. 4 (1969): 269-72. See also

Joe Thomas and Ricky Griffin, "The Power of Social Information in the Workplace," Organizational Dynamics 18, no. 2 (Autumn 1989): 63-75.

49  See Keith Davis, "Management Communication and the Grapevine," Harvard Business Review 31, no. 5 (1953): 43-9; "Communication Within Management," Personnel 31, no. 3 (November 1954): 212-18; and "Cut Those Rumors Down to Size," Supervisory Management (June 1975): 2-6.

50  John Glover, "Responsible Care: EniChem Addresses Its Poor Image," Chemical Week, July 1993.

51  Ellen Romano, "Retaining Tenants Against the Odds," Journal of Property Management, July/August 1992.

52  Karen Fawcett, "The (PR) Mouse That Roared—in Six Languages," Communication World, December 1991.

53  This section is based on Roy Lewicki and Joseph Litterer's book, Negotiation and Negotiator: Readings, Exercises, and Cases (Homewood, Ill.: Irwin, 1985).

54  L. Putnam, "Reframing Integrative and Distributive Bargaining: A Process Perspective," in B. Sheppard, M. Bazerman, and R. Lewicki, eds., Research on Negotiation in Organizations, Volume 2 (Greenwich, CT: JAI Press, 1990), pp. 3-5; and M. Neale and G. Northcraft, "Behavioral Negotiation Theory: A Framework for Conceptualizing Dyadic Bargaining," in L. Cummings and B. Staw, eds., Research in Organizational Behavior, vol. 13 (Greenwich, CT: JAI Press, 1991), pp. 147-90.

55  Ibid.

56  Ibid.

57  Ibid.

58  Mel Mandell, "Small Company Benefits from Corporate Castoffs," D&B Reports 42, no. 5 (September/October 1993): 50.

59  Ibid.

60  Ibid., p. 10.

61  M. Beschloss and S. Talbott, At the Highest Levels: The Inside Story of the End of the Cold War. (Boston: Little, Brown, 1993).

62  S. Coll, The Deal of the Century: The Break-up of AT&T (New York: Atheneum, 1986); and A. Von Auw, Heritage & Destiny: Reflections on the Bell System in Transition (New York: Praeger, 1983).

63  Coll, The Deal of the Century.

64  A. Dowd, "Let's Just Say Yes to NAFTA," Fortune, November 29, 1993, pp. 108-9.

65  Michael A. Verespej, "Bargaining in Layman's terms," Industry Week (February 15, 1993), p. 18.

66  Dennis Green and Casey Valdez, III. "Mutual-Gains Bargaining Assists Contract Negotiations," Personnel Journal (August 1993): 60.

67  Ibid.

68  Dan Cordtz, "Motown Showdown," Financial World, August 3, 1993, pp. 22-5.

69  Ibid.

70  Ibid.

71  Ibid.

72  Kathleen Morris, "Employee Retraining: Ford-AUW," Financial World, September 29, 1992, p. 47.

73  R. Lanham, "The Extraordinary Convergence: Democracy, Technology, Theory, and the University Curriculum," in D. Glenn and B.H. Smith, eds., The Politics of Liberal Education (Durham, N.C.: Duke University Press, 1992).

74  John R. Wilke, "Shop Talk: Computer Links Erode Hierarchial Nature of Workplace Culture," Wall Street Journal, December 9, 1993, pp. A1, A7.

75  Ibid.

76  Ibid., p. A7.

77  D. Kirkpatrick, "Groupware Goes Boom," Fortune, December 29, 1993, pp. 99-102, 106.

78  Wilke, "Computer Links Erode Hierarchial Nature of Workplace Culture," p. A1.

79  Ibid., p. A7.

80  D. Kirkpatrick, pp. 100-1.

81  Ibid., p. 100.

82  Wilke, "Computer Links Erode Hierarchial Nature of Workplace Culture," p. A7.

83  Ibid.

84  Ibid.

framework on the three-part division of managerial activities described by Robert N. Anthony in Planning and Control Systems (Boston: Harvard University Graduate School of Business Administration, 1965), pp. 15-21.

9   Charles R. Litecky, "Corporate Strategy and MIS Planning," Journal of Systems Management 32, no. 1 (January 1981): 36-9.

10  Suneel Ratan, "Why the Busters Hate the Boomers," Fortune, October 4, 1993, p. 58.

11  Brian O'Reilly, "Your New Global Workforce," Fortune, December 14, 1992, p. 64.

12  Our discussion in this section is based on G.W. Dickson and John K. Simmons, "The Behavioral Side of MIS," Business Horizons 13, no. 4 (August 1970): 59-71.

13  Dickson and Simmons, "The Behavioral Side of MIS," pp. 59-71.

14  Daniel Robey and M. Lynne Markus, "Rituals in Information System Design," MIS Quarterly 8, no. 1 (March 1984): 5-15; Michael Newman, "User Involvement—Does It Exist, Is It Enough?" Journal of Systems Management 35, no. 5 (1984): 34-8; and Blake Ives and Margrethe H. Olson, "User Involvement and MIS Success: A Review of Research," Management Science 30, no. 5 (May 1984): 586-603. Ives and Olson note there is a lack of research demonstrating the benefits of user participation, but they do suggest that participation is useful in unstructured situations and also in situations where user acceptance is important for MIS success.

15  Edwin B. Opliger, "Identifying Microcomputer Concerns," EDP Journal, no. 1 (1985): 42-67.

16  Paul E. Dascher and W. Ken Harmon, "The Dark Side of Small Business Computers," Management Account 65, no. 11 (May 1984): 62-7.

17  John F. Rockart and Lauren S. Flannery, "The Management of End-User Computing," Communications of the ACM 26, no. 10 (October 1983): 776-84.

18  Thomas E. Gallo, Strategic Information Management Planning (Englewood Cliffs, N.J.: Prentice Hall, 1988), p. 18.

19  Rockart and Flannery, "The Management of End-User Computing."

20  Steven Alter, in "A Taxonomy of Decision Support Systems," Sloan Management Review 19, no. 1 (Fall 1977): 39-59, describes seven different types of DSS, from systems that are heavily data-oriented to those that are heavily model-oriented. His taxonomy is based on the extent to which the system's outputs bear on decision making.

21  "Fourth-Generation Languages Make DSS Feasible for All Managers," Management Review 73, no. 4 (April 1984): 4-5.

22  Donald R. Wood, "The Personal Computer: How It Can Increase Management Productivity," Financial Executive 52, no. 2 (February 1984): 15.

23  Andrew T. Masland, "Integrators and Decision Support System Success in Higher Education," Research in Higher Education 20, no. 2 (1984): 211-33.

24  Hugh H. Watson and Marianne M. Hill, "Decision Support Systems or What Didn't Happen with MIS," Interfaces 13, no. 5 (October 1983): 81-8.

25  Jennifer E. Beaver, "Bend or Be Broken," Computer Decisions 16, no. 6 (1984): 43.

26  "What's Happening with DSS?" EDP Analyzer.

27  The discussion of expert systems is drawn mainly from Robert W. Blanning, "Knowledge Acquisition and System Validation in Expert Systems for Management," Human Systems Management 4, no. 4 (Autumn 1984): 280-85; Robert W. Blanning, "Expert Systems for Management: Possible Application Areas," Institute for Advancement of Decision Support Systems DSS-84 Transactions (1984): 69-77; and Robert W. Blanning, "Issues in the Design for Expert Systems for Management," Proceedings of the National Computer Conference (1984): 489-495.

28  Walter Reitman, "Artificial Intelligence Applications for Business: Getting Acquainted," in Walter Reitman, ed., Artificial Intelligence Applications for Business (Norwood, N.J.: Ablex Publishing, 1984), pp. 1-9. For an excellent discussion of AI, see Jeffrey Rothfelder, Minds Over Matter: A New Look at Artificial Intelligence (New York: Simon & Schuster, 1985). See also Karl W. Wiig, "AI: Management's Newest Tool," Management Review (August 1986): 24-8; and R. Kurzweil, "What Is Artificial Intelligence Anyway?" American Scientist 73 (1985): 258-64.

29  Michael W. Davis, "Anatomy of Decision Support," Datamation, June 15, 1985, pp. 201ff.

30  Kenneth Fordyce, Peter Norden, and Gerald Sullivan, "Review of Expert Systems for the Management Science Practitioner," Interfaces 17, no. 2 (March-April 1987): 64-77.

31  Robert C. Schank with Peter G. Childers, The Cognitive Computer: On Language, Learning and Artificial Intelligence (Reading, Mass.: Addison-Wesley, 1985), p. 33.

32  Jay Liebowitz, Introduction to Expert Systems (Santa Cruz, Cal.: Mitchell Publishing, 1988), pp. 3-21.

33  E. Andrews, "Ruling Frees Phone Concerns to Enter Cable TV Business," New York Times, August 25, 1993, pp. A1, D5; C. Farrell and M. Mandel, "What's Arriving on the Information Highway? Growth," Business Week, November 29, 1993, p. 40; "Calling All Channels," Business Week, September 27, 1993, pp. 130-38; E. Andrews, "When We Build It, Will They Come?" New York Times, October 17, 1993, Section 3, p. 5; C.E. Baker, "Tollbooths on the Information Superhighway," New York Times, October 26, 1993, p. A21; J. Huey and A. Kupfer, "What That Merger Means for You," Fortune, November 15, 1993, pp. 82-94; D. Clark, "Test Linking Pcs, Cable TV Lines To Be Slated by Several Big Firms," Wall Street Journal, December 1, 1993, p. B8; and A. Kupfer, "Look Ma! No Wires!" Fortune, December 13, 1993, pp. 147-52.

34  C. Sims, "The Uncertain Promises of Interactivity," New York Times, December 19, 1993, Section 3, p. 6.

35  Information is one resource in the emerging "resource dependence" view of strategic management.

36  These initial conflicts and stresses are described in Chris Argyris, "Management Information Systems: The Challenge to Rationality and Emotionality," Management Science 17, no. 6 (February 1971): B275-292.

37  Shelby Gilje, "Caller ID is Coming and in Some Ways is Already Here," Seattle Times, December 27, 1992, p. D15; "'Hello, Caller. You're on the Screen,'" Catalog Age, April 1993, p. 22.

38  Ibid.

39  Ibid.

40  This case is based on the following sources: G. Elsenstodt, "Information Power," Forbes, June 21, 1993, pp. 44-5; and W. Best, "Flexible Integrated Operations: The New Japanese Challenge," Planning Review (September-October, 1993): 49-50.

41  This case is based on the following sources: Kirk Johnson, "New Breed of High-Tech Nomads; Mobile Computer-Carrying Workers Transform Companies," New York Times, February 8, 1994, p. B1; Barbara J. Farrah and Cheryl D. Dagen, "Telecommuting Policies That Work," HRMagazine, July 1993, pp. 64-71; Shari Caudron, "Working at Home Pays Off," Personnel Journal, November 1992, pp. 40-9. In addition, the accompanying video case is "Technology in the Workplace, ABC News: Business World, March 28, 1993.

42  Johnson, "New Breed of High-Tech Nomads; Mobile Computer-Carrying Workers Transform Companies," p. B1.

43  Caudron, "Working at Home Pays Off," p. 40.

44  Ibid.

45  Ibid.

46  Ibid.

47  Ibid.

48  Ibid.

49  Johnson, "New Breed of High-Tech Nomads; Mobile Computer-Carrying Workers Transform Companies," p. B1.

# PHOTO CREDITS

**coaching** The training of an employee by his or her immediate supervisor, by far the most effective management development technique.

**coercive power** The negative side of reward power, based on the influencer's ability to punish the influencee.

**cohesiveness** The degree of solidarity and positive feelings held by individuals toward their group.

**collaborative management** Management through power sharing and subordinate participation; the opposite of hierarchical imposition of authority.

**collective bargaining** The process of negotiating and administering agreements between labor and management concerning wages, working conditions, and other aspects of the work environment.

**collective strategy** Occurs when people at different organizations collaborate to determine how organizations with common concerns will approach certain issues.

**command team** A team composed of a manager and the employees that report to that manager.

**committee** A formal organizational team, usually relatively long-lived, created to carry out specific organizational tasks.

**common morality** The body of moral rules governing ordinary ethical problems.

**communication** The process by which people attempt to share meaning via the transmission of symbolic messages.

**comparable worth** The principle that jobs requiring comparable skills and knowledge merit equal compensation even if the nature of the work activity is different.

**competitive benchmarking** The process of finding the best available product features, processes, and services and using them as a standard for improving a company's own products, processes, and services.

**competitiveness** The relative standing of one competitor against other competitors.

**competitive priorities** Four major criteria, including pricing, quality levels, quality reliability, and flexibility, on which products and services are evaluated.

**computer-assisted instruction (CAI)** A training technique in which computers are used to lessen the time necessary for training by instructors and to provide additional help to individual trainees.

**computer-based information systems (CBIS)** Information system that goes beyond the mere standardization of data to aid in the planning process.

**conceptual skill** The ability to coordinate and integrate all of an organization's interests and activities.

**conflict** Disagreement about the allocation of scarce resources or clashes regarding goals, values, and so on; can occur on the interpersonal or organizational level.

**confrontation meeting** A one-day meeting of all of an organization's managers in which they discuss problems, analyze the underlying causes, and plan remedial actions; typically used after a major organizational change, such as a merger or the introduction of a new technology.

**constancy of purpose** According to Deming, the view that an unwavering focus on an organization's mission of "continuously and forever" improving the quality of goods and services—combined with statistical quality control and achieving "joy in work"—is necessary for competitive survival.

**contingency approach** The view that the management technique that best contributes to the attainment of organizational goals might vary in different types of situations or circumstances; also called the situational approach.

**control** The process of ensuring that actual activities conform to planned activities.

**controlling** The process of ensuring that actual activities conform to planned activities.

**control system** Multistep procedure applied to various types of control activities.

**coordination** The integration of the activities of the separate parts of an organization to accomplish organizational goals.

**corporate-level strategy** Strategy formulated by top management to oversee the interests and operations of multiline corporations.

**corporate social performance** A single theory of corporate social action encompassing social principles, processes, and policies.

**corporate social responsibility** What an organization does to influence the society in which it exists, such as through volunteer assistance programs.

**corporate social responsiveness** A theory of social responsibility that focuses on how companies respond to issues, rather than trying to determine their ultimate social responsibility.

**corporate strategy** The idea about how people at an organization will interact with people at other organizations over time.

**cost argument** The argument that an organization's failure in managing multicultural issues results in higher costs, such as through the revolving door syndrome and having managers spend time and energy worrying about discrimination, harassment, and other issues instead of their jobs.

**cost-benefit model** A traditional approach to thinking about environmental solutions that says a proposed environmental regulation should be implemented if the potential benefits outweigh the potential costs.

**country club management** Management style characterized by high concern for employees but low concern for production; opposite of task or authoritarian management.

**creativity** The generation of a new idea.

**creativity argument** The argument that groups of people from diverse backgrounds can be more creative than groups with homogeneous backgrounds.

**critical incidents** Situations in which an employee displayed desirable or undesirable behavior.

**cultural relativism** The idea that morality is relative to a particular culture, society, or community.

**cultural system** The set of beliefs and the resulting behaviors that are shared throughout the organization; also called the social system.

**culture** The complex mixture of assumptions, behaviors, stories, myths, metaphors, and other ideas that fit together to define what it means to be a member of a particular society.

**current assets** Items such as cash, accounts receivable, marketable securities, and inventories—assets that could be turned into cash at a reasonably predictable value within a relatively short time period (typically, one year).

**current liabilities** Debts, such as accounts payable, short-term loans, and unpaid taxes, that will have to be paid off during the current fiscal period.

**D**

**dark green** Organizational approach to adopting environmental values that say we should live more in harmony with the earth; the environment should not be exploited for our own gain, particularly in non-renewable, non-sustainable fashions. This approach entails doing more than merely recycling; it generally involves taking an active role—such as through refusing to test products on animals—in protecting the environment.

**data** Raw, unanalyzed numbers and facts.

**decentralization** The delegation of power and authority from higher to lower levels of the organization, often accomplished by the creation of small, self-contained organizational units.

**decisional role** The type of role a person takes on when he or she enables a decision to be made, such as by discussing the allocation of resources.

**decision making** The process of identifying and selecting a course of action to solve a specific problem.

**decision support system (DSS)** Computer system accessible to nonspecialists to assist in planning and decision making.

**decoding** The interpretation and translation of a message into meaningful information.

**dedicated machines** Machines used to perform a specific task.

**delegation** The act of assigning formal authority and responsibility for completion of specific activities to a subordinate.

**democratic management** Management style characterized by a high concern for both production and employee morale and satisfaction; also called team management.

**departmentalization** The grouping into departments of work activities that are similar and logically connected.

**design for manufacture (DFM)** Technique that involves streamlining the design of products to simplify assembly.

**developmental program** A process designed to develop skills necessary for future work activities.

**devil's advocate method** A method of analysis in which a decision maker determines and negates his or her assumptions, and then creates "countersolutions" based on the negative assumptions; also called the dialectical inquiry method.

**dialectical inquiry method** A method of analysis in which a decision maker determines and negates his or her assumptions, and then creates "countersolutions" based on the negative assumptions; also called the devil's advocate method .

**differential rate system** Frederick W. Taylor's compensation system involving the payment of higher wages to more efficient workers.

**differentiation** Differences in attitudes and working styles, arising naturally among members of different departments, that can complicate the coordination of an organization's activities.

**direct-action elements** Elements of the environment that directly influence an organization's activities.

**direct investment** Investment in foreign assets whereby a company purchases assets that it manages directly.

**discipline** Actions taken when an employee violates company policy or falls short of work expectations, and managers must act to remedy the situation; it usually progresses through a series of steps—warning, reprimand, probation, suspension, disciplinary transfer, demotion, and discharge—until the problem is solved or eliminated.

**discretionary cost budget** Type of expense budget that is used for departments in which output cannot be accurately measured.

**dissatisfiers** According to the two-factor theory, the factors (which Herzberg called "hygiene" factors) that can inhibit work, such as salary, working conditions, and company policy—all of which are related to the context in which work is conducted.

**distributive process** Negotiation process in which each of the parties tends to seek maximum gains and wants to impose maximum losses on the other; also known as a win-lose situation or zero sum.

**division** Large organization department that resembles a separate business; may be devoted to making and selling specific products or serving a specific market.

**division of labor** The breakdown of a complex task into components so that individuals are responsible for a limited set of activities instead of the task as a whole. Often referred to as division of work.

**division of work** The breakdown of a complex task into components so that individuals are responsible for a limited set of activities instead of the task as a whole. Sometimes referred to as division of labor.

**dog** According to the portfolio framework, a business with a low relative market share in a slowly growing or stagnant market.

**downsizing** A version of organizational restructuring which results in decreasing the size of the organization and often results in a flatter organizational structure; one way organizations convert to leaner, more flexible structures that can respond more readily to the pace of change in global markets.

**downward mobility** A phenomenon referred to by Newman which describes the situation of many middle-level and upper-level managers whose jobs and departments and divisions have been eliminated and must therefore join the many non-managers whose jobs have disappeared due to restructuring.

**driving forces** According to Kurt Lewin's force-field theory, the forces that push for change.

**duties** Obligations to take specific steps or obey the law.

**dynamic engagement** The view that time and human relationships are forcing management to rethink traditional approaches in the face of constant, rapid change.

**E**

**earnings gap** The discrepancy between the earning power of workers of similar educational backgrounds but different races.

**economic variables** General economic conditions and trends that may be factors in an organization's activities.

**effectiveness** The ability to determine appropriate objectives: "doing the right thing."

**efficiency** The ability to minimize the use of resources in achieving organizational objectives: "doing things right."

**electronic data-processing (EDP)** Computerized data-processing and information management, including report standardization for operating managers.

**employee-oriented style** Style descriptive of managers who try to motivate rather than control subordinates; they seek friendly, trusting, and respectful relationships with employees, who often participate in decisions that affect them.

**employee survey** Procedure managers use to determine training needs of individuals in by asking managers as well as nonmanagers to describe what problems they are experiencing in their work and what actions they believe are necessary to solve them.

**empowerment** The act of delegating power and authority to a subordinate so that the goals of the manager can be accomplished.

**encoding** The translation of information into a series of symbols for communication.

**end-user computing** The creative use of computers by those who are not experts in data processing.

**engineered cost budget** Type of expense budget that describes material and labor costs of each item produced, including estimated overhead costs.

**enlightened self-interest** Organizations' realization that it is in their own best interest to act in ways that the community considers socially responsible.

**enterprise strategy (E-strategy)** A statement of values and principles that explains why an organization does what it does.

**entrepreneur** Either the originator of a new business venture or a manager who tries to improve an organizational unit by initiating product changes.

**entrepreneurship** The seemingly discontinuous process of combining resources to produce new goods or services.

**equal employment opportunity (EEO) requirements** The requirement of nondiscriminatory treatment in the workplace and enforcement of the provisions of Title VII of the Civil Rights Act that prohibit employment discrimination on the basis of race, sex, age, religion, color, or national origin.

**equal pay** The Equal Pay Act prohibits discrimination in which employers pay men more than women for performing jobs requiring substantially equal skill, effort, responsibility, and working conditions; it requires like pay for like jobs.

**equity** The assets left after liabilities are deducted.

**equity theory** A theory of job motivation that emphasizes the role played by an individual's belief in the equity or fairness of rewards and punishments in determining his or her performance and satisfaction.

**ergonomics** A new, biological approach to job design which represents a systematic attempt to make work as safe as possible.

**ERG theory** Theory of motivation that says people strive to meet a hierarchy of existence, relatedness, and growth needs; if efforts to reach one level of needs are frustrated, individuals will regress to a lower level.

**espoused values** The reasons given by an organization for the way things are done; according to Schein, the second level of organizational culture.

**ethics** The study of rights and of who is—or should be—benefited or harmed by an action.

**ethnocentric manager** Attitude that the home country's management practices are superior to those of other countries and can be exported along with the organization's goods and services.

**exchange transformation** The process of changing goods into money.

**expectancy model** A model of motivation that specifies that the effort to achieve high performance is a function of the perceived likelihood that high performance can be achieved, and that the reward will be worth the effort expended.

**expectancy theory** A theory of motivation that says that people choose how to behave from among alternative courses of behavior, based on their expectations of what there is to gain from each behavior.

**expense budget** Budget explaining where money was applied.

**expense center or cost center** Organizational units, such as administrative, service, and research departments, where inputs are measured in monetary terms, but outputs are not.

**expert power** Power based on the belief or understanding that the influencer has specific knowledge or relevant expertise that the influencee does not.

**expert system** A computer-based system using artificial intelligence techniques to diagnose problems, recommend approaches to solving or avoiding them, and provide a rationale for these recommendations.

**exporting** The selling of domestically produced goods in foreign markets.

**external audit** Verification process involving the independent appraisal of financial accounts and statements.

**external environment** All elements outside an organization that are relevant to its operation; includes direct-action and indirect-action elements.

**external stakeholders** Groups or individuals in an organization's external environment that affect the activities.

**extinction** The absence of reinforcement for undesirable behavior so that the behavior eventually stops recurring.

**extrinsic rewards** Reward that is provided by an outside agent, such as a supervisor or work group.

**F**

**family group** An existing or permanent team made up of a manager and his or her employees.

**feedback** The part of system control in which the results of actions are returned to the individual, allowing work procedures to be analyzed and corrected.

**financial budget** Budget detailing the money expected to be spent during the budget period and indicating its sources.

**financial statement** Monetary analysis of the flow of goods and services to, within, and from the organization.

**first-line (or first-level) managers** Managers who are responsible for the work of operating employees only and do not supervise other managers; they are

the "first" or lowest level of managers in the organizational hierarchy.

**fishbone diagram** Diagram used to organize and show visually the possible causes of a problem or event; also called the cause-and-effect diagram and the Ishikawa diagram.

**fixed assets** Incudes the monetary value of the company's plant, equipment, property, patents, and other items used on a continuing basis to produce its goods or services.

**fixed budget** The budget that expresses what individual costs should be at one specified volume

**fixed capital costs** Capital outlays that are not influenced by the amount of work accumulated in the responsibility center; for example, costs for construction, land, and equipment.

**fixed costs** Those expenses unaffected by the amount of work accumulated in the responsibility center.

**flat hierarchies** Organizational structures characterized by wide spans of management control and few hierarchical levels.

**flexible budget** Cost schedules that show how each cost should vary as the level of activity or output varies; also known as the variable budget, sliding-scale budget, and step budget.

**flows** Components such as information, material, and energy that enter and leave a system.

**force-field theory** Lewin's theory that every behavior is the result of an equilibrium between driving and restraining forces.

**formal authority** Power that exists when a subordinate or influencee acknowledges that the influencer has a "right" or is lawfully entitled to exert influence, within certain bounds; power rooted in the general understanding that specific individuals or groups have the right to exert influence within certain limits by virtue of their position within the organization; also called legitimate power.

**formal channel of communication** A means of communication that is endorsed, and probably controlled, by managers.

**formal systematic appraisal** A formalized appraisal process for rating work performance, identifying those deserving raises or promotions, and identifying those in need of further training.

**forming** According to Tuckman, the initial stage that groups go through, during which the members learn what behavior is acceptable to the group.

**franchise** A type of licensing arrangement in which a company sells a package containing a trademark, equipment, materials, and managerial guidelines.

**functional authority** The authority of members of staff departments to control the activities of other departments as they relate to specific staff responsibilities.

**functional-level strategy** Strategy formulated by a specific functional area in an effort to carry out business-unit strategy.

**functional manager** A manager responsible for just one organizational activity, such as finance or human resources management.

**functional organization** A form of departmentalization in which everyone engaged in one functional activity, such as marketing or finance, is grouped into one unit.

**functions** A classification referring to a group of similar activities in an organization, such as marketing or operations.

**G**

**game theory** The study of people making interdependent choices.

**general financial condition** The long-term balance between debt and equity.

**general manager** The individual responsible for all activities, such as production, sales, marketing, and finance, for an organization like a company or a subsidiary.

**generation gaps** Differences in sets of values held by different age groups.

**geocentric manager** Attitude that accepts both similarities and differences between domestic and foreign management policies and so attempts to strike a balance between those that are most effective.

**glass ceiling syndrome** The view that even though women and minorities can get hired into organizations, they have difficulty getting promoted, particularly to senior levels; it's as if there's an invisible barrier; they can see opportunities above, but they cannot reach them.

**globalization** The recognition by organizations that business must have a global, not local focus.

**global strategic partnership** Alliance formed by an organization with one or more foreign countries, generally with an eye toward exploiting the other countries' opportunities and toward assuming leadership in either supply or production.

**goal** The purpose that an organization strives to achieve; organizations often have more than one goal; goals are fundamental elements of organizations.

**goal-setting theory** A process theory of motivation that focuses on the process of setting goals.

**gossip chain** Type of grapevine chain that often occurs when information of an interesting but non-job-related nature is being conveyed and one person seeks out and tells everyone the information he or she has obtained.

**grapevine** In organizations, informal networks of communication that intersect at several points, circumvent rank or authority, and can link organization members in any combination of directions—horizontal, vertical, and diagonal.

**grapevine chains** The various paths through which informal communication is passed through an organization; the four types are the single strand, gossip, probability, and cluster chains.

**groupware** Software capabilities that enable two or more people to work together.

**H**

**Hawthorne effect** The possibility that workers who receive special attention will perform better simply because they received that attention: one interpretation of studies by Elton Mayo and his colleagues.

**heuristic principles** A method of decision making that proceeds along empirical lines, using rules of thumb, to find solutions or answers.

**hierarchy** A pattern of multiple levels of an organizational structure, at the top of which is the senior-ranking manager (or managers) responsible for the operations of the entire organization; other, lower-ranking managers are located down the various levels of the organization.

**hiring specification** A written description of the education, experience, and skills needed to perform a job or fill a position effectively.

**hostile environment** The type of sexual harassment that occurs when physical or verbal sexual conduct unreasonably interferes with an employee's performance in the work environment.

**human capital** An organization's investment in the training and development of its members.

**human relations** How managers interact with other employees or recruits, particularly subordinates.

**human resource management (HRM)** The management function that deals with recruitment, placement, training, and development of organization members.

**human resource planning** Planning for the future personnel needs of an organization, taking into account both internal activities and factors in the external environment.

**human skill** The ability to work with, understand, and motivate other people as individuals or in groups.

**I**

**impoverished management** Management style characterized by low concern for people and low concern for tasks or production; also called laissez-faire management.

**income statement** Summary of the organization's financial performance over a given interval of time.

**indirect-action elements** Elements of the external environment that affect the climate in which an organization's activities take place, but do not affect the organization directly.

**influence** Any actions or examples of behavior that cause a change in attitude or behavior of another person or group.

**informal communication** Communication within an organization that is not officially sanctioned.

**informal organizational structure** The undocumented and officially unrecognized relationships between members of an organization that inevitably emerge out of the personal and group needs of employees.

**informal performance appraisal** The process of continually feeding back to subordinates information regarding their work performance.

**information** Data that have been organized or analyzed in some meaningful way.

**informational role** The type of role a person takes on when he or she facilitates the gathering of information, such as by checking out market projections.

**information ownership** The possession by certain individuals of unique information and knowledge concerning their work.

**information transformation** The process of changing information from one form into another.

**infrastructure** Physical facilities needed to support economic activity; includes transportation and communication systems, schools, hospitals, power plants, and sanitary facilities.

**innovation** The translation of a new idea into a new company, a new product, a new service, a new process, or a new method of production.

**inputs** Resources from the environment, such as raw materials and labor, that may enter any organizational system.

**integration** The term Lawrence and Lorsch use in place of coordination, to designate the degree to which members of various departments work together in a unified manner.

**integrative process** Negotiation process in which the prospects for both parties' gains are encouraging; also known as a win-win situation.

**intelligent enterprises** What Quinn calls organizations whose most important product is knowledge, packaged as valuable services.

**internal audit** Audit performed by the organization to ensure that its assets are properly safeguarded and its financial records reliably kept.

**internal stakeholders** Groups or individuals, such as employees, that are not strictly part of an organization's environment but for whom an individual manager remains responsible.

**internship** Method of on-the-job training in which job training is combined with related classroom instruction.

**interpersonal role** The type of role a person takes on when he or she intermediates between people or groups of people, such as presiding over a meeting.

**intrapreneurship** Corporate entrepreneurship, whereby an organization seeks to expand by exploring new opportunities through new combinations of its existing resources.

**intrinsic reward** Psychological reward that is experienced directly by an individual.

**inventory** Supply of raw materials, work in progress, and finished goods an organization maintains to meet its operational needs.

**investment center** Organizational unit that not only measures the monetary value of inputs and outputs, but also compares outputs with assets used in producing them.

**J**

**job description** A written description of a non-management job, covering title, duties, and responsibilities, and including its location on the organization chart.

**job design** The division of an organization's work among its employees.

**job enlargement** The combining of various operations at a similar level into one job to provide more variety for workers and thus increase their motivation and satisfaction; represents an increase in job scope.

**job enrichment** The combining of several activities from a vertical cross section of the organization into one job to provide the worker with more autonomy and responsibility. An increase in job depth.

**job rotation** The practice of shifting workers from job to job within the same company so they can develop a variety of skills.

**job specialization** The division of work into standardized, simplified tasks.

**joint venture** Business undertaking in which foreign and domestic companies share the costs of building production or research facilities in foreign countries.

**just-in-time (JIT) inventory system** Inventory system in which production quantities are ideally equal to delivery quantities, with materials purchased and finished goods delivered just in time to be used; also known as kanban.

**K**

**kanban** Inventory system in which production quantities are ideally equal to delivery quantities, with materials purchased and finished goods delivered just in time to be used; also known as just-in-time (JIT) inventory system.

**key performance areas or key result areas** Aspects of a unit or organization that must function effectively if the entire unit or organization is to succeed.

**L**

**labor market** The pool of available people who have the skills to fill an open position; can be defined narrowly (locally) or more broadly (globally); changes over time in response to environmental factors.

**labor productivity index** Ratio of output to work-hours.

**laissez-faire management** Management style characterized by low concern for people and low concern for tasks or production; so labeled because the leader does not take a leadership role; also called impoverished management.

**large-batch production** The manufacture of large quantities of products, sometimes on an assembly line, such as computer chips. Also called mass production.

**lateral communication** Communication between departments of an organization that generally follows the work flow rather than the chain of command, and thus provides a direct channel for coordination and problem solving.

**law of effect** People's memory of past stimuli—response—consequence experience influence future behavior in that people are motivated to respond to stimuli in consistent patterns of behavior over time; people tend to alter behavior that results in negative consequences and continue behavior that results in positive consequences.

**leader-member relations** The quality of the interaction between a leader and his or her subordinates; according to Fiedler, the most important influence on the manager's power.

**leadership** The process of directing and influencing the task-related activities of group members.

**leadership functions** The group-maintenance and task-related activities that must be performed by the leader, or someone else, for a group to perform effectively.

**leadership styles** The various patterns of behavior

favored by leaders during the process of directing and influencing workers.

**leading** The process of directing and influencing the task-related activities of group members or an entire organization.

**least preferred co-worker (LPC)** Fiedler's measuring instrument for locating a manager on the leadership-style continuum.

**legitimate power** Power that exists when a subordinate or influencee acknowledges that the influencer has a "right" or is lawfully entitled to exert influence, within certain bounds; also called formal authority.

**liabilities** What an organization owes.

**liaison** The role a person takes on when he or she acts as a go-between.

**licensing** The selling of rights to market brand-name products or to use patented processes or copyrighted materials.

**line authority** The authority of those managers directly responsible, throughout the organization's chain of command, for achieving organizational goals.

**line-of-business strategy** Strategy formulated to meet the goals of a particular business; also called business unit strategy.

**liquidity** An organization's ability to convert assets into cash in order to meet current financial needs and obligations.

**locational transformation** The process of transporting goods from one location to another.

**long-run capacity changes** Changes in production capacity that result from more permanent changes, such as the adding or removing capacity by physical facility expansion (more press hammers, more lawyers) or contraction (fewer press hammers, fewer lawyers).

**long-term liabilities** Debts including mortgages, bonds, and other debts that are being paid off gradually.

**M**

**management** The process of planning, organizing, leading, and controlling the work of organization members and of using all available organizational resources to reach stated organizational goals.

**management by objectives (MBO)** A formal set of procedures that establishes and reviews progress toward common goals for managers and subordinates.

**management by walking around (MBWA)** The managerial technique of taking time to "walk around" through various departments and production facilities in order to observe operations and speak informally with employees.

**management information systems (MIS)** Computer-based information system for more effective planning, decision making, and control.

**management science school** Approaching management problems through the use of mathematical techniques for their modeling, analysis, and solution.

**management system** The processes through which an organization manages its human and physical resources and assets.

**manager** People responsible for directing the efforts aimed at helping organizations achieve their goals.

**Managerial Grid** Diagram developed by Blake and Mouton to measure a manager's relative concern for people and production.

**managerial performance** The measure of how efficient and effective a manager is—how well he or she determines and achieves appropriate objectives.

**marketing argument** The argument that organizations gain insight into markets consisting of minority group members and women by managing multicultural issues.

**market organization** The organization of a company into divisions that bring together those involved with a certain type of market.

**Maslow's hierarchy of needs** Theory of motivation that people are motivated to meet five types of needs, which can be ranked in a hierarchy.

**mass production** The manufacture of large quantities of products, sometimes on an assembly line, such as computer chips. Also called large-batch production.

**materials-requirements planning (MRP)** Operational planning system in which end products are analyzed to determine the materials needed to produce them.

**materials-resource planning (MRPII)** Operational planning system that extends MRP by comparing needs to known resources and calculates unit costs; can also be used with other computer programs to handle order entry, invoicing, and other operations tasks.

**matrix structure** An organizational structure in which each employee reports to both a functional or division manager and to a project or group manager.

**mechanistic system** According to Burns and Stalker, one characterized by a bureaucratic organization.

**message** The encoded information sent by the sender to the receiver.

**middle managers** Managers in the midrange of the organizational hierarchy; they are responsible for other managers and sometimes for some operating employees; they also report to more senior managers.

**middle-of-the-road management** Management style characterized by an intermediate amount of concern for both production and employee satisfaction.

**mission statement** Broad organizational goal, based on planning premises, which justifies an organization's existence.

**model** A simplified representation of the key properties of a real-world object, event, or relationship; can be verbal, physical, or mathematical.

**moral relativism** The idea that we cannot decide matters of right and wrong, good and evil, in any rational way.

**moral rules** Rules for behavior that often become internalized as moral values.

**motivation** The factors that cause, channel, and sustain an individual's behavior.

**multiculturalism** As applied to the workplace, the view that there are many different cultural backgrounds and factors that are important in organizations, and that people from different backgrounds can coexist and flourish within an organization.

**multidivisional firm** An organization that has expanded into different industries and diversified its products.

**multinational enterprise (MNE)** A large corporation with operations and divisions spread over several countries but controlled by a central headquarters.

**N**

**naive relativism** The idea that all human beings are themselves the standard by which their actions should be judged.

**need-achievement** According to McClelland, a social motive to excel that tends to characterize successful entrepreneurs, especially when reinforced by cultural factors.

**need theory** Theory of motivation that addresses what people need or require to live fulfilling lives, particularly with regard to work.

**negotiation** The use of communication skills and bargaining to manage conflict and reach mutually satisfying outcomes.

**negotiator** The role a person takes on when he or she helps to work out a compromise between two or more competing sides.

**net worth** The residual value remaining after total liabilities have been subtracted from total assets.

**new pay approach** An approach toward compensation that links it to the process of setting and achieving organizational objectives.

**noise** Anything that confuses, disturbs, diminishes, or interferes with communication.

**nonproductive facilities** Facilities where work does not take place, such as storage areas and maintenance facilities.

**nonprogrammed decisions** Specific solutions created through an unstructured process to deal with nonroutine problems.

**norming** According to Tuckman, the third stage that groups go through, during which the members address and hopefully resolve conflicts that occurred during the storming stage, establishing common goals, norms, and ground rules and allowing group unity to emerge.

**norms** Assumptions and expectations about how members of a group will behave.

**O**

**off-the-job training** Approach to training that takes place outside the workplace but attempts to simulate actual working conditions; the object is to avoid on-the-job pressures that might interfere with the learning process.

**okyakusama** In Japanese, a word meaning honored guest and customer; illustrates how Japanese companies treat customers.

**on-the-job training** An approach to training employees at work through such methods as job rotation, internship, and apprenticeship.

**open system** A system that interacts with its environment.

**operating budget** Budget indicating the goods and services the organization expects to consume in a budget period.

**operational auditing** The process of conducting internal audits to assist managers in evaluating the organization's operational efficiency and the performance of its control systems.

**operational plan** Plan that provides the details needed to incorporate strategy into day-to-day operations.

**operations** The production activities of an organization.

**operations management** Complex management activity that includes planning production, organizing resources, directing operations and personnel, and monitoring system performance.

**operations research** Mathematical techniques for the modeling, analysis, and solution of management problems. Also called management science.

**opportunity** Situation that occurs when circumstances offer an organization the chance to exceed stated goals and objectives.

**order backlog** The practice of taking orders well in advance of the time they will be needed or available; often used to stabilize production cycles.

**organic system** According to Burns and Stalker, one characterized by informality, working in groups, and open communication.

**organization** Two or more people who work together in a structured way to achieve a specific goal or set of goals.

**organizational analysis** Procedure managers use to determine training needs of individuals by analyzing the effectiveness of the organization and its success in meeting its goals to determine where differences exist.

**organizational culture** The set of important understandings, such as norms, values, attitudes, and beliefs, shared by organizational members.

**organizational design** The determination of the organizational structure that is most appropriate for the strategy, people, technology, and tasks of the organization.

**organizational development (OD)** A long-range effort supported by top management to increase an organization's problem-solving and renewal processes through effective management of organizational culture.

**organizational performance** The measure of how efficient and effective an organization is—how well it achieves appropriate objectives.

**organizational structure** The way in which an organization's activities are divided, organized, and co-ordinated.

**organization chart** A diagram of an organization's structure, showing the functions, departments, or positions of the organization and how they are related.

**organizing** The process of engaging two or more people in working together in a structured way to achieve a specific goal or set of goals.

**orientation** A program designed to help employees fit smoothly into an organization; also called socialization.

**outcome interdependence** The degree to which the work of a group has consequences felt by all its members.

**outplacement services** Services many companies provide to help separated employees find new positions.

**outputs** Transformed inputs that are returned to the external environment as products or services.

**P**

**paradox of authority** According to Smith and Berg, the paradox that the group derives its power from the power of its individual members, but in joining the group, members diminish their individual power by putting it at the group's disposal.

**paradox of creativity** According to Smith and Berg, the paradox that although groups must change in order to survive, change means the destruction of the old as well as the creation of the new.

**paradox of disclosure** According to Smith and Berg, the paradox that although the members of a group must disclose what is on their minds if the group is to succeed, fear of rejection makes them disclose only what they think others will accept.

**paradox of identity** According to Smith and Berg, the paradox that groups must unite people with different skills and outlooks precisely because they are different, while those people usually feel that the group diminishes their individuality.

**paradox of individuality** According to Smith and Berg, the paradox that a group can derive its strength only from the individual strengths of members who, when they participate fully in its work, might feel that their individuality has been threatened.

**paradox of regression** According to Smith and Berg, the paradox that although individuals usually join groups hoping to become more than they were before they joined, in order for the group to become more, individuals must become less.

**paradox of trust** According to Smith and Berg, the paradox that trust develops in the group after members trust each other, but members trust each other only after group trust develops.

**partial productivity** A measurement that relates the value of all output to the value of major categories of input, using the ratio total output/partial input.

**participative management** A management style that supports employees in taking on enhanced, empowered roles.

**path-goal model** A leadership theory emphasizing the leader's role in clarifying for subordinates how they can achieve high performance and its associated rewards.

**peer recruiter** Method of recruitment that uses employees with actual experience in the type of work for which applicants are being recruited.

**performance appraisal** Procedure managers use to compare an individual's job performance to the standards or objectives established for his or her job.

**performing** According to Tuckman, the fourth stage that groups go through, during which the members work effectively in achieving common goals within the ground rules established earlier.

**physical transformation** The process of changing raw materials into finished goods.

**planned change** The systematic attempt to redesign an organization in a way that will help it adapt to changes in the external environment or to achieve new goals.

**planned work activities** Training method that involves giving trainees important work assignments to develop their experience and ability.

**planning** The process of establishing goals and suitable course of action for achieving those goals.

**policy** A standing plan that establishes general guidelines for decision making.

**political action committees (PACs)** Groups organized to lobby and make campaign contributions to influence legislators.

**political variables** Factors that may influence an organization's activities as a result of the political process or climate.

**polycentric manager** Attitude that since a foreign country's management policies are best understood by its own management personnel, the home organization should rely on foreign offices.

**portfolio framework** An approach to corporate-level strategy advocated by the Boston Consulting Group; also known as the BCG matrix.

**portfolio investment** Investment in foreign assets whereby a company purchases share in companies that own those assets.

**position description** A written description of a management position, covering title, duties, and responsibilities, and including its location on the organization chart.

**position power** The power, according to Fiedler, that is inherent in the formal position the leader holds. This power may be great or small, depending on the specific position.

**positive reinforcement** The use of positive consequences to encourage desirable behavior.

**power** The ability to exert influence; that is, the ability to change the attitudes or behavior of individuals or groups.

**probability** A statistical measure of the chance a certain event or outcome will occur.

**probability chain** Type of grapevine chain that often occurs when the information is mildly interesting but insignificant and individuals are indifferent about whom they offer information to and therefore tell people at random, and those people in turn tell others at random.

**problem** Situation that occurs when an actual state of affairs differs from a desired state of affairs.

**problem solving argument** The argument that groups of people from diverse backgrounds are better at solving problems.

**problem-solving process** An organization's methods of dealing with the threats and opportunities in its environment.

**procedure** A standing plan that contains detailed guidelines for handling organizational actions that occur regularly.

**process** A systematic method of handling activities.

**process consultation** A technique by which consultants help organization members understand and change the ways they work together.

**process production** The production of materials that are sold by weight or volume, such as chemicals or drugs. These materials are usually produced with highly complex equipment that operates in a continuous flow.

**product flexibility** The situation in which product designs can be changed quickly and managers emphasize customized products to please individual customers.

**production organization** Organization that produces tangible goods that can be mass-produced and stored for later consumption.

**productive facilities** Facilities where work takes place, such as work stations and materials-handling equipment.

**productivity** Measure of how well an operations system functions and indicator of the efficiency and competitiveness of a single firm or department.

**product organization** The organization of a company into divisions that bring together those involved with a certain type of product.

**profitability** Measure of how well a system functions according to the profits it generates.

**Profit budget or master budget** Budget combining expense and revenue budgets in one unit.

**profit center** Organizational unit where performance is measured by numerical differences between revenues and expenditures.

**program** A single-use plan that covers a relatively large set of organizational activities and specifies major steps, their order and timing, and the unit responsible for each step.

**programmed decisions** Solutions to routine problems determined by rule, procedure, or habit.

**project** The smaller and separate portions of the programs.

**psychoanalytic view** View, originated by Sigmund Freud, that holds that much of human behavior is shaped by unconscious efforts to satisfy unfulfilled needs and drives.

**punishment** The application of negative consequences to stop or correct improper behavior.

**Q**

**quality** Quality in the workplace has gone beyond creating a better-than-average product at a good price, and now refers to achieving increasingly better products and services at progressively more competitive prices; this includes doing things right the first time, rather than making and correcting mistakes.

**quality circle** Work group that meets to discuss ways to improve quality and solve production problems.

**question mark** According to the portfolio framework, a business with a relatively small market share in a rapidly growing market.

**quid pro quo** The type of sexual harassment that occurs when sexual favors are requested or demanded in exchange for tangible benefits—advancement, pay increases—or to avoid tangible harm—loss of job, demotion.

**R**

**rational model of decision making** A four-step process that helps managers weigh alternatives and choose the alternative with the best chance of success.

**realistic job preview (RJP)** Information on a job provided by the organization to applicants and new employees that gives both the positive and negative aspects of the job.

**receiver** The individual whose senses perceive the sender's message.

**recruitment** The development of a pool of job candidates in accordance with a human resource plan.

**reengineering** This occurs when an organization conducts a significant reassessment of what it is all about.

**reference group** A group with whom individuals identify and compare themselves.

**referent power** Power based on the desire of the influencee to be like or identify with the influencer.

**refreezing** Transforming a new behavioral pattern into the norm through reinforcement and support mechanisms.

**reinforcement theory** An approach to motivation based on the "law of effect"—the idea that behavior with positive consequences tends to be repeated, while behavior with negative consequences tends not to be repeated.

**renewal process** The way managers adapt their problem-solving processes to the environment.

**research and development (R&D)** Entrepreneurial function devoting organizational assets to the design, testing, and production of new products.

**resource acquisition argument** The argument that

organizations effective in handling multicultural challenges will benefit from hiring advantages in the labor market, such as the positive impact already felt by companies such as Merck, Xerox, and Hewlett Packard.

**response** An individual's behavior provoked by a situation or event called a stimulus.

**responsibility center** Any organizational function or unit whose manager is responsible for all of its activities.

**restraining forces** According to Kurt Lewin's force-field theory, the forces that resist change and strive to maintain the status quo; forces of resistance include the existing organizational culture, individual employees' self-interests, and differing perceptions of organizational goals and strategies.

**revenue budget** Budget for projected sales revenue, used to measure marketing and sales effectiveness.

**revenue center** Organizational unit in which outputs are measured in monetary terms but are not directly compared to input costs.

**revolving door syndrome** Short tenure at work occurring, for example, when minorities can get into an organization but do not stay because they feel uncomfortable in the organization's environment.

**reward power** Power derived from the fact that one person, known as an influencer, has the ability to reward another person, known as n influencee, for carrying out orders, which may be expressed or implied.

**rights** Claims that entitle a person to take a particular action.

**risk** Decision making condition in which managers know the probability a given alternative will lead to a desired goal or outcome.

**role playing** Method of training in which people are assigned different organizational roles to play in order to improve their skills and understanding of various work situations.

**roving leaders** According to Max DePree, the people we look to as models, people who anticipate needs and respond, outside any formal position and hierarchy.

**rules** Standing plans that detail specific actions to be taken in a given situation.

**S**

**satisfice** Decision making technique in which managers accept the first satisfactory decision they uncover.

**satisfiers** According to the two-factor theory, the factors that can motivate work, such as achievement, recognition, responsibility, and advancement—all of which are related to the job content and the rewards of work performance.

**scientific management theory** A management approach, formulated by Frederick W. Taylor and others between 1890 and 1930, that sought to determine scientifically the best methods for performing any task, and for selecting, training, and motivating workers.

**selection** The mutual process whereby the organization decides whether or not to make a job offer and the candidate decides whether or not to accept it.

**self-managed team or self-managed work group** Teams that manage themselves without any formal supervision.

**semivariable costs** Those expenses, such as short-term labor costs, that vary with the amount of work performed but not in a proportional way.

**sender** The initiator of a communication.

**sense of potency** Collective belief of a group that it can be effective.

**sensitivity training** An early personal growth technique, at one time fairly widespread in organizational development efforts, that emphasizes increased sensitivity in interpersonal relationships.

**service organization** Organization that produces intangible goods that require consumer participation and cannot be stored.

**Seven-S model** According to Waterman and others, framework for change identifying seven key factors that can adversely affect successful change in an organization.

**sexual harassment** As applied in the workplace, any unwanted sexual behavior that can involve, for example, words, gestures, sounds, actions, or physical touching.

**short-run capacity changes** Changes in production capacity that result from temporary changes, such as scheduling overtime work, shifting existing personnel, subcontracting, and using inventories or back orders.

**shrinking** A version of organizational restructuring which results in decreasing the size of the organization and often results in a flatter organizational structure; often referred to as downsizing.

**single-strand chain** Least accurate type of grapevine chain that involves a person A who tells something to person B, who tells it to person C, and so on down the line.

**single-use plan** A detailed course of action used once or only occasionally to solve a problem that does not occur repeatedly.

**situational approach** The view that the management technique that best contributes to the attainment of organizational goals might vary in different types of situations or circumstances; also called the contingency approach.

**situational forces** Forces that influence a manager's choice of leadership style because they may affect organization members' attitudes toward authority; include the organization's preferred style, the size and cohesiveness of a specific work group, the nature of the group's tasks, the pressures of time, and even environmental factors.

**situational leadership theory** An approach to leadership developed by Hersey and Blanchard that describes how leaders should adjust their leadership style in response to their subordinates' evolving desire for achievement, experience, ability, and willingness to accept responsibility.

**sliding-scale budget** Cost schedules that show how each cost should vary as the level of activity or output varies; also known as the variable budget, flexible budget, and step budget.

**small-batch production** Products made in small quantities in separate stages, such as machine parts that are later assembled.

**small business** Businesses that are locally owned and managed, often with very few employees working at a single location.

**social audit** Report describing a company's activities in a given area of social interest, such as environmental protection, workplace safety, or community involvement.

**socialization** A program designed to help employees fit smoothly into an organization; also called orientation.

**social system** The set of beliefs and the resulting behaviors that are shared throughout the organization; also called the cultural system.

**social variables** Factors, such as demographics, lifestyle, and social values, that may influence an organization from its external environment.

**sociotechnical approaches** Approaches that attempt to improve performance by simultaneously changing aspects of an organization's structure and its technology. Job enlargement and job enrichment are examples of technostructural approaches to change; also called technostructural approaches.

**span of control** The number of subordinates reporting directly to a given manager. Also called span of management or span of management control.

**span of management** The number of subordinates reporting directly to a given manager. Also called span of control or span of management control.

**special group** A new group that either has been formed to solve a specific problem or has been cre-

ated through a merger or other structural change in the organization.

**special-interest groups (SIGs)** Groups of people who organize to use the political process to advance their position on particular issues, such as abortion and gun control.

**staff authority** The authority of those groups of individuals who provide line managers with advice and services.

**stakeholders** Those groups or individuals who are directly or indirectly affected by an organization's pursuit of its goals.

**standing plan** An established set of decisions used by managers to deal with recurring or organizational activities; major types are policies, procedures, and rules.

**star** According to the portfolio framework, a business with a high relative market share in a rapidly growing market.

**start-up** Business founded by individuals intending to change the environment of a given industry by the introduction of either a new product or a new production process.

**statement of cash flow or statement of sources and uses of funds** Summary of an organization's financial performance that shows where cash or funds came from during the year and where they were applied.

**statistical process control** Methods of measuring variation and continuously improving work processes before the final inspection stage to prevent the production of flawed products.

**step budget** Cost schedules that show how each cost should vary as the level of activity or output varies; also known as the variable budget, flexible budget, and sliding-scale budget.

**stereotype** The application of an assumed characteristic of a class of people (as defined by sex or race, for example) to an individual who belongs to the class, but may or may not have that characteristic.

**stewardship principle** Biblical doctrine that requires businesses and wealthy individuals to view themselves as stewards, or caretakers, holding their property in trust for the benefit of the whole society.

**stimulus** A situation or event that provokes an individual's own voluntary behavior, called a response.

**storming** According to Tuckman, the second stage that groups go through, during which the members begin to assert their individual personalities and often become hostile as they fight ground rules.

**strategic business unit (SBU)** Various business activities that produce a particular type of product or service are grouped and treated as a single business unit.

**strategic control points** Critical points in a system at which monitoring or collecting information should occur.

**strategic management** The management process that involves an organization's engaging in strategic planning and then acting on those plans.

**strategic partnering** When an organization builds long-term relationships with other organizations, such as suppliers, to enhance its products or services.

**strategic plans** Plans designed to meet an organization's broad goals.

**strategy** The broad program for defining and achieving an organization's objectives; the organization's response to its environment over time.

**strategy implementation** The basically administrative tasks needed to put strategy into practice.

**subsystems** Those parts making up the whole system.

**subunits** The smaller units into which an organization is broken down, such as division, departments, and so on.

**superteams or high-performance teams** Groups of 3 to 30 workers drawn from different areas of a corporation who get together to solve the problems that workers deal with daily.

**support facilities** Facilities that support the work taking place, such as offices, restrooms, waiting rooms, cafeterias, and parking lots.

**survey feedback** Can be used to improve the operations of the total organization; involves conducting attitude and other surveys and systematically reporting the results to organization members; members then determine what actions need to be taken to solve the problems and exploit the opportunities uncovered in the surveys.

**sustainable development** A more modern approach to thinking about environmental issues that says that organizations should engage in activities that can be sustained for a long period of time or which renew themselves automatically.

**symbolic communication** Communication such as gestures, sounds, letters, numbers, and words that can only represent or approximate the ideas that they are meant to communicate.

**synergy** The situation in which the whole is greater than its parts. In organizational terms, synergy means that departments that interact cooperatively are more productive than they would be if they operated in isolation.

**system** In an organization, the functions and activities that work together to fulfill the purposes of the organizations.

**System boundary** The boundary that separates each system from its environment. It is rigid in a closed system, flexible in an open system

**system flexibility** The argument that the ability to manage diversity increases the adaptability and flexibility of an organization.

**systems approach** View of the organization as a unified, directed system of interrelated parts.

**T**

**tall hierarchies** Organizational structures characterized by narrow spans of management control and many hierarchical levels.

**task force or project team** A temporary team formed to address a specific problem.

**task interdependence** The extent to which a group's work requires its members to interact with one another.

**task management** Management style characterized by high concern for production and efficiency but low concern for employees; opposite of country club management; also called authoritarian management.

**task-oriented style** Style descriptive of managers who closely supervise employees to be sure the task is performed satisfactorily.

**task structure** A work situation variable that, according to Fiedler, helps determine a manager's power. In structured tasks, managers automatically have high power; in unstructured tasks, their power is diminished.

**task-technology approach** An approach to organizational design which was first described in the 1960s, in which the production technology used strongly influences the organization's structure.

**team** Two or more people who interact with and influence each other toward a common purpose.

**team building** A method of improving organizational effectiveness at the team level by diagnosing barriers to team performance and improving interteam relationships and task accomplishments.

**team management** Management style characterized by a high concern for both production and employee moral and satisfaction; also called democratic management.

**technical skill** The ability to use the procedures, techniques, and knowledge of a specialized field.

**technical system** The factors, such as the technology and the physical infrastructure, and the capital investments necessary for an organization to achieve its goals.

**technological variables** New developments in products or processes, as well as advances in science, that may affect an organization's activities.

**technostructural approaches** Approaches that attempt to improve performance by simultaneously changing aspects of an organization's structure and its technology. Job enlargement and job enrichment are examples of technostructural approaches to change; also called sociotechnical approaches.

**theory** Coherent group of assumptions put forth to explain the relationship between two or more observable facts and to provide a sound basis for predicting future events.

**theory X** According to McGregor, a traditional view of motivation that holds that work is distasteful to employees, who must be motivated by force, money, or praise.

**theory Y** According to McGregor, the assumption that people are inherently motivated to work and do a good job.

**top managers** Managers responsible for the overall management of the organization; they establish operating policies and guide the organization's interactions with its environment.

**total productivity** A measurement that relates the value of all output to the value of all input, using the ratio total output/total input.

**Total Quality Management (TQM)** An organizational cultural commitment to satisfying customers through the use of an integrated system of tools, techniques, and training. TQM involves the continuous improvement of organizational processes, resulting in high-quality products and services.

**training positions** Selected jobs set aside for training managers, such as staff posts reporting directly selected managers; such assignments, often with the title of "assistant to", give trainees a chance to work with and model themselves after outstanding managers who might otherwise have little contact with them.

**training program** A process designed to maintain or improve current job performance.

**transactional leaders** Leaders who determine what subordinates need to do to achieve objectives, classify those requirements, and help subordinates become confident they can reach their objectives.

**transaction analysis (TA)** An approach to improving interpersonal effectiveness, sometimes used in organizational development efforts, that concentrates on the styles and content of communication.

**transformational leaders** Leaders who, through their personal vision and energy, inspire followers and have a major impact on their organizations; also called charismatic leaders.

**treatment discrimination** Involves practices unrelated to job performance that treat subgroup members differently from others once they are in the work force (less favorable work assignments, slower promotion rates).

**two-factory theory** Herzberg's theory that work dissatisfaction and satisfaction arise from two different sets of factors.

**U**

**uncertainty** Decision-making condition in which managers face unpredictable external conditions or lack the information needed to establish the probability of certain events.

**unfreezing** Making the need for change so obvious that the individual, group, or organization can readily see and accept that change must occur.

**unit production** The production of individual items tailored to a customer's specifications, such as custom-made clothes.

**university-sponsored management development programs** University programs ranging in length from a week to three months or up to one year, that provide full-time study opportunities for middle-level managers; these programs often provide a place for managers slated for promotion to go so that they can broaden their perspectives and prepare for movement into general (as opposed to functional) management; they often combine classroom instruction with case studies, role playing, and simulation.

**V**

**valence** The motivating power of a specific outcome of behavior; varies from individual to individual.

**values** Relatively permanent desires that seem to be good in themselves.

**variable budget** Cost schedules that show how each cost should vary as the level of activity or output varies; also known as the flexible budget, sliding-scale budget, and step budget.

**variable costs** Expenses that vary directly with the amount of work being performed.

**variable operation costs** Capital outlays that vary according to the amount of work, such as wages, taxes, energy and materials acquisition, and distribution.

**vertical communication** Any communication that moves up or down the chain of command.

**vertical integration** Broadening the scope of an organization's operations by buying a supplier or distributor that will contribute to efficient production of primary product or service offerings.

**vestibule training** Type of off-the-job training in which employees train on the actual equipment and in a realistic job setting but in a location different from the one in which they will be working.

**virtual corporation** A temporary network of independent companies, including suppliers and customers, that are linked by information technology that enables them to share skills, costs, and access to each another's markets, without organizational tools such as a central office, organization chart, hierarchy, or vertical integration.

**volume flexibility** The ability to make quick changes in the rate of production as the demand for a firm's product changes.

**W**

**win-lose situation** Negotiation process in which each of the parties tends to seek maximum gains and wants to impose maximum losses on the other; also known as a distributive process and zero-sum.

**win-win situation** Negotiation process in which the prospects for both parties' gains are encouraging; also known as an integrative process.

**Workforce 2000** A report published by the Hudson Institute in 1987 that identified key trends expected to become more important in the twenty-first century, particularly with regard to demographics, such as the aging of the population and the increased presence of women, minorities, and handicapped people in the workforce.

**workforce literacy** Knowledge and skills directly related to job performance.

**work in progress** Partially finished goods.

**Z**

**zero-sum** Negotiation process, so called because one party's gain and the other party's loss counterbalance and sum to zero; occurs when each of the parties tends to seek maximum gains and wants to impose maximum losses on the other; also known as a distributive process and a win-lose situation.

**zone of indifference (area of acceptance)** According to Barnard and Simon, respectively, inclinations conditioning individuals to accept orders that fall within a familiar range of responsibility or activity.

# Company Index

# Name Index

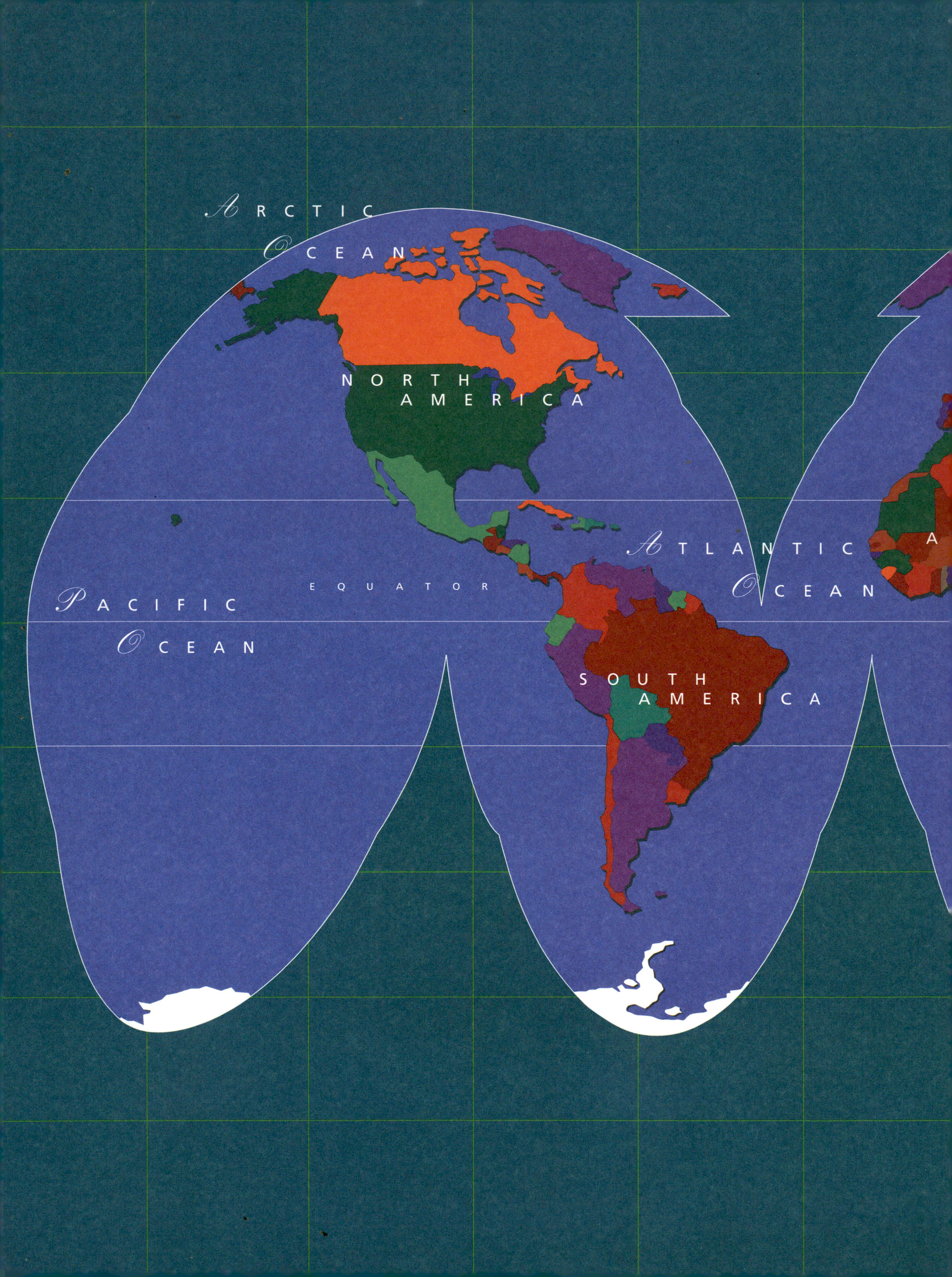
ARCTIC
OCEAN
NORTH
AMERICA
ATLANTIC
OCEAN
EQUATOR
PACIFIC
OCEAN
SOUTH
AMERICA
A